REAPPRAISALS IN CANADIAN HISTORY: PRE-CONFEDERATION

Third Edition

C. M. WALLACE

R. M. BRAY

Laurentian University

Prentice Hall Allyn and Bacon Canada
Scarborough, Ontario

To the memory of A.D. Gilbert

Canadian Cataloguing in Publication Data

Main entry under title:

Reappraisals in Canadian history, pre-confederation

3rd ed.
Includes bibliographical references and index.
ISBN 0-13-958828-0

1. Canada—History—To 1763 (New France). 2. Canada—History—1763–1867.
3. Canada—History—To 1763 (New France)—Historiography. 4. Canada—History—
1763–1867—Historiography. I. Bray, R. M. (Robert Matthew), 1944– .
II. Wallace, C. M. (Carl Murray), 1932– .

FC161.R38 1999   971   C99-932578-4
F1026.R38 1999

Prentice-Hall, Inc., Upper Saddle River, New Jersey
Prentice-Hall International (UK) Limited, London
Prentice-Hall of Australia, Pty. Limited, Sydney
Prentice-Hall Hispanoamericana, S.A., Mexico City
Prentice-Hall of India Private Limited, New Delhi
Prentice-Hall of Japan, Inc., Tokyo
Simon & Schuster Southeast Asia Private Limited, Singapore
Editora Prentice-Hall do Brasil, Ltda., Rio de Janeiro

ISBN 0-13-958828-0

Vice-President, Editorial Director: Laura Pearson
Acquisitions Editor: Dawn Lee
Developmental Editor: Jean Ferrier
Production Editor: Avivah Wargon
Copy Editor: Alex Moore
Production Coordinator: Peggy Brown
Cover Design: Lisa LaPointe
Cover Image: Photodisc
Page Layout: Janette Thompson (Jansom)

1 2 3 4 5   WEB   03 02 01 00 99

Printed and bound in Canada.

Visit the Prentice Hall Canada Web site! Send us your comments,
browse our catalogues, and more at **www.phcanada.com**.
Or reach us through e-mail at **phabinfo_pubcanada@prenhall.com**.

Contents

 **LIST OF WEBLINKS**

1   Native–Newcomer Interaction

kafka.uvic.ca/~vipirg/SISIS/sov/oh11500.html
A paper "500 Years of Indigenous Resistance" from *Oh-To-Kin* Vol. 1, No. 1, Winter/Spring 1992

kafka.uvic.ca/~vipirg/SISIS/Clarke/detente.html
A paper "Towards a Détente with History: Confronting Canada's Colonial Legacy" from *International Journal of Canadian Studies* 12, Fall 1995

odur.let.rug.nl/~usa/D/1601-1650/champlain/voyag.htm
A letter written in 1604 by Samuel de Champlain describing his encounters with North American natives

www.sgc.gc.ca/epub/abocor/e199408/e199408.htm
A book, *Conquest by Law,* by Christie Jefferson

2   Society in New France

www.mvnf.muse.digital.ca/default.htm
A site "Virtual Museum of New France"

odur.let.rug.nl/~usa/D/1651-1700/frame/seign.htm
An excerpt from the Marquis de Seignelay's memoirs "The Dangers that Threaten Canada and The Measures to Remedy Them, January 1687"

virtual-indiana.com/TAFDC/html/french_presence.html
An article "The French Presence in North America"

vc.lemoyne.edu/relations/relations_01.html
Volume One of "The Jesuit Relations and Allied Documents: Travels and Explorations of the Jesuit Missionaries in New France 1610–1791"

3   The Expulsion of the Acadians

ourworld.compuserve.com/homepages/lwjones/acadhist.htm
An article "History of the Acadians" by Bona Arsenault

www.cajunculture.com/Other/grandderangement.htm
The Encyclopedia of Cajun Culture (Louisiana) entry "Le Grand Derangement"

www.landryfamily.com/timeline_acadian.htm
An Acadian history timeline

www.geocities.com/BourbonStreet/Delta/6950/Acadia.html
An article "The Ancestors of the Louisiana Cajuns: From the Beginning of New France to 1671 and the Beginning of a Distinct Acadian Society" by Whitney Dartez

4   The French Military in New France During the Seven Years' War

www.miredespa.com/wmaton/Other/Legal/Constitutions/Canada/English/PreConfederation/Treaty_of_Paris_1763.html
French and English text versions of The Treaty of Paris

www.georgetown.edu/centers/CEPACS/alex_french.html
An article tracing the shifting alliances of irregular forces during the Seven Years' War

www.bedford.net/Tuor_Beleg/FBM/Map.htm
A map detaling several battles of the Seven Years' War

virtual-indiana.com/TAFDC/html/history.html
An article about the history of the French colonial Fife and Drum Corps.

5   The Meaning of the Conquest

www.upei.ca/~rneill/topic_6.html
A paper "Mercantilism, Settlement, New France" explores the economic history of New France pre and post conquest

www.upei.ca/~rneill/topic_4.html
A paper "The Legacy of Feudalism in America" identifies the conquest as a turning point for social and political life in North America

www.miredespa.com/wmaton/Other/Legal/Constitutions/Canada/English/ PreConfederation/rp_1763.html
Text of the Royal Proclamation, 1763, in which the British itemize territories and possessions ceded by the French

6   The Loyalist Experience

www.civilization.ca/cmc/cmceng/ca15eng.html
The Museum of Civilization's page on "Arriving in Upper Canada"

www.geocities.com/Athens/Delphi/4171/
An American site dedicated to revolutionary war activity in Upper New York

odur.let.rug.nl/~usa/E/novascotia/scotiaxx.htm
An article "Nova Scotia During the American Revolution"

www.miredespa.com/wmaton/Other/Legal/Constitutions/Canada/English/ PreConfederation/ca_1791.html
Text of the Constitutional Act, 1791

7   Invented Tradition: Laura Secord and the War of 1812

www.nmarcom.com/heritage/minutes/min6.htm
CRB Foundation's page for the Laura Secord "Heritage Minute"

www.norlink.net/~jkeigher/secord.html
A nine-year old scholar's site devoted to the Laura Secord story: "There was no cow...there was no chocolate."

www.niagara.com/~merrwill/
Site devoted to representations of women in Canadian history

www.miredespa.com/wmaton/Other/Legal/misc/jay.html
Text of the Jay Treaty

8   The Métis and Red River Society

www.ucalgary.ca/pubaff/Research/smith.html
An article about letters and manuscripts left by a Hudson's Bay Co. explorer

www.vcn.bc.ca/michif
The Michif Cultural Preservation Society's home page

www.cyberus.ca/~mfdunn/metis
The Confederacy of Métis Peoples' home page

library.usask.ca/northwest/
The NorthWest Resistance Database

9   The Rebellions of 1837–1838 in Upper and Lower Canada

www.geog.utoronto.ca/hacddp/plate13/p13.html
A map and statistics "Unrest in the Canadas" from the Historical Atlas of Canada

www.laurentian.com/morgan.html
An article "A Chronicle of Lower Canada" by Jan Henry Morgan

www.mbnet.mb.ca/~bphilli1/history/unit3e.html
An article detailing "Government in the British Colonies"

www.er.uqam.ca/nobel/k14664/patriote.htm
An article "Les Patriotes de 1837–38" (in French)

10   Travellers, Inns and Feasting

www.swcp.com/hughes/
The Food Museum

fortress.uccb.ns.ca/behind/food.html
An article "The Importance of Food in 18th Century Louisbourg"

www.civilization.ca/cmc/cmceng/ca08eng.html
A description of the inn located at the Place de la Nouvelle France from the Museum of Civilization

11   The Irish Come to Canada

www.bess.tcd.ie/diaspora.htm
A paper "The Irish Mind Abroad: The Attitudes and Experiences of the Irish Diaspora" from *The Irish Journal of Psychology*

avery.med.virginia.edu/~eas5e/Irish/Famine.html
A site devoted to the famine of 1845–1850.

www.kawartha.net/~jleonard/robinson.htm
An article "Irish Emigration to Peterborough"

www.bcpl.lib.md.us/~cbladey/orange.html
A site devoted to Battle of the Boyne Day celebrations and parades

12   The Social Contexts of Responsible Government

www.nlc-bnc.ca/confed/lowercan/elowrcan.htm
The National Library's page "Towards Confederation: Lower Canada (1791–1842)"

www.miredespa.com/wmaton/Other/Legal/Constitutions/Canada/English/PreConfederation/ua_1840.html
Text of the Union Act of 1840

www.geog.utoronto.ca/hacddp/plate6/p6.html
A map and statistics "Population of the Canadas and the Maritimes to 1851" from the Historical Atlas of Canada

www.canoe.ca/InDepthUnity/confederation.html
An article "The Road to Confederation" from the 1996 *Canadian Global Almanac*

13   Growing up in Pre-Industrial Canada

www3.ns.sympatico.ca/dmcclare/textld.htm
The edited text of "The 1815 Diary of a Nova Scotia Farm Girl"

www.worldweb.com/VertexCustomers/p/ParksCanada-Rocky/furtrade.html
An article "The Fur Trade in Canada"

www.geog.utoronto.ca/hacddp/plate54/p54_2.html
A map and statistics "The Developing Industrial Heartland, 1871–1891" from the Historical Atlas of Canada

dcs1.uwaterloo.ca/~marj/geneology/homeadd.html
An article "Youth Immigration to Canada"

www.mun.ca/rels/ang/texts/ang2.html
A paper "Bonavista's 'Hewers of Wood and Drawers of Water': The First School in Newfoundland" by Rollman/Power from *Bulletin of the Humanities Association of Canada*, 17/1 April 1989

14   Confederation

www.nlc-bnc.ca/confed/e-1867.htm
National Library's Confederation site

www.acs.ucalgary.ca/~dabrent/cbc/history.html
An article "Historical Highlights of US-Canada Relations"

www.solon.org/Constitutions/Canada/English/index.html
A legal history of Canadian constitutional documents

aims.ca/detour.html
An article "Confederation's Impact on Industrialization in the Maritimes"

Preface

The publication of this third edition of *Reappraisals in Canadian History* is a reflection of the dynamic nature of historical writing today. The trend towards fragmentation so obvious in the 1980s has matured to the point that it may be more appropriate to speak not of one but of several histories of Canada. We have attempted to incorporate much of this fractured climate into this edition, though we remain committed to the notion of one country with a common history. To this end we have consciously attempted to integrate the divergent strands into a united framework. This volume probes for a convergence of views in content areas. Each unit focuses on the diverse interpretations of a particular historical problem. A brief introduction establishes the context for the readings selected, and suggestions for additional sources are included for those who wish to delve further into the topic.

The vitality in Canadian historical studies since the 1960s has been remarkable, resulting in a profusion of new monographs and periodicals. While it was tempting to limit our selection of readings to that extensive literature, the important contributions of the previous generation of historians could not be neglected, nor should they be. It was those earlier views that spurred many of the debates included in this volume, though they are more and more likely to be ignored as their successors struggle among themselves for pre-eminence. The topical approach of this volume demanded that all interests, including such disparate ones as regions, women, political groups, minorities, the disadvantaged, the military, and victims be presented as part of the total fabric rather than in isolation.

In assembling this collection we have incurred a number of obligations. The imprint of the late A.D. Gilbert, our former co-editor, persists. Several colleagues across the country took the time to evaluate the previous edition and recommend changes, many of which have been incorporated in this volume; among these colleagues are Ernest Epp, Lakehead University; Douglas Leighton, Huron College, University of Western Ontario; Patrick Brennan, University of Calgary; and Dr. Linda Ambrose of the Department of History at Laurentian, who offered several thoughtful suggestions. The students in HIST 1406/1407 participated cheerfully as we experimented with these materials in classrooms and tutorials. Leo Larivière created the maps. Rose-May Demoré, our departmental secretary, responded to every call for help. Several editors at Prentice Hall Canada have worked with us over the years; for this edition Jean Ferrier and Avivah Wargon kept us on track, along with copy editor Alex Moore. Finally, we must thank the dozens of historians, editors and publishers who have generously given us permission to reprint this material.

We dedicate this edition to our wives, Jean and Diane, who over the years have endured several reappraisals with us.

C.M. WALLACE

R.M. BRAY

Laurentian University

Introduction

Canadian History and Historians

"Ignorance of history," observed Peter C. Emberley, "comes at a terrible cost."[1] Yet Canadian history is frequently ignored, trashed, corrupted or fabricated. Societies with a poor knowledge of their history routinely create imagined pasts for current needs and future objectives. Louis Riel, for example, has been reinvented several times, and the ingenuity goes on. This year he may well be found not guilty of any misdemeanour and named a Father of Confederation. While this has little to do with history, it has everything to do with what Desmond Morton calls heritage. History, writes Morton, "is a study of the past, pursued by those who try to get things right, even if they almost never succeed. Heritage is our attempt to exploit the past for present tastes and, therefore, by definition, has nothing to do with what actually happened."[2] The challenge for students is to know the difference between heritage and history. In this collection of *Reappraisals in Canadian History* you will read historians who try to get things right, although some are not above playing the heritage game. Keep this in mind as Riel proceeds through his rehabilitation. History, overall, is misunderstood more often than not. At a superficial level it appears to be one of the few immutables in an ever-changing world. That the past itself can never be altered is irrefutable, and students frequently choose history as an option at university believing that at least one subject will provide security when others mystify with unique concepts, vocabulary and content. That cozy view of history never lasts long, for, as a discipline, history is complex, malleable and imprecise, subject to changing conditions and perspectives. Far from being set in cement, history is continuously being recast. If R.G. Collingwood was correct, then "every new generation must rewrite history in its own way." Even in something as commonplace as hockey, a player like "Rocket" Richard may define the game to your grandfather, while you may consider Wayne Gretzky the great one, and your father may argue for Bobby Orr.

This characteristic of history causes much confusion for students and academics alike. A psychology professor at lunch with several historians recently declared that after she had taken world history in grade eight, further study was irrelevant. The subject, like Napoleon, was dead. One of the historians ventured the opinion that history had possibly changed more in the past twenty years than psychology. At that point she threw up her hands and left, unable to entertain such a ludicrous proposition. Yet it may be true.

The dynamic nature of the discipline of history, when compared to the permanence of past events such as the death of Napoleon, is the apparent paradox the psychology professor never unravelled. Over the past four decades a revolution has taken place in historical scholarship. In the era after the Second World War, historians reached a sort of plateau encompassing a broad consensus about the nature of the discipline. The traditional scholar worked for months or years in archives, poring over primary sources, and producing "revisionist" books or articles published in the handful of journals which all historians of Canada read. Triumphs were achieved with the discovery of new source material or a new angle on a known subject. Politics and biography were favoured, though economic, religious, military and international topics found their specialists. The overall nature of history as the study of the activities and ideas of elites, however, was rarely questioned.

This top-down view from the "court" became the textbook version of the Canadian past, and while there were divisions over some interpretations based on ideology, religion or even personal hostility, there was no division on what history itself was.

In Canada the small coterie of academics dominating the field included Marcel Trudel, Donald Creighton, A.R.M. Lower, W.L. Morton, Hilda Neatby, C.P. Stacey, W.S. MacNutt, Frank Underhill, Guy Fregault and Margaret Ormsby. A younger generation of "revisionists" from the same mould was expanding the content without challenging the structures. Among them were J.M.S. Careless, Peter Waite, Margaret Prang, W.J. Eccles, Ramsay Cook, Jean Hamelin, Ken McNaught, Blair Neatby and Jacques Monet. These people all knew each other personally, frequently comparing notes at the Public Archives of Canada then located on Sussex Drive beside the Royal Mint in Ottawa. At the annual meetings of the Canadian Historical Association they read papers to each other, and were never short of advice. The *Canadian Historical Review*, published by the University of Toronto Press, was the final authority in English Canada, while Abbé Groulx reigned over French Canada with the *Revue d'histoire de l'Amérique française*. It was from this more or less homogeneous group that the dominant view of Canada as presented in school textbooks emerged. The comfortable unity of this well-written version of Canada's past permitted it to survive its generation, which many regard as the "Golden Age" of Canadian historical scholarship.

By the late 1960s, however, several younger scholars began reacting against that veneration of the images of a previous generation. For these historians, the "Golden Age" of Canadian history represented a stifling force, an academic approach that had led to the historical imagination being crippled by consistency. More than that, the consensus version of the past, in their view, had no relevance for the current generation. One may admire a Rolls Royce "Silver Ghost," a 1955 Chevrolet, or even a Model T, the argument goes, but one must not confuse an abacus with a computer, a museum piece with modern needs.

It is the nature of history that the status quo does not survive long, and in the upheaval that characterized the whole mentality of the 1960s, several academics began to search for a more "usable past," one that abandoned the impressionistic views from the "court" and aimed at the reconstruction of a more meaningful society. The "New Social History" is the umbrella under which most of the innovations may be grouped. The dissatisfaction with a Canadian past dominated by political and economic factors led to a renovation with new methodologies, different approaches and alternate subject matter muscling in on the old school-tie network. Subjects once ignored moved to centre stage, including work on social classes and class relations, demography, literacy, the family, leisure, mobility, immigration, religion and education, though there was little cohesion among the disparate activities. Quantification and the computer found their place in the historian's toolbox. *Histoire sociale / Social History*, co-sponsored by the University of Ottawa and Carleton University in 1968, eventually provided a focus and emerged as an alternate journal, and its lack of coherent editorial policy was simply a reflection of the diversity of opinion within the discipline. In a sense, each historian could become a different school. The *Annales* of France, for example, were the source of inspiration for many French Canadians, while most English Canadians turned to American sociology for their models. Although there was considerable resentment over this "invasion of the barbarians" among the traditional historians, their own anecdotal and impressionistic approaches invited criticism from those who asked different questions of sources and approached the past from new perspectives.

By the 1970s a veritable floodgate had opened. The annual meetings of the Canadian Historical Association became not one but a dozen or more fragments meeting separately. There was the ethnic group, labour, Atlantic, Western, Arctic, Native, women, urban, local, material, oral – the divisions were endless. Each of these had the capacity to subdivide. Labour quickly separated into the "old-fashioned" and the "New Left," with the latter winning the day and mounting its own journal, *Labour/Le Travailleur*. Each segment, in fact, launched one or more journals, such as *Urban History Review, Canadian Ethnic Studies, Polyphony, Canadian Woman Studies, Journal of Canadian Studies, BC Studies, The American Review of Canadian Studies*. The range of topics and quality of scholarship were as varied as the hues of a rainbow. Some, like *Acadiensis: Journal of the History of the Atlantic Region*, founded in 1971 at the University of New Brunswick, established and maintained an enviable reputation. Others have been less successful.

As a consequence of this fragmentation over recent decades, a student is faced with not one but many versions of Canadian history. This confusion may be considered an unnecessary encumbrance to those who are content with the "good old stuff," but that implies the study of a dead subject. The reappraisal is never-ending, and the challenge for the student is not to learn a few facts and dates but to sample the literature and to recognize what the authors are doing with the subject and trying to do to the reader. Are they writing "history" or contributing to "heritage"? Drawing this distinction requires an agile and critical mind.

Reappraisals in Canadian History is intended to reflect this diversity of interpretation in Canadian history and to present it in such a way as to enable a student to make sense of it. This is not a "textbook" history of Canada, and makes no attempt to survey all of the main developments in that history. Nor is it simply a collection of readings randomly selected, with little or no relationship one to another. Rather, each of the chapters is devoted to a particular historical problem and the different ways in which historians have approached that problem. In some cases their conclusions stand in sharp contradiction to each other; in others they are complementary. In every case students should attempt, not merely to grasp the author's conclusions, but, of even greater importance, to understand how these conclusions were reached and what the author is attempting to do to the reader.

In order to do this, it is useful to understand the variety of reasons which may lead different historians to reach different conclusions about what appears to be the same historical problem. In one sense, of course, there is nothing new about this. The debate over "historical relativism" is an old one, and it is a truism that historians are influenced by the context in which they themselves live. It is, after all, hardly surprising that their view of the past is, to some degree at least, relative to their own time and place and circumstance, to their own preferences and prejudices. This may mean that they view historical evidence in a new light, or that they pose different questions of the past. It has long been accepted, therefore, that there will be differences of emphasis and interpretation, not only between different generations of historians, but also between historians of the same era.

The present fragmentation of the discipline, however, goes far beyond the traditional recognition of the relativity of historical knowledge. Implicit is fundamental disagreement over content and methodology, the meaning of history and its purpose. The one point on which historians do agree, however, is that not all historical interpretations are of equal validity. Certainly historians are less inclined than scholars in certain other disciplines to claim to have discovered any final "truths." This is understandable given the nature of the evidence with which historians deal and the problems with which they are concerned. The readings in this volume are in themselves testimony to the elusiveness of any final answers in history. Despite these limitations, historians do insist that historical scholarship can and must be subjected to critical scrutiny, that historical evidence and the use to which that evidence is put can be evaluated. The study of history at any kind of advanced level requires the development of these analytical skills, and never more so than with its current fragmentation. It is this, rather than the mastery of voluminous detail, which distinguishes the historian from the mere antiquarian. One of the purposes of this collection of readings is to assist students to develop their critical skills. Within each chapter, therefore, students should attempt to identify the interpretative thrust of each author, how the interpretation of one author differs from or complements that of another, what sources and methodologies have been employed, and, finally, how convincingly each author has based his or her interpretation on the historical evidence.

There are a number of fairly obvious points to look for. Has an author found new evidence which calls into question previous work on the subject? Is a new methodology being applied? Is the approach narrative and descriptive or is it analytical? Is anecdotal evidence, for example, being challenged by statistical analysis? Is a new type of historical evidence being brought to bear on an old problem? Does the author have an agenda or an obvious ideology? Is the historical problem itself being defined in an entirely new way?

The fourteen units in this volume are a selection from the history of New France and British North America. An attempt has been made to strike a balance between the various subjects and approaches. Although there are exceptions, generally speaking historical writing on the pre-Confederation period is more traditional and has been less influenced by the New Social History than that on the national period, perhaps because the historical sources are more intractable. The first five chapters of this volume explore the history of New France. Within these units students will encounter a diversity of opinion on a wide variety of subjects. The complexity of the cultural interaction between Amerindian and European is introduced in Chapter 1, Chapter 2 examines the debate over the nature of society in New France, while Chapter 3 reviews the frequently ignored expulsion of the Acadians in the 1750s. Regarding the same era, Chapter 4 offers two sharply contrasting views of the French military in the years leading to the Conquest, the meaning of which is debated in Chapter 5. Canadian history from the Conquest to Confederation is even more diverse and complex. Two chapters, 6 and 7, look at interaction with the United States and offer conflicting views on its results. Three chapters, 9, 12 and 14, are concerned with political changes. The four other chapters turn to the social spectrum, from family life, dining and drinking, to Irish immigrants, to Métis struggles on the prairies. In each unit there is a debate, a disagreement or an alternative perspective.

Of course, any rigid categorisation of the chapters is bound to be somewhat misleading since politics, economics, social dynamics and regional aspects pervade most studies about Canada in one way or another. The student must learn to stride through the variety, identifying the interpretations, the mind-sets, the biases, the methodologies and the mythologies. Each chapter in this collection offers a variety of interpretations which are frequently contradictory. At the same time, each chapter has a coherence which explains something about Canada, its history and its historians. Since history is what historians say it is, the student has both the opportunity and the responsibility to identify the perspectives and the objectives of the historians. History will undoubtedly continue to be misunderstood, and the student must know why.

Notes

1. Peter C. Emberley, "More volleys in the culture wars," *Globe and Mail*, 7 March 1998.

2. Desmond Morton, "Riel revisionist can't alter history," *Toronto Star*, 15 January 1998. Morton gives credit to David Lowenthal, *Possessed by the Past*, for the concepts. For another view on "The drive to rehabilitate Louis Riel" see Tom Flanagan, *The Globe and Mail*, 29 January 1998. He writes it "may sound like politicians enjoying a harmless game of historical revisionism, but it is also a serious game of contemporary politics."

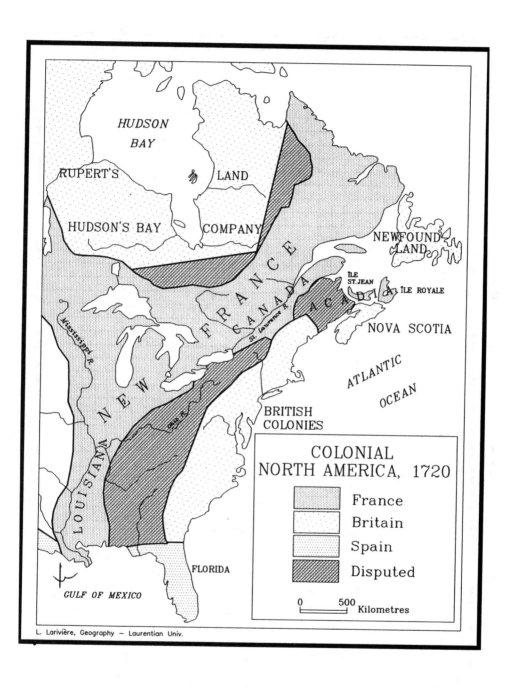

COLONIAL
NORTH AMERICA, 1720

France
Britain
Spain
Disputed

0   500 Kilometres

L. Larivière, Geography — Laurentian Univ.

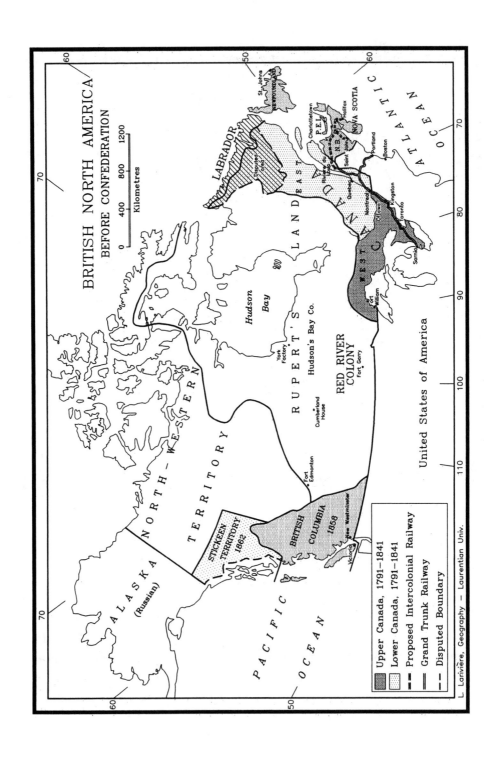

BRITISH NORTH AMERICA
BEFORE CONFEDERATION

Kilometres
0   400   800   1200

L. Larivière, Geography – Laurentian Univ.

Legend:
- Upper Canada, 1791–1841
- Lower Canada, 1791–1841
- Proposed Intercolonial Railway
- Grand Trunk Railway
- Disputed Boundary

ALASKA (Russian)

NORTH-WESTERN TERRITORY

STICKEEN TERRITORY 1862

BRITISH COLUMBIA 1858

PACIFIC OCEAN

Victoria
New Westminster

Fort Edmonton

RUPERT'S LAND

Cumberland House

Hudson's Bay Co.

York Factory

Hudson Bay

RED RIVER COLONY
Fort Garry

United States of America

Fort William

Sarnia
Toronto
Kingston
Ottawa
Montreal
Quebec
Rivière du Loup

CANADA WEST
CANADA EAST

Portland
Boston
Saint John
N.B.
P.E.I.
Charlottetown
NOVA SCOTIA
Halifax

LABRADOR

Disputed Area

NEWFOUNDLAND
St. Johns

ATLANTIC OCEAN

60
70
50
60
70
80
90
100
110
70
60
50

CHAPTER
1 NATIVE– NEWCOMER INTERACTION

The "New World" the Europeans thought they had discovered in North America had in reality already been inhabited for thousands of years. The first major theme in the early history of Canada is therefore the interaction between the First Nations, or Amerindians, and the Europeans. Not surprisingly, older historical writing on this subject reflects a Eurocentric perspective, describing a process in which a barbarous and inferior culture was inevitably overwhelmed by one much more civilized and technologically advanced. This view of the Amerindian as "Savage" permeated all the literature, especially that of the influential nineteenth-century American historian Francis Parkman, whose writings defined Canada for decades.

By the 1930s, the Parkman interpretation was under attack. The first reading in this unit, "The Problem of the Iroquois," by George T. Hunt, reflects this Eurocentric approach. Nevertheless, it was hailed as a major reinterpretation of the subject when it was first published in 1940. Completely rejecting Parkman's attribution of the seventeenth-century intertribal wars to the "homicidal frenzy" of the Iroquois, Hunt suggested instead that the wars were a direct result of European-Amerindian contact and, in particular, of the relationship between the Amerindians and the fur trade. Having become totally dependent upon European technology in the form of trade goods, the Iroquois had no option other than war once their supply of beaver fur became dangerously depleted by the 1640s.

Although this emphasis on the economic importance of the fur trade to the Amerindians has been influential and was typical of the economic deterministic literature predominant before the Second World War, more recent historical writing on early Amerindian-European contact suggests that the subject is much more complex than Hunt indicated. Hunt, in turn, has therefore been attacked. In the second reading, the "Conclusion" from his *Friend and Foe: Aspects of French-Amerindian Cultural Contact in the Sixteenth and Seventeenth*

Centuries, Cornelius Jaenan examines the more general question of the Amerindian-European cultural relationship. Acknowledging that this interaction had a powerful effect on both parties, he suggests that the process was one in which Europeans gained, but the natives lost. Although Amerindian culture was disastrously weakened, the native peoples remained unintegrated in the developing society of New France.

For any student of this subject, the lack of historical records and voices from the Amerindians themselves places severe limitations on analysis. Hunt represented a significant advance over the Parkman indignity; Jaenan, in turn, offered a much broader view than Hunt. All historical writing, however, is representative of the era in which it is written, and that was certainly true of Parkman, Hunt and Jaenan. The final reading is from the 1990s, by Huron academic Georges E. Sioui. In "The Destruction of Huronia" from *For An Amerindian Autohistory: An Essay on the Foundations of a Social Ethic, 1992* Sioui begins with a rejection of the Hunt thesis and then offers alternative voices and views.

Suggestions for Further Reading

Axtel, James, *The Invasion Within: The Contest of Cultures in Colonial North America.* New York: Oxford University Press, 1985.

Bailey, A.G., *The Conflict of European and Eastern Algonkian Cultures, 1504–1700* (2nd ed.). Toronto: University of Toronto Press, 1969.

Delage, Denys, *Bitter Feast: Amerindians and Europeans in the American Northeast, 1600–1664* (trans. by Jane Brierley) Vancouver: University of British Columbia Press, 1993.

Dickason, Olive, *Native Peoples and Cultures of Canada: An Anthropological Overview* (2nd ed). Toronto: McClelland and Stewart, 1992.

_____, *The Myth of the Savage and the Beginnings of French Colonialism in the Americas.* Edmonton: University of Alberta Press, 1984.

Krech, S., *Indians, Animals and the Fur Trade: A Critique of Keepers of the Game.* Athens, Georgia: University of Georgia Press, 1981.

Johnston, Susan, "Epidemics: the Forgotten Factor in Seventeenth Century Native Warfare in the St. Lawrence Region," in *Native People, Native Lands: Canadian Indians, Inuit and Metis*, ed. B.A. Cox. Ottawa: Carleton University Press, 1987, 14–31.

Martin, Calvin, "The European Impact on the Culture of a Northeastern Algonquin Tribe: An Ecological Interpretation," *William and Mary Quarterly*, 3d. ser. XXI (January 1974), 3–26.

Martin, Calvin, *Keepers of the Game: Indian-Animal Relationships and the Fur Trade.* Berkeley, California: University of California Press, 1978.

Schlieser, K.H., "Epidemics and Indian Middlemen: Rethinking the Wars of the Iroquois, 1609–1653," *Ethnohistory*, 23, no. 2 (Spring 1976), 129–45.

Trigger, Bruce, "The French Presence in Huronia: The Structure of Franco-Huron Relations in the First Half of the Seventeenth Century," *Canadian Historical Review*, XLIX, no. 2 (June 1968), 107–41.

_____, *Natives and Newcomers: Canada's 'Heroic Age' Reconsidered.* Kingston and Montreal: McGill-Queen's University Press, 1985.

THE PROBLEM OF THE IROQUOIS

George T. Hunt

In most respects the circumstances of the contact between white man and native in North America are unique in the history of such relationships. In other centuries and in other regions, where the frontiers of superior civilizations had long been in contact with the periphera of inferior civilizations, the conditions of these frontier-peripheral areas were well-established and relatively familiar, and the process of infiltration and conquest was comparatively gradual. The Russian advance into Siberia, the French and English movement into and beyond India, the penetration of the Orient by the peddling shipmasters of the West, all these were conditioned by the fact that each civilization had already considerable knowledge of the other. In Africa the Nile Valley and the Mediterranean shore had constituted a frontier area before historic times, and even in the southern part of the African continent contacts had been more or less continuous for nearly four hundred years before actual colonization and exploitation were begun.

In North America, on the other hand, a well-advanced civilization, in which the mechanism of exploitation was already highly developed, met the Stone Age face to face, in an invasion almost simultaneously continental in extent. There had been a few premonitory invasions along the St. Lawrence River, Coronado's horsemen had retreated from the far Southwest, a few mailed footmen had floundered through southern swamps to the Great River, a few Englishmen had died at Croatan, but these tentative ventures of the sixteenth century had come to nothing. The Wars of Religion cut short the beginning made by Cartier; Texas remained virtually uninhabited; and 130 years passed before another white man glimpsed the Mississippi.

In the thirty years following 1603 the whole Atlantic seaboard swarmed with settlement. Champlain established New France at Quebec and Three Rivers; Holland built forts far up the Hudson; England was at Plymouth, in Massachusetts Bay, Virginia, and Maryland, and struggling for a foothold in Maine. The entire coast was explored and mapped. The Stone Age faced the insistent seventeenth century on a fifteen-hundred-mile front which moved swiftly and relentlessly forward. This advance was no matter of slave raids, ivory, or gold. What these white men wanted was what every native had or could get, furs or land, and the trade that was opened was a trade in which every native could take part. As a matter of fact, he was usually frantically eager to take part in it.

From *The Wars of the Iroquois: A Study in Intertribal Relations* (Madison: University of Wisconsin Press, 1967), 3–12. Reprinted by permission of the University of Wisconsin Press.

The abundance of furs and the inexhaustible market for them made North America a unique theatre of interracial contacts. On other continents the desire of traders had been for materials or products considerably less plentiful and less easily obtained by individuals, but here the ease of acquisition, the apparently limitless supply, the ready market, and the permanence of the white settlements permitted the constant participation of every native, expanded the business of trade to unprecedented proportions, and changed, almost overnight, the fundamental conditions of aboriginal economy.

If it is true that "the relations into which the Europeans entered with the aborigines were decided almost wholly by the relations which they found to exist among the tribes on their arrival,"[1] it is certainly equally true that the intertribal relations of the aborigines were in the future to be decided almost wholly by the relations existing between them and the Europeans, especially in those areas in which the fur trade was the chief factor in those relations. On the question of land, the tribes could, and often did, cooperate, and yield or resist together, but the fur trade divided them immediately into groups—those who had fur and those who had none. The great desirability of the trade goods to the Indian who had once known them became shortly a necessity, a very urgent necessity that permitted no renunciation of the trade. As new desires wakened and old skills vanished, the Indian who had fur, or could get it, survived; he who could not get it died or moved away. But whatever he did, life for him could never again be what it had been: old institutions and economies had profoundly altered or disappeared completely at the electrifying touch of the white man's trade, which swept along the inland trails and rivers with bewildering speed and wrought social revolution a thousand miles beyond the white man's habitations, and years before he himself appeared on the scene. English powder burned on the Mississippi a half century before the English cabins reached Lake Ontario,[2] and the Ottawa tribe had fought a commercial war with the Winnebago of Wisconsin, forcing French trade goods upon them, ten years before the hesitant French settlement had reached Montreal.[3] In truth, the Indian world had in many respects already vanished before the white man saw it, and it is not strange that in his great hurry he formed opinions of it that were somewhat wide of the truth. Those who wonder at the foolishness of the Indians who fought each other to extinction instead of combining to stay the white man's advance are usually the same who attribute their intertribal wars to "insensate fury" and "homicidal frenzy."[4] Tribal motives must necessarily be mysterious to the historian who ignores the social and economic metamorphosis brought about by the trade.

The area in which the fur trade was most significant was the northeastern quarter of the continent, where two great waterways led through inhospitable mountains and highlands into a region which in the seventeenth century and long thereafter teemed with fur-bearers. The St. Lawrence-Ottawa and the Hudson-Mohawk routes led to the Great Lakes and the Mississippi-Ohio country, with their innumerable tributary streams where were to be found more beaver than in any similar area in the world. Commanding both these routes lay the Huron Iroquois, composed of a half dozen consanguine tribes which with the Algonquins of the upper St. Lawrence must have represented a population of nearly 100,000. Yet after only thirty years of intermittent warfare the Iroquois proper, probably the least numerous of the tribes, never numbering more than 12,000, were in sole possession of the region east of Lake Michigan, having dispersed, incorporated, or exterminated all their neighbours; they were even credited, though somewhat mistakenly, with a shadowy empire extending west to the Mississippi, and from Carolina to Hudson Bay. As to the importance of the Iroquois, it has been said that their steady alliance with the Dutch and English of the Hudson River colony was "the pivotal fact of early American history."[5]

With intertribal relations and activities centring as they did about the tribe most active in intertribal affairs, the Iroquois, the question, why did the Iroquois do the things that they did, becomes not only pertinent but vital to an understanding of colonial history. The answers thus far given by historians are three, none of which is in the least convincing.[6] The first of these is the theory that they were possessed of an "insensate fury" and "homicidal frenzy," a theory advanced by Parkman. The second is that a superior political organization, the League of the Iroquois, produced by a superior Iroquois intellect, rendered the Five Nations invincible. This thesis was propounded by Lewis H. Morgan, who even ascribed to the Iroquois the paradoxical motive of exterminating their enemies in order to establish universal intertribal peace.[7] To these may be added a third theory, that a great supply of firearms, furnished by the greedy Dutch West India Company and unavailable to their enemies, gave rein to a natural passion for conquest and butchery, which they indulged at random but with almost unimaginable enthusiasm.

Even a cursory contemplation of the generally known facts, however, will raise further questions. If a natural superiority or an innate fury was responsible, it is curious that neither of these traits was manifest in the very closely consanguine tribes, such as the Hurons, the Erie, the Neutrals, and others which the Iroquois conquered. Neither does this thesis explain why the naturally superior and ferocious Iroquois had fled from the Algonquins of the St. Lawrence in the years preceding the coming of Champlain, and were on the defensive, stockaded in invaded territory until after 1620. Even if there had been some virtues inherent in the Iroquois blood stream, that stream had changed very early and very completely, for as early as 1656 a priest found that there were more foreigners than natives in Iroquoia, eleven different nations being represented in the country of the Seneca.[8] In 1660 it would have been hard to find 1,200 Iroquois of pure blood, according to Lalemant, who anticipated Parkman by remarking, "It may be said that, if the Iroquois have any power, it is only because they are knavish and cruel."[9] Even the casual reader feels, after reviewing the achievements of the Iroquois, that knavery and cruelty could hardly have been the mainspring of their mighty and significant labours.

With respect to the great efficiency claimed for the League, a re-examination of only a few sources leads to the conclusion that in the period of Iroquois conquest the League was little if any more effectual in achieving unanimity of action than were the loose Powhatanic and Cherokee leagues, or even the Algonquin confederacy or the Choctaw republic. Despite the bluster of Mohawk orators, there is not a single recorded instance of unanimous or anywhere near unanimous action by the League prior to 1653, and none save in peace treaties thereafter. The Mohawk orators had a way, confusing to their enemies, as they well knew, of pretending, when on their own business, to speak for the League.[10] The habit has confused historians no less. Osgood, however, has recognized that the League could at best only prevent fratricidal strife among its members.[11] In any event, that result was achieved by the other, less celebrated, confederacies with more marked success than by the League of the Iroquois. The Hurons, for instance, kept peace with their Algonquin neighbors with no organization whatever, no ties of consanguinity, no common tongue or social institutions[12]—in fact, with nothing more in common than an economic interest—while throughout a series of five wars there was no such thing as unanimity among the Five Nations. Rarely did two of the cantons combine in an attack, and then only because their commercial interests were for the time identical. Never did two cantons combine for defense. Mohawks and Onondaga both cheered the French attack upon the Seneca, and Seneca and Onondaga were steadily antipathetic to the Mohawks, who, as the eastern canton, held the Hudson River country and the Dutch trade. The Mohawks sought ceaselessly to exploit their brothers, and were at swords' points with them half the time. All that prevented a vicious intra-Iroquois war was the fact that the common interest of all three in opposing the French and the French Indians was ever greater than their conflicting interests. At that, much Iroquois blood was spilled by Iroquois, and perhaps more embassies of peace travelled within Iroquoia than from Iroquoia to foreign tribes.

If all this is true, one may ask, why has the League been so celebrated by historians, and why has it for seventy-five years been given credit for accomplishing things it did not accomplish? The most important single reason is probably Lewis H. Morgan's book *The League of the Iroquois*. Morgan was a true scholar in spirit, a conscientious observer, and a tireless worker, but he was not a historian, and he had access to few or none of the sources which could have informed him on the history of the League he so carefully observed.[13] It is perhaps not strange that when he viewed the perfected League of 1850, knowing little of Iroquois history except tradition,[14] he should have assumed that the perfection of political organization he saw then was more than two centuries old. The League as he saw it in the nineteenth century offered a plausible explanation for a hitherto unexplained phenomenon of the seventeenth century, and without critical investigation it was temptingly easy to interchange result and cause. The very excellence of his general work unfortunately perpetuated this specific error, which was widely adopted by historians.[15] To those who read the sources, however, it becomes quite clear that the League as Morgan saw it did not wage the wars of the Iroquois nor make them possible, but that in a very real sense it was the wars that made the League which he and others were privileged to examine 200 years later. The League, then, cannot be an answer to the Iroquois problem.

In the matter of armament also, the assets of the Iroquois have been overstated. The 2,000 muskets which they are credited with having possessed in 1640[16] shrink upon investigation to a possible 400, and even this is probably too generous an estimate. In that year a French prisoner testified that a "heavily armed" war band of 500 Iroquois had exactly thirty-six arquebuses.[17] The supposed greed of the Dutch West India Company is called into serious question when it is discovered that they tried desperately to stop what trade in guns there was, and that both the Company and the settlement at Beverwyck passed and attempted to enforce ordinances against it, even going so far as to ordain the penalty of death. Among the Dutch on the Hudson and Connecticut the French were as bitterly accused of trading arms to Indians as were the Dutch in the French settlements on the St. Lawrence, and the justification was as ample in the one case as in the other. Moreover, the Susquehannah, whom the Iroquois conquered, were far better provided with arms than the Iroquois, possessing even artillery in their forts.

There is no denying that these conditions, to which is attributed the Iroquois phenomenon, existed in some measure and undoubtedly had an aggregate importance, but the fact still remains that although they were paralleled elsewhere, in fact were paralleled again and again all over the continent, the phenomenon itself was unparalleled. No other tribe ever did what the Iroquois did, and yet the three theories of inherent qualities, superior organization, and superior armament fail to explain their achievements or to suggest a motive which could have driven them so far and down so hard a road.

The explanation must lie in some fundamental condition which thus far has not received the attention of the relatively few students of Iroquois history. The search should be not for the ineluctable ultimate origin, but for a general condition of Indian life, readily ascertained and recognized, from which the motivation of the Iroquois should appear to proceed inevitably. Since this general condition was peculiar in its effect upon the Iroquois, it follows that unless the Iroquois were themselves peculiar, it must have some connection with geography or climate; and when it is recalled that the rise of the Iroquois to power coincided with the spread of the white trade throughout their region and the regions beyond them, a second inference follows, namely that some peculiarity of the Iroquois position and the spread of the white trade may well have combined to produce a motivation sufficiently powerful to drive the Iroquois through a half century of bloody intertribal conflict with their brother tribesmen, the closely related peoples that almost surrounded them. The inference gains in strength when it is recalled that throughout the wars there runs ceaselessly the theme of trade and commercial arrangement, and that even the merciless Indian oratory, punctuated by gifts made in frank expectation of counter-gifts, is wound tightly about a core of commercial negotiation—of proposal and counter-proposal.

Such wars as those of the Iroquois must have had not only an insistent motivation, but also a disastrous alternative, or at least an alternative that was regarded as disastrous by those who waged them. It is quite likely that if the white trade had become a social and economic necessity to them, their position had life and death as alternatives. That position would have permitted neither compromise nor inactivity, and would explain why their wars were the first truly national intertribal wars on the continent, there being now for the first time a truly national motive. It is possible that William C. Macleod may have struck the lost chord in intertribal relations when he wrote that "the same principles of economic science apply alike to the economy of modern Germany and of the Shoshone Digger Indians, or any like economic group."[18] If the Iroquois were either facing disaster or thought that they were, they may well have turned, as do "enlightened" nations, to war. What is true is never so important, historically, as what people think is true, and while it may be convincingly reasoned, with that keen hindsight which historians often call insight, that the Iroquois would have been better off economically had they done anything other than what they did, this reasoning need not mean that the ultimate facts were clear to the Iroquois or that their motive was not (perhaps mistakenly) economic.

The thesis that when the Iroquois made war on a national scale they did so with somewhat the same ends in view as have their Christian brothers, is admittedly attractive. Such a thesis, however, requires abundant and indisputable documentary evidence, if it aspires to solve the Iroquois problem.

Notes

1. George E. Ellis, "Indians of North America," in Justin Winsor, ed., *Narrative and Critical History of America* (8 vols., Boston and New York, 1884–89), 1:283.

2. The powder was burned by the Iroquois in their assault upon the Illinois in 1680. Oswego, the first English settlement on Lake Ontario, was founded in 1726.

3. Nicolas Perrot, *Memoir on the Manners, Customs, and Religion of the Savages of North America*, translated from the French by Emma H. Blair, in her *Indian Tribes of the Upper Mississippi Valley and Region of the Great Lakes* (Cleveland, 1911), 1:293. The date is not exact.

4. Francis Parkman, *The Jesuits in North America in the Seventeenth Century (France and England in North America*, pt. 2, Boston, 1867), 434, 444, 447; John A. Doyle, *Virginia, Maryland, and the Carolinas (English Colonies in America*, vol. 1, New York, 1882), 13–14. Doyle merely remarks upon the suicidal feuds and what the Indians could have done if they had united; he does not comment on the reason for the disunity. Parkman, in his *La Salle and the Discovery of the Great West* (12th ed., Boston, 1892), 204, again ascribes their actions to "homicidal fury," though he admits that once, in 1680, "strange as it may seem," there appeared to be another motive.

5. John Fiske, *The Dutch and Quaker Colonies in America* (2 vols., Boston, 1899), 2:172. For representative opinions see Frederic L. Paxson, *History of the American Frontier* (New York, 1924), 52; Herbert L. Osgood, *The American Colonies in the Seventeenth Century* (3 vols., New York, 1907), 1:420–421; Lewis H. Morgan, *League of the Ho-dé-no-sau-nee, or Iroquois* (new edition, edited by Herbert M. Lloyd, New York, 1904), II; Parkman, *Jesuits in North America*, 447; "Governor Dongan's Report on the State of the Province," in Edmund B. O'Callaghan, ed., *Documents Relative to the Colonial History of the State of New York* (15 vols., Albany, 1853–87), 3:393; "M. Du Chesneau's Memoir on the Western Indians," *ibid.*, 9:165; Andrew M. Davis, "Canada and Louisiana," in Winsor, *Narrative and Critical History*, 45:2.

6. For a critical estimate of the literature on the subject see page 185.

7. *League of the Iroquois,* 72.

8. Reuben G. Thwaites, ed., *The Jesuit Relations and Allied Documents* (73 vols., Cleveland, 1896–1901), 43:265.

9. *Ibid.*, 45:207, 211.

10. See, for example, Kiotsaeton to the Governor, in *Jesuit Relations*, 17:253: "Onontio, lend me ear. I am the mouth for the whole of my country; thou listeneth to all the Iroquois in hearing my words"; this when he had to return to his own country to get ratification for a peace concerning only his own people. See also Grangula to La Barre, in Louis A. Lahontan, *New Voyages to North-America*, edited by Reuben G. Thwaites (2 vols., Chicago, 1905), 1:82–83, 85. There are many more examples.

11. Osgood, *American Colonies*, 2:420–422; Parkman, *Jesuits in North America*, 344; John A. Doyle, *The Middle Colonies (English Colonies in America*, vol. 4, New York, 1907), 119.

12. See below, Chapters 3 and 4.

13. When Morgan wrote his *League of the Iroquois*, the *New York Colonial Documents* were only in the process of publication, and the *Jesuit Relations* were also as yet unpublished, so he took his background from Cadwallader Colden, who probably knew less about the subject than Morgan himself. For a discussion of Colden's work see below, page 185.

14. A great deal of nonsense has been written about the reliability of Indian tradition in factual matters. Charles Eastman was a full-blood Sioux, and his *Indian Heroes and Great Chieftains* is written mainly from information obtained directly from the older people of his tribe, but George E. Hyde, after checking it with known facts, says that "it presents a spectacle of poor and distorted memory that is appalling, as nearly every date and statement of fact is incorrect." *Red Cloud's Folk* (Norman, Oklahoma, 1937), 54. See also pages viii, ix, and 60 for other cases in point. Mr. Hyde is one of the regrettably few writers in the field of Indian history who has his feet on the ground, and who deals with source material in a scientific manner.

15. It was adopted by both Parkman and Fiske, and it influenced Channing, Doyle, and Turner. The youthful Turner writes, in his doctoral dissertation, that "thus by priority in securing firearms, as well as by their remarkable civil organization," did the Iroquois rise to power, citing Morgan directly. *The Early Writings of Frederick Jackson Turner* (University of Wisconsin Press, 1938), 97.

16. Louise P. Kellogg, *The French Régime in Wisconsin and the Northwest* (Madison, 1925), 85.

17. Testimony of Marguerie, transcribed by Le Jeune, in the *Jesuit Relations*, 21:37.

18. *The Origin of the State Reconsidered in the Light of the Data of Aboriginal North America* (Philadelphia, 1924), 41–42.

CONCLUSION From *Friend and Foe*

Cornelius J. Jaenan

The French established contact with the Amerindians on a casual basis through the Newfoundland fisheries as early as the fifteenth century, and probably earlier. In the sixteenth century, voyages of so-called discovery and abortive colonization schemes further acquainted the French with the aborigines whom the Spaniards and Portuguese were in the process of subjugating and exploiting. Swarthy American natives were taken as curios of the New World to be displayed in various public spectacles in Western Europe, raising disquieting theological and scientific questions.

In general, the French were less involved than their neighbours in great controversies about the origins of the American aborigines, their nature, and the possible sources of their civilizations. Indeed, Frenchmen did not contact the same highly developed Amerindian civilizations as did the Spaniards in Central and South America. The French judged the Amerindians in terms of their religious beliefs and their degree of civility. Just as there was no doubt that the tribes were heathen, so there was no doubt that, in terms of the classical distinction between Greeks and barbarians, they were also barbarians. These heathen barbarians were rough and unpolished, to be sure, but views differed as to whether they were men in savage and degenerate form, the prototype of the wild man, or whether they were primitive men without benefit of religion and social institutions. Montaigne observed that "everyone calls barbarian what is his own usage." In whatever way Amerindians were viewed, the consensus was definitely that they were unpolished *sauvages*, and therefore presented a challenge to Frenchmen to civilize them and impart to them the religion, arts and culture of Europe's leading civilization.

One of the early reactions was to equate the Amerindian societies with the lost Paradise of their literary and philosophical tradition. The liberty, equality and fraternity which travellers and missionaries, at least those who tended to

From *Friend and Foe: Aspects of French-Amerindian Cultural Contact in the Sixteenth and Seventeenth Centuries* (Toronto: McClelland and Stewart, 1976), 190–97. Reprinted by permission of the author.

be critical of their own society, reported in America provided a very powerful criticism of contemporary France. The Amerindians were apparently proof that Christian Europe did not have a monopoly on goodness and rationality. Those who looked for noble savages or native utopias as a means to criticize and castigate contemporary French manners, morals and government were well served. These precursors of the eighteenth-century deists and rationalists were, however, a minority whose influence must not be exaggerated.

The French discovery of America brought together many threads to form a twisted skein of perceptions of the New World and its peoples. Theories of lost continents and prehistoric migrations, mingled with myths of concurrent creations and cataclysmic displacements of populations, these in turn being overlaid by tales of fabled isles and monstrous lands given over to the devil, fed the imaginative and beckoned the venturesome. Religious revivalism, pious mysticism and eschatological undercurrents in France raised hopes of ushering in the millenial age, of building the spiritual church and New Jerusalem in the New World. From the excitement of early contact in the sixteenth and seventeenth centuries—for the fishermen never revealed their earlier experiences or their fishing grounds—and the contradictory reports of explorers and exploiters, there emerged a dominant French view of the world and of themselves which stood in sharp contrast to the views of the Amerindians.

Although there was a strain of romantic primitivism, the dominant French view of man was that he was a changer and overseer of nature: a husbandman, a builder, an inventor, a domesticator, a civilizer. As a steward of God in his relationship to other forms of life his normal and divinely ordained role was to change and control by his arts and his technology. Frenchmen regarded their intervention in nature as purposive. The Amerindians, on the other hand, saw themselves as having a contractual or symbiotic relationship with the forces of nature. The contractual relationships of the French were to various authorities—to God, to the king, to the *seigneur*, to the religious superior, to the monopolist. Amerindians saw themselves and their tribal society as a product of nature and they acknowledged this in the names they assigned their tribes and bands. The Amerindians saw themselves as intimately dependent on nature, while the French saw themselves as superior to nature, as destined to dominate it and to bend its forces to their own objectives and aspirations. Progress in French eyes consisted of manipulating, controlling and subordinating nature and society more and more to man's initiative and enterprise. Insofar as religion and nature were intimately related, Amerindian society was more theocentric than was French society in the seventeenth century.

All in all, the French experience differed markedly from the Spanish or English encounters in day-to-day relations with the aborigines. The conceptual frameworks of all Europeans closely resembled each other, whether they classified themselves as Latins or Anglo-Saxons, as Catholics or Protestants. When the contact with Amerindians did not involve displacing the native peoples or extensive European immigration, which was the French experience as contrasted to the English and Spanish experiences, relations remained friendly. Cooperation and intercourse resulted in a certain degree of interdependence and created an impression of successful accommodation and acculturation. Such impressions were superficial observations neglecting the deeper evidences of social disorganization. The fact that the British, who had such a poor reputation in cultural contact in the Anglo-American colonies, assumed and appropriated the apparently friendly French relationship with the tribesmen after the conquest of Canada and the American Revolution suggests the need for an environmental approach to the question of culture clash. The French contact experience with the sedentary agricultural Iroquoian tribes had been less amicable than had their contact with nomadic Algonkian tribes. In the seventeenth century, the Amerindians seem to have stereotyped the Englishman as a farmer or town-dweller whose activities gradually drove the original agriculturalists deeper into the hinterland, whereas the stereotype of the Frenchman was a trader or soldier laden with baubles and brandy who asked only for furs and hospitality.

These comparatively more amicable relations between Frenchmen and Amerindians resulted in more credence being given in France to the good qualities of native life. The view that they were filthy, depraved barbarians never became a dominant and obsessive view with the French, although it was always present as an undercurrent and occasionally surfaced as in the reaction to the so-called Iroquois scourge. When goodness and virtue were accepted as possible in aboriginal societies a number of purposes might be served: those who sought the lost Paradise found in America a hope of restoring it; those who deplored the evils of sophisticated civilization found in America the noble savages; those who chafed at political oppression and bureaucratic corruption saw in America a land of freedom and opportunity; those who wearied of religious turpitude and theological strife caught a vision of the New Israel in the New World and the imminent end of the world. But those who lived and worked in New France came to believe more in the New World of their own experience than in the America invented by the metropolitan French.

Frenchmen, as a result of contact with primitive peoples, were more convinced that they stood at the pinnacle of civilization. Their society, despite some defects such as religious wars, famines, rural unrest and unemployment, and bureaucratic corruption, was an orderly, rational and Christian one, which all peoples everywhere ought to adopt and emulate if they wished to progress and elevate themselves. Although the French did not discriminate against the Amerindians on strictly racial grounds, they did by their somatic norm image consider them inferior and infantile. Native barbarism and cruelty, which must be seen in the Amerindian religious and social context to be understood, was an important factor in the literature on captivity and the creation of a stereotype of cruel savages. This literary tradition and popular stereotype were largely responsible for later discrimination against the aboriginal peoples in both Canada and the United States.

The Amerindians, for their part, had their own somatic norm image in which Frenchmen were regarded as ugly, effeminate, weak, disorganized, improvident, excitable, domineering, and quite inconsistent in applying their ideals to their everyday living. The French regarded Amerindian societies as devoid of spirituality and basic religious concepts, but it turned out that native society was as religiously oriented as European society. Indeed, many of the aspects of Amerindian life which the French were slow to comprehend—torture of captives, significance of dreams, resistance to conversion—were spiritually based. In the final analysis, it was sometimes French Catholic society that emerged as this-worldly, materialistic and superstitious. True conversion for the Amerindians meant a renunciation of their culture and a loss of their identity, a fact which the French missionaries and civil officials, without realizing the full implications of social disorganization, found quite normal because the French and Catholic qualities of their own civilization were rarely dissociated or conceived as separable.

The fact that the continent was not an empty wilderness but a populated expanse required some accommodation with its inhabitants, and some state policy of occupation. The French response to this challenge came at two levels—the spiritual and the temporal. First, the Amerindians would have to be evangelized and take their place with the Christians of France. Secondly and concurrently, they would have to be assimilated into French society by a process of Frenchification and civilization. As conversion soon proved to be a very disruptive experience in the native communities, religious conversion and cultural assimilation became more closely entwined. Unless the whole community converted and the whole apparatus of French institutions and life-style were adopted, divisions became acrimonious, reversion was likely, and social disorganization always ensued.

In their contacts the French came to sense, although they never fully comprehended or openly acknowledged, that Amerindian societies were well-integrated units. Education, for example, was fully integrated into everyday living. Therefore, French attempts to introduce formal schooling as a means of civilizing and converting the natives cut across traditional belief systems, values, institutional forms and band aspirations. No two societies could have differed more in their conceptual frameworks than did the European and Amerindian. Religion also permeated all aspects of native life, probably to a greater extent than religion permeated French life because the French, unlike the Amerindians, did not always allow their religious convictions to interfere with their economic mores, their warfare, or their personal behaviour. Because the Amerindians sought to live in tune with nature and their religious perceptions, Catholicism as a new religion could only be a disruptive innovation undermining their spiritual concepts as well as their entire way of life, their value systems, and their moral assumptions.

The French considered the Algonkian nomadic peoples as idlers and vagabonds because they were not sedentary agriculturalists or village craftsmen; conversely, the natives occasionally were only too well informed about poverty and lower-class conditions in France. Amerindian concepts of communal property, hunting territories and kinship responsibilities found no precise equivalents in French views of property rights, legal jurisdictions, contractual agreements, monopolies and sovereignty. There was no common theoretical ground for accommodation. They did not clash, however, because they remained largely isolated and separated from each other. The French towns and *seigneuries* formed a riparian colony, whereas the majority of the Amerindians, except a small number of domiciled converts resettled on reservations, inhabited the hinterlands. Because of this physical separation, there were few if any confrontations or contests about property rights or civil jurisdiction.

The French in their contacts with the natives admired their ability to grapple with problems in a resourceful manner and often abandoned their abstract speculation to adopt native ways. This utilitarianism, born of a long experience in North America, did not conform to French concepts of artisanal organization, seigneurial subservience, or military logistics, but it gradually became one of the acquired qualities that distinguished a Canadian *habitant* from a metropolitan Frenchman. The superiority of European technology had profound consequences for the Amerindians. As their hunting and warfare became more effective and their artifacts became more sophisticated, their demands grew and correspondingly their dependence on the Europeans increased both for supplies and repairs. Interdependence developed between native hunter and French trader, between native canoeman and French soldier, between native catechist and French missionary.

The French contact experience does suggest that the behavioural patterns routinized and institutionalized among the aborigines were rational, at least in the sense that they applied the best available techniques to the resources at hand in order to obtain the greatest benefit and use from them. There is also another conclusion that clearly emerges. Traditional societies cannot respond so readily to external challenges to their institutional system. Since the French were more adaptable than the Amerindians, the transfer of French institutions to North America also involved a transformation as well as a transplantation. It was the French who gained most from the cultural contacts of the seventeenth century. The French learned new techniques for building, travelling, dressing, fighting, food-gathering and survival in the wilderness. They acquired new foods and medicines. They brought new areas under their domination and new peoples in contact with their trade and religion. French society was sufficiently cohesive and stable to absorb new elements while remaining basically itself. Amerindian societies, on the other hand, often became disorganized as a result of cultural contact and too frequently exhibited the worst elements adopted from French culture.

French culture in New France, however, lacked sufficient men, materials and money to act effectively as a host society for the assimilation of the socially disorganized Amerindians. The great failure of the French in seventeenth-century

America was their inability to integrate the native peoples in appreciable numbers into a new social order, thereby overcoming the continuing stresses of cultural clash and the nefarious consequences of social disorganization. As officials of church and state came to realize by 1685, their relatively insignificant and insecure colony could not acculturate the Amerindians. The French were unable to exert the kind of social control necessary to stamp out the brandy traffic or to prevent the exodus of *coureurs-de-bois* each year to the *pays d'en haut*. They could not, therefore, hope to exert much control over the vast territories in which their traders, soldiers and missionaries lived more as guests and dependents of the natives than as representatives of a ruling power.

What was the effect of cultural differences among Amerindian tribes when contact with the French influenced their traditional way of life? All the tribes contacted by the French showed a certain traditional inertia, an adherence to their ancestral beliefs and conceptualization. To live on good terms with the different tribes the French had to accept a degree of coexistence, which meant renouncing any plan of immediate assimilation of the natives. It was essential to accommodate a certain resistance, both conscious and subconscious and rooted in native religion, on the part of the Amerindians. The aborigines developed counter-innovative techniques when they sensed that their traditional society was threatened by the French intrusion. It was in this aspect of contact that the cultural differences emerged between nomadic and sedentary tribes, and between animists and polytheists. The more advanced Amerindian cultures assimilated more rapidly than the less advanced tribes, but they were also better able to preserve their traditional belief system and social organization. It was the less advanced, northern and eastern, nomadic Algonkian-speaking tribes who were most disorganized in the face of contact and who showed the most signs of social disintegration and cultural confusion.

Numerous Amerindians became zealous Catholics, some to the point of demonstrating excessive zeal in their self-mortifications and adorations, and some of them made genuine efforts to take up French agricultural life on the reservations administered for the state by the missionary clergy. But this should not obscure the evidence that the economic and social problems arising out of French competitive pressures, the new religious divisions, the inroads of drunkenness and diseases of epidemic proportions, and the introduction of a new technology were not resolved. The converted and resettled natives were no more immune than those who continued to hold to their traditional beliefs and lifestyle. Neither conversion nor resettlement seemed to reduce appreciably the cultural conflicts that engulfed their whole society.

Assimilation meant the adoption of a new belief and value system and the setting of new limits for behaviour. It meant that actions and thoughts considered good and moral in their traditional society might be censured in French society, and that sometimes what was formerly censured might now be permissible or approved. The problems attendant on assimilation arose out of the process of change and the admixture of beliefs and values, and often resulted in the confusion of individuals and whole societies. Assimilation efforts seemed essentially to produce dislocation; they were a breaking-down process in order to reconstruct a new order. But by attacking the value system of Amerindian societies in order to replace it with a new value system, the entire integrated way of life was upset, including folklore, religion and occupational patterns. As ambiguities and inconsistencies marked the changes, it was not unusual to find rather bizarre patterns of behaviour. Personal and social demoralization seemed to be reflected in alcohol addiction which became the curse, and often the identifying characteristic, of Amerindian communities.

Acculturation is a two-way process. The French were affected by contact too. When any culture is transplanted it changes and varies, but such adaptations are more marked when the society comes into contact and into conflict with other cultures. There follows an exchange and interaction of cultures which can, theoretically, enrich or impoverish both. Cultural *métissage* results, out of which a new culture can emerge. In a limited way, this is what began to occur in New France in the seventeenth century. The Amerindian societies were undermined and disoriented in several respects, as has been shown, without at the same time being afforded an opportunity to reorganize and consolidate themselves into Euro-Amerindian cultures. The French, on the other hand, did begin to develop a distinctive Canadian culture from a French Renaissance base, which was somewhat changed in both form and spirit by the North American environment and experience, and which was greatly enriched by and made the beneficiary of the centuries-old Amerindian experience in North America.

In the French experience, as in the Amerindian, paradoxes were to be found. The highest aboriginal civilizations were those which assimilated most readily to European society, but were also those best-equipped to retain their ancestral beliefs and social structures and so resist losing their identity. In French society, the paradox was that in the seminal development of a distinctive Canadian-French culture, owing much to transplantation and to contact with the Amerindians, the efforts to mould the colony in the image of metropolitan France increased with the passing of time. The optimum condition to assert an independent identity passed in the early phase of resource exploitation, missionary dominance, and social disorganization, but as the colony grew older and stronger efforts were made to fashion it more and more in the traditional cadres of the absolute monarchy, the Gallican church, mercantilism, and seigneurialism. A result of the important contacts with the indigenous tribes of New France—contacts which absorbed much evangelical zeal, which sustained the economy, and which threatened or assured military and political survival—was a growing Canadian ethnocentrism. The colonists turned to their culture, particularly their religion, as a source of identity. There they found a sense of stability and security. As New France became more like Old France it follows that the cultural gap between French and Amerindian widened rather than closed.

THE DESTRUCTION OF HURONIA

Georges E. Sioui

In recent decades, a certain number of researchers have been critically examining George T. Hunt's theory that the Iroquois waged war for economic reasons. For Bruce G. Trigger, there is both a cultural and an economic dimension to the matter: he maintains that because the Five Nations did not possess the entrepreneurial tradition of the Wendat, they tried to increase their trading power by acquiring new hunting territories rather than trade routes.

Most recent studies, however, are closer to the older, so-called "cultural" theory advanced in the writings of Francis Parkman, which attributed the wars waged by the Iroquois on so many other Amerindians to an enmity that, under certain favourable conditions (for example, the European invasion), would lead to the annihilation of one party.

In addition, revision of the earliest Amerindian demographic data has led other investigators to explain the nature of these conflicts differently. One of these, Wichita University historian Karl H. Schlesier, in a discussion of the "legend" of Amerindian middlemen, says that "the Iroquois never attempted to become middlemen in the fur trade: neither did other Indian tribes, including the Huron or Ottawa. They all were touched by far more powerful forces than European trade goods."[1] He explains that "smallpox (the main epidemic disease brought from the Old World) emerges as the most significant among those forces. Much of the historical and ethnological literature before and after Hunt propounds biases which not only do injustice to the Iroquois, but prevent a deeper understanding of the historical truth."[2] Most authors still present what we call "the myth of economic war," attributing to Native peoples on the brink of disaster the motives, interests, and intentions of people leading a normal existence. In fact, all Amerindians were waging desperate cultural war on an invader whose pathogenic allies made his very presence a disaster.

Interpreting the Facts According to Autohistory

Louis Hall Karaniaktajeh, a Mohawk artist and philosopher from Kahnawake, sums up the Amerindian's feelings about history with bitter-sweet humour: "Twistory," he says, "is written in such a way that you think that they [the colonizers] are heroes. They're out there plundering Indian land and looting, but it's their right, their God-given right ... and the Indians are not supposed to do anything about it, they're supposed to like it; they're supposed to even help the writers of these history books to plunder them."[3]

From *For an Amerindian Autohistory: An Essay on the Foundations of a Social Ethic*, trans. Sheila Fischman (Montreal and Kingston: McGill-Queen's University Press, 1992), 39–60, 118–20. Reprinted by permission of McGill-Queen's University Press.

Of all Amerindians, the Iroquois are those who have least wanted "to help" the Europeans to "plunder" them, and for that very reason they spread terror and animosity among the first generations of Europeans to establish themselves in north-eastern North America.

"The good Hurons were destroyed by the wicked Iroquois," we were led to believe from the time we were old enough to absorb prejudices, in order to distract an entire society from the real story of the grabbing of Amerindian land.

Always bearing in mind that microbes, not men, determined this continent's history, we shall use data provided by our Amerindian autohistorical analysis to try to elucidate the circumstances that enabled Europeans to destroy the order Amerindians had established for countless generations.

In 1492, the Wendat were situated geopolitically at the centre of a very important society of Amerindian nations. Wendake (the Wendat country) was the heartland that was the origin and focus of the main trade networks linking this vast extended family of societies, whose spirit perfectly reflected the Amerindian's social ideal: interdependence and redistribution around the common circle.

We may assume that communications networks in the original Amerindian world, free of national boundaries, while they were far less rapid than today's, were functional and reliable, and that news about the Spanish military and epidemiological devastations reached the northern peoples after a few years at most.

In 1498, the Italian John Cabot reported having visited Nova Scotia and Labrador, while in 1501 the Portuguese Gaspar Corte-Real captured fifty-seven Amerindians, probably Beothuks. When Jacques Cartier arrived in 1534, the Amerindians had already suffered from epidemic diseases brought by Europeans.

Some recent opinions, even when well-supported, do not sufficiently recognize the terrifying consequences for Amerindians of the Europeans' arrival. In "European Contact and Indian Depopulation in the North-East: The Timing of the First Epidemics," Dean Snow and Kim M. Lanphear attempt to invalidate the hypothesis put forward by Henry F. Dobyns in *Their Number Become Thinned*, where he postulates on pandemics in the north-east during the sixteenth century. Moreover, they also appear to dismiss three fundamental considerations:

- First, while inland peoples such as the Mohawk—living in what is now the state of New York—could defend themselves against epidemics, coastal nations such as the St. Lawrence Wendat-Iroquois, the Mi'kmaq, and the Montagnais, who inevitably came into contact with European crews, could not. In fact, while no ship went up the St. Lawrence to Stadacona (now Quebec) before Jacques Cartier, a good number certainly did so during the rest of the sixteenth century.

- Secondly, the epidemic that ravaged Stadacona during the winter of 1535–36 (and that may well have had more than the fifty victims Cartier reports) was undoubtedly not the only one that occurred over the 115 years between the arrival of the first ships in the Gulf of St. Lawrence around 1500 and the first "official" epidemic of 1616.

• Thirdly, both the very nature of the culture and way of life of these Amerindian societies, that is, their close union and the uniformity of their cosmo-political conception, encouraged the spread of contagious diseases.

Once these elements are considered, it is likely that the St. Lawrence Wendat-Iroquois disappeared in the sixteenth century because of the epidemics that raged in the St. Lawrence valley before the beginning of the seventeenth century.

In other words, depopulation of the northern part of North America had already begun in the sixteenth century, probably spreading panic through Amerindian society at large. Taioagny and Domagaya, the two sons of Donnacona, the "*seigneur* of Canada," made a forced journey to France in 1534, returning in 1535. Cartier thought that he could use them to disorganize the Amerindian country, but as it turned out they bore him a barely concealed suspicion. Better than anyone, these chief's sons were aware of the danger. Cartier left after having defied the Amerindian order, spurned their advice (which cost the lives of twenty-five members of his crew who, unprepared for the Canadian climate, died of scurvy at the beginning of winter), and captured the father of the two young men along with nine other members of their family, including at least one young girl.

While it is certain that the bulk of pre-contact Amerindian society did not live in perfect, constant harmony, archaeology informs us that those Amerindians did not experience significant conflicts, likely because they had the ideological and social means to maintain relative peace among themselves. "In every case," writes archaeologist James A. Tuck, "village and tribal movements A.D. 1000–1500 are devoid of drastic population shifts, conquests and the annihilation of whole prehistoric populations."[4]

It is very likely that the Wendat-Iroquois migrated north from southern countries, taking root fairly recently at the heart of the Algonquian world. Their way of life—they were farmers and traders with a remarkable gift for political organization—had enabled them, long before the Europeans arrived, to establish particularly harmonious relations with other nations. History and even prehistory prove beyond a doubt that the vast majority of the Algonquian nations had long since assigned the Wendat confederation a key role in the political, commercial, cultural, and religious sectors of a vast and strategically located territory.

It appears that at the time of European contact, the confederacy of the Five Nations Iroquois was the only one not yet integrated into this extensive trading system. Ironically, the people who originally were probably the least numerous and geopolitically the most marginal were the only ones able to resist the invader and provide a refuge for the survivors of previously stronger nations. In that way, the ideology common to all aboriginal nations was able to survive.

There is every reason to believe that the decimated residents of Stadacona, led to Wendake by Donnacona's descendants, as revealed by archaeology[5]— tried once they were resettled there to persuade the Wendats to form a great league of nations. It is conceivable that the central idea was open resistance to the pale and dangerous visitors and that, frustrated at having been ignored, a certain "prophet" named Deganawidah, a member of that ideological clan, had taken his message to the Iroquois nations. The latter, located outside the great Wendat trading network and thus spared the task of facing the Europeans head-on, were more receptive to the message.

According to Iroquois tradition, it was a Wendat—one "whose people had not wanted to listen to him"—who disclosed the prophetic message about the need to form the Iroquois league.

Most of the speculations by Elizabeth Tooker as to when the Iroquois confederacy was founded place it around 1540 to 1590, a period that corresponds fairly closely to the Wendat-Iroquoian exodus to Huronia.

In any case, the Wendat were traditionally considered as standard-bearers for the Amerindian ideology which claims that, if the world is to be and to remain what it is, it must be founded on communication and exchange between humans of all origins. The vision of a prophet of the resistance, no matter how enlightened, can never take ascendancy over the ideology of a society of nations that groups together hundreds of thousands of individuals, one that has always been nurtured at the inspiring, appeasing sources of the great circle.

In 1894, the historian J.N.B. Hewitt pointed out that "no league or confederation of peoples was perhaps ever formed without a sufficient motive in the nature of outside pressure."[6] We may assume that the Wendat, because of the refugees they took in by virtue of a clear cultural kinship (for example, the Stadaconans), or adopted, apparently by force (as seems to have been the case for at least part of the Hochelagans[7]), felt the need to reform their confederacy before the Five Nations Iroquois did, and this led to the consolidation of the Iroquois confederacy. As the Wendat were chiefs of the great Amerindian society of the north-east, they inevitably devised a union that was centred on trade. Naturally there was a place in it for the French and other Europeans, despite the disastrous consequences of their coming: it lasted about half a century, if we bear in mind that a pandemic in 1520 to 1524 had "almost certainly reached the Seneca"[8] and other neighbours of the Wendat long before its European carriers arrived, and that yet another, between 1564 and 1570, had made them abandon some of their villages.

The Iroquois, realizing the extent of the disaster, opted for defence. By allying themselves against the French-Amerindian force, they now declared their dissidence from prehistoric political and trading organization. The Iroquois made the difficult but inevitable decision to embark upon a war they knew would be very long and destructive, and whose logic was utterly foreign to Amerindian thinking.

According to Amerindian cultural logic, the Iroquois were the north-eastern nations best situated to resist the invasion, although they had virtually no chance of succeeding. Consequently, the Iroquois nations were no longer "the worst of all savages" or "the Indians of Indians" as they have so often been called. Instead, they were an extremely valorous people who, to enable the Amerindian race to survive, had to fight against the European powers, forcibly adopting nations that were already gravely decimated. For the Iroquois, the goal of this war was to extinguish the power of strangers in the way one extinguishes a raging fire. With extraordinary strength of character, they had to eliminate part of their own race so as to save it.

To explain the Iroquois' political offensive in relation to the French, historian John A. Dickinson quotes ethnohistorian Bruce G. Trigger: "The majority of Huron were killed or captured as a result of the general warfare that was going on between the Mohawk and the French; however, the emphasis that the Mohawk placed on capturing Huron prisoners reflected their long-term ambition to incorporate all of the Huron who had come to Quebec into their own society or, failing this, to kill them." "Thus," Dickinson observes, "the French would be deprived of allies."[9] He concludes by stating that when the Iroquois attacked Long Sault, they did not intend to destroy the colony by massacring settlers, but to paralyze it by abducting most of the remaining Huron warriors—mercenaries in the service of New France. "If the [Iroquois] army went up the Ottawa River," Dickinson explains,

> it is because their goal was to take Annaotaha [the chief of the Hurons] and his companions; Dollard's band was completely outside the Iroquois' preoccupations. For seven years, the Iroquois had been trying by every means possible to destroy [that is, to take away from the French] the whole Huron colony and here, at long last, was the chance to do it. Marie de l'Incarnation was amazed that the enemy's army was content with "so few people," but the reason is that this small group was the quarry the Iroquois had been looking for. For the Iroquois, the meaning of Long Sault was not the defeat of the seventeen Frenchmen, but the annihilation of the remaining Huron warriors. For them, it was a great victory.[10]

In the final analysis, both the Wendat and the Iroquois realized that they could not unite, because of the age-old order of the country. The Wendat noted impassively that the end was rapidly approaching. They would never accept the numerous peace overtures by their Iroquois cousins, nor would they make the choice—which seemed to the Jesuits so logical—of eliminating those priests who "established themselves in the heart of the Country [Wendake] to better bring about its ruin."[11] The Wendat, like any people, were ineluctably caught in the logic of their civilization. They had to trade until the end, like beavers who will get caught in traps until they are extinct: they were victims of their own nature.

The historiographic concept of "the destruction of Huronia by the Iroquois" is an axiom in the traditional history of the north-east that justifies North American sociopolitical attitudes. In the light of Amerindian autohistory, this cliché becomes an example of the manipulation of history, absolving Europe (particularly France) of the destruction of the most politically significant aboriginal people north of Mexico, a people who best represented the Amerindian interethnic fabric in north-eastern North America. This is a spectacular historic fraud: responsibility for the sociodemographic calamity in the north-east is assigned not to microbes, but to the Iroquois.

Karl H. Schlesier refers us to the Jesuits' pitiful descriptions of the Wendat and other nations in 1640, after several successive epidemics:

> Disease, war and famine are the three scourges with which God has been pleased to smite our Neophytes since they have commenced to adore him, and to submit to his Laws …. All these events have so greatly thinned the number of our Savages that, where eight years ago one could see eighty or a hundred cabins, barely five or six now can be seen; a Captain, who then had 800 warriors under his command, now has not more than thirty or forty; instead of fleets of three or four hundred canoes, we see now but twenty or thirty. And the Pitiful part of it is, that these remnants of Nations consist almost entirely of Women.[12]

Later, Schlesier asks, "Where after these tremendous losses, are the men supposed to have come from to fight continuous wars during this period? … These wars sprung only from the imagination of scholars."[13]

Traditional Amerindian Values of the Wendat-Iroquois in Lafitau's Time

Our twofold aim here is an historical rehabilitation of the Iroquois, and a demonstration of their profound adherence to the Amerindian value system. Even if the defensive action of the Five Nations towards the Europeans—particularly the French—was basically a fight to the finish between two civilizations, the Iroquois continued to live according to essential Amerindian values. From what we know of the present vitality of Amerindian social consciousness, we can study a particularly revealing description of Iroquois (and, in secondary fashion, Wendat) cultural consciousness at the beginning of the eighteenth century, left by the Jesuit Joseph-François Lafitau.

This missionary, who lived among the Wendat and then among the Iroquois, knew these peoples intimately. His *Customs of the American Indians* is an unusually valuable account of their philosophy and spirituality.

Lafitau, whose church was facing a rise in religious skepticism, drew from the Amerindian peoples a series of arguments to support a thesis of many contemporary theologians concerning the innate existence of a religious sense in man. For thinkers of the time, the "*sauvages amériquains*" were "the humans who show themselves in the most simple form in which they can be conceived to exist."

To an informed modern reader, Lafitau's work may seem to go beyond his original objective. In reality, he contributed to alleviating the Amerindians' crushing historical burden and was one of the rare individuals who conceded them any right to survival. Moreover, Lafitau's work provides a solid mass of arguments and evidence that help restore dignity to the people descended from the "savage" nations Lafitau describes. Even more, he enables modern men and women to acquire or rediscover respect and a salutary admiration for human nature.

"Deganawidah [founder of the league of the Iroquois] brought a message of peace, say the contemporary Iroquois ... . He devised the means of lifting up men's minds with the condolence ritual [addressing the emotions in order to attain reason], which provided for paying presents to the aggrieved. The same ceremony on a broader scale took former enemies into a network of alliances."[14]

The contemporary Seneca historian John Mohawk helps us penetrate deeper inside Iroquois thinking about their confederacy. He stresses the importance in Iroquois society of the development of oratorical art, since for them as for all Amerindians, no one has arbitrary power over any other person. Hence the importance of the art of persuasion. For John Mohawk, the "greatness" of the confederacy of the Five Nations comes from its high development of this art. He adds:

> This greatness [of the oratorical art] is the very idea of the Hodenosaunee: all human beings possess the power of rational thought; all human beings can think; all human beings have the same kinds of needs; all human beings want what is good for society; all human beings want Peace .... Out of that idea will come the power ... that will make the people of the Five Nations among the most influential thinkers in the history of human thought .... The basic fundamental truth contained in that idea is that so long as we believe that everybody in the world has the power to think rationally, we can negotiate with them to a position of Peace.[15]

Almost three centuries ago, Lafitau, like all contemporary observers of Amerindian society, emphasized how the Wendat and the Iroquois kept order in their councils. He was impressed by their confidence (which they still possess today) in the human's capacity for rational thought, provided that society respected individuality. "In general, we may say that they are more patient than we in examining all the consequences and results of a matter. They listen to one another more quietly, show more deference and courtesy towards people who express opinions opposed to theirs, not knowing what it is to cut a speaker off short, still less to dispute heatedly: they have more coolness, less passion, at least to all appearances, and bear themselves with more zeal for the public welfare."[16]

Faced with the Amerindians' choice of gentle persuasion in their relations with their fellows, as opposed to the coercive modes of European societies, Lafitau experienced the same sense of wonder as European chroniclers of all times:

> While the petty chiefs of the monarchical states have themselves borne on their subjects' shoulders and have many duties paid them, they have neither distinctive mark, nor crown nor sceptre nor consular axes to differentiate them from the common people. Their power does not appear to have any trace of absolutism. It seems that they have no means of coercion to command obedience in case of resistance. They are obeyed, however, and command with authority;

their commands, given as requests, and the obedience paid them, appear entirely free .... Good order is kept by this means; and in the execution of things, there is found a mutual adaptation of chiefs and members of society and a hierarchy such as could be desired in the best regulated state.[17]

By observing some of the social traits noted by Lafitau, we can better understand how the integrity of the human person, as well as the quality of relations between humans, are at the heart of Amerindian social ideology. He frequently contrasts Amerindian solidarity with the European competitive spirit:

> They should ... be done this justice, that among themselves, they spare each other more than Europeans do. They regard, with reason, as something barbarous and ferocious, the brutality of duels and the ease of mutual destruction introduced by a point of honour badly misunderstood .... They are no less astonished by the indifference of the Europeans for their fellow countrymen, by the slight attention paid by them to the death of their compatriots killed by their enemies.[18]

Lafitau openly admires the strength of the Amerindian social fabric, source of the individual's keen respect for the private life of others. This helps explain the gift-giving mechanisms for preventing and settling conflicts.

The Amerindian Conflict

In Lafitau's day, Amerindian societies, especially the Iroquois and Wendat, were in profound political disarray because of the European presence. In this stormy climate, the missionary was much better able to portray the Amerindian character than if the time had been peaceful. Much has been said about Amerindian cruelty and torture. As the Iroquois of that period were the prototype of the "cruel American savage," they contributed, in spite of themselves, to the elaboration of that image, one that was later applied to all Amerindians. Using Lafitau's descriptions and observations, we will now present a brief analysis of this historiographical "knot."

In the Amerindian ideological universe, "war for the sake of war," to use Lafitau's expression, does not exist. War—if the term can even be used with reference to Amerindian societies—is always the result of disruption of the political order, provoked by an enemy agent. The Iroquois, like all Amerindians, resigned themselves to war while being fully aware of its gravity: "The Council," Lafitau reports, "decides on war only after considering the plan for a long time and weighing with mature consideration all the factors pro and con."[19]

Because Amerindians saw their compatriots as the ultimate wealth, war assumed a meaning for them that compels admiration. In the conflict between Amerindians and Euroamericans, the Iroquois, as the most engaged Native people, were the ones who most often went to war, and consequently they lost the largest number of members. It was logical, then, for these nations to try to capture replacements for those who had been killed or seized; thus they did not simply indulge in murderous expeditions, as we are often led to believe.

"The loss of *a single person*," Lafitau writes, "is a great one, but one which must necessarily be repaired by replacing the person missing with one or many others, according to the importance of him who is to be replaced."[20]

On this matter, Lafitau shows us how, in a natural and matriarchal society, the women recognized as sages (matriarchs) have supreme control over even the nation's military affairs. When there is a loss of one or many persons,

> it is not up to the members of the same household [the longhouse, which among the Wendat and Iroquois could contain as many as 200 people] to repair this loss, but to all those men who have marriage links with that house, or their *Athonni*, as they say; and in that fact, resides the advantage of having many men born in it. For these men, although isolated at home and limited to themselves, marry into different lodges. The children born of these different marriages become obligated to their fathers' lodge, to which they are strangers, and contract the obligation of replacing them; in this way the "matron" (matriarch) who has the principal authority in this household, can force these children to go to war if it seems best to her, or keep them at home if they have undertaken a war displeasing to her.
>
> When, then, this "matron" judges it time to raise up the tree again, or to lay again on the mat someone of her family whom death has taken away from her, she addresses herself to some one of those who have their Athonni at her home and who she believes is most capable of executing her commission. She speaks to him by a wampum belt, explaining her intention of engaging him to form a war party. This is soon done.[21]

When it is time to set out and capture replacements, the leader of the expedition (still according to Lafitau) makes a public prayer, accompanied by all his relatives, who have dressed and adorned themselves in their best attire, as is done at the farewell feast for one who is about to die—for going to war is going towards death. All those who remain in the village hasten to obtain a relic from those who are leaving, and to give them some present. "Together," Lafitau tells us, "they exchange robes, coverings, or whatever other goods they may have. A typical warrior, before leaving the village, is despoiled more than twenty or thirty times."[22]

For Amerindians, no success or victory is great enough to make them forget, even for a moment, the value of one lost human life. In their society, the cult of the human, or of being (as opposed to the cult of having), assumes its full force and meaning. Lafitau is astonished at their respect for the dead:

> They have such respect for each other that, however complete may be their victory, and whatever advantage they may have gained from it, the first sentiment which they show is that of grief for those of their people whom they have lost. All the village has to participate in it. The good news of the success is told only after the dead have been given the first regrets which are their due .... The women do the same thing in regard to the men who have gone hunting or to war. For, at the moment of their return, they go to wait for them on the shore. And in place of showing (them) the joy which they must feel at seeing them arrive in good health, they begin by weeping for those of their relatives who died in the village during their absence.[23]

The Treatment of Captives

Of all the Amerindians, the Iroquois are known for the intensity of their defence against the crushing European invasion. For two centuries, from 1500 to 1700, they had to concentrate their strength in order to maintain the existence of a union of Amerindian nations. In response to the formidable onslaught of the epidemics, to say nothing of the European ideological assault, they developed a policy of adoption: as stated earlier, their "wars against the Wendat and their allies aimed above all at restoring their own numbers."

In Native societies in general, war, "established by the need to protect oneself from injustice, to repulse force by force and to right the injuries which the tribes might have received from each other, [is] also sanctified by religion."[24] Yet for the Amerindians, war, as made known to them by the white man, never became the exercise of destruction and extermination it represents for other cultures. In 1609, Champlain was indignant at the behaviour of the Wendat and Montagnais, who cried victory when the Mohawk fled after a French musket-shot cost them three of their chiefs. Champlain did not comprehend why his Amerindian allies did not set out in pursuit of the Iroquois, to exterminate them to the last man; he claimed that the Wendat and Montagnais were "cowards" who "know nothing about making war."

But it is the Amerindians, not the Europeans, who have been given the title of champions of cruelty in the history books. This view is wrong. Amerindians never inflicted torture on anyone because of religious or political ideas. During the two hundred years of the crusades, millions of people were killed because they did not share the crusaders' beliefs. To establish a point of comparison with America, the Dominican bishop Bartolomé de Las Casas wrote in 1552: "We furnish as a very sure and true number, that during the said forty years (1492–1532), have died because of the said tyranny and infernal works of the Christians, unjustly and in tyrannical manner, more than 12 million persons, men, women, and children, and I believe, trusting that I do not err that it was, in reality, more than 15 million."[25]

As for the Amerindians, if one of their warriors took a human life he did so only to gain respect for his nation, following a process always marked by the same humanity that characterizes his social vision of the great circle. Lafitau, in fact, recognized the rationality of the Amerindians' behaviour: "If they did not return the same treatment to those who treat them inhumanly, they would become their dupes, and their moderation would only serve to harden their enemies. The gentlest people are forced to put aside their natural gentleness when they see that it becomes a pretext for barbarous neighbours to become prouder and more intractable."[26]

The Iroquois themselves—and Lafitau supports them—deny being crueler than any other nation, white or Amerindian. Lafitau wrote: "The Iroquois, so fearsome to the French on account of the great number[27] of those they caused to perish in these frightful tortures, have gained an even worse reputation with us than all the other tribes .... To hear the Iroquois speak, however, they claim to be less cruel than the others and treat the captives thus only by reprisal."[28]

Their treatment of captives shows the very humane nature of the Iroquois people, even in the midst of the catastrophe represented by European interference in Amerindian society.

Returning from a capture expedition, those who had captives to offer clans who needed them gave them away ceremonially. "The warriors who give a slave [more correctly, a captive]," Lafitau recounts, "award him with their belt which has served as a symbol of his engagement in their enterprise, or serves them as parole, to say that they have fulfilled their obligation."[29]

Among the Iroquois in particular, it was very unusual for prisoners—who had been captured with such difficulty, and whose lives were eminently precious to a nation so frequently decimated—to be condemned to torture by fire. Indeed, their fate would have stirred the envy of more than one hostage of a "civilized" country. Lafitau tells us that, after being handed over, "the captives are led to the lodges to which they have been given and introduced .... There, they are immediately given something to eat. The people of this household, however, their relatives and friends, are still weeping for the dead whom these captives replace, as if they were losing them entirely, and in this ceremony shed genuine tears to honour the memory of those persons, to whom the sight of these captives recalls a bitter recollection, renewing their grief in their loss."[30]

The adoption was then formally carried out, in a way that shows that the Amerindian social ideal is based and focused on maintaining and developing relations between humans, as well as on faith in the capacity for reasoning of all humans, so long as their dignity is recognized. Lafitau observes:

> Among the Iroquois and Huron, it [the condition of "slave"] is gentler in proportion as that of those thrown into the fire is more cruel. The moment that he enters the lodge to which he is given and where he is to be kept, his bonds are untied .... He is washed with warm water to erase the colours with which his face was painted and he is dressed properly. Then he receives visits from relatives and friends of the family into which he is entering. A short time afterwards a feast is made for all the village to give him the name of the person whom he is resurrecting. The friends and allies of the dead man also give a feast to do him honour: and from that moment, he enters upon all his rights. If the captive is a girl, given to a household where there is nobody of her sex in a position to sustain the lineage, it is good fortune for this household and for her. All the hope of the family is placed in this captive who becomes the mistress of this family and the branches dependent on it. If the captive is a man who requickens an Ancient, a man of consequence, he becomes important himself and has authority in the village if he can sustain by his own personal merit the name which he takes.[31]

Cruelty

The severity of Amerindian punishment should not be seen as cruelty, madness, or blindness. On the contrary, it was compassionate, logical, and rational, and was dictated by the Amerindian's unshakeable morality, modelled on nature herself.

If we avoid sentimentality, cruelty can be evoked only in the context of aggression and domination, and not self-defence. It is therefore absurd—and unfair—to talk about the cruelty of persons who are only defending themselves, for such cruelty is a legitimate and noble act of physical self-protection, as well as an equally noble effort to safeguard the honour which has been imperilled by the assailant's deed. Cruelty is therefore an argument to justify aggression, which is itself linked to a desire for domination or, in other words, destruction, partial or total.

Among Amerindians, human sacrifice did not have the character of social diversion it had for the Romans. Even less did it represent a punitive act that was religious or political in nature. Torture was, indeed, intended to be a way of killing the war itself; to achieve this, harshness was the best guarantee of success. By aiming violently at the actual enemy, it imposed respect and restraint, and so can be considered a more humane response to violence than are the conventional means used by so-called civilized societies.

In 1626, in view of the difficulties presented by the conversion of Natives, Father Joseph Le Caron warned the young priests whose ambition was to die as martyrs in Canada: "The general opinion [of Amerindians] is that one must not contradict any one, but leave each one have his own thinking. There is, here, no hope of suffering martyrdom: the Savages do not put Christians to death for matters of religion; they leave every one to his belief."[32]

The cruelty of the Amerindian was simply political. Once again, Lafitau helps us penetrate to the core of Amerindian philosophy through a description of the scene preceding the torture of an enemy by the Iroquois. "From the appearance of everyone assembled around a wretch who is going to end his days in the most horrible torment, we should guess that there is no question of such a bloody tragedy as is about to take place before their eyes. All exhibit the greatest calm in the world. They are seated or lying on mats as they are in the councils. Each one talks loudly with his neighbour, lights his pipe and smokes with the most marvellous tranquillity."[33]

Among Amerindians, the sacrifice for political reasons of a human being was devoid of hatred or sadism. It was a considered, rational, and necessary act. The person to be tortured was fully aware of this and did not try to elude his fate. "In the intervals in which they are left in repose," reports Lafitau, "they talk coldly of different matters, of news, of what is happening in their country, or they inform themselves calmly of the customs of those who are busy burning them."[34]

The Amerindians' well-known heroic steadfastness under torture results from an unshakeable faith in their moral and spiritual values. Lafitau, like all missionaries, admires them for that: "This heroism is real and the result of great and noble courage. What we have admired in the martyrs of the primitive church which was, in them, the result of grace and a miracle, is natural to these people and the result of the strength of their spirit. The Savages, as I have already shown, seem to prepare for this event from the tenderest age."[35]

Just as victims showed great dignity and courage, so did those who had to sacrifice them show their compassion, proving once more the centrality of the human being in the Amerindian social vision: "When a captive is burned among the Iroquois," Lafitau notes, "there are few who do not pity him and say that he is worthy of compassion. Many ... have not the courage to be present at his execution .... Some ... give him relief when he asks for something."[36]

Cannibalism

The French philosopher Michel de Montaigne claimed that "there is nothing barbarous or savage in that nation [Amerindians], from what I have been told, except that each man calls barbarism, whatever is not his own practice; for indeed it seems we have no other test of truth and reason than the example and pattern of opinions and customs of the country we live in."[37]

The notion of cannibalism as practised by "primitive" cultures is a product of the racist thinking of so-called civilized societies. In a society where the human being was at the centre, how did one dispose of the body of the individual who had to be tortured? How was the dignity of the human race to be preserved?

We know that evoking the Amerindians' bloody cruelty was a powerful means used by the colonial (mainly religious) authorities to attract the favour, sympathy, and financial support of their country's upper classes. Aside from this self-seeking attitude, some sources, particularly oral accounts, indicate that torture and its corollary, cannibalism, never had the importance attributed to them. Besides, our autohistorical study of Amerindian philosophy has provided ample evidence to destroy this fable.

One fact is certain, however, and it deserves the greatest respect: Amerindians did sometimes consume one or several parts (for example, the heart) of the body of a prisoner who died a particularly courageous death. The Amerindian gesture of consuming human flesh was as consistent with their conception of the great circle as was their proverbial generosity. When they had to defend themselves against their fellow humans, they did not like to kill instantaneously or massively as is done with mechanical weapons. They preferred to glorify their captive enemies in death by giving them the chance to die courageously. The remains of a life thus ennobled until death and in death could not be simply thrown away as garbage; they deserved to be eaten. Amerindians had to treat with honour the flesh of those whose lives they had to take. They consumed it because they thought they must: they had been required to destroy persons who, deep down, they admired and loved because they were brothers whose hearts were filled with love, trust, and veneration for their Creator, and thus for their fellow human beings.

Morality

In his *Customs of the American Indians*, Lafitau compares Amerindian morality favourably with European. He maintains that Amerindian moral force invariably diminished upon contact with whites. He talks about the northern nomads as being "more distant peoples, who are fortunate enough not to know us [Europeans]."[38]

Amerindians practised to a high degree those individual and social virtues known as Christian. According to Lafitau, they were charitable: "If a household of famished people meets another whose provisions are not entirely exhausted yet, the latter share with the newly-arrived the little food which they have left, without waiting to be asked, although in so doing, they are left exposed to the same danger of perishing as those whom they are helping at their expense, with such humanity and nobility of soul. In Europe under similar circumstances, we would find little disposition to such noble and magnanimous generosity."[39]

Similarly, their courtesy to visitors should be edifying to people of any culture: "Whoever enters their home is well-received," Lafitau observes. "The one who arrives or comes to visit has scarcely entered than food is put before him, without saying anything: and he himself eats without ceremony, before opening his mouth to declare the subject which brings him."[40]

Respect Between the Sexes

The Amerindians' modesty and their discretion in matters of sex are well-documented. Lafitau recounts customs that fell into disuse because of the example of the French. One such custom, according to Lafitau, was "to pass the first year after the marriage without consummating it. Any advance made before that time would be insulting to the wife and would make her think that the alliance was sought less because of esteem for her than out of brutality."[41]

Another Amerindian custom, still practised among the Iroquois and others, does not allow an individual to marry another member of the same clan. This is true even if the person has been adopted by the clan, "for," as Lafitau explains, "since by giving them life the name of a particular person of this family is revived in them, they are given all the rights of adoption and represent those being resurrected as if they were those people themselves."[42]

The Amerindian of Lafitau's time would break off his intimate life with his wife as soon as a pregnancy occurred; "the general rule for all Savages is to stop living with their wives from the moment they declare themselves pregnant."[43]

Being Faithful to One's Word

Lafitau cites an "old Huron" who told him that "it was a law from time immemorial in their country that a village had a right to put to death anyone who ... did not fulfil the obligations of his pledge."[44] Friendship is sacred among Amerindians. The ties that bind friends together are stronger than the ties of blood. An individual cannot marry a friend's relative, since the bonds of their friendship make them kin. Usually, Lafitau tells us, "friends follow each other to the stake."[45]

Respect for Ancestors' Souls

Finally, Amerindians were admired by the first Euroamericans, especially the priests, because of their remarkable devotion to the souls of their dead. To the missionaries and perhaps more particularly to Lafitau because of the thesis he was defending, this natural disposition of the Amerindian was proof of the immortality of the soul, and so of the existence of God. Echoing numerous European observers, Lafitau wrote:

> It could be said that all their work, all their sweating and all their trade comes back almost solely to doing honour to the dead. They have nothing precious enough for this. And so they sacrifice their beaver robes, maize, axes, and wampum, in such quantity that it could be believed they attach no importance to them, although they constitute all the wealth of the country. They can be seen almost naked in the winter cold, while they have, in their chests, good fur or woolen robes destined for the funeral duties. On these occasions, each person makes it a point of honour or religion to appear liberal to the point of magnificence or prodigality.[46]

Conclusion

Despite historians' tendency to produce an image of the Amerindian that serves the interests of colonialist societies, Amerindian ideology has lost nothing of its essence. To cite historian Robert E. Berkhofer, "The remarkable persistence of cultural and personality traits and ethnic identity in Indian societies in the face of white conquest and efforts at elimination or assimilation"[47] is proof that America has never had and will never have any lasting spiritual culture other than its Native one. White America has lost the cultural battle it waged against the Amerindian people. Most ironically, the Iroquois nation, which has most often served as a pretext for whites to denigrate the aboriginal population, is now recognized even internationally as one of the most vibrant Amerindian cultures in the Americas. According to Mohawk historian and journalist Doug George, the Iroquois possess "an innate gift for organization." "You can find innumerable references in the historical documents that demonstrate the ability of the Iroquois people to pull it out of the fire, when things look their darkest, to create something out of that."[48] He points out that the Iroquois periodical *Akwesasne Notes*, founded in 1968, is "a device created [by the Iroquois] that has given stimulus to Indian movements across the hemisphere."[49]

Historically, the Iroquois' vision of peace was not limited to the Native people of North America, but has always been universal. To cite George again: "In 1656, a Mohawk delegation … went to Quebec City and asked the French [who had the technology to do it] to take this message of Peace throughout the world … to bring all the Nations together at Onondaga, under the Great Tree of Peace …. These were people who were gifted with world vision 300 years before the Europeans finally, after two World Wars, stumbled across it."[50]

Today, the Iroquois still acknowledge "the duty of trying to reach the non-Native world as well." George adds that "even on the other side of the [Atlantic] Ocean … we can see the influence of the Confederacy in movements like the Green Party that's taking hold among the young people of Europe, transcending national boundaries, an expression of the concern [in] those nations that they have 'a responsibility for their generations up until the seventh generation' [following the Amerindian maxim]."[51]

This triumph of Iroquois traditionalism, despite the fact that Amerindian culture has been severely undermined by the shock of contact, is proof enough in our opinion of the solid strength of America's original philosophy.

Notes

1. Karl H. Schlesier, "Epidemics and Indian Middlemen: Rethinking the Wars of the Iroquois," *Ethnohistory* 23, 2 (1976): 131.

2. *Ibid.*, 29.

3. Interview with Louis Hall Karaniaktajeh (aged sixty-eight), painter and writer of the Mohawk nation of Kahnawake, at Kahnawake, 5 July 1985, author's personal files.

4. James A. Tuck, "Northern Iroquoian Prehistory" in *Handbook of North American Indians*, vol. 15, *Northeast*, ed. Bruce G. Trigger (Washington, DC: Smithsonian Institution, 1978), 324.

5. Elizabeth Tooker, "The League of the Iroquois: Its History, Politics and Ritual" in *Handbook of North American Indians*, vol. 15, ed. Trigger, 419–22.

6. John Napoleon Brinton Hewitt, cited in ibid., 421–22.

7. William Douw Lightall, *Hochelagans and Mohawks* (Ottawa: J. Hope and Sons, 1899), 208–9.

8. Henry F. Dobyns, *Their Number Become Thinned: Native American Population Dynamics in Eastern North America* (Knoxville: University of Tennessee Press, 1983), 314–21.

9. Bruce G. Trigger, *The Children of Aataentsic: A History of the Huron People to 1660*, cited in "Annaotaha et Dollard vus de l'autre côté de la palisade," ed. John A. Dickinson, *Revue d'histoire de l'Amérique française* 35, 2 (1981): 171.

10. *Ibid.*, 177–78.

11. Reuben Gold Thwaites, ed., *The Jesuits' Relations and Allied Documents, 1610–1791*, vol. 15 (New York: Pageant Books, 1959), 171.

12. Schlesier, cited in *ibid.*, vol. 25, 105, 109.

13. *Ibid.*, 141.

14. William N. Fenton, "Northern Iroquoian Culture Patterns," in *Handbook of North American Indians*, vol. 15, ed. Trigger, 315.

15. Remarks by John Mohawk, Seneca historian and professor at the University of Buffalo, New York, during a conference on Iroquois communications, 11–12 April 1985, at the Native American Center for the Living Arts, Niagara Falls, New York, author's personal files.

16. Joseph-François Lafitau, *Moeurs des Sauvages américains comparées aux moeurs des premiers temps*, ed. Edna Hindie Lemay, vol. 2 (Paris: Maspéro, 1983), 88.

17. *Ibid.*, 83.

18. *Ibid.*, vol. 1, 99.

19. *Ibid.*, vol. 2, 12.

20. *Ibid.*, 6 (my emphasis).

21. *Ibid.*, 6–7.

22. *Ibid.*, 27.

23. *Ibid.*, vol. 1, 80.

24. *Ibid.*, vol. 2, 13.

25. Bartolomé de las Casas, *Brevisima Relacion de la Destruccion de las Indias*, trans. Georges Sioui (Santiago de Chili: Editorial Nascimiento, 1972), 30.

26. Lafitau, *Moeurs des Sauvages américains*, vol. 2.

27. Université de Montréal historian John A. Dickinson has carried out a critical study of the "great number" of French victims of the Iroquois during this period. See Dickinson, "La guerre iroquoise et la mortalité en Novelle-France, 1608–1666," *Revue d'histoire de l'Amérique française* 36, 1 (June 1982): 31–47.

28. Lafitau, *Moeurs des Sauvages américains*, vol. 2.

29. *Ibid.*

30. *Ibid.*

31. *Ibid.*, 111.

32. Joseph Le Caron, "Plainte de la Nouvelle-France dite Canada à la France sa germaine" (factum) (Paris, 1626).

33. Lafitau, *Moeurs des Sauvages américains*, vol. 2., 88.

34. *Ibid.*, 95.

35. *Ibid.*, 91.

36. *Ibid.*, 98.

37. Donald H. Frame, ed., *Montaigne's Essays and Selected Writings*, cited in *Friend and Foe*, ed. Cornelius J. Jaenen (Toronto: McClelland and Stewart, 1973), 122.

38. Lafitau, *Moeurs des Sauvages américains*, vol. 2., 31.

39. *Ibid.*, vol. 1, 234.

40. *Ibid.*, 232.

41. *Ibid.*, 157.

42. *Ibid.*, 145.

43. *Ibid.*, 146.

44. *Ibid.*, 23.

45. *Ibid.*, 182.

46. *Ibid.*, vol. 2, 151–52.

47. Robert E. Berkhofer, Jr., "The Political Context of a New Indian History," *Pacific Historical Review* 40, 3 (1971): 358.

48. Remarks by Doug George, historian and journalist of the Mohawk nation of Akwesasane (Quebec, Ontario, and New York), during a conference on Iroquois communications, 11–12 April 1985, at the Native American Center for the Living Arts, Niagara Falls, New York, author's personal files.

49. *Ibid.*

50. *Ibid.*

51. *Ibid.*

CHAPTER
2 SOCIETY IN NEW FRANCE

The structured society of New France, with the *habitant* toiling under the benign if firm hands of the seigneur, the *curé* and the royal officials, remains one of the strongest images in Canadian history. The feudal remnant drawn so vividly by Francis Parkman and George M. Wrong, among others, was transferred to the textbooks and repeated for generations, becoming true by repetition. This concept of a regimented colony became so entrenched in both historical studies and popular literature that forty years of revisionist scholarship failed to dislodge it. There was little sympathy for the paternalist French regime among the Whig historians who created the stereotype, and they found congenial readers. In the 1950s, historians rediscovered the history of New France. In the process, they reconstructed a significantly different *ancien régime*. The pastoral scenes and an official society of orders remained, but its personality was distinguished by its diversity and its irregularity. In the view of some, the typical *canadien* of the era was to be found in the bustling, urban communities rather than on the farm.

Among historians, the focus of the debate on the nature of society has ranged from the role of the state, to the role of the military, the church, the economy, the family and the environment. In the 1950s and 1960s no individual contributed more to the revision of the history of New France than W.J. Eccles, whose "The Society of New France, 1680's–1760" is included here. With the fervour of a possessed iconoclast, Eccles demolished cherished images about the colony, especially those of the imperious Parkman. Eccles was captivated by the *ancien régime* and its values. The advantages of that aristocratic state, when placed in juxtaposition with the English to the south, became self-evident in Eccles' prose. He did not reject the society of orders, but he did revise the picture, using the traditional sources and methodology of historians.

Jan Noël also toiled in those court records and travellers' accounts, but her interests were different from those of Eccles. Whereas Eccles envisioned a male, paternalistic society in which women were marginal but necessary, in "New France: Les femmes favorisées," Noël moved women out of the shadows and challenged several assumptions about women, family and, ultimately, society in New France. She began with the "pre-private" family of the non-industrial world, showing that in the "fluid situation" of New France, the demographic and economic circumstances permitted women to play many roles: "*Dévotes* and traders, warriors and landowners, smugglers and politicians, industrialists and financiers."

The third selection, "Individuals and Society," by Jacques Mathieu is from *La Nouvelle-France: Les Français en Amérique du Nord XVIe-XVIIIe siecle.* Mathieu has little tolerance for the impressionists who tell stories. Apparently, he considers Eccles to be just such an impressionist, since he ignores his work entirely. Mathieu turned instead to the sources and techniques of *l'Ecole des Annales* of France, examining demography, occupation, the economy, and mentality. The product is an alternative vision of the society of New France. Eccles was not impressed with this revision, and he wrote a very negative review of Mathieu's study in *Revue d'historique de l'Amerique francais* in the Autumn of 1992. In the next issue of that journal, Mathieu and Eccles squared off with competing and insulting missives. The student would be justified in questioning whether or not it was the nature of society in New France that was the real issue in such an exchange.

Suggestions for Further Reading

Bosher, John F., "The Family in New France," in *In Search of the Visible Past*, ed. Barry Gough. Waterloo: Wilfrid Laurier University Press, 1975. (Reprinted in Chapter 13 of this volume.)

Dechêne, Louise, *Habitants and Merchants in Seventeenth Century Montreal* (trans. by Liani Vardi). Montreal: McGill-Queen's University Press, 1992.

Desloges, Yvon and Marc Lafrance, "Dynamique de croissance et société urbaine: Québec au XVIIIe siècle, 1690–1759," *Histoire sociale / Social History*, XXI, no. 42 (novembre 1988), 251–68.

Eccles, W.J., *Canadian Society During the French Regime.* Montreal: Harvest House, 1968.

_____, *Essays on New France.* Toronto: Oxford, 1988.

_____, "The Social, Economic, and Political Significance of the Military Establishment in New France," *Canadian Historical Review*, LII, no. 1 (March 1971), 1–22.

Gadoury, Lorraine, Yves Landry and Hubert Charbonneau, "Démographie différentielle en Nouvelle-France: villes et campagnes," *Revue d'histoire de l'Amérique française*, 38, no. 3 (hiver 1985), 357–78.

Greer, Allan, *The People of New France.* Toronto: University of Toronto Press, 1997.

Lachance, Andre, "Women and Crime in Canada in the Early Eighteenth Century, 1712–1759," in *Crime and Criminal Justice in Europe and Canada*, ed. L.A. Knafla. Waterloo: Wilfrid Laurier University Press, 1981, 157–97.

Miquelon, Dale, *New France 1701–1744: "A Supplement to Europe."* Toronto: McClelland and Stewart, 1987.

THE SOCIETY OF NEW FRANCE, 1680's–1760

W.J. Eccles

In the middle of the eighteenth century, a Swedish gentleman named Peter Kalm travelled through the English and French colonies in North America. He wrote an endearing description of the Canadian *habitants* whom he met in the farms, villages and towns along the St. Lawrence River in the year 1749:

> The common man in Canada is more civilized and clever than in any other place of the world that I have visited. On entering one of the peasant's houses, no matter where, and on beginning to talk with their men or women, one is quite amazed at the good breeding and courteous answers which are received, no matter what the question is. One can scarcely find in a city in other parts, people who treat one with such politeness both in word and deed as is true everywhere in the homes of the peasants in Canada.

These people had been living under the direct supervision of the French kings since the year 1663. That was when Louis XIV turned what had been a struggling colony into a comparatively thriving royal province. Under this French regime, which lasted until 1760, the social and political framework of Canada took on some resemblance to that of today's welfare states.

Although it is true that the people had little say in how they were governed, yet they accepted this as being perfectly natural. At the same time, the officials appointed over them by the king and his ministers were always closely checked to ensure that they did not abuse their authority. The whole structure of society and government was paternalistic, based on responsibilities and duties rather than on freedom and privileges. The people had to obey the royal officials in all things, but these same officials were held responsible for their security and well-being.

In 1686, when Jean Bochart de Champigny was appointed Intendant of New France, he was given very detailed instructions governing all aspects of his responsibilities:

> His Majesty wishes him to know that his entire conduct must lead to two principal ends; the one to ensure that the French inhabitants established in that country enjoy complete tranquility among themselves, and are maintained in the just possession of all that belongs to them, and the other to conserve the said inhabitants and to increase their numbers by all means possible ...
>
> His Majesty wishes him to visit once a year all the habitations that are situated between the ocean and the island of Montreal, to inform himself of all that goes on, pay heed to all the inhabitants' complaints and their needs, and attend to them as much as he possibly can, and so arrange it that they live together in peace, that they aid each other in their necessities and that they be not diverted from their work.

From *The Ordeal of New France* (Toronto: Canadian Broadcasting Corporation, 1967), 96–106. Reprinted by permission of the author.

In other words, the Intendant, as the King's representative, was to act as the father of the king's large family of loyal subjects living on the banks of the St. Lawrence River.

That the king would not tolerate the abuse of his subjects by the officials was made plain in 1679. Complaints had been received that the Governor of Montreal had imprisoned people arbitrarily. Louis XIV issued an edict forbidding this practice. The officials were ordered on pain of severe penalties not to imprison anyone unless they had been duly charged by a court of law. Oddly enough, that same year, in England, Parliament passed a similar act under rather similar circumstances; the act known as *Habeas Corpus*. In fact, the common people of New France had as much, and likely more, personal freedom than had the people of England at this time, where only some 10 per cent of the population had a vote and parliament ruled in the interests of the land-owning class with far less solicitude for the common people than was shown by the appointed officials of New France for the Canadian *habitants*.

Another essential difference between seventeenth-century society in Canada and in England was that in Canada it might be described as essentially aristocratic, whereas society in England was coming more and more to be bourgeois in outlook. This may become clearer if we try to see what the chief aims of the people were, what they regarded as constituting the good life.

To the Canadians, as to the French in France, the good life was that of the noble who could appreciate the better things, had the means to enjoy them and made the most of them, without condescending to inquire too closely into the sordid mechanics of their procurement. The main aim was to live well, to enjoy the best available without counting the cost. But in England, as elsewhere in Protestant Europe, bourgeois standards were coming more and more to the fore. In this society work was an end in itself, a sign of virtue; pleasure was suspect, poverty was a mark of sin, and the surplus product of labour was not to be consumed but reinvested to create new wealth.

Before the end of the seventeenth century Canadian society had assumed the pattern that it retained to the end of the French regime. At the top were the royal officials; the Governor, the Intendant and the senior officers of the military establishment, all men sent out from France and who expected to return to France one day. Beside them were the clergy, but the Crown officials had far more authority over them than the state has today. After 1663, when the colony was taken over by the Crown from a private company, there was never any real doubt that the state was supreme in New France. For the most part the clergy of New France were, in comparison with those in France, singularly well-educated and many of them were persons of exceptionally strong character. But they had their thoughts and aspirations fixed more on the next world than this; thus they always remained a class apart.

Of the purely Canadian social groups the *seigneurs* ranked highest; some, but not all, were nobles; some had begun active life in the colony as peasants or soldiers and had achieved the rank of *seigneur* by sheer ability and drive. Many of them got their wealth from the fur trade. In the towns of Quebec, Montreal and Trois Rivières there was a sizeable middle class and urban working class; in fact, between 25 and 40 per cent of the colony's population were town dwellers or lived within easy reach of one or other of the three towns compared to 15 per cent in France. In the country, on the *seigneuries*, lived the remainder of the population, the *habitants*, who tilled their lands, paid their modest dues to their *seigneurs* and their tithe of one twenty-sixth of their grain to the church, and were far better off than the peasants of France, or indeed of England, where a third of the people existed at a bare subsistence level. In 1691 the Intendant, Champigny, reported to the minister in France:

> Those who try to make something of their land are rich, or at least live very comfortably, having their fields and fishing close by their homes and a goodly number of cattle in pasture.

In 1749, Peter Kalm, professor of natural history and economy at the University of Abo, toured the English colonies and New France and commented on how civilized the Canadian *habitants* were:

> I travelled in various places during my stay in this country. I frequently happened to take up my abode for several days at the homes of peasants where I had never been seen before, and who had never heard of or seen me, and to whom I had no letters of introduction. Nevertheless they showed me wherever I came a devotion paid ordinarily to a native or a relative. Often when I offered them money they would not accept it. Frenchmen who were born in Paris said themselves that one never finds in France among country people the courtesy and good breeding which one observes everywhere in this land. I heard many native Frenchmen assert this.

Thus the Swedish traveller in 1749. And the Marquis de Denonville, writing earlier in 1686, observed this of the Canadians:

> They are all big, well-built and firmly planted on their feet, accustomed whenever necessary to live on little, robust and vigorous, very obstinate and inclined to be dissolute, but quick-witted and vivacious.

By the middle of the eighteenth century it appeared to some Frenchmen that the Canadian *habitant* was, in fact, too affluent. In 1753 a French officer named Franquet, after a trip from Quebec to Montreal, noted in his journal:

> Stopped at Madame Lamothe's at La Chenaye and was very well received, a good dinner, and everything well served. We passed a very comfortable night in clean beds fit for a duchess ... Judging by the furnishings of that house, one would have to say that the country folk are too well off.

This same officer was, however, rather reactionary in his views. He declared that the colony was in danger of being ruined by the excellent education which the girls received from the grey nuns of the Congregation of Notre Dame:

The bad that results is like a slow poison that tends to depopulate the countryside; once educated, the girls wish to be ladies, they become affected in their manners, they want to live in the town, they will marry no one but a merchant and look down on the condition in which they were born.

The daughters of the *seigneurs* and more affluent merchant families were educated by the Ursuline nuns whose main aim was to turn out well-bred and learned young ladies. They were given the usual religious instruction, Latin and French grammar and literature, good penmanship and mathematics. In addition they were taught something of botany and chemistry in order to be able to prepare simple herbs and drugs; and also such things as drawing and embroidery. But more significantly, they were taught to be good conversationalists, to have charming manners, and to know how to please. Peter Kalm in 1749 was quick to remark on the manners of the Canadian girls:

> The difference between the manner and customs of the French in Montreal and Canada, and those of the English in the American colonies, is as great as that between the manners of those two nations in Europe. The women in general are handsome here; they are well-bred and virtuous, with an innocent and becoming freedom. They dress up very fine on Sundays; about the same as our Swedish women, and though on the other days they do not take much pains with other parts of their dress, yet they are very fond of adorning their heads. The hair is always curled, powdered and ornamented with glittering bodkins and aigrettes. Every day but Sunday they wear a little neat jacket, and a short skirt which hardly reaches halfway down the leg, and sometimes not that far. And in this particular they seem to imitate the Indian women ...
>
> The ladies in Canada, and especially at Montreal, are very ready to laugh at any blunders strangers make in speaking, but they are very excusable. People laugh at what appears uncommon and ridiculous. In Canada nobody ever hears the French language spoken by any but Frenchmen, for strangers seldom come there, and the Indians are naturally too proud to learn French, and compel the French to learn their language. Therefore it naturally follows that the sensitive Canadian ladies cannot hear anything uncommon without laughing at it. One of the first questions they put to a stranger is whether he is married; the next, how he likes the ladies in the country, and whether he thinks them handsomer than those of his own country; and the third, whether he will take one home with him ... Nobody can say that they lack either charm or wit.

Although the facilities in the colony were inadequate to give the entire populace an education, in the towns at least the emphasis was always on quality. At the Petit Séminaire in Quebec, at the Jesuit College or the Sulpician's seminary in Montreal, the boys received as good an education as could have been had in any provincial city in France. In 1687 the Abbé Dudouyt in Paris instructed the masters at the Petit Séminaire:

> You must limit yourself to thirty students, select them well and weed out those who do not apply themselves. It is far better to have a few students of high calibre than many indifferent ones.

In addition to education, the clergy were responsible for the hospitals, for alms houses for the poor and aged and indigent. Although the hospital at Quebec, the Hôtel Dieu, had an excellent reputation, its doctors followed the established rules of seventeenth- and eighteenth-century medicine. One had to be very hale indeed to survive that treatment.

If herbal remedies and a few well-known drugs failed to effect a cure, bleeding and purging were invariably inflicted on the patients.

When the superior of the Sulpicians, for example, was stricken with a very severe pain in his side, accompanied by fever and violent headaches, he was bled six times but, it was reported, he only became weaker. He was then thoroughly purged but, to everyone's regret, died two days later.

But the main concern of the clergy was, however, the spiritual and moral well-being of the people. It was in this last connection that, in the seventeenth century, they sometimes came into conflict with the secular authorities. At this time the clergy were very puritanical and tended to regard as sins matters that were accepted as quite normal elsewhere. Ladies' fashions, for example, frequently caused Bishop Laval and his successor, St. Vallier, to thunder denunciations from the pulpit. The ladies of Quebec and Montreal always insisted on dressing according to the latest fashions at the court of Versailles, which dictated very low-cut gowns and elaborate hair styles.

In 1682 Bishop Laval declared in a pastoral letter that women were appearing at mass in very luxurious garments, as though dressed for a ball; and what was far worse, some came dressed in a scandalous manner:

> They come wearing indecent gowns, revealing scandalous views of their nude shoulders and bosoms, or contenting themselves by covering their bare flesh with transparent veils which serve only to heighten the effect of their shameful nakedness. They come with their heads uncovered or with their curled and beribboned coiffures covered only by a piece of lace in a fashion most undignified for a Christian and which detracts from the sanctity of the church.

Such apparel was, the Bishop declared, forbidden. But the ladies appear to have paid no attention, for the complaints continued, and Bishop St. Vallier ordered the priests to refuse absolution to those who so comported themselves, not merely outdoors but also in their homes. To this stricture the ladies protested, and the secular authorities supported them, declaring that the clergy were going too far. The minister at Versailles and the clerical authorities in France quickly ordered the Canadian clergy to cease annoying the people in this fashion, and they had to obey. As any married man could have predicted, in their battle against female vanity the clergy were certain to go down to defeat.

The civil authorities had other more dreary problems to cope with—some of which are still with us today. In Montreal traffic was a continual source of annoyance. Most of the streets were only eighteen feet wide, and pedestrians were frequently run down by wagons or sleighs. The Intendant Raudot complained that those on horseback or driving vehicles paid no heed to pedestrians and expected them always to get out of the way. Present-day pedestrians in Montreal might well be inclined to remark: *"Plus ça change, plus c'est la même chose."*

In the country districts the depredations of goblins—the "lutins"—appear to have been a serious problem. They were reputed to sneak into barns at night and get into all kinds of mischief with the livestock. The *habitants*, however, had a method of curbing their activities which was reputed to be very effective; it consisted of placing a pail of cinders behind the stable door so that any goblin entering could not fail to upset it. The goblin then had to pick up the cinders piece by piece in order to remove all traces of his passage.

This took quite a time, and when the task was completed he, or it, had neither time, energy nor inclination to start tying horses' tails together. Very rarely did a goblin return to a stable where he had had this experience.

A more tangible problem in Montreal, Quebec and Trois Rivières was the excessive number of taverns. Any house became a tavern merely by hanging an evergreen branch over the door. In 1726 the Intendant Dupuy limited the number of licenses and issued stringent regulations which are quite revealing:

> It is hereby forbidden for tavern keepers, hotel keepers, and inn keepers to sell soldiers anything to drink in the morning except a little brandy or wine, nor to sell any liquor to lackeys or domestic servants, in or out of livery, at any hour of the day, without the written permission of their masters, on pain of fifty *livres* fine, and the closing of the establishment for a second offence ...
>
> It is forbidden for tavern keepers, hotel keepers and inn keepers to accept from any youth, valet or soldier, in payment for wine or other drinks, any table ware, cutlery or other utensils, on pain of being named accepters of stolen goods and of being punished as such.

The staple food of the Canadians was white bread. Plenty of it was available, and along with it went quantities of meat and fish. Early in December animals were slaughtered and game was brought in, enough to last the entire winter. The meat and game was then packed in barrels between layers of straw and left in the barns to freeze. If a mid-winter thaw lasted too long everyone went on short rations.

The Swedish visitor Peter Kalm was favourably impressed with the diet of the Canadians:

> The meals here are in many respects different from those in the English provinces. They breakfast commonly between seven and eight and the Governor-General can be seen at seven o'clock, the time when he has his levée. Some of the men dip a piece of bread in brandy and eat it; others take a dram of brandy and eat a piece of bread after it. Chocolate is likewise very common for breakfast, and many of the ladies drink coffee. I have never seen tea used here.
>
> Dinner is exactly at noon. People of quality have a great many dishes and the rest follow their example, when they invite strangers. The loaves are oval and baked of wheat flour. For each person they put a plate, napkin, spoon and fork. (In the English colonies a napkin is seldom or never used.) Sometimes

they also provide knives, but they are generally omitted, all the ladies and gentlemen being provided with their own knives. The spoons and forks are of silver, and the plates of Delft ware. The meals begin with a soup with a good deal of bread in it. Then follow fresh meats of various kinds, boiled and roasted, poultry, or game, fricassees, ragouts, etc., of several sorts, together with different kinds of salads. They commonly drink red claret at dinner, either mixed with water or clear; and spruce beer is likewise much in use. Each one has his own glass and can drink as much as he wishes, for the bottles are put on the table. Butter is seldom served and if it is, it is chiefly for the guest present who likes it. But it is so fresh that one has to salt it at the table. After the main course is finished the table is always cleared. Finally the fruit and sweetmeats are served, which are of many different kinds; walnuts from France or Canada, either ripe or pickled; almonds, raisins, hazelnuts, several kinds of berries, and cranberries preserved in treacle. Cheese is likewise a part of the dessert. Immediately after dinner they drink coffee without cream. They say no grace before or after their meals, but only cross themselves, a custom which is likewise omitted by some.

Peter Kalm, of course, visited the colony in the middle of the eighteenth century, a few years before the British conquest, and at a time when the Canadian economy was flourishing. The fur trade was bringing rich returns to the Montreal merchants; such industries as ship-building, mining and smelting, lumbering and fishing were now well-established. The population was beginning to grow rapidly, and had the conquest not intervened, New France would have begun to expand in every way. It appears just to have reached what a latter-day American economist has called the "take-off point." In both the towns and the countryside the people were well-housed. The churches, and in the older-established *seigneuries*, both the manor houses and the humbler homes of the *habitants*, were mostly built of stone. Inside they were well-enough furnished. The more well-to-do imported their furnishings from France; the *habitants* made do with locally-made products. This furniture was generally made of white pine, and frequently of a high order of craftsmanship. The Canadian craftsmen developed great skill in wood carving and wrought iron work, and the pieces that have survived are highly prized today in both Canada and the United States. The churches were adorned with fine carved figures and wood panelling, painted in light blues, terra cotta, creamy white, accented with gilt, giving the interiors a light, spacious and very pleasing—almost gay—appearance. In recent years numerous oil paintings, mainly of religious subjects, have come to light. Although rather primitive, many of them have great charm and some have considerable artistry. All things considered, New France by the mid-eighteenth century was quite an affluent society. In 1752 the French officer Franquet remarked of Montreal:

> The people there are generally very well off, they never travel on foot, in summer they ride in carriages and in winter use sleighs. They nearly all have horses. Usually they keep as many as there are boys in the family, who use them only for sport and to pay court to their lady friends.

And a few years later an Irish observer had this to say of the river empire's metropolis:

> On the fourteenth of this month I had an opportunity of viewing the interior parts of Montreal; and for delightfulness of situation, I think I never saw any town to equal it ... It stands on the side of a hill sloping down to the river with the south island of St. Helen, all in front; which forms a most agreeable landscape, the river here being about three miles across ... The streets are regular, the houses well-constructed ... and ... there are several pleasant gardens within the walls... Besides these, there are many other gardens and beautiful plantations without the gates ... at an agreeable distance, on the north side of the town... I saw no paintings, or anything remarkably curious, in their churches or other religious houses; everything carried an air of neatness, simplicity, and plainness.
>
> The inhabitants are gay and sprightly, much more attached to dress and finery than those of Quebec, between whom there seems to be an emulation in this respect; and, from the number of silk robes, laced coats, and powdered heads of both sexes, and almost of all ages, that are perambulating the streets from morning to night, a stranger would be induced to believe Montreal is entirely inhabited by people of independent and plentiful fortunes.

That was how Montreal appeared in September 1760 to Captain John Knox of the forty-third Regiment of Foot in General Amherst's invading army.

The calm and prosperity of New France could not last, could not survive untouched by the great struggle for domination between the European powers, chiefly France and Britain. In September of 1760, the Montreal described by Captain Knox had capitulated to victorious British armies. Fifteen years later, under British rule, the colony was to be invaded and partly occupied by a new breed of men from the south, calling themselves "Americans."

But these events, and many more to follow, would only attach the Canadians more firmly than ever to their great sources of strength: their families, their land, their language, their faith and their race.

NEW FRANCE: LES FEMMES FAVORISÉES

Jan Noël

> *You constantly behold, with renewed astonishment, women in the very depths of indigence and want, perfectly instructed in their religion, ignorant of nothing that they should know to employ themselves usefully in their families and who, by their manners, their manner of expressing themselves and their politeness, are not inferior to the most carefully educated among us.[1]*
>
> *Les femmes l'emportent sur les hommes par la beauté, la vivacité, la gaité [sic] et l'enjouement; elles sont coquettes et galantes, préfèrent les Européens aux gens du pays. Les manières douces et polies sont communes, même dans les campagnes.[a][2]*

From *Atlantis*, 6, no. 2 (Spring 1981), 80–98. Reprinted by permission of *Atlantis*.

... les femmes y sont fort aimables, mais extrêmement fières.[b][3]
... elles sont spirituelles, ce qui leur donne de la supériorité sur les hommes dans presque tous les états.[c][4]

Many a man, observing the women of New France, was struck by the advantages they possessed in education, cultivation and that quality called *esprit* or wit. Even an unsympathetic observer of colonial society, such as the French military officer Franquet, who visited New France in 1752–53, admitted that its women *"l'emportent sur les hommes pour l'esprit, généralement elles en ont toutes beaucoup, parlant un français épuré, n'ont pas le moindre accent, aiment aussi la parure, sont jolies, généreuses et même maniérées."*[d][5] He notes, albeit with disapproval, that women very commonly aspired to stations above those to which they were born.[6] The Swedish naturalist Peter Kalm, who deplored the inadequate housekeeping of Canadian women, nevertheless admired their refinement.[7]

Those for whom history is an exercise in statistics have taught us caution in accepting the accounts of travellers, which are often highly subjective. However the consensus (particularly that of seasoned observers such as Charlevoix and Kalm) on the superior education and wit of women in New France suggests that their views are founded on something more than natural male proclivity towards *la différence*. Moreover, historians' accounts of society in New France offer ample evidence that women did indeed enjoy an exceptionally privileged position in that colony. The position was so privileged, in fact, that it contrasts favourably not only with that of their contemporaries in France and in New England, but probably also with twentieth-century Canadian women as far as entrepreneurial activity is concerned.

How did the women of New France acquire a superior education? How did they come to be involved in commerce? What gave rise to their vaunted *esprit*? There is no single answer to these questions. The truth is a compound of three separate factors. First, studies of Western Europe under the *ancien régime,*[e] indicate that ideas about women's roles were surprisingly flexible and varied. Secondly, the particular demographic configuration of New France gave female immigrants a number of advantages not available to their counterparts in Europe. Thirdly, the colonial economy, with its heavy emphasis on war and the fur trade presented women with a special set of opportunities. Thus, as we shall see, cultural, demographic and economic conditions combined to produce the remarkable women of New France.

---

[a] The women surpass the men in beauty, liveliness, mirth and cleverness; they are flirts and forward, prefer men from Europe to those around them. Pleasant and polite manners are common, even in the countryside.

[b] ...the women are very agreeable but extremely proud.

[c] ...they are witty, which makes them superior to the men in almost every way.

[d] possess greater intelligence than the men, are generally quite intelligent, speak a refined French without the least accent, also like personal adornments, are pretty, generous and even genteel.

[e] the European political and social system before the French Revolution.

Women and the Family Under the *Ancien Régime*

The notion of "woman's place" or "women's role," popular with nineteenth-century commentators, suggests a degree of homogeneity inappropriate to the seventeenth century. It is true that on a formal ideological level men enjoyed the dominant position. This can be seen in the marriage laws which everywhere made it a wife's duty to follow her husband to whatever dwelling place he chose.[8] In 1650, the men of Montreal were advised by Governor Maisonneuve that they were in fact responsible for the misdemeanours of their wives since *"la loi les établit seigneurs de leurs femmes."*[f][9] Under ordinary circumstances the father was captain of the family hierarchy.[10] Yet, it is clear that this formal male authority in both economic and domestic life was not always exercised. Of early seventeenth-century France we are told that:

> si la prééminence masculine n'a rien perdu de son prestige, si elle n'a eu à se défendre contre aucune revendication théorique ... elle a dû ... souvent se contenter des apparences et abandonner devant les convenances et les exigences du public l'intérêt positif qu'elle défendait.[g][11]

The idea of separate male and female spheres lacked the clear definition it later acquired. This is in part related to the lack of communication and standardization characteristic of the *ancien régime*—along sexual lines or any others. Generalizations about women are riddled with exceptions. Contradicting the idea of female inferiority, for example, were the semi-matriarchal system in the Basque country, and the linen workers guild, in which a 1645 statute prevented a worker's husband from engaging in occupations unrelated to his wife's business, for which he often served as salesman or partner. More important, because it affected a larger group, was the fact that noblewomen were frequently exempt from legal handicaps affecting other women.[12]

One generalization, however, applies to all women of the *ancien régime*. They were not relegated to the private, domestic sphere of human activity because that sphere did not exist. Western Europeans had not yet learned to separate public and private life. As Philippe Ariès points out in his study of childhood, the private home, in which parents and children constitute a distinct unit, is a relatively recent development. In early modern Europe most of domestic life was lived in the company of all sorts of outsiders. Manor houses, where all the rooms interconnect with one another, show the lack of emphasis placed on privacy. Here, as in peasant dwellings, there were often no specialized rooms for sleeping, eating, working or receiving visitors; all were more or less public activities performed with a throng of servants, children, relatives, clerics, apprentices and

---

[f] the law makes them lords over their wives.

[g] if the male predominance has lost nothing of its authority, if it has not had to struggle against any theoretical claim, it has still had to be satisfied with appearances and make sacrifices to keep up appearances and to fulfil the requirements of the public good that it supports.

clients in attendance. Molière's comedies illustrate the familiarity of servants with their masters. Masters, maids and valets slept in the same room and servants discussed their masters' lives quite openly.[13]

Though familiar with their servants, people were less so with their children. They did not dote on infants as parents do today. It may have been, as some writers have suggested, that there was little point in growing attached to a fragile being so very apt, in those centuries, to be borne away by accident or disease. These unsentimental families of all ranks sent their children out to apprentice or serve in other people's homes. This was considered important as a basic education.[14] It has been estimated that the majority of Western European children passed part of their childhood living in some household other than their natal one.[15] Mothers of these children—reaching down, in the town, as far as the artisan class—commonly sent their infants out to nursemaids and in fact had very little to do with their physical maintenance.[16]

This lack of a clearly defined "private" realm relates vitally to the history of women, since this was precisely the sphere which they later were to inhabit.[17] Therefore it is important to focus on their place in the pre-private world. To understand women in New France one first must pass through that antechamber which Peter Laslett appropriately calls "the world we have lost." Its notions of sexuality and of the family apply to France and New France alike.

In this public world people had not yet learned to be private about their bodily functions, especially about their sexuality. For aid with their toilette, noblewomen did not blush to employ *hommes de chambre* [h] rather than maids. The door of the bedchamber stood ajar, if not absolutely open. Its inhabitants, proud of their fecundity, grinned out from under the bedclothes at their visitors. Newlyweds customarily received bedside guests.[18] The mother of Louis XIV held court and chatted with visitors while labouring to bring *le Roi Soleil* [i] into light of day. Humbler village women kept lesser court among the little crowd of neighbours who attended the midwife's efforts.[19] On the other side of the ocean, Franquet, arriving at Trois-Rivières in 1753, enjoyed the hospitality of Madame Rigaud de Vaudreuil who, feeling poorly, apparently received her visitors at bedside; farther west, he shared a bedroom with a married couple at Fort St. Jean.[20] From the seventeenth century to the colony's last days, clerics thundered more or less futilely against the *décolletage* of the *élite*.[j] [21] Lesser folk leaned towards short skirts[22] and boisterous public discussion of impotent husbands.[23] Rape cases also reveal a rather matter-of-fact attitude. Courts stressed monetary compensation for the victim (as if for trespass on private property) rather than wreaking vengeance on the lustful villain.[24] There was not the

---

[h] valets

[i] the Sun King

[j] necklines of the upper classes

same uneasiness in relations between the sexes which later, more puritanical, centuries saw, and which, judging by the withdrawal of women from public life in many of these societies, probably worked to their detriment.

Part of the reason these unsqueamish, rather public people were not possessive about their bodies was that they did not see themselves so much as individuals but as part of a larger more important unit—the family. In this world the family was the basic organization for most social and economic purposes.[25] As such it claimed the individual's first loyalty.[26] A much higher proportion of the population married than does today.[27] Studies of peasant societies suggest that, for most, marriage was an economic necessity:

> Le travail, particulièrement en milieu rural, était alors fondé sur une répartition des tâches entre les sexes: les marins et colporteurs sont absents plusieurs mois, leurs femmes font valoir les terres; les pêcheurs des marais vont au marché, les femmes à la pêche; le laboureur travaille aux champs, sa femme à la maison, c'est elle qui va au marché; dans le pays d'Auge, "les hommes s'occupent des bestiaux et les femmes aux fromages." Pour vivre il fallait donc être deux, un homme et une femme.[k] [28]

The family was able to serve as the basic economic unit in pre-industrial societies because the business of earning a living generally occurred at home. Just as public and private life were undifferentiated, so too were home and workplace. Agricultural and commercial pursuits were all generally "domestic" industries. We see this both in France and in New France. Removal of the man from home for most of the working day, an event which Laslett describes as the single most important event in the history of the modern European family,[29] was only beginning. The idea of man as breadwinner and woman as home-maker was not clearly developed. Women's range of economic activity was still nearly as wide as that of their husbands. Seventeenth-century France saw women working as bonesetters, goldbeaters, bookbinders, doubletmakers, burnishers, laundresses, woolfullers and wigmakers. Aside from their familiar role in the textile and clothing industries, women also entered heavy trades such as stoneworking and bricklaying. A master plumber, Barbe Legueux, maintained the drainage system for the fountains of Paris. In the commercial world, women worked as fishmongers, pedlars, greengrocers, publicans, moneylenders and auctioneers.[30] In New France, wives of artisans took advantage of their urban situation to attract customers into the taverns they set up alongside the workshop.[31] It was in farm work, which occupied most of the population, that

---

[k] Especially in rural areas, work was then based on the division of labour between the sexes. Since sailors and carters were absent for several months, their wives had to cultivate the land. Freshwater fishermen go to market while their wives go fishing. The ploughman works in the field while his wife works in the house as well as going to market. In the Auge region, "the men tend the animals and the women produce cheese." In order to survive, there had to be two, a man and a woman.

male and female tasks differed the least of all. *Habitantes* in New France toiled in the fields alongside the men; and they almost certainly—being better-educated than their French sisters—took up the farmwife's customary role of keeping accounts and managing purchases and sales.[32] Studies of Bordeaux commercial families have revealed that women also took a large role in business operations.[33] Marie de l'Incarnation's background as manager of one of France's largest transport companies,[34] shows that the phenomenon existed in other parts of France as well.

Given the economic importance of both spouses, it is not surprising to see marriage taking on some aspects of a business deal, with numerous relatives affixing their signatures to the contract. We see this in the provisions of the law which protected the property rights of both parties contracting a match. The fact that wives often brought considerable family property to the marriage, and retained rights to it, placed them in a better position than their nineteenth-century descendants were to enjoy.[35]

In New France the family's importance was intensified even beyond its usual economic importance in *ancien régime* societies. In the colony's early days, "all roads led to matrimony. The scarcity of women, the economic difficulties of existence, the danger, all tended to produce the same result: all girls became wives, all widows remarried."[36] Throughout the colony's history there was an exceptionally high annual marriage rate of eighteen to twenty-four per thousand.[37] The buildup of the family as a social institution perhaps came about because other social institutions, such as guilds and villages, were underdeveloped.[38] This heightened importance of the family probably enhanced women's position. In the family women tended to serve as equal partners with their husbands, whereas women were gradually losing their position in European guilds and professions.[39] We see this heightened importance of the family in the government's great concern to regulate it. At that time, the state *did* have a place in Canadian bedrooms (whose inhabitants we have already seen to be rather unconcerned about their privacy). Public intervention in domestic life took two major forms: the operation of the legal system and governmental attempts at family planning.

The outstanding characteristic of the legal system in New France—the *Coutume de Paris*[1]—is its concern to protect the rights of all members of the family. The *Coutume de Paris* is considered to have been a particularly benevolent regional variation of French law.[40] It was more egalitarian and less patriarchal than the laws of southern France which were based on Roman tradition. The *Coutume* reinforced the family, for example, by the penalties it levied on those transferring family property to non-kin.[41] It took care to protect the property of children of a first marriage when a widow or widower remarried.[42] It protected a woman's rights by assuring that the husband did not have power to alienate the family property (in contrast to eighteenth-century British law).[43]

---

[1] the body of customary law in force in the region of Paris.

The Canadians not only adopted the Parisian *coutume* in preference to the Norman *coutume,* which was harsher;[44] they also implemented the law in a way which maximized protection of all family members. Louise Dechêne, after examining the operation of the marriage and inheritance system, concludes that the Canadian application of the law was generous and egalitarian:

> Ces concentions matrimoniales ne nous apparaissent pas comme un marché, un affrontement entre deux lignées, mais comme un accord désintéressé entre les familles, visant à créer une nouvelle communauté, à l'assister si possible, à dresser quelques barrières à l'entour pour la protéger....
>
> La même simplicité, la même générosité président au partage des successions....[m] [45]

The criminal law, too, served to buttress family life with its harsh punishments for mistreatment of children.[46]

The royal administration, as well as the law, treated the family as a matter of vital public concern. The state often intervened in matters which later generations left to the individual or to the operations of private charity. Most famous, of course, is the policy of encouraging a high birth rate with financial incentives. There were also attempts to withdraw trading privileges from *voyageurs* who showed reluctance to take immigrant women to wife.[47] Particularly in the seventeenth century, we see the state regulating what modern societies would consider intimate matters. However, in a colony starved for manpower, reproduction was considered a matter of particularly vital public concern—a concern well demonstrated in the extremely harsh punishments meted out to women who concealed pregnancy.[48] We see a more positive side of this intervention in the care the Crown took of foundlings, employing nurses at a handsome salary to care for them, and making attempts to prevent children from bearing any stigma because of questionable origins.[49]

State regulation of the family was balanced by family regulation of the state. Families had an input into the political system, playing an important role in the running of the state. Indeed, it might be argued that the family was the basic political unit in New France. In an age when some members of the *noblesse* [n] prided themselves on their illiteracy, attending the right college was hardly the key to political success. Marrying into the right family was much more important. Nepotism, or rewarding one's kin with emoluments, seemed a most acceptable and natural form of patronage for those in power.[50] In this sense, a good marriage was considered a step upward for the whole family, which helps to explain why choice of spouse was so often a family decision.[51]

---

[m] These marriage agreements do not appear to us to be business arrangements or to turn the two families into adversaries. Rather, they are disinterested agreements between families and are intended to create a new household and, if possible, to help it erect a few defenses to provide protection.

The same simplicity and generosity apply when settling estates.

[n] nobility

These family lines were particularly tightly drawn among the military élite in New France. Franquet remarked that *"tous les gens d'un certain ordre sont liés de parenté et d'amitié dans ce pays."*[o] [52] In fact, with top military positions passing down from generation to generation, by the eighteenth century this élite became a caste.[53]

In this situation, where the *nom de famille* [p] was vastly more important than that of the individual, it was apparently almost as good for political (though not military) purposes to be an Agathe de Repentigny as a LeGardeur de Repentigny. Moreover, women's political participation was favoured by the large role of entertaining in political life. For the courtier's role, women were as well-trained as men, and there seems to have been no stigma attached to the woman who participated independently of her husband. Six women, Mesdames Daine, Pean, Lotbinière, de Repentigny, Marin, and St. Simon, along with six male officers, were chosen by the Intendant to accompany him to Montreal in 1753.[54] Of the twelve only the de Repentignys were a couple. It is surprising to see women from the colony's first families also getting down to what we would today consider the "business" end of politics. Madame de la Forest, a member of the Juchereau family, took an active role in the political cliques which Guy Frégault describes.[55] Mme. de la Forest's trip to France to plead the cause of Governor de Ramezay was inconsequential, though, in comparison with that of Mme. de Vaudreuil to further Governor Vaudreuil's cause in 1709. *"Douée d'un sens politique trés fin,"*[q] [56] she soon gained the ear of the Minister of Marine. Not only did she secure the Governor's victory in the long conflict with the Intendants Raudot (father and son) and win promotion for his patrons; she appears to have gone on to upstage her husband by becoming the virtual director of colonial policy at Versailles for a few years. Vaudreuil's biographer discusses the influence Madame de Vaudreuil exerted with the Minister Pontchartrain who so regularly sought her comment on colonial patronage that supplicants began to apply directly to her rather than to the minister.[57] Contemporaries agreed that her influence was vast:

> Pontchartrain, rapporte Ruette d'Auteuil, ne lui refuse rien, "elle dispose de tous les emplois du Canada, elle écrit de toutes parts dans les ports de mer des lettres magnifiques du bien et du mal qu'elle peut faire auprès de lui," et le ministre "fait tout ce qu'il faut pour l'autoriser et justifier ses discours." Riverin confirme que ... "ce n'est plus qu'une femme qui règne tant présente qu'absente."[r] [58]

---

[o] in this country, all the members of a certain class are connected by friendship and family relationships.

[p] family name

[q] Possessing a very subtle political sense

[r] Ruette d'Auteuil reports that Pontchartrain denies her nothing and that "she controls all the postings in Canada. She writes proud letters from every seaport that she can do anything with him," and that the minister "does everything necessary to give her authority and to support what she says." Riverin confirms that "this involves nothing more than a woman who rules whether she is present or not."

Governor Frontenac's wife (though not a *Canadienne*) also played an important role at court dispelling some of the thunderclouds which threatened her husband's stormy career.[59]

As for the common folk, we know even less about the political activity of women than that of men. That women participated in a form of popular assembly is hinted at in a report of a meeting held in 1713 (in present-day Boucherville), in which Catherine Guertin was sworn in as midwife after having been elected *"dans l'assemblée des femmes de cette paroisse, à la pluralité des suffrages, pour exercer l'office de sagefemme."*[s][60] Were these women's assemblies a general practice? If so, what other matters did they decide? This aspect of *habitant* politics remains a mystery, but women, as historians of "crowds" have found, were certainly part of the "pre-industrial crowd."[61] Along with their menfolk, they were full-fledged members of the old "moral economy" whose members rioted, took what was traditionally their rightful share (and no more) when prices were too high or when speculators were hoarding grain.[62] The women of Quebec and Montreal, who rioted against the horsemeat rations and the general hunger of 1757–58, illustrate this aspect of the old polity.[63]

In sum, women's position during the *ancien régime* was open-ended. Although conditions varied, a wide range of roles were available to women, to be taken up or not. This was so because the separate spheres of men and women in *ancien régime* societies were not so clearly developed as they later became. There was as yet no sharp distinction between public and private life: families were for most purposes the basic social, economic and political unit. Owing to the underdevelopment of other institutions (the guild, the *seigneurie*, the village), this situation was intensified in New France. The activities of breadwinner and home-maker were not yet widely recognized as separate functions belonging to one sex or the other. All members of the family also often shared the same economic functions, or at least roles were interchangeable. Nor had the symbolic, the honorific, the stylistic aspects of government yet been separated from the business end of politics and administration. These conditions, typical of most of pre-industrial France, were also found in New France, where particular demographic and economic conditions would enable the colony's women to develop their freedoms and opportunities to the fullest.

Demographic Advantages

Demography favoured the women of New France in two ways. First, the women who went there were a highly select group of immigrants. Secondly, women were in short supply in the early years of the colony's development, a situation that worked in their favour.

---

[s] in this parish's women's committee, with the majority of the votes, in order to carry out the duties of midwife.

The bulk of the female immigrants to New France fall into one of two categories. The first was a group of extremely well-born, well-endowed and highly dedicated religious figures. They began to arrive in 1639, and a trickle of French nuns continued to cross the ocean over the course of the next century. The second distinct group was the *filles du roi*,[t] government-sponsored female migrants who arrived between 1663 and 1673. These immigrants, though not as outstanding as the *dévotes*,[u] were nevertheless privileged compared to the average immigrant to New France, who arrived more or less threadbare.[64] The vast majority of the women (and the men) came from the Ile-de-France and the northwestern parts of France. The women of northern France enjoyed fuller legal rights, were better-educated, and more involved in commerce than those of southern France.[65] When they set foot on colonial soil with all this auspicious baggage, the immigrants found that they had yet another advantage. Women constituted a small percentage of the population. As a scarce resource, they were highly prized and therefore in an excellent position to gain further advantages.

The first *religieuses*[v] to arrive in New France were the Ursulines and Hospitallers who landed at Quebec in 1639. These were soon followed by women who helped establish Montreal in 1642. Their emigration was inspired by a religious revival in France, which is thought to have arisen in response to the widespread pauperism following the French civil wars of the sixteenth century. The seventeenth-century revival distinguished itself by tapping the energies of women in an unprecedented way.[66] Among its leaders were Anne of Austria and a number of the leading ladies at court.[67] In other parts of France, women of the provincial élite implemented the charity work inspired by Saint Vincent de Paul.[68] Occurring between 1600 and 1660, this religious revival coincided almost exactly with the period when the fledgling Canadian colony, besieged by English privateers and by the Iroquois, was most desperately in need of an injection of immigrants, money and enthusiasm.[69] It was at this moment that the Jesuits in Quebec appealed to the French public for aid. Much to their surprise, they received not a donation but a half-dozen religious zealots, in person. Abandoning the centuries-old cloistered role of female religious figures these nuns undertook missionary work which gave them an active role in the life of the colony.[70] Thus the great religious revival of the seventeenth century endowed New France with several exceptionally capable, well-funded, determined leaders imbued with an activist approach to charity and with that particular mixture of spiritual ardour and worldly *savoir-faire*[w] which typified the mystics of that period.[71] The praises of Marie de

---

[t] daughters of the King

[u] religious-minded women

[v] nuns

[w] sophistication

l'Incarnation, Jeanne Mance and Marguerite Bourgeoys have been sung so often as to be tiresome. Perhaps, though a useful vantage point is gained if one assesses them neither as saints nor heroines, but simply as leaders. In this capacity, the nuns supplied money, publicity, skills, and settlers, all of which were needed in the colony.

Marie de l'Incarnation, an extremely competent business woman from Tours, founded the Ursuline Monastery at Quebec in 1639. Turning to the study of Indian languages, she and her colleagues helped implement the policy of assimilating the young Indians. Then, gradually abandoning that futile policy, they turned to the education of the French colonists. Marie de l'Incarnation developed the farm on the Ursuline *seigneurie* and served as an unofficial adviser to the colonial administrators. She also helped draw attention and money to the colony by writing some 12,000 letters between 1639 and her death in 1672.[72]

An even more prodigious fund-raiser in those straitened times was Jeanne Mance, who had a remarkable knack for making friends in high places.[73] They enabled her to supply money and colonists for the original French settlement on the island of Montreal, and to take a place beside Maisonneuve as co-founder of the town.[74] The hospital she established there had the legendary wealth of the de Bullion family—and the revenues of three Norman domains—behind it. From this endowment she made the crucial grant to Governor Maisonneuve in 1651 which secured vitally needed French troops—thus saving Montreal.[75] Mance and her Montreal colleague Marguerite Bourgeoys both made several voyages to France to recruit settlers. They were particularly successful in securing the female immigrants necessary to establish a permanent colony, recruiting sizeable groups in 1650, 1653 and 1659.[76]

Besides contributing to the colony's sheer physical survival, the nuns materially raised the living standards of the population. They conducted the schools which were attended by girls of all classes, and from both of the colony's races. Bourgeoys provided housing for newly arrived immigrants and served in a capacity perhaps best described as an early social worker.[77] Other nuns established hospitals in each of the three towns. The colonists reaped fringe benefits in the institutions established by this exceptionally dedicated personnel. The hospitals, for example, provided high-quality care to both rich and poor; care which compared favourably with that of similar institutions in France.[78] Thus, the *dévotes* played an important role in supplying leadership, funding, publicity, recruits and social services. They may even have tipped the balance towards survival in the 1650s, when retention of the colony was still in doubt.

In the longer run, they endowed the colony with an educational heritage, which survived and shaped social life long after the initial heroic piety had grown cold. The schools that the *dévotes* founded created a situation very different from that in France, where education of women in the seventeenth century lagged behind that of men.[79] The opinion-setters in France sought to justify this neglect in the eighteenth century and a controversy began over whether girls should be educated outside the home at all.[80] Girls in Montreal escaped all this. Indeed, in 1663 Montrealers had a school for their girls but none for their boys. The result was that for a time Montreal women surpassed men in literacy, a reversal of the usual *ancien régime* pattern.[81] The superior education of women which Charlevoix extolled in 1744 continued until the fall of New France (and beyond)—a tendency heightened by the large percentage of soldiers, generally illiterate, among the male population.[82] The Ursulines conducted schools for the élite at Quebec and Trois-Rivières. This order was traditionally rather weak in teaching housekeeping (which perhaps accounts for Kalm's famous castigation of Canadian housewifery). Nevertheless they specialized in needlework, an important skill since articles of clothing were a major trade good sought by the Indians. Moreover the Ursulines taught the daughters of the élite the requisite skills for administering a house and a fortune—skills which, as we shall see later, many were to exercise.[83]

More remarkable than the Ursuline education, however, was that of the *Soeurs de la Congrégation,*[x] which reached the popular classes in the countryside.[84] Franquet was apparently shocked by the effect of this exceptional education on the colonial girls. He recommended that the *Soeurs'* schools be suppressed because they made it difficult to keep girls down on the farm:

> Ces Soeurs sont répandues le long des côtes, dans des seigneuries où elles ont été attirées pour l'éducation des jeunes filles; leur utilité semble être démontrée, mais le mal qu'en résulte est comme un poison lent qui tend à dépeupler les campagnes, d'autant qu'une fille instruite fait la demoiselle, qu'elle est maniérée, qu'elle veut prendre un éstablissement à la ville, qu'il lui faut un négociant et qu'elle regarde au dessous d'elle l'état dans lequel elle est née.[y] [85]

The second distinct group of female immigrants to New France was the famous *filles du roi*, women sent out by the French government as brides in order to boost the colony's permanent settlement. Over 900 arrived between 1663 and 1673.[86] If less impressive than the *dévotes*, they too appear to have arrived with more than the average immigrant's store of education and capital. Like the nuns, they were the product of a particular historical moment which thrust them across the sea. The relevant event here is that brief interlude in the 1660s and 1670s when the King, his Minister Colbert and the Intendant Talon applied an active hand to colonial development.[87]

---

[x] Sisters of the Order of the Congregation

[y] These nuns can be found all along the river, in the *seigneuries* where they have been attracted in order to educate the young girls. Their usefulness seems evident but the evil that results from their presence works like a slow poison that tends to reduce the rural population because a girl who has received an education begins to act above her station and to put on airs. She then wants to set herself up in town and to insist on marrying a merchant, eventually deciding that her social class at birth is now beneath her.

There has been much historical controversy about whether the *filles du roi* were pure or not.[88] More relevant to our discussion than their morality are their money and their skills. On both these counts, this was a very selective immigration. First of all, the majority of the *filles du roi* (and for that matter, of seventeenth-century female immigrants generally) were urban dwellers, a group which enjoyed better access to education than the peasantry did.[89] Moreover, the *filles du roi* were particularly privileged urbanites. Over one third, some 340 of them, were educated at the Paris Hôpital Général. Students at this institution learned writing and such a wide variety of skills that in France they were much sought after for service in the homes of the wealthy. 6 per cent were of noble or bourgeois origin. All the *filles* brought with them a 50–100 *livres* [z] dowry provided by the King; most supplemented this with personal funds in the order of 200–300 *livres*.[90] According to Lanctôt, among lay immigrants, these women constituted the immigration *"la plus stricte, la plus saine et la plus recommandable de toute cette époque."*[aa] [91] The Parisian origins of many *filles du roi*, and of the nuns who taught their children, probably account for the pure French accent which a number of travellers attributed to the colony's women.[92]

These two major immigrant groups, then, the nuns and the *filles du roi*, largely account for the superior education and "cultivation" attributed to the colony's women. Another demographic consideration also favoured the women of New France. As a result of light female emigration, men heavily outnumbered women in the colony's early days; a balance was not attained until 1710.[93] It might be expected that, as a scarce commodity, women would receive favoured treatment. The facility of marriage and remarriage, the salaries women received, and the leniency of the courts and the administrators towards women, suggest that this hypothesis is correct.

Women had a wider choice in marriage than did men in the colony's early days. There were, for example, eight marriageable men for every marriageable woman in Montreal in 1663. Widows grieved, briefly, then remarried within an average of 8.8 months after their bereavement. In those early days the laws of supply and demand operated to women's economic advantage, as well. Rarely did these first Montreal women bother to match their husband's wedding present by offering a dowry.[94] The colony distinguished itself as "the country of the *douaire* not of the *dot*."[bb] [95]

Other economic indicators suggest that scarcity served women well. Observers of women's salaries in the nineteenth and twentieth centuries are used to finding them ranging from one-half to two-thirds those of men. This list of 1744 salaries of New France therefore comes as something of a surprise:

---

[z] pounds

[aa] the most demanding, the healthiest and the most to be recommended for the whole period.

[bb] "the country of the marriage settlement not of the marriage portion."

Un professeur de collège	400 *livres*
Une institutrice	500 *livres*
Une sage-femme attachée à l'Hôtel-Dieu de Québec	400 *livres*
le prévot des maréchaux	500 *livres*
le lieutenant général de Montréal	450 *livres*
le procureur du roi (Mtl.)	250 *livres*
un conseiller ordinaire au Conseil Supérieur	300 *livres*
un Missionnaire au Poste de la mer de l'Ouest	600 *livres*[cc][96]

Perhaps the government, as in later centuries, led the way as an "equal opportunity" employer. At any rate, nursemaids hired by the government acquired not only the civil servant's dignity and job security but were paid, we are told, their salaries in cash, in advance, and at a rate "more than the townspeople were accustomed to pay for the nursing of their own children."[97]

In the social and legal realm we also find privileges which may have been attributable to the shortage of women. Perhaps it is due to the difficulties of replacing battered wives that jealous husbands in New France were willing to forego the luxury of uncontrolled rage. Some of the Intendants even charged that there were libertine wives in the colony who got away with taking a second husband while the first was away trading furs.[98] Recent indications that New France conformed rather closely to French traditions make it unlikely that this was common.[99] But the judgements of the Sovereign Council do offer evidence of peaceful reconciliations such as that of Marguerite Leboeuf, charged with adultery in 1667. The charge was dismissed when her husband pleaded before the Sovereign Council on her behalf. Also leaving vengeance largely to the Lord was Antoine Antorche, who withdrew his accusation against his wife even after the Council found her doubly guilty.[100] In this regard the men of New France differed from their Portuguese brothers in Brazil, who perpetrated a number of amorous murders each year; also from their English brethren in Massachusetts, who branded or otherwise mutilated their errant wives and daughters.[101] When such cases reached the courts in New France the judges, too, appear to have been lenient. Their punishments for adulterous women were considerably lighter

---

[cc] A male teacher in a college — 400 pounds
A female teacher — 500 pounds
A midwife working at the Hôtel-Dieu in Quebec City — 400 pounds
The provost marshall — 500 pounds
The lieutenant-general for Montreal — 450 pounds
The royal procurator (Montreal) — 250 pounds
An ordinary member on the Superior Council — 300 pounds
A missionary stationed at Western Posts — 600 pounds

than those imposed in New England. Other female offenders, such as the whiskey trader captured in 1661, received a much lighter punishment than men convicted of identical offences. A further peculiarity of the legal system in New France, which suggests that women were closer to being on an equal footing with men than in other times and places, was the unusual attempt to arrest not only prostitutes but their clients as well.[102]

Another indication of the lenient treatment Canadian women enjoyed is the level of insubordination the authorities were willing to accept from them. There was a distinct absence of timidity *vis-à-vis* the political authorities. In 1714, for example, the inhabitants of Côte St. Leonard violently objected to the Bishop's decision to cancel their membership in the familiar church and enrol them in the newly erected parish of Rivière-des-Prairies. A fracas ensued in which the consecrated altar breads were captured by the rebellious parishioners. An officer sent to restore order was assailed by angry women:

> L'huissier chargé d'aller assigner les séditieux, raconte que toutes les femmes l'attendaient "avec des roches et des perches dans leurs mains pour m'assassiner," qu'elles le poursuivirent en jurant: "arrête voleur, nous te voulons tuer et jeter dans le marais."[dd] [103]

Other women hurled insults at the Governor himself in the 1670s.[104] An even more outrageous case of insubordination was that of the two Desaulniers sisters, who by dint of various appeals, deceits and stalling tactics, continued to run an illegal trading post at Caughnawaga for some twenty-five years despite repeated orders from Governors, Intendants and the ministry itself, to close it down.[105]

A further indication of women's privileged position is the absence of witchcraft persecution in New France. The colony was founded in the seventeenth century when this persecution was at its peak in Western Europe. The New Englanders, too, were burning witches at Salem. Not a single Canadienne died for this offence.[106] It is not—as Marie de l'Incarnation's account of the 1663 earthquake makes clear[107]—that the Canadians were not a superstitious people. A scholar of crime in New France suggests that this surprising absence of witchcraft hysteria relates to the fact that *"depuis le début de la colonie une femme était une rareté trés estimée et de ce fait, protégée de la persécution en masse."*[ee] [108]

Thus, on the marriage market, and in their protection from physical violence, women seem to have achieved a favourable position because of their small numbers. Their relatively high wages and lighter court sentences may also have been related to the demographic imbalance. Moreover, the original female immigrants arrived in the colony with better-than-average education and capital, attributes which undoubtedly helped them to establish their privileged status.

[dd] The officer responsible for apprehending the troublemakers states that all the women were waiting for him "with rocks and sticks in their hands that they were going to kill me with," and that they chased him, swearing, "Stop, thief, we want to kill you and throw you in the pond."

[ee] "since the early days of the colony, women have not been numerous and have thus been greatly respected and, as a result, protected from mass persecution."

Economic Opportunities

Even more than demographic forces, the colonial economy served to enhance the position of women. In relation to the varied activities found in many regions of France, New France possessed a primitive economy. Other than subsistence farming, the *habitants* engaged in two major pursuits. The first was military activity, which included not only actual fighting but building and maintaining the imperial forts, and provisioning the troops. The second activity was the fur trade. Fighting and fur-trading channelled men's ambitions and at times removed them physically from the colony. This helped open up the full range of opportunities to women, whom we have already seen had the possibility of assuming a wide variety of economic roles in *ancien régime* society. Many adapted themselves to life in a military society. A few actually fought. Others made a good living by providing goods and services to the ever-present armies. Still others left military activity aside and concentrated on civilian economic pursuits—pursuits which were often neglected by men. For many this simply meant managing the family farm as best as one could during the trading season, when husbands were away. Other women assumed direction of commercial enterprises, a neglected area in this society which preferred military honours to commercial prizes. Others acted as a sort of home-office partner for fur-trading husbands working far afield. Still others, having lost husbands to raids, rapids or other hazards of forest life, assumed a widow's position at the helm of the family business.

New France has been convincingly presented as a military society. The argument is based on the fact that a very large proportion of its population was under arms, its government had a semi-military character, its economy relied heavily on military expenditure and manpower, and a military ethos prevailed among the élite.[109] In some cases, women joined their menfolk in these martial pursuits. The seventeenth century sometimes saw them in direct combat. A number of Montrealers perished during an Iroquois raid in 1661 in which, Charlevoix tells us, "even the women fought to the death, and not one of them surrendered."[110] In Acadia, Madame de la Tour took command of the fort's forty-five soldiers and warded off her husband's arch-enemy, Menou D'Aulnay, for three days before finally capitulating.[111]

The most famous of these seventeenth-century *guerrières* [ff] was, of course, Madeleine de Verchères. At the age of fourteen she escaped from a band of Iroquois attackers, rushed back to the fort on her parents' *seigneurie* and fired a cannon shot in time to warn all the surrounding settlers of the danger.[112] Legend and history have portrayed Madeleine as a lamb who was able, under siege, to summon up a lion's heart. Powdered and demure in a pink dress, she smiles very sweetly out at the world in a charming vignette in Arthur Doughty's *A Daughter of New France, being a story of the life and times of Magdelaine de Verchères*, published in 1916. Perhaps the late twentieth century is ready for her as she was: a swashbuckling, musket-toting braggart who extended the

---

[ff] warrior women

magnitude of her deeds with each successive telling, who boasted that she never in her life shed a tear; a contentious thorn in the side of the local curé (whom she slandered), and of her *censitaires,*[gg] (whom she constantly battled in the courts).[113] She strutted through life for all the world like the boorish male officers of the *campagnard* [hh] nobility to which her family belonged.[114] One wonders how many more there were like her. Perhaps all trace of them has vanished into the wastebaskets of subsequent generations of historians who, with immovable ideas of female propriety, did not know what on earth to do with them—particularly after what must have been the exhausting effort of pinching Verchères' muscled frame into a corset and getting her to wear the pink dress.

By the eighteenth century, women had withdrawn from hand-to-hand combat, but many remained an integral part of the military élite as it closed in to become a caste. In this system, both sexes shared the responsibility of marrying properly and of maintaining those cohesive family ties which, Corvisier tells us, lay at the heart of military society. Both also appealed to the Ministry for their sons' promotions.[115]

What is more surprising is that a number of women accompanied their husbands to military posts in the wilderness. Wives of officers, particularly of corporals, traditionally helped manage the canteens in the French armies.[116] Almost all Canadian officers were involved in some sort of trading activity, and a wife at the post could mind the store when the husband had to mind the war. Some were overzealous. When Franquet rode into Fort Saint Frédéric in 1752 he discovered a terrific row among its inhabitants. The post was in a virtual state of mutiny because a Madame Lusignan was monopolizing all the trade, both wholesale and retail, at the fort; and her husband, the Commandant, was enforcing the monopoly.[117] In fact, Franquet's inspection tour of the Canadian posts is remarkable for the number of women who greeted him at the military posts, which one might have expected to be a male preserve. Arriving at Fort Sault Saint Louis he was received very politely by M. de Merceau and his two daughters. He noted that Fort Saint Frédéric housed not only the redoubtable Madame Lusignan but also another officer's widow. At Fort Chambly he "spent the whole day with the ladies, and visited Madame de Beaulac, an officer's widow who has been given lodging in this fort."[118]

The nuns, too, marched in step with this military society. They were, quite literally, one of its lifelines, since they cared for its wounded. A majority of the invalids at the Montreal Hôtel Dieu were soldiers, and the Ursuline institution at Trois-Rivières was referred to simply as a *hôpital militaire*.[ii] [119] Hospital service was so vital to the army that Frontenac personally intervened to speed construction of the Montreal Hôtel-Dieu in 1695, when he was

---

[gg] tenants

[hh] rural

[ii] military hospital

planning a campaign against the Iroquois.[120] In the colony's first days, the Ursulines also made great efforts to help the Governor seal Indian alliances by attempting to secure Iroquois students who would serve as hostages, and by giving receptions for Iroquois chiefs.[121]

Humbler folk also played a part in military society. In the towns female publicans conducted a booming business with the thirsty troops. Other women served as laundresses, adjuncts so vital that they accompanied armies even on the campaigns where wives and other camp followers were ordered to stay home.[122] Seemingly indispensable, too, wherever armies march, are prostitutes. At Quebec City they plied their trade as early as 1667. Indian women at the missions also served in this capacity.[123] All told, women had more connections with the military economy than is generally noted.

While warfare provided a number of women with a living, it was in commerce that the *Canadiennes* really flourished. Here a number of women moved beyond supporting roles to occupy centre stage. This happened for several reasons. The first was that the military ethos diverted men from commercial activity. Secondly, many men who entered the woods to fight or trade were gone for years. Others, drowned or killed in battle, obviously never returned.[124] This left many widows who had to earn a livelihood. This happened so often, in fact, that when in 1710 women finally overcame the population imbalance due to their weak immigration, the tables turned quickly; they soon outnumbered the men, and remained a majority through to the Conquest.[125] Generally speaking, life was more hazardous for men than for women[126]—so much so that the next revolution of the historiographic wheel may turn up the men of New France (at least in relation to its women) as an oppressed group.

At any rate, women often stepped in to take the place of their absent husbands or brothers. A surprising number of women traders emerge in the secondary literature on New France. In the colony's earliest days, the mere handful of women included two merchants at Trois-Rivières: Jeanne Enard (mother-in-law of Pierre Boucher) who "by her husband's own admission" was the head of the family as far as fur-trading was concerned; and, Mathurine Poisson, who sold imported goods to the colonists.[127] At Montreal there was the wife of Artus de Sully, whose unspecified (but presumably commercial) activities won her the distinction of being Montreal's biggest debtor.[128] In Quebec City, Eleonore de Grandmaison was a member of a company formed to trade in the Ottawa country. She added to her wealth by renting her lands on the Ile d'Orleans to Huron refugees after Huronia had been destroyed. Farther east, Madame de la Tour involved herself in shipping pelts to France. Another Acadian, Madame Joybert, traded furs on the Saint John River.[129]

With the onset of the less pious eighteenth century, we find several women at the centre of the illegal fur trade. Indian women, including "a cross-eyed squaw named Marie-Magdelaine" regularly carried contraband goods from the Caughnawaga Reserve to Albany.[130] A Madame Couagne received Albany contraband at the other end, in Montreal.[131] But at the heart of this illegal trade were the Desaulniers sisters, who used their trading post on the Caughnawaga reserve as an *entrepô*[jj] for the forbidden English strouds, fine textiles, pipes, boots, lace, gloves, silver tableware, chocolate, sugar and oysters which the Indians brought regularly from Albany.[132] Franquet remarked on the power of these *marchandes*,[kk] who were able to persuade the Indians to refuse the government's request to build fortifications around their village.[133] The Desaulniers did not want the comings and goings of their employees too closely scrutinized.

These *commerçantes*,[ll] honest and otherwise, continued to play their part until the Conquest. Marie-Anne Barbel (*Veuve* [mm] Fornel) farmed the Tadoussac fur trade and was involved in diverse enterprises including retail sales, brickmaking and real estate.[134] On Franquet's tour in the 1750s he encountered other *marchandes* besides the controversial "Madame la Commandante" who had usurped the Fort Saint Frédéric trade. He enjoyed a more restful night closer to Montreal at the home of Madame de Lemothe, a *marchande* who had prospered so well that she was able to put up her guests in splendid beds which Franquet proclaimed "fit for a duchess."[135]

A number of writers have remarked on the shortage of entrepreneurial talent in New France.[136] This perhaps helps to account for the activities of Agathe de St. Père, who established the textile industry in Canada. She did so after the colonial administrators had repeatedly called for development of spinning and weaving, with no result.[137] Coming from the illustrious Le Moyne family, Agathe St. Père married the ensign Pierre Legardeur de Repentigny, a man who, we are told, had "an easygoing nature." St. Père, of another temperament, pursued the family business interests, investing in fur trade partnerships, real estate and lending operations. Then in 1705, when the vessel bringing the yearly supply of French cloth to the colony was shipwrecked, she saw an opportunity to develop the textile industry in Montreal. She ransomed nine English weavers who had been captured by the Indians, and arranged for apprentices to study the trade. Subsequently these apprentices taught the trade to other Montrealers on home looms which Madame de Repentigny built and distributed. Besides developing the manufacture of linen, drugget and serge, she discovered new chemicals which made use of the native plants to dye and process them.[138]

Upon this foundation Madame Benoist built. Around the time of the Conquest, she was directing an operation in Montreal in which women turned out, among other things, shirts and petticoats for the fur trade.[139] This is a case of woman doing business while man did battle, for Madame Benoist's husband was commanding officer at Lac des Deux Montagnes.

[jj] warehouse

[kk] women merchants

[ll] dealers

[mm] Widow

This absence of male entrepreneurs may also explain the operation of a large Richelieu lumbering operation by Louise de Ramezay, the daughter of the Governor of Montreal. Louise, who remained single, lost her father in 1724. Her mother continued to operate the sawmilling operation on the family's Chambly Seigneury, but suffered a disastrous reverse due to a combination of flooding, theft and shipwreck in 1725. The daughter, however, went into partnership with the Seigneuress de Rouville in 1745 and successfully developed the sawmill. She then opened a flour mill, a Montreal tannery and another sawmill. By the 1750s the trade was flourishing: Louise de Ramezay was shipping 20,000 *livres* loads, and one merchant alone owed her 60,000 *livres*. In 1753 she began to expand her leather business, associating with a group of Montreal tanners to open new workshops.[140]

Louise de Ramezay's case is very clearly related to the fact that she lived in a military society. As Louise was growing up, one by one her brothers perished. Claude, an ensign in the French navy, died during an attack on Rio de Janeiro in 1711, Louis died during the 1715 campaign against the Fox Indians, La Gesse died ten years later in a shipwreck off Ile Royale. That left only one son, Jean-Baptiste-Roch, and, almost inevitably, he chose a military career over management of the family business affairs.[141] It may be that similar situations accounted for the female entrepreneurs in ironforging, tilemaking, sturgeon-fishing, sealing and contract building, all of whom operated in New France.[142]

If military society was the warp for this network of trading women, family connections were the woof. Madame Benoist belonged to the Baby family, whose male members were out cultivating the western fur trade. Her production of shirts made to the Indians' specifications was the perfect complement. The secret of the Desaulniers' successful trade network may well be that they were related to so many of Montreal's leading merchants.[143] The fur trade generally required two or more bases of operation. We saw earlier in our discussion that this society not only placed great value on family connections but also accepted female commercial activity. It was therefore quite natural that female relatives would be recruited into business to cover one of the bases. Men who were heading for the west would delegate their powers of attorney and various business responsibilities to their wives, who were remaining in the colony.[144]

We find these husband-wife fur trade partnerships not only among *"Les Grandes Familles"*[nn] but permeating all classes of society. At Trois-Rivières women and girls manufactured the canoes which carried the fur trade provisions westward each summer. This was a large-scale operation which profited from fat government contracts.[145] In Montreal, wives kept the account-books while their husbands traded. Other women spent the winters sewing shirts and petticoats which would be bartered the following summer.[146]

[nn] The Leading Families

The final reason for women's extensive business activity was the direct result of the hazards men faced in fighting and fur trading. A high proportion of women were widowed; and as widows, they enjoyed special commercial privileges. In traditional French society, these privileges were so extensive that craftsmen's widows sometimes inherited full guild-master's rights. More generally, widows acquired the right to manage the family assets until the children reached the age of twenty-five (and sometimes beyond that time). In some instances they also received the right to choose which child would receive the succession.[147] In New France these rights frequently came into operation; and they had a major impact on the distribution of wealth and power in the society. In 1663, for example, women held the majority of the colony's seigneurial land. The *Veuve* Lemoyne numbered among the twelve Montreal merchants who, between 1642 and 1725, controlled assets of 50,000 *livres*. The *Veuve* Fornel acquired a similar importance later on in the regime. Some of the leading merchants at Louisbourg were also widows. The humbler commerce of tavernkeeping was also frequently a widow's lot.[148]

Thus, in New France, both military and commercial activities which required a great deal of travelling over vast distances were usually carried out by men. In their absence, their wives played a large role in the day-to-day economic direction of the colony. Even when the men remained in the colony, military ambitions often absorbed their energies, particularly among the upper class. In these situations, it was not uncommon for a wife to assume direction of the family interests.[149] Others waited to do so until their widowhood, which—given the fact that the average wife was considerably younger than her husband and that his activities were often more dangerous—frequently came early.

Conclusion

New France had been founded at a time in Europe's history in which the roles of women were neither clearly nor rigidly defined. In this fluid situation, the colony received an exceptionally well-endowed group of female immigrants during its formative stage. There, where they long remained in short supply, they secured a number of special privileges at home, at school, in the courts, and in social and political life. They consolidated this favourable position by attaining a major role in the colonial economy, at both the popular and the directive levels. These circumstances enabled the women of New France to play many parts. *Dévotes* and traders, warriors and landowners, smugglers and politicians, industrialists and financiers; they thronged the stage in such numbers that they distinguish themselves as *femmes favorisées*.

Notes

1. F.-X. Charlevoix, *History and General Description of New France* (New York: Harper, 1900), Vol. 3: p. 28.

2. Cited in R.-L. Séguin, "La Canadienne aux XVIIe et XVIIIe siècles," *Revue d'historie de l'Amérique français,* XIII, (mars 1960), p. 492.

3. Séguin, "La Canadienne," p. 500.

4. *Ibid.*

5. L. Franquet, *Voyages et mémoires sur le Canada* (Montréal: Editions Elysee, 1974), p. 57, recording a tour in 1752–53.

6. *Ibid.,* p. 31.

7. Séguin, "La Canadienne," pp. 492, 505.

8. G. Fagniez, *La Femme et la société française dans la première moitié du XVIIe siècle* (Paris: J. Gambler, 1929), p. 154.

9. Marcel Trudel, *Montréal, la formation d'une société* (Montreal: Fides, 1976), p. 216–217.

10. John F. Bosher, "The Family in New France," in *In Search of the Visible Past,* Barry Gough, ed. (Waterloo, Ont.: W.L.U. Press, 1976), p. 7.

11. Fagniez, *Femme et société française,* p. 121.

12. *Ibid.,* pp. 149, 104, 193.

13. Philippe Ariès, *Centuries of Childhood* (New York: Vintage 1962), pp. 392–406.

14. *Ibid.,* pp. 365–66.

15. Peter Laslett, "Characteristics of the Western Family Considered over Time," *Journal of Family History,* 2 (Summer 1977), pp. 89–115.

16. Richard Vann, "Women in Preindustrial Capitalism," in *Becoming Visible: Women in European History,* R. Bridenthal, ed. (Boston: Houghton Mifflin, 1977), p. 206.

17. *Ibid.,* pp. 206–8; Ariès, *Centuries of Childhood,* pp. 397–406.

18. Fagniez, *Femme et société française,* pp. 122–23; 179.

19. Vann, "Women in Preindustrial Capitalism," p. 206.

20. Franquet, *Voyages,* pp. 135 and 61.

21. Séguin, "La Canadienne," p. 499 and R. Boyer, *Les Crimes et châtiments au Canada française du XVIIIe au XXe siècle* (Montreal: 1966), p. 391.

22. Séguin, "La Canadienne," p. 506.

23. Boyer, *Crimes et châtiments,* p. 351.

24. *Ibid.,* pp. 344–46.

25. Laslett, "Western Family," p. 95.

26. I. Foulché-Delbosc, "Women of Three Rivers, 1651–1663," in *The Neglected Majority,* A. Prentice and S. Trofimenkoff, eds. (Toronto: McClelland and Stewart, 1977), p. 26.

27. Bosher ("The Family," p. 3) found the marriage rate in New France to be about three times that of modern-day Quebec.

28. This information is taken from a study of Normandy, which was the birthplace of many of the Canadian colonists. J.M. Gouesse, "La Formation du couple en Basse-Normandie," *XVIIe Siècle,* Nos. 102–3 (1974), p. 56.

29. Laslett, "Western Family," p. 106.

30. Fagniez, *Femme et société française,* pp. 99–104, 108, 111, 114–16.

31. Louise Dechêne, *Habitants et marchands de Montréal au XVIIe siècle* (Paris: Plon, 1974), p. 393.

32. Fagniez, *Femme et société française,* pp. 101, 1913, Séguin, "La Canadienne," p. 503; also G. Lanctôt, *Filles de joie ou filles du roi* (Montréal, 1952), m pp. 210–13.

33. Cf. Paul Butel, "Comportements familiaux dans le négoce bordelais au XVIIIe siècle," *Annales du Midi,* Vol. 88 (1976): pp. 139–157.

34. M.E. Chabot, "Marie Guyart de L'Incarnation, 1599–1672," in *The Clear Spirit,* M. Innis, ed. (Toronto: University of Toronto Press, 1966), p. 28.

35. Bosher, "The Family," p. 7; H. Neatby, *Quebec, The Revolutionary Age* (Toronto: McClelland and Stewart, 1966), p. 46.

36. Foulché-Delbosc, "Women of Three Rivers," p. 15.

37. Bosher, "The Family," p. 3. I have rounded his figures.

38. Dechêne, *Habitants et marchands,* p. 434, and Bosher, "The Family," p. 5.

39. Vann, "Women in Preindustrial Capitalism," p. 205; cf. also Alice Clark, *Working Life of Women in the Seventeenth Century* (London: Cass, 1968), chs. V, VI; and Fagniez, *Femme et société française,* for the scarcity of women's guilds by the seventeenth century.

40. *Ibid.,* p. 168 ff.

41. Y. Zoltvany, "Esquisse de la Coutume de Paris," *RHAF* (decembre 1971).

42. Foulché-Delbosc, "Women of Three Rivers," p. 19.

43. Neatby, *Quebec,* p. 46.

44. Fagniez, *Femme et société française,* p. 147.

45. Dechêne, *Habitants et marchands,* pp. 423–24.

46. A. Morel, "Réflexions sur la justice criminelle canadienne au 18e siècle," *RHAF,* 29 (septembre 1975), pp. 241–253.

47. Lanctôt, *Filles de joie,* p. 219.

48. Boyer, *Crimes et châtiments,* pp. 128–29.

49. W.J. Eccles, "Social Welfare Measures and Policies in New France," *Congreso Internacional de Americanistas,* IV, (1966), Seville, pp. 9–19.

50. J. Bosher, "Government and Private Interests in New France," in *Canadian History Before Confederation,* J.M. Bumsted, ed. (Georgetown, Ontario: Irwin-Dorsey, 1972), p. 122.

51. Bosher, "The Family," pp. 5–7; Fagniez, *Femme et société française,* p. 182.

52. Franquet, *Voyages,* p. 148; cf., also Frégault, *Le XVIIIe siècle canadien* (Montréal: Collection Constantes, 1968), pp. 292–293.

53. W.J. Eccles, "The Social, Economic and Political Significance of the Military Establishment in New France," *Canadian Historical Review,* LII (March 1971), pp. 8–10.

54. Franquet, *Voyages,* pp. 129–30. For another, similar trip, *cf.* pp. 140–42.

55. Frégault, *Le XVIIIe Siècle,* pp. 208–9, 216–21.

56. *Ibid.,* pp. 229–30.

57. Y. Zoltvany, *Philippe de Rigaud de Vaudreuil* (Toronto: McClelland and Stewart, 1974), p. 110; also p. 217.

58. Frégault, *Le XVIIIe Siècle,* pp. 228–30.

59. W.J. Eccles, *Frontenac: The Courtier Governor* (Toronto: McClelland and Stewart, 1959), p. 29.

60. *Rapport de l'archiviste de la province de Québec,* 1922–23, p. 151.

61. For example, George Rudé, *The Crowd in the French Revolution* (New York: Oxford, 1959).

62. Superbly described in E.P. Thompson, *The Making of the English Working Class* (London; Penquin, 1976), Ch. Three.

63. Séguin, "La Canadienne," pp. 498–99.

64. Jean Hamelin, "What Middle Class?" *Society and Conquest,* Miquelon, ed. (Toronto, 1977), pp. 109–110; and Dechêne, *Habitants et marchands,* p. 44, who concludes that the largest contingents of male immigrants arriving in seventeenth-century Montreal were *engagés* and soldiers.

65. H. Charbonneau, *Vie et mort de nos ancêtres* (Montréal: Presses de l'université de Montréal, 1975), p. 38; A. Burguière, "Le Rituel du mariage en France: Pratiques ecclésiastiques et pratiques popularies, (XVIe–XVIIIe siècle)," *Annales E. S. C.,* 33e annee (mai-juin 1978), p. 640; R. Mousnier, *La famille, l'enfant et l'éducation en France et en Grande-Bretagne du XVIe au XVIIIe siècle* (Paris: Sorbonne C.D.U., 1975); Fagneiz, *Femme et société française,* p. 97. Commercial activities, however, also prevailed among the women of Bordeaux, an important port in the Canada trade. (*Ibid.,* p. 196).

66. Fagniez, *Femme et société française,* pp. 267, 273–74, 311–12, 360–61.

67. Claude Lessard, "L'Aide financière de l'Eglise de France à l'Eglise naissante du Canada," in *Mèlanges d'histoire du Canada français offerts au professeur Marcel Trudel.* Pierre Savard, ed. (Ottawa: Editions de l'Université d'Ottawa, 1978), p. 175.

68. Fagniez, *Femme et société française,* pp. 311–321.

69. Marcel Trudel, *The Beginnings of New France,* (Toronto: McClelland and Stewart, 1973). For a gloomy assessment of the neglected colony during this period.

70. G. Brown *et al.,* eds., *Dictionnary of Canadian Biography* (hereafter *DCB*), (Toronto: U. of Toronto Press, 1966–) Vol. 1, p. 118; and J. Marshall, ed., *Word from New France* (Toronto: Oxford, 1967), p. 2.

71. Fagniez, *Femme et société française,* pp. 320–33, 358. Of course, not all *religieuses* were competent as leaders. Madame de la Peltrie, for example, patron of the Urusline convent, appears to have been a rather unreliable benefactress. Despite her firsthand knowledge of the difficulties under which the Ursulines laboured, her "charity" was quixotic. In 1642, she suddenly withdrew her support from the Ursulines in order to join the colonists setting off to found Montreal. Later she again held back her funds in favour of a cherished chapel project, even though the Ursulines' lodgings had just burned to the ground.

72. Chabot, "Marie Guyart de l'Incarnation," pp. 27, 37; *DCB,* 1, p. 353; Lessard, "Aide financière," pp. 169–70.

73. *DCB,* Vol. 1; pp. 483–87; also Lessard, "Aide financière," p. 175.

74. This is the interpretation given by G. Lanctôt in *Montreal under Maisonneuve* (Toronto: Clarke Irwin, 1969), pp. 20–24, 170.

75. *Ibid.,* p. 188.

76. Lanctôt, *Filles de joie,* p. 81 and Trudel, *Montréal,* p. 21. The Hôtel-Dieu de Montréal also sponsored immigrants from 1655 to 1662 (Lanctôt, *Filles de joie,* p. 81.)

77. Trudel, *Montréal,* p. 84.

78. Eccles, "Social Welfare Measures," p. 19; F. Rousseau, "Hôpital et société en Nouvelle-France: l'Hôtel-Dieu de Québec à la fin du XVIIe siècle," *RHAF,* Vol. 31 (juin 1977), p. 47.

79. Mousnier, *La famille l'enfant et l'éducation,* pp. 319–31.

80. Vann, "Women in Preindustrial Capitalism," p. 208.

81. Trudel, *Montréal,* p. 276, 87; P. Goubert, *The Ancien Régime* (New York: Harper, 1974), p. 262.

82. Neatby, *Quebec,* p. 237; French soldiers had a literacy rate of 3 to 4 per cent. A. Corvisier, *L'Armée française de la fin du XVIIe siècle au ministère de Choiseul* (Paris: Presses universitaires de France, 1964), p. 862.

83. Fagniez, *Femme et société canadienne,* p. 191.

84. Séguin, "La Canadienne," p. 501, lists nine of these schools in addition to the original one in Montreal.

85. Franquet, *Voyages,* pp. 31–32.

86. According to Lanctôt, (*Filles de joie,* pp. 121–30) there were 961. Silvio Dumas counts only 774 (*Les Filles du roi en Nouvelle France,* Québec, 1972, p. 164). Other estimates have ranged between 713 and 857.

87. J.-N. Fauteux, *Essai sur l'industrie au Canada sous le Régime Francais* (Quebec: Proulx, 1927), "Introduction."

88. For the record, it now seems fairly well established that the females sent to New France, unlike those sent to the West Indies, were carefully screened, and any of questionable morality returned by the authorities to France. Lanctôt (*Filles de joie*) and Dumas, (*Filles du roi*) agree on this. See also Foulché-Delbosc, "Women of Three Rivers," pp. 22–23.

89. Dechêne finds a majority of *Parisiennes* among the Montréal *filles* (*Habitants et marchands,* p. 96). Lanctôt states that one-half of the 1634–63 emigrants were urbanites and that two-thirds of the *filles* were from Ile-de-France (*Filles de joie,* pp. 76–79 and p. 124). On education in France see Mousnier, *La famille, l'enfant et l'éducation,* pp. 319–25.

90. Lanctôt, *Filles de joie,* pp. 110–130, 207.

91. *Ibid.,* p. 226.

92. Séguin, "La Canadienne," p. 492; Franquet, *Voyages,* p. 57.

93. J. Henripin, *La Population canadienne au début du XVIIIᵉ Siècle* (Paris: Presses universitaires de France, 1954). The overall population was sixty-three percent male in 1663 (Trudel, *Beginnings,* p. 261), an imbalance which gradually declined.

94. Trudel, *Montréal,* pp. 45–47, 108, 113.

95. Foulché-Delbosc, "Women of Three Rivers," p. 19.

96. Frégault, *Le XVIIIᵉ Siècle,* p. 144.

97. Eccles, "Social Welfare Measures," p. 18.

98. Cole Harris, *The Seigneurial System in Early Canada* (Québec: P.U.L., 1968), p. 163.

99. The richest single source for evidence along these lines is Dechêne's *Habitants et marchands.*

100. Boyer, *Crimes et châtiments,* p. 326.

101. Toronto *Globe and Mail,* 29 October 1979, p. 1; Boyer, *Crimes et châtiments,* pp. 329, 340. Cf. also N. Hawthorne's novel, *The Scarlet Letter,* based on an actual occurrence.

102. Boyer, *Crimes et châtiments,* p. 329, 350, 361–62; also Morel, "Justice criminelle canadienne."

103. Dechêne, *Habitants et marchands,* p. 464.

104. Séguin, "La Canadienne," pp. 497–99.

105. Jean Lunn, "The Illegal Fur Trade Out of New France 1713–60," *Canadian Historical Association Report,* (1939), pp. 61–62.

106. Boyer, *Crimes et châtiments,* pp. 286–87.

107. Marshall, *Word from New France,* pp. 287–95.

108. Boyer, *Crimes et châtiments,* p. 306.

109. Eccles, "The Social, Economic and Political Significance of the Military Establishment," *op. cit.*

110. Charlevoix, *New France,* Vol. 3, p. 35.

111. Ethel Bennett, "Madame de La Tour, 1602–1645," in *The Clear Spirit,* M. Innis, ed. (Toronto: U. of Toronto Press, 1966), p. 21.

112. *DCB,* Vol. 3, pp. 308–13.

113. *Ibid.,* pp. 308–13; and Boyer, *Crimes et châtiments,* pp. 338–39.

114. For a splendid description of the attitudes and lifestyle of this class in France, see p. de Vaissière, *Gentilhommes campagnards de l'ancienne France* (Paris, Perin 1903).

115. G. Frégault, *Le Grand Marquis,* (Montréal: Les Etudes de l'Institut d'Histoire de l'Amerique française, 1952), pp. 74–75 and Corvisier, *L'Armée française,* p. 777.

116. *Ibid.,* pp. 762–63, 826.

117. Franquet, *Voyages,* pp. 56, 67–68, 200.

118. *Ibid.,* p. 35, 76, 88.

119. Dechêne, *Habitants et marchands,* p. 398; Franquet, *Voyages,* p. 16.

120. *DCB,* Vol. 2, p. 491.

121. Marshall, *Word from New France,* pp. 27, 213, 222–23, 233.

122. Dechêne, *Habitants et marchands,* p. 393; Franquet, *Voyages,* p. 199; Foulché-Delbosc, "Women of Three Rivers," p. 25; Corvisier, *L'Armée française,* p. 760.

123. Boyer, *Crimes et châtiments,* pp. 349–51; Dechêne, *Habitants et marchands.* p. 41. Dechêne concludes that, considering Montreal was a garrison town with a shortage of marriageable women, the degree of prostitution was normal or, to use her term, *conformiste* (pp. 437–38).

124. Eccles, "The Social, Economic and Political Significance of the Military ...," pp. 11–17; Dechêne, *Habitants et marchands,* p. 121.

125. Séguin, "La Canadienne," pp. 495, 503.

126. Trudel, *Montréal,* pp. 30–33; and Charbonneau, *Vie et mort,* p. 135.

127. Foulché-Delbosc, "Women of Three Rivers," p. 25.

128. Trudel, *Montréal,* p. 163.

129. Bennett, "Madame de la Tour," p. 16; Madame Joybert was the mother of the future Madame de Vaudreuil. *DCB,* Vol. 1, p. 399. For E. de Grandmaison, see *DCB,* Vol. 1, p. 345.

130. Lunn, "Illegal Fur Trade," p. 62.

131. Eccles, *Canadian Society ..., op. cit.,* p. 61.

132. Lunn, "Illegal Fur Trade," pp. 61–75.

133. Franquet, *Voyages,* pp. 120–21.

134. Lilianne Plamondon, "Une femme d'affaires en Nouvelle-France: Marie-Anne Barbel, Veuve Fornel," *RHAF,* 31 (septembre 1977).

135. Franquet, *Voyages,* pp. 156–58.

136. For example, Hamelin in "What Middle Class?" The absence of an indigenous bourgeoisie is also central to the interpretation of Dechêne in *Habitants et marchands.*

137. Séguin, "La Canadienne," p. 494.

138. For accounts of Agathe de Saint-Père, see *DCB,* Vol. III, pp. 580–81; Fauteux, *Industrie au Canada,* p. 464–69; and Massicote, *Bulletin des Recherches historiques* (hereafter BRH), 1944, p. 202–07.

139. Neatby refers to this activity in the early post-Conquest era (*Quebec,* pp. 72–73); Franquet encountered Madame Benoist in 1753 (*Voyages,* p. 150).

140. For a discussion of the de Ramezay's business affairs Cf. Massicote, *BRH,* 1931, p. 530; and Fauteux, *Industrie au Canada,* pp. 158–59, 204–15, 442.

141. *DCB,* Vol. II, p. 548.

142. Fauteux, *Industrie au Canada,* pp. 158; 297, 420–21, 522; and P. Moogk, *Building a House in New France* (Toronto: 1977), pp. 60–64.

143. Lunn, *Illegal Fur Trade,* p. 61.

144. See Moogk (*Building a House,* p. 8) for one case of a husband's transfer of these powers.

145. Franquet, *Voyages,* p. 17.

146. Dechêne, *Habitants et marchands,* pp. 151–53, 187, 391; and Séguin, "La Canadienne," p. 494.

147. Charbonneau, *Vie et mort,* p. 184; Fagniez, *Femme et société française,* pp. 111, 182–84. A recent study by Butel ("Comportements familiaux") has documented the phenomenon of widows taking over the family business in eighteenth-century Bordeaux.

148. Trudel, *Beginnings,* p. 250. This was largely due to the enormous holdings of Jean Lauzon's widow. Dechêne, *Habitants et marchands,* pp. 209 and 204–5, 393; Plamondon, "Femme d'affaires." W.S. MacNutt, *The Atlantic Provinces* (Toronto: McClelland and Stewart, 1965), p. 25.

149. This happened on *seigneuries* as well as in town, as in the case M. de Lanouguère, "a soldier by preference," whose wife, Marguerite-Renée Denys, directed their *seigneurie* (*DCB,* Vol. 1, p. 418).

NEW FRANCE: THE FRENCH IN NORTH AMERICA, XVI–XVIIITH CENTURY

Jacques Mathieu

Individuals and Society

The relations between individuals and society in New France were more complex than the division into three orders (clergy, nobility and third estate) or the socio-professional classifications might lead one to believe. In the first place, there was no society of orders in Canada in the 18th century even though different individual statuses existed. The *Coutume de Paris* defined the legal frameworks which laid down for each individual, according to age and sex, rights and responsibilities within a family community and with respect to others. Less clear-cut legal situations existed, such as the status of natives, slaves, foreigners and, up to a certain point, Protestants.

From *La Nouvelle-France: Les Français en Amérique du Nord XVIe–XVIIIe siècle* (© Éditions Belin, Paris, 1991. Translation by Édition Électronique Niche). Reprinted by permission.

The French model, which persisted, had a profound effect on the social hierarchy. It influenced the nature of individuals' aspirations. On the other hand, *life in New France brought about changes*, notably in the distribution of wealth, which gave new dimensions to Canadian society. Between the characteristics of the society of orders and the equality of opportunity at the outset, there existed a considerable area of divergence where different social relationships were formed. Between the quarrels of precedence which marked the 17th century and the complaints which, in the 18th century, revealed the fact that domestics "spoke loudly," there appears to have been a significant development.

The junction of political and religious authority had resulted in the identification of those who belonged to society and those who were on its fringes. In this royal colony, only the King's subjects were entitled to his full protection. Only the children of God were admitted to society in this catholic, apostolic and Roman colony. *A number of individuals*, because of their membership in a different ethnic or religious group, were *just barely tolerated* in the hope that they would adapt and return to the ranks of society.

1. The Lower Statuses

a. Amerindians   The Amerindians, and particularly those who were the allies of the French, remained for the most part grouped in nations legally independent from the French, which did not mean that they were not politically or economically subjugated. But integration into French colonial society could be achieved only through assimilation. Since the charter of the *Compagnie des Cent-Associés* in 1627, the native, in order to be recognized as a French subject with the same rights, privileges and honours, had merely to accept baptism. In theory, this was the sole condition for entry into French society. In actual fact, even the Indians who were baptized and settled on reserves or in missions created for them and who had learned agriculture or a trade kept their way of life and their original ethnic affiliation. Only a few women, integrated into a family through adoption or marriage, eventually belonged to this colonial society. *The low percentage of interbreeding prevented integration of the two societies.* Despite intermittent economic exchanges and a certain domination by the French authorities, they lived side by side. Relationships were maintained through diplomatic channels, on a nation-to-nation basis. The Amerindians were not directly affected by the French institutions and administration. They received, with more or less dispatch, the notices sent through an intermediary, most often the missionaries who lived among them. The services which they accepted, or sometimes solicited, were dispensed as acts of charity or gestures of friendliness. Lastly, these nations had been dramatically affected by the effects of the French presence. Wars, epidemics and devastation of the hunting grounds had led to a considerable decrease in the Amerindian population in the St. Lawrence Valley. Numbering at least 8000 at the time of the discovery, the Amerindian population was reduced to 3000 individuals by the middle of the 18th century.

b. Slaves   *Slaves* did not even have political status. They were in a state of absolute dependance on their masters, who sold or bought them as they pleased, often for purposes of prestige or for specific needs. Marcel Trudel estimates that there were 4000 of them in the St. Lawrence Valley between 1627 and 1760. To the 1200 black slaves who came from Africa via the Antilles or from the English colonies, were added about 2400 Amerindians from the Mississippi Valley. *Their living conditions*, free from ill-treatment, *were similar to those of domestics* or servants. However, their life expectancy was less than 20 years.

c. Foreigners   *Some foreigners suffered other forms of discrimination.* About 100 British colonials were taken prisoner as a result of the wars of the early 18th century. In 1702, then in 1710, the King gave letters of naturalization to those who agreed to convert to Catholicism. From then on, they could marry, practise any trade and be granted land. The situation of Protestants was rather similar. They had been specifically excluded from the colonization venture as early as 1627; but 400 of them settled in New France. They were subject to the denunciations and pressures of the clergy, which was extremely hostile to these heretics. Deprived of ministers of religion, unable to practise their faith, excluded from certain professions such as doctor, notary, officer of the law as well as from all administrative functions, they could not marry or receive a religious burial without abjuring. The overwhelming majority therefore resigned themselves to this, although a certain number left no official record of their abjuration. One only notes that after having their children baptized in the Protestant church before leaving France, some Protestant parents had their children baptized in the Catholic faith once they had arrived in Canada.

d. Itinerant Vendors   The *itinerant vendors*, merchants who came to the colony every year during the commercial season, also were considered to be somewhat like foreigners. *Opposition to the itinerant vendors* intensified progressively during the 18th century. The merchants and traders of the colony succeeded in having their commercial rights restricted on the pretext of unfair competition. In any case, on the eve of the Conquest, a few Protestant merchants dominated colonial commerce and played a major economic role.

e. The Disadvantaged   Particular social conditions also affected the status of certain groups of persons, and appears to have deprived them, partially or temporarily, of their rights.

Like every society, that of New France included physically or mentally *handicapped persons, criminals, poor people* and lonely *old people*. They were generally shut away in the general hospital as a preventive measure or through charity. The institution sought to put everyone to work, to make each person play a role in order that he not be a burden to the community. The office of the poor also sought to eliminate mendicity by obtaining tools and work for each. Likewise, abandoned children were taken in charge by the Crown which tried to place them in a family. In short, the Administration favoured a system of social aid in which the most disadvantaged were taken in charge by persons and institutions in return for various compensations. These social contracts, often signed in the presence of a notary, enabled an individual to alienate his assets—most frequently his labour—in return for food, shelter and sometimes small favours. Thus, some persons, especially old people, alone and unable to provide for their needs, gave themselves to religious communities which agreed to take care of them until their death. Children "taken in charge by the King" were put in the care of a nurse for two years, then placed in a family until the age of 20. Likewise, the apprenticing or placing in domestic service of children at three or four years of age was similar to adoption. A work contract subordinated them to a family-type authority, to which they owed obedience in all that was lawful.

We know little about the fate of these persons, just as we often do not know about the circumstances which may have led to such a situation. It sometimes happened that some apprentices became well-known masters who were respected and relatively wealthy. The disadvantage of the initial situation is less well known. Apart from the handicapped, young orphans and old people without kin, what circumstances could have forced these people to place themselves entirely in the service of others? An analysis of female domestic service, based on the Quebec census of 1744, provides a few clues. Its geographical and social origin did not differ from that of the society as a whole. The proportion of rural and urban dwellers, of identified poor and of daughters of married persons corresponds to the general distribution. But we find an over-representation of people in an unfavourable family situation: widows, female orphans and illegitimate children. Above all, we discover the weight of family responsibilities: two-thirds of female domestics had from 6 to 14 brothers and sisters.

All these persons who hovered around the fringes of the principal social unit constituted nevertheless rather small minorities.

2. The Principal Social Statuses

The *Coutume de Paris* imposed on the family the principle of community of property. Under the quasi-absolute authority of the husband, the economic and social capital and the honour of the family community was administered in accordance with this principle. Hence *the importance of marriage agreements* for the possible purposes of sharing and passing on of an inheritance that was as much economic and social as it was cultural.

a. The Family In New France in the 18th century, the family was essentially conjugal. At the very most, some of the children took special care of parents who had become unable to provide for their own needs. It is also possible that the late marrying of young men (28.1 years on average) allowed for a phase of mutual aid. Living under the paternal roof, these young people were able to prepare for their future autonomy. But households consisting of two married couples remained the exception. When this situation occurred, it was always of a temporary nature. It did not constitute a way of life. *A family had 9 births on the average,* but only 5.1 children survived to adulthood. This average masks some considerable disparities. Families died out because all their children were cut down in their infancy or youth. Others lost few or no children. Above all, there was a great number of second and third marriages, constituting some 20% of marriages contracted. Deaths and remarriages brought dynamics into the family, particularly through marriage or the departure of the children.

b. **Men** Law and folklore combined to indicate the *preponderant position reserved for men* in the community between spouses. Article CCXXV of the *Coutume de Paris* made the husband "Lord over movable and immovable property." To this lord went all honours and all rights. He could dispose of the property of the community as he willed, even without the consent of his spouse. He could also dispose of the income from the personal property (separate estate) that his spouse had brought to the community. The only reservation concerned the impossibility of relinquishing the separate estate of his spouse without her consent.

If the woman who "took a husband" also "took a country," reality was less clear-cut. Many husbands delegated powers to their spouses by means of general and special powers of attorney signed in the presence of a notary. It was thus not rare that they had their wives represent them in court. Wives also had powers because of her responsibilities towards her children. The presence of the wife in court was most often related to family matters and the transmission of property. Lastly, whether it had to do with farmers or artisans, the family's source of income often took the form of a family enterprise in which each partner performed some of the tasks. But men, who came of age at 25, appeared to be undisputed masters, having the responsibility of respecting and treating properly those who depended on them.

c. **Women** Women came of age at 25; but at that age, most of the time, they had already replaced the guardianship of their fathers by the not less heavy-handed one of husbands. In this legal system, women enjoyed only certain protections specified in the law or marriage agreements. They had the power to renounce the community when their spouses died if they judged that they would get from it for themselves and their children more debts than property. They also could claim their separate estates, the dowers promised by their husbands or the share (rightful) falling to them, that is what they possessed prior to marriage and a sum (dower, rightful or preference legacy) equivalent to about a year's income depending on their station or that of their spouses. On the death of her husband, a woman could also continue the community of property until her children came of age or until she remarried. She then exercised the rights previously devolved upon her husband. We have thus seen a few widows who were very active in business make a name for themselves in major economic enterprises. But this was rather the exception than the rule.

In the social sphere, *the wives acquired their husbands' status*; hence complex and varied marriage and family strategies in the choice of spouses as in the creation of social networks. Social practices in this regard were defined according to material considerations, which were guarantees at that time of harmonious social functioning; after that, love and sensitivities could be taken into account. An example among others: the engineer in chief of the colony, in charge of fortifications, provided each of his daughters with 10,000 livres as an advancement of part of their inheritance (the average salary of a qualified craftsman at that time varied from 360 to 500 livres) and gave nothing to his sons. He thus settled matters of inheritance in advance. The sons, however, took advantage of the education they had received, of their fathers connections and of the opportunities that he provided them with to begin the practice of their chosen professions. The father's action was no doubt intended to attract husbands of quality. He would have succeeded in marrying his daughters to men of a high social status that they would inevitably share. We thus see, in urban areas, a kind of *general exchange between families of the same social standing*. Everywhere else, in each rural community, similar considerations appeared to be taken into account in the forming of marital unions. Children of seigneurs, militia officers and tradesmen married among themselves. Unions were formed among people of the "first rank" or families of the "top of the plateau" rather than with those of the hinterland or of the foot of the seigneurie. However, the situation was the same for men and women. A young man residing on good riverside land could marry a daughter of a family settled on the less attractive lands of the interior and thus raise her to his own social station. But the reverse was not true. A girl who married a young man of lower social status would be likely to go down in the social ladder.

d. Widows and Widowers A brief survey should now be given of the fate of widows and widowers. In New France in the 18th century *widowhood or widowerhood was frequently followed by a second marriage*. This even appears to have been encouraged by the civil and religious authorities. Family-centered enterprises, the dispersal of the settlement and the quasi-absence of villages would not have made it possible to create those places of sociability where a lonely individual would be able to survive through the rendering of small services to the community. Remarriage offered the simplest and most effective solution. Widows and widowers found new spouses rather easily. These were either unmarried persons or persons who had also lost their spouses. Despite the favour of the authorities, remarriage retained a particular nature in the minds of people. Depending on custom, widows sometimes remarried in the parishes of their spouses rather than in their own. In almost half of the marriages involving a widow and a widower, the future spouses requested and obtained a dispensal of banns, thus decreasing the attention surrounding their union. Lastly, woe betide widowers who took too young a wife: they exposed themselves to an uproarious hullabaloo.

e. Children   On the average, there were nine children per family, who were born every 28 months; but barely one out of two survived to adulthood. There were two mortality peaks in infancy: at birth or at the time of weening. Epidemics also killed a good number of young people in certain localities and age brackets, but never sufficiently to affect the demographic structure.

Children were always subject to a family-type authority, as indicated by the fate reserved for foundlings. If the father died, a guardian and a deputy guardian were appointed to look after the material, but also spiritual, interests of the child. Observers of the period agree that their education was less strict than in France. *The number of children who received an elementary education was somewhat limited.* There even appears to have been a decline in literacy from the 17th to the 18th century. Children were called upon very early, from the age of 5 or 6, to participate in the family work, whether on the farm or in a shop. When they reached the age of 15, they were considered to be capable of doing work comparable that of adults, without necessarily being responsible for it. The way in which boys were prepared for the life which awaited them is known to some extent. Some began to clear the land that they would occupy and that they sometimes already owned. Others went to learn a trade. A significant number, impossible to determine in the present state of research, would try, as we have seen, to build up a little nest egg by fishing or trading in furs.

In law as in mentalities, *equality among children appears to have been of prime importance*. Parents were even strictly forbidden to attempt to favour one child over another in the sharing out of property bequeathed. This egalitarian attitude appears to have been so well accepted that even the sharing of plots of land would sometimes be done by a drawing of lots in order to prevent any injustice and quarreling; which did not preclude compromises from time to time, while at the same time maintaining the values of fairness, if not of equality, at the end of the day. It was in this context that we must place the advancements of parts of an inheritance given to girls when they married.

The legal system that provided for a strictly egalitarian sharing of property and assets after the death of parents probably served as the basis for the social perception according to which equality reigned among *individuals who received equal chances at the outset*. In the main, fortunes were passed on to each generation and, in each family, assets were shared out just about equally among the children. In the absence of concentrations of wealth, whether movable or immovable, each had, so to speak, to recommence anew with very few vested interests and assets and on the same footing with his brothers and sisters. The system contained numerous loopholes and did not prevent the expression of family strategies. In addition, the initial social position, defined by the situation or the father's favour, clearly influenced the rest of the children's lives. Of course, good fortune, associated with skill, work and reputation, may have made it possible for some to rise rapidly in the social ladder. The majority, however, were obliged to live with the inertia and dilatoriness of the French hierarchy. Between this egalitarianism and this social organization into a hierarchy the destiny of each individual in New France was forged.

3. *Social Structuring*

The organization and functioning of society in the 18th century differed notably from the previous century. A certain oldness of the settlement—and especially its extension—favoured *the creation of more populated centres and, consequently, a tightening of the rules of life in society*. In absolute figures, the number of rural inhabitants quadrupled between 1690 and 1720. From that time on, there was more land being exploited and less attractive land to be cleared. Management and devolution of property methods became clearer. The colony's two urban areas, Quebec and Montreal, became cities in the true sense of the word. The offering of services such as education, law and hospitalization increased, but, above all, the urban area created its own needs and its own market. In the liberal professions, as among trades people, a system of competition was introduced. In these dense population centres, where the holders of political and economic power resided, the social strata were more sharply defined especially since New France experienced a long period of peace between 1713 and 1744.

The social spectrum was less open than in France. We find in the colony neither a higher clergy (except the bishop of Quebec), a nobility or great fortunes; at the other end of the spectrum free men had greater opportunities. Free from taxes (except for the rent) and tallage, the land was free and the achieving of the mastery in a trade remained accessible to all after 6 years of practice. A daughter of the Old World, this society adapted its structures to the New World.

In the image of the society of Old France, socio-professional groups enjoyed privileges or rights whose forms were inspired by those of the Middle Ages. The army, civil administration and religious communities in particular included a fair proportion of nobles. Traditional organizations into a hierarchy were accentuated there by the importance of the role of the State and of its administrative organization. *The context of a new country gave rise to a system of promotion* based on its new realities.

a. The Privileged Nobles, military officers, officers of the civil administration and upper middle-class persons grown rich through business and favoured by the political authorities shared an altogether similar way of life. They formed unions with each other through marriage, benefitted from the granting of seigneurial land and held simultaneously offices, titles and functions.

Since the end of the 17th century, the colonial authorities of the colony no longer gave out patents of nobility to colonials who performed acts or exploits worthy of reward. The *nobility* was replenished only through immigration or renewed itself through its descendants, especially as venality of offices did not exist in the colony. It tended to decrease relatively as it mingled increasingly with the other groups. Moreover, since 1689, it could, without losing rank and title, engage in commerce and various non-manual activities. A stage was reached where it was no longer possible to differentiate it clearly from the other elements of the society's élite.

The army, in which the majority of the nobles were to be found, constituted *one of the most powerful levers of social advancement*. Even during the long period of peace, New France resembled an entrenched camp. Forts were built on the threatened frontiers, fortifications were erected at Quebec and Montreal, and an imposing fortress stood at Louisbourg. A chain of fortified posts, also serving as fur trading posts, was placed under the responsibility of military officers. These post commanders, installed on the borders of the French possessions, enjoyed many advantages. Their promotion depended no more on their rank or seniority than on their titles. The favour of the colonial authorities, and in particular that of the Governor, appeared to be of prime importance. As a consequence, their membership in the dominant class, the excellence of their relations with the Amerindian nations and therefore their ability to conduct commerce and share the income therefrom favoured their social elevation. From the 17th to the 18th century, the positions occupied by native-born Canadians in this sector increased considerably. Officers were increasingly recruited in the colony. Their numbers went from a third of the strength at the beginning of the 18th century to the quasi-totality of the colony's regular troops at the end of the French regime. In the absence of war, career-advancement was rather slow. A cadet took 10 years to become an ensign, 15 years to be promoted to the rank of lieutenant, while promotion to the rank of captain—5 years later— occurred a few years prior to discharge from the army. A certain number were afterwards decorated with the Croix de Saint-Louis, an honour which assured its holders a pensioner's pay.

The officers of the civil administration experienced a system rather similar to that of military officers. Those who held the highest positions came from France. Their sojourn in the colony often constituted only a stage in their career.

The clergy of the colony *had the very great respect* of the authorities as well as of the population. Quite uniformly educated, it exerted a profound influence on the faithful, even though *its temporal power appears to have been somewhat reduced*. Religious devotion seems to have been constant and deviant practices rare. In the 18th century, there was an insufficient number of priests to celebrate all the masses paid for by the population. On the one hand, the Bishop did not succeed in having the tithe increased from one twenty-sixth to one thirteenth, the collection rate fixed in France. There subsisted notable differences in conduct, value and prestige among the communities who recruited their members exclusively in France and those who admitted Canadians to their ranks. Canadians, although increasingly numerous, succeeded seldom and with difficulty in obtaining positions of trust and responsibility. On the other hand, the power of the Bishop over the religious communities and the regular clergy was strengthened. The successor of François de Laval, Mgr. de Saint-Vallier, took away from the *Séminaire des Missions Étrangères* the appointment of parish priests and the management of cures. In the 18th century, parish organization developed.

A final group succeeded in carving out an enviable place for itself at the head of the colonial hierarchy. It was composed of the merchants who had benefitted from the favours of the authorities, obtained a seigneurie and sometimes a position in the administrative hierarchy. The support of the authorities, and of the Intendant in particular, often contributed to ensuring financial success and encouraged the creation of a network of relationships. *Power, money and relationships combined to glorify with a certain prestige persons who had come to belong to the best society.* The historian Cameron Nish has defined them as *bourgeois gentil-hommes* because of their degree of wealth, the positions they held concurrently, their relationships and their way of life. To their children, they sought less to bequeath assets than positions or titles in the military or civil administration: this was the means of making membership in a dominant group permanent.

b. Notables   Notables emerged as the colony's population increased: the local communities which came into being provided themselves with institutions which brought their incumbents a certain social superiority.

In the 18th century, *parish priests* became irremovable. They generally enjoyed the support of their congregations. Churches and presbyteries were quickly built despite occasional opposition concerning their cost and location. Parish priests had supreme control of temporal power, since the fabric and the church-wardens were completed devoted to them. Nevertheless, the Bishop sometimes had to intervene in order to improve the ordinary and have sacred vases of quality bought. The *churchwardens* were chosen by and from among the notables. They belonged to the leading families and the majority of them, born in the parish, had lived there for at least ten years and had a family of at least 5 children and more at the time of their election. Their education was not very different from that of the common people since only 20% of them could sign their name. However, but there was no doubt about their material wealth. They offered a dower or left property higher than one-third of the average. *Geographical stability, family network, relative wealth and irreproachable morality earned them the respect of the community of the faithful.*

The parish priest/churchwarden couple had its counterpart on the civil sphere in the *seigneur*, or his representative, and the *miller*. Even though three-quarters of the seigneurs did not reside in their seigneuries, they built a manor house on them, often of imposing dimensions, where their tenants had to go and pay feudal dues. In the 17th century, the unstable miller lived poorly from the service that the seigneur offered to his tenants. In the 18th century, the practice of the trade improved. The miller established greater permanence in the trade as well as in localization. Often more competent, he owned more property. Defined at the outset as a service to rural dwellers, his professional activity came more to resemble an urban-type commercial enterprise. The best millers, in the manner of business people, leased the construction and operation of the mill. Most of them knew how to write, and a number of them formed marriage unions with business people, thus forming a small local notability.

In a country like Canada, the *militia* played an important role. During periods of armed conflict, and particularly in the 18th century, it provided the colony with protection. Often led by former officers of the regular troops, it grouped, in theory, all able-bodied men from 16 to 60. They were subjected to periodic drills and participated, fifteen days a year, in fortification work. The militia officer who led them belonged to the rural community and maintained few relationships with urban dwellers. In the 18th century, the Intendants increasingly made them local agents of their authority, charging them with circulating their ordinances and having them complied with and managing the building of roads and bridges. The militia officer had the same education as the mass of the habitants. He stood apart from them through his seniority in the community, his family relationships and an enviable economic position. In the 18th century, the militia officer was less characterized by his military qualities than by his characteristics of notable. He could flaunt a certain social success and his average age, 55, offered guarantees of experience, maturity and credibility which made of him a natural intermediary between the population and the administrators of the colony.

c. *Range of Small Trades*

As a result of their level of wealth, way of life and limited social aspirations, *the farmers and craftsmen had comparable social status. Opportunities for social promotion were few.* A bad harvest or a year of famine, as occurred on about twenty occasions between 1700 and 1750, dampened hopes and slowed progress. A little luck, a lot of work on the land or in the shop made it possible for them to bequeath a little property to their children. In the towns, almost half of the craftsmen owned their homes, which included a shop. The other half lived from day labour. In the country, although the habitants were the owners of their land and a few of them could build up a modest surplus, almost half lived in debt and in an almost complete state of destitution. One out of every other child had to start out where his father or grandfather had begun, by clearing the forest.

At the bottom of the social ladder, the soldiers, enlisted men and the young men on apprenticeship divided their time between the hope of better days and acceptance of fate. The Indians, for their part, were subjected to the pressures of French policy. Living on reservations or urged to hunt, more or less subjected to the quest for French material goods, destroyed by epidemics and alcohol, subjected to the policy of alliances of the Europeans, they ceased seeing the Europeans as brothers and defined themselves as their children.

4. Social Reproduction   In this nascent society and expanding territory, *hopes of social promotion were still permitted* and they remained deeply rooted. The myth of the New World and of its wealth lived on. Observers of this period, the civil or religious authorities and visitors, did not fail to mention as a common mental characteristic *the tendency to "raise oneself up."* Everywhere was observed this affection of dressing up or believing oneself to be of a title or rank higher than was actually the case. Ordinary priests did not consider themselves to be inferior to canons when it was not the bishop. A number of bourgeois appropriated the title of master. In the industrial sectors of shipbuilding or the forges of Saint-Maurice, workers aspired to the mastery, shop foremen considered themselves to be as competent as the builder in chief. The day labourer declared himself to be an artisan, the artisan described himself as a specialized worker, the latter saw himself as a foreman, the carpenter claimed to be a builder, the stoker thought himself to be a caster and the mason defined himself as an architect. As for the farmer, we know that he would accept no other title than that of habitant. Even domestics, wrote an observer, reacted "indignantly" to the requests of their masters. The honorific epithet or the rank that was exhibited symbolized social aspirations.

These pretensions exemplified a certain perception of social reality. Only a very small number would win at this lottery in the 18th century, but it would not be for want of having tried. One of the most prominent characteristics of the society of New France was *mobility*: geographical, professional—indeed social.

The reasons for this mobility do not always appear to be positive. Some production sectors soon became saturated and many people such as leather workers, for example, sacrificed years of apprenticeship and acquired skills to turn to other more promising areas of activity. Thus the workers of the Saint-Maurice forges often came from outside the Government of Trois-Rivières and their former trade had no connection with the forge.

Mobility was not less great in rural areas. Of course, the historiography of New France emphasized the image of the farmer permanently attached to the soil and passing on his land to his children. *Every other child was one too many: to prevent the splitting up of the land, he had to leave the paternal property* and frequently the locality of his birth in order to find enough to live on elsewhere and start a family. Likewise, farmer families consisting of several adult children abandoned a cleared plot in order to acquire more extensive lands in *new areas of colonization.* Forty percent of the habitants who made up these new communities were composed of these large families; as for the rest, they were mostly young men, either recently married, or attracted by the opportunity of contracting a marriage in the area.

This social dynamic is observed at all levels of society. The senior officials of the colony's administration did not remain long in their posts. The authorities were appointed by the King or his Minister. In the colony, the positions giving access to wealth depended on the favour of the Intendant or the Governor.

Dependence on the authorities in place did not encourage tenure of status and function. Great fortunes generally appear to be of short duration. They were rarely transmitted from generation to generation.

The society of New France in the 18th century appeared to partake of two movements, two value systems, two social models. On the one hand, the legal bases of the social functioning, reinforced by the importance of the political, military, economic and administrative role of the State, favoured *an almost total transplantation of the French model* defining the station of persons. Adaptation to the new demographic and geographical context led to the introduction of new rules of social interplay: *the society was "canadianized"* and became aware of its differences.

The social élite, which obtained positions of trust and responsibility, still came mainly from France. Its presence was frequently of short duration. The sojourn in the colony constituted only a stage in a career plan which was resolutely France-oriented. But in order to meet the new challenges that adapting to the New World posed, nobles worked hard, commoners obtained seigneuries, merchants were given administrative responsibilities. The members of this apparently disparate élite formed close ties through marriage. They formed a group that was not hermetically closed, to be sure, but which was marked by a specific social identity. The mass of the population, from the apprentice to the master or from the enlisted man to the habitant, participated in the same collective destiny. The chances of rising considerably in the social hierarchy were rather slender. People did not, so to speak, leave their stations. This did not prevent claims from being asserted or living conditions from changing.

CHAPTER
3 THE EXPULSION
OF THE
ACADIANS

Although Champlain's decision in 1608 to establish a settlement at Quebec meant that henceforth French colonizing activity in North America would be centred on the St. Lawrence, a French presence stubbornly persisted in what became known as Acadia. Never very large in terms of population, and frequently handed back and forth between the French and British in the ongoing imperial rivalries of the age, Acadia gradually acquired a distinct character of its own. Its location meant both isolation from the main centre of French power at Quebec, and considerable contact with the colonies to the south. Although the fur trade was of some importance to Acadia, its economy was much more agriculturally based than that of New France.

Acadia changed hands for the last time during the War of the Spanish Succession. The Treaty of Utrecht, which formally ended that war in 1713, left Acadia in British hands. The British thus were confronted with the problem which would arise in a much greater way later in the century: the position of a French and Catholic colony in an Empire which was English and Protestant. This first experiment ended in 1755 with the forcible deportation of virtually the entire Acadian population, estimated at about 10,000 people.

The readings in this section place significantly different emphasis on that expulsion, though neither questions the immensity of the tragedy. The first was written in 1955 on the two-hundredth anniversary of the deportation by C. Bruce Fergusson, and may be considered a justification for the British action. Fergusson placed great emphasis on the question of the oath of allegiance. He argues that when the Acadians refused to choose between the only two options open to them—to remain French nationals and to leave Nova Scotia, or to become full and unqualified British subjects—the Acadians themselves were ultimately the authors of their own fate.

The second reading, "1748–1755: Community Devastated," is a chapter from *The Contexts of Acadian History, 1686–1784* by Naomi Griffiths. Griffiths has spent her career since her arrival from Britain in the 1950s studying the Acadians. This study is a synthesis of her work. If Fergusson looked at the Acadians through the eyes of the British, Griffiths has multiple vision, though her sympathies are solidly with the victims. She emphasized the complexity of not only the immediate issues, but also the nature of Acadian society itself. The Acadians were certainly helpless pawns in a struggle for imperial supremacy between Britain and France, but to Griffiths there "was no need for extraordinary measures of brutality to ensure a submissive population."

Suggestions for Further Reading

Barnes, Thomas Garden, "'Twelve Apostles' or a Dozen Traitors? Acadian Collaboration During King George's War, 1744–48," in F.M. Greenwood and Barry Wright, eds., *Canadian State Trials*. Toronto: Osgood Hall, 1996, 98–113.

Bertrand, Gabriel, "La culture des marais endures et le developpement de la solidarité militante en Acadie entre 1710 et 1755," *Les Cahiers*, 24, 1993, 318–349.

Brebner, J.B., *New England's Outpost: Acadia before the Conquest of Canada*. New York: Columbia University Press, 1927.

Daigle, Jean, "Acadia, 1604–1763: An Historical Synthesis," in *The Acadians of the Maritimes: Thematic Studies*, ed. Jean Daigle. Moncton: Centre d'études acadiennes, 1982.

Grant, Helen, "The Deportation of the Acadians," *Nova Scotia Historical Quarterly*, Special Supplement (1975), 101–19.

Griffiths, Naomi, "Acadian Identity: The Creation and Re-Creation of Community," *Dalhousie Review*, 73, 3, 1993, 325–349.

Griffiths, Naomi, *The Acadian Deportation: Deliberate Perfidy or Cruel Necessity?* Toronto: Copp Clark, 1969.

Griffiths, Naomi, *The Acadians: Creation of a People*. Toronto: McGraw-Hill Ryerson, 1973.

Reid, John G., "Acadia and the Acadians: In the Shadow of Quebec," *Beaver*, LXVII, no. 5 (October-November 1987), 26–31.

Reid, John G., *Six Crucial Decades: Times of Change in the History of the Maritimes*. Halifax: Nimbus, 1987.

THE EXPULSION OF THE ACADIANS

C. Bruce Fergusson

Some observers have said that Germany's annexation of Alsace-Lorraine was worse than a crime—it was a blunder; others have seemed to say that the expulsion of the Acadians was not a blunder but rather a crime. However that

From *Dalhousie Review*, XXV, no. 2 (1955), 127–135. Reprinted by permission of *Dalhousie Review* and Mrs. Evelyn Fergusson.

may be, history caught up with the Acadians in 1755, when 6,000 or more of them were uprooted from their beloved lands in Nova Scotia, placed on board ships and deported to British colonies to the south. Ninety-two years later, moreover, in a blend of fact and fancy, Longfellow caught them up in the unforgettable lines of the poem *Evangeline*. Since that time, it seems, the warp of fact and the woof of imagination have been so interwoven by poetic licence in a memorable mosaic of sentimentality and suffering, that it is difficult to separate fact from fancy and to get at the sober truth of the matter. Yet even the most aloof observer must feel sympathy for any group of people who experience the testing of exile from their accustomed place, no matter whose the responsibility for the exile, and no matter whether that forced expatriation was deserved or undeserved. That being the case, the heart goes out to the Acadians of 1755, without any need for the head to appreciate anything of the circumstances, or for any question to be asked of the why or the wherefore. But the two-hundredth anniversary of that event should provide the occasion for real attempts to understand what actually happened in 1755, and why and how it took place.

Was the expulsion of the Acadians a misfortune or was it a disaster? Were they the undeserved victims of misfortune, or did they reap disaster from their own folly? These are the salient questions which should be borne in mind whenever consideration is given to the fate of the Acadians in the year 1755. Their story, it is clear, is an admirable illustration of the relative strength of the ties that bind, and of the forces that influence, a people, as well as a supreme example of how a dramatic and colourful episode in the history of any people may be readily translated into the misty realm of romance, so that careful attention is needed for an adequate realization and a proper understanding. The story of the Acadians may be regarded as a tale that is told. But its versions differ, some of them are marred or distorted by emotion or bias, by artificial colouring or by unfounded judgements, and new appraisals are sometimes needed.

Centre or core of the Acadian problem was the oath of allegiance. One important factor was the fact that between the final capture of Port Royal by the British in 1710 and the fateful year 1755 most of the Acadians were unwilling to take the unconditional oath of allegiance. They refused to take the unqualified oath, insisted that they should not be required to take up arms in the event of war, and advanced the rather fantastic claim that they should be regarded as "French Neutrals."

Clearly the Acadian demand was an extraordinary one. It was the accepted conception then as now that the obligations incumbent upon those living within the bounds of the authority of a state included the taking of the oath of allegiance to that state. That was the case when New Sweden was obliged to submit to the New Netherlands in 1655, with those Swedes who desired to remain on the Delaware being expected to give an oath of unqualified allegiance to the new authority. That was also the case when the New Netherlands was obliged to submit to the English in 1664, and the Dutch about the Hudson and elsewhere were expected to do the same, if they remained beyond the period of a year. It was likewise the case, so far as France was concerned, when Frontenac received instructions respecting the expedition against New York, in the event of its capture, in 1689; and when the Duke d'Anville received instructions relating to his formidable but ill-fated expedition of 1746. Furthermore, this rule of broad international application was applied not only to the French in Canada after 1763, but also to those of Louisiana after 1803 when that territory became part of the United States, and to the Mexicans of northern Mexico after its cession to the United States in 1847.

Until the war was officially brought to a close by the Treaty of Utrecht in 1713 the situation was rather unsettled, with the articles of capitulation agreed upon at the surrender of Port Royal applying only to those within three miles of the fort and with the other Acadians anxious and uncertain about what the future held in store for them. One of the articles of capitulation provided that the inhabitants within the *banlieue*, an area having a radius of a cannon shot or three miles from the fort, should remain upon their estates, with their corn, cattle and furniture, for two years, if they were not desirous of leaving before the expiration of that time, they taking the oaths of allegiance to Her Britannic Majesty. In accordance with the terms of this article, the inhabitants within the *banlieue*—fifty-seven heads of families—did take such oaths by the end of the third week of January 1711, and that, in itself, seemed to portend auspiciously. But the war had not yet ended, French agents were active and the Acadians outside the *banlieue*, not being included in the articles of capitulation, were in a state of uneasiness and uncertainty. These Acadians applied to the British Governor for protection and offered to take the oath of allegiance. But the Governor who told them that by the arbitrament of war they had become prisoners, and who had collected a tribute from them, could give them no terms until Her Majesty's more particular orders were received. As a result of uncertainty over their situation the Acadians outside the *banlieue* became uneasy, tried to keep the Indians hostile to the English and attempted to stir up the Acadians within the *banlieue* who had already taken the oath of allegiance. Further apprehension was also caused by the hostile designs of the Indians and the French from Canada, as well as by the influence of the French missionary priests. That this apprehension was justified is clear from the fact that a party of sixty-five Englishmen which was sent in two flat boats and a whaleboat in June 1711 for the purpose of encouraging friendly Acadians in supplying wood and timber for the garrison was ambushed by a war party of French and Indians and all but one of them were killed or captured. Soon even those Acadians within the *banlieue* who had taken the oath of allegiance joined their compatriots in blockading the fort at Annapolis Royal, and the English were not only threatened with assault but with being one and all put to the sword.

The Treaty of Utrecht brought the war to an end. By it such of the Acadians as might choose to leave Acadia or Nova Scotia were free to do so within the space of a year,[1] taking with them their personal effects; while a letter of Queen Anne permitted such emigrants to sell their lands and houses. Those who remained in Nova Scotia were guaranteed freedom of worship under certain conditions. These were that they should accept the sovereignty of the British Crown, and that they and their pastors should keep within the limits of British law.

Now two roads lay before the Acadians, and it was a momentous question for themselves and for the local British authorities which one of them they would choose: whether they would remove themselves to French territory within the year stipulated in the Treaty of Utrecht, or remain in Nova Scotia and become British subjects. The one course meant their continuance as French nationals but their abandonment of their lands in Nova Scotia; the other meant the retention of their lands, the taking the oath of allegiance to the British monarch and the relinquishment of their French citizenship. Neither of these alternatives was their choice. Instead they tried for many years to combine what they wished of the two alternatives and eventually found themselves in an untenable position.

The best time to have settled the question of the oath was immediately after the Treaty of Utrecht. Then the Acadians numbered fewer than 2,000 and, if the interests of security, as well as international propriety, demanded that they take the oath or leave Nova Scotia and they persisted in refusing to do the one or the other, their deportation then would neither have been as formidable nor regarded with so much disfavour as forty-two years later when they had increased to five or six times that number. The reason why the question was not then settled was that the Acadians themselves were loath to leave their fertile meadowlands in Nova Scotia, whence they drew subsistence by means of cattle raising and farming, for uncleared and unknown or less fertile lands elsewhere, where much hard work would be needed, and the British authorities in Nova Scotia had neither the forces nor the resources to press the question to an issue. Other factors also supported the tendency to let matters drift; including the anxiety of the French authorities to maintain good relations with the British at a time when they were involved in difficulties with Spain.

Time and again the Acadians were given the opportunity to take the oath of allegiance. But the French authorities, who found that the Acadians were in the main reluctant to remove to Cape Breton Island, soon saw and seized advantages in the situation and employed French agents and French missionaries for the purpose of keeping the Acadians faithful to King Louis. This was indeed an anomalous state of affairs: the "year" of the Treaty of Utrecht soon passed; most of the Acadians remained in Nova Scotia; French missionaries, who were French agents as well as Roman Catholic priests, strove to keep the Acadians attached to both their religion and the French interest, and, on occasion, openly avowed that their object was to keep the Acadians faithful to the French monarch; none of these missionaries was ever molested by the British authorities, except when detected in practices alien to his proper functions and injurious to the government; freedom of worship continued to be accorded to the Acadians, notwithstanding the fact that most of them persisted in refusing to take the oath of allegiance, the condition on which they had acquired that privilege; and the British government, in spite of the concern of the British authorities in Nova Scotia, did nothing effective either to have the French missionaries in that colony give a pledge that they would do nothing contrary to the interests of Great Britain or to have them replaced by other priests to be named by the Pope at the request of the British government.

The chief reasons for this anomalous state of affairs were the feebleness of British authority in Nova Scotia, the neglect and the apathy of the British ministers and the fact that the Acadians leaned so heavily on their French spiritual and temporal advisers. For a while, it is true, the *imperium in imperio* which existed was such that the inner power seemed to wax and strengthen every day while the outer relatively pined and dwindled. But the time was to come when the British ministers would waken from their lethargy, bestir themselves and, warned by the signs of the times, send troops and settlers into the Province at the eleventh hour. Then it was that the Acadians were to find how deplorable their position really was. Perhaps the only thing that could have averted the danger of Acadian hostilities or revolt and have made unnecessary the harsh measures to which such conduct afterwards gave rise was for the British ministry to have sent out a force sufficient both to protect the inhabitants against French terrorism and to leave no doubt that the King of England was master of Nova Scotia in fact as well as in name. But such did not take place until after long delay and until the problem had attained greater proportions. In the meantime, although those Acadians who remained in Nova Scotia had been transferred by France to the British Crown by the Treaty of Utrecht, French officers on occasion denounced them as rebels and threatened them with death if they did not fight at their bidding against Great Britain, and British officers threatened them with expulsion if they did not remain loyal to King George. These were the horns of the dilemma for the Acadians; and while for a time they avoided both they were ultimately confronted with the necessity for a decision they had tried to avoid.

French policy after 1713 reveals that France was unwilling to reconcile herself to the loss of Acadia, although it had with its ancient limits been ceded to Great Britain by the Treaty of Utrecht. Nor was France to neglect Nova Scotia or Acadia, even if for years Great Britain was to do so. On Ile Royale the French not only built up a mighty base at Louisbourg, as the watchdog and protector of the Gulf and the approaches to Quebec, and as the base and the guardian for the fishery, but also established there a Governor who was charged with the management of Acadian affairs, and who had zealous and efficient agents among the Acadians in the missionary priests, who were sent into Nova Scotia by the Bishop of Quebec, or in a few cases by their immediate ecclesiastical superiors in Ile Royale, and whose services in keeping the Acadians in the French interest were recognized and acknowledged by French political leaders and officials. At first the French authorities endeavoured to induce the Acadians to migrate to Ile Royale, where the growing power of the fortress at Louisbourg was a symbol that France was preparing to contest the supremacy of the continent with Great Britain, and sent envoys into Nova Scotia, with the permission of the local British officials, to visit the Acadian settlements and to tell the Acadians what inducements they were prepared to give them to remove. A few of the Acadians did go to Ile Royale, and nearly all of them in the emotion of the moment signed declarations of their willingness to migrate to French territory, but it was soon seen that this mood quickly changed and that the Acadians in the main had no inclination to leave their homes. At the same time the British authorities, realizing the value of settlers in Nova Scotia, hopeful of having the Acadians become loyal British subjects, and having no desire to see them migrate to Ile Royale where they would greatly add to the numbers and the strength of a potential enemy near at hand, were almost as anxious to keep the Acadians in Nova Scotia as they were forty years later to get them out of it. Soon, moreover, the French authorities realized that the Acadians were of greater benefit to France by remaining in Nova Scotia, whence they could furnish Ile Royale with much-needed supplies, where religion and patriotism might be combined or confused in keeping them in the French interest, and where in time of war they might be a source of strength for French invaders aiming at the re-capture of old Acadia or a fifth column which would be a decisive factor in any test of strength. If the Acadians had really wished to emigrate, the British Governor could have done little to stop them for his authority hardly extended beyond gunshot of his fort at Annapolis Royal and all the Acadians except those of Annapolis and its immediate neighbourhood were free to go or stay at will.

While most of the Acadians maintained a careful neutrality in times of trouble, and Mascarene himself declared that their refusal to fight for the French besiegers was one reason for the success of his defence of Annapolis on one occasion, French designs involved the Acadians and some of them were implicated in hostile acts against the British in Nova Scotia. During the 1720s French authorities not only strove to foment trouble between the Indians and the English but they joined the Indians in a raid on Canso. On the outbreak of the War of the Austrian Succession, the French from Ile Royale seized Canso before the British on this side of the Atlantic were aware of the outbreak of hostilities. They then attacked Annapolis. In this attack Duvivier, the French commander, expected help from the Acadians who were French in blood, faith and inclination; and the latter, who would not join him openly lest the attack should fail, did what they could without committing themselves and made a hundred and fifty scaling ladders for the besiegers. To this seizure of Canso and this attack on Annapolis a contemporary French writer attributes the dire calamity which soon befell the French. When the capture of Louisbourg in 1745 by New Englanders with the aid of a British naval squadron was followed by French plans to retake it, reconquer old Acadia, burn Boston and lay waste to the other seaboard towns, French officials counted on aid from the Acadians for their designs. The result was the assembling of a vast armada, comprising nearly half the French navy, and carrying 3,150 veteran troops, under the Duc d'Anville, in 1746. This formidable expedition set out from France, and Ramesay, with a large body of Canadians, was sent to Acadia to cooperate with d'Anville's force. News of this design and the appearance at

Chebucto of part of d'Anville's ill-fated fleet caused great excitement among the Acadians, who undoubtedly expected that they would soon again come under the Crown of France. Fifty of them went on board the French ships at Chebucto to pilot them to the attack on Annapolis. To their dismay, however, they found that no such attack would then be made. Early in the next year, when Coulon de Villiers and his men in the depth of the winter led his men from Beaubassin to Grand Pré, where in the dead of night they attacked Colonel Arthur Noble and his force, who were quartered in Acadian houses, and killed many of them in their beds, a number of Acadians acted as guides for Coulon's band and assisted them in other ways. With the restoration of Louisbourg to France, the British Government founded Halifax as a counterpoise to it and commenced their first real attempt at settling Nova Scotia. By the time of the eve of the Seven Years' War it was clear that a showdown would soon be reached with respect to North America. In 1755 Braddock was defeated on the Monongahela and Beauséjour was captured by New England troops. At the siege of Beauséjour about 300 Acadians aided the French.

The developments of the 1740s, with French attacks on Canso and Annapolis, the d'Anville expedition, the massacre at Grand Pré, and other French designs, as well as the capture of Louisbourg and its restoration and the founding of Halifax, meant a heightened interest and an increased activity in Nova Scotia. New efforts to have the Acadians take the oath of allegiance to the British monarch had no better result than previous ones. British activity at the Isthmus of Chignecto, with a view to protecting the peninsula from French encroachments, were followed by two matters of very special significance. One, in 1750, was the first forcible removal of the Acadians: resolved that the Acadians at Beaubassin should be preserved from the contaminating influence of the British, Le Loutre, who had been unable to prevent the British from reaching that village, went forward with his Indians and set fire to it, in order to force its inhabitants to go to territory claimed by the French near Beauséjour, a short distance away. This was the beginning of the dispersal of the Acadians. Besides these, through great pressure from the French they migrated in such numbers that by 1752 2,000 of them were to be found in Ile St. Jean (Prince Edward Island), and about seven hundred in Ile Royale (Cape Breton Island). The other, in 1751, was an interesting commentary on the attitude of the French authorities towards the Acadian claim to neutrality which those authorities had encouraged while the Acadians remained under British sovereignty: this was the order of Governor La Jonquière that all Acadian refugees near Beauséjour who did not take the oath of allegiance to the French monarch and enlist in the militia companies would be branded as rebels and chased from the lands which they occupied.

Subsequently, just after the capture of Beauséjour in 1755, while the New England troops, who had achieved that victory, were still in Nova Scotia, and British ships of the line still lay in Halifax harbour, Governor Lawrence of Nova Scotia and his council at Halifax decided that the safety of the colony required that the Acadians should take the oath of allegiance, which they had so often refused to do, or be deported from the province. They again refused, and they were thereupon deported to British colonies. In the circumstances, and particularly after the attacks on Annapolis Royal in 1744 and 1745 and the deeds done at Grand Pré in 1747, it seems both unfair and inappropriate to attempt to pin the chief responsibility for this decision on either Lawrence of Nova Scotia or Shirley of Massachusetts.

Lack of space prevents an account of the hardships experienced by those Acadians who were expelled or a description of the efforts made by the British authorities to keep families and people from the same community together. Suffice it to say that it might appear that the expulsion was unnecessary, for if the old situation had persisted for but another few years until the French menace on the continent had been eradicated the problem would no longer have existed, or if the Acadians could have taken the oath of allegiance prior to 1755, as those who remained in the Province and those who returned to it afterwards did, those harsh deeds would not have been done. Not many years after 1755, at any rate, probably about 2,000 of the exiled Acadians returned to Nova Scotia, where, along with a like number who escaped the expulsion, they received grants of land, took the oath of allegiance and assumed their full place in the life of the Province. On the two hundredth anniversary of that catastrophe which emerged from the vicissitudes of war and threats of war, all Nova Scotians of every racial origin rejoice with those of Acadian descent in marking the great achievements of the last two centuries.

Note

1. There have been different views as to the beginning and the end of the "year" of this Treaty, and some have held the untenable one that it was still in effect at the time of the founding of Halifax.

1748–1755: COMMUNITY DEVASTATED

Naomi E.S. Griffiths

The main theme of this monograph is that the building and development of Acadian society was a much more complex process than has usually been thought, and that a great deal more investigation is needed about a wide variety of questions of Acadian history. This theme was developed in [my] first two chapters by the description of the two powerful and contrasting polarities in Acadian life: that of the wider world and that of the Acadian community itself.

From *The Contexts of Acadian History, 1686–1784* (Montreal and Kingston: McGill-Queen's University Press, 1992), 62–94. Reprinted by permission.

Much about Acadian society not only links that society to experiences of other societies made up of newcomers to the North American continent but is also a consequence of the very existence of these other societies. Further, the emergence of Acadia is obviously related to the broader story of the European migration to North America, and a good part of Acadian developments can be best understood in the context of North American and European history. At the same time, however, Acadia is neither Quebec nor New England, and Acadian life is not just a transposition of European customs. There is a unique Acadian experience, developed partly because of the particular combination of European migrants who came to the colony, partly because of the very environment of the lands settled, and partly because of the peoples already on the territory claimed, the Micmac and Malecite. Acadian life in the late seventeenth and early eighteenth centuries produced a distinct society. Local conditions produced particular problems which were solved by distinctively Acadian methods.

In many ways, it is inevitable that the impact of the forces outside the small settlements of early Acadia should be seen as being more powerful in the early decades of Acadian history, and the internal strengths of this growing community visibly gain power with its very development. In the period that is the subject of this chapter, 1748–55, however, Acadian history is determined by an almost equal balance of internal and external forces. This most traumatic period of Acadian history, the era of exile and proscription, is an era dominated by a major world war. That the Acadians survived the death and destruction that the world war brought them is due, above all, to the nature of the Acadian community itself. Bitter imperial rivalry between England and France brought the suffering. It was the strength of the Acadians that allowed them to endure the years of deportation, to preserve a measure of social coherence and identity in exile, and to re-root their community, after a generation of turmoil, once again in the Maritimes.

The theme of the complexity of Acadian history—the contention that the Acadians are no simpler than the rest of humankind—is crucial for an understanding of the period 1748–84, the period of this chapter and the following. Much of what is considered general knowledge about the Acadian deportation is more myth than history. Had the Acadians been a society of simple and devout peasantry, who were ignorant victims of imperial policies they were too naive to understand, their community would never have survived the attempt to destroy it between 1755 and 1764.[1] It is important to be clear at the outset that these years really did see a policy, not for the physical extermination of those who were Acadian, but for the eradication of the idea of an Acadian community. Charles Lawrence, Lieutenant-Governor of Nova Scotia in 1755 and the person who must bear the major responsibility for the policy of the exile and proscription of the Acadians, was quite clear as to what he wanted.[2] He wrote a circular which was dispatched from Halifax on 11 August 1755[3] to inform the other governors of British colonies in North America that the deportation of Acadians was under way. After listing the reasons why he considered the deportation necessary, he stated that, "it was judged a necessary and the only practicable measure to divide them [the Acadians] among the Colonies where they may be of some use, as most of them are healthy strong people; and as they cannot easily collect themselves together again it will be out of their power to do any mischief and they may become profitable and it is possible, in time faithful subjects."

The Acadians were to be exiled from the lands they thought their own, and divided among other British colonial societies in North America where it would be impossible for them to organize themselves as a distinct and separate community. They were to be assimilated within the context of each separate colony, from Massachusetts to Georgia, and become undifferentiated from the majority within each colony, unique as individuals but not as a distinct group. Lawrence had an unsophisticated perception of the unity of the other colonial societies in British North America, and certainly no conception of the individuality of, for example, German settlement groups in Pennsylvania or the Scots-Irish in Connecticut.[4] But his main purpose was clear and his judgement unequivocal: the Acadians must cease to exist as a coherent and separate society and become, in terms of political and civic standing, absorbed into the mass of the other culture.

Surprisingly, Lawrence's ambition failed. While many an individual Acadian perished and many indeed did find themselves assimilated into some other society, an Acadian group identity continued to exist. While there were circumstances in the nature of the exile and proscription which contributed, the continuation of an Acadian identity was largely due to the characteristics that had become the hallmark of Acadian identity before 1755. Any assessment of why exile did not triumph has to start from an appreciation of the nature of the Acadian community before 1755.

The size of Acadian population in 1755 has still not been established, even after the splendid work by Jean Daigle and Robert Leblanc published in the first volume of *The Historical Atlas of Canada*.[5] But disagreement about how many people should be numbered as part of the community that year—15,000, 18,000, or even 20,000—is less important than what we do know: the whereabouts of the major concentrations of this population and the main thrust of their expansion.

The older settlements of the Acadian population, those in the neighbourhood of Annapolis Royal, Cape Sable, and La Heve, whose roots are in the 1630s, while significant, are by 1755 much less so than those of the Minas Basin and Chignecto Isthmus, which were established in the 1670s and 1680s. The Acadian population of Annapolis Royal in 1755 was probably 2,000 and the other settlements—Cape Sable and La Heve—would number at most 400 people.[6] The most populous centres of Acadian life at that time were to found through the stretch of country from the Minas Basin to the valleys of the Memramcook, the Petitcodiac, and the Shepody. Settlements along the Minas Basin, communities which ran from the base of Blomindon to the gentle hills of what was then called Cobequid (Truro), traced their beginnings back to the 1680s. In 1755 their combined population was in the region of 5,000.[7]

Similarly, the families of Beaubassin, whose houses looked out on the Chignecto Basin from the higher terraces near present-day Amherst and Sackville, lived on land settled at around the same time as the Minas Basin. Bishop St. Vallier had visited the area in 1686, finding it a charming region and estimated that 150 people lived on the edges of what he described as *"un des plus beaux havres du monds."*[8] In 1755 the population there was probably 3,000.[9]

The most recently established settlements of the Acadians in 1755 were those of the area known to them as "Trois-Rivières": the valleys of Shepody, Petitcodiac, and Memramcook.[10] Small hamlets grew of there from 1731 onwards, when Blanchards, Legers, Dubois, and other families moved out from the Minas Basin, just as earlier members of their families had once moved from the Port Royal settlements to the Minas Basin. The "Trois-Rivières" settlement was the most considerable new expansion of Acadian settlement after 1730. By 1755, the population of these river valleys probably totalled between 200 and 300.

While the settlements just enumerated are the most populous of the Acadian community, they represent just that. They are not the totality of the Acadian people in 1755. There were also Acadians settled along the coast from the Baie des Chaleurs to Baie Verte on sites first explored in the 1630s and 1640s, the time of Nicholas Denys and his imaginative enterprises. The most important of these were around the mouth of the Miramichi and at Cocagne and Shediac, also tidewater sites. Further, while there is some dispute as to whether there was year-round settlement by Acadians on the Madeleine Islands at this time, there is ample evidence that these were known and exploited as rich fishing grounds by both Acadian and Micmac.[11] The Acadian interest in Canso should not be overlooked, nor that there were also Acadians along the Saint John River Valley, as far inland as Jemseg. Acadians had settled, along with more recent French migrants, on Ile St. Jean and in parts of Ile Royale. Linked by direct kinship ties to people living within the major centres of Acadian population, as well as by ties of trade and custom, language, religion and common experience, these people numbered close to 3,000.

The Acadian demographic experience was not that different from the pattern of demographic development elsewhere in colonial North America. The growth of the Acadian population, from roughly 3,000 in 1713 to at least 15,000 in 1755, may have been slightly more rapid than that experienced generally in colonial America, but not overwhelmingly so. Jim Potter has pointed out that "different colonies experienced very different growth rates at different periods."[12] For example, in the eighteenth century the average decennial growth rate in New England was 27 per cent. The comparable demographic studies of Acadians have not yet been completed, but it is unlikely that their population growth would be much greater than this.[13] Similarly, the way in which the settlements of the Acadians moved from the Annapolis Basin, along the river valleys and through the marshlands of the Bay of Fundy, as well as to the river mouths along the Atlantic coast, has a striking similarity to patterns of expansion found elsewhere—in Maine and other New England colonies, as well as in Quebec.

The variation of settlement patterns to be found within the colony was much the same as that of New France. Mid eighteenth-century Kamouraska, Quebec City, and Montreal, for example, had as much distinctiveness from each other as they had features in common. Similarly, as has been outlined in the previous chapter, Acadian life in different parts of the territory revealed subtle distinctions between settlements, as well as clear similarities of experience. The Annapolis Valley Acadians had lived dominated by farming, hunting, and fishing, but a fair number of them were connected to the comings and goings of the officials of the small colony. Acadians were pilots for the incoming ships from Europe and, occasionally, part of the tiny bureaucracy.[14] Some pursued commerce and trade, or small-scale home industries in woodwork or textiles.

The settlers of the Minas Basin had lives which were shaped by dyke-building and an agriculture rich enough to allow for exports, not only to other communities within the colony, but also to Louisbourg and to Boston.[15] There is some evidence that trade was also carried on with the West Indies.[16] This meant a very different daily round than that of those settled along the Atlantic shore north of Cape Tormentine, or newly arrived on Ile St. Jean. The inhabitants of one such outpost, Mirliguesch, were referred by Le Loutre as a mixed collection of "Acadians and ... Savage."[17] Lives in these settlements would be dominated by hunting and fishing, with subsistence agriculture producing no surplus for trade.

The Acadian society was strengthened, as were the other European colonies in North America, by a wide variance of lifestyles.[18] However, there were a number of significant features which helped to give those who lived in the different settlements of particular colonies a strong sense of common purpose. One of the most important of such unifying factors for the Acadians was external pressure arising from the fact that Acadians were considered colonials, and their lands, a colony. While this is true for all European settlements in North America at this time, the Acadians had a particularly complex colonial status. A large part of Acadian distinctiveness arose from the impact upon the Acadian polity of the imperial policies of both France and England. The alternating administration of their society by French and English officials, each for considerable periods, helped to produce that mindset among the Acadians which led them to develop a distinctive policy of neutrality. French and English attempts to control the lands the Acadians settled were accompanied by international boundary commissions and the development of military installations. The founding of Louisbourg and the establishment of Beauséjour by the French were matched by the establishment of Halifax and the organization of Fort Lawrence and Fort Edward by the English. The living space of the Acadians was one of the centres in North America for the conflicting territorial ambitions of two great empires, England and France.

I have suggested elsewhere that one of the keys to understanding the development of Acadian identity is recognizing the reality of their experience as a border people.[19] It is important to realize that the political status of this border varied. In the seventeenth century and until the 1740s, "Acadia or Nova Scotia" was at one of the most important junctions of Anglo-French claims in North America. The colony was a border that made part of the frontier between empires and saw frequent skirmishes which greatly hindered development of the settlements. But, until 1744, "Acadia or Nova Scotia" as a whole was not a battlefield. After 1744, however, the Acadians saw an episode of the war between the Empires involve the heartlands and peripheries of their communities simultaneously. Military historians have noted that by the early 1740s the Missaquash river was the effective boundary between French and English control.[20] It was a boundary that, in the expansion of their communities, the Acadians had ignored when their colony was the meeting place of empires. They continued to ignore it when the colony became an actual battleground of imperial forces.

In the eyes not only of London and Paris but also of officials in New England and New France, Acadia and the Acadians were a disputed resource. Their lands were seen as a legitimate area for control both by London and by Paris. France and England both considered the Acadians' male population as a possible source of military strength.[21] In sum, Acadia was perceived as a colony and the Acadians as colonials. This is not surprising, for it was partly true. For the Acadians, however, their colonial status was less a central and deciding factor of their political being than it was just another aspect of life, something with which one coped, not something by which one was controlled. Even the system of deputies, a system first structured by the English solely for the purpose of communicating their commands to the scattered settlements,[22] served to reinforce the Acadian sense of their own independence. Over the decades since 1710, the delegates, originally chosen to act as representatives of official direction from Annapolis Royal, became officials themselves. They, not the clergy, became the indispensable arbiters of community life. Occasionally constables and officers of the court at Annapolis, they were more often, as Brebner has summarized it, "registrars-general for their district, [those who] recorded titles, sales, and other transfers, marriage settlements and inheritances, and were rewarded by a commission of 15 per cent on the seigneurial fees they collected and small fees for executing deeds."[23] This organization of local government gave the Acadian population considerable experience in self-leadership. We do not know precisely how the delegates were elected by the community, but we do know that they were elected. Thus, before exile, the Acadian people were accustomed to select spokesmen to present their views to others who considered themselves more powerful. This situation could not help but encourage the Acadians to think of themselves having very considerable political rights, even if they were not entirely self-governed.

Further, the Acadian sense of control over their daily lives was enhanced by the fact that, as in most North American colonial settlements, the family was the most important social institution.[24] For the majority of Acadians the family and the household not only formed the basis of their daily experience but also structured their relationships to the wider community and their working world.[25] Throughout the length and breadth of the Acadian settlements the family and household shaped life for most individuals, whether one looks at the traditional patterns of life on farms in the Annapolis Valley, the mixed trading and farming economies of the Minas basin, or the new ways of life being tried in the Trois-Rivières area; or whether one analyses the Beaubassin settlements and considers the outposts of Acadian life at the mouth of the Miramichi or in Merliguesch. In the two most fundamental aspects of the community, landholding and religion, family and kin connections played the most significant roles.

To deal with kinship ties first: family relationships within and among the Acadian communities made a close net of interconnections. It was a net, not a solid piece of cloth. Before exile, as afterwards, the Acadians showed a considerable ability to absorb newcomers into their community. Even in the older settled Acadian parishes of Annapolis, Minas, and Beaubassin, newcomers accounted for a significant percentage of marriage partners.[26] Within a particular Acadian hamlet or village one can find an intricate series of intermarriages, brothers in one family marrying sisters from another, marriages within the then-forbidden relationship of second-cousin. However, such a pattern of relationships existed alongside families who had no ties to their neighbours, not even by marriage of distant relatives. There has been little comparison of the kin structure of Acadian villages with contemporary villages elsewhere, either in North America or in Europe, and it is not yet possible to say whether the kin lines of Acadian parishes were closer than those to be found in south-western France, in New England, or along the St. Lawrence. One can assert, however, that in 1755 Acadian family life was flourishing and as vital to the Acadian sense of community as was family life elsewhere in British North America.

The Acadian family and household were the economic arbiters of the community, made more powerful because of very lax official control of the Acadians' exploration and settlement of new lands. After 1713 landholdings were granted to individuals directly and Acadians in many settlements paid quit-rents for their property.[27] But the officials at Annapolis Royal and later at Halifax were in no hurry to grant any obviously unchallengeable titles to property since the tenure of land was, as Clark wrote, inextricably linked in the official mind with an unqualified oath of allegiance which the Acadians showed no sign of accepting.[28] The result was predictably chaotic. But land claims by

Acadians were registered and suits between Acadians about land were judged by the officials at Annapolis Royal.[29] At the same time, especially in the Trois-Rivières region, Acadians, in the words of their own deputies, "[took] possession of and improved large portions of lands"[30] claimed as timberland reserves by the Crown, and ignored any and all demands made by officials to cease and desist. The first settlers in the present-day Dieppe-Moncton region were, as Paul Surette has discovered, two kin groups of families linked by marriage among siblings and cousins.[31] The organization of the plans of these hamlets along the Petitcodiac was not by official survey and land grant: it was by agreement between the pioneers themselves. The Acadian family was the arbiter of plans for new settlements, and it was between kin groups and households that boundaries were claimed and agreed.

As well as being the real authority behind land clearance and distribution, the family was crucial in the maintenance of religious belief. Catholic life gained its daily reality in the practices of the home. Few of the Acadian settlements had resident priests. In 1748, there were five priests reported in action, excluding Le Loutre whose activities were mostly peripatetic and centred upon the Micmac. There was de Miniac, "half blind," de la Goudalie, "quite old and a little deaf," and Desenclaves, who suffered "from a weak chest." This left Chauvreulx and Girard, who were apparently hale and hearty.[32] Basically, each Acadian settlement could count on a visit from a priest annually, and those in the three main regions of Acadian life—the Annapolis Valley, the Minas Basin, and Beaubassin—could also count on a priest residing in the region most years. Weekly Mass was the privilege only of those living within an hour or so's journey of the major parish churches, and priestly blessing or weddings and baptisms took place only when a priest came to a particular neighbourhood. This was a common practice for eighteenth-century Catholicism. A great deal more must be written about Acadian religious practices, based on archival records, including those of the Archdiocese of Quebec, rather than the wishful thinking of nineteenth- and twentieth-century myth makers.[33] It is no slur on the devotion of the Acadians to point out that the rites of the Church were less easily available to them before 1755 than they were after 1830, nor that Acadian interpretation of Catholicism before 1755 was based as much upon individual faith as upon clerically imposed discipline. During the years of exile among mostly Protestant communities of the British colonies in North America, the family framework of Catholic belief proved to be a major factor in Acadian survival.

This crucial importance of family within Acadian society has been unaccountably neglected, given the immense interest in genealogy that has characterized Acadian studies.[34] The archival resources have rarely been examined in detail to discover whether members of particular families played consistently dominant roles in the Acadian settlements.[35] Were the Leblancs unusual in being linked to British interests, given the number of men of that name who acted as notaries and delegates throughout the settlements? What would an analysis of landholding size and numbers of herds and flocks tell us about the economic stratification among the Acadians? The work to answer such questions remains to be done,[36] as does the work to tell what place trading, hunting, and fishing held in each of the Acadian communities at this time.[37] At the moment, one has merely the major outlines of Acadian life on the eve of the deportation. Much of the process of Acadian life has yet to be uncovered.

But even with such a host of questions yet unanswered, it is clear that in 1755 the Acadians were seen as a distinctive society by those who considered themselves their rulers. Sent out by London to govern "Acadia or Nova Scotia" in 1749, Edward Cornwallis informed the delegates who had been brought to meet him that "It appears to me that you think yourselves independent of any government; and you wish to treat with the king as if you were so."[38]

The new Governor was right. By the mid eighteenth-century the Acadians did indeed consider themselves a people. Further, they considered that this meant they had definite political rights in society. Acadian policy throughout the years leading up to the deportation was largely based on this conviction that they had, at the very minimum, a negotiating strength in any confrontation with officials, whether military, civil, or clerical, English or French. As late as 10 June 1755, the people of Minas offered to promise "our unshaken fidelity to his Majesty, provided that His Majesty shall allow us the same liberty that he has granted us."[39] This sense of political existence is not without parallel in colonial societies: it is similar to one of the motivating forces behind the American revolution.

It is unlikely that the Acadians ever envisaged exile as a likely fate, even during the tumultuous decade that preceded their deportation. Their tactics were strongly influenced by a belief that the worst that could occur would be a temporary dislocation into French-controlled territory. Ever since 1713 the possibility of Acadian emigration had been part of the rhetoric political discussion between the English and the Acadians. Such movement had almost always been envisaged in terms of Acadian wish and English opposition. But towards the end of the war of the Austrian succession (usually known in North America as King George's War), the then Lieutenant-Governor of Nova Scotia, Paul Mascarene, reported that there were rumours among the Acadian settlements that "a great force was coming from New England to transport or destroy them."[40] He also reported that every effort was immediately taken to scotch the report. Governor Shirley of Massachusetts[41] issued a proclamation in the fall of 1746 in which he declared

> in His Majesty's name, that there is not the least foundation for any Apprehensions of His Majesty's intending to remove the said Inhabitants of Nova Scotia from their settlements and Habitations: but that on the contrary it is His Majesty's Resolution to protect and maintain all such of 'em as have adhered to, and shall continue in their Duty and Allegiance to him in the quiet and peaceable Possession of their respective Habitations and Settlements and in the Employment of all their rights and Privileges as his Subjects.[42]

Given the Acadian belief that they had demonstrated their loyalty very adequately in recent years, it would not be surprising for their delegates to consider that their policy of independent neutrality needed no particular adjustment after 1749.

In fact, once open warfare between England and France had been brought to a halt by the treaty of Aix-la-Chapelle in 1748, the relationship between the majority of the Acadian settlements and English officials became much as it had been before fighting gave red snow to Grand-Pré.[43] In 1749, both England and France immediately set about reorganizing their forces and England, in particular, looked to the strengthening of her position in North America. Louisbourg had been returned to France, causing thunderous criticism from Boston.[44] Plans were now made in London to strengthen the British hold on Nova Scotia. A new regime was inaugurated to oversee the foundation of Halifax as well as the establishment of Lunenburg with Protestant migrants.[45] Acadia was to become Nova Scotia, a colony that would be a reliable outpost of the British Empire instead of a region of doubtful security inhabited by people with questionable loyalty to His Britannic Majesty.

Edward Cornwallis arrived, as has been noted, to take over as Governor of the colony on 21 June 1749.[46] While he managed to fulfil a fair number of the aspirations of those who had appointed him, his attempt to make the Acadians take an unqualified oath of loyalty—without any provision for their remaining neutral during an Anglo-French confrontation—was met with a replay of past Acadian responses.[47] On 31 July 1749 the assembled delegates from the Acadian settlements heard Cornwallis proclaim that their position within the colony must be regularized by the swearing of an unqualified oath. On 6 September 1749 the Acadians presented the Governor and his council with a petition that requested a renewal of the oath administered to them twenty years earlier by Governor Phillips, an oath which in Acadian eyes had never been repudiated by them nor annulled by the British. Should this petition be denied, the Acadians stated, they would then quit the colony. Cornwallis and his administration made the same response to this reply that their predecessors had done to previous similar rejoinders: inaction. This could be fairly taken as tacit acceptance of the Acadian terms. As Brebner wrote, "the relations between Governor and *habitants* had fallen into the old ruts and were wearing them deeper."[48] In these circumstances, it is unlikely that many Acadians envisaged being sent into exile as a distinct possibility even as late as spring 1755. At any rate no alteration can be discerned in Acadian attitudes about the oath during the years 1749–55.

However, if the general outlines of Acadian politics towards the English did not change, the converse is not true. Despite the similarity of official policy on the question of the oath itself, there were fundamental differences between the regimes of Mascarene and his predecessors and of Edward Cornwallis and his successors. John Bartlett Brebner opened his chapter on these years, which he called "Caught between the duellists," with a striking description of the meeting of Mascarene and five of his councillors with Cornwallis, on the deck of the HMS *Beaufort* in Chebucto Bay, 12 July 1749.[49] For Brebner this meeting represented the start of a radically new policy for the colony, which was "to be prosecuted vigorously and with generous financial support."[50]

This new policy was a direct consequence of the Treaty of Aix-la-Chapelle which had been signed in 1748. During negotiations, the British diplomats had given back Ile Royale and its "great fortress" of Louisbourg to the French, in return for concessions elsewhere. Now came London's attempt to redress the balance in British North America. The policy decided upon had three major features: the establishment of an English stronghold on the Atlantic coast of the colony to offset Louisbourg, the general enhancement of the military presence of the English within centres of Acadian population, and a scheme for the assisted emigration of Protestants to the colony. The establishment of Halifax was the most dramatic sign of the new order. Clark called its building "the greatest public porkbarrel yet opened in North America" and cited the parliamentary votes for the construction of the city between 1749 and 1753 as a measure of the opportunities created. They were "1749, £40,000; 1750, £57,583; 1751, £53,928; 1752, £61,493; 1753, £94,616; and 1755, £49,418."[51] While construction proceeded neither as smoothly nor as swiftly as its planners had hoped, proceed it did.[52] Despite its reputation as a place where one-half of the city lived by selling rum to the other, by 1750 it was asserted that there were 750 brick houses in Halifax.[53] Its population fluctuated wildly, because it was a port of entry for new migrants to the colony. Clark estimates that at one point in 1750 there were as many as 6,000 people living about its streets.[54] Its core population during the period 1749–55 was somewhere in the region of 3,000.[55] During the early years, many migrants moved on to other British colonies. From the outset, however, Halifax attracted a small but steady flow of immigrants from New England. Many opportunists came for the government contract, to sell rum, or to further the smuggling trade between Boston and Louisbourg. Just as many came because they saw a chance for their long-term betterment in the changing circumstances of Nova Scotia. As traders, fishermen, merchants, craftsmen, and even lawyers, they brought a great deal of experience and ability to the new society. At the very least, Halifax gave Cornwallis a strength that no previous English administration in the colony had possessed.

The establishment of Halifax was crucial for the success of the new policy for Nova Scotia, but it was only part of the scheme evolved by London and Boston.[56] The general strengthening of English military presence throughout the colony that took place at the same time was equally important. The Annapolis garrison was reorganized, and Fort Edward was built at Pisiquid, with a road connecting it to Halifax. In September of 1750, Major Charles Lawrence built a fort, which he named after himself, on the south side of the Misseguash. All these actions brought the reality of the English possession of the colony to the heart of the Acadian settlements in a new and vivid manner.

The third feature of the policy that Cornwallis and his successors pursued was the foundation of Lunenburg and the settlement by 1754 of upwards of

2,000 "Foreign Protestants" there and in the immediately surrounding area. This neighbourhood was that known to the Acadians as Merligash and La Heve. Winthrop Pickard Bell wrote the classic study of this project.[57] He disentangled the mixture of motives that lay behind London's willingness to assist foreign Protestant migration to Nova Scotia at that time and illuminated the complex history of their establishment there. Bell made it clear that after 1749 the officials concerned with these migrants envisaged them as being established in townships of their own. Whatever might have been the dream of Governor Shirley of Massachusetts—that mingling English settlements among the Acadian villages "as contiguous to theirs as maybe" would enhance their loyalty to Great Britain—this vision was no more than advice and advice not followed.[58] Again, as in the case of Halifax, the settling of new migrants proved much more difficult in practice than had been anticipated. But, like Halifax, by 1754 something considerable had been achieved: the foundations of the new community had been laid. The new town of Lunenburg had been laid out, with no concessions made to the steep hillside on which it was built. The grid-iron plan had been used, yielding roughly horizontal streets running parallel to a narrow waterfront and cross streets running at right angles straight up the hill.[59] While the years 1755 to 1763 were hard for these new migrants, in 1754 a settlement was in place, with sawmills in operation, some houses built, some farms laid out, and a number of craftsmen plying their trades.

All this action meant a major change in the political situation of the Acadians. Before 1749, while their lands were the border between two empires, it seemed clear, from an Acadian point of view, that one of these empires, France, was more concerned with the territory than the other. "Acadia or Nova Scotia" could be considered as a distant outpost of the British empire. But it could also be seen as the moving frontier of the French. France had the most impressive military establishment at Louisbourg. Small English trading vessels might ply the waters off the coasts of the colony, but French shipping was more visible. French military action brought war directly into the Acadian settlements in the 1740s. Until the conclusion of hostilities and the fall of Louisbourg, from the Acadian perspective French military force could be considered the more daring and often the more successful. With the foundation of Halifax and the establishment of new forts, this situation was radically altered.

Further, until 1749, it had also seemed clear that Acadian development would set the pattern for the future of the colony. The Acadians had been the clear majority of the population within "Acadia or Nova Scotia" since sometime in the 1720s, when their numbers surpassed the Micmac population. Acadians were the settlers of the colony. Their lifestyle was its economy. With the arrival of migrants for Halifax and Lunenburg, this no longer seemed obvious. Whilst the English military presence could be dismissed as a temporary phenomenon, the establishment of new villages and towns presaged a more enduring transformation.

If the Acadians seemed to react slowly to these new elements in the life of the colony, the French and the Micmac responded rapidly. As John Reid has pointed out, the French had few grounds on which to object to this outburst of energetic action by the English.[60] But this did not stop an attempt by France to lay *de facto* claim to as much territory in the area as possible. While peace supposedly reigned between the two empires throughout the world as a result of the treaty of 1748, and while an international commission was working to establish the boundaries of "Acadia or Nova Scotia,"[61] the day-to-day life on the frontiers of that colony was punctuated by raid and counter-raid, ambush and seige.[62] Fort Lawrence would soon be faced by Fort Beausejour, whose construction was begun in April 1751 scarcely more than a kilometre from the earlier fortification. In the Anglo-French struggle for dominance in North America, 1748 marked a truce rather than a peace.

The Micmac aided the French by exerting their own pressure on both the English and the Acadians during these years. Throughout the years of the European exploration and settlement of "Acadia or Nova Scotia," the Micmac had never stopped considering themselves the rightful tenants of the land. In 1720 they had affirmed their rights of possession by saying: "This land here that God has given us which we can be accounted a part as much as the trees are born here.... We are masters independent of everyone and wish to have our country free."[63] The Micmac were not so much allies of the French in the 1750s as they were a people convinced of their autonomy and taking all means to ensure their continued independence. England seemed a greater threat than France to this goal. So the Micmac not only mounted raiding parties against Halifax and Lunenburg, they also helped the French make the Acadian communities of Beaubassin a war zone. In 1750 the Micmac, accompanied and abetted by the French missionary priest, Jean-Louis Le Loutre, helped to force some Acadian migration from the Beaubassin villages by setting fire to both houses and church.[64]

The extent to which the Acadians remained strictly neutral in these years has been hotly debated. In my view, there is no doubt that the bulk of the Acadians adhered to the policy. There is no evidence of a major rejection of British rule throughout the Acadian settlements. But there is also no doubt in my mind that some Acadians not only traded with Louisbourg and neglected to supply local English garrisons but also supported French activities against the English. There is documentary evidence about the participation of young Acadian men, in particular, in French and Micmac raiding parties.[65] Once more, the key to understanding Acadian action is to consider them as a normal human society, hence as a polity that would contain a variety of views even though a majority would finally unite in support of a common policy. Cornwallis concluded his term of office in August 1752, handing over to Colonel Peregrine Hopson. This latter gentleman only remained in the colony until October 1753, but retained the governorship of the colony until 1755. When he sailed for England, Colonel Charles Lawrence was appointed as Lieutenant-Governor. Lawrence had had a long career in the military, in the colonial service, and in the colony. He was thirty-eight when he was gazetted major and had joined his regiment in the 1747 occupation of Louisbourg.[66] Whatever one may think of his political abilities, his career shows considerable military perspicacity. There is no doubt that he framed his policies as Lieutenant-Governor in the light of his military experiences, as will become clear below.

International events are of paramount importance for understanding what happened to Acadian society as Lawrence entered upon his term of office. The new policy introduced by Cornwallis, a policy of increased English interest and presence within the colony, was largely the result of international concerns. It was a policy that prepared for war. It had been framed in the context of a bitter struggle between the English and French colonies in North America. This flamed into open warfare in the spring of 1754 with the clash of the French and American militia in the Ohio Valley. The French were quite as much concerned for boundaries of their empire as were the English and appointed Roland-Michel Barrin de la Galissonière as "commander in chief" of New France. His mission was the "restructuring" of the French empire in North America, a "restructuring" that would necessitate stopping "the undertakings of the English."[67] 1755 was the last year of prologue, the final year of preparatory clash and skirmish the outbreak of worldwide war, a war which would involve battles between France and England not only in North America and Europe but also in Asia. This war became known as the Seven Years' War and the peace treaties that brought it to a close in 1763 effectively ended the power of the French empire in North America. In the declaration of war issued from Kensington on 18 May 1756, England put in pride of place the "usurpations and encroachments made by the French upon the English territories and settlements ... in the West Indies and North America ... particularly in the province of Nova Scotia."[68] France issued her declaration from Versailles on 9 June 1756. The events of exile and proscription, which would so profoundly shape the identity of the Acadian community for the next centuries had their immediate cause in the tensions of the New World. Although European men and money were deeply involved in the strategy and tactics of the war effort in North America before 1756, the deportation of the Acadians was, fundamentally, rooted in North American realities and perceptions.

The most obvious of these realities is a matter of political geography: the tactical and strategic possibilities to both sides of the land settled by the Acadians. Moreover, by 1755 "Acadia or Nova Scotia" was not only the border between two rival empires but also in itself a region with considerable tactical importance for both powers.

We have a great deal of information on how Lawrence saw his own policy. There is no doubt that for him military matters were an understood priority. He shaped his policy for the colony accordingly. He wrote, at length, to Governor Shirley of Massachusetts, to other Governors of British colonies in North America, and to the authorities in London.[69] Lawrence's policy resulted from the wish to make Nova Scotia a secure and flourishing outpost of the British Empire in North America. He was convinced by 1753, when he was made lieutenant-governor of the colony, that the refusal of the Acadians to take an unqualified oath of loyalty to the

British crown made them a major obstacle to the fulfilment of this ambition.[70] He held two completely different, but in his view interdependent, objectives: first, the preservation of British possessions in North America, and, second, the strengthening of Nova Scotia as a crucial and significant part of those possessions.

By the spring of 1755, Lawrence had become thoroughly convinced that his colony could not become a reliable outpost of the British Empire while the Acadians were among its people. Thus the best possible solution was to send them to be assimilated among the populations of the other British North American colonies. In the circular to the governors of these colonies quoted from earlier, this was made plain.[71] Lawrence informed his fellow governors of the unique opportunity now available: "The success that has attended his Majesty's arms in driving the French from the Encroachments they had made in this province," he wrote, "furnished me with a favourable opportunity of reducing the French inhabitants of this Colony to a proper obedience to His Majesty's Government or forcing them to quit the country." He went on to state that "I offered such of them as had not been openly in arms against us, a continuance of the Possession of their lands, if they would take the Oath of Allegiance, unqualified with any Reservation whatsoever." "But this," he also stated, "they have most audaciously as well as unanimously refused." Lawrence therefore turned to the council of the colony "to consider by what means we could with the greatest security and effect rid ourselves of a set of people who would forever have been an obstruction to the intention of settling this Colony and that it was now from their refusal to the Oath absolutely incumbent upon us to remove." The circular continued: "As their numbers amount to near 7000 persons the driving them off with leave to go whither they pleased would have doubtless strengthened Canada with so considerable a number of inhabitants; and as they have no cleared land to give them at present, such as able to bear arms must have been immediately employed in annoying this and neighbouring Colonies. To prevent such an inconvenience it was judged a necessary and the only practicable measure to divide them among the Colonies."

Lawrence may have known what he was about and why, but the debate that has raged over the deportation of the Acadians ever since has been bitter and wide-ranging.[72] Whose influence ensured that the proposal of deportation became reality? Governor Shirley of Massachusetts?[73] What part did London play?[74] Was the determining factor the opinions of the British admirals Boscawen and Mostyn who arrived that spring? Can the whole episode really be summed up, as Guy Fregault believed, as an act of war, and be accepted in that context?[75]

For the Acadians in 1755 such questions must have been of considerably less importance than the events of the dispersion itself. Perhaps the only such matter that would have been argued among them would have concerned their own tactics. The crucial meetings between Acadian and English officials took place in early July, but these meetings were the culmination of an eventful spring. The incident that provided Nova Scotia with the opportunity to deport the Acadians, and to which Lawrence referred in his circular, was the fall of

Beausejour, which had capitulated on 16 June 1755. While the campaign to capture the fort had been in progress, efforts had also been made to ensure that the Acadian population, as a whole, would remain quiet. In April and May orders were sent out to the Minas Acadians to surrender not only any weapons they might possess but also their boats.[76] A petition from the Acadians for the return of their possessions was written on 10 June and received in Halifax at the time when Lawrence received the news that Beausejour had fallen and that about 300 Acadians had been found in arms within the fort.[77]

A meeting of the Council, presided over by Lawrence, took place at the Governor's House on 3 July 1755.[78] The petition sent from Minas was discussed with a number of the signatories. The Council took the Acadians point by point through the petition and concluded by asking the Acadians to take an unqualified oath of loyalty to the King. It is obvious from the Minutes of this meeting that the Councillors found the petition "an Insult upon His Majesty's Authority." In it the Acadians had insisted that they had not only not violated their oaths but had kept faithful "in spite of the solicitations and dreadful threats of another power." They had affirmed their intentions of so keeping faith "provided that His Majesty shall allow us the same liberty that we have enjoyed formerly." In sum, the attitude of the Acadians was that they had proved their political neutrality to the government by their past actions and should now be rewarded. The Council was completely unpersuaded by the proofs offered and demanded further assurances. The Acadians, by such phrases as "Permit us, if you please, Sir, to make known the annoying circumstances in which we are placed, to the prejudice of the tranquillity we ought to enjoy," showed that, in their own eyes, they had the right to argue with English officials. The Acadians had held this attitude from the time of Françoise Perrot in 1688. It was a point of view consistently repudiated by those sent from Europe to govern them. It was the attitude that was maintained by all of the Acadian delegates throughout the July meetings of 1755. Polite, unafraid, and obdurate the Acadians offered a qualified oath. The council minutes for 28 July conclude as follows:

> As it had been before determined to send all the French Inhabitants out of the Province if they refused to Take the Oaths, nothing now remained to be considered but what Measures should be Taken to send them away, and where they should be sent to.[79]

There is one indication that other tactics might have been considered among the Acadians. When finally convinced that exile was imminent, some of the delegates from the Minas Basin did offer an unqualified oath of allegiance. The offer was made on 4 July 1755 only to be rejected by Lawrence and the Council on the grounds that "there was no reason to hope their proposed compliance proceeded from an honest Mind and could be esteemed only the Effect of Compulsion and Force."[80]

But such discussions among the Acadians in 1755 would have been overshadowed completely by the events of the deportation itself. The vast majority of the population was shipped away, either in the last six months of 1755 or at some point over the next six years. The last attempt at completing the deportation came in 1763.[81] Those who remained mostly took refuge along the river banks of the Saint John and the Miramichi, or survived more or less as prisoners of war within Nova Scotia. In 1764 Acadians were once more permitted to own land in Nova Scotia.[82] Some 165 families are noted as being in the colony at the time, a population of perhaps a thousand.[83] The size of the pre-deportation population of the Acadians is a matter of considerable debate, with estimates ranging from around 13,000 to more than 18,000. I now consider the second figure to be the more likely. In their work for *The Historical Atlas of Canada*, Jean Daigle and Robert Leblanc present a lower figure, 13,000. They have published the following table of the distribution of the Acadian population at the time of the Peace of Paris in 1763: Massachusetts, 1,000; Connecticut, 650; New York, 250; Maryland, 810; Pennsylvania, 400; South Carolina, 300; Georgia, 200; Nova Scotia, 1,250; St. John river, 100; Louisiana, 300; England, 850; France, 3,500; Quebec, 2,000; Prince Edward Island, 300; Baie des Chaleurs, 700. The total is 12,660.[84]

Again, as with the estimation of the total population of the Acadians in 1755, the numbers can only be taken as approximate, as their authors themselves remark. Questions remain not only about the actual figures, but also about possible groupings of Acadians that have been overlooked: what about the Acadians who had arrived in Santo Domingo?[85] What about the Acadians in the Channel Islands? The more important question, however, is the reconciliation of these statistics with the pre-deportation figures and with the available figures for death tolls among the exiles between 1755 and 1763. Whatever the precise figures may be, there is no doubt that the Acadian community was devastated. The breaking of a people from lands where they had been established for more than three generations was a matter of force and coercion. The Acadians were now officially regarded by the English as a hostile population, whose only rights were to be deported. Lawrence, basing his instructions on work done sometime earlier by surveyor Morris,[86] on 31 July 1755 sent out his explicit directions for the officers who would carry out the operation.[87] There has been considerable debate about whether these instructions show a criminal mind or merely a painstaking administrator at work.[88] The immediate consequence of the instructions being sent was that the military set about their implementation. For the officers who received them, their duty was plain. As John Winslow, the army officer in charge of the removal of the Acadians from the Grand-Pré area, wrote to Lawrence, "altho this is a Disagreeable Part of Duty we are Put Upon I am Sensible it is a Necessary one."[89]

This judgement was the common opinion shared by most of those engaged in carrying out the task. In the words of Major Handfield, the officer in charge of the Annapolis Royal area, it was a "most disagreeable and troublesome part of the Service."[90] But it was policy; the work was to be done. Though Winslow would write to Captain Murray, the officer engaged in the deportation from

Fort Edward, that "Things are very heavy on my Harte and hands," he would conclude the sentence, "But as it is shall I question not be able to Skuffell Throh."[91] Once the decision had been taken, the deportation was set in motion and the military carried it out with the inevitable infliction of considerable suffering. But there is no evidence that the cruelty of circumstances was generally augmented by a planned policy of terror.

There was no need for extraordinary measures of brutality to ensure a submissive population. The Acadians were stunned by events. Winslow considered that even when gathered together on the shores, waiting to embark on the transports, the Acadians were not even then fully persuaded that they were "actually to be removed."[92] The reality, even if it had been fully expected, would have been psychologically stunning. Settlements burned, cattle driven off, lives now entirely at the command of soldiery: within days the Acadians were turned from a free and flourishing people into a crowd of refugees. Winslow has left us an account of the first embarkation from the Minas Basin: his journal reads, "October 8th: began to Embarke the Inhabitants who went of very Solentarily and unwillingly, the women in Great Distress Carrying off Their Children in their Arms, Others Carrying their Decrepit Parents in their Carts and all their Goods moving in Great Confusion and appeared a scene of Woe and Distress."[93] This "Woe and Distress" was only the beginning.

The Acadians suffered appalling losses in consequence of the deportation, first on board ship and second on arrival at their various destinations. Shipboard conditions in the eighteenth century were dreadful.[94] Those who sailed with the naval squadron under the command of Admirals Boscawen and Mostyn, which had arrived in Halifax on 28 June 1755, were so severely battered by scurvy, typhus, and yellow fever that they could scarcely manoeuvre the ships into Halifax harbour. The condition of soldiers and sailors arriving at Quebec City in the 1750s was much the same.[95] Conditions for civilians were no better. One traveller of 1734 recorded that passengers were lumped together regardless of sex. He continued, "We were crammed into [this] dark foul place like so many sardines; it was impossible to get into bed without banging our heads and our knees twenty times.... The motion of the vessel would dismantle the apparatus, slinging people into each others' cots."[96]

The circumstances which the exiles experienced were equally as bad, though probably not worse. The condition of the ships putting into Boston, but bound for colonies further south, was reported as bad, the Port authorities remarking that, "The vessels in general are much too crowded; their allowance of Provisions short being 1lb of Beef 5lb of Flour & 2lb of Bread prt men [sic] per week and too small a quantity to that allowance to the Ports they are Bound to especially at this season of the year; and their water very bad."[97]

Half of the 415 people shipped on the *Edward Cornwallis*, destination South Carolina, died en route.[98] While this is the largest number of known deaths for one ship, tolls of 20 and 30 per cent were not uncommon. At least two of the ships, the *Violet* and *Duke William*, carrying Acadians to Europe, sank with the loss of all on board.[99] Ocean-going travel was hazardous in the eighteenth century, and the Acadians were not spared any of its dangers.

The impact of disease on the Acadians, once they had arrived at their destination, was almost equally devastating. The Acadian communities had relatively little acquaintance with epidemics of smallpox, typhoid, yellow fever, and other such infectious diseases before exile, and thus no real community immunity to these illnesses. Further, the resistance to infection of those exiled, after the physical conditions of their journeyings, was very weak. The ravages of smallpox, for example, were severe among those who arrived in Pennsylvania.[100] The disease was even more brutal to those who arrived in England by way of Virginia. The death toll was so great, about 25 per cent of their number, as to lead to a charge of genocide by France against England.[101]

Causing up to 50 per cent death-rates on shipboard, with diseases cutting a further swathe through those who landed among strangers, the actual physical consequences of the deportation of the Acadians sent into exile were ruinous. It must also be remembered that the policy of deportation and exile, begun in 1755, continued until the Peace of Paris. As late as 1762, Jonathon Belcher, who had been the Attorney-General of the colony under Lawrence and who succeeded him as Lieutenant-Governor,[102] was still attempting to deport those Acadians who had somehow escaped earlier efforts. Belcher was convinced that "it will by no means be safe to suffer the Acadians to remain in this Province as settlers,"[103] and so more shiploads of Acadians were sent to Boston in the spring of 1762. That jurisdiction promptly sent them back to Halifax.[104]

Between 1755 and 1762, the majority of the Acadian community that had been built up throughout the present-day Nova Scotia, New Brunswick, and Prince Edward Island over a course of some 150 years was uprooted. In spite of what became a policy of eradication during these years, some Acadians remained in Nova Scotia at the close of the war in 1763. The Acadian people still existed, they still considered themselves distinct as a community, and they still sought to control their own destiny. As soon as their proscription was ended, in 1764, exiles began to return and rebuild the Acadian community.

Notes

1. The historiographical debate has produced countless volumes, but much of the argument can be found summarized in N.E.S. Griffiths, *The Acadian Deportation: Deliberate Perfidy or Cruel Necessity?* (Toronto, 1969).

2. I should note here that in making this judgement, I am not trying to answer the vexed question of who was responsible for the Acadian deportation. I merely assert that it was Lawrence who accepted the policy as viable though he did not invent it, and who, from 1755 until his death in 1760, initiated and followed through its implementation.

3. "Circular letter from Governor Lawrence to the Governors on the Continent," *Report Concerning Canadian Archives for the Year 1905*, 3 vols. (Ottawa: Public Archives of Canada, 1906), 2: App. B, 15–16.

4. The literature on colonial British America is both extensive and excellent. However, on this issue see in particular Walter Allen Knittle, *Early Eighteenth Century Palatine Emigration: A British Government Redemptioner Project to Manufacture Naval Stores* (Baltimore, 1970); and N.D. Landsman, *Scotland and Its First American Colony, 1683–1675* (Princeton, 1985) especially chapter 6, "A Scots' Settlement or an English Settlement: Cultural Conflict and the Establishment of Ethnic Identity," 163 ff.

5. Jean Daigle and Robert Leblanc, in R. Cole Harris, ed., *Historical Atlas of Canada: From the Beginning to 1800* (Toronto, 1987), 1: Plate 30.

6. The French government called for a report on the Acadian settlements in 1748. This is printed in *Le Canada Français* (1889), 1: 44. It estimates that Port Royal had 2,000 communicants. The original document is in the Archives de la Marine, Paris. I put these figures forward very tentatively. The document of the Archives de la Marine gives ninety families for these settlements, roughly 450 people. My estimate is derived from deportation figures rather than from earlier parish records, and it needs verification. It is interesting to note the extent to which the obvious predominance of the Minas Basin and Chignecto Isthmus has left the Acadian population of these older areas (e.g., Port Royal) relatively unexamined by scholars.

7. *Le Canada Français* gives 4,850, which I would accept as a minimum.

8. H. Têtu and C.O. Gagnon, eds., *Mandements, lettres pastorales et circu laires des évèques de Quebec* (1887), "Voyage de St. Vallier," 216.

9. *Le Canada Français* cites 2,500, but the population of the settlements of the Memramcook, the Petitcodiac, and the Shepody areas may be included in that figure.

10. I am much indebted to the recent work on this development by Paul Surette, *Petitcoudiac: Colonisation et destruction, 1731–1755* (Moncton, 1988).

11. Aliette Geistdoerfer, *Pêcheurs Acadiens, Pêcheurs Madelinots: Ethnologie d'une communauté de pêcheurs* (Quebec, 1987); Frederic Landry, *Pêcheurs de métier* (Iles de la Madeleine, 1987); and Charles A. Martin, ed., *Les Micmacs et la mer* (Montreal, 1986).

12. Jim Potter, "Demographic Development and Family Structure," in Jack P. Greene and J.R. Pole, eds., *Colonial British America: Essays in the New History of the Modern Early Era* (Baltimore, 1984), 139.

13. On population rates and their methodology during this period see F. Ouelett, "L'accroissement naturel de la population catholique québecois avant 1850: aperçus historiques et quantitatifs," *L'Actualité économique. Revue d'analyses économique*, 59 no. 3 (1983).

14. One was even a clerk to the Justices of the Peace. J.B. Brebner, *New England's Outpost* (New York, 1927), 150.

15. Clark, *Acadia: The Geography of Nova Scotia* (Madison, 1968), 230 ff.

16. Captain Charles Morris, "A Brief Survey of Nova Scotia," NA, MG18, D10, cap. 5, p. 4.

17. "Biographie de Jean-Louis Le Loutre," Archives Departementales de la Vendée, Papiers Lanco, vol. 371, 2.

18. The archaeological work is know being done on Upper Belle Isle marsh, as well as the imaginative work by Azor Vienneau for the film "Premières Terres Acadiennes," will help us to visualize the richness of Acadian life. It will complement work already

completed for the Acadian Village on the outskirts of Caraquet. The work of Jean Claude Dupont, *Histoire d'Acadie* (Moncton, 1977) and Dupont, *Histoire Populaire de l'Acadie* (Moncton, 1979) needs to be read with an eye to the author's own caution as to the applicability of his information. Time and place are not constant throughout these volumes, and the works need to be read carefully bearing this in mind.

19. N.E.S. Griffiths, *Creation of a People* (Toronto, 1973); and Griffiths, "The Acadians," *DCB*, 4: xxvii–xxxi.

20. George F. Stanley, *New France: The Last Phase, 1744–1760* (Toronto, 1968), 74–75.

21. Their assumptions do not answer our question about Acadian attitudes. Duvivier certainly considered that the neutrality of the Acadians had been responsible for his defeat and lack of success in the expeditions of 1744. See Griffiths, "The Acadians." As far as both British and French policy-makers were concerned, however, the Acadian men were seen as a possible military force.

22. Brebner, *New England's Outpost*, 62 and 149 ff.

23. *Ibid.*, 152.

24. "It is hardly an exaggeration to say that until the late eighteenth century the major social and economic organization in Massachusetts was the family ... Lacking a state bureaucracy, standing army and police force, implementation of state policy depended on the family ... The family was also the centre of economic activity, for there were no banks, insurance companies, corporations or other formal economic organizations." P.D. Hall, "Family Structure and Economic Organization: Massachusetts Merchants, 1700–1850," in T. Hareven, ed., *Family and Kin in Urban Communities, 1700–1930* (New York, 1977), 39.

25. The relationship between family and household is one of the most interesting questions being discussed by those working in the field of family history. The work of Michael Mitterauer and Reinhard Sieder—*The European Family Patriarchy to Partnership* (Chicago, 1983)—in disentangling the change from "whole house" to family household leads to a demand for detailed analysis of Acadian kin relationships within a household, as well as for description of ties between households within settlements and from settlement to settlement.

26. Clark, *Acadia*, 203–4.

27. Lists of quit-rents paid in Grand-Pré and elsewhere in the 1750s can be found in the Brown Manuscripts, "Papers relating to Nova Scotia, 1720–1791," additional Mss. 19071, f. 138–48, British Museum. One of the best analyses of Acadian land-ownership claims is Winthrop Pickard Bell's The *"Foreign Protestants" and the Settlement of Nova Scotia* (Toronto, 1961), 79 and the footnotes for same, 80–3.

28. Clark, *Acadia*, 197.

29. See, for example, "Petition of Reny and Francois Leblancs Against Antoin Landry" Council Minutes, Garrison of Annapolis Royal, 7th January, 1731/2, PANS *Original Minutes of His Majesty's Council at Annapolis Royal, 1720–1739* (Halifax, 1908), 207.

30. PANS, *Nova Scotia Archives II: A Calendar of Two Letter-books and One Commission Book in the Possession of the Government of Nova Scotia* (Halifax, 1900), 221.

31. Paul Surette, *Petcoudiac*, 17. The author defines marriage through male partici-
    pation, and by so doing overlooks the more complex reality of interrelationship
    between households.

32. "Description de l'Acadie avec le nombre des paroisses et le nombre des habi-
    tants—1748," *Le Canada français*, 1: 44.

33. Micheline Dumont Johnson: *Apôtres ou agitateurs: la France missionaire en Acadie*
    (Quebec, 1970) makes a good beginning in attempting to assess the influence of the
    priests on the Acadians during the eighteenth century.

34. This includes the work in progress by Stephen White (see above, chapter 1, n. 33);
    Placide Gaudet, "Acadian Genealogy and Notes," *Report for 1905*; and Bona
    Arsenault, *Histoire et genealogie des Acadiens* (Moncton, 1965).

35. Maurice Bosc is undertaking, for an MA at the University of Moncton, a study of mar-
    riage alliances which should tell us something about the pattern of social hierarchy
    among the settlements at this time.

36. While the work demands a painstaking trek through a wide variety of archival
    holdings, material that suggests patterns of economic holdings is available. The
    theoretical advances in family studies made by scholars such as John Demos, *Past,
    Present and Personal: The Family and Life Course in American History* (Oxford,
    1986); and Tamara Hareven and Andrejs Plakens, eds., *Family History at the
    Crossroads: A Journal of Family History Reader* (Princeton, 1987) should be used to
    provide a clearer understanding of questions concerning Acadian social stratifica-
    tion, the economic activity within households, and the ways in which education,
    and social welfare are reinforced by political attitudes.

37. We have, for example, documents giving trade at Louisbourg from Acadie in livestock,
    wood and flour: in 1740 such exports were valued at 26,940 *livres*, inclusive of some
    5,423 *livres* of furs and skins. New England exports to Louisbourg for the same
    year were valued at 48,447 *livres*, including some 4,448 *livres* of axes and hatch-
    ets. J.S. McLennan, *Louisbourg From Its Foundation To Its Fall, 1713–1758* (1918)
    contains relevant colonial documents outlining this trade.

38. "Minutes of the Council, Wednesday the 6th of October, 1749," T.B. Akins, *Selections
    from the Public Documents of the Province of Nova Scotia* (Halifax, 1869), 174.

39. *Ibid.*, "Minutes of the Council," 247.

40. "Mascarene to Newcastle, Annapolis Royal, 23rd January 1746–47," *Report for
    1905*, 2: App. C, 46.

41. The role of Massachusetts in Nova Scotia history is both important and complex.
    Brebner in *New England's Outpost* presents a masterly analysis of the relation-
    ship from the point of view of imperial policy. George Rawlyk's *Nova Scotia's
    Massachusetts: A study of Massachusetts-Nova Scotia Relations, 1630 to 1784*
    (Montreal, 1978) is a complex monograph, centring upon the intricacies of colonial
    interaction. For present purposes, it is necessary to understand only that, without
    any hierarchy being stated, the relationship between the colonial administrators
    of Massachusetts and Nova Scotia was frequently one of senior and junior officials.

42. "Enclosure in letter of 20th October, 1747, Mascarene to Newcastle," *Report for
    1905*, 2: App. C, 47.

43. Accounts of the impact of the hostilities during the 1740s upon the Acadians abound. One of the best is in R. Rumilly, *Histoire des Acadiens* (Montreal, 1955), 1: 286–344, but see also G.F. Stanley, *New France.*

44. The most politic expression of these views is contained in "Governor Shirley to the Duke of Bedford, February 18, 1748/9," PRO, NSA, 148–49. For interpretations see Brebner, *New England's Outpost*, 118 ff.; and L.H. Gipson, *The British Empire Before the American Revolution, Zones of International Friction: The Great Lakes Frontier, Canada, The West Indies, India, 1748–1754* (New York, 1942), 5: 180.

45. The work of Winthrop Pickard Bell, *The "Foreign Protestants" and the Settlement of Nova Scotia*, already cited, is a seminal work of meticulous scholarship on this subject.

46. Murray Beck, "Edward Cornwallis," *DCB*, 4: 168–71.

47. The papers to this exchange are in, *Report for 1905*, 2: App. C, 49 ff. A full analysis of the interchange is given by Brebner, *New England's Outpost*, 181 ff. Brebner's opinion of the Acadians, however, is that they had little sophisticated appreciation of the probable consequences of their actions.

48. Brebner, *New England's Outpost*, 183.

49. *Ibid.*, 166.

50. *Ibid.*

51. Clark, *Acadia*, 338 and 339 n. 24.

52. There is an account of the first year of Halifax in *Northcliffe Collection, Reports* (Ottawa: Public Archives of Canada, 1926), 68–76. See also Winthrop Pickard Bell, *The "Foreign Protestants,"* 347 ff.

53. Hugh Davidson, "Description of Conditions [1750] in Nova Scotia," in Adam Shortt, V.K., Johnston and Gustave Lanctot, eds., *Documents relating to Currency, Exchange and Finance in Nova Scotia with Prefatory Documents, 1675–1758* (Ottawa, 1933), 319.

54. Clark, *Acadia*, 338.

55. Thomas B. Akins, "History of Halifax City," *Collections of the Nova Scotia Historical Society 8* (1895): 3–272.

56. Rawlyk, *Nova Scotia's Massachusetts*, 190 ff.

57. Winthrop Pickard Bell, *The "Foreign Protestants."*

58. *Ibid.*, 318.

59. *Ibid.*, 426.

60. For one of the most perceptive discussions of events in "Acadia or Nova Scotia" at this time see John G. Reid, *Six Crucial Decades: Times of Change in the History of the Maritimes* (Halifax, 1987), 29–60.

61. This commission provoked a great many pamphlets, arguing for one viewpoint or another, and a massive collection of documents; but it achieved nothing. However, see *Memoires des Commissaires du Roi et du Ceux de Sa Majeste Britannique* (Paris, 1755); and *Memorials of the English and French Commissaries Concerning the Limits of Nova Scotia* (London, 1755).

62. Stanley, *New France*, gives the most detailed account of this period but A.G. Doughty, *The Acadian Exiles: A Chronicle of the Land of Evangeline* (Toronto, 1916), 72–82 is very clear about the sequence of incidents.

63. "Antoine and Pierre Couaret to Governor Philipps, 2 October 1720," PRO, CO 217/3, f 155–56, cited in L.F.S. Upton, *Micmacs and Colonists: Indian—White Relations in the Maritimes, 1713–1867* (Vancouver, 1972), 199, n. 41.

64. One of the best accounts of this action is in D.C. Harvey, *The French Regime in Prince Edward Island* (New York, 1970), 137 ff.

65. N.E.S. Griffiths, *The Acadian Deportation*.

66. Dominick Graham, "Charles Lawrence," *DCB*, 3: 361–66.

67. La Galissoniere to the Minister, 25 July 1749. NA C-11-A: 93, 138; on this gentleman's career see Lionel Groulx: *Ronald-Michel Barrin de La Galissoniere 1693–1756* (Toronto, 1970).

68. Cited in B. Murdoch, *A History of Nova Scotia or Acadia*, 2: (Halifax, 1865), 310.

69. Almost all of this correspondence has been printed in Akins, *Nova Scotia Documents*, and *Report for 1905*.

70. "Tho I would be very far from attempting such a step [imposing the unqualified oath] without Yourships approbation, yet I cannot help being of the opinion that it would be much better, if they refuse the oaths, that they were away," in "Lawrence to the Lords of Trade, August 1st, 1754," 55, p. 187 ff., and partially printed *Nova Scotia Archives* 1, 212–14.

71. "Circular letter from Governor Lawrence to the Governors on the continent," *Report for 1905*, 2: App. B., 15–16.

72. See the comments of the Abbé Raynal in his *Histoire philosophique et politique de l'etablissement dans les deux Indes* (La Have, 1760), 360. A generation ago there were more than two hundred books and articles in print about the deportation of the Acadians. See the bibliographic guides published by the Centre d'études Acadiennes particularly Helene Harbec and Paulette Leversque eds., *Guide bibliographique de l'Acadie, 1976–1987* (Moncton, 1988).

73. While this has been a favourite conclusion of historians such as Brebner, George Rawlyk hotly contested this judgement in *Nova Scotia's Massachusetts*, 199 ff.

74. On this question see Placide Gaudet, *Le Grand Dérangement* (Ottawa, 1922).

75. "Nova Scotia is at war and is engaged in a movement of intense colonization. The dispersion of the Acadians constitutes an act of war and is a factor in this movement" [translation], *La Guerre de la Conquête* (Montreal, 1955), 272.

76. *Le Canada francais*, 1: 138–39.

77. On this episode and its impact on Lawrence see Brebner, *New England's Outpost*, 199–202 and 212–213.

78. Akins, *Nova Scotia Documents*, 247 ff.

79. "Council Minutes," PANS, RG 5, vol. 187.

80. The issue is discussed extensively by Brebner, *New England's Outpost*, 216 ff.

81. Murdoch, *History of Nova Scotia*, 2: 426.

82. The Lords of Trade were very hesitant about admitting the Acadians as subjects after the Peace of Paris, 1763. However, as of 5 November 1764, Governor Wilmot offered those remaining in Nova Scotia the opportunity to take an oath of allegiance to the British Crown and to be granted land. The correspondence between Wilmot

and the Lords Commissioners for Trade and Plantations on this issue is partially published in *Report for 1905*, App. J., 210–16.

83. A report of 1767 estimates the Acadian population of Nova Scotia as 1,265. *Ibid.*, App. L, 255–56.

84. Jean Daigle and Robert Leblanc, in R. Cole Harris, ed., *Historical Atlas of Canada*, Plate 30. A report to the French government of 1763 estimates the total Acadian population in 1763 as 12,866: some 866 divided among the British sea-ports, some 2,000 in France and 10,000 among the British colonies in North America, *Report for 1905*, 2: App. G, 156.

85. G. Debien, "Les Acadiens à Saint Dominique," in Glenn Conrad, ed., *The Cajuns: Essays on Their History and Culture* (Louisiana, 1978), 255–330.

86. Brown Mss., Add. Mss. 19071–19073, British Museum. There is considerable debate about whether these instructions had been prepared as early as 1751.

87. Printed in toto in the *Northcliffe Collection*, 80–83.

88. For the first view see E. Lauvrière, *La Tragédie D'une Peuple* (Paris, 1922), 1: 465, for the latter, Brebner, *New England Outpost*, 225. It has been demonstrated for the late twentieth century that these characteristics are not necessarily mutually exclusive.

89. Printed in *Report for 1905*, 2: App. B, 17. John Winslow had been born in Massachusetts in 1703 and at the time of the deportation he was a captain in the British army, stationed in Nova Scotia. He has left a journal of the summer and autumn of 1755 which has been fully printed in *Collections*, Nova Scotia Historical Society, 3: 71 ff. See biography of him by Barry Moody in *DCB*, 4: 774.

90. Major John Handfield to Winslow, 3 September 1755: Boston, MA, Municipal Library.

91. Winslow to Murray, 5 September 1755: *Report for 1905*, 2: App. B., 29.

92. Winslow to Lawrence, 17 September 1755: *Report for 1905*, 2: App. B., 12.

93. Winslow's Journal in *Collections* (Nova Scotia Historical Society, 1888), 3: 166.

94. "The number of seamen in time of war who died by shipwreck, capture, famine, fire or sword are but inconsiderable in respect to such as are destroyed by the ship diseases and the usual maladies of intemperate climates," wrote Dr. James Lind at the beginning of the Seven Years' War. The figures for that war bear him out: 133,708 men were lost by disease or desertion, compared with 1,512 killed in Action," N.R.S. Lloyd, *The Health of Seamen* (1965), cited in Christopher Lloyd, *The British Seaman, 1200–1860: A Social Survey* (Paladin, 1968), 234.

95. Gilles Proulx, *Between France and New France: Life Aboard the Tall Sailing Ships* (Toronto, 1984), in particular the tables for sickness of sailors arriving in Quebec, 1755–59, 114.

96. "Rev. Father Nau to Rev. Father Richard, Québec City, 20 October, 1734," *Rapports des Archives de l'Archévêque du Québec, 1926–1927* (Quebec, 1927), 267.

97. *Report for 1905*, 2: App. E, 81.

98. "Report of the Edward Cornwallis," Andrew Sinclair, Master, 17 November 1755; "210 dead, 207 in health," in Council Records (Columbia, S.C.), 480.

99. Brown Manuscripts, Add. Mss. 19071, British Museum.

100. "Commissioners of the Poor, Report October 1756," in J. MacKinney, ed., *Votes and Proceedings, Pennsylvania* (Harrisburg, 1931), 6: 4408.

101. Much of this story is covered in N.E.S. Griffiths, "The Acadians of the British Sea-Ports" *Acadiensis* 4 (1976): 67–84.

102. "March 20th 1760, Order-in-Council," PANS, RG 5, vol. A, 70.

103. "Jonathon Belcher to His Excellency Governor Murray, Halifax March 25th, 1762," *Report for 1905*, 2: App. L, 263.

104. The correspondence on this issue from Belcher to the Board of Trade and also to Lord Egremont, Secretary of State, has been partially printed in Akins, *Nova Scotia Documents* 329 ff.

CHAPTER

4 THE FRENCH MILITARY IN NEW FRANCE DURING THE SEVEN YEARS' WAR

The Battle of the Plains of Abraham on 13 September 1759 is one of the few world-class events in Canadian history. Usually included in lists such as the One Hundred Most Important Battles in History, it marked the zenith of the first British Empire. In Britain to this day, General James Wolfe remains a magical name to school children. In Canada there is an ambivalence about the siege, the soldiers, the generals and the outcome. Francis Parkman created icons for Canadians with his two-volume *Montcalm and Wolfe* (1884), the story of a battle between valiant heroes on both sides. The tragic Shakespearean ending provided the necessary grief and the glimmer of a better world. Regardless of any reality, that image of brave French and British soldiers fighting for survival and supremacy suited Canadian needs for over half a century.

Since the Second World War, the picture of the battle and the participants has been renovated. Guy Frégault's *La Guerre de la conquête* (1955) was a major reappraisal from a Canadian perspective. The Marquis de Montcalm and the Europeans emerged as inferior, if not incompetent, soldiers, while the *canadiens*, as epitomized by Pierre de Rigaud, Marquis de Vaudreuil, were pictured as inspired worthies obstructed by Montcalm, François Bigot and other Europeans. Wolfe, a bully and a terrorist who won by default, was vilified. C.P. Stacey took a less ideological position in his military analysis, *Quebec, 1759: The Siege and the Battle* (1959). His study of generalship, however, found Montcalm and Wolfe both wanting. A competent strategist, Montcalm made disastrous tactical errors, while Wolfe, a dismal strategist, saved himself from disgrace by successful tactics on the field of battle. W.J. Eccles rejected even that praise for Wolfe. He delighted in telling his students that anybody except the British could have taken Quebec in half the time. Like Frégault, he depicted the *canadiens* as soldiers *par excellence*. In "The French Forces in North America During the Seven Years' War," the first selection, Eccles provided an overview of French military activity over much of the life of the colony.

Neither old soldiers nor wars are ever laid to rest, however, and it was not long before the battle was joined. Peter E. Russell in 1978 rescued the British regulars in a study of warfare in both Europe and America during the 1740s and 1750s (see *Suggestions for Further Reading*). Recently, Martin L. Nicolai examined the French military in both its European and North American theatres, and arrived at similar conclusions in "A Different Kind of Courage: The French Military and the Canadian Irregular Soldier During the Seven Years' War." He rejected the criticisms of the European military as unwarranted, and offered a less sanguine but perhaps more realistic view of the *canadien* soldier.

Suggestions for Further Reading

Frégault, Guy, *Canada: The War of the Conquest*. Toronto: Oxford University Press, 1969.

Lawson, Philip, "The Conquest of Quebec and Peace Making, 1759–63," Chapt. 1 of *The Imperial Challenge: Quebec and Britain in the Age of the American Revolution*. Montreal and Kingston: McGill-Queen's Press, 1989, 3–24.

McCulloch, Ian, " 'But the King Must Be Obeyed': Montcalm at Quebec, 1759." *Beaver*, 72, 5, 1992, 4–15.

Russell, Peter E., "Redcoats in the Wilderness: British Officers and Irregular Warfare in Europe and America, 1740–1760," *William and Mary Quarterly*, XXXV, no. 4 (October 1978), 629–152.

Stacey, C.P., *Quebec, 1759: The Siege and the Battle*. Toronto: Macmillan of Canada, 1959.

————, "The British Forces in North America during the Seven Years' War," *Dictionary of Canadian Biography*, Volume III. Toronto: University of Toronto Press, 1974, xxiv–xxx.

Stanley, George F.G., *New France: the Last Phase, 1744–1760*. Toronto: McClelland & Stewart, 1968.

Steele, I.K., *Guerillas and Grenadiers: The Struggle for Canada, 1689–1760*. Toronto: Ryerson, 1969.

Steele, I.K., *Warpaths: Invasions of North America*. New York: Oxford University Press, 1994.

THE FRENCH FORCES IN NORTH AMERICA DURING THE SEVEN YEARS' WAR

W.J. Eccles

From 1713 to 1744 France and England were at peace, the span of one generation. During those years French overseas trade steadily increased. Trade with the French colonies rose from 25 million *livres* a year in 1710 to 140 million by 1741. In the latter year the total of French overseas trade was valued at 300 million *livres,* that is £12.5 million sterling. Much of this trade was with the Spanish empire, one half to seven-ninths of the goods shipped from Cadiz being French in origin. France now supplied all continental Europe with sugar and coffee, and in addition French fishermen were garnering the lion's share of the fisheries on the Grand Banks and in the Gulf of St Lawrence. But while French trade had expanded during the 1730s, that of England had remained stationary. Moreover, a sizable proportion of England's overseas commerce consisted of contraband trade with the Spanish colonies. Thus, when Spain began taking effective measures to curb this illicit traffic the English commercial community became alarmed; half of the world's maritime commerce might still be under the British flag but were its trade to continue to stagnate while French industry and commerce kept on expanding, then England, its population less than half that of France, might well go the same way as the Netherlands, and eventually be reduced to the status of a fourth-rate power. It was to forfend this possibility that England went to war with Spain in 1739, and with France in 1744.

The British government did not pursue that war, the War of the Austrian Succession, known to the English colonies as King George's War, effectively. It chose to engage France on the continent where the poorly officered British army proved no match for the Maréchal de Saxe, the foremost soldier of his age. In North America a combined Anglo-American and British naval force captured Louisbourg in 1745 (*see* William Pepperrell and Peter Warren), but it was not until 1747 that the Royal Navy gained the upper hand and succeeded in severing temporarily France's communications with her colonies. By 1748 the belligerents were exhausted and in October of that year the treaty of Aix-la-Chapelle was signed, which merely restored the *status quo ante bellum.* France recuperated rapidly and her overseas trade quickly recovered. The English commercial community now became convinced that a better-conducted spoiling war was essential to prevent the French overtaking them in the struggle for supremacy. The French, on the other hand, had no desire for a maritime war—they had too much to lose; nevertheless, they still had to prepare for it.

Although the West Indies were the great prize—by 1740 the exports of the French islands were valued at 100 million *livres* a year and their imports, mainly

---

slaves, at 75 million—the north Atlantic fisheries were also extremely valuable, particularly since they were regarded as vital by both Britain and France for the training of seamen needed to man their fleets. In 1754, 444 ships from France fished in these waters, employing some 14,000 sailors. In addition the resident maritime population of Île Royale (Cape Breton Island), Îles de la Madeleine, and Gaspé provided a large number of mariners. It was estimated that the loss of these fisheries would cost France 15,000 experienced seamen, nearly a third of her total supply. Canada, on the other hand, produced little except furs, in good years some wheat for export to Louisbourg, and a few ships built at Quebec by the crown at great expense (*see* Pierre Lupien, *dit* Baron, and Louis-Pierre Poulin de Courval Cressé). This colony was, in fact, an economic liability much of the time. Politically and militarily, however, Canada was regarded as valuable to curb the expansion of the English colonies, hence of England's commercial strength, and to protect Louisiana for whose resources great hopes were entertained. Moreover, it was calculated that in time of war the Canadians, with the aid of a few reinforcements from France, would be able to tie down a much larger British army and a sizable part of the Royal Navy, thus preventing their deployment elsewhere. The success enjoyed by the Canadians against the Anglo-Americans in the previous wars gave every reason for confidence in this policy.

The fortress of Louisbourg was therefore strengthened to serve as a naval base for a fleet to protect the fisheries, guard the entrance to the St. Lawrence, and prey on British shipping. When an influential group of Anglo-American land speculators began to implement their scheme to seize the Ohio valley, thereby threatening the French hold on the west, a Canadian force was dispatched, on orders of the Minister of Marine, to drive the Americans out (*see* Paul Marin de La Malgue). Forts were then built in the region. In 1754 came the first clash of arms near Fort Duquesne (Pittsburgh, Pennsylvania). Although war between England and France was not declared until 1756, this skirmish in the wilderness marked the beginning of the Seven Years' War (*see* Joseph Coulon de Villiers de Jumonville).

Unfortunately for France the government, its personnel, and methods, were to prove inadequate to meet the challenge offered by Great Britain and her new-found ally, Prussia. Louis XV could rarely bring himself to make decisions and when he attended council meetings he concerned himself with trivia. Moreover, until 1761 when the Duc de Choiseul was given charge of the ministries of War, Marine, and Foreign Affairs, the ministers, all of them mediocrities or worse, did not remain long in office. During the course of the war there were four Ministers of Foreign Affairs, four Controllers-General of Finance, four Ministers of War, and five Ministers of Marine. Their ministries were grossly understaffed and overworked, which resulted in interminable delays and too often in non-decisions. To cap it all, the entire decision-making process was beset by intrigue of Byzantine proportions, the king being to the fore in this activity.

Nor were the instruments of government policy, the armed forces, in better condition. Under Louis XIV, and later under Napoleon, the French army was the best in Europe. Under Louis XV it sank to a low level of efficiency. After the demise of the Maréchal de Saxe its commanders were incompetent. Defence predominated over offence in their thinking. Here too intrigue was rife. Every general in the field knew that many about him, and at the court, were scheming to have him removed. At the regimental level also officers were not distinguished by competence, the military capacity of most of the colonels being virtually nil. Commissions were purchased; money and family connections, not merit, governed advancement.

As is always the case, military tactics were dominated by the principal weapon employed, in this instance the smooth-bore, flint-lock, muzzle-loading musket, mounted with a bayonet, making it both a fire and a shock weapon. Even well-trained soldiers could fire no more than two or three rounds a minute; loading and firing required some twelve movements executed to command and drum beat. At close range, under eighty paces, a musket volley could be murderous, but at that distance there was barely time to reload before the enemy's charge, if it were not checked, reached the line. In battle two basic formations were employed, the line and the column. The line, three ranks deep, depended on the fire power of the musket followed by a bayonet charge against the shattered foe. Attack by column depended on the shock effect of an attack on a narrow front to pierce and shatter the enemy's line. Deployment in line demanded the most rigorous discipline to make the men stand fast and deliver measured volleys against the charging foe. Attack by column also required discipline to have the men press on into the hail of fire. The swifter their advance, the fewer volleys they had to endure. The British army relied on the line; the French at this time still had a predilection for the column, believing that the charge with the *arme blanche* was better suited to their poorly trained troops with their impetuous temperament.

To manoeuvre the troops on the battlefield, and have them attack either in line or in column, required that they receive at least eighteen months of basic training on the drill ground until they became virtually automatons. After that, five years' experience was deemed necessary to produce a good, dependable soldier. Iron discipline was the essence of it all, instilled by fear and by *esprit de corps*. The men had to be rendered more afraid of their own officers than of the enemy, and to be willing to stand and die rather than turn and run. Everything depended on the ability of the officers to manoeuvre their troops, and on the discipline and training of the men once battle was joined. Compared to other European armies the French army was deficient on both counts. Its officers lacked spirit and professional training, its men were badly instructed, poorly drilled, and wretchedly disciplined; its equipment, with the exception of the Charleville musket, was inferior. The supply system and the cannon were both antiquated, essentially the same as in the time of Louis XIV. All attempts at reform had been blocked by reactionary elements or vested interests.

The French navy was in a better state than the army. Its ships were superior to those of the Royal Navy. They could outsail and outgun the British ships. A French ship of fifty-two guns was a match for a British seventy-two. The reverse was true of the officers of the two navies. The British officers were better trained and more aggressive. Although the Royal Navy was in poor shape at the onset of the war it had twice as many ships as the French and its reserve of seamen was much greater. To make matters worse for the French, before war was declared the Royal Navy seized 800 French merchant ships and 3,000 seamen. This was a crippling blow. Moreover, during the course of the war epidemics in the French ports took a heavy toll. At Brest alone, in 1757–58, 2,171 sailors died in a four-month period. Many others fled the ports to avoid the contagion. The navy was reduced to impressing landsmen who had never been afloat to work their ships. Yet despite the superiority of the Royal Navy supply ships reached Quebec every year until 1760 (*see* Jacques Kanon), after the city had been taken by Wolfe's army.

When hostilities began the French had three distinct military forces at their disposal in North America: the colonial regular troops (*troupes de la Marine*), the militia, and the Indian allies. The colonial regulars were infantry units raised for guard duty in the naval ports of France and for service in the colonies. They were the creation of Louis XIV's great minister Jean-Baptiste Colbert and were under the control of the Ministry of Marine, not of the Ministry of War, hence were known as the *troupes franches de la Marine*. To obviate the abuses rampant in the regimental organization of the army Colbert had incorporated these marines in independent companies rather than in regiments. Commissions were not purchased but were obtained on merit and, of course, influence. A good reference was essential. Each company consisted of a captain, a lieutenant, a brevet ensign, a second ensign, two cadets, two sergeants, three corporals, two drummers and forty-one soldiers. By 1758, twenty companies of these marines were stationed at Louisbourg and twenty-one in Louisiana. In Canada there were thirty companies in 1756. In that year their strength was increased to 65 non-commissioned ranks per company, and the following year their number was raised to forty companies with a nominal strength of 2,760 officers and men.

During the half-century following the establishment of the colonial regulars, the officer corps became Canadian although the other ranks were nearly all recruited in France. By the 1740s commissions were reserved for the sons of serving officers, who were invariably *seigneurs*. Unlike the regiments of the French army the colonial regulars gave no direct entry into the commissioned ranks, except for such privileged persons as the son of a governor general (*see* Joseph-Hyacinthe and Louis-Philippe de Rigaud de Vaudreuil). With that notable exception, every would-be officer had to serve in the ranks for several years as a cadet. Despite this arduous training, so eager were the Canadians for commissions that in 1728 the age for entry as cadets was lowered to fifteen, and the waiting list became ever longer. Promotion could not be accelerated by purchase, only by a display of exceptional valour in action, and even then, *only* when a vacancy occurred through death or retirement. This condition served to inculcate a very aggressive spirit in the corps.

When the Seven Years' War began most of the officers of the colonial regulars had had years of military experience at the western posts, in the Fox and Chickasaw campaigns, and in savage raids on the frontier settlements of the English colonies (*see* Louis Coulon de Villiers, Jacques Legardeur de Saint-Pierre, François-Marie LeMarchand de Lignery, Nicolas-Joseph Noyelles de Fleurimont). In addition to their training in the drill manoeuvres demanded in European style warfare these troops had had to master the art of guerilla fighting both against and alongside the Indian nations. They could travel long distances, winter or summer, living off the land if need be, strike swiftly, then disappear before the enemy could muster a force to counter attack. Against them the American provincial troops and militia were no match. Great mobility, deadly marksmanship, skilful use of surprise and forest cover, high morale and, like the Royal Navy, a tradition of victory, gave the colonial regulars their superiority. Just how effective they could be was demonstrated when, in 1755, 250 Canadians with some 600 Indian allies destroyed Edward Braddock's army of 1,500 (*see* Jean-Daniel Dumas).

Supporting, and frequently serving alongside, the colonial regulars were the militia units. In 1669 Louis XIV had ordered the establishment of militia companies for colonial defence. Each company comprised all the able-bodied men between fifteen and sixty in a parish and was commanded by a captain of militia (who also had important civil functions), with a lieutenant, one or two ensigns, and sergeants. They all served without pay. During the wars against the English colonies and hostile Indian nations the militia was called out for war parties, to repel invading forces, for *corvées* to supply the frontier fortresses, or for the building of military roads.

When properly utilized this Canadian militia was a formidable fighting force, but its men were of little use in European-style warfare. Faced with regular army units in the open, firing massed volleys, they took cover or fled. They would not stand and be shot at while waiting for an order to fire back. There were other limits to the use that could be made of these *habitant* soldiers; many of them had to be released for work on the land in the spring and in late summer for the harvest; others had to serve in the canoe brigades to the western posts. A muster roll of 1750 lists 165 companies varying in number from 31 to 176, comprising 724 officers, 498 sergeants, 11,687 men; in all, 12,909. This total may well be too low, by as much as 25 per cent; it gives for one company a total strength of fifty-five whereas a separate muster roll of that particular company lists seventy-six names, half of whom are noted as fit to go on detachment. An important factor with these militiamen was their high morale. When they were ordered to Quebec in 1759 to help defend the city against Wolfe's army, Montcalm and his staff were astounded by the number that appeared, boys of twelve, old men of eighty-five, all demanding muskets and the right to serve. The contrast with the militia of the English colonies could not be more marked.

In addition to the colonial regulars and the militia the French had the aid of a horde of Indian allies, Micmacs, Abenakis, Ottawas, Algonkins, Delawares,

Shawnees, to mention a few. The British, significantly, had virtually none. The operative word here is "allies," for these nations would take orders from no one—indeed their own chiefs had no authority over the warriors. They did not regard themselves as an auxiliary force of the French, but as allies in a joint effort against a common foe. Another inducement was the liberal supplies of food, clothing, arms, and munitions provided by the French, as well as the bounties paid for scalps and prisoners. Although they proved to be highly effective in guerilla warfare, the Indians could never be relied on. They were subject to whims that appeared strange to Europeans. After being well supplied a war party would set out but, *en route*, suffer a change of heart and quietly disperse. Yet mixed war parties of Canadians and Indians did wreak havoc on the Anglo-American settlements and tied down enemy forces vastly superior in numbers. The enemy's supply lines were constantly threatened, his advanced bases frequently destroyed. The mere knowledge that a French force had Indians with it was sometimes enough to cause a large Anglo-American force to flee or surrender. As scouts and intelligence agents the Indians were particularly useful. Although their verbatim reports were, on occasion, imaginary tales of things not seen, they could take prisoners far behind the enemy's lines who revealed much when questioned by the French. By such means the French were usually better informed than were the British of the opponent's dispositions and intentions.

When, in 1754, the British government decided to launch an all-out assault on New France without the formality of a declaration of war, it detached two battalions of regular troops for service in America. France had to counter this threat by reinforcing its units at Louisbourg and in Canada. A serious military and administrative problem immediately emerged. The colonies were in the charge of the Ministry of Marine but its colonial regular troops could not be expanded rapidly enough to meet the emergency. Recourse had to be had to the regiments of the French regular troops (*troupes de terre*, so called because most of them took their titles from the provinces of France where they were raised) under the Ministry of War, and the mutual hostility of these two ministries was extreme. Moreover, the Governor-General of New France, always an officer in the Marine, was commander-in-chief of all the French forces in North America whether stationed at Louisbourg, in Canada, or Louisiana. The council of ministers, however, agreed that divided responsibility would be fatal, and that unity of command, at such a remove from the centre of authority, was essential. It was therefore concluded that the reinforcement of six army battalions from the regiments of La Reine, Artois, Bourgogne, Languedoc, Guyenne, and Béarn, 3,600 officers and men all told, would be placed under the orders of the Ministry of Marine, which would be responsible for their pay and maintenance.

Two of the battalions, Artois and Bourgogne, went to Louisbourg. The other four went to Canada. In 1756 a battalion each from the La Sarre and Royal Roussillon regiments were shipped to Quebec, and in 1757 two more battalions from the Régiment de Berry were sent to Canada. Each battalion had an officer corps made up of a lieutenant-colonel in command, an adjutant (*aide-*

major), and a surgeon major; a captain, a lieutenant, and a sub-lieutenant (*sous-lieutenant*) of grenadiers; twelve fusilier captains, twelve lieutenants, and two ensigns. The other ranks consisted of the grenadier company comprising two sergeants, two corporals, two lance-corporals, one drummer, thirty-eight grenadiers; twenty-four fusilier sergeants, twenty-four corporals, twenty-four lance-corporals, twelve drummers, and 396 fusiliers; a total strength of 557. The grenadier company in each battalion was an élite group of shock troops, men chosen for their superior physique, martial appearance, and training. One of their functions was to stand directly behind the line in battle to prevent, with their bayonets, the fusiliers from turning tail—as occurred at Carillon in 1758 when some of the de Berry regiment made to bolt. If a section of the line reeled under an assault, the grenadiers stepped into the breach.

Separate from both the French regular troops and the colonial regulars were the engineers, represented by two French officers, Nicolas Sarrebource de Pontleroy and Jean-Nicolas Desandrouins, and a company of artillery. At this time the artillery was the weakest branch in the French army. The unit in Canada, commanded by François Le Mercier, comprised eight officers, three of them Canadians, four sergeants, ten cadets, and eighty-six gunners. The engineers were mainly concerned with fortifications. Pontleroy agreed with Montcalm that all the fortifications in the colony, including Quebec, were worthless and could not resist an assault let alone bombardment. On some points, however, Pontleroy's testimony is palpably false, for example his statement that there was no dry moat beneath the walls of Quebec. After Quebec fell to the British the French officers, including Desandrouins, deemed its defences virtually impregnable. As for the frontier fortresses, in their criticisms the French officers ignored the fact that they had been built to fend off the feeble Anglo-American forces and hostile Indians, not a British army which, although its engineers were poor, had in the Royal Regiment of Artillery one of the finest artillery corps in the world.

At Louisbourg the four battalions from the regiments of Artois, Bourgogne, Cambis, and Volontaires Etrangers, along with 1,000 colonial regulars and 120 gunners, all came under the orders of the commandant, Augustin de Boschenry de Drucour. For the battalions serving in Canada, however, a general staff had to be appointed. Baron Jean-Armand de Dieskau accepted the appointment as commanding officer with the rank of major-general (*maréchal de camp*)—making him one of 170 holding that rank in the French army. He was given a staff consisting of a second in command, an adjutant (*major*), an aide-de-camp, a war commissary (*commissaire des guerres*) in charge of supplies, and two partisan officers for detached duties.

Great care was taken in the drafting of Dieskau's instructions to prevent any conflict or misunderstanding between him and the newly appointed Canadian-born Governor-General, Pierre de Rigaud, Marquis de Vaudreuil. They carefully spelled out that the Governor-General was in full command of all the military forces. Dieskau was to take his orders from Vaudreuil, and whether he liked them or not he had no alternative but to obey them to the letter. The governor general was required to leave the details of the command of the army battalions to Dieskau but the latter had to keep the commander-in-chief informed of their strength, deployment, and everything else needed to enable him to make the most effective use of them in any operations he chose to undertake. When, in 1756, the Marquis de Montcalm replaced Dieskau he received the same instructions and the same restricted authority. He and his officers were also subordinate to the governments at Montreal and Trois-Rivières, which consisted of a local governor, a king's lieutenant (*lieutenant du roy*), a town major, and an adjutant (*aide-major*). The army battalions were there for one main purpose, to defend the colony, and they had to take their orders from the colonial authorities.

The council of ministers also decreed, not only that the French regular troops would, contrary to custom, be paid during the Atlantic voyage but that they would be paid over double the normal rate while serving in America. It was anticipated that the colonial regulars would protest, since the increase was not accorded them, but it was pointed out that they were defending their homeland. Their officers, and some of the men who had married in the colony, could enjoy the pleasures of their own homes and attend to their personal and business affairs when not campaigning. The French officers, on the other hand, had to face the prospect of years of exile from their families and friends in a colony where life was harder, and more expensive, than in France. Unfortunately, there was friction between the army and marine officers at the outset, and the pay differential aggravated the problem. More specifically it caused trouble when replacements for both corps were sent from France. The men all wanted to be incorporated into the higher paid French battalions.

Many of the French officers found campaigning in the North American wilderness not at all to their liking. The tedium of garrison duty at the remote frontier forts sapped their morale. Some of them were physically incapacitated and nearly driven out of their minds by the clouds of mosquitoes and stinging flies. Receiving news from home only once a year, and being unable to cope at such a remove with trouble that might arise, was hard to bear. Some of them were repelled by the seeming barbarism of the Indians and wanted nothing to do with them. The guerilla tactics of the Canadians, both regulars and militia, were remote from their concepts of how war should be waged. Even by European standards the French army was seriously deficient in reconnaissance and light infantry units trained for skirmishing and scouting duties. When army companies were detached to serve with the Canadians on their frontier raids their officers were disconcerted to discover that no mobile field hospitals or baggage trains went with them. Were they to be wounded they would have to make their way back to a French base as best they could before receiving medical attention. Their food supplies and equipment they had to carry on their backs like common soldiers. When rivers were encountered they had to wade or swim across. Resentful Canadians who were ordered to carry them across on their backs had an unfortunate habit of tripping in mid-stream. Some of the French officers declared that this was not warfare at all, and they refused to have any part in it. For them military operations required a secure, comfortable base, with servants, camp followers, clean linen, well-prepared food, and wine, close by the chosen field of battle or fortified place, where all the paraphernalia of siege warfare could be brought into play.

The Canadians formed a low opinion of the French officers, and the latter thought that the Canadians had far too high an opinion of themselves. The Canadians thought the French troops displayed too great a reluctance to seek out the enemy, preferring to remain on the defensive and let the enemy come to them. The defeatist attitude of Montcalm and several of his officers did nothing to ease the situation. While the French troops were employed in garrison duty, taking part in a campaign each summer, then remaining in their dispersed quarters all winter, many of the Canadians were fighting on the enemy's frontiers all year round. Vaudreuil felt constrained to complain to the Minister of Marine that the French officers were too loath to abandon their comforts for active campaigning. He also complained that some of these officers, including Montcalm, abused the Canadians shamefully, and that unless a stop were put to it there could be serious trouble. He stated bluntly that the moment hostilities ended he wanted the French troops shipped back to France. One cause of this problem, attested to in considerable detail by an official of the Marine recently arrived from France, may well have been that the French army in Europe, since the days of Louis XIV, had fought its wars on foreign soil and was accustomed to live largely off the land, treating the hostile population of the occupied territory with scant regard.

In this controversy one thing stands out clearly: the calibre of the French officers was much lower than that of the Canadians. Among the senior regimental officers physical and mental competence was not always in evidence. In 1758 Montcalm informed the Minister of War that the commandants of the Béarn and Royal Roussillon battalions were *hors de combat* and ought to be retired. In fact, only one lieutenant-colonel, Étienne-Guillaume de Senezergues de La Rodde of the La Sarre regiment was fit for active campaigning. After the battle of Carillon Montcalm had to ship nine officers back to France as quietly as possible. One, a knight of Malta and scion of an illustrious family, had been insane for some time and it had become impossible to conceal his condition; five others were sent back for displaying a want of courage—or as Montcalm put it, *"pour avoir manqué à la première qualité nécessaire à un soldat et à un officier"*—two for stealing from their fellow officers and one for having displayed considerable talent as a forger. Two other officers were allowed to resign their commissions, for good cause. Montcalm pleaded with the minister to see to it that replacements not be sent merely because their regiments, or their families, wanted to be rid of them. Meanwhile, he was obliged to fill the vacancies by granting the sons of Canadian officers lieutenants' commissions. Vaudreuil, although he sanctioned this solution, pointed out that it had established a bad precedent since these young officers entered the service with a higher rank than the Canadians in the colonial regular troops who had had several years of active campaigning. He added that too many of them could never have hoped to obtain commissions in the Canadian regulars.

Because the population of New France was only a fraction of that of the English colonies, some 75,000 compared to over 1.5 million it is frequently assumed that the outcome of the war was a foregone conclusion. If numbers alone were what counted then Britain's ally, Prussia, also could not have escaped destruction. Such comparisons can be misleading since the size of the forces that either side could bring to bear was governed by the nature of the terrain, communications, and supply routes. The British had 23,000 regulars in America by 1758, but they were not able to make very effective use of their provincial levies. The largest force they could deploy in a campaign against Canada was 6,300 regulars and 9,000 provincials at Lake Champlain in 1758. That army was routed by Montcalm's 3,500 regulars. Similarly, at Quebec in 1759 Wolfe arrived with 8,500 troops, mostly British regulars. By September his force was reduced to 4,500 effectives. To oppose them the French had over 15,000 men—regulars, militia, and Indians. It was not numerical superiority that conquered Canada but poor generalship on the part of Montcalm that lost Quebec in one battle.

During the course of the war, however, as the effectiveness of the British army improved, that of the French declined. On the British side the introduction of short-term enlistments and the popularity of the war brought forth higher-quality recruits for the regulars. Officers who proved to be too incompetent were weeded out; in some instances they were replaced by highly competent Swiss professional soldiers who, ironically, introduced the Canadian methods and tactics in the wilderness campaigns that the French officers sneered at. On the French side the quality of the reinforcements sent from France was low. They were mostly raw recruits, the sweepings of the streets. Some of them were even cripples who had to be shipped back. To make matters worse they brought disease with them that spread through the ranks and among the civilian population in epidemic proportions. In 1757, 500 troops were hospitalized and more than half of them died. Thus as the number of veteran trained soldiers dwindled through the wastage of war the quality of the regulars declined badly. By 1759 both the French battalions and the colonial regulars were not of the calibre they had been three years earlier. Among the French regulars discipline was not maintained; there were mutinies; morale sank to a low ebb. Thieving, looting, and other crimes became rampant. The war commissary was kept busy sending men before the council of war. He complained, "We spend our life having the rogues punished." The effectiveness of the French battalions was further reduced by Montcalm's decision to bring them up to strength by drafting Canadian militiamen into their ranks. It required more than the grey-white uniform of the French army to make regular soldiers out of them, capable of fighting in line. They did not receive the harsh, intensive, parade-ground training that that type of warfare demanded. The lack was to prove fatal on the Plains of Abraham.

Another frequently-stated reason for the conquest of New France is inadequate supplies. The question requires more critical scrutiny than it has received to date. Far too much tainted subjective evidence has been accepted at face value. Owing to crop failures and the greatly increased number of mouths to feed, estimated to be 17 per cent, the colony could not produce enough food to supply its needs. It was dependent on supplies shipped from France, but the supply ships reached Quebec every year up to 1759. In 1757 Montcalm reported that a three years' supply of clothing for the troops had arrived and there was nothing to worry about on that score. Moreover, sizable quantities of food and other military supplies were captured by the French; enough to maintain the army for months were captured at Oswego (Chouaguen) and Fort William Henry (Lake George, New York). There is no viable evidence that military operations were curtailed by a shortage of supplies. Poor distribution and the *habitants'* distrust of inflated paper money obliged the urban population to tighten its belt and eat unpalatable food at times, such as horse meat, but no one starved.

Account also has to be taken of the fact that the British had supply problems. The chicanery of their colonial supply contractors and the provincial assemblies was notorious. At Quebec in 1759 over a quarter of Wolfe's army was on the non-effective list, suffering from the dietary diseases, dysentery and scurvy. Moreover, owing to the military ineptitude of the Anglo-Americans, the British had to import in far larger numbers than the French the most essential military commodity of all, fighting men. Had no regular troops been imported by either side, the Canadians would certainly not have been conquered.

In 1758 Vaudreuil had contrasted the attitude of the colonial regular troops towards the war with that of the French regulars. For the Canadians, he wrote, the colony was their homeland; it was there that they had their families, lands, resources, and aspirations for the future. The French troops on the other hand, being expatriates, wanted only to return home with their honour intact, without having suffered a defeat, caring little what wounds the enemy inflicted on the colony, not even about its total loss.

The events of 1759 and 1760 made all too plain that there was more than a little truth in these charges. After the *débâcle* on the Plains of Abraham the French officers refused to give battle again, despite the fact that they outnumbered the British three to one and still held Quebec. The following year their failure to recapture the city they had abandoned and to block the British drive up Lake Champlain, the arrival of three British armies at the portals of the colony, the failure of reinforcements to arrive from France, all meant that further resistance was completely hopeless. James Murray, advancing up the river from Quebec, ravaged and burned the homes of the Canadians who had not laid down their arms. At one point his men got out of hand and some Canadian women were violated. Yet Lévis and his staff still demanded that the British be resisted for the honour of the army, which meant their personal honour and future careers. When many of the Canadians deserted to protect their homes and families the French officers wanted them apprehended and shot. French troops were sent to seize at gunpoint the last remaining cattle of the *habitants*, who resisted vigorously since this was all that was left them to feed their families during the coming winter.

Even when the British stood at the gates of Montreal in overwhelming strength, and although the sacking of the town might ensue, Lévis demanded that the capitulation terms be rejected because Jeffery Amherst had churlishly refused to grant the French the honours of war. Vaudreuil would not heed him and capitulated to spare the colony further devastation. The king subsequently declared, in a savagely worded letter from the Minister of Marine, that Vaudreuil should not have accepted the terms; that he should have heeded Lévis and continued to resist, come what may, for the honour of French arms. The missive made plain that the loss of the colony and the plight of the Canadians were of no consequence compared to the army's having surrendered without receiving the right to march out of Montreal bearing its arms, flags unfurled, and drums beating.

After the surrender arrangements had to be made for the transport of the regular troops, the civil officials, and the Canadians who chose to quit the colony rather than remain under the British, some 4,000 in all. Of the 2,200 French regular troops who remained on strength, 500 to 600 opted to stay in the colony; upwards of 800 had previously deserted to that end. Among them were 150 British deserters who had enlisted in the French forces. Vaudreuil and Lévis allowed these deserters to make themselves scarce before the capitulation, but most of them were subsequently rounded up by the British. Some French soldiers were persuaded to enlist in the British army, but one of their officers remarked that now they had discovered they were to be transported to serve elsewhere few would be tempted to follow their example.

The officer corps of the colonial regular troops, with the exception of those too severely wounded to make the voyage, crossed to France where they were retired from the service on half pay. With the conclusion of peace in 1763 twenty-one officers returned to Canada to settle their affairs, then went back again to France hoping to receive appointments on the active list. Others quietly gave up and returned to Canada to eke out a living on their seigneurial lands. Those who held the cross of the order of Saint-Louis were in a difficult position as the oath of the order prevented them becoming subjects of His Britannic Majesty without the consent of the king of France. Several of those who chose to remain in France eventually received active appointments in the service, in Gorée, the West Indies, or Guiana. Louis-Thomas Jacau de Fiedmont, for example, the brave gunner captain who, at Jean-Baptiste-Nicolas-Roch de Ramezay's council of war that opted to surrender Quebec, declared that they should hold out until the ammunition was exhausted, eventually became Governor of Guiana. Another, Gaspard-Joseph Chaussegros de Léry, returned to Canada and became a member of the Legislative Council of Quebec but sent his young sons to France. One of them, François-Joseph, gained entry into the reformed and prestigious corps of engineers. He ultimately rose to be commander-in-chief of the engineers in Napoleon's Grande Armée. His name is engraved on the Arc de Triomphe along with those of Napoleon's other great generals. For some of these Canadian officers the career was all important; for others, it was their homeland that mattered. Some, at least, who chose the latter did so because, owing to age or lack of means and influential connections, they saw no future for themselves in the service of their king. Their cause was truly lost.

As for the soldiers of the colonial regular troops who returned to France, when an attempt was made to have them enlist in French regiments not one of them would do so. Their almost unanimous response was that they knew the route to Halifax and they could easily find their way back to Canada from there. The Maréchal de Senneterre commented: "All those who have returned from Quebec and Montreal appear to have a great love for that country."

A DIFFERENT KIND OF COURAGE: THE FRENCH MILITARY AND THE CANADIAN IRREGULAR SOLDIER DURING THE SEVEN YEARS' WAR

Martin L. Nicolai

In recent decades two historians of Canada during the Seven Years' War, Guy Frégault and William J. Eccles, have attacked their predecessors' adulation of Louis-Joseph, Marquis de Montcalm, by portraying him as a poor strategist, a mediocre tactician, and a defeatist. However true this might be, they also portray the French officer corps, including their commander, as contemptuous of Canadians and irregular warfare.[1] During the course of the Canadian campaign, Montcalm and his officers did demonstrate a general lack of respect for the petty raiding of *la petite guerre* and an ambiguous attitude towards the Canadian soldier. This, however, was less a rejection of irregular warfare than an expression of their belief that a more structured and sophisticated use of irregular tactics was necessary when the enemy was no longer simply a colonial militia but a large, well-organized army complete with highly trained regiments of heavy and light infantry. As Ian Steele makes clear, the Seven Years' War in North America marks the end of the days of small-scale raiding and the advent of professional armies on the continent. The war, he states, was won by conventional, European-style battles and sieges, not by skirmishes in the woods.[2]

At first complacent in their use of Canadian irregulars, relying on local practice and their knowledge of the use of light troops in Europe during the War of the Austrian Succession, the French eventually attempted to bring Canadian soldiers onto the conventional battlefield not simply as sharpshooters roaming on the flanks but as actual light infantry operating on the central line of battle in close cooperation with the heavy infantry of the French *troupes*

From *Canadian Historical Review*, LXX, no. 1 (March 1989), 53–75. Copyright 1989 by University of Toronto Press. Reprinted by permission of University of Toronto Press.

de terre. There is every sign that the Frenchmen finished the campaign convinced by the success of Canadian light troops that units of properly led and disciplined light infantry were a valuable part of a European army.

The War of the Austrian Succession (1740–48) was the training ground of most of the French officers who came to Canada with the Baron von Dieskau and the Marquis de Montcalm, and it was during this war that irregular troops were first employed on a large scale by modern armies. In 1740–41 the young Austrian empress Maria Theresa mobilized her Croatian and Hungarian military borders on the Ottoman frontier and moved them for the first time to the central European front in an attempt to eject Frederick the Great's troops from Silesia. They performed invaluable service in every campaign, and in 1744 Field Marshal Traun successfully forced the Prussians out of Bohemia by threatening Frederick's supply lines and harassing his foraging parties. Over 40,000 Serbo-Croatian "Grenzer" would serve in the Habsburg armies during the War of the Austrian Succession and about 88,000 during the Seven Years' War.[3] These fierce soldiers were usually dispatched on independent operations against enemy outposts and communications, but sometimes they played a small part on the battlefield as sharpshooters posted on the flanks. Faced by these irregulars, the French, Prussians, and British responded by recruiting some light troops of their own. In the Seven Years' War all of the major European armies raised units of irregulars and light infantry and cavalry, and their use gradually became more sophisticated.[4]

The French army began very early to adapt to this new aspect of warfare. Although the use of skirmishers had disappeared in France at the end of the seventeenth century because of the widespread obsession with the firepower of the line, interest in these troops slowly revived during the following decades. There were experiments with skirmishers in military exercises as early as 1727, but only necessity during the 1740s forced the French to raise light troops in any numbers. During the winter of 1744, the Maréchal de Saxe, who had extensive previous experience with light troops in eastern Europe and had written the first modern treatise to deal with the subject, raised a number of *compagnies franches* or free companies for the French army, and would have formed more if the minister of war had approved. He eventually commanded five regiments of light troops, usually combining infantry and cavalry in these units, and by 1748 there were 5,000 of them in the French army. At Fontenoy in 1745 Saxe used his irregulars on the battlefield itself, sending a screen of skirmishers against the British centre while he deployed his army. He also stationed Monsieur de Grassin's new 1,200-strong Régiment des Arquebusiers in the Bois de Berry on his left flank, where their deadly independent fire or *feu de chasseur* made a British attempt to secure their flank exceedingly difficult. Saxe also used skirmishers at Laufeld in 1747. The tactics of this general, who was one of the greatest commanders of the eighteenth century, were studied with great care by other French officers. Although the French did not make extensive use of skirmishers during the War of the Austrian Succession itself, their presence was customary during the peacetime military exercises of 1748 to 1755 and no French military writer of this period neglected to discuss them.[5]

Montcalm and François-Gaston, Chevalier de Lévis, both served in Bohemia and Piedmont during the War of the Austrian Succession, and had more than enough experience with irregulars on both campaigns.[6] During the operations around Prague in late 1742 and during the subsequent retreat to Germany, Hungarian hussars and other light cavalry constantly harassed French foraging parties and other units, greatly hampering the ability of the Maréchal de Belle-Isle to supply his troops, obtain information about the main Austrian army, or easily manoeuvre his forces.[7] In Piedmont, Charles Emmanuel III organized his Piedmontese mountaineers or *barbets* in militia units, and these men fought beside the king's regular troops in the endless mountain battles of this campaign, also overrunning the French communications outposts in the mountain valleys, taking few prisoners in the process. Throughout most of 1745 and 1746 Montcalm protected sections of the French communications in the Ligurian Alps against repeated attacks by the *barbets*, and in one daring night operation the French colonel led his troops, some of whom were mountain fusiliers, over "impracticable paths" to surprise and capture 150 *barbets* in a village. To counter the Piedmontese militia, the Franco-Spanish recruited two battalions of Catalonian mountaineers from the Pyrenees called *Miquelets*—many of whom were former bandits—and equipped them with carbines.[8]

The exposure of many members of the officer corps to irregular warfare in Europe made them appreciate the effectiveness of this type of military activity. Irregulars could severely hamper reconaissance, slow an army's advance, and harry an enemy's communications so severely that large numbers of fighting men had to be withdrawn from the main body simply to guard the army's baggage and lines of supply and communication. There was, as a result, a general recognition among military men by the end of the 1740s that irregular troops, fortunately or unfortunately, had a role to play in wartime, if only to defend one's own force against enemy irregulars.

What impressions did French officers have of Canadian soldiers during the first few years of the Seven Years' War? One prominent characteristic of the Canadian *habitants*, noted by all of the officers, was their willingness to perform military service, an attitude which was in striking contrast to that of the average French peasant. The long wars against the Iroquois in the seventeenth century, which forced all Canadian males to take up arms and learn Indian methods of irregular warfare, engendered a military ethos among Canadians which was fostered by intermittent campaigns against the English in company with Canada's Indian allies.[9] The reputation of Canadians as a "race of soldiers" was confirmed by the French officers, whose constant refrain in their writings was to contrast the Canadians' skill and courage with their indiscipline.[10] Colonel François-Charles de Bourlamaque, for instance, believed that Canada possessed far more "naturally courageous men" than any other country, and although

Canadian militiamen were not accustomed to obedience, when they found firmness and justice in their officers they were quite "docile."[11] They possessed a different "kind of courage," wrote Louis-Antoine de Bougainville, for like the Indians, Canadians exposed themselves little, organized ambushes, and fought in the woods behind a screen of trees, defeating in this way an entire British army under General Braddock.[12] Despite his criticisms of Canadian indiscipline, Bougainville was careful to qualify his remarks: "God knows we do not wish to disparage the value of the Canadians ... In the woods, behind trees, no troops are comparable to the natives of this country."[13] Some of the least charitable comments on Canadians came from the Baron von Dieskau's second-in-command, Pierre-André de Gohin, Chevalier de Montreuil, who, blaming the irregulars for his commander's humiliating defeat at Lake George in 1755, declared sarcastically that the "braggart" Canadians were well adapted for skirmishing, being "very brave behind a tree and very timid when not covered."[14]

Despite a tendency among many officers to make generalizations about Canadian soldiers, most realized that not all Canadian males were experienced irregulars. Stereotypes may have been reinforced, however, by the presence of several hundred *coureurs de bois* and other experienced woodsmen among the militia companies and transport troops, especially before 1785. Captain Jean-Guillaume-Charles de Plantavit de La Pause de Margon, Chevalier de La Pause, found that there was no proper system of drafting soldiers in the parishes, with the result that the same men were chosen each year to fill the parish militia quota. These, according to La Pause, were the poorest *habitants*, presumably men with little land and a greater inclination towards hunting, long-term work as *coureurs de bois*, or related activities which provided the military skills useful for irregular warfare.[15] Bougainville differentiated between the men of the districts of Montreal and Trois-Rivières, who were considered more warlike and accustomed to voyages in the west, and those of the Quebec area, who tended towards proficiency in fishing and other nautical pursuits.[16] Similarly, Lieutenant Jean-Baptiste d'Aleyrac and Montcalm's junior aide-de-camp, Captain Pierre Marcel, made fun of the militia of the cities of Montreal and Quebec, "composed of all kinds of workers, wholesale merchants, who never go to war."[17] Despite these views, however, the officers felt that their generalizations about Canadians were justified.

Constant contact with Indian allies in wartime and the success of their tactics resulted in Canadians adopting not only Indian methods of fighting but also their attitudes towards war, such as the idea that victory involved inflicting losses on the enemy without incurring any and that the campaigning season was over when a victory, however insubstantial, had been achieved and honour gratified. In addition, native ritual boasting of prowess in war may have encouraged some Canadian soldiers to advertise their military talents in a flagrant manner. French officers noticed these characteristics, and generally realized that they were cultural borrowings from the Indians, but they were too ethnocentric and accustomed to professional military conduct to sympathize very much with this type of behaviour.

The Canadian penchant for boasting was of minor concern. Boasts "after the Canadian fashion, that one of their number could drive ten Englishmen" only boosted morale, and this behaviour was considered no more than a minor annoyance.[18] The Canadian and Indian custom of returning home *en masse* every time a "coup" was made, however, was subjected to considerably more criticism. La Pause recounted how the comical race of Canadians departed after the Battle of Carillon, rushing off in their boats within hours, moving "day and night, forgetting, losing and often leaving people behind if they did not embark fast enough." After visiting their families, he noted, they would return at an exceedingly leisurely pace to resume the campaign.[19] At other times, as when muskets had to be fired in an attempt to stem the exodus of Canadian officers and men after the fall of Fort William Henry—a factor which may have influenced Montcalm's decision to discontinue the offensive—the French were even less amused.[20] This behaviour at Oswego and on other occasions decidedly undermined the French officers' respect for Canadian soldiers. Even though they recognized the special nature of the Canadian "race," they expected them, as Frenchmen, to be more amenable to discipline than the Indians.

During the early years of the war the French officer corps simply accepted the traditional role of their Canadian militia and Indian allies. The recent battle on the banks of the Monongahela proved that the Canadians already had considerable potential, and there did not seem to be any immediate need to do more than instil Canadians with obedience and a basic orderliness. Captain Pierre Pouchot regarded Braddock's defeat on the Monongahela as an "impressive lesson" for regular troops who could not fire steadily and were unacquainted with the style of fighting of their opponents, although he did not believe that properly organized and trained regular soldiers should be defeated by irregulars.[21] Training Canadians as heavy infantry was pointless because they already performed satisfactorily as scouts, raiders, and sharpshooters, duties which admirably suited the "natural spirit" of the local people.[22] French officers, accustomed to the mosaic of provinces which made up their country, each with its own distinct culture and identity, saw Canadians as a very peculiar set of fellow Frenchmen. It was easiest to adapt to their particular nature and use their skills rather than try to make them more like other Frenchmen and amenable to European-style heavy infantry training. As Pouchot's companion-in-arms Captain Nicolas Sarrebource de Pontleroy of the Royal Corps of Engineers pointed out, Canadians were brave, but without discipline they could not be expected to fight in open fields against regular troops; they were not even equipped for such an eventuality.[23] The war was not yet desperate enough to require a complete rethinking of the role of irregular troops.

Baron Johann Hermann von Dieskau, who was one of Saxe's aides-de-camp and had experience with light troops in eastern Europe, undoubtedly derived much of his confidence in irregulars from his former commander.[24] However, he learned the limitations of irregular infantry during his campaign against

William Johnson in 1755. Leaving behind most of his French troops, he forged ahead with a mixed force of regulars, Canadian militia, and Indians to mount a surprise attack on Fort Edward. He properly posted flank guards of Canadians and Indians to prevent his small column from being ambushed, but was obliged to give up his plans to attack Fort Edward when the Iroquois refused their assistance. He was soundly beaten in an assault on Johnson's entrenchments at the foot of Lake George. Dieskau had not foreseen that Johnson's force would be both entrenched and alerted, for under these conditions he required more regular troops and a few cannon. His Canadians and Indians were simply unable to participate in a conventional assault. While irregulars were occasionally capable of capturing forts and other fortifications if they had the advantage of surprise, they could do little if the garrison was prepared for their attack.[25]

The Marquis de Montcalm, who arrived in New France in 1756 to take command of the French forces, was by a combination of experience, necessity, and advice persuaded to employ the regulars and irregulars in the separate roles to which they were most accustomed. The Chevalier de Montreuil, who condemned the "blind confidence" of Dieskau in his Canadian advisers, made certain to instruct Montcalm to rely upon his regulars and to employ his Canadians and Indians only in harassing the enemy.[26] Montcalm viewed raiding expeditions, especially those directed against military targets, as useful in harassing enemy troops and lowering their morale. He also believed that successful raids maintained the offensive spirit in his troops and encouraged the Canadian civilian population, although he abhorred the atrocities committed by his aboriginal allies just as he had hated the tortures inflicted on prisoners by the Slavic Pandours and Italian *barbets*.[27]

Irregulars were perceived to have a particular role: they tied down large numbers of enemy militia on the frontiers and lines of communication, carried out reconaissance, ambushed detachments of enemy troops, and provided some firepower during sieges and other engagements. Both Captain Jean-Nicolas Desandroüins and Lévis wrote approvingly concerning the contributions of the militia during the sieges of Oswego in 1756 and Fort William Henry the following year. Desandroüins found that the Canadians and Indians showed great enthusiasm at Oswego, and while they wasted a great deal of ammunition firing all day, they did succeed in lowering the garrison's morale. It obviously did not occur to him, however, that they might have captured the fort by themselves, or that the irregulars were anything more than auxiliaries.[28]

The year 1758 was a turning point in the war and in French tactics. For this campaign the British massed an army of 6,000 regulars and 9,000 provincials at Fort William Henry and advanced on Fort Carillon. Among these regulars were several new specially trained light infantry regiments and Robert Rogers' Corps of Rangers.[29] Few Canadians arrived in time for the Battle of Carillon, and the shortage of irregulars obliged the French to station two companies of *volontaires* in front of the abattis while it was under construction—*volontaires* being the contemporary French term for light infantry. These regular soldiers, probably the pickets from each of the battalions, skirmished all day with the enemy's abundant light troops, and successfully held them at bay while the abattis was hastily completed. Just as the battle opened, the French *volontaires* withdrew to the protection of the abattis or to the army's left flank.[30] A group of 300 Canadians who were present were ordered to leave the protection of the abattis and open independent fire on the flank of one of the attacking British columns, but refused to do so. A few had to have shots fired over their heads to prevent their fleeing the field, although in the latter case Bougainville admitted that "It is true that these were not Canadians of the good sort."[31] Canadians were not accustomed to fighting on the open battlefield and, having only *habitant* militia officers and occasionally a Canadian colonial regular officer of the *troupes de la Marine* to lead them, could not easily be coerced into exposing themselves to enemy fire. Even worse than the refusal of the Canadians at Carillon to follow orders was the rout of Canadian troops during a forest encounter in August 1758 with Roger's Rangers.[32]

Montcalm resolved at the end of this campaign that a higher level of discipline and cooperation was needed from his Canadian soldiers. His aide-de-camp and close friend Bougainville concluded, correctly, that "Now war is established here on a European basis of campaign plans, armies, artillery, sieges, battles. It is not a matter of making *coup*, but of conquering or being conquered. What a revolution! What a change!"[33] Indeed, the arrival of large regular armies in America had changed the nature of war on the continent. Montcalm believed that a concentration of his forces was necessary to confront the English along the major invasion routes, and he advocated a release of as many of the troops in the garrisons in the west as possible without undermining the Indian war effort. He saw that the Indians tied down large numbers of enemy militia on the frontiers, but doubted that a major French presence in the west had much effect in diverting British regular troops—the chief danger to New France, in his opinion—away from the central front.[34] The British were better able to respond to attacks by irregulars, and raids against military targets in the Lake George area were becoming more and more costly. Irregulars now found it more difficult to defeat regulars without the support of French or French colonial heavy infantry, and these troops had to be conserved for the principal engagements. Montcalm felt that large-scale raids no longer paid off in terms of the manpower, supplies, and effort invested, and he hoped that the Indians and small numbers of Canadians could maintain sufficient pressure on the English to keep them more or less on the defensive. By the fall of 1758 Montcalm knew that no ambush or raid was going to stem the advance of massive English armies against Montreal or Quebec; what he needed were large numbers of regular soldiers and disciplined light infantry who could be depended on to fight in a series of conventional battles.[35]

Montcalm believed that masses of poorly equipped and undisciplined Canadian militiamen who consumed his extremely limited food supplies were of minimal assistance to his army; rather, he needed regulars to reinforce his depleted battalions, which even at full strength were outnumbered approximately four to one by the British.[36] He therefore obtained Vaudreuil's consent to select 4,000 of the best militiamen and divide them into three groups. The first group was to be incorporated into the regular battalions of the line, the second into the *troupes de la Marine,* and the third was to be organized separately in the customary militia brigades. A total of approximately 3,000 Canadians were intended for the incorporations.[37]

This reorganization was intended to serve several purposes. First, each company of the *troupes de terre* and *troupes de la Marine* would be augmented by fifteen men, and would therefore add good shots, canoeists, and workers to the existing body of regulars, improving the ability of these troops to fight, travel, and build fortifications. Montcalm hoped to have the French and Canadian soldiers teach each other what they knew, making the regulars better woodsmen and the Canadians more dependable infantrymen. The Canadians, who customarily fell sick in large numbers on campaign because they lacked clothing, proper shelter, and enforced camp sanitation, would now live with the regulars in tents and receive uniforms, food, and other supplies. In addition, there had always been a serious lack of officers among the militia—sometimes only one for every 200 men—which resulted in a lack of supervision, discipline, and leadership in battle. Incorporated troops would receive abundant attention from the numerous officers and sergeants of the French line troops and *troupes de la Marine,* thereby, it was hoped, improving discipline and reducing desertion. Montcalm and his fellow officers claimed to have no worries that Canadians would be mistreated in their new companies, for "They live very well with our soldiers whom they love," and their complaints would be addressed by the general himself.[38] The militia and the French-recruited *troupes de la Marine* already camped together, so it was not expected that there would be any serious difficulty in uniting Canadians and the *troupes de terre.*[39]

The 1,000 remaining militiamen would be organized in their customary "brigades" of approximately 150 men, each theoretically comprising five companies of thirty men. Three soldiers of the *troupes de la Marine* were usually attached to each company as sergeants, and they gave the Canadians a modicum of discipline and military training.[40] According to Montcalm's plans for 1759, his picked militiamen would be placed under the best militia officers, subjected by special ordinance to the same rules of discipline as the regulars, and since there were fewer militiamen on continuous service, they could be better fed, clothed, armed, and even possibly paid for their longer period on campaign. As a further incentive, Montcalm proposed that distinguished Canadian soldiers receive marks of honour, including gratuities, and that small pensions be granted to those crippled by their wounds. The rest of the militia would remain at home prepared at a moment's notice to assemble and join the troops in the field.[41] All of these ideas centred around an attempt to organize and obtain the most efficient performance possible from irregular troops, either as raiders or as sharpshooters on the edges of the battlefield.

The decision to organize this special militia force to act independently of or in concert with regular troops had the full support of Montcalm's regular officers. Parscau du Plessis and Pouchot both noted the potential of Canadians to form "light companies," and in 1757 La Pause had the idea of establishing four companies of *partisans* composed of French and Canadian troops and guided by Indians; at any one time one or two of these companies could be in the field harassing the enemy. Bourlamaque made a similar proposal that a troop of 150 volunteer *chasseurs* adept at *la petite guerre* be maintained in the colony in peacetime, usefully employing the *coureurs de bois* whom he believed usually resided in unproductive debauchery among the Indians.[42]

Montcalm's intention to create a new army for the campaign of 1759, however, was only partially fulfilled. The *levée en masse* of the Canadian militia and the need to arm, feed, and supply thousands of these soldiers resulted in an abandonment of the plan to organize a set of elite militia brigades. The only special Canadian units to be formed were a small cavalry detachment led by French officers and the *réserve de Repentigny,* which was attached to Bougainville's command to patrol the riverbank upstream from Quebec during the siege. Neither unit took part in the Battle of the Plains of Abraham.[43] The planned militia incorporations, however, did take place in the late spring, just before the arrival off Quebec of the first ships of a fleet bearing a large British and American colonial army under Major-General James Wolfe. The number of Canadians actually incorporated is unknown, but it is doubtful whether more than 500 or 600 men joined the 3,000 or more regulars at Quebec.[44] Montcalm had only three months to train his Canadian regulars, simply an insufficient amount of time to produce the kind of soldier he wanted. Judging by the behaviour of the incorporated Canadians on the Plains of Abraham, it seems that very little effort had been made to drill them at all, and the abysmal performance of the regulars suggests that drill was not a high priority in the French army in Canada. After the battle, one of Montcalm's aides wrote in Montcalm's journal that "The French soldier no longer knew any discipline, and instead of molding the Canadian, he assumed all of his faults."[45]

The French officers were extremely pleased by the behaviour of the Canadian militia in the Battle of Montmorency on 31 July, for the militiamen were chiefly responsible for repelling a landing by 500 British grenadiers and Royal Americans. Lining the top of the slope overlooking the river, the militia opened a vigorous fire on the climbing troops, inflicting heavy casualties and forcing them to retreat to their boats. The French regulars, held in reserve immediately behind the Canadians, did not have to be committed to the action.[46] According to Captain Pierre Cassagniau de St. Félix of the Régiment de Berry, the French generals lacked "any great dependence on the prowess of the Canadians" until this action, "for they intermixed them with their regulars, and gave the latter public orders to shoot any of them that should betray the least timidity: however, they behaved with so much steadiness throughout the whole cannonading, and, upon the approach of [the enemy] troops up the precipice, fired with such great regularity, that they merited the highest applause and confidence from their Superiors."[47] This experience may have encouraged the officers to believe that the incorporated Canadians and militia would show more steadiness in any upcoming engagements.

On the morning of 13 September 1759, as Wolfe's army assembled on the Plains of Abraham and the French brought up their main force, platoons from the districts of Quebec, Montreal, and Trois-Rivières were detached from their militia brigades and sent forward with the pickets of the Régiment de Guyenne to harass the British troops from behind rocks and bushes all along the front of their line. After pushing back some British advance posts, these soldiers kept up a galling fire on the British regulars. Canadian militia and some Indians scattered in the woods on the two edges of the battlefield also kept up a steady fire from the cover of trees and underbrush.[48] Then, at about ten in the morning, Montcalm ordered the advance. In the centre, the battalions of Béarn and Guyenne formed a single deep column. On their right and left, at some distance, two other bodies of regulars formed shallower columns with a much wider frontage than the central formation. In the columns the incorporated Canadians were sandwiched in the second rank, no doubt to keep them in order. There were almost certainly more of them in the ranks further back in the columns.[49] Montcalm was clearly following the military ordinance of 1755, which recommended that attacks be made by a series of two-battalion columns.[50]

The officers lost control of their men almost immediately. The enthusiastic soldiers surged forward at an excessively fast pace, and as they marched over the rough terrain without pausing to dress ranks, they quickly lost cohesion.[51] As they approached the British line they began to collide with the advanced platoons of Canadian militia, which because of the rapidity of the advance had no time to retire in the intervals between the columns, two of which had very wide frontages. This caused further havoc in the French formations.[52] The columns began to move obliquely towards the British flanks, and at a distance of about 130 metres, extreme musket range, the French troops came to a sudden halt and fired several ineffectual volleys. The incorporated Canadians dropped to the ground to reload, as was their custom in an exposed position, and as the French officers urged the troops to advance, many if not all of the Canadians suddenly deserted their units and retired to the right where the platoons of skirmishers were joining the Canadians and Indians who lined the woods on the British flank.[53] This unorthodox behaviour—which left the regular officers somewhat nonplused—demonstrates just how little instruction the Canadian troops had received or accepted.

Pouchot commended the resistance of the militiamen on the right flank, but he also explained that the main attack "confused the [incorporated] Canadians who were little accustomed to find themselves out of cover." This was, however, the kindest assessment of the incorporated Canadians to be made by the French officers whose records are extant. Malartic accused them of cowardice, and others blamed them for setting the French regulars in disarray and abandoning their proper place in the line. The Canadians were shielded from further criticism by the fact that almost immediately after the Canadians left the ranks, the French regulars, who advanced in places to within approximately forty metres of the enemy line, broke under the impact of devastating British volleys and fled madly to the walls of Quebec and across the St. Charles River.[54]

At the conclusion of the Battle of the Plains of Abraham, as the French regulars abandoned the battlefield in complete disorder, the Canadians went far in redeeming themselves for their somewhat weak performance during the main encounter, this time in their traditional role as irregular soldiers. A quarter of Fraser's Highlanders were shot down as they attempted in vain to drive the Canadian rearguard from the woods, and they were obliged to retreat and regroup. A further attack by 500 British regulars from three regiments finally drove the Canadians back to the St. Charles.[55] The Chevalier de Johnstone, who observed this half-hour-long rearguard action, had nothing but lavish praise for their performance.[56] Pouchot and several other officers mentioned this resistance with approval, although they deplored the indiscipline among the Canadians in the columns.[57]

The French officers had underestimated the extent to which Canadians were attached to the tactics which they had practised for over four generations. Like the Indians, Canadians firmly believed that they should fight in their traditional manner, even if they recognized that conventional heavy infantry tactics might be appropriate for Europeans. Pre-industrial societies are extremely resistant to change because survival is so closely linked to practices—passed on by an oral tradition—which have been proven effective by generations of experience. Also, unlike the American colonists to the south, Canadians had no tradition of training in conventional tactics to make them open to such ideas. As usual, Canadians did their best in their traditional role fighting as skirmishers, and this would be taken into account when the tactical role of Canadians was reassessed for the next campaign, that of 1760.

The Chevalier de Lévis was not present at the Battle of the Plains of Abraham, but the news of the Canadian rearguard action confirmed his already high opinion of the effectiveness of Canadian militiamen when they fought under conditions for which they were trained. Ever since his arrival in Canada he had shown great interest in the use of irregular troops, and this goes far to explain why he was so popular with Vaudreuil and the Canadian officers. As early as 1756, Lévis had outlined the role he expected his light troops to play. In a directive he specified, first, that the *troupes de la Marine* and those of the colony will fight in their manner on the flanks of the *troupes de terre*."[58] This role of light troops in guarding the flanks was relatively orthodox in the French army, and was practised from Fontenoy to the middle of the Seven Years' War in both Europe and Canada. Second, Lévis attempted to work out a system whereby regulars and irregulars could support each other in battle and compensate for their respective weaknesses. Of particular significance is the fact that he designated some regular troops to serve as light infantry: "M. de Montreuil will also detach all the good shots of his regiment, who will fight *à la canadienne*, and will keep together only a part of his detachment to receive those who fight *à la canadienne*," so that, in case they were obliged to withdraw, they could do so with security behind the detachment, which, being in order, would face the enemy and give the troops who had fought as skirmishers [*à la légère*] time to rally and recommence the fight.[59] Light infantry depended on line troops for protection on the open battlefield because they lacked the density to deliver the concentrated firepower of a large body of men. In the days when one musket meant one bullet, a few men could do little harm to an advancing infantry unit unless they continually retreated to a new position and renewed their fire.

Meanwhile, parallel tactical developments were taking place in Germany, where light troops were employed by the French army at Sundershausen and Lutternberg in 1758 and at Bergen, Lippstadt, and Minden the following year. Until 1759 grenadiers, pickets, and entire line battalions detached as *volontaires* were used as light infantry, but during the winter of 1758–59 several regiments decided of their own accord to form detachments of fifty men to serve as light infantry, and these soldiers proved so useful at Bergen, in the retreat from Minden, and in other engagements that at the end of the 1759 campaigning season a number of officers successfully urged the Maréchal de Broglie to institute light infantry companies throughout his army. This allowed a battalion to be a self-contained unit which could depend on itself and not on special light infantry battalions elsewhere in the army when it met the enemy during or between major battles. Despite opposition from the Duc de Choiseul, battalion light infantry companies were confirmed by Broglie's French army drill instructions of 1764 and 1769 and officially instituted in 1776, just in time for the Comte de Rochambeau's campaign in America.[60]

It seems unlikely that Lévis knew of Broglie's reforms of the autumn of 1759, since the British blockade of the St Lawrence began in May and communications with France via Acadia were tenuous in the extreme. This makes it especially interesting that he should organize battalion light infantry companies at exactly the same time as Broglie. Both generals, however, were carrying the primarily post-1748 practice of detaching battalion grenadiers and pickets as skirmishers to its logical conclusion.

During the winter of 1759–60 Lévis decided to continue the incorporation of Canadian troops into the regular battalions, but on a significantly different basis than that envisioned by his later commander. Lévis's instructions for the organization of his army in 1760 specified that three companies of militia would be attached to each regular battalion, and to command these companies he designated "a captain who would be the best for this assignment and to manage the *habitants* with gentleness, and three lieutenants to command the said companies."[61] It is especially important to note that these Canadian troops were to be attached to the battalion in independent companies and not merely assimilated into the ranks of the regulars. Their role on the battlefield was explained in detail: "When it is necessary to march in column, they will march by companies or by half-company at the head of the brigade, and when it is necessary to place themselves in order of battle to fight, they will go forward forming a first line, leaving from one division to the next an equal distance to occupy the entire front of the line."[62] In other words, the light infantry would spread out to form a skirmishing line in front of the regular troops. "Once they are thus formed, they will march forward and seek to make use of the most advantageous situations to approach as closely as possible and fire on the enemy, and follow him closely if he withdraws."[63] Lévis further explained that if the skirmishers were pushed back, they would rally and form line in the intervals between the two-company divisions and then march forward with the whole army, firing volleys and then charging with the bayonet.[64]

We see here the final development of the light infantryman, no longer an irregular sharpshooter roaming on the edges of the battlefield but a regular soldier trained to prepare the way for the decisive attack. This not only required a high degree of training and flexibility, but also called for an intelligent, motivated soldier quite different from the automatons advocated by most of the leading generals of the day.[65] Each regular battalion was equipped with light infantry and could employ them offensively or defensively whenever the need arose.

In the spring of 1760 the Chevalier de Lévis incorporated 2,264 Canadian militiamen into his eight battalions of *troupes de terre* and two battalions of *troupes de la Marine*.[66] A full 38 per cent of the rank and file of the average battalion was Canadian, with 226 Canadians and 361 regulars in this "average" unit combining to raise its strength to 587 men. There were, however, significant variations from unit to unit, especially in terms of the proportion of Canadians to Frenchmen. In the case of the Régiment de Languedoc, the incorporated Canadians slightly outnumbered the regulars.[67] At the Battle of the Plains of Abraham, the incorporated Canadians had constituted only about 10 per cent of the regulars present. Lévis's militiamen, who wore their traditional costumes and were accompanied by their Canadian *habitant* militia officers and French regular NCOs under the command of French regular officers, were organized in units separate from the French troops in the battalions and, of course, were not officially enlisted in the regular army. While it was usual for three strong companies to be attached to each battalion, in a number of cases more were involved; this is probably due to the fact that Canadian militia companies varied widely in size, and Lévis was reluctant to amalgamate companies from different localities.[68]

The French met the British at Sainte-Foy, on the edge of the Plains of Abraham, and a fierce, desperate battle ensued which left four times as many men dead and wounded as the more celebrated engagement of the previous September.[69] The Canadian militia companies, stationed in front and in the intervals between their battalions, kept up a relentless, accurate fire on the British regulars who, despite repeated attacks, failed to make any impression on their French opponents. The effectiveness of the Canadian troops greatly impressed Malartic: "The Canadians of the four brigades of the right, those who were in the intervals or in front of the brigades, fired a long time and most opportunely. They did a lot of harm to the English."[70] A reserve battalion composed of the townsmen of Montreal and Trois-Rivières under Repentigny of the colonial regulars advanced to fill a gap in the line accidentally created by the withdrawal of a battalion of the Régiment de La Reine, and fighting in a semblance of close order kept a battalion of Germans of the Royal American Regiment and other British regulars at bay.[71] The Canadians showed great steadiness and bravery in this battle, and took part in the set-piece attacks which drove in the British flanks and forced General Murray to order a hasty retreat with the loss of all of his guns.[72] Lévis singled out Dominique Nicolas de Laas de Gustede, a captain in the Régiment de La Reine and commander of the 223 Canadians of his battalion, for distinguished conduct. Although Laas never received orders to advance, when he saw Royal Rousillon and Guyenne marching against Fraser's brigade on the British left flank, he led his Canadian soldiers forward to join in the successful attack.[73] Canadian militiamen had already cleared this flank of Murray's light troops by nearly annihilating the force of American and Highland Rangers sent into the woods to operate against the French right.[74] The fact that nearly one-fifth of the French casualties at Sainte-Foy were Canadians suggests just how heavily engaged they were.[75]

Companies of Canadian skirmishers under French officers had formed a long line in front of their battalions, covering both the French heavy infantry and the gaps between the battalions and remaining in position despite British artillery and musket fire at close range. Joined to their respective battalions by French regular officers, they were able to offer valuable assistance to the heavy infantry and were supported by their fire. A Canadian militia battalion under a Canadian colonial regular officer had actually replaced a battalion of regulars in the line of battle, and other Canadian light troops covered the flanks and defeated trained enemy light infantry. Canadian troops had therefore performed in several roles: as skirmishers in front of the heavy infantry preparing and taking part in the decisive attack, as skirmishers acting offensively and defensively on the flanks, and as heavy infantry in the line of battle.

French officers, including Lévis, Malartic, and artillery lieutenant Joseph Fournerie de Vezon, were unanimous in praising the steadiness, effectiveness, and dash of the Canadian soldiers, and there is little doubt that the officers considered the military reforms of 1760 a great success.[76]

On both sides of the Atlantic, French military men faced the problem of how to increase the efficiency of irregular soldiers while retaining their special attributes of initiative and independence and their unique fighting skills.

On each continent they met the problem in a similar way by giving their irregulars more discipline and better leadership, while at the same time cultivating their special *esprit de corps*. Conventional discipline and irregular tactics were combined to produce a new soldier with the ability to deal with a variety of opponents and battlefield situations. They also increased the cooperation between conventional and light troops until the latter, instead of being employed in a completely auxiliary role as scouts and raiders, became an effective tool on the classic, eighteenth-century battlefield.

The French officers who served in Canada during the Seven Years' War were obliged to fight under conditions which were very different from those which they had known in Europe, but their past experience and awareness of important trends in military tactics helped to prepare them for this new campaign. The growing ability of the enemy to deal with irregulars on their line of march and the likelihood of major encounters between the British and French armies meant that Canadians had to expand their skills by learning to fight on the conventional battlefield against enemy light and heavy infantry. Montcalm displayed a lack of judgment in filling the ranks of his regulars with undrilled Canadians, and was not sufficiently imaginative or ambitious enough to develop a closer cooperation between his regulars and irregulars. This job was left to Lévis to accomplish by placing militia units under regular officers and carefully linking these new light infantry units to his regular battalions so as to ensure close mutual support between these two corps—a change which paralleled reforms taking place simultaneously in the French army in Germany. The result was a decisive victory at Sainte-Foy, and this accomplishment justified the faith French officers had in the potential of Canadian militiamen to become what even they might have considered professional soldiers.

Notes

1. For historians who favour Montcalm see Francis Parkman, *France and England in North America,* part 7: *Montcalm and Wolfe,* 2 vols. (Boston 1884); Henri-Raymond Casgrain, *Guerre du Canada, 1756–1760: Montcalm et Lévis,* 2 vols. (Quebec 1891); and Lionel-Adolphe Groulx, *Histoire du Canada depuis la découverte,* 2 vols. (Montreal 1950). For highly critical perceptions of the French general see Guy Frégault, *La Guerre de la conquête* (Montreal 1955); William J. Eccles, "The French Forces in North America during the Seven Years' War," *Dictionary of Canadian Biography* (DCB), III, xv–xxiii; W.J. Eccles, "Montcalm, Louis-Joseph de, Marquis de Montcalm," DCB, III: 458–69; and W.J. Eccles, "Rigaud de Vaudreuil de Cavagnial, Pierre de, Marquis de Vaudreuil," DCB, IV: 662–74. Charles P. Stacey, *Quebec, 1759: The Siege and the Battle* (Toronto 1959), and George G.F.G. Stanley, *New France: The Last Phase, 1744–1760* (Toronto 1968), maintain a more neutral attitude.

2. Ian K. Steele, *Guerrillas and Grenadiers: The Struggle for Canada, 1689–1760* (Toronto 1969). I use the term "irregular" to denote light troops without extensive formal military training. "Light infantry" I define as formally trained light troops, who were often regulars rather than militia or auxiliaries.

3. With the addition of the Hungarian hussars, these light troops formed a very substantial proportion of the Habsburg forces. John F.C. Fuller, *British Light Infantry in the Eighteenth Century* (London 1925), 46–9; Gunther E. Rothenberg, *The Military Border in Croatia, 1740–1881* (Chicago 1966), 18–20; John Childs, *Armies and Warfare in Europe, 1648–1789* (New York 1982), 116–17; and Hew Strachan, *European Armies and the Conduct of War* (London 1983), 30.

4. For further discussion of Austrian, Prussian, and British light troops in the European theatre during the Seven Years' War see Fuller, *British Light Infantry,* 59–75; Strachan, *European Armies,* 30–5; Childs, *Armies and Warfare in Europe,* 118–20; Rothenberg, *Military Border in Croatia,* 40–52; and Christopher Duffy, *Frederick the Great: A Military Life* (London 1985), 314, 319–20.

5. Maurice de Saxe, *Reveries on the Art of War,* trans. Thomas R. Phillips (Harrisburg, Penn. 1944), 1–11. The *Reveries* were written in 1732 and circulated in manuscript long before they were published in 1757. Saxe deals extensively with irregular infantry and cavalry on pages 40–1, 48, and 50. See also Jean Colin, *L'Infanterie au XVIIIe siècle: La Tactique* (Paris 1907), 47–51, 71; Robert S. Quimby, *The Background of Napoleonic Warfare: The Theory of Military Tactics in Eighteenth-Century France* (New York 1957), 84–5; Jon M. White, *Marshal of France: The Life and Times of Maurice, Comte de Saxe* (London 1962), 129, 147, 157–8; Fuller, *British Light Infantry,* 49–54; Strachan, *European Armies,* 31; and Childs, *Armies and Warfare in Europe,* 118.

6. Thomas Chapais, *Le Marquis de Montcalm (1721–1759)* (Quebec 1911), 16–22, and Lévis, *Journal, Collection des manuscrits du maréchal de Lévis* (*Lévis* MSS), I, 24. Montcalm was aide-de-camp to the Marquis de La Fare in Bohemia, and was colonel of an infantry regiment in Piedmont. Lévis served as a captain in Bohemia and as an adjutant (*aide-major*) with the army in Piedmont; in 1748 he was promoted colonel. Both men displayed extraordinary bravery, and Montcalm suffered wounds on a regular basis.

7. Rohan Butler, *Choiseul,* I: *Father and Son* (Oxford 1980), 304–5, 343, 363.

8. Spenser Wilkinson, *The Defence of Piedmont 1742–1748: A Prelude to the Study of Napoleon* (Oxford 1927), 163–4, 208, 309–17; Butler, *Choiseul,* I, 500–52; White, *Marshal of France,* 222; Fuller, *British Light Infantry,* 54; and Strachan, *European Armies,* 31.

9. See William J. Eccles, "The Social, Economic, and Political Significance of the Military Establishment in New France," *Canadian Historical Review* 52 (1971): 1–22, for an examination of the impact of war and the military establishment on Canada's inhabitants.

10. Georges-Marie Butel-Dumont, *Histoire et commerce des colonies angloises dans l'Amérique septentrionale, où l'on trouve l'état actuel de leur population, & des détails curieux sur la constitution de leur gouvernement, principalement sur celui de la Nouvelle-Angleterre, de la Pensilvanie, de la Caroline & de la Géorgie* (Paris 1755), 40.

11. François-Charles de Bourlamaque, "Memoire sur le Canada," *Lévis* MSS, V, 102. See also James Johnstone, "The Campaign of Canada, 1760," *Collection de manuscrits contenant lettres, mémoires, et autres documents historiques relatifs à la Nouvelle-France, recueillis aux archives de la Province de Québec ou copies à l'étranger* (MRNF), IV, 254, 262; Pierre Pouchot, *Memoir Upon the Late War in North America between*

the French and English, 1755–60, 2 vols., ed. and trans. Franklin B. Hough (Roxbury, Mass. 1866), II, 45; Louis-Guillaume de Parscau du Plessis, "Journal de la campagne de *la Sauvage* frégate du Roy, armée au port de Brest, au mois de mars 1756 (écrit pour ma dame)," *Rapport de l'archiviste du Province de Québec* (RAPQ) (1928–9), 221; and Peter Kalm, *Travels into North America,* trans. John R. Foster (Barre, Mass. 1972), 492, for further comments on the warlike spirit of Canadians.

12. Louis-Antoine de Bougainville, "Mémoire sur l'etat de la Nouvelle-France," RAPQ (1923–4), 58.

13. Bougainville to Mme Hérault, 20 Feb. 1758, Louis-Antoine de Bougainville. *Adventure in the Wilderness: The American Journals of Louis Antoine de Bougainville, 1756–1760,* ed. and trans. Edward P. Hamilton (Norman, OK 1964), 333.

14. Montreuil to d'Argenson, Montreal, 12 June 1756, *Documents Relative to the Colonial History of the State of New York* (NYCD), ed. E.B. O'Callaghan (Albany 1859), x, 4 9. See also anonymous, "Situation du Canada en hommes, moyens, positions," RAPQ (1923–4), 9, a memoir probably by Bougainville, and the account by La Pause, who uses almost the same words as this anonymous officer in describing the inability of Canadians to "defend themselves with countenance." Jean-Guillaume-Charles; Plantavit de La Pause, chevalier de La Pause, "Mémoire et observations sur mon voyage en Canada," RAPQ (1931–2), 66.

15. La Pause, "Mémoire et observations sur mon voyage en Canada," 10.

16. Bougainville, "Mémoire sur l'état de la Nouvelle-France," 58.

17. Jean-Baptiste d'Aleyrac, *Aventures militaires au IXVIIIe siècle d'après les mémoires de Jean-Baptiste d'Aleyrac,* ed. Charles Coste (Paris 1935), 131; Pierre Marcel, "Journal abrégé de la campagnes de 1759 en Canada par M. M[arcel] ayde de camp de M. le Mis. de Montcalm," in Arthur C. Doughty and G. W. Parmelee, *The Siege of Quebec and the Battle of the Plains of Abraham* (Quebec 1901), V, 299.

18. Pouchot, *Memoir,* I, 35, 37, and II, 45

19. La Pause, "Mémoire et observations sur mon voyage en Canada," 66.

20. Bougainville, *Journals,* 174; Stanley, *New France,* 162; Steele, *Guerillas and Grenadiers,* 108; La Pause, "Journal de l'entrée de la campagne 1760," RAPQ (1932–3), 384; and Lévis, *Journal,* 1, 12.

21. Pouchot, *Memoir,* I, 41–3.

22. This common philosophy of the time was best illustrated by Montesquieu, who in *De l'esprit des lois* explained the idea that people in a particular environment develop a special character which the laws had to be made to fit rather than making people fit the laws.

23. Nicolas Sarrebource de Pontleroy, "Mémoire et observations sur le project d'attaquer les postes ennemis en avant de Québec, et sur celui de surprendre la place ou de l'enlever de vive force," 18 Jan. 1760, *Lévis* MSS, IV, 199.

24. J.R. Turnbull, "Dieskau, Jean-Armand (Johan Herman?), Baron de Dieskau," DCB, III, 185–6. Dieskau's first name is sometimes erroneously given as Ludwig August.

25. Steele, *Guerillas and Grenadiers,* 91; Stanley, *New France,* 102–3; and Guy Frégault, *Canada: The War of the Conquest,* trans. Margaret M. Cameron (Toronto 1969), 103–6. This latter book is a translation of *La Guerre de la conquête* (Montreal 1955).

26. Chevalier de Montreuil, "Detail de la marche de Monsieur de Dieskau par Monsieur de Montreuil," MRNF, IV, 1–4; Montreuil to d'Adabie, St Frédéric, 10 Oct. 1755, MRNF, IV, 9; Montreuil to d'Argenson, Montreal, 2 Nov. 1755, MRNF, IV, 13; and Montreuil to d'Argenson, Montreal, 12 June 1756, NYCD, X, 419. Montcalm, La Pause, and Pouchot shared similar ideas regarding the cause of Dieskau's defeat. See Montcalm to d'Argenson, 28 Aug. 1756, National Archives of Canada (NA), MG 4, A1, vol. 34 7, no 208; La Pause, "Mémoire et observations sur mon voyage en Canada," 20; and Pierre Pouchot, *Memoir,* I, 46–7.

27. Montcalm to Moras, Quebec, 19 Feb. 1758, NYCD, X, 686–7. See also Bougainville, *Journals,* 42.

28. Charles Nicolas Gabriel, *Le Maréchal de camp Desandroüins, 1729–1792: Guerre du Canada, 1756–1760, Guerre de l'indépendence américaine, 1780–1782* (Verdun 1887), 50–64, and W. J. Eccles, "Lévis," DCB, IV, 477–82

29. The French officers had a consistently high opinion of British regulars and a consistently low opinion of American provincials. They referred to the provincials only in order to point out their numbers and incompetence. They did, however, have respect for the Royal American Regiment and Rogers' Rangers—both regular units—even though they enjoyed recounting the numerous abortive or disastrous operations mounted by the Rangers. For the development of light infantry tactics in the British army in North America during the Seven Years' War see Peter Russel, "Redcoats in the Wilderness: British Officers and Irregular Warfare in Europe and America, 1740 to 1760," *William and Mary Quarterly* 3rd ser. 35 (1978): 629–52; Fuller, *British Light Infantry,* 76–110; Hugh C.B. Rogers, *The British Army in the Eighteenth Century* (London 1977), 73; Strachan, *European Armies,* 28; and for a long-term view, Peter Paret, "Colonial Experience and European Military Reform at the End of the Eighteenth Century," *Bulletin of the Institute of Historical Research* 37 (1964): 47–59.

30. Bougainville, *Journals,* 230. In the French army, pickets were not selected on a rotational basis; instead, they formed permanent units which were often detached for special duties.

31. Bougainville, *Journals,* 238. See also Gabriel, *Desandrouins,* 182, and Doreil to Belle-Isle, Quebec, 28 and 31 July 1758, RAPQ (1944–5), 138 and 150–2. In these last two letters, war commissary André Doreil passed on to the minister of war confidential information which he had obtained from Montcalm.

32. For French reactions to this incident see Gabriel, *Desandrouins,* 203–6; Bougainville, *Journals,* 261–2, and Montcalm to Moras, Montreal, 11 July 1757, MRNF, IV, 105–6. In 1756 1900 Canadian militiamen served in the ranks, but another 1100 were needed for transport work and for building fortifications. By 1758 1500 Canadians were employed on the western supply routes alone. George F.G. Stanley, *Canada's Soldiers: The Military History of an Unmilitary People,* rev. ed. (Toronto 1960), 23.

33. Bougainville, *Journals,* 252. Henderson believes that Bougainville may have copied passages from Montcalm's journal into his own, rather than the contrary, since duplicated passages often have a later date in Bougainville's journal. In my opinion, however, Bougainville authored parts of the general's official journal, then copied his handiwork into his own a few hours or days later. The style of the common passages seems more characteristic of Bougainville than of Montcalm. I have therefore ascribed the quoted passage to Bougainville and not to Montcalm, who also records it: Montcalm, *Journal, Lévis* MSS, VII, 419. Susan W. Henderson. "The French Regular Officer Corps in Canada, 1755–1760: A Group Portrait" (PhD thesis, University of Maine, Orono, 1975), 115–16.

34. Stanley, *New France,* 220–1; Steele, *Guerillas and Grenadiers,* 109; Henderson, "The French Regular Officer Corps in Canada," 102; Montcalm to Vaudreuil, Carillon, 26 July 1758, NYCD, X, 760–1; Montcalm to Cremille, Montreal, 12 April 1759, MRNF, IV, 224–5; and Montcalm to Le Normand, Montreal, 12 April 1759, NYCD, X, 966.

35. Montcalm, "Réflexions générales sur les mesures à prendre pour la défense de cette colonie," 10 Sept. 1758. *Lévis* MSS, IV, 45–6, and Stanley, *New France,* 220–1. Eccles claims, incorrectly, that Montcalm believed that "the guerrilla warfare on the English colony's frontiers had to cease." Eccles, "Montcalm," 463.

36. Bougainville, *Journals,* 199.

37. Montcalm, "Réflexions générales sur les mesures à prendre pour la défense de cette colonie," 45–8.

38. Ibid.; anonymous, "Milices du Canada: inconvenients dans la constitution de ces milices qui empêchent leur utilité; moyens d'en tirer partie, la campagne prochaine," Jan. 1759, RAPQ (1923–4), 29–31; and anonymous, "The Siege of Quebec in 1759," *The Siege of Quebec in 1759: Three Eye-Witness Accounts,* ed. Jean-Claude Hébert (Quebec 1974), 52. Canadian officers of the *troupes de la Marine* were especially plentiful, for at the beginning of the war sixty of them commanded 900 soldiers. Stanley, *Canada's Soldiers,* 27.

39. D'Aleyrac, *Adventures militaires,* 33, 58.

40. Montcalm, "Réflexions générales sur les mesures à prendre pour la défense de cette colonie," 45–8, and d'Aleyrac, *Aventures militaires,* 58.

41. Montcalm, "Réflexions générales sur les mesures à prendre pour la défense de cette colonie." 45–8, and anonymous, "Milices du Canada," 29–31.

42. Parscau du Plessis, "Journal de la campagne de *la Sauvage,*" RAPQ (1928–9), 221. Pouchot, *Memoir,* I, 37; La Pause, "Mémoire sur la campagne à faire en Canada l'année 1757," RAPQ (1932–3), 338; and François-Charles de Bourlamaque, "Memoir on Canada," NYCD, X, 1149.

43. Stacey, *Quebec, 1759,* 117

44. See Lévis, *Journal,* I, 209, and H.-R. Casgrain, *Montcalm et Lévis,* II, 97, for an indication of the numbers incorporated; Casgrain suggests several hundred. See Doughty and Parmelee, *Siege of Quebec,* III, 154, and John Knox, *An Historical Journal of the Campaigns in North America For the Years 1757, 1758, 1759, and 1760,* ed. Arthur G. Doughty (Toronto 1914), II, 105–6, for estimates of the size of the French army on the Plains of Abraham.

45. Montcalm, *Journal,* VII, 613.

46. For the Battle of Montmorency see Casgrain, *Montcalm et Lévis,* II, 133–4; Lévis, *Journal,* I, 187–8; anonymous, "Memoirs of the Siege of Quebec, from the Journal of a French Officer on Board the Chezine Frigate," Doughty and Parmelee, *Siege of Quebec,* IV, 249–50; Gordon Donaldson, *Battle for a Continent: Quebec 1759* (Toronto 1973), 138–40; Stanley, *New France,* 226–7, and Chapais, *Montcalm,* 610–11.

47. Pierre Cassagniau de St Félix, cited in Knox, *Historical Journal,* II, 6.

48. Armand Joannès (Hermann Johannes), "Mémoire sur la campagne de 1759 depuis le mois de mai jusqu'en septembre," Doughty and Parmelee, *Siege of Quebec,* IV, 226, and Marcel, "Journal abrégé de la campagne de 1759 en Canada," ibid., V, 296.

49. Doughty and Parmelee, *Siege of Quebec,* III, 160; Foligné, "Journal de Foligné," ibid., IV, 205; and La Pause, "Mémoire et observations sur mon voyage en Canada," 97. For scholarly accounts of the battle see Stacey, *Quebec, 1759,* 145–8; Donaldson, *Battle for a Continent,* 175–83; William J. Eccles, "The Battle of Quebec: A Reappraisal," *Proceedings of the Third Annual Meeting of the French Colonial Historical Society* (1977), 70–81. Also, Stanley, *New France,* 299–32; Doughty and Parmelee, *Siege of Quebec,* III, 131–72; and Philippe-Baby Casgrain, *Les Batailles des Plaines d'Abraham et de Sainte-Foye* (Quebec 1908), 1–68.

50. Quimby, *The Background of Napoleonic Warfare,* 86. The Ordinance of 1755 was influenced by both Folard and Saxe.

51. H.-R. Casgrain, *Montcalm et Lévis,* II, 249; Lévis, *Journal,* I, 209; and Marcel, "Journal abrégé de la campagne de 1759 en Canada," Doughty and Parmelee, *Siege of Quebec,* V, 296.

52. Joannès, "Mémoire sur la campagne de 1759," 226, and Marcel, "Journal abrégé de la campagne de 1759 en Canada," 296.

53. Joannès, "Mémoire sur la campagne de 1759," 226, and Anne-Joseph-Hippolyte de Maurès de Malartic, Comte de Malartic, *Journal des campagnes au Canada de 1755 à 1760 par le comte de Maurès de Malartic,* ed. Gabriel de Maurès de Malartic and Paul Gaffarel (Paris 1890), 285.

54. Pouchot, *Memoir,* I, 217; Malartic, *Journal,* 285; Joannès, "Mémoire sur la campagne de 1759," 226; and Marcel, "Journal abrégé de la campagne de 1759 en Canada," 296.

55. Stacey, *Quebec, 1759,* 152; P.-B. Casgrain, *Plaines d'Abraham et Sainte-Foye,* 53–6; Donaldson, *Battle for a Continent,* 187–9; Stanley, *New France,* 232; Chapais, *Montcalm,* 662; and Doughty and Parmelee, *Siege of Quebec,* III, 151, 171–2.

56. Doughty and Parmelee, *Siege of Quebec,* III, 164, 172.

57. Pouchot, *Memoir,* I, 217.

58. Lévis, *Journal,* I, 51.

59. Ibid.

60. Colin, *L'Infanterie au IXVIIIe siècle,* 75–80, 106–13, 126; Quimby, *The Background of Napoleonic Warfare,* 92, 98–9; Fuller, *British Light Infantry,* 69–70, 118–23; and Eugène Carrias, *La Pensée militaire française* (Paris 1960), 170.

61. Lévis, "Instructions concernant l'ordre dans lequel les milices attachées à chaque bataillon seront formées pour camper et servir pendant la campagne," *Journal,* I, 248.

62. Ibid., 250. The divisions Lévis mentions here include two companies, each about thirty men strong.

63. Ibid., 250–1.

64. Ibid., 251. See also Lévis, "Instruction concernant les dispositions et ordre de bataille qui doivent suivre toutes les troupes," and "Instructions concernant l'ordre dans lequel les milices attachées à chaque bataillon seront formées pour camper et servir pendant la campagne," ibid., 243–54, as well as Lee Kennett, *The French Armies in the Seven Years' War: A Study in Military Organization and Administration* (Durham, NC 1967), 29–30.

65. Strachan, *European Armies,* 23–5.

66. Data derived from table in Lévis, *Journal,* I, 257. Lévis lists 6,910 troops, including 2,264 incorporated militia and militia officers (who were *habitants,* not professionals) 3,610 regulars, and 266 regular officers. There was also a battalion of Montreal militia, 180 Canadian cavalry, and 270 Indians.

67. Ibid., 257.

68. Ibid., 253, and La Pause, "Mémoire et observations sur mon voyage en Canada," 107.

69. For scholarly accounts of the battle see Jean-Claude Lizotte, Jacques Gervais, and Carl Lavoie, "La Bataille de Sainte-Foy," *Mémoire: Magazine d'histoire et patrimoine,* nos 2–3 (1985): 4–21; P.-B. Casgrain, *Plaines d'Abraham et Sainte Foye,* 69–90; George M. Wrong, *The Fall of Canada: A Chapter in the History of the Seven Years' War* (Oxford 1914), 143–54; Stanley, *New France,* 244–8; Parkman, *Montcalm and Wolfe,* II, 348–51; and H.-R. Casgrain, *Montcalm et Lévis,* II, 350–6.

70. Malartic, *Journal,* 319.

71. P.-B. Casgrain, *Plaines d'Abraham et Sainte-Foye,* 69, 87.

72. H.-R. Casgrain, *Montcalm et Lévis,* II, 351, 355; Malartic, *Journal,* 319 note: and anonymous, "Narrative of the Expedition against Quebec, under the orders of Chevalier de Lévis, *Maréchal des Camps et Armées* of the King," NYCD, X, 1083. This last account is Canadian, and is attached to one of Vaudreuil's letters to Berryer, dated Montreal, 3 May 1760.

73. Lévis, *Journal,* I, 267; H.-R. Casgrain, *Montcalm et Lévis,* II, 355–6; Vaudreuil to Berryer, Montreal, 3 May 1760, NYCD, X, 1076; and Stanley, *New France,* 248.

74. Stanley, *New France,* 247–8.

75. Casgrain's casualty figures are not completely reliable, but they indicate that about 17 per cent of the French casualties were Canadian, or 150 men. Casgrain, *Montcalm et Lévis,* II, 356.

76. Lévis, *Journal,* I, 267; Malartic, *Journal,* 319; and Fournerie de Vezon, "Evénements de la guerre en Canada depuis le 13 7bre 1759 jusqu'au 14 juillet 1760," RAPQ (1938–9), 6–7.

CHAPTER
5 THE MEANING
OF THE
CONQUEST

No subject has generated more controversy, particularly among French-Canadian historians, than the impact of the Conquest on *la société canadienne*. In the modern, post-1945 era, that controversy centred on two conflicting interpretative approaches. One was the neo-nationalist Montreal school, heir to the Abbé Lionel Groulx tradition, composed of men such as Maurice Séguin, Guy Frégault, Michel Brunet and Cameron Nish. A proponent of the "decapitation thesis," this school viewed the Conquest as catastrophic, eliminating by 1800 the middle-class élites so vital to the economic and national development of the colony. Challenging this interpretation was the Laval "liberal" school of historians consisting of individuals such as Jean Hamelin, Fernand Ouellet and Marcel Trudel. While agreeing that by 1800 Quebec lacked a dynamic bourgeoisie, these historians found the explanation not in the Conquest but in the flawed nature of the society of New France itself. What had never existed, they argued, could not be decapitated.

More recently, this debate has taken a somewhat different turn. Applying modified Marxist analyses to the issue, a younger generation of Québecois political scientists has concluded that the traditional historical interpretations, nationalist and liberal alike, have missed the mark. What was really important about the Conquest, argue individuals such as Gerald Bernier and Vinh Ta Van, is that it caused a "structural rupture" in the economy of New France. The sudden, rapid and external imposition of capitalism onto an essentially feudal society, they believe, was both cataclysmic and far-reaching in its consequences.

Because of its nationalistic overtones, the debate between the Montreal and Laval schools of historians is as much about the future of Quebec as about the history of New France, and no final "winner" can ever be declared. Keeping this in mind, the readings in this unit move beyond theory to fact, evaluating the traditional interpretations of the Conquest by reference to specific historical circumstances. In "A Change in Climate: The Conquest and the *Marchands* of Montreal," José Igartua tests the decapitation thesis by examining the impact of the new socio-economic order of the post-Conquest world on the merchants of Montreal. Generally his findings substantiate the thesis, although Igartua acknowledges that if Canada had remained in French hands "there is no guarantee that other changes would not have affected the Montreal merchants."

French historian John Bosher also examines the impact of the Conquest on the merchant class, but from a much broader cosmopolitan perspective. Indeed, Bosher has long argued that both the Montreal and Laval schools interpret the Conquest within a too-narrow North American framework; New France, in his view, was first and foremost a colony whose fate very much depended upon the fortunes of the mother country. In *The Canada Merchants, 1713–1763*, from which the second reading has been excerpted, he places the Conquest and its legacy for the Canada merchants in the context of the critical eighteenth-century commercial and religious policies of the French government. "France," he concludes, "lost Canada in the course of financial, military and religious crises that simultaneously undermined Bourbon official society by revealing its weaknesses."

Suggestions for Further Reading

Bernier, Gerald, "Sur quelques effets de la rupture structurelle engendrée par la Conquête au Québec: 1760–1854," *Revue d'histoire de l'amérique-française*, 35, no. 1 (juin 1981), 69–95.

Blain, Jean, "Economie et société en Nouvelle-France—L'Historiographie au tournant des années 1960: La réaction à Guy Frégault et à l'école de Montréal—La voie des sociologues," *Revue d'histoire de l'amérique-française*, 30, no. 3 (décembre 1979), 323–62.

Bosher, John F., *Business and Religion in the Age of New France*. Toronto: Canadian Scholars' Press, 1994

Bosher, John F., *The Canada Merchants, 1713–1763*. Oxford: Clarendon Press, 1987.

Brunet, Michel, *French Canada and the Early Decades of British Rule*. Ottawa: Canadian Historical Association, 1971.

Igartua, José, "A Change in Climate: The Conquest and the *Marchands* of Montreal," CHA *Historical Papers* (1974), 115–35.

_____, "Le comportement démographique des marchands de Montréal vers 1760," *Revue de l'histoire de l'amérique-française*, 33, no. 3 (décembre 1979), 427–45.

_____, "The Merchants of Montreal at the Conquest: Socio-Economic Profile," *Histoire Sociale / Social History*, VIII, no. 16 (November 1975), 275–93.

Miquelon, Dale, ed., *The Debate on the Bourgeoisie and Social Change in French Canada, 1700–1850*. Toronto: Copp Clark Publishing, 1977.

Ouellet, Fernand, "Michel Brunet et le problème de la conquête," *Bulletin des Recherches historiques*, 62 (avril-mai-juin 1956), 92–101.

Sanfilippo, Matteo, "Du féodalisme au capitalisme? Essai d'interprétation des analyses marxistes de la Nouvelle-France," *Histoire Sociale / Social History*, XVIII, no. 35 (mai 1985), 85–98.

Séguin, Maurice, "La conquéte et la vie économique des Canadiens," *Action nationale*, XXVIII, no. 4 (1946–1947), 308–26.

Standen, S. Dale, "The Debate on the Social and Economic Consequences of the Conquest: A Summary," in Phillip P. Boucher, ed., *Proceedings of the Tenth Meeting of the French Colonial Historical Society*, University Press of America, 1985.

Ta Van, Vinh, "La Nouvelle France et la Conquête: Passage du Féodalisme au Capitalisme," *Cahiers d'histoire de l'Université de Montréal*, II, no. 2 (printemps 1982), 3–25.

A CHANGE IN CLIMATE: THE CONQUEST AND THE *MARCHANDS* OF MONTREAL

José Igartua

When the British government issued the Royal Proclamation of 1763, it assumed that the promised establishment of "British institutions" in the "Province of Quebec" would be sufficient to entice American settlers to move north and overwhelm the indigenous French-speaking and Papist population. These were naive hopes. Until the outbreak of the American Revolution, British newcomers merely trickled into Quebec, leading Governor Carleton to prophesy in 1767 that "barring a catastrophe shocking to think of, this Country must, to the end of Time, be peopled by the Canadian Race ..."[1] But the British newcomers, few though they were, had to be reckoned with. By 1765 they were powerful enough to have Governor Murray recalled and by 1777 they would be strong enough to command the majority of investments in the fur trade.[2] Did their success stem from superior abilities? Did the British take advantage of the situation of submission and dependence into which the Canadians had been driven by the Conquest? Did the newcomers gain their predominance from previous experience with the sort of political and economic conditions created in post-Conquest Quebec?

Historians of Quebec have chosen various ways to answer these questions. Francis Parkman was fond of exhibiting the superiority of the Anglo-Saxon race over the "French Celt."[3] More recently the studies of W.S. Wallace, E.E. Rich, and D.G. Creighton took similar, if less overt, positions.[4] One of the best students of the North West fur trade, Wayne E. Stevens, concluded: "The British merchants ... were men of great enterprise and ability and they began gradually to crowd out the French traders who had been their predecessors in the field."[5]

The French-Canadian historian, Fernand Ouellet, attributed the rise of the British merchants to the weaknesses of the Canadian trading bourgeoisie: "*Son attachement à la petite entreprise individuelle, sa répugnance à la concentration,*

From *Historical Papers* (The Canadian Historical Association, 1974), 115–34. Reprinted by permission.

son goût du luxe de même que son attrait irrésistible pour les placements assurés étaint des principaux handicaps." ["Its attachment to small personal businesses, its aversion to amalgamation, its taste for luxury, along with its irresistible attraction to safe investments were major handicaps."] No evidence is given for this characterization and the author hastens to concede that before 1775 "*le problème de la concentration ne se pose pas avec acuité,*" ["amalgamation did not come into focus as an issue,"] but for him it is clear that the economic displacement of the Canadians resulted from their conservative, "*ancien Régime*" frame of mind, bred into them by the clergy and the nobility.[6] Ouellet painted British merchants in a more flattering light as the agents of economic progress.[7]

Michel Brunet has depicted the commercial competition between the British newcomers and the Canadian merchants as an uneven contest between two national groups, one of which had been deprived of the nourishing blood of its metropolis while the other was being assiduously nurtured. For Brunet the normal and natural outcome of that inequality was the domination of the conqueror, a situation which he sees as prevailing to the present day.[8]

Dale B. Miquelon's study of one merchant family, the Babys, shed new light on the question of British penetration of Canadian trade. It outlined the growth of British investments in the fur trade and the increasing concentration of British capital. The author concluded:

> The French Canadians dominated the Canadian fur trade until the upheaval of the American Revolution. At that time they were overwhelmed by an influx of capital and trading personnel. English investment in the top ranks of investors jumped by 679 per cent and was never significantly to decline. Even without explanations involving the difference between the French and English commercial mentalities, it is difficult to believe that any body of merchants could recover from an inundation of such size and swiftness.[9]

This conclusion had the obvious merit of staying out of the murky waters of psychological interpretations. But Miquelon's own evidence suggests that the "flood theory" is not sufficient to account for the Canadians' effacement; even before the inundation of 1775–83, British investment in the fur trade was growing more rapidly than Canadian. By 1772, to quote Miquelon, the "English [had] made more impressive increases in the size of their investments than [had] the French, and for the first time [had] larger average investments in all categories."[10]

It is difficult not to note the ascendancy of the British in the fur trade of Canada even before the American Revolution. The success of the British merchants, therefore, was rooted in something more than mere numbers. It was not simply the outcome of an ethnic struggle between two nationalities of a similar nature; it was not only the natural consequence of the Canadians' conservative frame of mind. It arose out of a more complex series of causes, some of them a product of the animosities between Canadians and British, others inherent to the differences in the socio-economic structures of the French and British Empires; together, they amounted to a radical transformation of the societal climate of the colony.

The aim of this paper is to gauge the impact of the Conquest upon a well-defined segment of that elusive group called the "bourgeoisie" of New France. It focuses on Montreal and its Canadian merchants. Montreal was the centre of the fur trade and its merchants managed it. Historians of New France have traditionally seen the fur trade as the most dynamic sector of the colony's economy; by implication it is generally believed that the fur trade provided the likeliest opportunities for getting rich quickly and maintaining a "bourgeois" standard of living.[11] It is not yet possible to evaluate the validity of this notion with any precision, for too little is known about other sectors of the economy which, in the eighteenth century at least, may have generated as much or more profit. Research on the merchants of Quebec should provide new information on the wealth to be made from the fisheries, from wholesale merchandising, and from trade with Louisbourg and the West Indies. But if one is concerned with the fate of Canadian merchants after the Conquest, one should examine the fate of men involved in the sector of the economy of Quebec which was the most dynamic *after* the Conquest, the fur trade. The paper examines the impact of the arrival of (relatively) large numbers of merchants on the Montreal mercantile community, the attitude of British officials towards the Canadians, and the changing political climate of the colony. It is suggested that it was the simultaneous conjunction of these changes to the "world" of the Montreal merchants, rather than the effect of any one of them, which doomed the Canadian merchants of Montreal.[12]

The Montreal Merchants at the End of the French Regime

In 1752 a French Royal engineer passing through Montreal remarked that "*la plupart des habitants y sont adonnés au commerce principalement à celui connu sous le nom des pays d'en haut*" ["most of the inhabitants are involved in trade, chiefly in what is known as the 'upcountry' trade"].[13] It was only a slight exaggeration. By the last year of the French regime one could count over 100 *négociants*, merchants, outfitters, traders, and shopkeepers in Montreal. The overwhelming majority of them had been in business for some years and would remain in business after the Conquest. Over half were outfitters for the fur trade at some time or other between 1750 and 1775; these men comprised the body of the merchant community of Montreal. Above them in wealth and stature stood a handful of import merchants who did a comfortable business of importing merchandise from France and selling it in Montreal to other merchants or directly to customers in their retail stores. Below the outfitters a motley group of independent fur traders, shopkeepers, and artisans managed to subsist without leaving more than a trace of their existence for posterity.[14]

The fur trade, as it was conducted by the merchants of Montreal before 1760, had little to do with the glamorous picture it sometimes calls to mind. For the outfitter who remained in Montreal, it was not physically a risky occupation; its management was fairly simple and the profits which it produced quite meager. For the last years of the French regime the fur trade followed a three-tier system. Fort Frontenac (present-day Kingston) and Fort Niagara were king's posts; they were not lucrative and had to be subsidized to meet English competition. The trade of Detroit and Michilimackinac, as well as that of the posts to the south-west, was open to licencees whose numbers were limited. Some *coureurs de bois* (traders without a licence) also roamed in the area. The richest posts, Green Bay and the posts to the north-west past Sault Sainte Marie, were monopolies leased by the Crown to merchants or military officers.[15] The export of beaver was undertaken by the French *Compagnie des Indes*, which had the monopoly of beaver sales on the home market. Other furs were on the open market.

The system worked tolerably well in peacetime: there was a stable supply of furs, prices paid to the Indians had been set by custom, the prices paid by the *Compagnie des Indes* were regulated by the Crown, and the prices of trade goods imported from France were fairly steady. There was competition from the Americans at Albany and from the English on the Hudson Bay, to be sure, but it appeared to be a competition heavily influenced by military considerations and compliance with Indian customs.[16]

The system faltered in wartime. Beaver shipments to France and the importation of trade goods became risky because of British naval power. Shipping and insurance costs raised the Canadian traders' overhead, but the Indians refused to have the increase passed on to them. This was the most obvious effect of war, but it also produced general economic and administrative dislocations which led H.A. Innis to conclude that it " ... seriously weakened the position of the French in the fur trade and contributed to the downfall of the French *régime* in Canada.[17]

Nevertheless, outside of wartime crises, the fur trade of New France was conducted with a fair dose of traditionalism. This traditionalism resulted from two concurrent impulses: Indian attitudes towards trade, which were untouched by the mechanism of supply and demand and by distinctions between commercial, military, political or religious activities; and the mercantilist policies of France, which tried to control the supply of furs by limiting the number of traders and regulating beaver prices on the French market. While the fur trade structure of New France had an inherent tendency towards geographic expansion, as Innis argued, it also had to be oligopolistic in nature, if investments in Indian alliances, explorations, and military support were to be maximized. Open competition could not be allowed because it would lead to the collapse of the structure.[18]

It is not surprising, therefore, that most outfitters dabbled in the fur trade only occasionally. On the average, between 1750 and 1775, the Canadian merchants of Montreal invested in the trade only four times and signed up about eleven *engagés* each time, not quite enough to man two canoes. Few merchants outfitted fur trade ventures with any regularity and only six men hired an average of twelve or more *engagés*, more than twice before 1761 (see Table 1).

TABLE 1   Largest Canadian Fur Trade Outfitters in Montreal, 1750–1760

Name	Total No. of Years	No. of Hirings	Yearly Average
CHARLY, Louis Saint-Ange	6	85	14.1
GODET, Dominique	5	85	17.0
LECHELLE, Jean	4	130	32.5
LEMOINE MONIERE, Alexis	7	300	42.8
L'HUILLIER CHEVALIER, François	7	90	12.6
TROTIER DESAUNIERS, Thomas-Ignace "Dufy"	5	129	25.8

Source: "Répertoire des engagements pour l'ouest conservés dans les Archives judiciaires de Montréal," *Rapport de l'Archiviste de la province de Québec*, 1930–31, pp. 353–453; 1931–32, pp. 242–365; 1932–33, pp. 245–304.

Three of these were unquestionably wealthy: Louis Saint-Ange Charly, an import merchant who, unlike his colleagues, had a large stake in the fur trade, realized 100,000 *livres* on his landholdings alone when he left the colony for France in 1764; Thomas-Ignace Trotier Desauniers "Dufy," who in a will drawn up in 1760 bequeathed 28,000 *livres* to the Sulpicians; the illiterate Dominique Godet, who in a similar document of 1768, mentioned 5,000 *livres* in cash in hand, land in three parishes in the vicinity of Montreal, "*Batiment & Bateaux qui en dependent*," around 5,000 *livres* in active debts, and two black slaves.[19] Two other large outfitters left relatively few belongings at the time of their death: Alexis Lemoine Monière left less than 1,000 *livres*, all of it in household goods, and François L'Huillier Chevalier just slightly more.[20] Little is known about the sixth man, Jean Léchelle.

If the fur trade made few wealthy men among those who invested heavily in it, it would be hard to argue that less considerable investors were more successful. It is not unreasonable to conclude that the fur trade was not very profitable for the overwhelming majority of outfitters and that it only sustained a very limited number of them each year. Yet the French had reduced costly competition to a minimum and had few worries about price fluctuations. How would Canadian outfitters fare under a different system?

The Advent of the British Merchants

With the arrival in Montreal of British traders, the workings of the fur trade were disputed. At first, the licensing system was maintained and some areas were left to the exclusive trade of particular traders.[21] But from the very beginning the trade was said to be open to all who wanted to secure a licence, and the result could only be price competition. With individual traders going into the fur trade, the organization of the trade regressed. The previous division of labour between the *Compagnie des Indes*, the import merchants and outfitters, the traders, the *voyageurs*, and the *engagés* was abandoned and during the first years of British rule the individual trader filled all of the functions previously spread among many "specialists."

The story of Alexander Henry, one of the first British merchants to venture into the upper country, illustrates the new pattern of trade. A young man from New Jersey, Alexander Henry came to Canada in 1760 with General Amherst's troops.[22] With the fall of Montreal Henry saw the opening of a "new market" and became acquainted with the prospects of the fur trade. The following year, he set out for Michilimackinac with a Montreal outfitter, Etienne Campion, whom he called his "assistant," and who took charge of the routine aspects of the trip.[23] Henry wintered at Michilimackinac. There he was urged by the local inhabitants to go back to Detroit as soon as possible for they claimed to fear for his safety. Their fears were not without foundation, but Henry stayed on. His partner Campion reassured him: " ... the Canadian inhabitants of the fort were more hostile than the Indians, as being jealous of British traders, who ... were penetrating into the country."[24] At least some of the Canadians resented the British traders from the outset and a few tried to use the Indians to frighten them away.[25]

Henry proceeded to Sault Sainte Marie the following year. In the spring of 1763, he returned to Michilimackinac and witnessed the massacre of the British garrison during Pontiac's revolt.[26] He was eventually captured by the Indians and adopted into an Indian family with whom he lived, in the Indian style, until late June 1764. Undaunted, Henry set out for the fur trade again, exploring the Lake Superior area. He was on the Saskatchewan River in 1776, tapping fur resources which the French had seldom reached.[27] Finally he settled down in Montreal in 1781 and while he did join the North West Company after its formation, he seldom returned to the upper country himself.[28]

Henry was not the first British merchant to reach the upper country. Henry Bostwick had obtained a licence from General Gage before him in 1761,[29] and the traders Goddard and Solomons had followed Henry into Michilimackinac in 1761. By early 1763 there were at least two more British merchants in the area.[30] In Montreal alone there were close to fifty new merchants by 1765. Governor Murray's list of the Protestants in the district of Montreal gives the names, the origins, and the "former callings" of forty-five.[31] Over half of them came from England and Scotland and 20 per cent were from Ireland. Only 13 per cent came from the American colonies and an equal number came from various countries (Switzerland, Germany, France, Guernesey). In the proportion of more than three to one, the newcomers had been merchants in their "former calling." The others had been soldiers and clerks. Many of the newcomers were men of experience and enterprise. Among them were Isaac Todd, Thomas Walker, Lawrence Ermatinger, Richard

Dobie, Edward Chinn, John Porteous, William Grant, Benjamin Frobisher, James Finlay, Alexander Paterson, Forrest Oakes, and the Jewish merchants Ezekiel and Levy Solomons, all of whom became substantial traders.[32]

The arrival of so many merchants could only mean one thing: strenuous competition in the fur trade. Competition ruthlessly drove out those with less secure financial resources or with no taste for sharp practices. Among the British as among the French, few resisted the pressures. The story of the trader Hamback is not untypical. Out on the Miami River in 1766 and 1767, he found that competition left him with few returns to make to his creditor William Edgar of Detroit. "I live the life of a downright exile," he complained, "no company but a Barrel of drunken infamous fugitives, and no other Comfort of Life."[33]

The Canadian merchants of Montreal had competition not only from British merchants in their town, but also from American merchants moving into Detroit and Michilimackinac. William Edgar, a New York merchant, was at Niagara in late 1761.[34] In 1763 he was established at Detroit, where he conducted a brisk trade supplying individual traders at Michilimackinac and in the South-West District.[35] From Schenectady, the partnership of Phyn and Ellice also carried on a profitable supply trade for the fur traders of the interior.[36]

Competition also came from the French on the Mississippi, who were trading in the Illinois country and the Lake Superior region. These French traders could all too easily link up with French-speaking traders from Canada, whose help, it was feared, they could enlist in subverting the Indians against British rule.[37] This always troubled Sir William Johnson, the Superintendent for Indian Affairs, who refused to abandon his suspicions of the French-speaking traders from Canada.

This many-sided competition produced a climate to which the Canadian merchants were not accustomed. The increased number of fur traders led to frictions with the Indians, smaller returns for some of the traders, and unsavory trade practices.[38] Even the retail trade was affected. Merchants from England flooded the market at Quebec "with their manufactures, so much so that they are daily sold here at Vendue Twenty per Cent below prime Cost."[39] In 1760 alone, the first year of British occupation, £60,000 worth of trade goods had been brought into Canada.[40] From 1765 to 1768 the pages of the *Quebec Gazette* were filled with notices of auctions by merchants returning to England and disposing of their wares after unsuccessful attempts to establish themselves in the trade of the colony.[41]

By 1768 some thought the Canadians still had the advantage in the fur trade, even though there was "Competition" and a "strong Jealousy" between Canadian and English. The Canadians' "long Connections with those Indians," wrote General Gage, "and their better Knowledge of their Language and Customs, must naturaly for a long time give the Canadians an Advantage over the English ... "[42] Sir William Johnson had expressed a similar opinion the previous year and had deplored the British merchants' tactics: "The English were compelled to make use of Low, Selfish Agents, French, or English as Factors, who at the Expence of honesty and sound policy, took care of themselves whatever became of their employers."[43]

Another observer, the Hudson's Bay Company trader at Moose Factory, complained of "Interlopers who will be more Destructive to our trade than the French was." The French had conducted a less aggressive trade: they "were in a manner Settled, their Trade fixed, their Standards moderate and Themselves under particular regulations and restrictions, which I doubt is not the Case now."[44] Competition was forcing the British merchants in Montreal into ruthless tactics, a development which upset the Hudson's Bay Company man and which would unsettle the Canadians.

The pattern of British domination of the fur trade began to emerge as early as 1767. Trading ventures out of Michilimackinac into the North-west were conducted by Canadians, but British merchants supplied the financial backing. The North-west expeditions demanded the lengthiest periods of capital outlay, lasting two or three years. British merchants, it seems, had better resources. Of the fifteen outfitters at Michilimackinac who sent canoes to the North-west in 1767, nine were British and six were Canadian; the total value of canoes outfitted by the British came to £10,812.17, while the Canadians' canoes were worth only £3,061.10. The British outfitters—most notably Alexander Henry, Isaac Todd, James McGill, Benjamin Frobisher, Forrest Oakes—invested on the average £1,351.12 and the Canadians only £510.5. The average value of goods invested in each canoe stood at £415.17 for the British and £278.6 for the Canadians.[45] The Canadians' investment per canoe was only two-thirds that of the British and the Canadians were already outnumbered as outfitters in what would become the most important region of the fur trade.[46]

Open competition was not conducive to the expansion of the fur trade and an oligopolistic structure reminiscent of the French system soon reappeared as the only solution.[47] This led to the formation of the North West Company in the 1780s but already in 1775, those Montreal merchants who had extended their operations as far as the Saskatchewan felt the need for collaboration rather than competition. Again developments in the more remote frontiers of the fur trade foretold of events to occur later in the whole of the trade: the traders on the Saskatchewan were almost all of British origin.[48] The fur trade was returning to the structures developed by the French, but during the period of competition which followed the Conquest the Canadians were gradually crowded out. There was some irony in that. Why had the Canadians fared so badly?

The Attitude of Government Officials

Much has been made of the natural sympathies of Murray and Carleton towards the Canadians and their antipathies towards the traders of their own nation. Yet for all their ideological inclinations there is no evidence that the governors turned their sentiments into policies of benevolence for Canadians in trade matters. Rather, it is easier to discover, among the lesser officials and some of the more important ones as well, an understandable patronizing of British rather than Canadian merchants. Colonial administrators may not have set a deliberate pattern of preference in favour of British merchants. But the Canadian merchants of Montreal, who put great store by official patronage, cared not whether the policy was deliberate or accidental; the result was the same.

Official preferences played against the Canadian traders in many ways. First, the lucrative trade of supplying the military posts was given to British and American merchants as a matter of course, and this occasion for profit was lost to the Canadians. Under the French regime some of the Montreal merchants, notably the Monières and the Gamelins, had profited from that trade.[49] Now it fell out of Canadian hands. This advantage did not shift to the sole favour of the British merchants of Quebec. New York and Pennsylvania traders were also awarded their share of the trade. The firms of Phyn, Ellice of Schenectady and Baynton, Wharton, and Morgan of Philadelphia received the lion's share of that business while the upper country was under the jurisdiction of Sir William Johnson.[50] But this was of little comfort to the Canadians.

Less tangible by-products of the British occupation of the former fur trading areas of New France are more difficult to assess than the loss of the supply trade; they were, however, quite real. One was the British military's attitude towards Canadians. The military were wary of French-speaking traders in Illinois and on the Mississippi. Although the French from Canada had been vanquished, French traders in the interior could still deal with France through New Orleans. No regulations, no boundaries could restrain French traders operating out of Louisiana from dealing with the Indians, and the Canadians who were confined to the posts protested against the advantage held by the French traders.[51] But who were these French traders? Did they not include Canadian *coureurs de bois* and wintering merchants? How could one really tell a French-speaking trader from Canada from a French-speaking trader out of New Orleans? Were not all of them suspect of exciting the Indians against the British, promising and perhaps hoping for France's return to America?[52] As late as 1768, when Indian discontent in the West threatened another uprising, General Gage failed to see any difference between French-speaking Canadians and the French from New Orleans.

> There is the greatest reason to suspect that the French are Endeavouring to engross the Trade, and that the Indians have acted thro' their Instigation, in the Murders they have committed, and the Resolutions we are told they have taken, to suffer no Englishman to trade with them. And in this they have rather been Assisted by the English Traders, who having no Consideration but that of a present gain, have thro' fear of exposing their own Persons, or hopes of obtaining greater influence with the Indians, continualy employed French Commissarys or Agents, whom they have trusted with Goods for them to Sell at an Advanced price in the Indian Villages.[53]

Gage's suspicions of the French traders were nurtured by Sir William Johnson, who had to keep the Indians on peaceful terms with one another and with the British. It was part of Johnson's function, of course, to worry about possible uprisings and about subversive individuals. His job would be made easier if he could confine all traders to military posts where they could be kept under surveillance. But the traders had little concern for Sir William's preoccupations. If British traders were irresponsible in their desires of "present gain," the Canadian traders' vices were compounded by the uncertainty of their allegiance to the British Crown:

> Since the Reduction of that Country [Canada], we have seen so many Instances of their [the Canadian traders'] Perfidy false Stories & C[a]. Interested Views in Trade that prudence forbids us to suffer them or any others to range at Will without being under the Inspection of the proper Officers agreeable to His Majesty's Appointment ...[54]

Johnson's attitude spread to the officers under him, even though Carleton had found nothing reprehensible in the Canadians' behaviour.[55] Johnson's deputy, George Croghan, believed there was collusion between the French from Canada and the French from Louisiana.[56] In 1763 the commandant at Michilimackinac, Major Etherington, had displayed a similar mistrust of the Canadians.[57] Major Robert Rogers, a later commandant at Michilimackinac, checked the Canadians by trading on his own account.[58]

The British military's mistrust of the French traders from Canada was understandable. Before 1760, one of the major reasons for the American colonials' antagonism towards New France had been the French ability to press the Indians into their service to terrorize the western fringes of American settlement. Thus there was an historical as well as a tactical basis for the military's attitude towards the Canadians. But British officers failed to recognize that not all Canadian traders were potential troublemakers and that there was indeed very little tangible evidence, as Carleton had reminded Johnson, of any mischief on their part. The military's attitude was directed as much by ethnic prejudice as by military necessity.

The Canadian traders could not fail to perceive this prejudice, and it dampened their spirits. Perhaps the military's attitude, as much as competition, forced the Canadians into partnerships with British merchants. (The express purpose of the bonds required for the fur trade was to ensure loyal conduct; what better token of loyalty could there be for a Canadian trader than a bond taken out in his name by a British partner?) The military's mistrust of the Canadian traders did not lessen with time. The advantage which this prejudice gave British traders would continue for some twenty years after the Conquest, as the American Revolution rekindled the military's fears of treasonable conduct by the Canadians.

Other patronage relationships between British military officials and British traders also deprived the Canadians of an equal chance in the competition for furs. It is hard to evaluate precisely the effect of such patronage; only glimpses of it may be caught. Later in 1763 a Philadelphia merchant who had lost heavily because of Pontiac's uprising wrote to William Edgar in Detroit that Croghan was in England where he was to "represent the Case of the Traders to his Majesty" and that General Amherst had "given us his faithful promise that he will do everything in his power in our behalf."[59] In 1765 Alexander Henry was granted the exclusive trade of Lake Superior by Major Howard, the military commandant at Michilimackinac. Nine years later Henry received the support of such patrons as the Duke of Gloucester, the consul of the Empress of Russia in England, and of Sir William Johnson in an ill-fated attempt to mine the iron ore of the Lake Superior area.[60]

These were obvious examples of patronage; other forms of cooperation were less visible. Another correspondent of William Edgar, Thomas Shipboy, asked Edgar to represent him in settling the affairs of a correspondent at Detroit and at Michilimackinac where, he added, "if you find any Difficulty in procuring his effects I dare say the Commanding officer will be of Service to you if you inform him in whose [sic] behalf you are acting ... "[61] Benjamin Frobisher also asked Edgar to "use your Interest with Capt. Robinson" to put a shipment of corn aboard the government vessel which sailed from Detroit to Michilimackinac.[62] Such shipping space was scarce and was only available through the courtesy of military officers or the ships' captains. Here again British traders put their social connections to good use. A last resort was sheer military force. Out on the Miami River, the trader Hamback saw "little hope of getting any thing from [Fort] St. Joseph at all, if I don't get protected, by the Commanding Officer, who might easily get those [Canadian] rascals fetch'd down to Detroit if He would ..."[63]

None of this patronage appears to have been available to Canadians. It is impossible to ascertain the degree to which military suspicions and patronage lessened the Canadians' chances in the fur trade. But more important, perhaps, than the actual loss of opportunities was the psychological handicap imposed upon the Canadians. What heart could they put in the game when the dice were so obviously loaded?

The Merchants' Political Activities

The enmity between British merchants and the military, the merchants' growing agitation in favour of "British liberties" and their sentiments of political self-importance have been ably told by others and need not be retold here.[64] What needs to be underlined is that political agitation was unfamiliar to the Canadians. They had had no experience in these matters under French rule. Only on rare occasions during the pre-Conquest years had the Canadian merchants engaged in collective political representations; such representations were elicited by the Governor or the Intendant to obtain the merchants' advice on specific issues.[65] As French subjects, the Canadian merchants of Montreal had lacked the power to foster their economic interests through collective political action.

After 1760, the Canadian merchants would gradually lose their political innocence under the influence of the British merchants. During the thirty years which followed the Conquest they would make *"l'apprentissage des libertés anglaises"* and in 1792 they would take their place in the newly-created legislative assembly more cognizant of the workings of the British constitution than the British had expected.[66] But that is beyond the concern here. In the years preceding the American Revolution the Montreal merchants were still looking for bearings. They showed their growing political awareness by following in the *Quebec Gazette* the political and constitutional debates which were rocking the British Empire. The merchants also began to voice their concerns in petitions and memorials to the authorities in the colony and in London.

The *Quebec Gazette* was the province's official gazette and its only newspaper before 1778. The paper published public notices for the Montreal district and occasional advertisements sent in by Montrealers as well as matters of concern to Quebec residents. It also made an effort to publish Canadian news of a general character. It closely followed the debates raging across the Atlantic over the Stamp Act and the general issues of colonial taxation. It reported on changes in the Imperial government and on contemporary political issues in England, notably the Wilkes affair.[67]

The pages of the *Gazette* also served on occasion as a forum for political discussion. In September 1765 a "Civis Canadiensis" declared his puzzlement at all the talk of "British liberties" and asked for enlightenment. The following year, a Quebec resident wrote a series of letters arguing that the colony should not be taxed.[68] In 1767, a debate arose on the British laws relating to bankruptcy and their applicability in Quebec.[69] Because of the pressures of Governor Carleton the *Gazette* stifled its reporting of controversial issues after 1770 and thereafter had little to print about American affairs.[70] In 1775 the *Gazette*'s political outpourings were directed against the American rebels and towards securing the loyalty of those Canadians who might be seduced by revolutionary propaganda.[71] The paper had become more conservative in its selection of the news but those Canadians who read the *Gazette* had been made familiar with the concepts of personal liberty, of "no taxation without representation," of the limited powers of the sovereign, and of the rights of the people. The *Gazette*'s readers most probably included the leading merchants of Montreal.

The *Gazette* was not the only instrument for the learning of British liberties. Anxious to give the appearance of a unanimous disposition among all merchants in Montreal, the British merchants often called on their Canadian *confreres* to add their names to various memorials and petitions dealing with the political and the economic state of the colony. The Canadian merchants who signed these petitions and memorials represented the top layer of the Canadian mercantile group in Montreal. Those who signed most often were the import merchants and the busy outfitters.

These Canadian merchants followed the political leadership of the British merchants. From 1763 to 1772 their petitions were either literal translations or paraphrased equivalents of petitions drafted by British merchants. It was only in December 1773 that they asserted views different from those of their British counterparts.[72] They petitioned the king that their "ancient laws, privileges, and customs" be restored, that the province be extended to its "former boundaries," that some Canadians be taken into the king's service, and that "the rights and privileges of citizens of England" be granted to all.[73]

The Canadians were becoming aware of their own position and were seeking to consolidate it against the attacks of the British element. The demand for the maintenance of the "ancient laws" was designed to counter British demands for British laws and representative institutions. The Canadians opposed the latter since, in their view, the colony was "not as yet in a condition to defray the expences of its own civil government, and consequently not in a condition to admit of a general assembly."[74] The demand for "a share of the civil and military employments under his majesty's government" came naturally to those who had lived under the French system of patronage. The Canadians had been accustomed to seek official patronage as the main avenue of upward mobility. The prospect of being denied such patronage was "frightful" to them, since they had little familiarity with alternate patterns of social promotion.[75]

In style as well as in content the Canadian merchants' petitions and memorials revealed differences in attitudes between Canadians and British. British memorials and petitions were rarely prefaced by more than the customary "Humbly showeth" and went directly to the point. In their own memorials and petitions, the Canadians first took "the liberty to prostrate themselves at the foot" of the royal throne and surrendered themselves to the "paternal care" of their sovereign. They often appealed to the wisdom, justice, and magnanimity of the king.[76] Their formal posture of meekness contrasted sharply with the self-assertion of the British. The Canadians' "Habits of Respect and Submission," as one British official put it,[77] may well have endeared them to Murray and Carleton, but those habits constituted a psychological obstacle against their making full use of their new-found "British liberties" to foster their own economic interest.

Conclusion

With the fall of Montreal to British arms in September 1760 something was irrevocably lost to the Canadian merchants of that city. More than the evil effects of the war, the tribulations over the fate of the Canada paper, or the post-war commercial readjustments, the most unsettling consequence of the Conquest was the disappearance of a familiar business climate. As New France passed into the British Empire, the Montreal outfitters were thrown into a new system of business competition, brought about by the very numbers of newly-arrived merchants, unloading goods in the conquered French colony and going after its enticing fur trade. In opening up the trade of the colony to competition, the British presence transformed Canadian commercial practices. The change negated the Canadian merchants' initial advantage of experience in the fur trade and created a novel business climate around them.

Competition in trade, the new political regime, the Canadian merchants' inability to obtain the favours of the military, all these created a mood of uncertainty and pessimism among the Montreal merchants. The merchants could only conclude from what was happening around them that the new business climate of the post-Conquest period favoured British traders at their expense. They can be understood if they were not eager to adapt their ways to the new situation.

It may be argued, of course, that the changes which produced the new situation are subsumed under the notion of "Conquest" and that the previous pages only make more explicit the "decapitation" interpretation advanced by the historians of the "Montreal school."[78] It is true enough that the new business climate described here may not have been created after the Seven Years' War had Canada remained a French possession. But there is no guarantee that other changes would not have affected the Montreal merchants. During the last years of the French regime they had reaped few profits from the fur trade. After the Conquest they continued in the fur trade much on the same scale as before. The Montreal merchants were not "decapitated" by the Conquest; rather, they were faced in very short succession with a series of transformations in the socio-economic structure of the colony to which they might have been able to adapt had these transformations been spread over a longer period of time.

This paper has attempted to show that the fate of the Canadian merchants of Montreal after the Conquest followed from the nature of trade before the Conquest and from the rate at which new circumstances required the merchants to alter their business behaviour. But it should be remembered that the decapitation hypothesis still remains to be tested in the area of the colony's economy which was most heavily dependent upon the control of the metropolis, the import-export trade of the Quebec merchants. Only a detailed examination of the role and the activities of the Quebec merchants, both before and after the Conquest, will fully put the decapitation hypothesis to the test.

Notes

1. Public Archives of Canada [hereafter PAC], C.O. 42, vol. 27, f. 66, Carleton to Shelburne, Quebec, 25 November 1767; quoted in A.L. Burt, *The Old Province of Quebec* (2 vols. Toronto, 1968), 1, p. 142.

2. See Burt, *Old Province*, I, Chapter VI; Dale B. Miquelon, "The Baby Family in the Trade of Canada, 1750–1820" (Unpublished Master's thesis, Carleton University, 1966), pp. 145–46.

3. Francis Parkman, *The Old Regime in Canada* (27th ed. Boston, 1892), Chapter XXI, especially pp. 397–98.

4. W. Stewart Wallace, ed., *Documents Relating to the North West Company* (Toronto, 1934); Wallace, *The Pedlars From Quebec and Other Papers on the Nor'Westers* (Toronto, 1954); E.E. Rich, *The Fur Trade and the Northwest to 1857* (Toronto, 1967); Rich, *The History of the Hudson's Bay Company*, II (London, 1959); D.G. Creighton, *The Empire of the St. Lawrence* (Toronto, 1956).

5. Wayne F. Stevens, *The Northwest Fur Trade 1763–1800* (Urbana, Ill., 1928), p. 25.

6. Fernand Ouellet, *Histoire économique et sociale du Québec 1760–1850* (Montreal, 1966), p. 77.

7. *Ibid.*, pp. 104–6.

8. Michel Brunet, *Les Canadiens après la Conquête, 1759–1775* (Montreal, 1969), pp. 173–74, pp. 177–80.

9. Miquelon, "The Baby Family," p. 158.

10. *Ibid.*, p. 142.

11. The implication is unwarranted. A given economic sector can be dynamic and even produce the largest share of marketable commodities and still provide individual entrepreneurs with meager profits. The macro-economic level of analysis should not be confused with the micro-economic level. Jean Hamelin showed that only around 28 per cent of the profits from the beaver trade remained in Canada. Since the Canadians had an assured market for beaver, one can wonder how much more profitable it was for them to deal in other peltries. See Hamelin, *Economie et Société en Nouvelle-France* (Quebec, 1960), pp. 54–56.

12. The obvious economic explanation for the downfall of the Canadian merchants after the Conquest has to be dismissed. The liquidation of Canadian paper money by France hurt most of all those British merchants who bought it from Canadians for speculation. Canadian merchants had already compensated in part for the anticipated liquidation by raising prices during the last years of the Seven Years' War. Those Montreal merchants who had the greatest quantity of French paper were not driven out of business; on the contrary the most prominent merchants were able to open accounts with British suppliers soon after the Conquest without too much difficulty. See José E. Igartua, "The Merchants and *Négociants* of Montreal, 1750–1775: A Study in Socio-Economic History" (Unpublished Ph.D. thesis, Michigan State University, 1974), Chapter VI.

13. Franquet, *Voyages et mémoires sur le Canada en 1752–1753* (Toronto, 1968), p. 56.

14. For a more elaborate description of the size and the socio-economic characteristics of the Montreal merchant community at this time, see Igartua, "The Merchants and *Négociants* of Montreal," Chapter II.

15. See H.A. Innis, *The Fur Trade in Canada* (Rev. ed. Toronto, 1956), pp. 107–13.

16. See Abraham Rotstein, "Fur Trade and Empire: An Institutional Analysis" (Unpublished Ph.D. thesis, University of Toronto, 1967), p. 72.

17. Innis, *Fur Trade*, p. 117. For his discussion of the impact of war on the fur trade and on New France, see pp. 114–18.

18. In theory, the French licensing system set up to restrict the trade remained in operation from its re-establishment in 1728 to the end of the French regime; only twenty-five *congés* were to be sold each year. In practice, military officers in the upper country could also acquire for a modest fee exclusive trade privileges for their

particular area. With some care, concluded one author, they could make an easy fortune. See Emile Salone, *La Colonisation de la Nouvelle-France* (Trois-Rivières, 1970), p. 390, pp. 392–93. No clear official description of the licensing system was found for the period from 1750 to 1760, but the precise way in which the fur trade was restricted matters less than the fact of restriction.

19. On Charly see PAC, RG 4 B58, vol. 15, 19 September 1764, pass by Governor Murray to "Monsr. Louis Saint-Ange Charly [and his family] to London, in their way to France agreeable to the Treaty of Peace ... "; Archives Nationales du Québec à Montreal [formerly Archives judiciaires de Montréal; hereafter ANQ-M], Greffe de Pierre Panet, 16 août 1764, no. 2190. Trotier Desauniers "Dufy's" will is in *ibid.*, 29 juillet 1760, no. 1168, and Godet's will is in *ibid.*, 28 décembre 1768, no. 3140.

20. The inventory of Monière's estate is in *ibid.*, 28 décembre 1768, no. 3141; that of L'Huillier Chevalier's in *ibid.*, 15 [?] juin 1772, no. 3867.

21. See Alexander Henry, *Travels and Adventures in Canada* (Ann Arbor University Microfilms, 1966), pp. 191–92.

22. W.S. Wallace, *Documents Relating to the North West Company*, Appendix A ("A Biographical Dictionary of the Nor'Westers"), p. 456.

23. See Henry, *Travels*, pp. 1–11, p. 34.

24. *Ibid.*, p. 39.

25. *Ibid.*, p. 50. Cf. the rosier picture painted by Creighton, *The Empire of the St. Lawrence*, p. 33.

26. Henry, *Travels*, pp. 77–84. The Indians killed the British soldiers but ransomed the British traders, giving to each according to his profession.

27. Henry, *Travels*, pp. 264–92.

28. See Wallace, *Documents*, p. 456; Milo M. Quaife, ed., *Alexander Henry's Travels and Adventures in the Years 1760–1776* (Chicago, 1921), pp. xvi–xvii.

29. Henry, *Travels*, p. 11; *Henry's Travels*, p. 12 n. 6.

30. Rich, *History of the Hudson's Bay Company*, II, p. 9.

31. See PAC, C.O. 42, vol. 5, ff. 30–31, Murray's "List of Protestants in the District of Montreal," dated Quebec, 7 November 1765.

32. See Miquelon, "The Baby Family," pp. 181–87.

33. PAC, MG 19 A1, 1, William Edgar Papers, vol. 1, p. 97, F. Hamback to W. Edgar, 2 November 1766. See also *ibid.*, p. 95, Hamback to D. Edgar, 29 October 1766, and pp. 104–6, same to Edgar, 23 March 1767.

34. *Ibid.*, vol. 1, p. 12.

35. See *Ibid.*, vols. 1 and 2.

36. R.H. Fleming, "Phyn, Ellice and Company of Schenectady," *Contributions to Canadian Economics*, IV (1932), pp. 7–41.

37. See Marjorie G. Jackson, "The Beginnings of British Trade at Michilimackinac," *Minnesota History,* XI (September, 1930), 252; C.W. Alvord and C.E. Carter, eds., *The New Regime 1765–1767* (Collections of the Illinois State Historical Library, XI), pp. 300–1; Alvord and Carter, eds., *Trade and Politics 1767–1769* (Collections of the Illinois State Historical Library, XVI), pp. 382–453.

38. See "Extract of a Letter from Michilimackinac, to a Gentleman in this City, dated 30th June," in *Quebec Gazette*, 18 August 1768; see also Rich, *History of the Hudson's Bay Company*, II, p. 26: "The suspicions between the Pedlars [from Quebec], and their encouragements of the Indians to trick and defraud their trade rivals, especially by defaulting on payments of debt, were widespread and continuous."

39. *Quebec Gazette*, 7 January 1768.

40. Burt, *Old Province*, I, p. 92.

41. The flooding of the Quebec market by British merchants was part of a larger invasion of the colonial trade in North America. See Marc Egnal and Joseph A. Ernst, "An Economic Interpretation of the American Revolution," *William and Mary Quarterly*, Third Series, XXIX (1972), pp. 3–32.

42. Quoted in Alvord and Carter, eds., *Trade and Politics*, p. 288.

43. *Ibid.*, p. 38.

44. Quoted in E.E. Rich, *Montreal and the Fur Trade* (Montreal, 1966), p. 44.

45. These figures are somewhat distorted by the inclusion of a single large British investor, Alexander Henry, who outfitted seven canoes worth £3,400 in all. See Charles E. Lart, ed., "Fur Trade Returns, 1767," *Canadian Historical Review*, III (December, 1922), pp. 351–358. The definition of the North West as including Lake Huron, Lake Superior, and "the northwest by way of Lake Superior" given in Rich, *Montreal and the Fur Trade*, pp. 36–37, was used in making these compilations. The French traders were "Deriviere," "Chenville," St. Clair, Laselle, "Guillaid [Guillet]," and "Outlass [Houtelas]."

46. See Rich, *Montreal and the Fur Trade*, pp. 36–37.

47. Jackson, *Minnesota History*, XI, pp. 268–69.

48. Rich, *History of the Hudson's Bay Company*, II, p. 68.

49. On the Monières, see Igartua, "The Merchants and *Négociants* of Montreal," Chapter II. On the Gamelins, see Antoine Champagne, *Les La Vérendrye et les postes du l'ouest (Quebec, 1968), passim.*

50. See R.H. Fleming, *Contributions to Canadian Economics*, IV, 13; on Baynton, Wharton and Morgan, see *The Papers of Sir William Johnson* [hereafter *Johnson Papers*], 14 vols. (Albany, 1921–1965), V, VI, XII, *passim*.

51. PAC, C.O. 42, vol. 2, ff. 277–80, petition of the "Merchants and Traders of Montreal" to Murray and the Council, Montreal, 20 February 1765; *Johnson Papers*, V, pp. 807–15, memorial and petition of Detroit traders to Johnson, 22 November 1767; XII, pp. 409–14, 1768 trade regulations with the merchants' objections.

52. See Alvord and Carter, eds., *The New Regime*, pp. 118–19, and *Trade and Politics*, p. 39, p. 287; see also Stevens, *The Northwest Fur Trade*, p. 44.

53. *Johnson Papers*, XII, p. 517, Thomas Gage to Guy Johnson, New York, 29 May 1768.

54. *Ibid.*, V, p. 481. See also Alvord and Carter, eds., *The New Regime*, pp. 118–19; *Johnson Papers*, V, p. 362; Alvord and Carter, eds., *Trade and Politics*, p. 39; *Johnson Papers*, V, pp. 762–64; XII, pp. 486–87; Stevens, *The Northwest Fur Trade*, p. 28.

55. PAC, C.O. 42, vol. 27, ff. 81–85, Carleton to Johnson, Quebec, 27 March 1767.

56. *Johnson Papers*, XII, pp. 372–75, Croghan to Johnson, 18 October 1767.

57. Henry, *Travels*, pp. 71–72.

58. See PAC, C.O. 42, vol. 26, f. 13, Court of St. James, Conway [Secretary of State] to the Commandants of Detroit and Michilimackinac, 27 March 1766. See also Alvord and Carter, eds., *Trade and Politics*, pp. 207–8, Gage to Shelburne, 12 March 1768; p. 239, Johnson to Gage, 8 April 1768; p. 375, Gage to Johnson, 14 August 1768; p. 378, Gage to Hillsborough, 17 August 1768; p. 384, Johnson to Gage, 24 August 1768; p. 599, Gage to Hillsborough, 9 September 1769. More than trading on his own account, Rogers was suspected of setting up an independent Illinois territory. He was eventually cleared. See "Robert Rogers," *Dictionary of American Biography*, XVI (New York, 1935), pp. 108–9, and *Johnson Papers*, V, VI, XII, XIII, *passim*.

59. PAC, William Edgar Papers, vol. 1, pp. 43–44, Callender to Edgar, n.p., 31 December 1763.

60. Henry, *Travels*, pp. 191–92, p. 235.

61. PAC, William Edgar Papers, vol. 1, p. 90, Thos. Shipboy to Rankin and Edgar, Albany, 21 August 1766.

62. *Ibid.*, p. 201, Benjamin Frobisher to Rankin and Edgar, Michilimackinac, 23 June 1769.

63. *Ibid.*, pp. 104–6, F. Hamback to Edgar, 23 March 1767.

64. The most detailed account is given in Burt, *Old Province*, I, Chapters VI and VII. See also Creighton, *Empire of the St. Lawrence*, pp. 40–48.

65. See for instance E.Z. Massicotte, "La Bourse de Montréal sous le régime français," *The Canadian Antiquarian and Numismatic Journal*, Third Series, XII (1915), pp. 26–32.

66. See Pierre Tousignant, "La Genèse et l'avènement de la Constitution de 1791" (Unpublished Ph.D. thesis, Université de Montréal, 1971).

67. See the *Quebec Gazette* of 15 September 1766 and the issues from June to September 1768.

68. See *Quebec Gazette*, 26 September 1765. Tousignant, "La Genèse," pp. 21–39, points out the political significance of this letter.

69. See texts by "A MERCHANT" in the 10 and 17 December 1767 issues, and rebuttals in the 24 and 31 December 1767 and 7 and 21 January 1768 issues.

70. Tousignant, "La Genèse," p. 39.

71. See issues of 13 and 27 July, and 5 October 1775.

72. Canadian notables of Quebec broke with the "Old Subjects" earlier: a petition, thought to date from 1770 and signed by leading Canadians of that city, asked for the restoration of Canadian institutions. See Adam Shortt and Arthur G. Doughty, *Documents Relating to the Constitutional History of Canada* (2nd ed. Ottawa, 1918) [hereafter *Docs. Const. Hist. Can.*], I, pp. 419–21.

73. The petition and the memorial are reproduced in *Docs. Const. Hist. Can.*, I, pp. 504–6, pp. 508–10.

74. *Ibid.*, I, p. 511. The British merchants of Montreal signed a counter-petition in January 1774, requesting the introduction of an assembly and of the laws of England. See *ibid.*, I, pp. 501–2.

75. Recent historians have highlighted the influence of the military and civil adminis-
trations as sources of economic and social betterment in New France. See Guy
Frégault, *Le XVIIIe siècle canadien* (Montreal, 1968), pp. 382–84; W.J. Eccles, "The
Social, Economic, and Political Significance of the military Establishment in New
France," *Canadian Historical Review*, LII (March, 1971), pp. 17–19; and Cameron
Nish, *Les Bourgeois-Gentilhommes de la Nouvelle-France* (Montreal 1968), *passim*.

76. See PAC, C.O. 42, vol. 24, ff. 72–73v.; *ibid.*, ff. 95–95v; *ibid.*, vol. 3, f. 262; *Docs.
Const. Hist. Can.*, I, pp. 504–8.

77. See *Docs. Const. Hist. Can.*, I, p. 504.

78. Maurice Séguin, of the History Department of the Université de Montréal, was the
first to present a systematic interpretation of the Conquest as societal decapitation. His book, *L'Idée d'indépendance au Québec: genèse et historique* (Trois-Rivières,
1968), which contains a summary of his thought, was published twenty years after
its author first sketched out his thesis. Guy Frégault's *Histoire de la Nouvelle-
France, IX. La guerre de la Conquête, 1754–1760* (Montreal, 1955) is a masterful
rendition of that conflict, cast as the *affrontement* of two civilizations. Michel Brunet,
the most voluble of the "Montreal school" historians, has assumed the task of pop-
ularizing Séguin's thought. See Brunet, "La Conquête anglaise et la déchéance de
la bourgeoisie canadienne (1760–1793)," in his *La Présence anglaise et les Canadiens*
(Montreal, 1964), pp. 48–112. Brunet developed the point further in *Les Canadiens
après la Conquête, I: 1759–1775* (Montreal, 1969). An abridged version of Brunet's
position is provided in his *French Canada and the Early Decades of British Rule,
1760–1791* (Ottawa, 1963). For a review of French-Canadian historiography on the
Conquest up to 1966, see Ramsay Cook, "Some French-Canadian Interpretations of
the British Conquest: Une quatrième dominante de la pensée canadienne-française,"
Canadian Historical Association *Historical Papers*, 1966, pp. 70–83.

MERCHANTS AT THE CONQUEST

John F. Bosher

For most merchants in the Canada trade, the conquest of Canada by Great Britain
in 1759–60 was a catastrophe. But this platitude does not do justice to the complexity of the crisis brought on by the War of the Austrian Succession (1743–48) and
the Seven Years' War (1756–63). The naval and military defeats were partly the
result of weaknesses in a financial system dependent on the credit of government
financiers. Unable to pay its debts and defeated in battle, the government suspended the Canada bills on 15 October 1759 and soon went bankrupt altogether.

These catastrophic events led to three more crises. First, the Crown blamed
the events in Canada, financial and military, on its own officials, and put about
fifty of them on trial in the noisy *affaire du Canada*, which gave the Crown an excuse to reduce its Canadian debts, but publicized the essential corruption of

Bourbon official society. Secondly, most Canada merchants who had not gone bankrupt earlier, notably the big Huguenot merchants, now collapsed one after the other. Thirdly, the Society of Jesus, one of the pillars of the Counter-Reformation, was dragged into the bankruptcy of its Martinique trading firm and assaulted by the Jansenist Parlements. Having abandoned the cause of the Counter-Reformation in the 1750s, the Crown was persuaded to outlaw the Society in 1762–64 at the same time that it was turning its back on that other pillar of the Counter-Reformation, the colony of New France. These events marked a profound change in religious policy that matched the changes wrought by the British government in New France. The Crown began to set itself against the persecution of Huguenots, and to give way to the Atlantic trading society that had grown so powerful in the eighty-five years since the revocation of the Edict of Nantes. Bourbon official society was doomed in old France as well as in New France. So brief a summary of such startling events leaves much to be explained.

Louis XV's government, dogged throughout the mid-century wars by a shortage of funds, was soon unable to pay sailors and their families, or merchants for goods and services, and went bankrupt in October and November 1759.[1] This bankruptcy was not merely a result of momentary weakness owing to unfortunate circumstances or to mistakes in judgement. Nor was it a result, as so many historians have thought, of fighting on too many fronts at once. The French financial system was fundamentally and inherently weaker than those of Great Britain, the Dutch Republic, and even perhaps of Brandenburg-Prussia. Its weaknesses, as I have explained elsewhere, were to bring it before long to the brink of the French Revolution.[2] Already in the 1750s and 1760s the Crown was hampered in its war effort and discredited among its own people, especially its merchants, because it could not pay its way as well as its British, Dutch, and Prussian enemies could.

Merchants in the Canada trade suffered directly from their government's inability to pay. As early as March 1748, a partner in Dugard's *Société du Canada* reported from Paris that Maurepas, the Secretary of State, and Mouffle de Géorville, the naval Treasurer General, kept putting him off with promises. "It seems that we have to have ourselves listed on the *État de distribution*" he wrote. "Furthermore, *chez* Monsieur de Maurepas I saw a list of more than twenty merchants in the same case as we are in ... *C'est le diable pour tirer de l'argent du Roy.*"[3] Ten years later, on 18 October 1758, the Crown appointed five magistrates, the famous "Fontanieu Commission," to examine and settle the debts of the Ministry of Marine and Colonies totalling some 42 million *livres* of which 12 million were for the War of the Austrian Succession (1743–48), 3 million for the inter-war years (1748–55), and 27 million for the years 1755 to 1758. Some officials put the debt much higher than that.[4]

Among the ministry's creditors were most of the shipping merchants in the Canada and Louisbourg trades. These had engaged their ships at one time or another to transport soldiers, munitions, supplies, or food to Canada. When the Crown had engaged certain vessels, such as *La Complaisante, Le Pacquet de*

Londres, Le Cytoen, La Maréchale de Broglie, and *La Badine*, for transport to Canada in 1758, and then delayed and sent the ships to the West Indies, the merchant owners naturally claimed compensation. Not only had the Crown deferred its debt to them, but the Commission set up to deal with these debts now proceeded to reduce many of them on the grounds that the Crown had been a victim of wartime profiteering when it had signed the original contracts. By the end of 1759, the Commission had received creditors' claims to a total of 4,338,734 *livres*, and had cut them down to 3,368,137 *livres*.[5]

This was excessively arbitrary considering that there were two sides to the question of wartime contracts. We know from much scattered evidence that wartime freight rates to Quebec and other transatlantic destinations rose steeply as a result of British naval supremacy. *Paillet et Meynardie* wrote to François Chevalier of Montreal on 26 April 1758, "our enemies are ready to come out with immense forces, with which they threaten to blockade our ports of France, which is very easy for them ... our warships think only of saving themselves ...," etc.[6] Marine insurance premiums rose from about 5 per cent in peacetime to 40 per cent in the early years of both mid-century wars, and by the later years insurance was practically unobtainable in France. "Insurance is eating up profits," Pierre Guy wrote from Montreal as early as 1747.[7] French losses in shipping were extremely heavy, especially in the Seven Years' War. Crews and ships became scarce. Return cargoes could seldom be found, as merchants often complained. As any merchant could see, the wartime shipping market had naturally imposed high freight rates: 240 *livres* and then 400 *livres* per ton soon became normal for Canadian cargoes, this without any profiteering. "Freight rates at Bordeaux amount to 400 *livres* a ton, and it is impossible to buy insurance," Meynardie *jeune* wrote on 19 May 1758.[8] Early the next year, *Paillet et Meynardie* reported from La Rochelle, "We wanted to freight an entire ship for 550 *livres* a ton, but we were refused."[9] Even while the Fontanieu Commission was at work in spring 1760, the Minister approved freight rates to Canada of 400 *livres* per ton.[10]

On receiving objections, argued along these lines, to the Crown's refusal to honour its contracts, the Commission showed a typical eighteenth-century misunderstanding of the inflationary process. Fontanieu himself remarked that merchants who complained were merely piqued at losing their ill-gotten profits. "It seems that the avarice of a considerable number of the merchants at our ports led them to form a sort of conspiracy among themselves to profit from the urgent needs of the Kingdom, and to make immense gains by extorting exorbitant prices for ships which the *ordonnateur* and the Ministers of Marine had to hire (*affréter*) to take defenders and munitions of all kinds to the colonies, and goods which these same merchants supplied for prices just as exorbitant."[11] In this belief the Fontanieu Commission cut down many of the Crown's debts.

Among the debts to merchants were wartime loans to the naval establishments at certain ports. For instance, in 1757 four merchants of Le Havre had lent 124,000 *livres* to the Marine Intendant, Ranché, at 6 per cent annual

interest. Two years later, the Fontanieu Commission was examining the five
credit notes with suspicion, inquiring whether the loans had been authorized
by the minister, and so on. When they decided that 6 per cent interest was
"against the general laws of the State," and that Ranché had no business bor-
rowing on his own personal signature but should have arranged for the naval
treasurer's agent to borrow, they were putting the merchant lenders in an
awkward position.[12] Furthermore, they were ignoring the desperate circumstances that must have driven Ranché, even in 1757, to borrow as he did. We
have no records concerning the treasurer's agent at Le Havre, but the agents
at Lorient and Rochefort were already in difficulties.[13] At the end of the previous war, to take another example, the Intendant at Rochefort had borrowed
126,000 *livres* from various merchants of La Rochelle, the Treasurer General
being some 176,000 *livres* behind in the payments authorized for that port,
and had been begging for permission to borrow a great deal more.[14]

More damaging for the Canada merchants was the government's suspension
and reduction of the Canadian bills; that is, the bills of exchange and promissory notes that had been common currency in Canada. These had long been
issued in all French colonies by the governing authorities in payment for goods
and services. According to the Bourbon financial system, an Intendant or other
responsible official authorized payments in the form of signed *ordonnances* but
did not make payments. To be cashed, an *ordonnance* had to be taken to the
agent of a Treasurer General for Marine and Colonies who was one of those
venal financiers or *comptables* entrusted with the management of all government
funds from the collection of taxes to the payment for goods and services. The
Treasurer General's agent at Quebec might cash *ordonnances* with silver coin
if he had it, as in 1755 and 1756 when coin had been shipped out from France,
but he usually issued his own promissory notes (*billets de caisse*) or the famous
playing-card money which he later took back in exchange for the bills of exchange he would draw once a year on his employer in Paris, the Treasurer
General. These payments in paper need careful study because much nonsense
has been written about them, chiefly in the antiquated belief that the only
sound currency is gold or silver coin.

The Crown paid merchants at Quebec in somewhat the same way that one
merchant paid another. For most debts of more than a few *livres*, merchants
everywhere used some form of paper payment because coin was awkward and
costly to transport, scarce and consequently hoarded, and kept in reserve for a
few special purposes: dowries for daughters marrying or entering convents; advances to the crews of departing ships; occasional household spending to maintain
the family's local credit; and paying certain local debts, such as bills of exchange
presented when due, also in order to maintain personal credit. The credit thus
maintained was the basis for business transactions. Merchants usually opened
current accounts with one another, as with their suppliers far and near, and
their local tradesmen. Accounts were reckoned up and settled periodically.

Otherwise, a payment might be made with a promissory note or a bill of exchange, and these were endorsed from one person to another until they fell due. Most notes and bills—millions of them—were thrown away when they had served their purposes, but in notarial minutes we find copies of those few that were rejected, protested, or not honoured for one reason or another, and these show that this type of payment was scarcely any different from bills drawn by the treasurer's Quebec agent on the Treasurer General in Paris.[15] The only real difference was that the Treasurer General, like a dead, dishonest, or bankrupt merchant, failed to honour the bills drawn on him at Québec. He failed, first, because the Crown could not supply him with the funds he needed and, secondly, because on 15 October 1759 the Crown ordered him to accept no more of them, and publicly suspended all Canadian bills.

This was the first step in a general financial disaster that amounted to the bankruptcy of the French government. On 26 October, the Crown was obliged to suspend the *rescriptions* of the Receivers General of Finance and the notes of the General Farm of Taxes, and on 14 November the notes of the consortium of *Beaujon, Goossens et Compagnie* that had been financing the Marine and Colonies since the beginning of the year. But these were the principal paper currencies with which the Crown had been paying merchants and others in France, the metropolitan equivalent of the Canadian bills. Its paper notes discredited, the government was now bankrupt; that is, unable to pay its debts or to meet its commitments. Had it been a private firm, its creditors would now have assembled to press its debtors, sell its property, cash its other assets, and generally recover whatever they could from the wreckage. That is, in fact, what the revolutionary National Assembly began to do in 1789. In 1759, however, the Crown was still determined to defend itself with its own absolute authority. It dismissed the Controller General of Finances, Étienne Silhouette, on 21 November. By royal decree it defended *Beaujon, Goossens et Compagnie* and the other paying services from prosecution in the courts, took stock of its own debts, decided which to honour and which to repudiate, marshalled the funds accumulating meanwhile from tax revenues, slowly resumed payments with some of the suspended notes, and by such authoritarian means gradually restored its normal financial procedures and the public confidence that depended on normalcy. On 2 February 1760, Berryer told the naval Intendant at Bordeaux to be ready to send to Canada three boxes containing 30,000 printed bills of exchange and 18,000 *billets de caisse* that were to arrive shortly from the director of royal printing, Anisson Duperron.[16] Normal payments were never resumed, however, on the Canadian bills in which so much of the profit from the Canada trade was still held.

For at least three reasons, the Crown made a special case of the Canadian bills. First, Canada being now in British hands, the holders of bills that were still there were likely to become British subjects, and their payment was a contentious diplomatic issue. Secondly, the Crown, unfamiliar with the phenomenon or even the concept of inflation, was convinced that the enormous sums paid out at Quebec during the war had been fraudulent, and acted on that conviction by arresting its officials in the *affaire du Canada*. The third reason was to cut down government debt. The Crown was able to use the *affaire* as a moral justification for deferring and reducing its payments on the Canadian bills. Of the original 90-odd million *livres*, only 37,607,000 *livres* were eventually recognized, and this sum was converted into *reconnaissances* bearing interest at 4 per cent per annum, a rate at which the French government could not borrow on the money markets at the time. This policy had a devastating effect on many of the Canada merchants, and its consequences were also felt throughout Europe. "Nothing has been paid since 18 October 1759," *Paillet et Meynardie* wrote to their Montreal agent on 1 February 1761, "and so long as the war lasts nothing will be paid. At the peace, arrangements will be made but not sooner, from which you see how distressing this is for those who counted on being paid."[17] From the merchants' point of view, this was the most discreditable of the crises that racked France in the years 1759–63, and it was remembered years later on the eve of the French Revolution.[18]

The bankruptcies that ensued among some of the biggest Canada merchants are attributable partly to the suspension of the Canada bills, partly to wartime losses of ships and cargoes, partly to the loss of Canada and Louisbourg, and partly to unpaid accounts of bankrupt debtors. *Bérard et Canonge* of Bordeaux, in whose firm Testas of Armsterdam held a one-third interest, collapsed on 22 November 1759, listing among their bad debts some 3,841 *livres* due from Bossinot, Denel, Giron and Quenel (*sic*), all of Quebec.[19] When Jacques Garesché of La Rochelle went bankrupt on 28 July 1760 he claimed among his assets 12,000 *livres* owing by the Crown for ships rented, 40,000 *livres* owing at St. Domingue, and 23,000 *livres* owing by insurers on *Gracieuse*, seized on 7 February 1758 returning from Canada and St. Domingue. He also claimed a staggering loss of 38,000 *livres* owing by the bankrupt Canada merchant Pierre Blavoust.[20] At Montauban, Étienne Mariette soon went bankrupt, pulling down other merchants with him, and turned over all his assets to his creditors on 18 April 1760.[21] At Bordeaux, Étienne Caussade failed on 2 August 1762.[22] Pierre Boudet was immediately in difficulties in the autumn of 1759, but managed to stave off bankruptcy until 31 December 1764 when his creditors forced him to retire on an allowance of 600 *livres* a year, and his sons went off to seek their fortunes, one to Louisiana, the other to Pondicherry.[23] Simon Lapointe's widow at La Rochelle failed on 9 March 1764, unable to recover from the loss of her well-established trade with friends and relatives in Canada.[24] When the Bordeaux firm of *Fesquet et Guiraut* failed in 1765, they claimed losses of 40,800 *livres* on three vessels sailing to Quebec, *La Fortune*, *Le Rostan*, and the schooner, *Les Bons Amis*.[25]

On 3 March 1766, *Paillet et Meynardie* of La Rochelle reported to their creditors that they were forced to stop making payments owing to "the misfortunes that have affected their trade since the seizure of Canada by the English, either by losses suffered, by the delay of funds in royal paper, of funds in America, or by the scarcity of money which prevents the recovery of what is owing to them."[26] Seven years later, Jean-Mathieu Mounier, who had returned from Canada with a fortune of 300,000 *livres*, intending to continue his trade at La Rochelle, ascribed his bankruptcy of 8 November 1773 to many causes, but prominent among them were the loss of Canada and the Crown's failure to honour the Canadian bills.[27]

The financial collapse of the French government had led directly to the collapse of many Canada merchants, but it had also led indirectly to that end. That is, the war was lost in 1759–60, and Canada was not relieved, partly because the Crown could no longer make payments. By 1758, the war in all its theatres was being fought on credit, not only the organized credit of the Estates of Languedoc, Brittany, and other provinces, but the short-term, haphazard, private credit of the government's own financiers, including the Treasurers General for the Navy and Colonies. As early as 1750, indeed, they had raised a loan of 4 million *livres* that was still outstanding in 1758, by which time the accumulated interest totalled nearly 2 million *livres*.[28] In 1758, the Treasurers General and their agents in the ports were being pressed for more and more payments at a time when they could not recover their money by the usual method of negotiating rescriptions drawn by the Receivers General of Finance on their own agents in provincial towns. The correspondence of Laurent Bourgeois, naval treasurer's agent at the small ports of Lorient and Port Louis, shows him advancing more and more of his own and his friends' money to settle naval debts with such merchants as Robert Dugard of Rouen, whose sailors, he reported, "have been in the most frightful misery for a long time."[29] By October 1758 he was desperately begging for funds and quoting his own advances in thousands of *livres*.

His personal predicament reflected a general situation. A naval official wrote to the Intendant of finance charged with assigning tax revenues to the spending departments, "Our poor navy is already in disorder by its inability to cope with an infinity of essential payments.... "[30] The ministers were particularly alarmed at the enormous sums the colonial Intendants were drawing in bills of exchange. If these bills were ever to be suspended, the Secretary of State for Marine and Colonies wrote to the Controller General of Finance as early as February 1758, the navy would be discredited and unable to carry on.[31] Some of the bigger Canada merchants in France were aware of the danger. "Paper on the treasury is being scorned," Admyrault *fils* wrote to a correspondent at Quebec on 28 January 1759, "No one wants to take it, though it is being paid punctually at maturity. People fear a distressing emergency (*un évènement fâcheux*); may this serve you as a warning."[32]

It was in these difficult circumstances, and to avoid discredit, that the firm of *Beaujon, Goossens et Compagnie* were called in to assist in financing the navy and colonies. At the same time, a merchant banker of Bayonne, Jean-Joseph Laborde (1724–94), was called in to furnish a million *livres* a month to the army by a contract of 3 December 1757; then, by another contract of 13 October 1758, to take charge of military financing in general up to 50 million livres or more a year; and finally, as Court Banker, to pay French diplomats abroad, subsidies to foreign allies, and other such obligations, this beginning on 4 February 1759 with the retirement of the previous Court Banker, Jean Paris de Montmartel.[33] When the crisis came the next autumn, *Beaujon, Goossens et Compagnie* went bankrupt, on 14 November 1759, and Laborde nearly did. The French government, now unable to pay for goods and services, called upon old friends and anyone it could think of in a desperate effort to send out ships and men.

Early in December, the Minister, Berryer, composed a letter proposing to that old friend of the ministry, Abraham Gradis at Bordeaux, that he send a military expedition to Canada disguised as a trading expedition because "at the moment the navy has not enough vessels to detach a force sufficient for that expedition."[34] He soon thought better of this idea, and decided on 10 December not to send the letter. But in January 1760, Berryer hatched another scheme for a privateering expedition to Canada to consist of three ships of the line, a frigate, and two fly-boats to be financed by selling 400 shares worth 4,000 *livres* each and so producing 1,600,000 *livres*. The Crown was to take 150 shares, Gradis 50, and the banking firm of *Banquet & Mallet* were to sell the remaining 200 shares in Paris.[35] This scheme, too, was dropped. The tiny merchant fleet that sailed for Canada from Bordeaux in April 1760 accompanied by *Le Machault*, a royal naval vessel, was a subject of hard bargaining between the minister and some merchants of Bordeaux, notably Lamalétie recently returned from Quebec, to make them pay for as much as possible.[36] In this "violent crisis in French finances," as Berryer afterwards called it, funds were so desperately scarce that he refused all unnecessary expenses, such as a subsidy the Abbé Reignière requested for his new invention of "an inflammable and inextinguishable firework suitable for being thrown by arrows, cannon or mortar on the enemy vessels."[37]

The crisis was compounded by the reluctance of investors to place money in French government funds. Foreign investors tended to avoid French loans. "The last loan in England in December [1759]," Bertin, the new Controller General of Finance, wrote to Miromesnil on 23 June 1760, "was subscribed by capitalists whose funds had been intended for our loans; this is established by details I have from Holland, from Switzerland and from Germany that would make you tremble.... "[38] In a humbler way, French loans were being abandoned in Canada also. When Guy *fils* stopped for a month in London on his way home to Montreal in May 1763, he decided to have Goguet send the family's funds from France so that he could invest them "in the public funds or annuities on the company for which the State is responsible, and therefore nothing is more secure," as he wrote to his mother. "This money will yield at least 3 per cent in the worst circumstances. It would have yielded up to 5 per cent, 10 per cent or even

15 per cent if I had been here two months ago. I might have bought into some of those funds that would have yielded up to 15 per cent and better. There is another advantage. This is that the exchange rate is at thirty-two and one-eighth *deniers sterling* for a crown (*écue*) ... etc."[39]

Canada was lost in battle and in bankruptcy. But it was also abandoned, as historians have pointed out. Choiseul foresaw the possibility of a rupture between Great Britain and its North American colonies once the threat of attack from New France was removed.[40] However, a policy of abandoning Canada, for whatever reason, could only have been adopted by abandoning the religious policy that had sustained the colony since Cardinal Richelieu's time in the early seventeenth century. To Church and State, Canada was a Roman Catholic imperial outpost. The French Church supported the Canadian Church as a mission; most of the Canadian clergy came from France; and the Crown paid them.[41] Supporting Canada and persecuting Huguenots were parts of the same religious policy, much weakened in the eighteenth century, but still established. In the 1750s, however, the Crown gave up its old religious policy. This was a profound change.

The change was first visible when the enlightened Chancellor, Lamoignon, and other royal officials began to urge the bishops to adopt a more lenient policy towards Protestants.[42] The bishops remained firmly opposed to recognizing Protestant marriages and baptisms, but in the middle 1750s—in 1757, according to Dale Van Kley—the Crown washed its hands of the *dévot* clergy's repressive cause and ceased to enforce the declaration of 1724 against Protestants and the edict of 1695 against Jansenists.[43] In the 1750s, Protestants at La Rochelle and Bordeaux were unofficially allowed to worship in private and to keep parish registers for the first time since the seventeenth century. The humiliating brass plaque that a royal Intendant had fixed on the door of the Minimes church at La Rochelle, to celebrate the king's defeat of the town in 1628, was ceremonially removed by royal orders on 1 November 1757.[44] At Versailles during the 1750s, Lamoignon de Malesherbes, the Chancellor's son, directed the government censorship service in a new liberal spirit.[45] In the 1760s, certain ministers and officials of the Crown responded sympathetically to Voltaire's appeal on behalf of the abused Huguenot merchant, poor Jean Calas, and his English Huguenot wife. Here and there during these years, some authorities began to remove the dangers and anxieties that had beset Protestants for more than a century. In the 1770s, the tolerant Turgot and the Protestant Swiss banker, Necker, were destined to become ministers of the Crown, and in 1787, a royal decree was at last to take the first step towards offering Protestants legal recognition as citizens.

Already, thirty years earlier, Huguenot merchants from Canada found Bordeaux and La Rochelle less oppressive than before the War of the Austrian Succession (1743–48). A certain relaxing of the old anti-Protestant laws made life less insecure and less disagreeable. When Jean-Mathieu Mounier returned from Quebec at the Conquest, he lived for a few years like a minor *philosophe*, accumulating a library of some 1,500 works, many of them in several volumes, and a collection of scientific instruments with which he made experiments in the manner of the age. In 1760 and again in 1764–65, he visited several French towns, and he also spent two years in Paris. By 1774 and doubtless earlier, he had learned to use the deists' expression, *"l'être suprême."*[46] For him and other Huguenots, France was becoming less oppressive and less dangerous. In a famous study, Daniel Mornet saw a major change after 1748 when Montesquieu of Bordeaux published his influential *De l'esprit des lois* based on a comparative study of different civilizations.[47] One of Montesquieu's friends, Mathieu Risteau, was a Huguenot merchant at Bordeaux who sometimes sent ships and goods to Canada. Risteau and his wife, Marie Renac, were in close touch with other Huguenot merchants, such as the Goudal, Rauly, and Dumas families. These and their friends cannot have been ignorant of the changing climate of opinion which Montesquieu expressed and which this later phase of Mounier's life illustrates.

One of the forces that helped to create that climate was the famous movement of Jansenists and Richerists among the clergy and magistrates. This movement triumphed just as the Seven Years' War was coming to an end, when the Society of Jesus, so powerful in France and Canada alike, was brought to trial and soon afterwards suppressed.[48] The triumphant followers of Edmond Richer (1560–1631) and Cornelius Jansen (1585–1638) had not forgotten how Louis XIV and the Jesuits had crushed them in obedience to papal orders expressed in bulls like *Unigenitus* (8 September 1713). *Unigenitus* had condemned 101 Jansenist propositions which read like the theology of a Protestant group in favour of simplicity of worship, Bible-reading in the vernacular, the voice of the laity, the power of divine grace, and much else.[49] When Louis XIV died in September 1715, many opponents of *Unigenitus* were recalled from exile or pardoned and began their teaching again, especially in the Faculty of Theology in Paris. In the 1720s and 1730s some tried to bring about a union with the Anglican and Russian Churches.[50] Meanwhile, radical Richerists still in exile, a sort of French presbyterian movement, secretly circulated Jansenist books printed in Holland, and a weekly journal, *Nouvelles ecclésiastiques*, and drew the support of many *parlementaires*.[51]

They eventually succeeded in discrediting their worst enemies, the Jesuits, in a celebrated affair that began in 1755 when British ships seized several French ones that happened to be carrying goods to France for the Jesuit West Indian mission on the island of Martinique. As a result of these losses at sea, the Jesuits' correspondents at Marseille, *Jean Lioncy et Gouffre*, went bankrupt in February 1756. Their assembled creditors tried to make their debtors pay, according to the usual procedures of the times, and soon discovered that the biggest debtor was Antoine de La Valette, the head of the Jesuit mission at St. Pierre, Martinique, who managed large plantations and a considerable transatlantic trade. As the many legal cases arising from this bankruptcy proceeded, de La Valette's superiors and the entire Society of Jesus were dragged in. The Paris Parliament held them responsible for de La Valette's unredeemed bills of exchange and so declared in a decision of 8 May 1761. By then the struggle had blossomed into a noisy political affair in which Jansenist magistrates succeeded in having the Paris Parlement condemn the Society, on 6 April 1761, as illegal and dangerous because of its "vicious nature" and "anarchical, murderous and parricidal doctrines."[52] Other Parlements rallied to this view, and after much deliberation and negotiation, Louis XV and his council issued an Edict in November 1764 which finally suppressed the Society of Jesus throughout the kingdom. Their many houses, colleges, and estates were confiscated, and this once-great Catholic agency disappeared from France, and, after Clement XIV's encyclical, *Dominus ac Redemptor Noster* (21 July 1773), from the world. One of the greatest pillars of the Counter-Reformation, and of clerical power in New France, had been laid low.

This great revolution—for such it was—fascinated all observers at the time. A clerk in the offices of the Treasurer General of the Marine reported on it to the Treasurer's agent at La Rochelle, while also reporting news of the *affaire du Canada*. "Monsieur de Vaudreuil, Governor-General of Canada, was put in the Bastille a few days ago," he wrote on 3 April 1762, "and they say he was arrested with fifteen other people who are not named. That is all the news I can tell you except about the Jesuits who are at last *[outus]*. They shut up shop on the first of this month and they are all in their house on the rue Saint Antoine."[53] The suppression of the Jesuits was a step towards the destruction of the Church's power that was accomplished in Canada at this time by the British conquest, and in France thirty years later by the French Revolution.[54]

While the affair of the Jesuits was in full swing, another affair held the French administration of Canada up to public scrutiny in a general arrest and investigation of some fifty colonial officials. This, the famous *affaire du Canada*, exposed the greedy machinations of the Intendant, the naval controller, the purveyor, a long list of king's storekeepers and military and naval officers.[55] The Minister of Marine and Colonies, a former Lieutenant-General of Police, was already talking in 1759 of giving orders "to stop the calamities that bad administration has brought upon that colony, or at least to have those who have taken part in them punished."[56] For the observing public, this affair began on 17 November 1761 when the Purveyor General, Cadet, and the Intendant, Bigot, were arrested with many other officials from New France, high and low, about the same time. On 12 December, a commission or tribunal of the Châtelet criminal court was named to investigate and to judge the various crimes of which the arrested men were to be accused.

During the next two years, a very black picture of the colonial administration was gradually revealed and summed up at last in the final judgement of 10 December 1763, printed and published in many copies. Bigot was banished from the realm forever, Bréard for nine years, and immense fines were imposed on most of the principal accused in order to extract their ill-gotten gains from them. Meanwhile, other colonial officials were under scrutiny, and several were arrested, denounced, and sentenced to various punishments. For instance, the treasurer's agent in Louisiana, Destrehan, was dismissed in 1759, and their former agent at Louisbourg, Jean Laborde (1710–81), for many years a busy transatlantic shipping merchant on the side, was imprisoned in the Bastille on 16 March 1763 and held until 25 August 1764 after he had signed over all his assets to the Crown in a detailed notarial document.[57] The Intendant at Martinique and such scriveners in his service as Lachenez were suspected of trading and cheating like their colleagues in Canada.[58]

The *affaire du Canada* was intended to persuade the French public that the defeat of the French forces in Canada was owing to corrupt, self-seeking officials. The *affaire* was timed, furthermore, to coincide with the negotiations that ended with the ignominious Peace of Paris signed on 10 February 1763. If much public opinion easily blamed the condemned officials, some observers saw them as mere scapegoats for the failures and misdeeds of higher officials and financiers in Paris. "You know that the Sieur Cadet, Purveyor General in Canada, has been put in the Bastille," wrote François Havy to Robert Dugard on 14 February 1761. "There are at present a great many in Paris who would deserve it much more than he because they were the cause of the trouble."[59] In the words of Mouffle d'Angerville, nephew of a Treasurer General for the Marine and Colonies, the government made scapegoats of the Canadian officials because it was "too weak to attack the abuses at their source and to punish the big culprits."[60] The biggest "culprit" of all, as the revelations of these *affaires* suggested, was Bourbon society itself, anchored as it was to the absolute authority of Church and State.

When the trade and graft of royal officials and financiers was shown together with the official and financial connections of Catholic merchants, the fabric of Bourbon society appeared as tainted with corruption as Guy Frégault, Cameron Nish, and others have presented it.[61] But most Huguenot or New Convert merchants had only the most superficial connection with it, and were scarcely part of it all, being social outcasts. The principal exceptions to this general statement were a few New Converts like François Maurin, Pierre Glemet, and Abraham Gradis. Maurin's name appears in connection with the depredations of the officer, Péan, the Purveyor General, Cadet, the Intendant, Bigot, and several king's storekeepers. A relative of the Mouniers, Maurin had served as Cadet's Montreal manager under Péan's direction from 1756 to 1760, married a Dagneau Douville de Quindre in 1758, generally blended with Bourbon society, and returned to France in 1760 with a fortune of nearly 2 million *livres*. He was sentenced with the rest, banished from Paris for nine years and heavily fined. So well did he mix with Bourbon society that his twentieth-century biographer apparently did not know he was a Huguenot.[62]

Glemet had a somewhat similar connection with the condemned officials, though he made less profit and accordingly suffered less. Abraham Gradis had been deeply involved with Bigot, Bréard, and the rest, and was saved from incrimination only by Choiseul's repeated intervention on his behalf. On 12 October 1762, for instance, Choiseul wrote to Sartine to stop any further investigation of Gradis' affairs: "I desire that the last documents Sieur Gradis sent me, and which I gave you yesterday, should suffice for Messieurs the Commissioners."[63] Gradis had served the Crown during the war, as well as the colonial officials, and was to go on being useful to Choiseul in the future. But such cases as these were exceptions. The few Jews and Huguenots who had been in business with the condemned officials from Canada had not been related to them in the way that Catholic merchants had. Merchants such as those whom Cadet had used as his correspondents at Bordeaux and La Rochelle had not intermarried with officials and financiers.

Choiseul and Sartine thought well enough of several New Converts during the *affaire* to consult them in establishing standard prices for the decade 1749–59. By an order of 6 September 1762, the Châtelet court in Paris and the *Présidial* court at La Rochelle ordered the police to consult *Meynardie frères*, Thouron the younger, François Havy, Admyrault, and Jean-Mathieu Mounier.[64] The Catholic, Soumbrun, was mentioned, but not consulted. At Montauban, the Huguenot merchants Pierre de Lannes, Jean-Jaques Gauthier, and Joseph Rouffio were also trusted in establishing standard prices.[65] One Catholic merchant, but only one, Lamalétie of Bordeaux, was asked for his account books.[66] Thus, in seeking honest merchants seriously engaged in the Canada trade, but not too deeply involved with the criminal officials of the colony, the Crown eventually consulted seven Huguenots and only one Catholic. We can easily see why as we follow the French authorities in their investigation of the Canadian officials and their business partners, merchants such as Guillaume Estèbe, Jean-Patrice Dupuy, Denis Goguet, Louis Pennisseault, Lemoine Despins, and the many who had become king's storekeepers.

Much of their shady business is revealed in the biographies of Estèbe, Pennisseault, Bréard, Cadet, Bigot, and others in the *Dictionary of Canadian Biography*, volume iv (Toronto, 1979). By way of example, let us here sketch the business dealings of one who does not appear therein, Jean-Patrice Dupuy (1732–86) of Bordeaux. He served his cousin, Lamalétie, and Lamalétie's partner, Admyrault, as a commission agent at Montreal from 1754 to 1756; and in 1757, back in Bordeaux, he sent consignments of merchandise out to Lamalétie and Estèbe, still in Quebec.[67] Meanwhile, on 20 October 1756 he formed a company with Péan, the notorious adjutant at Quebec, and Jean-Baptiste Martel, the royal storekeeper at Montreal. It was a transatlantic trading company founded for seven years beginning on 1 January 1757 under the name of *Dupuy fils et compagnie,* and Dupuy directed it and had a one-third interest in it representing 133,333 *livres* of the total capital fund of 400,000 *livres,* whereas

Péan had a one-quarter interest, or 100,000 *livres* investment. It seems that Martel was to put up five-twelfths of the capital fund and hold the largest interest, but in any event the company dissolved on 14 May 1760 and re-formed without Martel on the basis of an equal sharing of profits and losses. This new partnership was to continue without term until either Péan or Dupuy decided to withdraw, and when at last they wound up their affairs on 30 May 1768, Dupuy in effect bought out Péan with payments totalling just over 51,000 *livres* and a promise to take over all the company's debts as well as its assets.[68]

Long before this, in 1759, even before the Crown had begun to prosecute the Canadian officials and others of the *grande société*, Dupuy had begun to serve as a business agent for two of those officials who were later arrested, prosecuted, and sentenced to heavy fines. For one of them, the aforementioned Martel, Dupuy purchased for 100,000 *livres* a furnished house "with six statues in the garden, each on its pedestal, a little mutilated and blackened by time," in the expensive Chartrons district of Bordeaux, this in his own name to conceal the identity of Martel for whom he acted as *prête-nom*.[69] And three years later, after Martel's arrest, Dupuy rented the house for him to another Bordeaux merchant for seven years at a rent every six months of "3,800 *livres* while the present war lasts and 4,500 *livres* in peacetime." Meanwhile, by a formal agreement of 9 February 1760, Martel paid another 100,000 *livres* for a one-third interest in Dupuy's share in the *Régie ou ferme générale des droits réunis*, a tax-collecting agency founded in September 1759 by the Controller General of Finance to help in meeting the financial crisis of the time. Already, on 20 October 1759, Dupuy had sold another third interest, also for 100,000 *livres*, to Jean-Victor Varin de la Mare, the notorious former *commissaire de la Marine* at Montreal. A royal commission set up to deal with the property of Bigot, Varin, and the other major criminals of the *affaire du Canada* traced this transaction in 1764 and soon recovered from Dupuy what he still held of Varin's 100,000 *livres*, but I have no evidence that they knew of Martel's share.[70]

As if this were not enough, on 31 December 1760 Dupuy went to one of the business agents (*prête-nom*) of Péan and Bigot, and others from Canada, a certain Nicolas-Félix Vaudive, who was an *avocat au Parlement et greffier de l'audience du grand conseil du Roi*, and the son of a merchant jeweller and goldsmith of Paris, and borrowed 50,000 *livres* to invest in the tax farm of the *Devoirs de Bretagne*. The Crown confiscated this sum in 1764 as being part of Bigot's estate and Dupuy handed it over.[71] Another of Dupuy's unsavoury business arrangements showing how widely he cast his net in the field of maritime and colonial business was made in 1762 with a well-known financier, the *régisseur des économats*, Marchal de Sainscy, who managed the Crown's funds from vacant benefices and other ecclesiastical property. De Sainscy took a one-quarter interest in a project of Dupuy's for buying large quantities of the sort of merchandise that would sell in the colonies, and two ships, *Le Casque* and *Le Cheval Marin*, but by 1771 this project had proved to be a failure.[72]

Notwithstanding Dupuy's shady dealings with officials arrested in the *affaire du Canada*, he was not himself arrested. But he was denounced to the investigating commission, evidently by someone who knew much about his affairs. The denunciation illustrates the hostile public feelings the *affaire du Canada* aroused against what I have called, for convenience, Bourbon official society. It runs,

> The most important man to arrest in the *affaire du Canada* is a certain Dupuy, merchant, living at Bordeaux in the Chartron quarter, formerly a clerk in Canada. He is the secret confidential agent of Messieurs Bigot, Péan, Varin, and Martel. It is he who has cashed for them, in France and here the Treasury bills of exchange they have entrusted to him.
>
> He used to return to France almost every year with these gentlemen's papers. He would collect the sums from the Treasurer General and with that money would buy a prodigious quantity of notes of the royal lottery. He has bought thirteen millions worth of thousand-*livre* shares in the general farms [of taxes] from the late Monsieur du Vergier, cashier to Monsieur de Montmartel. He has bought all the good bearer notes (*papier au porteur*). He has bought land for these gentlemen. He has bought Martel's house in Bordeaux which is rented in his name. In a word, that man is informed of all the money they have invested. The Commission would learn more from that man alone in a week than they could learn in six months by a lot of research.[73]

Dupuy was one of those Canada merchants from a family that was a part of Bourbon official society, related to the Lee, O'Quin, and Bennet families who had come to Bordeaux from Ireland in the seventeenth century, and related also to the Lamalétie family which had married into the Foucault family of officials in Canada. He was typical, then, of the merchants linked in business and marriage with officials and financiers.[74]

To sum up, France lost Canada in the course of financial, military, and religious crises that simultaneously undermined Bourbon official society by revealing its weaknesses. The Crown went bankrupt, owing to faults in the financial system from which the English and Dutch systems did not suffer. The ministry blamed the huge Canadian debts and the loss of the colony on the rapacity of its own officials, and tried them in a noisy affair that revealed widespread corruption in Bourbon official society. The odium this trial brought upon the colonial administration helped the Crown to abandon New France without losing face altogether. When the Crown gave up Canada it was turning its back on a Roman Catholic imperial mission, and it could do this in the 1750s because it had at last given up leading the Counter-Reformation. As another result of the same change, the Crown also abandoned the Society of Jesus to its enemies and eventually banished it. As the Age of the Enlightenment dawned, Bourbon official society, always founded on royal policy, began to crumble. The old differences between Catholic and Protestant merchants were ceasing to matter in old France as well as in what had been New France.

***

Conclusion

France gave up Newfoundland and Acadia in 1713 and the rest of New France half a century later. This was the same half-century in which the aggressive Roman Catholic empire of Louis XIV was transformed into the crumbling, tolerant monarchy of the pre-revolutionary Enlightenment. At the beginning of it, Catholic families with branches on both sides of the Atlantic had a monopoly of trade and shipping to New France; at the end, Huguenot families had a large share, perhaps most of it. At the beginning, the typical Canada merchant was a man with relatives in the magistracy, in the priesthood, in the ranks of the government financiers, and so was part of the society that had formed around the ruling families at court, part of the hierarchy of patronage created by the Bourbon kings. At the end, the typical Canada merchant was related to other merchants in Amsterdam, London, Hamburg, Geneva, even Boston, and some belonged to the cosmopolitan world of maritime business that had grown up in the Protestant seaports. In the early eighteenth century Church and State kept Protestant merchants out of the Canada trade unless they disguised themselves as Roman Catholics; in mid-century the State abandoned the Church's cause, even abandoned the Society of Jesus, and tolerated Protestants who conformed to Catholic practices.

A social study of merchants in that half-century, those in the Canada trade at any rate, shows basic religious differences. Most Huguenots and Catholics, like most Jews, married within their own religious communities. A marriage in that age was a family treaty based on a negotiated contract, just as a business partnership was. Contracts in marriage or in business were usually founded on the trust that grew out of a common religious tradition. For merchants, the two religious traditions were, moreover, profoundly different in that French Catholics were part of the approved, legal society of Bourbon France in which the clergy were extremely powerful. French Protestants, on the other hand, were outcasts and outlaws who survived by submitting themselves and their children to Catholic baptism, marriage, and other sacraments.

The two traditions were politically different also: a Catholic merchant belonged to the authoritarian hierarchy of Church and State; whereas a Huguenot merchant was part of the Calvinist or reformed Church that had no priestly hierarchy and had not submitted to secular authority. In addition, the Huguenot merchant had strong ties with the communities of Huguenot refugees in Protestant cities. Merchants had a strong voice in the governments of those cities, and also in the central governments of Holland and Great Britain. The cosmopolitan business world of those countries, which for convenience we may call Atlantic trading society, was much freer than society in France, where Church and State censored the press, interfered in municipal government, and even controlled people's movements between France and the colonies. Religious differences were thus linked with different political traditions.

The Huguenot merchants who stayed in France did so for a variety of reasons. Some were from families too poor and numerous to emigrate. Lands and houses, kith and kin, kept others in those Huguenot communities which survived collectively at La Rochelle, Bordeaux, Rouen, Nîmes, Montauban, Paris, and other towns. The *abjuration* or "conversion" that was rewarded with official posts or advantageous marriages kept some in France, apparently "New Converts" but often merely trimming to the political winds and hoping for better times later. Historians have been too quick to think that any Huguenot who abjured had truly converted. Then, in the eighteenth century many Huguenots found profit in their position as French "agents" of Atlantic trading society. With relatives in the ports of the Protestant Baltic and North Sea, and the Protestant Atlantic, they were well-placed to export wine and brandy, woollens, furs, and colonial sugar, and to import American tobacco, Baltic naval stores, and Irish foodstuffs. These trading families found life easier in France as persecution died down gradually here and there after Louis XIV's death.

The Canada trade was opened to them, it is clear, in the 1730s. In the 1740s the Crown began to call on them, and on Jews also, to transport men, munitions, and foodstuffs to the colonies. Long wars at sea against heavy odds drove the French ministers to rely more and more on New Converts with their foreign trading networks and their ample resources. Religious scruples began to be set aside, and the Canada trade became increasingly cosmopolitan, less and less in the hands of the old Catholic trading families. German, Swiss, and Austrian fur buyers began trading with New France. The established Catholic families were hard-pressed. Those who could—Pascaud, Goguet, Lamalétie, Trottier Désauniers—bought offices and married their children to noble or office-holding families, which had always been their inclination in any case. Others failed and went bankrupt: Bourgine, Blavoust, Soumbrun, Jung, Guillaume Pascaud, and more. Still others carried on in partnership with government officials in Canada, as indeed did a few New Converts, Jewish and Protestant.

Army officers, naval officers and storekeepers, and government financial agents had always traded in the colonies, adding to their meagre and uncertain emoluments by using their power for profit. They have to be counted as part-time merchants in any serious study of the Canada trade. After all, officials and financiers dominated the business life of Paris and the great monopoly companies, and had much authority in Bourbon official society. The mid-century wars offered them unprecedented opportunities in New France, where the Crown was spending more and more in the imperial cause. In old France, too, agents of the Treasurers General of Finance went into maritime trade. Government financiers invested in privateering ventures or speculated, like Prévost, in marine insurance.

The French government depended on its financiers for loans as well as for services, and in the Seven Years' War strained their resources beyond the limit. Efforts to supplement the financiers' resources with the funds of merchant bankers could not save the rickety Bourbon credit system, and its collapse in autumn

1759 began on 15 October when it suspended the Canadian bills. As a result, the Crown could no longer send out ships and men, or command the services of merchants in the Canada trade. Nor could it pay its debts to them. Added to the cruel blow of the colony's loss to Great Britain, the government's bankruptcy set off a series of failures among the Canada merchants. To save money and to save face, the government blamed its own officials in Canada for the Canadian debts and defeats. The trial of these scapegoats revealed much corruption in Bourbon official society, and some of the big merchants were implicated.

The revelations of the notorious *affaire du Canada*, beginning in 1761, helped the government to turn its back on New France, an expensive white elephant it then seemed, and no efforts were made to recover the colony thereafter. The Huguenots who stayed in Canada suddenly found themselves free and respectable, eligible for offices from which Catholics were now excluded. But the trade between New France and old France was just as suddenly stopped. Many a cargo intended for Canada, in a warehouse at La Rochelle or Bordeaux, had to be disposed of elsewhere. "There is still no news concerning the shipping of the merchandise in storage here belonging to Canadians," Goguet wrote from La Rochelle to Madame Guy at Montreal on 1 May 1763, and went on to explain that the British government would allow no such shipments.[75]

Suddenly passengers between Canada and France had to go by way of British ships and British ports, like young Guy who spent some weeks in London in May 1763 on his way home to Montreal from La Rochelle, "which will give me the time," he wrote to his mother, "to make acquaintances here, which is very easy to do."[76] Suddenly the ships in the Canada trade were British or British-American ships, such as the *Nettleton* which reached Dartmouth from Quebec on 1 January 1760, the *Experiment* which landed on the same day in Virginia, having come from Quebec, and the *Peter Beckford* which landed at New York on 11 January; and the sixteen vessels at the Downs, not far from London, announced by *Lloyd's List* on 11 April 1760 as "remains for Quebec." The ports in the Canada trade were soon established as London, Bristol, Cowes, Falmouth, Plymouth, Cork, Greenock, and a dozen colonial ports. The Canada merchants now had names like William and Robert Hunter, William and John Grant, John Schoolbred, Robert Ellice, James Phyn & Co., Muir & Co., Buchanan, and John Cochrane.[77] But theirs is another story.

Notes

1. These financial difficulties of the French government I have discussed in various articles such as "Les Trésoiriers de la Marine et des Colonies sous Louis XV: Rochefort et La Rochelle," *Revue de la Saintonge et de l'Aunis*, tome v (1979), pp. 95–108, "The French Government's Motives in the *affaire du Canada*, 1761–63," *English Historical Review*, vol. xvci (1981), pp. 59–78; and "Financing the French navy in the Seven Years' War: *Beaujon, Goossens et Compagnie*," *Business History* (London), vol. 28 (July 1986), pp. 115–33.

2. J.F. Bosher, *French Finances 1770–1795: From Business to Bureaucracy* (Cambridge, 1970), 370 pp.

3. AN, 62 AQ 35, France (Paris) to Dugard (Rouen), 14 Mar. 1748 and 28 Apr. 1748.

4. Henri Legohérel, "Une Commission extraordinaire du Conseil d'État du Roi: La Commission de Liquidation des Dettes de la Marine et Colonies (1758–68)," *Faculté de Droit et Sciences économiques de Dakar* (Paris, 1968), 32 pp., and AN, Colonies E 45, "Précis concernant la dette du Roy pour le Canada (29 June 1764)"; BN, ms. fr. 11340, Le Normand de Mézy.

5. BN, ms. fr. 11337, Berryer to Fontanieu, 18 May 1759; BN, ms. fr. 11338, Fontanieu to Berryer, 31 Dec. 1759.

6. Bibl. mun. de La Rochelle, ms. 1954.

7. Université de Montréal, Collection Baby, U 5113.

8. *Ibid.* U 8503; AN, Colonies, B 108, Minister to the Marseille Chamber of Commerce, 18 Feb. 1758.

9. Collection Baby, U 9256 (1 Feb. 1759).

10. J.F. Bosher, *Business and Religion in the Age of New France, 1600–1700: Twenty-two Studies* (Toronto, Canadian Scholars' Press, 1994), Chapter 21, "Shipping to Canada in Wartime," pp. 464–486.

11. BN, ms. fr. 11336, fols. 14 ff.

12. BN, ms. fr. 11337, Fontanieu to Berryer, 27 Apr. 1759.

13. Arch. de la Marine, Lorient, 1E5 I, Laurent Bourgeois (Lorient) to de Selle (Paris), 14 June 1758.

14. Arch. de la Marine, Rochefort, 1E 145, Maurepas to de Givry, 14 July 1748 and 17 Nov. 1748.

15. I have found copies of about forty such bills of exchange from Quebec in the minutes of half a dozen Bordeaux notaries between 1716 and 1756: Bernard, Lagénie, Lamestrie, Parran, Rauzan, and Séjournée *l'ainé*.

16. AN, Colonies B 112, fol. 35, Min. to Rostan, 2 Feb. 1760.

17. Bibl. mun. de La Rochelle, ms. 1954, *Paillet et Meynardie* (La Rochelle) to François Chevalier (Montréal), 1 Feb. 1761.

18. Simon-Joseph-Louis Bonvallet des Brosses, *Moyens de simplifier la perception et la compatibilité des deniers royaux*, 1789 (Bibliotheque nationale Lb^{39} 7248), p. 89 note.

19. ADG, 7 B 428; Butel, "La Croissance commerciale," vol. i, pp. 176, 687–88.

20. A.D. Ch. Mar., Fredureaux-Dumas (LR), 28 July 1760, *Traité du sieur Jacques Garesché ..., [sic]*.

21. A.D. Tarn-et-Garonne, David Delmas (Montauban), 22 Dec. 1762, *Accord*, 13 pp.

22. ADG, 7 B 528.

23. A.D. Char. Mar., 4J 5, notes Garnault, and Tardy (LR), 31 Dec. 1764 to 16 June 1765, *abandon de biens*.

24. A.D. Ch. Mar., Tardy (LR), 9 Mar. 1764, *abandon de biens*.

25. ADG, 7 B 429. For details of these and other voyages, see J.F. Bosher, *Men and*

Ships in the Canada Trade: A Biographical Dictionary (Ottawa: Environment Canada, 1992), *passim.*

26. A.D. Ch. Mar., Tardy (LR), 3 and 10 Mar. 1766, *Réunion des créanciers*, 7 pp.

27. A.D. Ch. Mar., B 1757, *État à peu près ….*

28. AN, f⁴ 1008, *Mémoire: situation du Sieur de Géorville*, 3 Feb. 1762; Armand Rébillon, *Le États de Bretagne de 1661–1789* (Paris, 1932), p. 730, shows six million *livres* lent to the Crown in 1758 and another six million in 1760, all at 5 per cent interest.

29. Arch. de la Marine (Lorient), 1 E⁵ 1, Bourgeois to Mouffle de Géorville, 23 Jan. 1758 etc.

30. AN, Colonies B 108, Le Normand de Mézy to Boullogne, Intendant of Finance.

31. AN, Colonies B 108, fols. 64–67. By April 1758, the Treasurers General for the Colonies were unable to find a million *livres* to pay Simon Darragory, a French merchant in Spain, for shiploads of food sent to Canada on Spanish ships with false neutral passports.

32. Université de Montréal, Collection Baby, U 21.

33. On *Beaujon, Goossens et Cie* see Bosher, "Financing the French navy"; Laborde's career is explained in his memoirs, edited by Yves-René Durand, in *Annuaire-Bulletin de la Société de l'Histoire de France, année 1968–1969* (Paris, 1971), pp. 75–162.

34. AN, Colonies B 110, Berryer to Gradis, a letter dated only December 1759 with a note added, "Le 10 Dec. 1759 monseigneur a suspendu l'expédition de cette lettre et de l'état dont il y est question."

35. Jean de Maupassant, "Abraham Gradis et l'approvisionnement des colonies (1756–63)," *Revue historique de Bordeaux*, 2e année (1909), pp. 250 ff.

36. AN, Colonies B 112, *passim* from Jan. to Apr.

37. AN, Marine B² 362, Berryer to Regnières, 23 Nov. 1759.

38. Marcel Marion, *Histoire financière de la France* (Paris, 1914), vol. i, p. 209.

39. Université de Montréal, Collection Baby, U 5065, Guy (London) to Mme Guy (Mtl.), 20 May 1763.

40. For example, Marcel Trudel, *Louis XVI, Le Congrès américain et le Canada, 1774–1789* (Quebec, 1949).

41. Guy Frégault, *Le XVIIIᵉ siècle canadien* (Montreal, 1968), ch. 3, "L'Église et la société canadienne"; Cornelius J. Jaenen, *The Role of the Church in New France* (Toronto, 1976), ch. 3.

42. Grosclaude, *Malesherbes*, ch. 15, "Les Affaires des Protestants."

43. Dale Van Kley, *The Damiens Affair and the Unravelling of the ancien régime, 1750–1770* (Princeton, 1984), pp. 269, 351 note 17; and see above, pp. 116–18.

44. Père B. Coutant, *Les Minimes* (La Rochelle, 1968), ch. 4, "L'Affaire des plaques."

45. Grosclaude, *Malesherbes*, ch. 3.

46. A.D. Ch. Mar., B 1757, *État à peu près de mes malheureuses affaires*, 28 Jan. 1774.

47. Daniel Mornet, *Les Origines intellectuelles de la Révolution française, 1715–1787* (1933), 4th ed. (Paris, 1947), part ii, ch. 1, p. 71; ADG, Rauzan (Bx.), 27 Oct. 1753; Bernard (Bx.), 7 Aug. 1718, marriage contract of Risteau and Renac.

48. Jean Egret, "Le Procès des Jésuites devant les Parlements de France 1761–1770," *Revue historique*, vol. cciv (1950), pp. 1–27; D.G. Thompson, "The Fate of the French Jesuits' Creditors under the ancien régime," *English Historical Review*, vol. 91 (1976), pp. 255–77.

49. Anne Fremantle, *The Papal Encyclicals in their Historical Context* (NY, 1956), p. 99.

50. Edmond Préclin, *Les Jansenistes du XVIIIᵉ siècle et la Constitution Civile du Clergé* (Paris, 1929), p. 545.

51. *Ibid.*, p. 132.

52. Van Kley, *The Jansenists and the Expulsion of the Jesuits from France*, pp. 92, 134.

53. A.D. Ch. Mar., B 4055, Couteau (Paris) to Brunet de Béranger (LR), 3 Apr. 1762.

54. Hilda Neatby, *Quebec, The Revolutionary Age, 1760–1791* (Toronto, 1961), 300 p. p.19; Marcel Trudel, *L'Église canadienne sous le régime militaire, 1759–1764*, 2 vols. (Quebec, 1956–57).

55. Bosher, "The French Government's Motives in the *affaire du Canada, 1761–63*."

56. AN, Colonies B 110, fol. 220, Berryer (Paris) to Péan (Que.), 22 July 1759.

57. AN, MC, Étude XXXIII 553, 12 July 1764, *Compte de transport de créance au Roy le Sieur La Borde*.

58. AN, Colonies B 111, fol. 65, Minister to Le Mercier de la Rivière, 13 Oct. 1761 and 31 Oct. 1761.

59. AN, 62 AQ 36, Havy to Dugard, 14 Feb. 1761.

60. Moufle d'Angerville, *Vie privée de Louis XV*, vol. iv, p. 71.

61. Frégault, *François Bigot, Administrateur francais*; Nish, *Les Bourgeois-gentilshommes de la Nouvelle-France, 1719–1748*.

62. *DCB* vol. iii, pp. 441–42.

63. Bibl. de l'Arsenal (Paris), Bastille ms. 12, 145, fols. 83–84, 323, 374; Bibl. nat., ms. fr. 11338, Berryer to Fontanieu, 25 Jan. 1760.

64. A.D. Ch. Mar., B 1796, *Procès-verbal destinés des négotiants faisant le commerce du Canada*, 14 Sept. 1762, 35 pp.

65. Bibl. de l'Arsenal, Bastille ms. 12, 144, fol. 162, Choiseul to Sartine, 28 June 1762.

66. ADG, 3 B 248, Sénéchaussée-présidial, *Procès-verbal transport*, 14 Sept. 1762, 5 pp.

67. Dupuy's story is told in another context in J.F. Bosher, "A Quebec merchant's Trading Circles in France and Canada: Jean-André Lamalétie before 1763," *Histoire sociale* (Ottawa), vol. ix (1977), pp. 24–44.

68. ADG, Faugas (Bx.), 30 May 1768, *Cession et dissolution de Sossiété (sic) Péan et Dupuy*, 8 pp.

69. ADG, Guy (Bx.), 16, 17 Feb. 1769, and 8 oct. 1762.

70. AN, MC, Étude XXX, 9 Feb. 1760, *société*, and 20 Oct. 1759, *société* with attached notes; V⁷ 353, entry for 3 Apr. 1764.

71. AN, MC, étude LVII, 8 May, 31 Dec. 1760, and 20 Feb. 1761.

72. AN, MC, Cordier (Paris), 18 Mar. 1771, *procuration* of which a copy in ADG, Faugas (Bx.), 6 Apr. 1771.

73. Bibl. de l'Arsenal, Bastille ms. 12, 145, fol. 6; 12, 143, fol. 313.

74. Bosher, "A Quebec Merchant's Trading Circles," genealogical chart.

75. Université de Montréal, Collection Baby, U 4663.

76. *Ibid.* U 5065, Guy (London) to Mme Guy (Mtl.), 20 May 1763.

77. R.H. Fleming, "Phyn, Ellice and Company of Schenectady," *University of Toronto Studies in History and Economics*, vol. iv (1932), pp. 7–41; Jacob M. Price, "Buchanan & Simson, 1759–1763: A Different Kind of Glasgow Firm Trading to the Chesapeake," *William and Mary Quarterly*, 3rd series, vol. xl (1983), pp. 3–41; David Geddes, "How Habeas Corpus Came to Canada: the Bills on Credit Scandal in Quebec, 1783," *Three Banks Review* (London), no. 112 (Dec. 1976), pp. 50–65; and "John Cochrane's Troubles," *ibid.*, no. 111 (Sept. 1976), pp. 56–60.

CHAPTER
6 THE LOYALIST EXPERIENCE

The American Revolution was among the most important wars in Canadian history. While the Seven Years' War gave unquestioned supremacy to the British in North America, Canada was marginalized in the aftermath. The American Revolution, on the other hand, rescued Canada from that vast Anglo-American empire and created not just one new nation but two. It also defined the nature of what became known as British North America. The Catholic, French Canada of the *ancien régime* became a bilingual, bicultural, multidenominational colony with the arrival of thousands of United Empire Loyalists, the losers in that American War of Independence. The Loyalists spread across the old French empire, from the eastern tip of Cape Breton Island to western outposts like Detroit. They became the dominant population in the newly created colonies of Upper Canada, New Brunswick and Prince Edward Island. Even in Lower Canada, they occupied whole regions and challenged French dominance.

Since they were the first to reject the American Dream, the Loyalists fascinate historians in the United States, who have analysed those untypical ancestors in an attempt to understand who they were and why they pursued their un-American activities. This has also attracted Canadians, since the Loyalist mentality was transported north during and after the Revolution. Wallace Brown, author of the first article, has written widely on what he calls *The King's Friends: The Composition and Motives of the American Loyalist Claimants* (1965). In "'Victorious in Defeat': The American Loyalists in Canada," he offers the traditional, sympathetic overview of the Canadian experience. Others have been less kind, and there is a significant body of "Loyalist Myth" literature that describes in both positive and negative terms the convolutions of the Loyalist image in Canada over time. The ups and downs are usually tied to attitudes about monarchy, empire, imperialism, anti-Americanism, and the increasing obscurity of the Loyalists with the passage of time.

In most of this Loyalist literature the role of women, both during and after the Revolution, has rarely been considered. With the rethinking of Canada's past from several perspectives over the past quarter-century, Loyalist women have finally been rediscovered. Janice Potter examines several in "Patriarchy and Paternalism: The Case of Eastern Ontario Loyalist Women." Their courageous activities in the Revolutionary War went unrecognized later in British North America, because of "a well-defined power structure in which there were clearly prescribed social roles." This is the position of modern feminist historians, who expose the concept of natural order implicit in the oppressive patriarchal systems.

Suggestions for Further Reading

Bell, David, "The Loyalist Tradition in Canada," *Journal of Canadian Studies*, V, no. 2 (May 1970), 22–33.

Brown, Wallace and Hereward Senior, *Victorious in Defeat: The Loyalists in Canada*. Toronto: Methuen, 1984.

Condon, Ann Gorman, *The Envy of the American States: The Loyalist Dream for New Brunswick*. Fredericton: New Ireland Press, 1984.

Condon, Ann Gormon, "The Family in Exile: Loyalist Social Values After the Revolution," in Margaret Conrad (ed.) *Intimate Relations: Family and Community in Planter Nova Scotia, 1759–1800*. Fredericton: Acadiensis Press, 1995, 42–53.

Errington, Jane, "Loyalists in Upper Canada: A British American Community," in *"None was ever better ..." The Loyalist Settlements of Ontario*, ed. S.F. Wise, D. Carter-Edwards and J. Witham. Stormont, Dundas and Glengarry Historical Society, 1984.

MacKinnon, Neil, *The Unfriendly Soil: The Loyalist Experience in Nova Scotia, 1783–1791*. Kingston and Montreal: McGill-Queen's University Press, 1986.

MacNutt, W.S., "The Loyalists: A Sympathetic View," *Acadiensis*, VI, no. 1 (Autumn 1976), 3–20.

McCalla, Douglas, "The 'Loyalist' Economy of Upper Canada, 1784–1806," *Histoire sociale/Social History*, XVI, no. 32 (November 1983), 279–304.

Mills, David, *The Idea of Loyalty in Upper Canada, 1784–1850*. Kingston and Montreal: McGill-Queen's University Press, 1988.

Moore, Christopher, *The Loyalists: Revolution, Exile, Settlement*. Toronto: Macmillan of Canada, 1984.

Potter-MacKinnon, Janice, *While the Women Only Wept: Loyalist and Refugee Women*. Kingston and Montreal: McGill-Queen's Press, 1993.

Stewart, Ian, "New Myths for Old: The Loyalists and Maritime Political Culture," *Journal of Canadian Studies*, 25, 2, Summer 1990, 20–43.

Rawlyk, George, "The Federalist-Loyalist Alliance in New Brunswick, 1784–1815," *Humanities Association Review*, XXVII, no. 1 (Spring 1976), 142–160.

Upton, L.S.F. (ed.), *The United Empire Loyalists: Men and Myths*. Toronto: Copp Clark, 1967.

Wise, S.F., "The Place of the Loyalists in Ontario and Canadian History," *"None was ever better ..." The Loyalist Settlements of Ontario*, ed. S.F. Wise, D. Carter-Edwards and J. Witham. Stormont, Dundas and Glengarry Historical Society, 1984.

VICTORIOUS IN DEFEAT: THE AMERICAN LOYALISTS IN CANADA

Wallace Brown

> *"They [the Loyalists] would rather go to Japan than go among the Americans where they could never live in peace."*
>
> Col. John Butler, a New York Loyalist who emigrated to Canada.

As the War for Independence drew to a close, thousands of American Loyalists were looking for new homes.[1] The most attractive location because of proximity, availability of land and continuing royal rule, was what was left of British North America, constituting in 1783 three colonies: Nova Scotia, which included the future New Brunswick; the Island of St. John, renamed Prince Edward Island in 1799; and the ancient province of Quebec, which since 1774 stretched west to include the Great Lakes region. The term Canada, except as a synonym for Quebec, is an anachronism before 1867 (the date of Confederation); but it will be used in this essay to designate the entire area. The Maritimes refers to Nova Scotia, New Brunswick and Prince Edward Island.

Most Loyalists arrived in Nova Scotia by ship, at government expense, from New York City, the last great British stronghold in the "lost thirteen" colonies. The invasion began in October, 1782, with the descent of 300 Americans on the Annapolis Valley. Thousands more soon followed into the peninsula where the greatest concentration, perhaps 10,000, was at Port Roseway, renamed Shelburne, after the man who was the patron of Governor John Parr, but by no means a hero to the Loyalists on account of the generous peace terms he had negotiated with the rebels. A Spring and a Fall fleet in 1783 brought a host of refugees to the St. John valley, some of whom founded the city of Saint John at the river's mouth and Fredericton, seventy miles upstream. Other settlements were made at Passamaquoddy Bay (notably St. Andrews), Sackville, Bay Chaleur and the Miramichi River. Other Loyalists were lured to the Island of St. John, mainly the Malpeque-Bedeque isthmus, where Summerside, the island's second largest town, was founded.

The results of the influx into the Maritimes were dramatic. A new province, New Brunswick, was split off from Nova Scotia, the 15,000 Loyalists swamping the pre-Loyalist population of about 4,000 New Englanders and Acadians. Nova Scotia was further partitioned—temporarily, in this case—when hitherto little-developed Cape Breton Island, acquired from France in 1763, became a separate colony as a result of the arrival of 400 Loyalists who more than doubled the existing population. The Americans could not take over the rump of Nova Scotia;

From *History Today,* 27, no. 2 (1977), 92–100. Reprinted by permission of *History Today.*

but, numbering at least 15,000, they slightly outweighed the old inhabitants. On the Island of St. John the up to 1,000 immigrants, almost equalling the existing population, were a force to be reckoned with.

Arrival in Quebec was much more sporadic than in the Maritimes as the Loyalists, often pushing hand-carts, trickled in by various water-assisted routes, including the St. Lawrence and Hudson-Mohawk rivers, and Lakes Oneida and Champlain. Some sailed across Lake Ontario, frequently to the Bay of Quinte; others followed the southern shore to the Niagara peninsula; others pushed on to the Thames River and the northern shore of Lake Erie; a few even ascended the Mississippi and settled at Detroit. Again the results were the founding of new towns including New Johnstown (now Cornwall) and Cataraqui (now Kingston), and partition when the western area became Upper Canada (the future Ontario) in 1791. In Upper Canada, as in New Brunswick, the Loyalists, numbering perhaps 7,000, took over a wilderness area from a small pre-Loyalist population of only a few hundred; but in the original colony of Quebec 70,000 French Canadians were not directly threatened by the 1,000 Loyalist immigrants, half of whom settled in the outlying Gaspé peninsula, and half in the old inhabited area, mainly at Sorel and Machiche. Later, the Eastern Townships received some Loyalists.

Government was ill-prepared for the arrival of the Tories, though Governor Frederick Haldimand in Quebec proved much more capable and sympathetic than Governor Parr in Nova Scotia. Halifax and Saint John were severely overcrowded. In the former, churches and warehouses served as temporary quarters, and in both tent-cities sprang up. Congestion, but not always hardship, was relieved when many refugees moved to take up government land grants. Contemporary accounts are few, but some evidence about life in early Fredericton survives. All too soon the Loyalists faced the hard Canadian winter in tents covered with boughs or in half-finished log cabins. Some unfortunates froze to death; others only escaped by organizing shifts through the night to keep the fires going. The want of bedding might be supplied by heated boards. Even in 1787 the Reverend Jacob Bailey, a talented Loyalist from Massachusetts, reported from Annapolis County, Nova Scotia, that: "Many families are confined to a single apartment built with sods, where men, women, children, pigs, fleas, bugs, mosquitoes and other domestic insects mingle in society."

In western Quebec there was also much hardship. In July 1784, it was stated that "the settlers at Cataraqui are in great disorder, not having yet got upon their land, many of them unprovided with a Blanket to cover Them, scarce any Turnip seed and neither Axes nor Hoes for Half of Them." Brighter reports soon followed; but 1789 was known as the "hungry year" when "dreadful circumstances" were noted: "one spoonful of meal per day, for one person" was the ration; wild leaves, such as beech, were eaten; famished domestic animals were bled Masai-style; one family "leaped for joy at one robin being caught, out of which a whole pot of broth was made."

The Canadian land was quite capable of supplying a living at a simple farming level, but first came the back-breaking work of clearing the forest. Even Beverly Robinson Jr., scion of one of the richest New York families, recounted in 1784 that: "He is now settling a new farm in Nova Scotia by beginning to cut down the first tree and erect a loghouse for the shelter of his wife and two small children, and to accomplish that is obliged to labour with *his own* hands" (my italics). We see here the influence of the frontier at work in a Turnerian way.

Under the strain of the new environment, grown men wept like children and some cracked up completely. Filer Diblee and his family came from a prosperous middle class background in Connecticut. Their Loyalism resulted in an odyssey of flight, imprisonment and persecution which ended with their arrival at the Kingston peninsula, New Brunswick, where they survived the winter of 1783–84 in a log cabin. But Diblee's "fortitude gave way" at the prospect of imprisonment for debt; he "grew Melancholy, which soon deprived him of his Reason"; and one day in March, 1784, "he took a Razor from the Closet, threw himself on the bed, drew the Curtains, and cut his own throat." Though she lost her house twice by fire, his widow struggled on in what she called "this frozen Climate and barren Wilderness."

Groups as well as individuals were unfortunate. The Loyalist boomtown, Shelburne, had a magnificent harbour, but otherwise was so badly located that it rapidly declined to a hamlet. Port Mouton, Nova Scotia, was settled by over 2,000 refugees, mainly disbanded soldiers, in 1783 and quickly the town of Guysborough was built, and a road hacked through the woods to Liverpool. But in 1784 the town was destroyed by fire, a fate that struck several Loyalist settlements. Most of the inhabitants left and founded the present Guysborough on Chedabucto Bay, Nova Scotia, while some others founded St. Stephen in New Brunswick. Typically, most Loyalist set-backs were temporary. Most Shelburners found new homes. Even the Diblee family endured.

The arrival of the Loyalists in Canada marks the beginning of a great epic tale insufficiently appreciated by historians or the public. It ranks with the history of the Jesuit missionaries and the *coureurs de bois*, but has never found its Parkman.

Although plagued with difficulties, the Loyalists had many advantages. The environment was not completely hostile. Trees that had to be removed also supplied fuel and material for houses, tools and furniture; winters that inflicted frostbite also provided a free "deep-freeze" for the abundant game and fish; governments that were cursed for incompetence and ingratitude granted tax exemptions, issued provisions, medicines, clothes, tools, seeds, boards, and, most important of all, surveyed and granted, free of charge, land—the basis of survival for most people in those days. For a fortunate minority government largesse went further. Ex-officers received half pay for life; some Loyalists got pensions and lump-sum grants in compensation for losses sustained by the Revolution; all of this injected much-needed capital into Canada and ultimately benefited all the inhabitants. A very small minority got government offices, especially in the new provinces of New Brunswick and Upper Canada, but there were never enough to satisfy the vociferous Loyalists' demands. The scorned pre-Loyalist inhabitants were helpful as suppliers and informants. For example, in New Brunswick the Acadians sold cleared land and provisions to the Loyalists, while the Indians introduced them to fiddlehead greens (the edible shoots of a wild fern that are still a local delicacy). Though some observers noted the "vice of every kind, incident of the camp," that prevailed among the many Loyalists who settled as groups of disbanded regiments, particularly at Niagara, on the St. John River and the upper St. Lawrence, others stressed the advantages that military discipline and cohesiveness gave.

It has nurtured the self-esteem of some Canadians, especially New Brunswickers, to consider the Loyalists as mainly colonial aristocrats and Harvard graduates, in the same way it has flattered Virginians to consider themselves the progeny of Cavaliers. In fact, the vast majority of Loyalists were modest farmers (plus some artisans) who were well-suited to pioneering. But the Loyalist myth of gentility has a grain of truth; there *was* a significant minority of the "better sort," again especially in New Brunswick. Sergeant-Major William Cobbett, on duty in New Brunswick in the 1790s, was amazed to find "thousands of captains ..., without soldiers, and of squires without stockings or shoes," some of whom were happy to serve him a glass of grog. There were few fee-paying clients for doctors or lawyers. Not surprisingly a number of gentlemen Loyalists left Canada. For example, no less than six members of New Brunswick's first assembly, which met in 1785, had returned to the United States before the session was completed!

Nevertheless the contribution of the élite Loyalists to Canada, especially to government, politics, the law, religion and culture, must be acknowledged and can be suggested by listing a few names. Edmund Fanning (North Carolina) and Sir John Wentworth (New Hampshire) became the lieutenant-governors of the Island of St. John and Nova Scotia respectively; John Saunders (Virginia) and William Smith (New York) became chief-justices of New Brunswick and Quebec; Philip Marchington and Richard Cartwright (both from New York) were leading merchants in Nova Scotia and Upper Canada respectively; Sir John Johnson and Gabriel Ludlow (both from New York) became prominent office-holders in Quebec and New Brunswick; the Reverend Jonathan Odell (a poet of distinction from New Jersey) became the long-serving provincial secretary of New Brunswick; and so it went even to succeeding generations—Simon Fraser, the great explorer, was the son of a Loyalist; Sir Leonard Tilley, a father of Confederation, was a grandson.

Most Loyalists were subsistence farmers; but there were other areas of economic endeavour. Canada was slated by the British government to replace the former thirteen colonies as the purveyor of fish, timber and other supplies to the British West Indies. Indeed, some so-called Loyalists only migrated when they learned that the Navigation Acts would be applied against the

United States. The West Indian market encouraged Canadian agriculture, fishing and lumbering; but supply never equalled demand, and the British frequently had to open the West Indian trade to the United States. Even much of the early Nova Scotia and New Brunswick timber exports were American, frequently illegally obtained. The French Revolutionary and Napoleonic wars stimulated the Maritime mast trade; but much of it was not in Loyalist hands, and people tended to be diverted from agriculture, which partly explains why the Maritimes were chronically short of food.

The Loyalists dreamed of making the new provinces "a showcase for the continent," "the envy" of the United States; but sometimes the dream fell short. The Maritimes were poor by American standards. In 1790 William Pitt, influenced by *laissez-faire* principles and the United States policy of selling public lands, ended free land grants in British North America. Lord Dorchester, the Governor of Quebec, ignored the order; little land worth having remained in Nova Scotia; but the ban, which lasted seventeen years in New Brunswick, stunted development. On the Island of St. John most Loyalists could not get clear title to their land because of a complicated matter of absentee ownership. Some refugees bought new land; many simply squatted; others moved away. The issue, which was not resolved until 1875, cast a pall over the island, but stimulated reform politics during the first half of the nineteenth century. Upper Canada suffered from isolation and the barrier of the rapids of the St. Lawrence; but the rich soil presaged a prosperous future in what became the wealthiest part of Canada.

There is a chorus of contemporary testimony that most Loyalists, apart from a few who had "contracted ... rum and idle habits ... during the war," made good settlers. For example, Patrick Campbell visiting Upper Canada in the early 1790s, was impressed with the "immense industry" of the Loyalists, who, he claimed, had cleared more land in eight years than the French had in one hundred; James MacGregor visiting Prince Edward Island in the early nineteenth century found the Loyalists "industrious and independent," very well-suited to coping with "a country in a state of nature." In 1802 Edward Winslow, a descendant of the Pilgrim Father of the same name, looked back at the history of his fellow New Brunswick Loyalists with modest satisfaction. "Immense labour" had transformed a wilderness into a prosperous farming community. "Enquire among 'em. Are you oppressed with taxes? No. Does anybody interrupt you in matters of conscience? No. Do the laws afford you sufficient protection. Why yes." After a few years the Loyalists were strung out along a line of permanent, mainly agricultural, settlements from Cape Breton to Detroit,[2] and they had created two new provinces and several important towns. This is their prime contribution to Canada. They are the English founding fathers, analogous to the Virginians and Puritans of the early seventeenth century.

There remain two questions to be answered: what kind of society did the Loyalists create; and what was their legacy to Canada? The Loyalists were essentially good Americans, rarely docile Tories. As early as May, 1783, the royal surveyor, Benjamin Marston, a Loyalist himself, was complaining about the "curs'd Republican Town meeting Spirit" that made his life in Shelburne a trial. Bishop Charles Inglis was appalled by the democratic implications of "free pews" (i.e., not assigned according to rank) at Trinity Church, Kingston, New Brunswick. The Maritimes were (and are) susceptible to United States frontier-style revivalism; and from the start the hopes of the élite for a strong, established, Anglican Church were disappointed, despite the appointment in 1787 of Inglis as Bishop of Nova Scotia with jurisdiction over New Brunswick and Quebec, and the setting aside of "clergy reserves" of land in the Maritimes and Upper Canada. Too many Loyalists were Erastian. Élite hopes for an hereditary aristocracy were frustrated, and it was even difficult to live in gentlemanly style. Thus, the very wealthy John Saunders sat on his great estate, the Barony, near Fredericton, unable to attract tenants—men naturally preferred to work their own land.

The single characteristic common to the Loyalists was quarrelsomeness. The old inhabitants could not be expected to relish the intrusion, even if the refugees had been exceptionally reticent. Generally the Loyalists disliked the old inhabitants of Canada whom they considered had been too friendly to the American Revolution. "Languid wretches," said Edward Winslow in New Brunswick; "exulting in their beloved Ignorance," said Jacob Bailey in Nova Scotia; "idle" and "indolent," said Benjamin Marston in the Island of St. John; "the Darkest Corner of the Dominion," said William Smith in Quebec.

But the most bitter quarrels were between Loyalists, usually between the élite and the rest. The tone was set even before the evacuation of New York when a group known as the Fifty-Five, on account of their high social standing, petitioned for special large land grants of 5,000 acres each in Nova Scotia. A howl of protest resulted and the scheme was thwarted. The first New Brunswick election in November 1785 led to rioting in St. John which crystallized two parties: the minority, aristocratic Upper Covers, versus the majority, plebeian Lower Covers. In 1787 Lord Dorchester had to send a committee to investigate Loyalist unrest in the future Upper Canada. The committee reported "a very dangerous Jealousy and want of Confidence ... between the Majority of the settlers and their late officers." In New Brunswick the political dispute culminated in "the Glenie affair," in which James Glenie, a Scottish timber merchant, not a Loyalist, led the opposition to Governor Thomas Carleton and the official clique in Fredericton which in 1792 lost its majority in the assembly. The affair finally turned on whether the council had the constitutional right to interfere with the initiate money bills. From 1795 to 1798 an impasse meant no revenue was collected at all until a compromise allowed both houses to initiate.

In Nova Scotia the situation was complicated by a powerful segment of "old comers," and no real Loyalist party developed. But the Loyalists were in the thick of politics and led a thrust against the council. A Halifax by-election of 1788 was marked by rioting and murder; and, a year later, the Loyalists were charged with rebellion. Order was restored in 1791 when Governor Parr, who had long complained about the Americans—they "almost wish to take over the government"—died and was replaced by a Loyalist, Sir John Wentworth.

W. S. MacNutt, the best historian of the Maritimes, comments on the early political history of Nova Scotia and New Brunswick that it was firmly in the tradition of the former American colonies, that "replicas of the constitutional struggles ... of New York and Massachusetts were ... the common lot of the two provinces."

Now to consider the Loyalist legacy. It must be stressed that only in New Brunswick did the Loyalists remain a majority for very long, and even there they were engulfed by other immigrants after the War of 1812. They and their descendants retained political power almost until Confederation; but from the early years the economy was dominated by Scots. Direct Loyalist influence was much more ephemeral elsewhere in Canada. In Upper Canada by 1812 only one-fifth of the population of 100,000 were Loyalists or their children, although most of the remainder were American-born; these were the so-called "late Loyalists," American frontiersmen who were simply attracted by Governor John G. Simcoe's offer of free land in an area where the land was very good. Many Canadians with no Loyalist background, however, have acquired Loyalist attitudes. For example, John Strachan arrived in Upper Canada from Scotland in 1799 with pro-American convictions, but by 1809 was convinced that "true liberty" did not exist in the United States; later in the nineteenth century in New Brunswick, Protestant Irish immigrants became "Loyalized," a process aided by intermarriage.

The Loyalists helped establish Canada's tradition of a "cultural mosaic," which is held to contrast with America's alleged, homogenizing melting pot. From the start most Loyalists preferred to leave the French alone, and their own settlements were frequently fragmented; for example, in the Upper Canadian Townships Roman Catholic Scots and Presbyterian Scots kept apart. The Loyalist influx also brought many loyal Iroquois, who settled along the Grand River, and a number of black Loyalists who founded settlements in the Maritimes that persist to this day.

The Loyalists and the British government set the political structure of English Canada which was only in embryo in Nova Scotia before 1783. The aim was to avoid the "mistakes" that had caused revolution to the south. New Brunswick may serve as a model that was generally copied. The lower houses were believed to have become too powerful; so the powers of the appointed council and the Governor, who was made financially independent, were strengthened. The élite were encouraged by appointment to the council and government office, and as JPs in the counties—the New England township was scrupulously avoided. The colonial government of New Brunswick was made less dependent on the home-country; more internal self-government was allowed than had been the case in America. Conservative social institutions, like the Church of England, were supported; and with sad memories of Revolutionary agitation in the American cities still vivid, the capital was moved from Saint John to the inland village of Fredericton. (Many Loyalists had a Jeffersonian dislike of commerce and cities.) But the tone in New Brunswick was far from entirely conservative; the British never attempted to tax the North American colonies directly; thus the essential early goal of the Revolution was secured. In the words of W. S. MacNutt, "democracy ran riot in the Loyalist citadel"; the suffrage was for all men, and the city government of Saint John, with its annual elections, was one of the most democratic bodies of its kind in North America. The Revolution not only made Americans free, but also Canadians, who found that "subjects" could be just as happy as "citizens."

French-Canadians owe much to the Loyalists. The Constitutional Act of 1791, partly because of Loyalist agitation, began representative government in Quebec and introduced freehold land tenure. At the same time, the French way of life, including legal and religious systems, was maintained. The Loyalist numbers doomed the French to become a minority; but the Loyalist strength enabled Canada to withstand the onslaught of American imperialism. It is doubtful if French culture could have survived within the American union.

The Loyalist tradition is often decried in Canada because it has been held responsible for the development of aristocratic governing cliques, known as the Family Compacts. In fact, the Family Compacts were not a Loyalist phenomenon. True, in Upper Canada about half of the leading members of the compact were second-generation Loyalists, men like Sir John Beverley Robinson; but Loyalists' descendants were an important component of the opposition, and the rebellion of 1837 similarly found them on both sides. In New Brunswick the Loyalists were also on both sides of the compact question. Lemuel Allen Wilmot, a grandson of a Poughkeepsie Loyalist, led the struggle, successful in 1836, for New Brunswick to gain control of Crown lands, an important landmark on the road to full self-government. During the same period Joseph Howe, whose father was a loyal Massachusetts newspaper editor, played a similar role in leading the forces of Nova Scotia democracy. Nevertheless, the aristocratic British proclivity of some Loyalists and their descendants has frequently gone against the Canadian grain. The tone was set in 1789 when the Quebec Council resolved to have the Loyalists and their posterity discriminated, from future settlers, "giving them a Marke of Honor," the right to put UE (Unity of Empire) after their names, hence the expression United Empire Loyalists.

New Brunswick is *par excellence* the Loyalist province; and a brief account of some influences there may be appropriate. On the positive side, there is a cultural tradition. In 1784 the Loyalists laid the foundations of the University of New Brunswick at Fredericton, where the residence of the poet, Jonathan Odell, began a literary tradition that leads directly to Bliss Carman and others. On the negative side, we find an over-dependence on government, a scramble for office and patronage, a morbid absorption in politics that sapped more wholesome initiative, particularly economic. Writing in this vein in 1904, John Davidson, a Scottish professor, now perhaps understandably forgotten, at the University of New Brunswick, found the Loyalist tradition baleful. He quoted a local: "in this country men think five dollars of government money is worth ten dollars from anybody else," and added that New Brunswick was the only country he knew where professional and business men had to do their legitimate work at night because politics took up the day.

Discussion of the efforts of the Loyalists often centres on explanations of why Canada is so different from the United States. Such items as law, Parliamentary government and the monarchy are obvious; but Canada's relatively peaceful western expansion, and a general lack of lynching, are also listed. It is even argued that several Canadian provinces have elected mild socialist governments during the last few decades because of the Loyalists. More of a class structure was maintained in Canada, and Canadians, far from starting with a distrust of government authority, positively embrace it.

The Loyalists offered a valid critique of the Revolutionary ideals and moral absolutism. The Nova Scotian writer, Thomas C. Haliburton, the grandson of a Loyalist and a popular satirist, had Sam Slick say simply "there is no tyranny on airth equal to the tyranny of a majority." Similar sentiments were expressed by the Reverend Mather Byles, who, watching the hysteria surrounding the funeral of a victim of the Boston "massacre" in 1771, opined: "They call me a brainless Tory; but tell me ... which is better to be ruled by one tyrant three thousand miles away, or by three thousand tyrants one mile away?"

The Loyalists have profoundly influenced Canadian nationalism. They began an abiding love-hate attitude toward the Great Republic. During the War of 1812, by opting out, the Maritimes demonstrated the love; but there was a bitter struggle in Upper Canada. The Loyalists took pride in victory of sort; but more important were the myths and symbols established: the Loyalist militia had beaten the Yankees; Laura Secord had led her cow through the American lines. Fear of the United States has remained, and Unity of Empire has frequently been invoked as a shield, as in the 1880s which witnessed one of several Loyalist revivals.

It is true that there is a certain Canadian dourness resulting from three losing traditions: French, Scottish and Loyalist. But a Canadian poet's description of the latter is also apt:

> Not drooping like poor fugitives they came
> In exodus to our Canadian wilds
> But full of heart and hope, with heads erect
> And fearless eyes victorious in defeat.

Notes

1. For a general account see my article "Escape from the Republic: The Dispersal of the American Loyalists," *History Today,* February, 1972.

2. Detroit, although legally in the United States by the peace treaty of 1783, was not evacuated until after the signing of Jay's Treaty in 1794, when the Loyalists moved across the border into Canada.

PATRIARCHY AND PATERNALISM: THE CASE OF THE EASTERN ONTARIO LOYALIST WOMEN

Janice Potter

Although the American Revolution did not alter the legal or political rights of women, it changed their lives dramatically in other ways.[1] With the men away fighting, women were forced to shoulder the burden of running the farm, the estate, or the business, and as a result there was less rigidity in the sexual division of labour, women gained confidence in their abilities, and men had more respect for women and their contributions to society. Those experiences were reinforced by public recognition of women's contribution to the Revolution and by the ideology of the Revolution. For example, boycotts of British cloth meant that wearing homespun became a sign of patriotism and that spinning, one of the most time-consuming and clearly feminine domestic chores, was raised in status. Moreover, there was an antipatriarchal aspect of the Revolution that fostered less authoritarian and more reciprocal relationships between men and women. Republican ideology, with its emphasis on voluntary consent, also allowed more scope for women. There was "greater mutuality and reciprocity" in marriages and in some cases "more egalitarian marital relationships."[2] The belief in the need to raise a moral and upright citizenry also enhanced the status of motherhood and made it easier for women to obtain an education, since it was they who would be raising the children. The result was more confident, self-reliant women, some of whom decided not to marry, and a society that valued more highly the domestic sphere generally and women specifically.

But what was the situation of Loyalist women, whose actions did not receive the same recognition and for whom there was no equivalent to republican ideology? The existing material on Loyalist women includes books about individuals, papers about specific groups, such as Loyalist women who filed claims for compensation, and an interesting thesis discussing Loyalist women in general terms.[3] This paper, however, considers in a preliminary way the effect of the Revolution on one specific group of Loyalist women—those who lived on the frontiers of New York, New England, and Pennsylvania and eventually settled in the townships created along the St. Lawrence River and Lake Ontario between Longueuil and the Bay of Quinte in what is now eastern Ontario.

Despite the diversity of their ethnic origins, the eastern Ontario Loyalist women shared a common background characterized by paternalism and patriarchy, and their experiences during the Revolution were similar. Virtually all went through several stages in the course of becoming refugees: they were

From *Ontario History*, LXXXI, no. 1 (March 1989), 3–24. Reprinted by permission of the author, the Ontario Historical Society and *Ontario History*.

harassed or persecuted, they were forced to flee to British bases for protection, they lived under British military rule in what might be called refugee camps, and with aid from the British they were eventually resettled.

Information about these women can be found in the few personal letters and diaries that have survived, in the claims Loyalists made for compensation from the British government, and in the records of the Patriot committees that interrogated Loyalists and of the British authorities who had to supervise and provision them. And, from records such as military registers, provisioning lists, returns of Loyalists, and land grants, it is possible to compile a reasonably precise statistical profile of the eastern Ontario Loyalists.

The 1786 census reveals that the 1,800 families, or 4,661 individuals, living along the St. Lawrence River and the eastern end of Lake Ontario were an ethnically diverse group that included many recent immigrants. Of the eastern Ontario Loyalists whose birthplace is known, about 45 per cent were foreign and about 45 per cent American-born.[4] Many of the American-born belonged to ethnic groups that had retained their native language, group cohesiveness, and other aspects of their culture. The largest of the ethnic minorities were the Germans, who accounted for about 30 per cent of the total and of whom one-quarter were immigrants and the rest Americans of German ancestry. About 5 per cent were Dutch, mostly more traditional members of the Dutch Reformed Church who had kept their culture and language.[5] Another group of American-born Loyalists who had retained their distinctive culture were the Mohawk Indians, who had played an important military role in the Revolution.

The largest of the immigrant groups, constituting 24 per cent of the total, were the Scots. Many were Highlanders and Jacobites who had emigrated because of poverty and the enclosure of their lands. In the colonies they retained their Gaelic language, Catholic religion, and other aspects of their culture.[6]

Whether American- or foreign-born, the vast majority of eastern Ontario Loyalists had lived on the frontiers of colonial society and were farmers. Over 70 per cent came from the northern New York counties of Tryon, Charlotte, and Albany. About 2 per cent came from each of New Jersey, Connecticut, and Pennsylvania, and many of the Pennsylvanians were from the frontier settlements along the Susquehanna River.[7] They had all been part of the mass movement to the frontiers after the Seven Years' War.

A common theme in the social relationships of many eastern Ontario Loyalists was paternalism. Paternalism has been variously defined as interference with people's liberty for their own good and as the determination by one person what is in the best interests of another. A paternalistic relationship need not be harsh, however, and can even be cooperative in that it is a close and affectionate relationship in which the dependent party feels the need for guidance and is willing to exchange some independence or security.[8] But in such a relationship there is a hierarchy or at least inequality—there are superiors and subordinates, leaders and followers—and the dominant party feels an obligation to protect the interests of the subordinate in return for loyalty and deference.

Eighteenth-century paternalism was exemplified in the relationship between some New York landlords and their tenants. In spite of the rush to the
frontiers for land, not all colonial Americans managed to acquire land of their
own. In the case of the eastern Ontario Loyalists, only 20 per cent had held
their land in freehold, and some had shared land or squatted on disputed land,
but the vast majority had been tenants on the northern New York manorial
estates owned by families like the Johnsons; indeed, at least 20 per cent of the
Loyalist claimants who settled in what is now eastern Ontario had been tenants
of the Johnsons.

The Johnsons ran their 20,000-acre estate like quasi-feudal lords. They
helped their tenants financially, burned the debtor bonds of over-extended tenants, and helped artisans like Richard Mandevell, a "Breeches Maker" who
later settled in eastern Ontario, establish themselves in the local village. They
also built roads, schools, and mills; introduced sheep and new crops; and at
Johnstown, the county seat, established a county fair and built the local jail,
courthouse, and Anglican church.[9] In return for looking after the interests of
their tenants, the Johnsons expected loyalty and deference—letters to them
from tenants and others, for example, often began, "May it Please your Lordship."
When the Revolution came, the Johnsons' tenants formed an armed guard to protect their landlord, and when he fled to Canada, they followed.[10]

There were also other paternalistic relationships between eastern Ontario
Loyalists and various authorities. Many of the colonists, of German Palatinate
or French Huguenot ancestry, were Protestants who had fled to England in
search of religious freedom and who revered George III as a defender of
Protestantism. The Highlanders were accustomed to an authoritarian society,
and their family and clan structure was patriarchal. And the Mohawk, although
they considered themselves an independent people, spoke of the king as a father
and looked to the British government to protect them from the rapaciousness of
the powerful New York landlords who spent much of the eighteenth century
defrauding the Indians of their land. As they fled the frontiers of the colonies for
Canada, the Loyalists who later settled in eastern Ontario did so in groups
and as families. This can be seen by comparing them to the immigrants who had
come to the colonies in the mid-eighteenth century. As the table below illustrates, 74.3 per cent of the immigrants were male and 25.7 per cent female,
whereas 70.6 per cent of the adult eastern Ontario Loyalists were male and
29.4 per cent female.

	Percentage of Males	Percentage of Females
Immigrants	74.3	25.7
Eastern Ontario Loyalists	70.6	29.4

Even these statistics underestimate the female Loyalists in that boys as young as ten belonged to the Loyalist regiments and could be listed as adult male settlers rather than as children, whereas girls of the same age were considered children. Moreover, whereas the number of children per adult female in early eighteenth-century New York had been only 1.88, among eastern Ontario Loyalists there were about 2.4 children per adult woman.[11]

The social and family structure in which these Loyalists and other colonial Americans lived was also patriarchal if we take patriarchy to mean "the manifestation and institutionalization of male dominance over women and children in the family and the extension of male dominance over women in society in general. ... [It] implies that men hold power in all the important institutions of society and that women are deprived of access to such power."[12] Colonial American society was patriarchal in several senses. Women could not participate in the political process, they could not get a higher education, and men controlled the most basic commodity in the society—land. Not only was the title to the family's property in the man's name, but a widow who remarried lost ownership of her property to her new husband. A married woman's identity was subsumed in that of her husband's. "A married couple," in the words of one historian, "became like a legal fiction: like a corporation, the pair was a single person with a single will"—the husband's. Even within the household it was common for the man to make all of the major decisions about finances and even about raising the children, and in any marital separation the man retained custody of the children.[13]

Patriarchal relationships, like paternalistic ones, did not mean that there could not be affection between husband and wife. To cite one example, a 1776 letter from Alexander McDonald, a captain in the Royal Highland Emigrants stationed in Halifax, to his wife in the colonies began, "My dear Susannah" and ended tenderly, "I have no time to write more. ... Kiss the children for me and believe the one forever to be yours." Yet the patriarchal nature of the relationship was revealed in the instructions he gave her about all aspects of her life: "Keep the Child always clean and well dress'd and you must appear in yr best Colours yourself." Of a fellow soldier, he wrote, "Keep the old gentleman always at a distance from you and never let him again appear in the House."[14]

The subordination of women in the colonial American family was revealed in the diary of Dothe Stone, sister of the eastern Ontario Loyalist, Joel Stone. As Dothe's list of births illustrates, marriage and childbirth were central to women's lives. The average woman was married in her early twenties to a man from one to five years older; she could expect to be pregnant within twelve months, and her childbearing years became a cycle of pregnancy, birth, and lactation.[15]

The birth and care of children, combined with women's other tasks, meant that their life centred on the home. The family farm was the basic economic and social unit on the frontier, and although some women did have to help with clearing and farming the land, women's jobs were more often milking the cows, taking care of the chickens, planting and tending the garden, and harvesting the orchard. As well, they cared for the house, salted beef and pork, preserved fruit and stored vegetables, made cider and cheese, and dried apples. A major chore was making clothing: Dothe writes of spending days with her sisters at spinning wheels. Whereas her husband might get away from home by going fishing or hunting or by travelling to town for supplies or to do business, the woman, especially if she had small children (which was almost always), was tied to the home.[16]

Colonial women found security in what was familiar to them—their homes, their families, and their circle of community friends and relatives. Dothe wrote fondly of her favourite room, her "once loved chamber," and her diary is full of excitement when describing social events, such as weddings, or gatherings at which a fiddler led the party in singing and dancing. Dothe also relied heavily on female companionship. Tasks like spinning were done in the company of other women; women helped each other in childbirth and child rearing, and most of them lived in the same house as, or close to, other female relatives. Some of Dothe Stone's sweetest memories were of times spent with her sisters: "Sunday afternoon Sister Hannah and I have been walking to the far part of Davis' South lots, being very tyred, I lyed down under a pretty bush, I tied my long pocket handkerchief about my head, and took a stone for a pillow and never did I rest more sweetly, while Sister Hannah set by me making some excellent verses about the gracefullness of my appearance."[17] Home, family, and female companionship were what mattered most to colonial women.

Patriarchy was also evident in the Stone family. Whether unmarried and living in her father's or brother's house, or married and in her husband's, Dothe Stone's life was run by men. Her brother, whom she lived with for nine years, "supported and directed" her and made all the decisions, including the one to move, without consulting her. The image of the father as patriarch was captured by Dothe when she described "my Dad an old gentleman ... in the other room with a large family of likely children gathering round and looking to him for support."[18]

Relationships within the colonial family were patriarchal, and even women themselves spoke of their own inferiority and dependence. Widows, like the strong-minded Patriot, Mary Fish, for example, described themselves as "a poor weak and helpless creature, [who] could do nothing but lie at the foot of mercy and look for direction." "What," she asked rhetorically, "Could a feble [*sic*] woman do."[19] Statements like these do not necessarily mean that women inwardly accepted the notion of their helplessness and inferiority. What they do mean, however, is that the social norms were such that women felt the need to express their feminine dependence and weakness.

But the notions of female helplessness and dependence were brought into question by the Revolution, which posed new challenges for Patriot *and* Loyalist women and forced many to adopt new roles. To Loyalist women, attached to their homes and local surroundings, accustomed to the security of friends, relatives and neighbours, and used to relying on men to direct their lives and make important decisions for them, the Revolution was a shattering experience. Patriot women, it is true, were left to manage the family and farm or business in their husbands' absence; but at least most remained in their homes and communities. Many Loyalist women, however, lost everything they valued most. Their families were scattered and the men who had directed their lives, gone. Many were also wrenched from all that was familiar—their homes, their relatives, and their communities. What all Loyalist women shared was their experiences as refugees, which were far more challenging than those of most Patriot women.

The pattern was set in May 1776, when Sir John Johnson fled from his northern New York estate with 170 tenants to escape arrest by the Patriots and to seek refuge in Canada, leaving behind his wife, Lady Mary Watts Johnson, who was pregnant and already the mother of two children under two. Mary, or Polly, who was from a prosperous New York city merchant and banking family, had married Sir John in 1773 at the age of nineteen and moved north to live in Tryon County. When her husband fled, Polly could not accompany him because of her condition, the hastiness of his departure, and the extraordinary rigours of the trip. Disappointed at the escape of Sir John, the Patriots forced her to turn over the keys to "every place"; her husband's private papers were seized, his "books distributed about the country," and their home, Johnson Hall, plundered and "made a Barrack." Lady Johnson was held hostage in Albany, although she was in touch regularly with her husband through "Indian and white men ... sent through the Woods." After some twenty months in captivity, Lady Johnson escaped, travelling through enemy territory in the cold winter. Although she finally reached the British base in New York City, her youngest child died as a result of its traumatic experiences.[20]

Within months of Lady Johnson's escape the war that was to rage on the frontier for more than four years began, and the hostages in this vicious conflict were the women and the children. As the Patriots attempted to assert their control over the region by forcing suspected Loyalists to take oaths of allegiance or join the militia, many able-bodied Loyalist men were either arrested or followed Sir John Johnson's lead by escaping to British lines, reluctantly leaving their families behind. Once in Canada, most had to join the various Loyalist regiments that collaborated with the Indians to launch retaliatory raids on the American frontier. For the British, the raids had a military purpose: to harass the enemy and destroy food supplies for Patriot forces. For many Loyalist soldiers, the raids were an opportunity to seek revenge on their foes in the colonies, find new recruits, make contact with their families, and occasionally bring the families back to Canada. For the families, the raids complicated their already troubled lives by intensifying Patriot hatred of the Loyalists and compromising them even further, since the families often harboured or helped the raiding parties. As the raiding parties retreated to the safety of Canada, they left their families behind.[21]

With the men in their lives gone, Loyalist women were forced to assume new responsibilities, and some even actively engaged in the war effort. For example, three women were implicated in a plot to kidnap the mayor of Albany, and one, an Indian woman, confessed to having lured the mayor to the woods by reporting that she had found a dead body there.[22] Another woman was arrested and jailed along with twenty men for "having assisted in the destruction of Currey Town."[23] Women were arrested and some imprisoned for taking part in robberies, which were especially common at the manor of Rensselaerwyck in the late 1770s.[24] Loyalist women also provided intelligence and passed messages between the British in New York City and Canada.[25]

Two eastern Ontario Loyalist women who were unusually active in the war effort were associated with the Mohawk Indians. This is not surprising in light of the status of women in the matrilineal Mohawk society, where children belonged to the mother's rather than the father's clan and women chose and deposed the chiefs. The local economy of the predominantly agrarian Mohawk was controlled by the women, who were responsible for planting, harvesting, and distributing the crops. Mohawk matrons were also influential in war councils and in determining the fate of captives.[26]

One very influential Mohawk woman was Molly Brant, or Konwatsi'tsianienni. A member of a high-ranking Mohawk family, sister of the famous Mohawk chief, Joseph Brant, and a matron who had a great influence in the matrilineal Iroquois society, Molly Brant "was a person of great prestige in her nation and throughout the Confederacy." Her power and influence were heightened after 1759, when she became the wife in all but name of Sir William Johnson, superintendent of Indian affairs, with whom she had eight children. Equally at home in the Indian village, in the war council, as the charming and gracious hostess at Johnson Hall, or in running Johnson's huge estate during his frequent absences, Molly Brant was a remarkable woman.[27]

She helped many Loyalists escape to Canada, provided intelligence to the British, and played a decisive part in fostering the ties of loyalty, self-interest, and history that underpinned the Mohawk support for the British during the Revolution. After her home was plundered by the Patriots and she was forced to flee with her family to the safety of the Iroquois villages, Brant came to Canada in 1778 and moved from one British base to another, cementing the Mohawks' loyalty to the British. Daniel Claus, Indian agent and son-in-law of the late Sir William Johnson, said of Molly Brant, "One word from her is more taken notice of by the five nations than a thousand from any white man without Exception." The commanding officer at Carleton Island attributed the good behaviour of the Indians there to Brant's influence: "The Chiefs were careful to keep their people sober and satisfy'd, but their uncommon good behaviour is in a great Measure to be ascribed to Miss Molly Brant's influence over them, which is far superior to that of all their Chiefs put together, and she has in the course of this Winter done every thing in Her power to maintain them strongly in the King's interest." Brant's stature was recognized by the British government, which awarded her one of the largest pensions ever given to any Indian and built her a house at present-day Kingston, where she spent her last years.[28]

Another woman influential among the Mohawk was Sarah Kast McGinnis, an American-born Palatinate German, who as a child in northern New York lived with the Mohawks, was adopted by them, and learned their language. In the 1740s Sarah married an Irishman, Timothy McGinnis, who became involved with Sir William Johnson in the fur trade and as a captain in the Indian Department. After her husband was killed in the Seven Years' War, the widow McGinnis carried on his trading business.[29]

When the Revolution broke out, both sides courted Sarah because of her close association with the Iroquois, the Patriots offering her twelve shillings York currency a day and a guard of fifteen men. But Sarah and her family sided with the British and worked to cement the Iroquois' loyalty, actions that caused them to be persecuted by the Patriots. In 1777, as news spread of Burgoyne's expedition from Canada through northern New York, the Patriots considered it necessary to neutralize Loyalists like Sarah and her family. In Sarah's case, this involved arresting her son-in-law and then confiscating all her property. Sarah, her daughters, and grandchildren watched helplessly as their belongings were sold at public auction; they were then arrested and "so harshly used" that one granddaughter died. When the Patriots mistakenly concluded that the British had the upper hand in the region, Sarah and her family were released. Before they could be recaptured, they "escaped at night with only what they could carry on their backs" and left for Canada with British troops, although Sarah had to leave behind a son "who was out of his senses and bound in chains ... and who some time afterward was burnt alive."[30]

After arriving in Canada, Sarah agreed to a British request to return to northern New York, winter with the Iroquois, and try to counter the harmful effects of Burgoyne's defeat. On her arrival at "the most central village of the Six nations," the Indians "flocked to her from the remotest villages and thanked her for coming ... to direct and advise them in that critical time." Soon after her arrival, the Patriots sent messages to the Iroquois, "with a most exaggerated account of General Burgoyne's disaster" and "belts," inviting them to join the Patriots along with "threats" in case the Indians refused. In response to the Patriot overtures, the Indians "consulted with" Sarah and sought her "opinion and advice": "Then after that with an Authority and privilege allowed to women of Consequence only among Indians, [she] seized upon and cancelled the [Patriot] Belts, telling them such bad news came from an evil Spirit and must endanger their peace and union as long as it was in their sight and therefore must be buried underground."[31] When Sarah spent this long and difficult winter in the Indian villages, she was sixty-four years old.

Although Sarah Kast McGinnis's relationship with the Indians and her active participation in the Revolution were extraordinary, her other experiences were typical of those of other Loyalist women. As able-bodied Loyalist men on the frontiers either were arrested or fled, leaving their families behind, the sins of the fathers and husbands were visited on the wives and children. Patriot committees and mobs assumed, unless there was evidence to the contrary, that families were accomplices in the guilt of one member. If one member of a family fled or was arrested, the rest were vulnerable either to official interrogation by committees or to unofficial harassment by mobs or Patriot neighbours.

The case of the Cartwright family was not unusual. The father, Richard, Sr., a prosperous innkeeper landowner, and deputy postmaster of Albany, had shown his support for the Patriots in 1775 when he gave money to the Patriot expedition against Ticonderoga. But his daughter, Elizabeth, who was married to a British soldier and lived in Niagara, was in touch with his son, Richard, Jr., and when the local committee of correspondence discovered this in February 1777, it forced Richard, Jr., to give security for his future good behaviour. By October 1777 he could no longer give this guarantee, and with his young niece, Hannah, he left on a difficult journey through the northern New York wilderness to Canada. The parents, tainted by the Loyalism of their children, were mistreated, their property was confiscated, and within a year of their son's departure they were taken under guard to the border.[32]

The Cartwrights' experiences were shared by many Loyalist women who had to live with the consequences of their husbands' actions. With the men in their lives gone, the women not only had to assume responsibility for running the farm and taking care of their families, but also had to deal with Patriot harassment or persecution and in many cases they were forced to leave their homes to seek refuge behind the British lines. When Garnet Dingman, who was a squatter on land on the Susquehanna River, joined the British in 1781, he left his cattle, utensils, and furniture to his wife and friends; however, shortly after his departure, the "rebels," in the words of an observer, "stript [his wife] of every thing." Another Susquehanna River squatter was Jane Glasford, whose "husband was to [sic] old to serve, but he sent his Sons to serve" with Joseph Brant, whose troops took some of their stock and grain. Jane described what happened to her and her husband because of their son's military service: "The Rebels came in '79 & plundered them, & stript them of everything. She was almost starvd in her own house. They were all obliged to come away. ... Their house was burnt as soon as they left it." A similar fate was meted out to Mary Waldec, wife of a tenant in Tryon country who fled to Canada with Sir John Johnson in 1776. In 1777 the "rebels ... took most" of her "things ... and sold them at Vendue," and later Mary fled to Canada.[33] The wife of Philip Empy, who had refused to sign a Patriot oath and whose sons had joined the British, was jailed along with her children and then "beat," "abused" by four men, and left on the road. Friends rescued her, but she died soon after.[34]

The severity of the treatment meted out to Loyalist women depended on their husbands' connections and reputation among the dominant faction in the community. The case of two Vermont Loyalist women illustrates this point. Sarah Bottum was the wife of Justus Sherwood, a Vermont landowner, speculator, and entrepreneur in the timber business. Originally from Connecticut,

Justus had received his land in Vermont from the New Hampshire govern-ment, and he supported Ethan Allen and his brothers, the dominant faction in the disputed territory. When Justus fell afoul of the local Patriots for refusing to take an oath of allegiance and allegedly corresponding with the British, he was threatened with execution and imprisoned, although he escaped and fled to Canada. The Patriots ransacked the Sherwoods' cabin and destroyed some of their belongings, but Sarah could look to her parents for help, and she was al-lowed to remain in Vermont until she decided to seek permission from the Patriots to join her husband in Canada.[35]

The treatment of another Vermont Loyalist, Mary Munro, was much harsher because her husband belonged to an unpopular faction in Vermont. John Munro, originally from Scotland, had been granted large tracts of land by New York, and this put him at odds with the dominant faction in Vermont, whose land grants came from New Hampshire. Munro became even more unpopular when he was ap-pointed justice of the peace and given the unenviable task of imposing law and order on Ethan Allen and the Green Mountain Boys, who harassed New Yorkers in Vermont. When the Revolution came and Munro supported the British, the Council of Safety drove him from his home and seized all his property, except "a few personal articles left for the support of his wife." Unlike Sarah Sherwood, who had the support of her family, Mary Munro was treated very harshly by her neigh-bours and shunned by her own family. She wrote to her husband of her plight:

> I am in a poor state of health and very much distresst. I must leave my house
> in a very short time and God knows where I shall get a place to put my head in,
> for my own relations are my greatest enemies. ... They have distrest me be-
> yond expression. I have scarcely a mouthful of bread for myself or children. ...
> Is there no possibility of your sending for us? If there is no method fallen upon
> we shall all perish, for you can have no idea of our sufferings here ... my heart
> is so full it is ready to break.

Luckily, Mary Munro and her eight children did make their way to Canada within a few months of this letter.[36]

Flight may have represented an end to persecution for many Loyalist women; yet, it was also difficult for them to leave their homes and cut their ties with their families, friends, and communities. Simon Schwartz, the son of tenants of the Johnson family, who described his father's flight to Canada with Sir John in 1776 and the harassment of other family members, stressed that his mother had left only when she had to; she "would not come in [to Canada] be-fore the House & builds [*sic*] were burnt." Women like Mrs. Schwartz usually had no choice but to leave. If they left voluntarily, it was usually because their prop-erty had been confiscated or their homes destroyed and there were no relatives or neighbours to protect them.

Some Loyalist women simply fled, but many others sought permission to leave from Patriot committees. Either permission was granted and the women escorted to the frontiers, or they were exchanged for Patriot prisoners being held in Canada. Mary Cruger Meyers had been alone with seven children under thirteen since the summer of 1777, when her husband, John Walden Meyers, left to join Burgoyne. In October 1778 she and another Loyalist woman requested permission to go to New York.[37] After being dispossessed of their property, the wives of Loyalists in Tryon County petitioned the local Patriot committee to be either taken care of or allowed to join their husbands. Their latter request was eventually granted.[38] When women left, they could only take children under twelve with them; boys twelve and over were considered capable of bearing arms and had to be left behind.[39] Those going to British lines also had to pay all the costs of being escorted there and take fourteen days' provisions with them.[40]

By the late 1770s, however, many Loyalist women were forced to leave. Some were sent to Canada because they were destitute and "subsisted at public Expense." A more common reason for removing the women was that they had assisted the enemy. When their husbands, relatives, or friends returned to the frontiers from Canada to gather intelligence, to recruit, or to raid, the women provided food, shelter, and other forms of assistance, which only further incriminated them in the eyes of the Patriots. Rachel Ferguson and her daughters, for example, were brought before the local Patriot committee in 1779 "for harbouring and entertaining a Number of Tories who came down from Canada with an inte[n]tion of Murdering the Defenceless Inhabitants on the Western Frontiers."[41] For their efforts the Ferguson women were jailed and later forced to leave.

By July 1780 it was official policy in New York to "remove families of persons who [had] joined the Enemy." The families were given twenty days to prepare for their departure, their goods and chattels were to be sold to pay the costs, and any who ignored the edict were to "be liable to be proceeded against as Enemies of this and the United States."[42] Some women asked for and received a reprieve; but this required that "sundry well affected inhabitants" had to testify that the woman had "behaved herself in a becoming manner."[43] In other words, it was up to the woman to prove innocence by having well-known Patriots testify on her behalf. In the absence of such testimony, the woman was assumed to share the guilt of her husband.

Exile was the last stage in a process that profoundly altered the role and responsibilities of many Loyalist women. Like their Patriot counterparts, Loyalist women assumed the responsibility for running the household and farm in the absence of their husbands. But Loyalist women also had to endure harassment, persecution, and often poverty because of the actions of their husbands. Most difficult of all, perhaps, was the necessity of abandoning their homes, relatives, and communities.

In facing these adversities, women were often forced to assert themselves and assume what were generally considered to be male responsibilities. The more public and assertive role of women was illustrated by Polly Watts Johnson, who had the audacity, after being captured by the Patriots, to write directly to General George Washington to complain of being treated "with severity."[44] When an exchange had to be arranged for the prominent New York Loyalist Alexander White, it was his wife who undertook the negotiations with the British. Isabel Parker, who had "aided and succoured his Majesty's Scouts on secret service by procuring them provisions and intelligence and encouraging Sundry persons to join his Majesty's service at her great expense, peril and risk," interceded with the governor of Quebec on behalf of her son, who had been in the British secret service and had been arrested by the Patriots. Mrs. Jeremiah French, whose husband had joined the British and had all his property confiscated and his "cattle driven away and sold," was brought to the attention of the Vermont governor and council because she was "very turbulent and troublesome and refused to obey orders." Known for her "bitter tongue," Mrs. French proved so troublesome that the Patriots dispatched her to the British lines.[45]

Women were also forced to take more responsibility for looking after themselves and families. A group of New York Loyalist women who had established themselves near Saratoga petitioned the Patriots in 1780 for permission to go to Canada; in 1781 they were still on the frontier and regarded as a serious enough threat that they were ordered to move to the interior. The sixteen-year-old daughter of John McDonell, a Scots Loyalist from Tryon county, "was obliged to hire herself to an old Dutch woman to spin in order to prevent starving." And there was the case of Elizabeth Bowman, who, after her house on the Susquehanna River had been sacked by the Patriots and her husband and eldest son carried off, was left to care for eight children. The Indians helped them through the winter, and in the spring she moved to the Mohawk River and joined other Loyalist women to grow corn and potatoes. When the British rescued them in the fall and took them to Canada, there were five women, thirty-one children, and one pair of shoes.[46]

Exile marked the end of one stage of Loyalist women's refugee experience and the beginning of another. The women had left the American colonies as disaffected citizens considered a threat to the security of the new nation. In British territory they were burdens, mouths to be fed and bodies to be clothed and housed. When they reached Canada, they were usually destitute and the British unprepared for their arrival. In 1777 an officer in Niagara described the refugees flocking to that base: "They are almost naked and have been so long hiding in the woods, and almost famished that it is distressing to behold them.... I am informed that 50 are on their way, but so weak they can scarcely crawl. I wish your excellency's direction on how to dispose of them."[47] From Crown Point, a base at the other end of the outer perimeter of British defences, came similar accounts of the arrival of Loyalists who "had fled from persecution," especially in the winter when the lakes and rivers could be crossed by sleigh. Often British officials were uncertain what to do with the refugees, and families arriving in Niagara were often sent on to Montreal.[48]

When the women arrived at the bases, they were in need of food, clothing, and shelter. Most had been stripped of their property and many of their possessions before their flight. The journey itself across the wilderness of northern New York was gruelling. Reaching Canada involved either crossing one of the many lakes in an open boat or perhaps a sleigh in winter, or travelling along rugged trails since "there [was] no road by land to go with a carriage." Sir John Johnson and his tenants who fled from northern New York in 1776 travelled for nineteen days, during which they almost starved, going nine days without provisions, except "wild onions, Roots and the leaves of beech trees." When they reached Canada, their shoes were worn through and their clothes ragged.[49]

Sarah Bottum Sherwood's greatest ordeal during the Revolution was her trip to Canada, which began with a wagon ride over trails to the shores of Lake Champlain. Next was a boat trip across the lake and a thirty-mile trek through the bush to the closest British outpost. When Sarah undertook the trek, it was November; she had with her a slave, a child of three, and a baby; and she was seven months pregnant. But she succeeded and was reunited with her husband.[50]

When Loyalists arrived at British bases, penniless and exhausted by the rigours of their journey, they were at the mercy of paternalistic and patriarchal British military regimes. Even Sarah McGinnis, the tough sixty-four-year-old who had wintered with the Iroquois in 1777, was "in dire need" in Montreal the following year. Her daughter was "so scantily lodged" that her mother could not stay with her. She was also refused firewood by the officer in charge, who said that only the Governor could make such a decision. Sarah and her family were left "without any money or income except what they could earn by the needle."[51] Thus, Loyalists had to look to the British government to provide shelter, clothing, and rations and at the end of the war to chart their future.

The British government took care of its charges but expected deference and service in return. The British regimes were military ones that dealt quickly and harshly with dissenters. In return for their keep, men had to fight in the Loyalist regiments and women had to do washing and other domestic chores for the army. Questioning of the regime was neither common nor tolerated. When a group of Loyalists in Quebec petitioned the governor for more aid, for example, they were informed that if the governor's plans for them were not acceptable, they could go to Nova Scotia.[52]

Patriarchy and paternalism were also apparent in the last phase of the Loyalists' experience—their resettlement in what is now eastern Ontario. Under the direction of British officials, the Loyalists were transported into the interior and provided with food, clothing, agricultural equipment, and seeds. They were settled on land surveyed by British officials, and British army officers were there to preserve order and ensure that the governor's instructions were obeyed. Although the new communities were on the frontier, from the beginning there was a structure and hierarchy. In a society where land ownership was central to status, the size of one's land grant varied according to one's military rank, the British government compensated Loyalists for their losses on the basis of the value of their former assets in the American colonies, and Loyalist officers received half pay after their regiments were disbanded.[53]

Thus, when Loyalist women reached British lines, they were reintegrated into a paternalistic and patriarchal power structure. Within this paternalistic order there was a hierarchy. There were those who needed to be cared for and those responsible for administering the care, those in leadership roles and those who were clearly subordinates. Deference to authority was built into the military regimes, and deference was accorded to those dispensing benevolent care and expected of those receiving it. Even more so than the civil regimes in the American colonies, the military regimes in Quebec and New York City had no place for women and even shunned them as extra mouths to be fed and families to be housed. Women could only fit into such paternalistic and patriarchal power structures as subordinates needing care and protection.

This subordination was reflected in the Loyalist women's petitions for rations, subsistence, or compensation for losses. The very act of petitioning those in authority for aid cast all Loyalists in the role of supplicant; "the formulation of a petition," in the words of Linda Kerber, "begins in the acknowledgement of subordination."[54] Moreover, many Loyalist petitions were stylized litanies of loyalty, service, and sacrifice. But there was a difference in the substance of women's petitions: women based their claim to British assistance on their feminine frailty and on the service of their husbands. In fact, some did not even petition on their own behalf but had men request aid for them. When Catherine Peck, wife of one of Sir John's tenants who had fled to Canada in 1776, arrived in New York City "in hope of getting a Passage to Canada" and found herself and her child "destitute of any Sort of Support," it was an official from Indian Affairs who appealed to British officials to assist her.[55] Even Molly Brant, who had been so active in maintaining the loyalty of the Mohawk, had to seek male help when it came to approaching the British for support. She sought advice from her brother in 1779, and in 1780 two members of the Johnson clan and another associate discussed helping Molly and her daughters to get a pension from the British.[56] Of the twenty-six eastern Ontario Loyalist women who sought compensation from the British for their losses, four had men file their claims.[57]

Whether Loyalist women petitioned themselves or had others do it for them, what was stressed was their weakness, helplessness, and dependence. Citing a "numerous, small and helpless family" as his main burden, one Loyalist appealed to the governor of Quebec for subsistence, while another asked for aid for his "chargeable family." The Loyalist Jean McConell summed up perfectly the notion of female incapacity when she described herself as "feeble" and added that she also had "a family of daughters."[58] Feeble and helpless were the adjectives used most often by Loyalist women to describe themselves.[59]

These professions of feebleness were very much at odds with Loyalist women's recent experiences. The case of Phoebe Grant, or Grout, illustrates this point nicely. When her husband and son joined Burgoyne in 1777, the "rebels" seized his property and "effects" and turned her "and three helpless Female children Out of Doors destitute." She then had to "fly" to Quebec "for protection." Within days of her arrival in Quebec, her husband drowned and she was "obliged to provide for herself and her three children without an allowance from government which ceased on the death of her husband." After her husband's death she did "everything in her power to support herself," even though she was "in a country far from a single Friend and a stranger to the language." When Phoebe finally had to throw "herself and poor family at your Excellency's feet praying" for subsistence, she could not revel in her accomplishments and seek praise for even surviving such ordeals; all she could do was tell her story as a tale of suffering and depict herself, in her own words, as "a Feeble Woman."[60]

Why did Loyalist women describe themselves as feeble or helpless when their recent experiences suggested just the opposite? One reason was a practical reality. What the British needed from the Loyalists were able-bodied males to raid the frontiers, spy on the Patriots, bring in new recruits, supply British troops, or build fortifications. What they did not need or want was women and children, who, it was assumed, could perform none of these services and would be a burden to the British because they had to be fed, clothed, and housed. Thus, the only way for women to appeal to the British was to cite their husband's valued services, rather than their own undervalued ones, and to invoke the paternalism of the military regimes by stressing their vulnerability and need for protection.

Another reason, however, was that when they reached British lines, Loyalist women confronted a well-defined power structure in which there were clearly prescribed social roles. In the colonies during the Revolution, traditional relationships were disrupted and lines of authority far from clear. Women could and did do things they might have never dreamed of doing in peacetime, and their actions were of necessity considered socially acceptable, if only because the boundaries of socially acceptable behaviour are more flexible in wartime. However, at British bases lines of authority were not only clear, but were better defined than they had been in the colonies. Though there had been elements of paternalism and patriarchy in the pre-Revolutionary experiences of many Ontario Loyalists, the British regimes were much more patriarchal and paternal. And women could fit into such a power structure only as frail subordinates.

But the fact that women used the language of enfeeblement does not mean that they themselves accepted their own weakness. They were supplicants who had to petition for assistance and "the rhetoric of humility is a necessary part of the petition as a genre, whether or not humility is felt in fact."[61] Women had no choice but to stress their dependence and helplessness; whether they actually believed it is another matter.

Yet, whether or not women accepted their own weakness is beside the point. The language they used expressed accurately their position in the power structure. Whether or not they were weak and dependent, they were assumed to be so for all public purposes and were outwardly treated as such. On the other hand, the consistent use of certain words cannot be divorced from one's attitudes about oneself: if women were forced by circumstances to reiterate their helplessness again and again, how long was it before they came either to accept that helplessness was basic to their femininity or to allow their actions to be limited by their supposed weakness? The fact that the eastern Ontario Loyalist women were never allowed to speak of their achievements with pride meant that they never received in any measure the recognition accorded to Patriot women.

It is ironic that many eastern Ontario Loyalist women, though they overcame greater obstacles and met more devastating challenges during the Revolution than their Patriot counterparts, received less recognition. As well as having to take charge of their families and farms in the absence of their husbands, Loyalist women were dispossessed of their property, thrown out of their houses, and even jailed by the Patriots. They had to leave what was most dear to them—their homes, their relatives, and their friends—and travel through the wilderness to the British lines.

Yet these remarkable and heroic accomplishments were never recognized. When they reached British lines, they had to fit once again into a patriarchal power structure in which their inferiority and dependence were assumed. Needing British support, they had to stress their dependence and weakness to appeal to the paternalism of the British regime. Only their suffering and their husband's service counted with the British. Whereas republicanism at least potentially offered more scope to women, paternalism assumed inequality and deference. There were the weak and the strong, the leaders and the followers. Within such a framework, women could only be the weak followers.

Not only were the accomplishments of eastern Ontario Loyalist women not recognized by the British; they were also ignored by later generations. After the Revolution, myths grew up about the Loyalists' undying devotion to the British Empire or their upper class backgrounds, and tales were told of the men's heroism. Virtually ignored, however, were the heroic feats of the Loyalist women. Whereas the contributions of Patriot women, such as their spinning of homespun cloth, became part of the American folklore, the memories of the *travails* and victories of the eastern Ontario Loyalist women died with them.

These women were also ignored by Canadian historians, who, by focusing on the Revolutionary war on the frontier as it was run by the British and fought by the Loyalist regiments, have overlooked the essential fact that the war was a civil war in which women and children were of necessity participants. The experiences of the eastern Ontario Loyalist women and their part in the civil war that raged on the frontiers are an important part of Canadian history. Recognition of their accomplishments is long overdue.

Notes

1. Mary Beth Norton, *Liberty's Daughters: The Revolutionary Experience of American Women, 1760–1800* (Boston: Little, Brown, 1980); Linda Kerber, *Women of the Republic: Intellect and Ideology in Revolutionary America* (Chapel Hill, N.C.: Univ. of North Carolina Press, 1980). For another view, see Joan Hoff Wilson, "The Illusion of Change: Women and the American Revolution," In Alfred F. Young, ed., *The American Revolution: Explorations in the History of American Radicalism* (DeKalb: Northern Illinois Univ. Press, 1976), pp. 383–446.

2. Jay Fliegelman, *Prodigals and Pilgrims: The American Revolution against Patriarchal Authority, 1750–1800* (Cambridge: Cambridge Univ. Press, 1982); Norton, *Liberty's Daughters,* pp. 235, 229; Jacqueline S. Reinier, "Rearing the Republican Child: Attitudes and Practices in Post-Revolutionary Philadelphia," *William and Mary Quarterly,* 3rd ser., 39 (1982), 150–63.

3. See, for example, Mary Beacock Fryer, "Sarah Sherwood: Wife and Mother, an 'Invisible Loyalist'," in *Eleven Exiles: Accounts of Loyalists of the American Revolution,* Phyllis R. Blakely and John N. Grant, eds. (Toronto: Dundurn, 1982), pp. 245–64; Mary Beth Norton, "Eighteenth-Century American Women in Peace and War: The Case of the Loyalists," *William and Mary Quarterly,* 3rd ser., 33 (1976), 386–409; Katherine M.J. McKenna, " 'Treading the Hard Road': Some Loyalist Women and the American Revolution" (M.A. thesis, Queen's Univ., 1979).

4. M.S. Waltman, "From Soldier to Settler: Patterns of Loyalist Settlement in 'Upper Canada,' 1783–1785" (M.A. thesis, Queen's Univ., 1981), p. 58.

5. Waltman, "From Soldier to Settler," p. 60; Walter Allen Knittle, *Early Eighteenth Century Palatinate Emigration: A British Government Redemptioner Project to Manufacture Naval Stores* (Baltimore: Dorrance, 1937): Eula C. Lapp, *To Their Heirs Forever* (Picton: Picton Publishing Co., 1970); Alice P. Kenney, *Stubborn for Liberty: The Dutch in New York* (Syracuse: Syracuse Univ. Press, 1975); "The Albany Dutch: Loyalists and Patriots," *New York History,* 42 (1961).

6. Waltman, "From Soldier to Settler," p. 62; I.C.C. Graham, *Colonists from Scotland: Emigration to North America, 1707–1783* (Ithaca: Cornell Univ. Press, 1956); Hazel C. Mathews, *The Mark of Honour* (Toronto: Univ. of Toronto Press, 1965).

7. Waltman, "From Soldier to Settler." pp. 39–42.

8. Gerald Dworkin, "Paternalism," in Rolf Sartorious, ed., *Paternalism* (Minneapolis: Univ. of Minnesota Press. 1983), pp. 19–34; Donald Van De Veer, *Paternalistic Intervention: The Moral Bounds of Benevolence* (Princeton: Princeton Univ. Press, 1986), pp. 16–23; John Kleinig, *Paternalism* (Totow, N.J.: Rowman and Allaneld, 1984). pp. 4–5; Jack D. Douglas, "Cooperative Paternalism versus Conflictual Paternalism," in Sartorius, *Paternalism,* pp. 171–200; David Roberts. *Paternalism in Early Victorian England* (New Brunswick, N.J.: Rutgers Univ. Press, 1979), pp. 4–6.

9. Abbott Collection, Ms. 420, Letter and Reference for Richard Mandevell, Sir William Johnson, June 11, 1771. Quoted in Robert William Venables, "Tryon County, 1775–1783: A Frontier in Revolution" (Ph.D. thesis, Vanderbilt Univ., 1967), pp. 72, 64; Edward Countryman, *A People in Revolution: The American Revolution and Political Society* (Baltimore: Johns Hopkins Univ. Press, 1981), pp. 21, 33.

10. Countryman, *A People in Revolution,* p. 33.

11. Bernard Bailyn, *Voyagers to the West: A Passage in the Peopling of America on the Eve of the Revolution* (New York: Knopf, 1986), pp. 192–234; National Archives of Canada [hereafter NAC], *Haldimand Papers,* [hereafter HP], MG 21, B 168, p. 100, "Return of Loyalists, October, 1784"; Robert V. Wells, *The Population of the British Colonies in America before 1776* (Princeton: Princeton Univ. Press, 1975), p. 315.

12. Gerda Lerner, *The Creation of Patriarchy* (New York: Oxford Univ. Press, 1986), p. 239.

13. Kerber, *Women of the Republic,* p. 120; Joan R. Gundersen and Gwen Victor Gampel, "Married Women's Legal Status in Eighteenth-Century New York and Virginia," *William and Mary Quarterly,* 3rd ser., 39 (1982), 114–34.

14. NAC, Fraser Papers, MG 23, B 33, Alexander McDonald to his wife, in "Letters Extracted from the Letter Book of Capt. Alexander McDonald of the Royal Highland Emigrants written from Halifax, Windsor and Cornwallis between 1775 and 1779."

15. Archives of Ontario [hereafter AO], Joel Stone Papers, Dothe Stone Diary, 1777–1792 [hereafter Stone Diary]; Joy Day Buel and Richard Buel, Jr., *The Way of Duty: A Woman and her Family in Revolutionary America* (New York: Norton, 1984); Robert V. Wells, "Quaker Marriage Patterns in a Colonial Perspective," in Nancy F. Cott and Elizabeth Peck, eds., *A Heritage of Her Own: Toward a New Social History of American Women* (New York: Simon and Shuster, 1979), pp. 81–106; Norton, *Liberty's Daughters,* pp. 71–72; Laurel Thatcher Ulrich, *Good Wives: Image and Reality in the Lives of Women in Northern New England, 1650–1750* (New York: Knopf, 1982).

16. See, for example, Stone Diary; Norton, *Liberty's Daughters,* pp. 3–14.

17. Stone Diary, Oct. 22, 1783, p. 5; May 30, 1784, p. 11.

18. Stone Diary, Oct. 22, 1783, p. 5; Dec. 3, 1783, p. 8.

19. New Canaan Historical Society, Noyes Family Papers, pp. 39–47, Mary to Joseph and Rachel Fish, Aug. 6, 1769, May 30, 1772, privately owned, quoted in Buel, *The Way of Duty,* pp. 62–63, p. 67.

20. NAC, Claus Papers, C-1478, vol. 1, Sir John Johnson to Daniel Claus, Jan. 20, 1777.

21. Jack M. Sosin, *The Revolutionary Frontier, 1763–1783* (New York: Holt, Rinehart and Winston, 1967).

22. Victor Hugo Palsits, ed., *Minutes of the Commissioners for Detecting and Defeating Conspiracies in the State of New York: Albany County Sessions, 1778–1781,* 3 vols. (New York: J.B. Lyon, 1909), Aug. 13, 1781, vol. 2, 762–63.

23. *Ibid.,* July 25, 1781, vol. 2, 751–52.

24. *Ibid.,* Sept. 4, 1778, vol. 1, 224; May 20, 1778, vol. 1, 122; June 17, 1778, vol. 1, 146; Aug. 3, 1779, vol. 1, 398; Oct. 3, 1778, vol. 1, 252.

25. *Ibid.,* Nov. 8, 1780, vol. 2, 563; Jan. 29, 1781, vol. 2, 624; June 9, 1781, vol. 2, 733.

26. Barbara Graymont, *The Iroquois in the American Revolution* (Syracuse: Syracuse Univ. Press, 1972), pp. 17, 21–23.

27. Graymont, *The Iroquois in the American Revolution,* p. 47; *Dictionary of Canadian Biography,* vol. 4, 416–19; H. Pearson Gundy, "Molly Brant, Loyalist," *Ontario Historical Society Papers and Records,* 45 (1953), 97–108.

28. NAC, HP, vol. 21, p. 774, Daniel Claus to Governor Haldimand, Aug. 30, 1779; NAC, HP, vol. 21, p. 787, Captain Frazer to Haldimand, Mar. 21, 1780.

29. NAC, HP, vol. 21, p. 774, Daniel Claus to Governor Haldimand, Nov. 5, 1778.

30. NAC, HP, vol. 27, p. 302, Petition of Sarah McGinn, Audit Office 14.

31. *Ibid.*

32. Janice Potter and George Rawlyk, "Richard Cartwright, Jr.," *Dictionary of Canadian Biography,* vol. 5, 167–72.

33. *Report of the Public Archives of Ontario* [hereafter *PAO Report*], (Toronto: 1904), Claim of Garnet Dingman, p. 1038; claim of John Glasford, p. 1112; claim of Martin Waldec, p. 1121.

34. Petition by Philip Empy, Mar. 1, 1780, HP, vol. 21, p. 874.

35. *PAO Report,* Claim of Justus Sherwood; Ian Cleghorn Pemberton, "Justus Sherwood, Vermont Loyalist, 1747–1798," (Ph.D. thesis. Univ. of Western Ontario, 1973); Mary Beacock Fryer, *Buckskin Pimpernel: The Exploits of Justus Sherwood, Loyalist Spy* (Toronto: Dundurn, 1981), "Sarah Sherwood: ...," " *Eleven Exiles,* pp. 245–64; Queen's University Archives, H.M. Jackson, *Justus Sherwood: Soldier, Loyalist and Negotiator* (Kingston: n.p., 1958).

36. AO, John Munro Papers, Undated document; NAC, HP series B, vol. 214, p. 35.

37. Palsits, *Minutes of the Commissioners,* Oct. 1, 1778, vol. 1, 248.

38. "Petition of sundry women wives of tories for relief," n.d. Tryon County Committee of Safety Papers, in Kerber, *Women of the Republic,* p. 50.

39. Palsits, *Minutes of the Commissioners,* Aug. 1, 1778, vol. 1, 190.

40. *Ibid.,* Introduction, vol. 1, 57.

41. *Ibid., Minutes of the Commissioners,* Sept. 21, 1778, vol. 1, 237–38; Sept. 8, 1779, vol. 1, 441.

42. *Ibid.,* vol. 3, 795.

43. See, for example, the case of Elizabeth Hogel, in Palsits, *Minutes of the Commissioners,* vol 2, 540.

44. Mrs. Johnson to General Washington, June 16, 1776, Peter Force, *American Archives,* 9 vols. (Washington, D.C., 1837–53), 4th series, vol. 6, 930.

45. Palsits, *Minutes of the Commissioners,* Aug. 15, 1778, vol. 1, 206; NAC, HP, vol. 21, p. 875, Petition of Isabel Parker, AO, French Papers, Loveland Munson, "The Early History of Manchester."

46. Palsits, *Minutes of the Commissioners.* Oct. 29, 1780, vol. 3, 558; Apr. 30, 1781. vol. 3, 696; NAC, HP, vol. 73, p. 54, John McDonell to Mathews, Mar. 20, 1780; "A Letter from Mrs. Elizabeth Bowman Spohn," in J.J. Talman, *Loyalist Narratives from Upper Canada* (Toronto: Champlain Society, 1946). 315–22.

47. NAC, Colonial Office 42 [hereafter CO 42], vol. 36, B 33, pp. 2–3, R.B. Lernoult to Haldimand, Apr. 28, 1777.

48. CO 42, Q13, vol. 36, B 33, Sir Guy Carleton to Lord G. Germaine, May 27, 1777; NAC, Claus Papers, vol. 25, C 1485, Taylor and Diffin to Daniel Claus, Nov. 11, 1778, Claus Papers.

49. Claus Papers, C 1478, vol. 1, Johnson to Claus, Jan. 20, 1777.

50. Fryer, "Sarah Sherwood: ...," *Eleven Exiles,* pp. 245–64.

51. NAC, HP, vol. 21, p. 774, Claus to Haldimand, Nov. 19, 1778.

52. NAC, HP, vol. B 211, pp. 133–34, Memorial: Michael Grass and Loyalists from New York, Sorel, Jan., 1784. NAC, HP, vol. B 63, pp. 109–10, Mathews to Stephen DeLancey. Mar. 2, 1784.

53. H.V. Temperley, "Frontierism, Capital and the American Loyalists in Canada," *Journal of American Studies,* 13 (1979), 5–27.

54. Kerber, *Women of the Republic,* p. 85.

55. NAC, British Headquarters Papers, vol. 16, microfilm, reel M-348, [Name illegible] to Lt. Col. Roger Morris, Apr. 22, 1779.

56. NAC, Claus Papers, C 1478, Mary Brant to Joseph Brant, Oct. 5, 1779; C 1485, Captain Frazer to Daniel Claus, June 26, 1780.

57. Lydia Van Alstine, Flora Livingston, widow Obenholt, Margaret Hare.

58. NAC, HP, vol. 21, p. 875, Petition to Haldimand, Jan. 3, 1783; HP, vol. 21, p. 874, Petition of George Christie, Dec. 16, 1778; HP, vol. 21, p. 874, Petition of Jean McDonell, Nov. 30, 1782.

59. Mary Beth Norton, "Eighteenth-Century American Women in Peace and War: The Case of the Loyalists," *William and Mary Quarterly,* 3rd ser., 33 (1976), 386–409.

60. NAC, HP, A 776, Phoebe Grout, Petition.

61. Kerber, *Women of the Republic,* p. 85.

CHAPTER

7 INVENTED TRADITION: LAURA SECORD AND THE WAR OF 1812

"Laura Secord," Cecilia Morgan writes in the final selection in this chapter, "is best-known as the figurehead of a candy company." Just as one is confronted by a multiplicity of choices over flavour, content, shape, colour or wrapping in one of those stores, Laura Secord herself can be regarded as a "variety pack." While some have considered her a heroine extraordinaire, others have dismissed her claim as "too absurd for further discussion."[1] As recently as 1986, on the other hand, she was called *"la plus celebre des espionnes canadiennes,"*[2] yet a textbook with a strong feminist bias, published in 1993, does not even mention her.[3] Over the almost two centuries since the battle of Beaver Dams, for which she became famous, controversy has swirled about Laura Secord as each generation embellished the legend, fabricated a new Laura, rejected a previous Laura, or attacked those who wrote about her. In the process she has gone from profound obscurity, to mythological heroine, to questionable woman, to symbol for a movement.

It is unlikely that the Laura Secord conundrum will ever be resolved, for people will continue to make choices about her just as they make choices in the candy stores. The readings offered here represent three of those choices. The details of her life are quite straightforward, as presented by Ruth McKenzie in the first selection from the *Dictionary of Canadian Biography*. McKenzie had previously written the very sympathetic *Laura Secord: The Legend and the Lady*.

The second reading, by George C. Ingram, on "The Story of Laura Secord Revisited," is typical of the revisionist perspective that dominated historical writing into the 1960s. Ingram examined the previous literature critically, and offered new details as evidence to provide a modified analysis of the subject. The third selection is by contemporary feminist Cecilia Morgan on " 'Of Slender Frame and Delicate Appearance': The Placing of Laura Secord in the Narratives of Canadian Loyalist History." Morgan is concerned not about the actual historical events or even about Secord herself, but about the use of the Secord image over time. She begins with "the deeply gendered notions and assumptions" of world view that are dominant with males then follows the Secord legacy by "linking gender, race, nation, and empire in both past and present." It is the use of history, rather than history itself, that concerns Morgan.

Notes

1. W.S. Wallace, *The Story of Laura Secord: A Study in Historical Evidence* (Toronto, 1932), p. 25.

2. Hugh Halliday, "Secret Professionnel," *Holiday Canada*, no. 50, Vol. 5, 1986, p. 1697.

3. Margaret Conrad, Alvin Finkel and Cornelius Jaenan, *History of the Canadian Peoples: Beginnings to 1867* (Toronto: Copp Clark Pitman Ltd., 1993).

Suggestions for Further Reading

Errington, Jane, *The Lion, the Eagle and Upper Canada: A Developing Colonial Ideology*. Kingston and Montreal: McGill-Queen's University Press, 1987.

McKenzie, Ruth, *Laura Secord: The Legend and the Lady*. Toronto: McClelland and Stewart, 1971.

Mills, David, *The Idea of Loyalty in Upper Canada, 1784–1850*. Kingston and Montreal: McGill-Queen's University Press, 1988.

Robinson, Helen Caister, *Laura: A Portrait of Laura Secord*. Toronto: Dundurn, 1981.

Sheppard, George, "'Deeds Speak': Militiamen, Medals, and the Invented Traditions of 1812," *Ontario History*, LXXXIII, no. 3 (September 1990), 207–32.

Sheppard, George, *Plunder, Profit, and Paroles: A Social History of the War of 1812 in Upper Canada*. Kingston and Montreal: McGill-Queen's University Press, 1994.

Stanley, G.F.G., *The War of 1812: Land Operations*. Toronto: Macmillan of Canada in collaboration with the National Museum of Man, 1983.

Turner, Wesley, *The War of 1812: The War that Both Sides Won*. Toronto: Dundurn, 1990.

Wise, S.F., "Colonial Attitudes from the Era of the War of 1812 to the Rebellion of 1837," in S. Wise and R.C. Brown, *Canada Views the United States*. Toronto: Macmillan of Canada, 1967.

Zaslow, Morris, (ed.), *The Defended Border: Upper Canada and the War of 1812*. Toronto: Macmillan, 1964.

INGERSOLL, LAURA (SECORD)

Ruth McKenzie

INGERSOLL, LAURA (Secord), heroine; b. 13 Sept. 1775 in Great Barrington, Mass., eldest daughter of Thomas Ingersoll and Elizabeth Dewey; d. 17 Oct. 1868, at Chippawa (Niagara Falls, Ont.).

When Laura Ingersoll was eight, her mother died, leaving four little girls. Her father remarried twice and had a large family by his third wife. In the American War of Independence, Ingersoll fought on the rebel side, but in 1795 he immigrated to Upper Canada where he had obtained a township grant for settlement. His farm became the site of the modern town of Ingersoll. He ran a tavern at Queenston until his township (Oxford-upon-the-Thames) was surveyed. Within two years, about 1797, Laura married James Secord, a young merchant of Queenston. He was the youngest son of a loyalist officer of Butler's Rangers, who had brought his family to Niagara in 1778. James and Laura Secord were to have six daughters and one son.

They lived first at St. Davids but soon settled in Queenston. Early in the War of 1812, James, a sergeant in the 1st Lincoln militia, was wounded in the battle of Queenston Heights and was rescued from the battlefield by his wife. The following summer, when neither side had a firm hold of the Niagara peninsula, Laura heard on 21 June 1813, probably by listening to the conversation of some American officers dining at her house, that the Americans intended to surprise the British outpost at Beaver Dams and capture the officer in charge, Lieutenant James Fitzgibbon. It was urgent that someone warn Fitzgibbon and, since James was disabled, Laura resolved to take the message herself early the next morning.

The distance to the outpost by direct road was twelve miles but Laura feared she would encounter American guards that way and chose a roundabout route. She went first to St. Davids where she was joined by her niece, Elizabeth Secord, and then to Shipman's Corners (St. Catharines). Elizabeth became exhausted and Laura continued alone, uncertain of the way but following the general direction of Twelve Mile Creek through fields and woods. That evening, after crossing the creek on a fallen tree, Laura came unexpectedly on an Indian encampment. She was frightened, but after she explained her mission to the chief he took her to Fitzgibbon. Two days later, on 24 June 1813, an American force under Colonel Charles Boerstler was ambushed near Beaver Dams by some 400 Indians led by Dominique Ducharme and William Johnson Kerr. Fitzgibbon then persuaded Boerstler to surrender with 462 men to his own fifty men. In the official reports of the victory no mention was made of Laura Secord.

From the *Dictionary of Canadian Biography*, Vol. IX (Toronto: University of Toronto Press, 1976), 405–7. Reprinted by permission.

The Secords lived in poverty in the postwar years until 1828 when James, who had received a small pension because of his war wound, was appointed registrar, then judge (in 1833), of the Niagara Surrogate Court. In 1835 he became collector of customs at Chippawa. He died in 1841 leaving Laura without financial resources. She ran a school for children in her Chippawa cottage for a brief period. Petitions to the government for a pension and other favours were unsuccessful.

Laura Secord was eighty-five before she achieved wide public recognition for her heroic deed. While visiting Canada in 1860, the Prince of Wales (the future Edward VII) learned of Laura's twenty-mile walk. She had prepared a memorial for the prince describing her wartime service, and she also had placed her signature among those War of 1812 veterans who presented an address to him. After Albert Edward returned to England, he sent Mrs. Secord a reward of £100. She died in 1868, at the age of ninety-three, and was buried beside her husband in Drummond Hill Cemetery, Niagara Falls.

Laura Secord became celebrated as a heroine in history, poetry, and drama, after 1860. Legends grew; the favourite was that she had taken a cow with her on her walk, for camouflage, and that she had milked it in the presence of American sentries before leaving it behind in the woods. In fact, Mrs. Secord never mentioned a cow and it is unlikely that she encountered an American sentry. William F. Coffin apparently invented the episode for his book *1812, The War And Its Moral* (1864). According to another story, Laura had walked through the woods at night, on her bare feet. But she herself said, "I left early in the morning," and though she may have lost a slipper in the woods or fields, she was far too sensible to have started out barefoot. Her popular fame was such that two monuments were erected in her honour, one at Lundy's Lane in 1901, the other on Queenston Heights in 1910. Her portrait was hung in the parliament buildings in Toronto, and a memorial hall was established in the Laura Secord School at Queenston.

Some twentieth-century historians, however, have questioned her place in history. For example, W. Stewart Wallace in *The Story Of Laura Secord: A Study In Historical Evidence* (1932) concluded from the available documents that Mrs. Secord had undoubtedly taken a message to Fitzgibbon, probably on 23 June, but that she had arrived too late for her information to be of value. Lieutenant Fitzgibbon had said in his report on the battle of Beaver Dams: "At [John] De Cou's this morning, about seven o'clock, I received information that...the Enemy...was advancing towards me..." It was argued that this information, brought by Indian scouts, was Fitzgibbon's first warning. Wallace also cited a certificate written by Fitzgibbon in 1837 testifying that Mrs. Secord had brought warning of an American attack; unfortunately Fitzgibbon gave no specific date, and he wrote, he said, "in a moment of much hurry and from memory."

The puzzle of the chronology and of Laura's role in the events was solved when two earlier testimonials came to light, both written by Fitzgibbon, in 1820 and 1827, to support petitions the Secords had made to the government.

In the 1827 certificate, Fitzgibbon said that Mrs. Secord had come "on the 22nd day of June 1813," and that "in consequence of this information" he had placed the Indians in a position to intercept the Americans. Thus he made it clear that Laura's warning had indeed made the victory possible at Beaver Dams. It was a significant victory, and for her part in it Laura Secord became justly known as the heroine of the War of 1812.

Laura Secord typified pioneer women in her courage, endurance, and resolution in the face of adversity. Fitzgibbon remembered her as a person of "slender frame and delicate appearance," but underneath was a strong and persistent will.

THE STORY OF LAURA SECORD REVISITED

George C. Ingram

Scorned by her own generation, Laura Secord was enthroned as the queen of Upper Canadian pioneer womanhood in the last half of the nineteenth century and the first part of the twentieth century. Her claim to renown was her perilous journey to warn James Fitzgibbon of an impending American attack on Beaver Dams, an attack that came on 24 June 1813. Before Laura herself died in 1868, she had modestly asserted that her contribution had enabled Fitzgibbon to save the country. Her case was then taken up by poetic nationalists, ardent feminists, and uncritical historians who revelled in the romantic qualities of Laura's sylvan ramble and unhesitatingly added a few flourishes of their own. By 1913, a century after the fact, an impressive edifice had been constructed around Laura's walk.

By this time, the folklore surrounding Laura contained so many undocumented details that it became an easy target for the critical historian. Accordingly, in the next few decades Laura was stripped of all her achievements and left a shivering "myth"[1] who "played no part in determining the issue of the Battle at the Beaver Dams."[2]

Newly-discovered evidence shows that the "debunking" has gone too far. Laura Secord did give an early warning. She likely encountered an American sentry, and did undertake a perilous and lengthy walk, although the specific length of this walk cannot be known. With the debunkers, however, it must be agreed that Laura played only a limited role in the battle, not because she arrived too late, as her foremost critic W.S. Wallace has maintained,[3] but because Fitzgibbon and the Indian leaders chose to ignore her warning after it failed to come true exactly as expected. This circumstance becomes evident from an examination of the battle and an analysis of Laura's role in it.

From *Ontario History*, Vol. LVII, no. 2 (1965), 85–96. Reprinted by permission.

Even those recent historians who are taking a long critical second look at the War of 1812 agree that the Battle of Beaver Dams fought on 24 June 1813, was an "important victory for the British."[4] It followed a number of significant events. On 27 May, the Americans had launched an amphibious attack against Fort George, forcing the hopelessly outnumbered British troops and militia under General John Vincent to retreat first to Beaver Dams and then to the British keep on Burlington Heights. The Americans had pursued rapidly, reaching Stoney Creek on 5 June. That night, an ingenious attack by the British forces completely routed the Americans and forced them to retreat first to the Forty, and then to Fort George. By 9 June, the Americans had abandoned all their newly-won positions on the peninsula and had concentrated their troops in Fort George. The British immediately cordoned the fort with centre-positions at De Cou's and St. Catharines.

At De Cou's there was a detachment of forty-six men of the 49th Regiment under Lieutenant James Fitzgibbon and a considerable body of Indians under Captains Ducharme, Kerr, and Norton. The latter harassed and molested the enemy's pickets and even fired on American troops at Queenston. Their activities probably led the American commander to decide to despatch a troop of 550 men under Lieutenant-Colonel Boerstler to eliminate this thorn in the side of the American position.

Boerstler set out from Fort George on the twenty-third of June and arrived in Queenston "about eleven o'clock p.m."[5] The next morning, "after daybreak,"[6] the detachment advanced, making contact with the British Indians "between eight and nine o'clock in the morning of the twenty-fourth."[7] The three-hour engagement that followed was fought solely between the Americans and the Indians. The latter surrounded, harassed and terrified the American troops. By the time that Fitzgibbon with his regulars came "to our aid,"[8] he was able to demand and obtain a surrender from Boerstler, who feared that his troops might face the bloody reprisals of the "tomahawk and the scalping knife"[9] if the Indians were allowed to continue. The entire American force capitulated and, with the exception of the militia men who were paroled, fell into the hands of the British. Captain De Haren, the senior officer for the area, arrived with reinforcements from his position at St. Catharines only after the American army had capitulated.

The victory was significant. This was the last time that the Americans ventured outside of Fort George with a force of any size. The Indians, who now had a free hand around the fort, effectively contained the American troops. "This army," wrote Porter of the American militia a month later, "lies panic-struck, shut up and whipped in by a few hundred miserable savages...."[10] In December, after months of virtual inaction, McLure, the American commander, fired Newark and abandoned Fort George.

What part did Laura Secord play in the actual events of the Battle of Beaver Dams? There can be no doubt that Laura did walk to De Cou's and did talk to James Fitzgibbon. Three certificates issued in 1820, 1827, and 1837 by Fitzgibbon attest to this fact.[11] It also appears quite certain that Laura arrived "on the twenty-second day of June 1813...after sun set"[12] and "on the morning of the second day after the information was given...[the] detachment was captured."[13]

If Laura walked on 22 June she either obtained her information that morning, which is highly unlikely because she set out very early, or the night before, that is, the twenty-first. In 1827, Fitzgibbon explained that "her husband had learned from an American officer the preceding night...that a detachment from the American army then in Fort George would be sent out the following morning [the twenty-third]...."[14] This testimony would immediately rule out Boerstler as the source of information as he did not arrive in Queenston with his troops until around 11:00 p.m. on the twenty-third.[15]

At least two possibilities arise as alternative sources. A detachment of the 13th Regiment under Colonel Chrystie had been stationed at Queenston "for a few days" and "was ordered back two days previous to the marching of the detachment [Boerstler's]."[16] This fact means that it left Queenston on the twenty-first or twenty-second depending on how one dates the "two days." Here was a possible source of information. And, if the detachment did not leave until the twenty-second, here is an explanation of the American picket which played such a prominent role in subsequent accounts of Laura's trials. Another source could have been the renegade Captain Chapin, whose raiders were circulating in the neighbourhood at this time and might have stopped for a meal in Queenston (a meal also crops up in most of the accounts). Certainly Chapin seems to have been prominent in recommending the attack of Beaver Dams.[17]

Both of these sources would have been mere speculation at this time because the American plan was not officially revealed until the twenty-third.[18] Professor Moir has suggested that "it is quite conceivable that the American plan for a surprise attack was common knowledge to the officers at Fort George."[19] The detachment at De Cou's was a thorn in the side of the American position, and if there was talk of moving against it, quite naturally officers close to the area of trouble would be discussing the matter as a form of wishful thinking, or perhaps armchair generalship. This talk would have been vague and uncertain on the twenty-first. Certainly it would not have been definite regarding times and numbers. This is probably the type of information that Laura carried to De Cou's.

Fitzgibbon himself was guarded in his assessment of the information. In 1820, he described it as "substantially correct,"[20] implying a general validity. But in 1827 he was more definite when he explained that "Colonel Boerstler, their commander, in a conversation with me confirmed fully the information communicated to me by Laura Secord."[21] At the very least, Laura Secord told Fitzgibbon of "an intended attack to be made by the Enemy upon the detachment"[22] and might have been more specific and reported that "a detachment from the American army then in Fort George would be sent out on the following morning (the twenty-third)...."[23]

What effect did Laura's information have on the outcome of the battle? It definitely gave an early warning. Fitzgibbon apparently took it very seriously at first and acted upon it:

> In consequence of this information, I placed the Indians under Norton together with my own Detachment in a situation to intercept the American Detachment and we occupied it during the night of the twenty-second.[24]

But he made no attempt that night to tell De Haren, his superior officer at St. Catharines, of the impending attack. The latter does not seem to have heard of the Americans' approach until the morning of the actual battle.[25] Certainly no attempt was made to rush in reinforcements until that time. Perhaps due to ambition or through suspicion of Laura's account, Fitzgibbon decided not to relay the news.

After maintaining the position during the night of the twenty-second, the troops disbanded again. On the morning of the twenty-fourth Fitzgibbon's men were not with the Indians.[26] One can imagine the ill-temper of the British troops after staying up all night chasing "paper tigers"! Fitzgibbon must have been an unpopular man around camp on the twenty-third. The Indians in Queenston on the twenty-third[27] might have been sent to discover if the enemy was approaching. They were there in the afternoon, well before Boerstler arrived, and their report probably heaped more suspicion on Laura's warning. The expectation of an attack quite likely then dwindled, bringing in turn a relaxation in vigilance.

Certainly neither the Indians nor Fitzgibbon's detachment was well-prepared on the morning of the twenty-fourth. Ducharme discovered the enemy's approach only at about 8:00 that morning when an Indian scout brought back word, while Fitzgibbon heard shortly after.[28] Only then was a messenger despatched to De Haren.[29] The engagement had already begun and had almost finished by the time that Fitzgibbon was able to move his men into position. In other words, in spite of, or because of Laura's early warning the installation was caught off guard. The failure of her prognostication to develop a forecast might have led Fitzgibbon "to doubt the veracity of Mrs. Secord's information";[30] furthermore, it could have lulled the detachment into false confidence. On the other hand, the installation could still have been kept on a sharper guard than usual; that is, the scouts which gave the crucial warning might not have been circulating under normal conditions.

Caught off guard as they were, neither Ducharme nor Fitzgibbon could very well stress in the official reports that they received information of an impending American attack a full two days before.[31] Instead, both mentioned the much more dramatic day-of-the-battle report brought in by the Indian scout. However, why did other accounts of the battle, even the informal ones, fail to mention advance information? Perhaps Fitzgibbon wished to keep Mrs. Secord in the background for fear of her life. She had come from behind the enemy lines and returned the next day. If her name was revealed, it would circulate, become known to the Americans, and the Secords in Queenston would suffer.

Mrs. Secord did come to Fitzgibbon on the twenty-second with information that an American attack would come on the twenty-third. Her information might have aided somewhat in bringing about the subsequent British victory, but it did not have the effect that it might have had simply because "the enemy did not come until the morning of the twenty-fourth."[32] In each of the certificates Fitzgibbon stressed this time lag as though he were attempting to explain some doubt which existed at the time. Only once did Fitzgibbon concede that "I am personally indebted to her for her conduct upon that occasion."[33] But never did he attribute the victory directly to her information.

* * *

Based on this shaky information, Laura Secord's story eventually achieved a tremendous popularity. The *fons et origio*, as Wallace maintained, rested with the Secord family and especially Laura in her later years. The explanation for the story's continued popularity and expansion after her death must be looked for elsewhere. Laura Secord was a woman and this in itself accounts for the avid interest shown by those of her own sex whose whimsical approach to historical study added details of decidedly doubtful validity. But Laura's walk must also be viewed within the larger context of the War of 1812 which has itself been surrounded by an aura of folklore. Central to this has been the myth of the militia, the tenacious idea, only recently attacked, that Upper Canada ensured her own survival.

In 1813, Bishop Strachan gave what was probably the earliest statement of the belief:

> It will be told by the future historians that the province of Upper Canada without the assistance of man or arms except a handful of regular troops repelled its invaders, slew or took them all prisoners, and captured from its enemies the greater part of the arms by which it was defended....And never, surely was greater activity shown in any country than our militia have exhibited, never greater valour, cooler resolution, and more resolved conduct; they have emulated the choicest veterans and they have twice saved the country.[34]

Strachan accurately predicted the viewpoint that historians would take. For almost a century and a half Upper Canadians and later Ontarians gloried in the fact that they alone had repulsed the neighbour to the South. The myth lived on through the nineteenth century, receiving strength and vigour with periodic appearances of histories of war and a barrage of shorter articles published in the journals of local historical societies.

When she conveyed her message to Fitzgibbon at Beaver Dams, Laura Secord became the only Upper Canadian involved in what was a significant battle of the campaign of 1813 on the Niagara peninsula. James Fitzgibbon, in charge of the small detachment of regulars, had fought in the 19th and 61st Regiments of Great Britain and only after the war became a resident of Upper Canada, although the fact that he did become a resident might have undermined Laura's earlier claims. The company under him was of the 49th Regiment, a troop of British regulars. The Indians, natives though they were, actually fought and won the battle, but could scarcely be considered for a position in the Canadian War of 1812 folklore. Of course, there was Captain Chapin. But he was a turncoat Upper Canadian who was fighting for the Americans, and the myth conveniently attempts to play down or reject such exceptional characters. Laura then, was the only true-blue Canadian eligible for veneration. The fact that she was a woman placed her in a category in which few dramatic examples could be found. She became the symbol of the pioneer Upper Canadian women sturdily defying the American invader—a symbol which at least made the Canadian resistance heterosexual.

Not until the middle of the twentieth century was the "myth of the militia" really challenged; and then, it was heartlessly swept aside by a military historian, C.P. Stacey, who maintained that the war had been won mainly by the British regulars. The new interpretation clashed vigorously with the already shaken "Whiggery" of Canadian historiography. No longer could the "victory" in 1814 be viewed as the first assertion, albeit weak, of a Canadian nation, which had almost single-handed and certainly without significant help from the mother country, repulsed an aggressive United States. Laura Secord, a significant part of the general myth of the War of 1812, has also fallen prey to the onslaught against the war.

* * *

The Secords were not very reticent about Laura's feat. In the course of the next three decades, it was used at least four times in attempts by the Secords to obtain concessions from the provincial government. In 1820, James Secord petitioned Lieutenant Governor Maitland for a grant of the military reserve at Queenston listing among his family's contributions the fact that

> [the petitioner's] wife embraced an opportunity of rendering some service at the risk of her life, in going through the Enemies' lines to communicate information to a detachment of His Majesty's troops at the Beaver Dams in the month of June 1813.[35]

Accompanying the petition was a certificate of proof from James Fitzgibbon.[36] The very fact that Secord felt obliged to include a certificate documenting the trip shows that the journey was not yet common knowledge. Fitzgibbon had received all of the credit for the victory in the battle, because of his official report and the fact that he had negotiated the surrender. Only two years earlier on 30 March 1818, Fitzgibbon had issued a similar document for W.J. Kerr, explaining that "with respect to the affair with Captain Boerstler, not a shot was fired on our side by any but the Indians."[37] But James Secord did not make any extravagant claims here, concerning the outcome of the battle. He merely noted, as did all of Fitzgibbon's certificates, that Laura communicated information to the detachment at De Cou's.

When the second certificate appeared in 1827,[38] James Secord was again "an applicant for some situation."[39] Maitland apparently turned down his request but did have "a favourable opinion of the character claims of Mr. Secord and his wife...and suggested to her that when the Brock's monument was completed she might have charge of it...."[40] The Secords seem to have refused this position.

By 1839, the June day walk had become the only card which the Secords played. Mrs. Secord petitioned for the grant of the

> Ferry at Queenston with Rent free. That your Excellency will be pleased to affix a small Rent upon the same as you in your judgement may seem just and right, say 50 per year, leaving therefore all herein stated and considering her great claim, and your memorialist indifferent circumstances, your Excellency will give her case Just and equitable consideration.[41]

By this time Laura's claim was much stronger. She gave, she argued:

> important entelligence of a meditated attack of the Americans upon our troops, and by which means 550 of the enemy were captured...and for which performance your Excellency's memorialist has never received the smallest compensation....[42]

The memorial was not even answered. This was harsh testimony of the shock that "officialdom" in Upper Canada placed in Laura's feat.

Undaunted as ever, Laura applied in 1841 for pensions for herself and her husband, who died in that year. This time the plea was more desperate and the claim much stronger:

> But for such information your Excellency's Petitioner is fully convinced the British troops must have been captured and by that means would have lost an important station.[43]

Again a certificate was appended to the petition, presumably the certificate of 1837. The Governor, Sir George Arthur, did not think the plea even warranted the placing of the petition before the Legislature. "In reply," wrote the Civil Secretary, "I am commanded to inform you, that His Excellency regrets that he does not feel himself warranted under all the circumstances of your case, in bringing it under the notice of the Legislature."[44] Again official disdain was shown for the contribution of Mrs. Secord.

A few years later, in 1845, the story of Laura Secord first appeared in print in the form of a letter written by Laura's son, Charles B. Secord, to the *Church*. The occasion was a debate in the House of Assembly "relative to the propriety of granting Col. Fitzgibbon £1,000 for his services in lieu of a grant of land."[45] A member of the Legislature, Mr. Aylwin, had protested that a Major Delormier, and not Fitzgibbon, deserved the credit for the British victory. Secord now set out to settle the record. His mother had been instrumental in the battle. She had overheard enemy officers plotting, had carried the message to Fitzgibbon, and the latter "in consequence of this information prepared himself to meet the enemy; and soon after, the attack being made, the American troops were captured.... Col. Fitzgibbon was the only officer who appeared to be in command, to whom my mother gave the information, and who acted the part he so nobly did on that occasion."[46] Fitzgibbon was returned to the spotlight and Mrs. Secord now added.

Laura's role now became public property and from this point can be dated the unrestrained elaboration of the Secord story. At first Laura herself, with her memory romanticized by the fancies of old age, provided the innovations. Gilbert Auchinleck's *History of the War Between Great Britain and United States of America During the Years 1812, 1813, 1814*, appeared in the *Anglo-American Magazine* of 1853. Laura's venture was not included in the actual text; but in a footnote the author quoted a long narrative by Laura herself, including, as had the account of 1845, the American sentries and the awesome Indians. When it came to an evaluation of her contribution, she was relatively subdued: "Benefiting from this information, Capt. Fitzgibbon, formed his plans accordingly and captured about 500 American infantry."[47]

Eight years later, in February 1861, Laura wrote her account for another history of the war, this time for Benson J. Lossing's anecdotal and highly personal *Pictorial Field Book of the War of 1812*. The strongest claim to date, both for the Battle of Beaver Dams and Laura's role, was advanced: "With the intelligence I gave him [Fitzgibbon] he formed his plans and saved his country...."[48] More interesting was the account of Lossing of the visit of the Prince of Wales in 1860. A list of signatures of veterans of the War of 1812 was being prepared to present to him and "Mrs. Secord applied for permission to place her name on the list."[49] The strange part was that she had to explain why her name should be on such a list. "Wherefore? was the natural question. She told her story...."[50] In other words, the story of Laura's contribution was not yet common currency, even in her own district. It was in the next half-century that Laura's feat received popularization.

Laura herself, in claiming in 1861 that Fitzgibbon had "saved his country" and that she had been the power behind the scene, went as far on the basic issue as any account that followed. But the attendant circumstances, the events surrounding Laura's walk, received an elaboration and romanticization that went far beyond even the imaginative mind of Laura's later life. Furthermore, Laura's exploit, like so many heroic deeds of the past, was called in to serve a variety of causes.

W.F. Coffin's *1812, The War and its Moral* was one of the first works to appear. In what seems to be in the main an inferential account, he gave many flourishes to the story. A cow is added to give Laura some protection in her walk, and Laura herself is described in far more detail than previously. The bovine extension, now an essential part of the folklore surrounding Laura, was solely a product of Coffin's imagination.[51]

Later Charles Mair—poet, author, and Canadian nationalist—saw in Laura Secord's exploit a way of whipping up nationalist fervour sadly lacking in the new dominion. His "Ballad for Brave Women," based mainly on information found in William Coffin, provided a moral example for all Canadian women:

> For a moment her Reason forsook her; she raved,
> She laughed, and she cried— "They are saved! they are saved!"
> Then her senses returned, and with thanks, loud and deep
> Sounding sweetly around her, she sank into sleep
> And Boerstler came up; but his movements were known.
> His force was surrounded, his scheme overthrown,
> By a woman's devotion—on stone be't engraved!
> The foeman was beaten, and Burlington saved.
>
> Ah! faithful to death were our women of Yore,
> Have they fled with the past, to be heard of no more?
> No, No! though his laurelled one sleeps on the grave;
> We have maidens as true, we have matrons as brave;
> And should Canada ever be forced to the test—
> To spend for our country the blood of her best—
> When her sons lift the linstock and brandish the sword
> Her daughters will think of brave Laura Secord.[52]

What better way could one find for kindling a spirit of unity than by reference to Canada's only war for survival and to the frail and yet heroic Laura?

Others who followed did not have such a grand aim, or, at least, the aim was considerably more parochial. Laura was taken up with enthusiasm by the members of the movement for equality of women. Mrs. Sarah A. Curzon, for instance, was a "Champion in Canada of woman's rights."[53] Her play, *Laura Secord*, ends with Fitzgibbon attributing his victory to "a brave woman's glorious deed,"[54] and in her preface Mrs. Curzon made her feelings even more explicit:

> But surely we who enjoy the happiness she [Laura] so largely secured for us, we who have known how to honour Brock and Brant, will also know how to honour Tecumseh and LAURA SECORD; *the heroine as well as the heroes of our Province—of our common Dominion*—and will no longer delay to do it, lest Time should snatch this happy opportunity from us.[55]

Mrs. E.A. Currie, authoress of *Laura Secord and Canadian Reminiscences*, was a member of the Women's Club of St. Catharines, the Daughters of the Empire, and the W.C.T.U.[56] "Always a Reformer," states her biographical note, [she] "has ever believed that the women of Canada are entitled to the same political privileges as the men; they have earned them by industry and self-sacrifice; was instrumental in securing a grant from Parlt. Towards erecting a memorial to Laura Secord on Queenston Heights."[57]

Miss Machar, a poetess, was "officially connected with the National Council of Women."[58] Her final stanza in *Laura Secord* waxes strongly:

> How British gallantry and skill
> There played their noblest part,
> Yet scarce had won if there had failed
> One woman's dauntless heart.[59]

Finally, Mrs. E.J. Thompson, important in establishing a memorial to Laura Secord at Queenston, was a member of the Daughters of the Empire, and the Woman's Canadian Club.[60]

All of these women were active in Women's associations—natural enough for women of their calibre, all were interested in the study of history, and some were descendants of United Empire Loyalists. Almost all of them were active in the movement for women's rights which was just gathering momentum in the 1890s and early 1900s. What better subject for such strong feminists than Laura Secord; one of their own sex whose contribution gave women a role in the War of 1812 and called history to their side? Their flair for dramatization and poetic licence added many new features to the story, while their feminine instincts introduced detailed, although poorly documented, appreciations of Laura's attire. Who but a woman could write that:

> She wore a cottage bonnet tied under her chin. She had balbriggin stockings with red silk clocks on the side, and low shoes with buckles.[61]

Miss Thompson added another movement, that of negro rights. Laura was able to overhear the American officers discussing plans of the campaign because she was forced to serve the Americans a meal herself. They had been abusive to her two coloured servants, Pete and Floss, and this simple Upper Canadian housewife who spent the next thirty years attempting to obtain a sinecure with a plea of poverty, had to don an apron herself. At the turn of the century as now, Canadians could not resist an opportunity of informing the Americans that they had "solved" their peculiar problem.

Since World War I, and since the formal achievement of women's rights, Laura has been ridiculed or neglected. Colonel William Wood, editor of *Select Documents of the Canadian War of 1812* declared of the Battle of Beaver Dams that "the result would have been the same without her."[62] In his *The War of 1812 on the Niagara Frontier*, L.L. Babcock concluded "it seems fairly clear that her good intentions were fruitless."[63] Finally Dr. Milo M. Quaife heartlessly indexed Laura as "SECORD, Mrs. Laura, myth."[64]

W.S. Wallace in his scholarly work, *The Story of Laura Secord: A Study in Historical Evidence*, presented what seemed to be the capping stone of debunking. Basing his conclusion mainly on the certificate of 1837, he found that

> Mrs. Secord did in the month of June 1813, make an attempt to convey information to the British troops at Beaver Dams; and it must be confessed that her picture of her encounter with the Indians has about it a strong air of verisimilitude. Of her courage and patriotism there is no question. But truth compels one to say that the story she told from memory in later years (and no doubt

sincerely believed) was seriously at variance with the facts, and that she played no part in determining the issue of the battle at the Beaver Dams.[65]

The Laura-ites reeled only temporarily from the attack, and the defence of Laura's virtues was soon taken up. It was helped by the discovery of further historical evidence. The certificate of 1820, published in 1934, and rediscovered by Dr. J.S. Moir in 1962,[66] and the certificate of 1827 published by Dr. Moir in 1959,[67] clear up a problem which had been central for Wallace.

From the vague 1837 certificate alone, Wallace could not see how Laura could have arrived in time to give Fitzgibbon valuable information. She came, but she came too late to have any effect on the outcome of the battle. The certificates of 1820 and 1827 are quite explicit on the matter. Laura took her walk on 22 June, leaving plenty of time to reach and to warn Fitzgibbon.

Wallace's charge that "Mrs. Secord's claim that she enabled Fitzgibbon to 'save the country' is too absurd for further discussion,"[68] is more serious. The Indians, not Fitzgibbon, won the Battle of Beaver Dams...by Fitzgibbon's own admission; they received their information and acted independently of Fitzgibbon's detachment. Therefore, Wallace would conclude, Laura's warning to Fitzgibbon, even if it came before the battle, had no impact on the battle's outcome.

However, Fitzgibbon's certificate of 1827, not available to Wallace, claimed that "the Indians under Norton together with my own detachment [occupied] a situation to intercept the American Detachment... during the night of the twenty-second."[69] This evidence would indicate that the Indians as well as Fitzgibbon had knowledge of the intentions of the Americans supplied by Laura Secord. They too were not well-prepared on the day of the battle, but it was in spite of Laura's warning. Again the possibility looms up that the scouts who gave the 7:00 warning of attack on the twenty-fourth were sent out because an attack was expected. But it is difficult to believe that such scouts or pickets would have been out as a normal procedure.

Up to this point, the argument seems to support the main contention of the debunkers: namely that Laura's mission had no influence on the eventual outcome of the battle. But it seems that the debunking of Laura has gone too far. Certainly the fictitious accoutrements of her walk—the cow, the milkstool, the servants, the various forms of dress—must be abandoned. There is simply no concrete evidence to support them. But the assessment of Laura's actual contribution to the Battle of Beaver Dams must be restated. She did arrive a full two days before the battle and did warn that the Americans were coming. Unfortunately her speed was not matched by the Americans whose tardiness brought them to Beaver Dams on 24 June, a day later than expected. By this time Fitzgibbon had already stayed up all night in ambush formation and, probably quite annoyed, rejected as false the information of that interfering woman. When the Americans finally arrived, the British troops and Indians had to organize themselves hastily. Only the fighting of the Indians and the Americans' great fear of the Indians won the day.

Laura Secord's information should have played a greater part in the outcome of the battle. As events turned out, it brought at most only a slightly increased precaution. But it was not Laura's fault that the British were not prepared. She arrived in plenty of time to warn Fitzgibbon and gave him information which was "substantially correct." Ironically, a defeat of the British force at De Cou's would have made the potential of her visit evident. Her testimony at a subsequent court-martial, revealing her early warning, would have brought out the sloppiness of Ducharme and Fitzgibbon. However, the British victory, left unnecessarily to chance, clouded over the British leaders' neglect of Laura Secord's message. For this reason, Laura was destined to struggle first with "officialdom" and now historians for a place in history which her walk well deserved.

Notes

1. See, for instance, Milo M. Quaife, *The John Askin Papers* (Detroit, 1931) as quoted in W.S. Wallace, *The Story of Laura Secord: A Study in Historical Evidence* (Toronto, 1932), p. 4.

2. Wallace, *op. cit.*, p. 26.

3. *Ibid.*, p. 23.

4. G.F.G. Stanley, "The Indians in the War of 1812," *Canadian Historical Review*, XXXI (1950), p. 158.

5. Boerstler's narrative, in General E. A. Cruikshank, *A Documentary History of the Campaign upon the Niagara Frontier in 1813*, pt. II (Welland, n.d.) p. 131.

6. *Ibid.*, p. 131.

7. *Ibid*, p. 151.

8. John Askin, *ibid.*, p. 203.

9. Captain W.J. Kerr's memorial, *ibid.*, 120–21.

10. Porter to Tompkins, July 27, 1813, *ibid.*, p. 283.

11. See *Appendices I, II*, and *III*.

12. Certificate of 1827.

13. Certificate of 1820.

14. Certificate of 1827.

15. Boerstler's narrative, *Cruikshank*, p. 131.

16. *Ibid.*, p. 135.

17. *Ibid.*, p. 130.

18. *Ibid.*, pp. 130–31.

19. J.S. Moir, "An Early Record of Laura Secord's Walk," *Ontario History*, LI (1959), 106.

20. Certificate of 1820.

21. Certificate of 1827.

22. Certificate of 1820.

23. Certificate of 1827.

24. Certificate of 1827.

25. Ducharme's Report in Cruickshank, *op. cit.*, p. 126.

26. W.J. Kerr's memorial, *ibid.*, p. 120.

27. *Ibid.*, p. 126 and p. 165. The Indians fired on some American troops in a boat on the Niagara River and killed two men.

28. *Ibid.*, p. 126. He mentions 7:00 but it is highly unlikely that he heard before Ducharme. They probably shared their source of information.

29. *Ibid.*, p. 126.

30. J.S. Moir, *op. cit.*, p. 107.

31. For Ducharme's Report see in Cruickshank, *op. cit.*, p. 126, and for Fitzgibbon's see *ibid.*, p. 111.

32. Certificate of 1827.

33. *Ibid.*

34. From the *Report of the Loyal and Patriotic Society*, quoted in C.P. Stacey, "The War of 1812 in Canadian History," *Ontario History*, L (1958), 156.

35. Petition of James Secord, 1820.

36. See *Appendix I.*

37. Fitzgibbon to Kerr in Cruickshank, *op. cit.*, pp. 120–21.

38. See *Appendix.*

39. Memorandum of J.B. Robinson quoted from J.S. Moir "An Early Record of Laura Secord's Walk," *Ontario History*, LI (1959), 108.

40. *Ibid.*, p. 108.

41. From Laura Secord's memorial of 1839, as quoted in Wallace, *op. cit.*, p. 10.

42. *Ibid.*, p. 9.

43. As quoted in *ibid.*, pp. 10–11.

44. *Ibid.*, p. 12.

45. Letter to the editor, *Church*, April 18, 1845.

46. *Ibid.*, April 18, 1845.

47. *The Anglo-American Magazine*, No. 5. III (November, 1853), p. 467. Also printed in *op. cit.*, pp. 127–28.

48. Benson J. Lossing, *Pictorial Field Book of the War of 1812* (New York, 1868) n., p. 621.

49. *Ibid.*, p. 621.

50. *Ibid.*, p. 621.

51. The story of the cow has apparently been "indignantly contradicted by a granddaughter." See Wallace, *op. cit.*, p. 17.

52. Charles Mair, "A Ballad for Brave Women," *Tecumseh: A Drama and Canadian Poems* (Toronto, 1901), p. 147.

53. W.S. Wallace, *The Macmillan Dictionary of Canadian Biography*, 3rd ed. (Macmillan, 1963), pp. 167–68. Also entry in H.J. Morgan, *Canadian Men and Women of the Time* (Toronto, 1898), p. 235–36.

54. Sarah A. Cruzon, *Laura Secord, the Heroine of 1812: A Drama and other Poems* (Toronto, 1887), p. 66.

55. *Ibid.*, p. vi (Italics mine).

56. Entry in H.J. Morgan, ed., *Canadian Men and Women of the Time: A Hand-book of Canadian Biography of Living Characters*, 2nd ed. (Toronto, 1912), p. 289.

57. *Ibid.*, p. 289.

58. Entry in H.J. Morgan, *Types of Canadian Women* (Toronto, 1903), p. 226.

59. A.M. Machar, *Lays of the True North and Other Poems* (Toronto, 1887), p. 35.

60. Morgan, *Canadian Men and Women*, p. 1095.

61. E.J. Thompson, "Laura Ingersoll Secord," *Niagara Historical Society*, No. 25 (Niagara, 1913), p. 3.

62. As quoted in Wallace, *op. cit.*, p. 4.

63. *Ibid.*, p. 4.

64. *Ibid.*, p. 4.

65. *Ibid.*, pp. 25–26.

66. The certificate was published in the *Mail and Empire*, June 23, 1934. J.S. Moir makes a note of it in "Laura Secord Again," *Ontario History*, LIV (1962), p. 190.

67. Published in J.S. Moir. "An Early Record of Laura Secord's Walk," *Ontario History*, LI (1959), pp. 105–9.

68. Wallace, *op. cit.*, p. 25.

69. Certificate of 1827.

"OF SLENDER FRAME AND DELICATE APPEARANCE": THE PLACING OF LAURA SECORD IN THE NARRATIVES OF CANADIAN LOYALIST HISTORY

Cecilia Morgan

To most present-day Canadians, Laura Secord is best-known as the figurehead of a candy company, her image that of a young, attractive woman wearing a low-cut ruffled white gown.[1] Some may even harbour a vague memory from their high-school courses in Canadian history of her walk in 1813 from Queenston to Beaver Dams, to warn British troops of an impending American attack. From the mid-nineteenth century, the story of that walk has been told by a number of Canadian historians of the War of 1812 in Upper Canada. Its military implications in assisting the British during the War of 1812 have been the subject of some rather heated debate. Did Laura Secord actually make a valuable contribution to the war? Did her news arrive in time and was it acted

From *Journal of the Canadian Historical Association*, no. 5 (1994), 195–212. Reprinted by permission.

upon? However, another and as yet little-discussed issue is the way in which late nineteenth- and early twentieth-century historians attempted to transform Secord into a heroine, a symbol of female loyalty and patriotism in this period's narratives of Loyalist history.

As historian Benedict Anderson argues, the formation of modern national identities has involved more than the delineation of geographically-defined boundaries and narrow political definitions of citizenship. Nations, Anderson tells us, are "imagined political communities," created by their citizens through a number of political and cultural institutions and practices: shared languages, newspapers, museums, and the census. Furthermore, as Anderson (and others) have emphasized, it is also within narratives of "the nation's" history that these imagined communities are formed and national identities are created.[2] To the promoters of late nineteenth-century Canadian nationalism and imperialism, such narratives were of critical importance in understanding Canada's link to Britain and British political, social, and cultural traditions. As Carl Berger argues in *The Sense of Power*, "history in its broadest cultural sense was the medium in which [these traditions were] expressed and history was the final and ultimate argument for imperial unity."[3] Those who wrote these historical narratives also worked diligently to create national heroes who symbolized loyalty and the preservation of the imperial link. Historians interested in early nineteenth-century Ontario history found that a cast of such figures lay conveniently close to hand: Major-General Sir Isaac Brock and the Upper Canadian militia, the colony's saviours during the American invasion of 1812.

But Brock and the militia were not the only significant figures to be commemorated and celebrated, for it was during this period that Laura Secord became one of the most significant female symbols of Canadian nationalism. As feminist historians have pointed out, the formation of imagined national communities has been frequently, if not inevitably, differentiated by gender. While Anderson's work has been extremely influential on historians' understanding of national identities, he fails to recognize "that women and men may imagine such communities, identify with nationalist movements, and participate in state formations in very different ways."[4] And, in their use of iconography, monuments, or written narratives of the nation's history, proponents of nationalism have frequently relied upon gender-specific symbols and imagery.[5] Yet in these textual and visual representations of nationalities, gender as an analytic category has also varied according to its context and has been influenced by other categories and relationships, particularly those of race, class, religion, and sexuality. By looking at the process whereby Secord became a national heroine and at the narratives that were written about Secord's walk, we can further our understanding of the links between gender, race, and imperialism in late nineteenth-century Canadian nationalism and feminism.[6]

Secord became part of the narratives of Loyalist self-sacrifice and duty to country and Crown primarily—although not solely—because of the attempts of women historians and writers who, from the 1880s on, strove to incorporate women into Canadian history and to dislodge the masculine emphasis of the nineteenth-century Loyalist myths of suffering and sacrifice. Women such as Sarah Curzon, the feminist writer, historian, and temperance advocate, insisted that white Canadian women, past and present, had something of value to offer the nation and empire and that their contribution as women to the record of Canadian history be acknowledged and valued. Secord, she (and others like her) argued, was not outside the narrative of Canadian history and she (and other women) therefore had a place in shaping the "imagined communities" of Canadian nationalist and imperialist discourse. Unlike that of other, potentially unruly and disruptive women in Canadian history, Laura Secord's image could be more easily domesticated to accord with late Victorian notions of white, middle class femininity.[7] It could also be moulded by feminists to argue for a greater recognition of the importance of such femininity to Canadian society. Moreover, Laura Secord was not an isolated figure. Ranged behind and about her was a whole gallery of women in Canadian history, from Madeleine de Verchères of New France to the anonymous, archetypal pioneer woman of the backwoods of Upper Canada; women, these "amateur" historians insisted, who were historical figures as worthy of study as their male contemporaries.[8]

Before discussing the writing of Laura Secord into Loyalist history, however, it is crucial to outline the gendered nature of the nineteenth-century narratives of the War of 1812. Historians who have studied Upper Canadian politics have duly noted that assertions of loyalty and sacrifice during the war became the basis for many claims on the Upper Canadian state, in the competition for land and patronage appointments and for compensation for war losses.[9] Donald Akenson, for example, has pointed to the way in which claims to loyal duty during the war were used in attempts to justify the access of some residents to certain material benefits. Such claims were also made to legitimate the exclusion of others from such rewards.[10] Yet what has not been included in these historians' analysis of sacrifice in the war as a bargaining chip in the struggle for material gains in Upper Canada, is the gendered nature of the narratives that were used. In Upper Canadians' commemorations of the War of 1812, the important sacrifices for Country and monarch were made by Upper Canadian men, frequently in their capacity as members of the militia who risked life and limb to protect women and children, homes and hearths, from the brutal rampages of hordes of bloodthirsty Americans. During the war, and in its aftermath, women's contributions to the defence of the colony were either downplayed or ignored, in favour of the image of the helpless Upper Canadian wife and mother who entrusted her own and her children's safety to the gallant militia and British troops.[11]

Personifying the whole, of course, was the masculine figure of Isaac Brock, the British commander who made the ultimate sacrifice for the colony when he died at the Battle of Queenston Heights in 1812. Brock provided those who shaped the history of the war with a dualistic image of nationalism, one that managed to celebrate both Upper Canadian identity and colonial loyalty to Britain. He was also a Christ-like figure, a man who had given both his troops and the colony beneficent paternal guidance and wisdom but who had not spared himself from the physical dangers of war—physical dangers that really only threatened men in the military. Those who contributed to the glorification of Brock claimed that he had provided an invaluable means whereby the colonists might resist the enemy's encroachments. Brock had inspired Upper Canadian men, who might emulate his deed or manly patriotism, and he had reassured Upper Canadian women that, come what may, they could look to their husbands, fathers, sons, and brothers for protection.[12]

This kind of narrative, which emphasized masculine suffering, sacrifice, and achievements, was not unique to that of the War of 1812. As Janice Potter-MacKinnon argues, the history of Upper Canadian Loyalism focused on male military service and the political identification of male Loyalists with the British Crown and constitution:

> Well into the twentieth century, loyalty was a male concept in that it was associated with political decision-making—a sphere from which women were excluded. The same can be said of the idea that the Loyalists bequeathed conservative values and British institutions to later generations of Canadians: women have had no role in fashioning political values and institutions. The notion that the Loyalists were the founders of a nation had obvious and unequivocal gender implications, the amateur historian William Caniff was right when he equated the "founders" with the "fathers."[13]

Admittedly there was no automatic and essential connection between military activities and masculinity in Canadian history for, as Colin Coates has pointed out, the woman warrior tradition was not unknown to nineteenth-century Canada.[14] But specific female images (or images of femininity in general) as symbols of loyalty and patriotism in Upper Canada are almost completely lacking in the discourses of the period, and they display a general reluctance to admit that women could have contributed to the war effort as civilians.[15] This silence about women, and the feminine—except as helpless victims to which the masculine bravery of Upper Canadian men was inextricably linked—was quite the opposite of the discourses of the French Revolution, with their glorification of Marianne; the American Patriot's figure of the republican mother; or even the more conservative use of the British figure of Britannia.[16]

The earliest efforts to call attention to Secord's contribution to the war were made by her husband James, by her son, and by Laura herself. In a petition written 25 February 1820 and addressed to Lieutenant-Governor Sir Peregrine Maitland, James Secord requested a licence to quarry stone in the Queenston military reserve. After mentioning his own wartime service—he had served as a captain in the militia—his wounds, and the plundering of his home by American troops, Secord claimed that "his wife embraced an opportunity of rendering some service, at the risk of her own life, in going thru the Enemies' Lines to communicate information to a Detachment of His Majesty's Troops at the Beaver Dam in the month of June 1813."[17] A second, similar petition was turned down in

1827 but Maitland did propose that Laura apply for the job of looking after Brock's monument. It is not clear whether Maitland was aware of the gendered and nationalist symbolism of a Canadian woman caretaking the memory of a British General; he did, however, have "a favourable opinion of the character and claims of Mr. Secord and his wife."[18] However, Maitland's successor, Sir John Colborne, was apparently not as well-disposed toward the family and the job went to Theresa Nichol, the widow of militia Colonel Robert Nichol.[19]

When James died in 1841, Laura submitted two petitions to Governor Sydenham: one that asked that her son be given his father's post as customs' collector and another that asked for a pension. Both cited her poverty, her lack of support since her husband's death, and her need to support her daughters and grandchildren. While her petitions used the language of female dependency noted by Potter-MacKinnon in Loyalist women's submissions, they also featured her service to her country in 1813 and her new position as the head of a household.[20] Her son Charles' article, published in an 1845 edition of the Anglican paper, *The Church*, publicized her walk, calling attention to his mother's service to her country and the British Crown.[21] Eight years later Laura Secord wrote her own account of her trek to warn the British Lieutenant James Fitzgibbon, in a piece that appeared in the *Anglo American Magazine* as part of a larger narrative of the war. While this article would be used and cited by others from the 1880s on, it was written in a straightforward manner, with few of the rhetorical flourishes or personal details that would characterize later accounts. And, while Secord concluded her story with the observation that she now wondered "how I could have gone through so much fatigue, with the fortitude to accomplish it," she did not stress her need to overcome physical frailty in reaching Fitzgibbon.[22]

Secord achieved some success in her campaign for some financial recognition on the part of the state in 1860, when she presented her story to the Prince of Wales during his tour of British North America. She was also the only woman whose name appeared on an address presented by the surviving veterans of the Battle of Queenston Heights to the Prince, in a ceremony attended by 500 visitors and at which a memorial stone was laid on the site where Brock fell. Her "patriotic services," claimed the *Niagara Mail* in 1861, were "handsomely rewarded" by the Prince with an award of £100.[23] One of her more recent biographies argues that the Prince "provided the magic touch that transformed the 'widow of the late James Secord' into the heroine, Laura Secord."[24]

However, Secord did not become a heroine overnight. Her own efforts to draw attention to the service she had rendered to her country should not be seen as attempts to create a cult for herself, but rather as part of the Upper Canadian patronage game, in which loyal service to Crown and country was the way to obtain material rewards.[25] Furthermore, she died in 1868, almost twenty years before her popularity began to spread. Still, references to Secord had begun to appear in a few mid nineteenth-century accounts of the War of

1812. For example, the American historian Benson J. Lossing's *The Pictorial Field-Book of the War of 1812* devoted a page to Secord and the Battle of Beaver Dams. The page's caption read "British Troops saved by a Heroine," and Laura's own written account was the voice that supplied Lossing with his information.[26] The Canadian historian and government official, William F. Coffin, elaborated on her story by adding the cow—which, he claimed, she had milked in order to convince the American sentry to let her pass. While some regard Coffin's account as yet another example of a romantically-inclined nineteenth-century historian playing fast and loose with the facts, his placing of Secord in a context of pioneer domesticity foreshadowed subsequent stories appearing two decades later.[27] Secord thus was not rescued from complete obscurity by Curzon and others in the 1880s and '90s; she was, however, given a much more prominent place in their narratives of the war and Upper Canadian loyalty.

Sarah A. Curzon has become known in Canadian women's history as a British-born suffrage activist and a founding member of the Toronto Women's Literary Society (which would later become the Canadian Woman's Suffrage Association) and the editor of a women's page in the prohibition paper, the *Canada Citizen*. But she was also an avid promoter of Canadian history and was one of the co-founders of the Women's Canadian Historical Society of Toronto (WCHS) in 1885, along with Mary Agnes Fitzgibbon, a granddaughter of Lieutenant James Fitzgibbon. Furthermore, Curzon and Fitzgibbon were supporters of Canada's "imperial connection" to Britain, a link which they believed would benefit Canada both economically and culturally.[28] Emma Currie was another major contributor to the campaign to memorialize Secord. Indeed, her book, *The Story of Laura Secord and Canadian Reminiscences*, was published in 1900 as a fund-raiser for a monument to the "heroine" of Upper Canada. Currie lived in St. Catharines, helped found the Women's Literary Club in that city in 1892, and would later join the Imperial Order of the Daughters of the Empire (IODE). She too was a supporter of the Women's Christian Temperance Union and women's suffrage.[29]

But these women were not alone in their crusade to win recognition for Secord. Other Canadian nationalist writers like Charles Mair, Agnes Maule Machar, and William Kirby praised Secord's bravery in their poetry and prose,[30] while local historical societies and those who purported to be "national" historians, such as Ernest Cruikshank, also published papers that focused on the Battle of Beaver Dams and acknowledged Secord's role in it.[31] Much of their work, as well as that of Curzon and Currie, was part of late Victorian Canadian imperialist discourse, which perceived the past as the repository of those principles (loyalty to Britain, respect for law and order, and the capacity for democratic government) that would guide the nation into the twentieth century.[32] As Berger has argued, the local history societies that spread in the 1880s and 1890s were part of this "conservative frame of mind" in which loyalism, nationalism, and history were inextricably linked.[33]

Tributes in ink comprised the bulk of this material but they were not the only efforts to memorialize Secord. As Currie's book indicates, printed material might be used to raise funds and spread awareness in order to create more long-lasting, substantive reminders, such as monuments and statues. On June 6, 1887, W. Fenwick, a grammar school principal in Drummondville, wrote to the *Toronto World and Mail* asking for better care for the Lundy's Lane graveyard, a national monument to be erected to honour those who had died there, and a separate monument to Laura Secord. Curzon joined in a letter-writing campaign, calling for the women of Canada to take up the matter, and petitions were presented to the Ontario Legislature. When these were unsuccessful, the Lundy's Lane and Ontario Historical Societies mounted fund-raising drives for the monument, sending out circulars asking Canadian women and children to contribute ten cents and one cent respectively to the cause.[34] A competition for the sculpture was held and won by a Miss Mildred Peel, an artist and sculptor who also would paint the portrait of Secord hung in 1905 in the Ontario Legislature.[35] After fourteen years of campaigning, the monument was unveiled 22 June 1901 at Lundy's Lane. In 1911, the Women's Institute of Queenston and St. David's felt that the village of Queenston (site of the Secord home during the War of 1812) had not done enough to honour Secord's memory and built a Memorial Hall as part of Laura Secord school. The gesture that ensconced her name in popular culture came in 1913, when Frank O'Connor chose Secord as the emblem for his new chain of candy stores.[36]

While it was not suggested that celebrating Secord's contribution was the sole responsibility of Canadian womanhood, many aspects of this campaign were shaped by deeply gendered notions and assumptions about both past and present. The idea that women might have a special interest in supporting the subscription drive, for example, or petitioning the Legislature, linked perceptions of both womanhood and nationalism, drawing upon the underlying assumptions of self-sacrifice and unselfishness that lay at the heart of both identities.[37] Groups such as the WCHS, with their "unselfish patriotism," were exactly what the country needed, Kirby told Mary Agnes Fitzgibbon upon being made an honorary member of the society, adding "let the women be right and the country will be might!"[38] Moreover, while male writers and historians certainly expressed an interest in Secord, it is important not to overlook the significance of the participation of Anglo Celtic, middle and upper-middle class women in the writing of Canadian history, a task they frequently undertook as members of local historical societies. Such women scrutinized historical records in order to find their foremothers (in both the literal and metaphorical sense).[39] However, they also were fascinated with the entire "pioneer" period of Canadian history, both French and English, and with both male and female figures in this context. For the most part, women members of historical societies researched and presented papers on as many Generals and male explorers as they did "heroines."[40]

There was, however, a difference in their treatment of the latter. They insisted that Canadian women's contributions to nation-building be valued, even though they had not achieved the fame and recognition of their male counterparts. To be sure, they did not offer alternative narratives of early Canadian history and tended to place political and military developments at its centre. Nevertheless, they sought to widen the parameters of male historians' definitions of these events in order to demonstrate their far-reaching effects on all Canadian society. In the meetings of organizations such as Canadian Women's Historical Societies of Toronto and Ottawa, papers were given on topics such as "Early British Canadian Heroines" or "Reminiscences" of pioneer women.[41] Women such as Harriet Prudis, who was active in the London and Middlesex Historical Society during this period, believed that while the history of the pioneer women of the London area

> records no daring deed ... nor historic tramp, like that of Laura Secord, yet every life is a record of such patient endurance of privations, such brave battling with danger, such a wonderful gift for resourceful adaptability, that the simplest story of the old days must bear, within itself, the sterling elements of romance. While they took no part in the national or political happenings of the day, it may be interesting to us, and to those who come after us, to hear from their own lips how these public events affected their simple lives.[42]

Their efforts were shared by male novelists and historians who not only glorified Secord but also wished to rescue other Canadian women of her era and ilk from obscurity.[43] However, as more than one honorary member of the WCHS told Fitzgibbon, Canadian women should have a special desire to preserve records of their past. According to Mair, "the sacred domestic instincts of Canadian womanhood will not suffer in the least degree, but will rather be refreshed and strengthened" by the Society's "rescuing from destruction the scattered and perishable records of Ontario's old, and, in many respects, romantic home life."[44] The collection of material concerning this latter area, Mair and others felt, should be the special work of Canadian women.[45]

The extent to which this relegation of the "social" realm to women historians set a precedent for future developments, whereby "romantic home life" was perceived as both the preserve of women and the realm of the trivial and anecdotal, is not entirely clear.[46] Certainly it does not appear to have been Mair's intention that these areas be perceived as trivial or unworthy of male historians' attention, while women such as Mary Agnes Fitzgibbon were as eager to research battles and collect military memorabilia as they were concerned with "primitive clothing, food cookery, amusements, and observances of festivals attending births and wedlock or the *charivari*."[47] Yet it was probably no coincidence that the first historian to seriously challenge the military value of Secord's walk was the male academic W.S. Wallace, who in 1930 raised a furor amongst public supporters of Secord with questions concerning the use of historical evidence in documenting her walk.[48]

This, then, was the context in which Laura Secord became an increasingly popular symbol of Canadian patriotism: one of feminism, history, patriotism, and imperialism. While many of these histories were, as Berger has pointed out, local and might seem incredibly parochial in their scope, their authors saw locally-based stories as having a much wider emotional and moral significance in the narratives of the nation.[49] Hence, narratives of Secord's contribution to the War of 1812 and to the colonial link with the British Empire were marked by the interplay of locality, nationality, and gender. First, Laura and James Secord's backgrounds were explored and their genealogies traced, in order to place them within the Loyalist tradition of suffering and sacrifice. For those writers who were concerned with strict historical accuracy, such a task was considerably easier for the Secords than for Laura's family, the Ingersolls. James' male ancestors had fought in the Revolutionary war for the British Crown and the many military ranks occupied by the Secord men were duly listed and acclaimed. Moreover, the Secords could claim a history of both allegiance to the British Crown and a desire for the protection of the British constitution; they were descended from Huguenots who arrived in New York from La Rochelle in the late seventeenth century.[50]

But it was not only the Secord men that had served their country and suffered hardships. The loyalist legacy inherited by both Laura and James had, it was pointed out, been marked by gender differences. As Curzon told her audiences, James Secord's arrival in Canada had been as a three-year-old refugee, part of his mother's "flight through the wilderness, with four other homeless women and many children, to escape the fury of a band of ruffians who called themselves the 'sons of Liberty.' After enduring frightful hardships for nearly a month, they finally arrived at Fort Niagara almost naked and starving." Curzon went on to comment that these were by no means "uncommon experiences." Frequently, she pointed out, Loyalist men had to flee "for their lives" and leave their women and children behind (as well as their "goods, chattels, estates, and money"). Their loved ones were then left to endure the terrors of the wilderness:

> unprotected and unsupported, save by that deep faith in God and love to king and country which, with their personal devotion to their husbands, made of them heroines whose story of unparalleled devotion, hardships patiently borne, motherhood honourably sustained, industry and thrift perseveringly followed, enterprise successfully prosecuted, principle unwaveringly upheld, and tenderness never surpassed, has yet to be written, and whose share in the making of this nation remains to be equally honoured with that of the men who bled and fought for its liberties.[51]

Unfortunately for Laura's popularizers, the Ingersoll family did not fit as neatly into the Loyalist tradition. Her father, Thomas, had fought against the British in 1776 and had seen his 1793 land grant cancelled as a result of British efforts to curb large-scale immigration of American settlers into Upper Canada.[52]

As J.H. Ingersoll observed in 1926, Laura's inability to claim the United Empire Loyalist pedigree "has been commented upon." However, some historians argued that Thomas Ingersoll came to Upper Canada at Lieutenant-Governor Simcoe's request.[53] For those poets and novelists who felt free to create Laura's loyalism in a more imaginative manner, her patriotism was traced to a long-standing childhood attachment to Britain. They insisted that she chose Canada freely and was not forced to come to the country as a refugee.[54] Moreover, despite these historians' fascination with lines of blood and birth, they were equally determined to demonstrate that the former could be transcended by environment and force of personality. The loyal society of Upper Canada and the strength of Laura's own commitment to Britain were important reminders to the Canadian public that a sense of imperial duty could overcome other relationships and flourish in the colonial context.[55]

Accordingly, these historians argued, it should come as no surprise that both Laura and her husband felt obliged to perform their patriotic duty when American officers were overheard planning an attack on the British forces of Lieutenant Fitzgibbon.[56] However, James was still suffering from wounds sustained at the Battle of Queenston Heights and it therefore fell to Laura—over her husband's objections and concern for her safety—to walk the twenty miles from Queenston to warn the British troops at Beaver Dams. (Here the linear chronology of the narratives was frequently interrupted to explain out that Laura had come to his aid after the battle when, finding him badly wounded and in danger of being beaten to death by "common" American soldiers, she had attempted to shield him with her own body from their rifle butts—further evidence that Laura was no stranger to wifely and patriotic duty.[57])

Laura's journey took on wider dimensions and greater significance in the hands of her commemorators. It was no longer just a walk to warn the British but, with its elements of venturing into the unknown, physical sacrifice, and devotion to the British values of order and democracy, came to symbolize the entire "pioneer womanish experience in Canadian history."[58] Leaving the cozy domesticity and safety of her home, the company of her wounded husband and children, Secord had ventured out into the Upper Canadian wilderness with its swamps and underbrush in which threatening creatures, such as rattlesnakes, bears, and wolves, might lurk.[59] And even when Sarah Curzon's 1887 play permitted Laura to deliver several monologues on the loveliness of the June woodland, the tranquillity of the forest was disrupted by the howling of wolves.[60]

But most serious of all, in the majority of accounts, was the threat of the "Indians" she might meet on the way. If Secord's commitment to Canada and Britain had previously been presented in cultural terms, ones that could be encouraged by the colonial tie and that might transcend race, it was at this point that her significance as a symbol of white Canadian womanhood was clearest. While her feminine fragility had been the subject of comment throughout the stories, and while her racial background might have been the underlying sub-text for this fragility, it was in the discussions of the threat of native warriors that her gender became most clearly racialized.[61] Unlike the contemporary racist and cultural stereotypes of threatening black male sexuality used in American lynching campaigns, however, her fears were not of sexual violence by native men—at least not explicitly—but of the tactics supposedly used by native men in warfare, scalping being the most obvious.[62]

To be sure, some stories mentioned that Secord had had to stay clear of open roads and paths "for fear of Indians *and* white marauders" (emphasis mine).[63] But even those who downplayed her fear of a chance encounter with an "Indian" during her journey were scrupulous in their description of her fright upon encountering Mohawks outside the British camp. Secord herself had stated that she had stumbled across the Mohawks' camp and that they had shouted "woman" at her, making her "tremble" and giving her an "awful feeling." It was only with difficulty, she said, that she convinced them to take her to Fitzgibbon.[64] As this meeting with the natives was retold, they became more menacing and inspired even greater fear in Secord. In these accounts, at this penultimate stage in her journey she stepped on a twig that snapped and startled an Indian encampment. Quite suddenly Secord was surrounded by them, "the chief throws up his tomahawk to strike, regarding the intruder as a spy."[65] In some narratives, he shouted at her "woman! what does woman want!" Only her courage in springing to his arm is the woman saved, and an opportunity snatched to assure him of her loyalty.[66]

Moved by pity and admiration, the chief gave her a guide, and at length she reached Fitzgibbon, delivered and verified her message—"and *faints*."[67] Fitzgibbon then went off to fight the Battle of Beaver Dams, armed with the knowledge that Secord had brought him and managed to successfully rout the American forces. In a number of narratives, this victory was frequently achieved by using the threat of unleashed Indian savagery when the Americans were reluctant to surrender.[68] While the battle was being fought, Secord was moved to a nearby house, where she slept off her walk, and then returned to the safety of her home and family. She told her family about her achievement but, motivated by fear for their security (as American troops continued to occupy the Niagara area) as well as by her own modesty and self-denial, she did not look for any recognition or reward. Such honours came first to Fitzgibbon.[69]

Women such as Curzon and Currie might see Secord's contribution as natural and unsurprising (given her devotion to her country) but they also were keenly aware that their mission of commemoration necessitated that their work appeal to a popular audience. These narratives were imbued with their authors' concerns with the relations of gender, class, and race and the way in which they perceived these identities to structure both Canadian society and history. For one, Secord's "natural" feminine fragility was a major theme of their writings. As a white woman of good birth and descent she was not physically suited to undertake the hardships involved in her walk (although, paradoxically, as a typical "pioneer woman" she was able to undertake the hardships of raising a family and looking after a household in a recently-settled area). Her delicacy and slight build, first mentioned by Fitzgibbon in his own testimony of her walk, was frequently stressed by those who commemorated her.[70] Her physical frailty could be contrasted with the manly size and strength of soldiers such as Fitzgibbon and Brock.[71] Nevertheless, the seeming physical immutability of gender was not an insurmountable barrier to her patriotic duty to country and empire. The claims of the latter transcended corporeal limitations. Even her maternal duties, understood by both conservatives and many feminists in late nineteenth-century Canada to be the core of womanly identity, could be put aside or even reformulated in order to answer her country's needs.[72] While her supporters did not make explicit their motives in stressing her frailty, it is possible to see it as a subtext to counter medical and scientific arguments about female physical deficiencies that made women, particularly white, middle class women, unfit for political participation and higher education.[73]

Furthermore, there were other ways to make Secord both appealing and a reflection of their own conceptions of "Canadian womanhood," and many historians treated her as an icon of respectable white heterosexual femininity. Anecdotes supposedly told by her family were often added to the end of the narratives of her walk—especially those written by women—and these emphasized her love of children, her kindness and charity towards the elderly, and her very feminine love of finery and gaiety (making her daughters' satin slippers, for example, and her participation as a young woman in balls given by the Secords at Newark). Indeed, they went so far as to discuss the clothing that she wore on her walk. Her daughter Harriet told Currie that she and her sisters saw their mother leave that morning wearing "a flowered print gown, I think it was brown with orange flowers, at least a yellow tint …."[74] Elizabeth Thompson, who was active within the Ontario Historical Society and was also a member of the IODE, also wrote that Secord wore a print dress, adding a "cottage bonnet tied under her chin … balbriggan stockings, with red silk clocks on the sides, and low shoes with buckles"—both of which were lost during the walk.[75]

For her most active supporters, the walk of Laura Secord meant that certain women could be written into the record of loyalty and patriotic duty in Canadian history, and female heroines could gain recognition for the deeds they had committed. In the eyes of these historians, such recognition had heretofore been withheld simply because of these figures' gender, for in every other significant feature—their racial and ethnic identities, for example—they were no different than their male counterparts. But such additions to the narrative were intended to be just that: additions, not serious disruptions of the story's focus on the ultimate triumph of British institutions and the imperial tie in Canada. Like her walk, Secord herself was constructed in many ways as the archetypical "British" pioneer woman of Loyalist history, remembered for her willingness to struggle, sacrifice, and thus contribute to "nation-building." These historians also suggested that patriotic duties and loyalty to the state did not automatically constitute a major threat to late nineteenth-century concepts of masculinity and femininity. Secord could undertake such duties, but still had to be defined by her relations to husband and children, home and family. She did not, it was clear, take up arms herself, nor did she use her contribution to win recognition for her own gain.

In the context of late nineteenth- and early twentieth-century debates about gender relations in Canadian society, Secord was a persuasive symbol of how certain women might breach the division between "private" and "public," the family and the state, and do so for entirely unselfish and patriotic reasons. The narratives of Laura Secord's walk helped shape an image of Canadian womanhood in the past that provided additional justification and inspiration for turn-of-the-century Canadian feminists. These women could invoke memory and tradition when calling for their own inclusion in the "imagined community" of the Canadian nation of the late nineteenth century.[76] Furthermore, for those such as Curzon who were eager to widen their frame of national reference, Secord's legacy could be part of an imperialist discourse, linking gender, race, nation, and empire in both the past and the present.

Acknowledgement

Much of the research and writing of this paper was conducted with the financial assistance of Canada Employment. I would also like to thank Colin Coates, Mariana Valverde, and the *Journal's* anonymous readers for their much-appreciated suggestions and encouragement. The members of the gender, history, and national identities study group have provided invaluable comments and support: Lykke de la Cour, Paul Deslandes, Stephen Heathorn, Maureen McCarthy, and Tori Smith.

Notes

1. A Dorion Gray-like image that, as the company has enjoyed pointing out, becomes younger with the passage of time. See the advertisement, "There must be something in the chocolate," *Globe and Mail*, 25 November 1992, A14.

2. This term has been an invaluable methodological tool in thinking about the narratives of Secord. See Benedict Anderson, *Imagined Communities: Reflections on the Origin and Spread of Nationalism*, Revised Edition (London and New York, 1991). See also Eric Hobsbawm and Terence Ranger, (eds.) *The Invention of Tradition* (New York, 1983). Like Anderson's work, however, this collection does not address the complex relationships of gender, nationalism, and the "invented traditions" it analyses.

3. Carl Berger, *The Sense of Power: Studies in the Ideas of Canadian Imperialism 1867–1914* (Toronto, 1970), 78.

4. Catherine Hall, Jane Lewis, Keith McClelland, and Jane Rendall, "Introduction," *Gender and History: Special Issue on Gender, Nationalisms, and National Identities* 5:2 (Summer 1993): 159–64, 159.

5. Recent work by historians of Indian nationalism explores the use of female images, particularly that of the nation as mother. See, for example, Samita Sen, "Motherhood and Mother craft: Gender and Nationalism in Bengal," *Gender and History: Special Issue on Gender, Nationalisms and National Identities*, 231–43. See also the essays in *History Workshop Journal, Special Issue: Colonial and Post-Colonial History* 36 (Autumn 1993) and Mrinalini Sinha, "Reading *Mother India*: Empire, Nation, and the Female Voice," *Journal of Women's History* 6:2 (Summer 1994): 6–44.

6. One of the few Canadian historians to point to these connections has been George Ingram, in "The Story of Laura Secord Revisited," *Ontario History* LVII: 2 (June 1965): 85–97. Other works tackling these questions have looked at such areas as social reform. See Angus McLaren, *Our Own Master Race: Eugenics in Canada, 1885–1945* (Toronto, 1990) and Mariana Valverde, *The Age of Light, Soap, and Water: Moral Reform in English Canada 1885–1925* (Toronto, 1991).

7. For a heroine who was not so easily domesticated, see Colin M. Coates, "Commemorating the Woman Warrior of New France: Madeleine de Verchères, 1696–1930," paper presented to the 72nd Annual Conference of the Canadian Historical Association, Ottawa, June 1993; also Marina Warner, *Joan of Arc: The Image of Female Heroism* (London, 1981).

8. See, for example, the *Transactions* of both the Women's Canadian Historical Society of Ottawa and those of the Women's Canadian Historical Society of Toronto, from the 1890s to the 1920s.

9. David Mills, *The Idea of Loyalty in Upper Canada, 1784–1850* (Montreal and Kingston, 1988).

10. Donald H. Akenson, *The Irish in Ontario: A Study in Rural History* (Montreal and Kingston, 1984), 134.

11. See Cecilia Morgan, "Languages of Gender in Upper Canadian Politics and Religion, 1791–1850" (Ph.D. Thesis, University of Toronto, 1993), Chapter 11. It is interesting that, while the militia myth has been challenged by many historians, its gendered nature has received very little attention. See, for example, the most recent study of the War of 1812., George Sheppard's *Plunder, Profit, and Paroles: A Social History of the War of 1812 in Upper Canada* (Montreal and Kingston, 1994).

12. Morgan, 56–60; see also Keith Walden, "Isaac Brock: Man and Myth: A Study of the militia myth of the War of 1812 in Upper Canada 1812–1912" (M.A. Thesis, Queen's University, 1971).

13. Janice Potter-MacKinnon, *While the Women Only Wept: Loyalist Refugee Women in Eastern Ontario* (Montreal and Kingston, 1993), 158.

14. Coates, "Commemorating the Heroine of New France."

15. Morgan, chap II.

16. On the French Revolution, see Maurice Agulhon, *Marianne into Battle: Republican Imagery and Symbolism in France, 1789–1880* (Trans. by Janet Lloyd. Cambridge, 1981). For republican motherhood, see Linda Kerber, "The Republican Mother: Female Political Imagination in the Early Republic," in *Women of the Republic: Intellect and Ideology in Revolutionary America* (Chapel Hill, 1980); for Britannia, see Madge Dresser, "Britannia," in Raphael Samuel (ed.), *Patriotism, the Making and Unmaking of British National Identity*, Volume III: *National Fictions* (London, 1989), 26–49.

17. The petition is reprinted in Ruth McKenzie's *Laura Secord: The Legend and the Lady* (Toronto, 1971), 74–75. To date, McKenzie's book is the most thorough and best-researched popular account of the development of the Secord legend.

18. *Ibid.*, 76.

19. *Ibid.*, 76–77; also Sheppard, 221.

20. McKenzie, 84–85.

21. *Ibid.*, 49ff.

22. *Ibid.*, 91–92; also in Benson J. Lossing, *The Pictorial Field Book of the War of 1812* (New York, 1869), 621.

23. McKenzie, 102.

24. *Ibid.*, 103–4.

25. For an analysis of patronage in nineteenth-century Ontario, see S.J.R. Noel, *Patrons, Clients, Brokers: Ontario Society and Politics 1791–1896* (Toronto, 1990).

26. Lossing, 621.

27. William F. Coffin, *1812: The War, and Its Moral: A Canadian Chronicle* (Montreal, 1864), 148.

28. See Sarah A. Curzon, *Laura Secord, the Heroine of 1812: A Drama and Other Poems* (Toronto, 1887). For biographical sketches of Curzon and Fitzgibbon, see Henry James Morgan, *The Canadian Men and Women of the Time: A Hand-Book of Canadian Biography* (Toronto, 1898 and 1912), 235–36 and 400. Curzon's work is briefly discussed in Carol Bacchi's *Liberation Deferred? The Ideas of the English Canadian Suffragists, 1877–1918* (Toronto, 1981), 26–27 and 44, but Bacchi's frame of reference does not take in Curzon's (or other suffragists') interest in history as an important cultural aspect of their maternal feminism and imperialism.

29. Morgan, 1912, 288–89; see also Mrs. G.M. Armstrong, *The First Eighty Years of the Women's Literary Club of St. Catharines, 1892–1972* (n.p., 1972); Emma A. Currie, *The Story of Laura Secord and Canadian Reminiscences* (St. Catharines, 1913).

30. Charles Mair, "A Ballad for Brave Women," in *Tecumseh: A Drama and Canadian Poems* (Toronto, 1901), 147; William Kirby, *Annals of Niagara*, ed. and intro. by Lorne Pierce (Toronto, 1927, first ed. 1896), 209–10. Kirby had been Currie's childhood tutor in Niagara and both she and Curzon continued to look to him for advice, support, and recognition (Archives of Ontario [AO], MS 542, William Kirby Correspondence, Reel 1, Curzon and Currie to Kirby, 1887–1906). Kirby and Mair were made honorary members of the WCHS (AO, MU 7837–7838, Series A, WCHS papers, Correspondence File 1, William Kirby to Mary Agnes Fitzgibbon, April 11, 1896, Charles Mair to Fitzgibbon, May 8, 1896). For Machar, see "Laura Secord," in her *Lays of the True North and Other Poems* (Toronto, 1887), 35. See also Ruth Compton Brouwer, "Moral Nationalism in Victorian Canada: The Case of Agnes Machar," *Journal of Canadian Studies*, 20: 1 (Spring 1985): 90–108.

31. See, for example, "The Heroine of the Beaver Dams," *Canadian Antiquarian and Numismatic Journal* VIII (Montreal, 1879): 135–36. Many thanks to Colin Coates for this reference. See also Ernest Cruikshank, *The Fight in the Beechwoods* (Lundy's Lane Historical Society: Drummondville, 1889), 1, 13, 14, 19.

32. Berger, 89–90.

33. *Ibid.*, 95–96.

34. Janet Carnochan, "Laura Secord Monument at Lundy's Lane," *Transactions of the Niagara Historical Society* (Niagara, 1913), 11–18.

35. Carnochan, 13.

36. McKenzie, 118–19.

37. Marilyn Lake has made a similar argument about Australian nationalist discourse during World War I. See her, "Mission Impossible: How Men Gave Birth to the Australian Nation—Nationalism, Gender and Other Seminal Acts," *Gender and History: Special Issue on Motherhood, Race and the State in the Twentieth Century* 4:3 (Autumn 1992): 305–22, particularly 307. For the theme of self-sacrifice in Canadian nationalism, see Berger, 217. The links between the discourses of late-Victorian, white, bourgeois femininity and that of Canadian racial policy have been explored by Valverde in *The Age of Light, Soap, and Water*, in the contexts of moral reform, the white slavery panic, and immigration policies. See also Bacchi, *Liberation Deferred?*, ch. 7. For gender and imperialism in the British and American contexts, see Vron Ware, *Beyond the Pale: White Women, Racism and History* (London and New York, 1992). The seminal article on imperialism and British womanhood is Anna Davin, "Imperialism and Motherhood," *History Workshop Journal* 5 (Spring 1978): 9–65.

38. WCHS papers, MU 7837–7838, Series A, Correspondence File 1, Kirby to Fitzgibbon, April 14, 1896.

39. See, for example, Mrs. J.R. Hill, "Early British Canadian Heroines," *Women's Canadian Historical Society of Ottawa Transactions*, 10 (1928): 93–98; Harriet Prudis, "Reminiscences of Mrs. Gilbert Ponte," *London and Middlesex Historical Society Transactions* (1902, pub. 1907): 62–64.

40. Harriet Prudis, "The 100th Regiment," *L & M H S Transactions*, V (1912–1913), n.p.; Agnes Dunbar Chamberlin, "The Colored Citizens of Toronto," *WCHS of Toronto Transactions*, 8 (1908): 9–15; also the biography of Brock by Lady Edgar, one of the first presidents of the WCHS [*Life of General Brock* (Toronto, 1904)].

41. See note 37 above.

42. Prudis, 62.

43. See Ernest Green, "Some Canadian Women of 1812–14," *WCHS of Ottawa Transactions* 9 (1925): 98–109.

44. WCHS papers, MU 7837–7838, Series A, Correspondence File 1, Mair to Fitzgibbon, May 8, 1896.

45. *Ibid.*; see also WCHS papers, MU 7837–7838, Series A, Correspondence File 1, John H. to Fitzgibbon, May 6, 1896.

46. As Linda Kerber argues, it was precisely this relegation that women's historians of the 1960s and '70s had to confront in their attempts to lift women's lives from the "realm of the trivial and anecdotal." See her "Separate Spheres, Female Worlds, Woman's Place: The Rhetoric of Women's History," *The Journal of American History* 75: 1 (June 1988): 9–39, especially 37.

47. Mair to Fitzgibbon, May 8, 1896.

48. W.S. Wallace, *The Story of Laura Secord* (Toronto, 1932). For a response to Wallace, see "What Laura Secord Did," *Dunnville Weekly Chronicle*, 35 (1932), reprinted from Toronto *Saturday Night*, June 22, 1932.

49. Berger, 96. As M. Brook Taylor has pointed out about the work of nineteenth-century writers such as John Charles Dent, Francis Hincks, and Charles Lindsey, "National historians were essentially Upper Canadian historians in Masquerade." See his *Promoters Patriots, and Partisans: Historiography in Nineteenth-Century Canada* (Toronto, 1989), 231.

50. Currie, 21–33.

51. Curzon, *The Story of Laura Secord, 1813* (Lundy's Lane Historical Society, July 25, 1891) 6–7.

52. See Gerald M. Craig, *Upper Canada: The Formative Years 1784–1841* (Toronto, 1963), 49, for a discussion of this shift in policy. McKenzie also argues that Ingersoll did not fulfill his settlement obligations (29). See also Currie, 38–39.

53. J.H. Ingersoll, "The Ancestry of Laura Secord," *Ontario Historical Society* (1926): 361–63. See also Elizabeth Thompson, "Laura Ingersoll Secord," 1. Others argued that Ingersoll was urged by Joseph Brant to come to Upper Canada (Ingersoll, 363). The Brant connection was developed most fully and romantically by John Price-Brown in *Laura the Undaunted: A Canadian Historical Romance* (Toronto, 1930). It has also been pointed out that Price-Brown picked up the story, "invented out of whole cloth" by Curzon, that Tecumseh had fallen in love with one of Secord's daughters. See Dennis Duffy, *Gardens, Covenants, Exiles: Loyalism in the Literature of Upper Canada/Ontario* (Toronto, 1982), 61. In Price-Brown's account, Tecumseh proposes just before he is killed; Laura, however, disapproves of the match (259–69).

54. Price-Brown, 16–17, 180–82.

55. Just as French-Canadians could overcome other ties (see Berger, 138–39).

56. Thompson, 2; Currie, 48; Ingersoll, 362.

57. Price-Brown's "fictional" account is the most colourful, since one of the American officers who did not intervene to save the Secords was a former suitor of Laura's, whom she had rejected in favour of James and Canada (252–5). See also Currie, 53–54.

58. Norman Knowles, in his study of late nineteenth-century Ontario commemorations of Loyalism, argues that pioneer and rural myths subsumed those of Loyalism ("Inventing the Loyalists: The Ontario Loyalist Tradition and the Creation of a Usable Past, 1784–1924," Ph.D. thesis, York University 1990). To date, my research on women commemorators indicates that, for them, both Loyalism (particularly people, places, and artifacts having to do with 1812) and the "pioneer past" were closely intertwined; both were of great significance and inspirational power in their interpretations of the past. See Elizabeth Thompson, *The Pioneer Woman: A Canadian Character Type* (Montreal and Kingston, 1991) for a study of this archetype in the fiction of Canadian authors Catherine Parr Trail, Sara Jeanette Duncan, Ralph Connor, and Margaret Laurence.

59. The most extensive description is in Curzon's *The Story of Laura Secord*, 11–12.

60. Curzon, *Laura Secord: The Heroine of the War of 1812*, 39–47.

61. While examining a very different period and genre of writing, I have found Carroll Smith-Rosenberg's "Captured Subjects/Savage others; Violently Engendering the new American" to be extremely helpful in understanding the construction of white womanhood in the North American context. See *Gender and History* 5: 2 (Summer 1993), 177–95. See also Vron Ware, "Moments of Danger: Race, Gender, and Memories of Empire," *History and Theory* Beiheft (1992); 116–37.

62. See Ware, "To Make the Facts Known," in *Beyond the Pale* for a discussion of lynching and the feminist campaign against it. Smith-Rosenberg points to a similar treatment of native men in Mary Rowlandson's seventeenth-century captivity narrative (183–84). While the two examples should not be conflated, this issue does call for further analysis.

63. Cruikshank, 13.

64. Secord in Thompson, 4–5.

65. See, for example, Blanche Hume, *Laura Secord* (Toronto, 1928), 1. This book was part of a Ryerson Canadian History Readers series, endorsed by the IODE and the Provincial Department of Education.

66. *Ibid.*, 15.

67. Curzon, *The Story of Laura Secord*, 13.

68. See, for example, Cruikshank, 18.

69. Currie, 52–53. Fitzgibbon supposedly took full credit for the victory, ignoring both Secord's and the Caughnawaga Mohawks' roles (McKenzie, 66–67). He later became a Colonel in the York militia and was rewarded for his role in putting down the 1837 rebellion with a £1,000 grant (89–90).

70. Fitzgibbon in Thompson, 6.

71. Hume, 4.

72. For example, in Curzon's play Secord is asked by her sister-in-law, the Widow Secord, if her children will not "blame" her should she come to harm. She replies that "children can see the right at one quick glance," suggesting that their mother's maternal care and authority is bound to her patriotism and loyalty (34).

73. See Wendy Mitchinson, *The Nature of their Bodies: Women and Their Doctors in Victorian Canada* (Toronto, 1991), especially "The Frailty of Women."

74. Currie, 71.

75. Thompson, 3. Balbriggan was a type of fine, unbleached, knitted cotton hosiery material.

76. See Hobsbawm and Ranger, "Introduction: Inventing Tradition," particularly their argument that invented traditions are often shaped and deployed by those who wish to either legitimate particular institutions or relations of authority or to inculcate certain beliefs of values (9). In this case I would argue that the Secord tradition served very similar purposes, although it was used to both legitimate and, for certain groups of women, to subvert.

CHAPTER
8 THE MÉTIS AND RED RIVER SOCIETY

In the eighteenth century the expansion of the fur trade into what is today the Canadian west brought into existence at least one and, depending upon the interpretation, possibly two new societies. The larger and more easily identifiable group was the Métis, the sons and daughters of the French, Roman Catholic traders and their native wives. Their English-speaking, mainly Protestant, counterparts, known variously as "half-breeds," "mixed-bloods," "country-born" and "Métis Anglais," were less numerous but still important, especially in the nineteenth century history of the Canadian prairies, and especially that of the Red River.

While the Métis played a central role in the history of pre-1870 western Canada, until quite recently they have not been well served by the country's historians. Often ignored, or even worse, treated with thinly disguised contempt as losers in the Whiggish story of Canadian progress, the issues relevant to the Métis have only just begun to be fully examined. Of critical importance is the nature of the Métis and their Red River society, including the attendant question of the interaction between the two linguistic sub-groups. The traditional interpretation was spelled out by G.F.G. Stanley in *The Birth of Western Canada*, first published in 1936 but re-issued as late as 1970. In Stanley's view, while the Métis exhibited many admirable qualities such as honesty and hospitality, "the French half-breeds were indolent, thoughtless and improvident, unrestrained in their desires, restless, clannish and vain."[8] In contrast, he characterized the English-speaking mixed-blood population as, "for the most part, economical, industrious and prosperous."[9] Proof, he believed, was to be found in the very different attitudes of the French and English-speaking Métis toward the agrarian way of life. While the former "inclined to the roving life of the *coureur de bois*" and persisted in following the buffalo hunt, the latter often "settled down to farm and to take a leading role in the life of their community," a sure sign of a more advanced civilization.[8]

Several more recent studies have disputed Stanley's interpretation in its entirety. Far from seeing the Métis choice of the buffalo hunt over agricultural as evidence of indolence or improvidence, both W. Leland Clark and George Herman Sprenger argue that, given the environmental and technological state of mid-nineteenth century agriculture in the Red River area, this was the only rational decision.

Although neither addresses this debate directly, the two readings presented here bear tangentially on it, and students should attempt to identify their respective points of view. At issue, rather, is a related but equally fascinating point of contention. Both Ens and Pannekoek present a portrait of the Red River community in the 1830s, though that having been said, the similarity between the two ends abruptly. Indeed, at times it is difficult to comprehend that the two are discussing essentially the same subject. In the first, a chapter excerpted from his 1996 study entitled *Homeland to Hinterland The Changing Worlds of the Red River Métis in the Nineteenth Century*, Gerhard Ens paints a picture of relative homogeneity and harmony. In contrast, Frits Pannekoek, in a chapter from his 1991 work, *A Snug Little Flock The Social Origins of the Riel Resistance, 1869–70*, portrays the Red River society as deeply divided ethnically and fragmented socially. In assessing the relative merits of the conflicting perspectives of these two readings, students should examine carefully both the nature and use of sources by their authors.

Suggestions for Further Reading

Clark, W.L., "The Place of the Metis Within the Agricultural Economy of the Red River during the 1840s and 1850s", *Canadian Journal of Native Studies*, 3, 1, 1983, 69–84.

Ens, Gerhard, "Dispossession of Adaptation? Migration and Persistence of the Red River Metis, 1835–1890", Canadian Historical Association *Historical Papers*, 1988, 120–144.

Ens, Gerhard, *Homeland to Hinterland The Changing Worlds of the Red River Métis in the Nineteenth Century*. Toronto: University of Toronto Press, 1996.

Foster, John, "Wintering, the Outsider Adult Male and the Ethnogenesis of the Western Plains Métis," *Prairie Forum*, 19, 1, 1994, 1–13.

Hough, Brenda, "Prelates and Pioneers: The Anglican Church in Rupert's Land and English Mission Policy," *Journal of the Canadian Church Historical Society*, 33, 1, 1991, 51–63.

Mailhot, P.R., and D.N.Sprague, "Persistent Settlers: The Dispersal and Resettlement of the Red River Metis, 1870–1885", *Canadian Ethnic Studies*, XVII, 2, 1985.

Pannekoek, Frits, "The Anglican Church and the Disintegration of Red River Society, 1818–1870," in Carl Berger and Ramsay Cook, eds., *The West and the Nation*. Toronto: McClelland & Stewart, 1976, 72–90.

Pannekoek, Frits, "The Flock Divided: Factions and Feuds at Red River," *The Beaver*, 70, 6, 1990–1991.

Pannekoek, Frits, *A Snug Little Flock The Social Origins of the Riel Resistance, 1869–70*. Winnipeg: Watson and Dwyer Publishing, 1991.

Sprenger, George H., "The Metis Nation: Buffalo Hunting versus Agriculture in the Red River Settlement, 1810–1870", in B.A.Cox, *Native People*. Ottawa: Carleton University Press, 1987, 120–135.

Spry, Irene, "The Metis and Mixed-Bloods of Rupert's Land Before 1870", in J. L.Peterson, *The New Peoples*. Winnipeg: University of Manitoba Press, 1985, 95–118.

Stanley, G.F.G., "The Metis and the Conflict of Culture in Western Canada", *Canadian Historical Review*, XXVIII, 1947.

Stanley, G.F.G., "The Old Order of Red River", in *The Birth of Western Canada*, Toronto, 1970, 3–18.

St.Onge, Nicole J.M., "Variations in Red River: The Traders and Freemen Métis of Saint-Laurent, Manitoba," *Canadian Ethnic Studies*, 22, 2, 1997, 193–212.

THE RED RIVER PEASANTRY: MÉTIS ECONOMY AND SOCIETY IN THE 1830s

Gerhard Ens

By 1835 the Metis communities of Red River had settled into a new way of life. Residence in the colony was, in fact, central to their involvement in the hunting, farming, tripping, and provisioning niches in the fur trade. In the absence of other economic opportunities and competitive markets, the culturally diverse communities came to share remarkably similar characteristics. Regardless of their origins, all Red River Metis came to be united by common land tenure, economy, and social structure.

Semi-autonomous village communities and cultures were the primary elements of their way of life. Land tenure was based on grants and sales from Lord Selkirk and the Hudson's Bay Company, on squatters' rights, and on a tradition of communal jurisdiction. Its economic basis was a household economy comprising small-scale agriculture, the buffalo hunt, and seasonal labour for the Hudson's Bay Company. It was, in effect, a type of peasant society and economy whose primary aim was meeting the subsistence needs of the family rather than making a profit. Economic activity was dominated by the need to satisfy the requirements of each production unit. Each production unit was, at the same time, a consumer unit. Therefore budgeting was to a high degree qualitative; it balanced family subsistence needs with a substantive distaste for manual labour that determined the intensity of cultivation and the size of the net product. As soon as the equilibrium point was reached, continuing to work was pointless.[1]

From *Homeland to Hinterland: The Changing Worlds of the Red River Métis in the Nineteenth Century* (Toronto: University of Toronto Press, 1996). Reprinted by permission of the author and University of Toronto Press Incorporated. © University of Toronto Press Incorporated 1996.

Although the Red River Settlement was connected to commercial capital-ism through the Hudson's Bay Company, a parallel and contradictory economic system existed at the household level. This peasant or subsistence economy should not, however, be considered as 'subsistence' in the strict sense of the word. As in most peasant economies, there was a dual orientation to market and household.[2] Each Metis family not only used produce from the buffalo hunt and the farm to feed itself, but also exchanged it in Red River for other goods. The Metis also engaged in other activities, such as occasional wage labour. They participated to a limited degree in the wage labour system of the Hudson's Bay Company by hiring on for a specific period (boat trip, cart brigade), for which they received a credit in the company's account books that was usually spent for provisions or goods in the following months. As Gerald Friesen has noted, 'this labour system might be described as typical of a non-industrial society, and, in its informal work discipline and rough measures of time, not far removed from that of the casual farm labourer or cottage artisan in 17th century England.'[3]

Most Metis families aimed at subsistence rather than re-investment. They might sell a portion of their crop or hire themselves out to the Hudson's Bay Company, but they used the proceeds chiefly to buy the goods and services they needed to subsist and maintain their social status. The family remained the main unit of production in a non-capitalistic mode of production.[4] Although the Hudson's Bay Company routinely purchased pemmican, dried meat, and agricultural produce from the settlers of Red River, its annual demand varied little even though the population of the colony increased rapidly.[5] By the 1830s the growth of Metis population, and the attendant increase in the production of pemmican and dried meat, had so saturated the limited market that the Hudson's Bay Company refused to buy much of the pemmican offered to it.[6] The company was also not able to absorb much of the agricultural produce of the settlement. The demand of the trading posts was small and easily satisfied. Company grain purchases seldom amounted to more than 1,000 to 1,330 bushels. These purchases initially amounted to 16 bushels of grain per settler, but as the population grew this fell to 12 bushels, then to 8 bushels; by 1845 it was even below this level.[7] In later years the company further depressed demand by maintaining large company-run farms at both Lower Fort Garry and St François Xavier to supply its provisioning needs.

Although trade with the Hudson's Bay Company in the 1830s enabled the Metis to purchase manufactured clothing and commodities, their production from the hunt and the farm remained oriented mainly to household consump-tion. In 1893, when William Keating travelled through the settlement, he noted there were no cash transactions in the colony. Wheat, along with other com-modities, was 'traded in the way of exchange for some other commodity.'[8] Given the level of technology at the time and the absence of any real market, this was a rational course of action.

The *Nor'Wester,* looking back on the agricultural history of the colony, com-mented in 1859:

In one respect, however, the farmers appear to have been generally agreed. We refer to their determination to raise little more than enough of produce for home consumption; and so strictly did they carry out their resolves—so nicely did they gauge the needed home supplies—that last year the temporary presence in the Settlement of a couple of exploring parties and a few batches of fortune-hunters ... almost created a famine.[9]

While it is true that the Metis were already participating in an illicit fur trade, until the 1840s this trade was largely circumscribed by the efforts of the Hudson's Bay Company, the inaccessibility of alternative markets, and the lack of capital and marketing skills on the part of the Metis. James Sinclair and Cuthbert Grant, and perhaps one or two other Metis, operated small trading concerns, but these few individuals were allowed to trade only with the permission of the Hudson's Bay Company and depended on getting most of their supplies via HBC ships. One of the conditions the company set in allowing Grant to trade was that he keep other Metis out of the business.

Land Tenure in Red River

The basis of land tenure in the Red River Settlement was as complex as it was inconsistent. Although the Selkirk settlers had settled in Red River in 1819, five years passed before they concluded a treaty with the resident Cree and Saulteaux Indians. It was only the dispute with the North-West Company over the legitimacy of the colony that moved Selkirk to treat with the Indians at all, as he believed a treaty necessary to remove the threat of Indian violence.[10] When Selkirk arrived at Red River, the Saulteaux Indians resident there informed him that they did not own the land, having only arrived in the area some thirty years before. According to them, it belonged to the Cree. They agreed to sell only when Selkirk informed them that, since they were living on the soil, he considered them masters of it.[11] By this treaty Peguis, a chief of the Saulteaux, ceded to Selkirk a two-mile-wide strip on either side of the Red River from Lake Winnipeg to the junction of the Red and the Assiniboine. Although the treaty reads two 'English Statute Miles,' it was later argued that the Indians had no concept of measurement in miles, and that the actual agreement made with the Indians stipulated land extending back from the river bank 'as far as a man standing on the bank could see under the belly of a horse out into the plain.'[12] Les Grandes Oreilles, another Saulteaux chief, ceded a similar strip from the Forks to Pembina. La Robe Noire sold two miles on either side of the Assiniboine River from the Forks to a point beyond Portage La Prairie. Finally, the Red Lake chief sold a strip on either side of the Red River from Pembina south to the Red Lake River. In return the various chiefs were to receive a quit-rent consisting of one hundred pounds of tobacco each year.[13]

This treaty dealt only with two miles on either side of the Assiniboine and Red Rivers; there remained some confusion as to who owned the land outside the two miles. According to Andrew McDermott, a former HBC servant and prominent independent trader in the settlement,[14] the Hudson's Bay Company claimed all the land beyond the two miles as well, except that which they had sold.[15] Clearly, settlers felt they had rights to land outside the two-mile limit. In 1858 Eske-puck-a-koos, who styled himself as the chief of the heathen Indians at Red River, as opposed to the Christian Indians under Peguis, published a manifesto asking remuneration in return for permission to cut hay outside the two-mile limit. He also threatened to burn the hay if this were not respected. Peguis intervened and asserted that the settlers had a right to cut hay by his permission.[16]

Under Lord Selkirk's direction, lands were granted freehold to colonists in plots of up to one hundred acres. As Red River increasingly became a refuge for retired Hudson's Bay Company servants in the 1820s, Governor Simpson retained joint power with Selkirk's representatives to grant and sell lands.[17] Grants to former servants of the company varied from as little as 3 chains (60.35 metres) of river frontage, with as few as 30 acres, to 12-chain lots containing upwards of 200 acres for former chief factors. In 1822 the Council of the Northern Department of the Hudson's Bay Company recommended that grants of lands to former servants be restricted to 30 acres or 3 chains.[18] Settlers usually supplemented this by purchasing an additional 3 chains from the company. By 1833 Rev. William Cockran, the Anglican clergyman in charge of the Rapids congregation (later to become the Parish of St Andrew's) commented on the usual practice there: 'He receives gratis a piece of land, 33 yards in breadth, and two miles in length. This is too narrow to fence and make a farm of. Therefore the dust of the balance, which has been collecting for 30 years, must be swept out at once to procure another piece, to add to his gratuity.'[19]

In return for a grant of land, the settler was also required to fulfil some obligations. In 1822 the governor of Assiniboia, Andrew Bulger, informed the bishop of St Boniface that the one condition applying to all land grants in Assiniboia stipulated that the grantee had to settle upon the land and cultivate a portion of it. He noted that many former French-Canadian and Metis company servants were also bound by their HBC land grants to pay an annual rent of five bushels of wheat per hundred acres. Additionally, grants were accompanied by the obligation to provide six days of labour for the upkeep of the colony's roads and bridges. Alternatively, settlers could buy their land outright for the fixed price of five shillings sterling per acre.[20] When the Hudson's Bay Company took over administration of the colony in 1835, this was the established policy towards land tenure. The company then ordered a re-survey of the settled portions of the settlement and began entering land grants and sales in a land register. In 1823 William Kempt had prepared a survey and plan of the Red River Settlement, but it was inaccurate. Ten years later there were few traces left of Kempt's survey, as the flood of 1826 had obliterated most of them. Lots ran into each other, and no one was certain about their own boundaries. The re-survey of 1836 was meant to quiet these disputes and bring order to the settlement process.[21]

Land regulations changed little over the years, except that by the 1850s the price of land had risen to 7s 6d sterling per acre and title was given in the form of a lease for 999 years. The conditions in the lease were:

> 1st. That one-tenth of the land is to be brought into cultivation within five years; 2nd. That trading or dealing with Indians or others so as to violate the chartered privileges of the Company, be forsworn; 3rd. Obedience to all laws of the Company; 4th. Contributions to expenses of public establishments in due proportion; 5th. All trade or traffic in any kind of skins, furs, peltry, or dressed leather, except under licence of the Company, forbidden; 6th. Land not to be disposed of or let, or assigned without Consent of the Company.[22]

While this was the official policy of the Hudson's Bay Company, there was also a tradition of land tenure based on occupation. Those inhabitants who squatted on lands unclaimed by another were left undisturbed. Governor Simpson considered it inadvisable to interfere with this practice until real purchasers appeared, as any attempt to remove the squatters was bound to result in resistance.[23] By 1857 Governor Simpson stated that the company could not prevent squatting nor should it endeavour to try to prevent it. By the 1860s, it was recognized that beyond the surveyed limits of the settlement, squatters could settle without paying for the land, although claims were not to exceed 12 chains.

The method of land disposition in the Parish of St François Xavier was another exception to the official policy of the Hudson's Bay Company. Cuthbert Grant viewed this land as his personal seigneury and had parcelled out the land to the displaced Metis of Pembina in 12-chain lots.[24] This method of disposition later created a good deal of confusion as the company officers still regarded themselves as proprietors, whereas settlers laboured under the belief that they owned the land through Cuthbert Grant.[25]

This hodgepodge system of land tenure was generally accepted by all groups in the settlement. It was only during periods of tension and uncertainty that some Metis rose to speak out against the consensus. In 1835, when the Hudson's Bay Company took over the administration of the colony from Selkirk's heirs, some Metis feared this change in administration might threaten their unofficial claims to land. They petitioned Governor Simpson for assurances of legal title to their lands.[26] Simpson's reply stated simply that those who had received grants or bought their land from the Hudson's Bay Company would be assured of a title deed. He made no mention of squatters' rights, but he likewise failed to indicate that the Company was about to change its administration of lands.[27] When the Metis realized that no action would be taken against those who had squatted on unoccupied lands, the matter was dropped. The issue came up again in 1860 when the possibility arose that Red River might become a crown colony. At that time, a dispute developed about whether Peguis had ever actually sold the land on which the settlement was located. Through an interpreter, Peguis claimed that the Indians had only rented or allowed Selkirk and his settlers to reside on it. The bargain that had been struck was, in his view, only preliminary to a final bargain. The Metis who took this view argued that the Hudson's Bay Company therefore had no legal title to the land, and that its system of land registration was void. The issue was widely debated in the settlement with Metis on both sides of the question.[28] When crown colony status proved illusory, the matter was dropped, but briefly flared up again in 1861 when the Hudson's Bay Company tried to exact payment for all lands occupied in the colony at the rate of 7s 6d per acre. If not paid, the company threatened to sell these lands to the first purchaser. This set off 'indignation' meetings in several parishes, at which the Metis decided that no monies should be paid, that the Hudson's Bay Company had no right to the land, never having purchased it, and that the Metis had a right to it, being 'the descendants of the original lords of the soil.'[29] In the face of this opposition, the company backed down. It was this type of protest that was resuscitated in the summer of 1869 when it became apparent that the Hudson's Bay Company was preparing to transfer Rupert's Land to Canada.[30]

Land holding in Red River thus followed a pattern of peasant tenure. The inhabitants of Red River managed their river-lot farms as they wished, but were subject to the leasehold requirements of the Hudson's Bay Company that deprived them of uncontested ownership.[31] Visitors to Red River stressed the organic nature of this community. J. Wesley Bond, a secretary to Governor Alexander Ramsey of Minnesota Territory, visited the settlement in 1851 and described Red River as a long, serpentine village:

> Farmhouses, with barns, stables, hay, wheat, and barley-stacks, with small cultivated fields or lots, well fenced, are [sic] stretched along the meandering river, while the prairies far off to the horizon are covered with herds of cattle, horses, & c., the fields filled with a busy throng of whites, half-breeds and Indians—men, squaws, and children—all reaping, binding, and stacking the golden grain.[32]

For his part, Governor Ramsey wrote that the Red River Settlement resembled nothing so much as a long suburban village typical of those in pictures of English country villages.[33]

These river-lot villages combined elements of the French-Canadian river-lot survey and the Scottish system of infield-outfield agriculture.[34] In this old Celtic mode of land management, the house and barn of the farmstead stood by the infield, often at the edge of a stream in a valley. The infield was usually cropped, while the outfield, lying to the rear, was most often reserved for pasture land. Beyond this, in the hills, farmers could send their cattle out to graze during the summer. As W.L. Morton has noted,

> in Red River cottage and byre had risen by the river side and the little 'parks' on the banks, cropped year after year, recalled the infields of the old land. The back portion of the two-mile-deep lot was pastured as the outfield was; ... And a further two miles behind each lot had become the 'hay privilege' of the owner of the lot, with all possessing right of common to hay and pasturage on the outer plain.[35]

A variation on this pattern were 'park lots' located in the outer two miles of unoccupied lots. These consisted of choice pieces of prairie land on which the settler would break and cultivate a few acres. Often the claimant would also build a cabin on the lot and live on it in the summer, taking his calves and cows out for better pasturage. There were many of these park lots in St Andrew's, varying from 2 to 100 acres. If left uncultivated for a number of years, these lots were sometimes claimed by others. Usually an absence of three to four years was enough for the lot to be considered abandoned. Others in the settlement claimed that the period was to eight years, and still others claimed that ceasing to cultivate or occupy these park lots did not invalidate the claim. This resulted in many disputes between claimants, but there had been no judicial decision on the question before 1870.[36]

The Metis Economy

Although the Metis supplemented the produce of their buffalo hunts and river-lot farms with seasonal labour for the Hudson's Bay Company, duck hunting, and fishing in Lakes Winnipeg and Manitoba, farming and buffalo hunting remained their economic focus until the 1840s. The settlers first harvested good crops in 1824,[37] but it was not until 1827—the year after a disastrous flood—that agriculture became established in the colony. Between 1827 and 1835, a succession of good crops stabilized the colony's economy. This was evident in the construction, by 1830, of 204 new houses, barns, and enclosures.[38] Land under cultivation rose from 2,152 acres in 1831 to more than 3,500 acres in 1835.[39] Establishing farms on the banks of the Red and Assiniboine Rivers was, according to one observer, much less difficult than in many other places. Father Laflèche, a Roman Catholic missionary stationed at St François Xavier in the 1840s, observed that at most locations in the settlement, all that was necessary to put a plough into the ground was to clear or burn off some brush. In many places, it was only necessary to erect an enclosure around a field and plough it.[40] The necessity of enclosing all cultivated fields to protect the crops from cattle roaming at large, and the increasing scarcity of wood needed to build these enclosures, kept fields small. Five acres was considered a large plot in Red River. Cultivated plots were also kept small by the level of farm technology and the absence of a market for surplus production. Before 1850, broadcast sowing on roughly ploughed and harrowed land was the usual method of planting, while harvesting was carried out with a sickle. The marshy state of the back land, and the inability of the iron-tipped wooden plough to cut through the heavy soil and grass growth of the meadow lands, tied cultivation and settlement to the loamy silt soils of well-drained river lots.[41]

While most scholars agree that agriculture and the hunt were supplementary to each other in Red River, recourse is occasionally made to the 'attraction of the hunt' as a way of explaining the varying degrees of commitment to agri-

culture among the Metis. In most such accounts, the French Metis are identified as buffalo hunters, while the English Metis are portrayed as serious
farmers.[42] The censuses of Red River from the mid to late 1840s are the basis
of this interpretation. Typically, these scholars ignore earlier census data and
thus miss the crucial economic transition that occurred in the 1840s.

It is clear from census figures that by 1835 small-scale peasant agriculture
was customary in most Red River parishes. There appears to have been little difference in cultivated acreage among the various communities in the settlement.
Most families cultivated five to six acres, which works out to about one acre
per person. In the parishes of St François Xavier and St Andrew's, the number
of cultivated acres per family and individual were almost identical. The number of larger farms in the two parishes is also very similar, with twenty-two
families (23 per cent of the parish's families) cultivating ten or more acres in St
Andrew's, and twenty-six families (27 per cent of the parish's families) in St
François Xavier. Within both St François Xavier and St Andrew's there was a
discrepancy in cultivation between families headed by Europeans and those
families headed by Metis. While most family members (wives and children)
were Metis, families headed by European males generally cultivated about
twice as much as families headed by Metis males. One explanation for this was
that European heads of family were usually older, had larger families, and
hence more sons at home to help farm.

The staple crop of the colony by the 1850s was an early maturing spring
wheat,[43] which produced high yields. According to H.Y. Hind, the University of

TABLE 1 Population and Cultivation in Red River, 1835

	St Andrew's	St François Xavier	Red River
Total population	547 (15%)*	506 (13.8%)	3,646
No. of single adults	3	5	–
No. of families	94 (14.3%)	97 (14.7%)	658
Average family size	5.79	5.16	5.55
% Metis (family heads)	53.6	74.5	–
Cultivated acreage	566 (16.2%)	594 (17%)	3,504
Cult. acreage per family	6.02	6.12	5.33
Cult. acreage per person	1.03	1.17	0.96
No. cultivating more than 10 acres	22	26	–
Cult. acreage per Metis fam. head	4.04	4.62	–
Cult. acreage per Eur. fam. head	7.93	9.34	–

Source: Census of Red River. While the 1835 census did not break down the population by parish,
this was accomplished by using parish registers, the HBC land register, and other censuses.
* In parentheses: the percentage of the total for the entire settlement

Toronto geologist hired by the government of Canada to explore the Northwest during 1857–8, yields of forty bushels per acre were common on new ground in the Red River Settlement.[44] Father LaFlèche noted that wheat fields were the height of a man, and that a farmer harvested about twenty-two bushels of wheat for every one sown.[45] Harvest season began in late August and ran into September. Cut with a sickle, the wheat was gathered into sheaves and then assembled into 'shocks' by the women and children, who followed behind the men. The sheaves were carted from the field to the farmyard and stacked, to be threshed in winter when more time was available. The grain was threshed by flailing the wheat stalks on the floor in the barn. It was then winnowed from the chaff by the cross draught of the two-doored barn. The threshing season lasted throughout the winter, grain being threshed as it was needed, for food or sale.[46] Because of the absence of any external market, most of this wheat was ground into flour for colony consumption at one of the thirteen wind- and water-mills in the settlement in the 1830s.[47] Other crops included barley, oats, corn, potatoes, and turnips, but there was little use for them other than as animal feed. Some barley was malted for home brewing of beer, but all attempts to establish a distillery failed.[48] Wheat and other grain production remained at subsistence levels until the 1870s. In 1849 there were still only 6,392 acres under cultivation in the colony—less than 1.2 acres per person. In St Andrew's, one of the more agricultural parishes after 1849, the average cultivation per person remained under 1.3 acres per person until 1870.

After 1822–3, cattle and pigs were introduced to the settlement. But before 1827, livestock husbandry met with limited success as the severity of winters and attacks by wolves reduced returns. Even more serious was the lack of winter fodder, which arose because the settlers had little experience in haying in the 1820s.[49] As settlers gained experience in harvesting hay from the plains, livestock became increasingly important in the subsistence economy of Red River.[50] For winter fodder, each farmer could count on the yield of his lot and the two-mile hay privilege. This he mowed when he thought fit and his other work allowed. If he required more hay, he had recourse to the plains. Competition for the hay of the wild land behind the hay privilege became so intense that the Council of Assiniboia regulated the cutting of hay on the plains. Livestock provided motive power and meat for household consumption. Some cattle were exported to the United States in the period after 1830, but this was never an important economic factor. By 1835 most settlers had a horse for riding and pulling the ubiquitous Red River cart, a pair of oxen for ploughing,[51] and some cattle and pigs for meat. The larger number of cattle and pigs in St Andrew's, in comparison to St François Xavier, stemmed from the greater reliance of the St François Xavier Metis on buffalo for meat (see Table 2).

The biannual buffalo hunt provided a great deal of the colony's provisions. Contrary to W.L. Morton's position that agriculture and the hunt acted as fatal checks on each other, with one depressing the price of the other's produce,[52] subsistence agriculture and the buffalo hunt were more complementary than

TABLE 2   Livestock Production in Red River, 1835

	St Andrew's	*St François Xavier*	*Red River*
Total livestock	1,223 (16%)*	884 (11.6%)	7,617
Average per family	12.87	8.93	11.6
Total horses	87 (12.1%)	131 (18.2%)	718
Average per family	0.93	1.35	1.1
Total cattle**	824 (16.9%)	555 (11.4%)	4,874
Average per family	8.76	5.72	7.40
Total pigs	312 (15.4%)	198 (9.7%)	2,025
Average per family	3.28	2.0	3.07

Source: Red River census of 1835
* In parentheses: the percentage of the total for the entire settlement
** Includes oxen and calves

competitive. Whenever the hunt failed, the produce of the farm helped provide the needs of the Metis hunters, and vice-versa. Census returns also indicate that most Metis in the various parishes had some cultivated land in the 1830s, dispelling the notion that the hunting and farming economies originated in different sections of the population. The 1835 census shows, for example, that 80 of the 94 families (85.1 per cent) in the parish of St Andrew's cultivated at least one acre, and that in St François Xavier 76 of 97 families (78.35 per cent) cultivated at least one acre.

In the 1820s, organized buffalo hunts began to replace the more individualized hunting out of the Red River Settlement.[53] Prior to this, the buffalo were found so close to the settlement that individuals and small groups could secure their food supply without leaving the colony. As the settlement's population increased and the level of hunting intensified, the buffalo herds roamed farther from Red River, obliging hunters to go out in groups or bands. In part, this was a result of the necessity of making a common approach to the herds, but it also arose because the largest herds were found southwest of the settlement in hostile Sioux territory. By the late 1820s, two separate hunts originated in Red River. The first and largest hunt left the settlement in early June and returned in late July or August. The proceeds of this hunt, largely dried meat and pemmican, were usually traded to the Hudson's Bay Company for clothing and other supplies.[54] For this reason, the summer hunt was also known as the 'dried meat hunt.' The second and smaller hunt left the settlement in September, with the hunters returning after the first cold spell in late October or early November. This hunt was smaller (about one-third the size of the summer hunt) because many Red River Metis who could not afford to winter in the settlement had by then left for their wintering camps, where they subsisted by hunting deer and moose.[55] The size of the fall hunt was also affected by the fact that it occurred during harvest and haying, which were important to the welfare of many families. This hunt produced some dried meat and pemmican, but the colder weather permitted the Metis to return with large quantities of frozen meat as well. As such, the fall hunt was commonly referred to as the 'green meat hunt.' Meat from this hunt was used mainly to feed the Metis families through the winter. The hunt also provided the Metis with most of the thick buffalo robes they used as blankets before the 1850s.

As the population of the settlement increased, the size of the summer hunts increased. The first hunts in the 1820s comprised 500 to 600 carts; by the mid-1830s this had increased to nearly 1,000; and by 1840 more than 1,200 carts accompanied the summer hunt. Whole families went with the hunters, as the Metis women were crucial in the production of pemmican and dried meat, and in the curing of the buffalo robes and skins. Alexander Ross, who accompanied the 1840 hunt that originated at Pembina, noted that in addition to the 620 hunters, there were 650 women and 360 children in the caravan.[56] The summer hunt attracted both the English and French Metis. During June and July, the Red River Settlement was almost deserted. The only remaining residents were the elderly, very young children, and the Scottish settlers of Kildonan.[57] The extent to which the hunt was complementary to the agricultural economy in Red River is attested to by William Cockran, the Anglican missionary at St Andrew's. An avowed opponent of the hunt because he thought its nomadic character uncivilized, Cockran himself sent a cart along in 1837 to gather provisions for his Indian school as there was no prospect of reaping a grain crop that year.[58]

The buffalo hunt out of Red River comprised three different parties. One was the Pembina Metis who had not moved to St François Xavier in the 1820s. Pembina was not only the rendezvous where all three parties met in council before heading out onto the plains, it was also the home of Jean Baptiste Wilkie, a famous hunt chief of the late 1830s and 1840s. The second group was the 'main river party,' which consisted of those Metis who lived along the Red River northward from St Boniface. The third group was the Metis hunters of St François Xavier. By the 1850s, the size of the hunt had increased to such an extent that the St François Xavier hunters formed a separate expedition. They did, however, remain in contact with the main group because they feared Sioux hostilities.[59]

The three parties normally met at Pembina in early June to choose leaders and set rules for the hunt. These rules included prohibitions on running the buffalo before the general order was given, or going off alone to hunt or lagging behind the main party—rules that protected the interests of the whole group. Ten captains were chosen by lot to enforce these rules and to protect the caravan on the march. Each captain, in turn, had ten soldiers under his command, who acted as the police force. The senior captain was considered the chief of the hunt and he, along with the other captains, formed the council of the hunt. In the 1820s, Cuthbert Grant was usually the chief of the hunt. In the

1830s and 1840s, prominent chiefs included Jean Baptiste Wilkie from Pembina and William Hallet from the 'main river' group. Besides being captains, such men were regarded as great chiefs or heads of the camp. The chief was the final arbiter of disputes while on the march; his decisions were not questioned.

Ten or twelve men were also selected to guide the camp and choose the direction the march would take. These guides were usually hunters of experience, as it was not easy to avoid marshes, go around lakes, or find a path between precipitous hills. Each guide led the hunt for a day at a time. The guide for the day was responsible for hoisting the camp flag in the morning as a signal for the march to begin and for lowering the flag as the signal for a new camp to be struck. While the flag was raised, the guide was understood to be the chief of the expedition. All captains were then subject to him, and the soldiers served as his messengers. When the flag was lowered and camp struck, however, authority reverted to the captains of the hunt.[60]

The Metis would leave their rendezvous site for the buffalo plains in a controlled and orderly manner because at any time the expedition might encounter hostile Sioux or a herd of buffalo. Typically, the march began at daybreak, and the cart brigade proceeded in two to four columns depending on the number of carts. The line of march was often five or six miles long. At the head of the column rode the guide of the day, carrying the flag and giving direction to the moving camp. Four groups of mounted scouts and soldiers protected the caravan. They formed advance and rear guards and protected both flanks. Any intelligence they gathered about Sioux or buffalo herds was relayed to the guide of the day. When the first alarm was sounded, the carts immediately formed into two columns and the whole formation wheeled, joining the extremities of the columns and forming a circle. Wheel to wheel, the carts formed a corral for the horses and oxen. This prevented stampedes. If no hostile Sioux or buffalo were encountered, the march would not break off for lunch until two in the afternoon. It then resumed until 5:00 or 6:00 p.m. By that time, the expedition would have travelled about twenty miles. When camp was struck for the night, a council of all the leading men would be held to discuss the day's activities and to decide the line of march for the next day.

If the scouts spotted a buffalo herd, they signalled the guide and a camp was immediately struck. Once camped, the hunters mounted their fastest horses and awaited the orders of the chief. Normally, they approached the herd slowly upwind as short-sighted buffalo have an excellent sense of smell. They advanced at an easy canter in a long line with the hunt chief leading the way. Anyone who passed the chief faced a heavy fine. When within 400–500 yards of the buffalo, they broke into an easy gallop, keeping a long unbroken line. When the herd noticed the hunters, usually at a distance of a few hundred yards, it usually wheeled about and galloped off. The chief then gave the 'advance' signal and it became every man for himself. The hunters would ride into the herd with their mouths full of shot and their pockets full of powder. A hunter with a good horse often got to within three or four yards of the buffalo before firing. His trained buffalo runner, as the horses were known, would leap to the side to avoid stumbling over the falling animal. The Metis would immediately reload by pouring a handful of powder down the gun barrel, spitting a ball into the muzzle, and striking the gun-stock on his saddle to set the bullet. By this time, his horse would have brought him alongside another buffalo. Bringing his gun down across his saddle, he would fire from the waist. An experienced hunter with a fast horse could kill ten to twelve animals in a run, while a hunter with a less adept horse might kill only two or three. Much depended on the roughness of the terrain. Within an hour or two, the hunt would be over.[61]

While brief, the hunt was very dangerous. Scratched faces, sprains, contusions, dislocated shoulders, and broken legs and arms were common injuries as the ground was often rough and hilly and honeycombed with badger and fox holes. Men were killed during most hunts. In 1860, for example, Alexander Swain was one of the fatalities. While reloading his firearm, Swain put his mouth over the muzzle to spit a ball down the barrel. The hot barrel ignited the powder and the gun discharged in his mouth. While he survived the explosion and fall from his horse, his severely burned throat prevented him from eating and drinking and he died within two days.[62]

When the chase was over, the hunters immediately dismounted and began skinning and butchering the animals. The Metis were renowned for being able to identity their individual kills. Soon the women of the camp brought the carts to the place of the kill. They helped with the butchering and loaded the meat into the carts so that it could be hauled back to camp. Once in camp, the women assumed responsibility for the preparation and preservation of the meat. They would cut the meat into thin strips, which they dried over a fire for two or three days. The best of this dried meat would be folded up and tied into sixty- or seventy-pound bales. They made the rest pemmican, a nutritious form of buffalo meat that would keep for several years. In 1845 Father Belcourt, a Catholic missionary from Red River, wrote an eye-witness account of the making of pemmican:

> This meat, having previously been exposed to strong heat upon a drying frame of green wood, has become brittle and easy to reduce to powder. The fat of the interior, having been cut up and melted in large cauldrons of sheet iron, is poured out upon the threshed meat which is stirred up with spades until all the parts are well saturated; then this mixture is poured in skin sacks from which they have not even taken the trouble to remove the hair. The sacks so filled are called bulls *(taureaux)* or *pimikenhigen (pemmican)*. If the fat that has been used is fat of the udder, they are called fine bulls *(taureaux fins)*. Some mix with them dried fruits such as plums, or cherries; then they are called bulls with grains *(taureaux á graines)*. The gastronomic experts esteem the first kind as good, the second better, and the third very good.[63]

These methods of curing the buffalo meat not only preserved it for later consumption but considerably reduced its volume. An entire buffalo yielded just a sack of pemmican or three-quarters of a bale of dried meat. Once the meat had been processed, the march resumed. This pattern of activity was repeated until the carts were filled. It has been estimated that one cart-load comprised the dried meat, pemmican, and hides of eight to ten buffalo.

In the 1830s, the other main occupation of the Red River Metis was as hired labour, or 'tripmen,' on Hudson's Bay Company boats. This job was an integral part of the HBC transportation system. When the company moved inland from its coastal factories in the last quarter of the eighteenth century, its chief form of transportation was a York boat that developed out of the traditional Orkney fishing craft. On the western rivers, the York boat could carry more than twice the load of the Nor'Westers' canoes with the same number of crew. York boats required crews of youthful 'tripmen,' who were capable of managing the large craft around rapids and on lakes. To man their boats, the company turned to the native sons of servants and officers. With the formation of the Red River Settlement and the move of the Hudson's Bay Company's administrative and distribution centre from York Factory to Fort Garry, the company increasingly recruited tripmen from the Metis of the colony. Each York boat was usually manned by nine men and carried three to four tons of freight. Tripmen fell into three categories: steersman, bowsman, and middlemen or rowers. The main duty of the steersman—the best paid of the tripmen—was to steer the boat, an ability that involved a thorough knowledge of dangerous water along the entire route. He would also lift the bales of goods or furs from the boat and place them on the backs of the carriers at the portages. The bowsman, in addition to the rowing, and carrying he had to do, would stand in the bow of the boat at the rapids or shoals and signal the steersman about the nature of the course ahead. Using a long pole, he also helped keep the boat on course and away from rocks. The duties of the middlemen included rowing, 'tracking' or dragging the boats with ropes around rapids on the upstream journey, and carrying the goods across portages. Later, in the 1850s and 1860s, when the Hudson's Bay Company replaced many of their York boat brigades with overland cart transport, the term 'tripman' also came to refer to those men who hired themselves out to man these cart brigades. In the 1830s, the company hired about 260 tripmen yearly to work the York boats. By the late 1850s and early 1860s, the Hudson's Bay Company and private traders hired fully a thousand tripmen annually to work on boats or cart brigades.[64]

By the 1830s, the Red River Metis worked on two main boat routes. The York brigades plied the route between Fort Garry on the Red and York Factory on Hudson Bay. Brigades made up of four to eight boats passed and repassed each other during the season of open water. With a round trip taking about sixty days, a tripman made two trips per season. The York trip, however, was less significant than the Portage La Loche brigades, which were responsible for carrying the yearly supplies to HBC posts in the Northwest. By the 1830s, this brigade numbered seventeen or eighteen boats. It left Fort Garry in three divisions, staggered at one-week intervals to avoid crowding or confusion at portages and camping places. Wages for the Portage la Loche tripmen were more than double those of the York brigades, but only one trip could be made per season and the work was harder. Given these conditions, most Metis preferred working on the York brigades. It was usually difficult to sign up enough tripmen to fill the complement needed for the Portage brigade.

The Portage brigades left Red River with dried meat, pemmican, and farm produce as soon as ice left Lake Winnipeg. At Norway House on Lake Winnipeg, they exchanged their cargo of food for European trade goods brought down from York Factory during the previous season. They then proceeded westward across the lake and up the Saskatchewan River. Reaching Ile-á-la-Crosse and Portage la Loche by August, the tripmen carried their cargo half-way across the twelve-mile portage, where they exchanged their European goods for cargoes of furs brought down from the Mackenzie River and Athabasca districts. They then retraced their route to Norway House, collected any furs left there, and proceeded to York Factory, usually reaching the bayside post in early September. After resting and celebrating for a week to ten-days, they started back for Norway House laden with English trade goods that had been shipped to York Factory by the Hudson's Bay Company's annual boat from England. They left these goods at Norway House for the next year's brigades and returned to Red River by mid-October.

As the tripping season lasted from May to October, few tripmen farmed. One historian has pointed out that the hardships, slavish work, and the thrilling experiences common to these trips coloured a tripman's life for the rest of the year: 'Once or twice repeated, it left him a tripman and nothing else. The nature of the work unfitted him for the more prosaic walks of life, even if he had any inclination for them, which was not often.'[65] At the end of the season, some tripmen left the settlement to winter on the plains, where they hunted buffalo, but most idly spent the cold season among friends. In this way, the proceeds of the season's work were quickly spent, and by December they were ready to re-engage for the next year. In general, about half the wages were paid out in instalments before the trip started. Once caught in this economic cycle, many Metis remained tripmen for their entire working lives.

The Social and Seasonal Round

The social life of the Red River Metis revolved around settlement-wide gatherings during the summer buffalo hunt, the winter festive season, and the more mundane activities of visiting and gossiping. Like peasants everywhere, the Metis looked forward to those times when food and drink were plentiful and they could forget the hard labour of the farm, the hunt, and the freighting trip. Weddings, feasts, horse racing, and dancing were in a real sense what men and women, whether old or young, lived for. Bishop Taché noted with a disapproving tone that 'the most striking fault of the Half-breeds appears to me to be the ease with they resign themselves to the allurements of pleasure. Of lively disposition, ardent and playful, gratification is a necessity to them, and if a source of pleasure presents itself they sacrifice everything for its enjoyment.'[66]

The winter festive season was the highlight of the year. It lasted from the week before Christmas until a week after New Year's. The isolation of the Northwest made Red River the place to be at Christmas, and many Metis travelled hundreds of miles to be there then. This was the best time for social intercourse of all kinds, and, as Margaret Arnett MacLeod has noted, 'not a man in the settlement however poor or idle, but possessed some kind of horse or pony, and at this season the whole settlement vied with each other in gay carioles (sleighs), bright embroidered saddle-cloths and harness, and fine or gaudy clothes.'[67] In the week before Christmas, sleigh bells rang continually up and down the frozen Red and Assiniboine Rivers, which served as winter roads, as the Metis made the round of houses throughout the settlement. No one felt a need to extend invitations, except to the most exclusive balls, and houses and kitchens were open to all. There was always a pot of tea brewing, and often the fiddling and dancing continued till dawn.

On Christmas Eve, many Catholic Metis attended midnight Mass in the Cathedral of St Boniface, while Protestants held their Christmas service on the morning of the twenty-fifth. A large Christmas dinner, consisting of various combinations of roast beef, whitefish, buffalo meat, and mutton, was considered essential. Particular delicacies included boiled buffalo hump, dried moose nose, and smoked or salted buffalo tongue; the better off also served plum or Christmas pudding.[68]

New Year's was another high point of the season. While the blue bloods of the settlement gathered at Fort Garry for a revel and dance, the majority of the Metis gathered in private homes for dancing and merrymaking of their own on New Year's Eve. The next day was considered 'kissing day.' From early morning until dusk, the men travelled from house to house in their best capotes, sashes, and hats to receive a New Year's kiss from the women and girls of the settlement. After the obligatory kiss, they received the best food and spirits the house had to offer. Women who did not comply with this ritual were considered 'stuck up.' Another practice, often followed by the French Metis, was to visit the parental home on New Year's Day to receive their father's blessing. Invariably this was followed by a breakfast of New Year's 'tortiere' (meat pie). During the day, it was also common to hold horse races on the Red River adjacent to Fort Garry. A course was laid out on the ice, and, regardless of the temperature, spectators lined the banks to watch. Many Red River couples also took advantage of the winter to marry, as this was a season of abundance among family and friends with time on their hands. Both were essential for the week-long celebration that marked Red River weddings.[69]

Following the winter festive season, life in Red River returned to a more prosaic and relaxed pace. Some residents, like Peter Garrioch, went out onto the plains with a few friends to restore his supply of fresh meat. In the 1830s and

1840s, buffalo still wintered within a few days' travel of the settlement.[70] Others trapped in the north, or cleaned and ground their wheat for home consumption. But hauling wood was the most common activity for the remainder of the winter. While some Metis had woodlots adjacent to their river lots, most Red River residents had to travel far for firewood and building and fencing materials. If it was to burn properly, wood had to be dried for at least two summers.[71] Much wood was needed. In 1827 William Cockran noted that to heat his house on a cold day he burnt a cord of wood (a stack of wood 2.44 metres long, 1.22 metres high, and .91 metres broad).[72] In February of 1849, Rev. Smithurst employed twenty persons to cut the wood he needed for his Indian school at St Peter's.[73] Wood could be cut at any time of the year, but it was easiest to haul in winter. Favoured woodlots included those in the vicinity of Portage la Prairie, 'the Pines' (a tract of coniferous forest northeast of Winnipeg near what today is Bird's Hill Park), 'the Far Pines' (near the present-day town of Selkirk), and 'Davie's Pines' (a tract of coniferous forest where cedar could be found located south of Beausejour some 56 kilometres east of Winnipeg).[74] As the woodlots along the Red and Assiniboine Rivers became exhausted in the 1850s and 1860s, such excursions became even more frequent.

With spring came the duck and goose hunts on Lake Manitoba and Shoal Lake (April and May) and preparations for spring seeding. Land newly converted to cropland had to be fenced and ploughed. Seeding usually began in May. By the end of May, the HBC boats manned by Metis tripmen began leaving for York Factory and Portage La Loche. Depending on when the ice left Lake Winnipeg, these brigades departed between May 30 and June 10. Early June was also the time when the Metis began leaving the settlement to rendezvous at Pembina for the large summer buffalo hunt. They would not be back until late July. Most Metis families participated in the buffalo hunt, but usually left behind some older men and women along with the younger children to take care of the crops and farm animals.

Those who remained in the settlement during the hunt initiated haying. While hay could be cut at any time on one's own river lot, this source seldom produced enough to feed more than a few animals through the winter. Most Red River residents had to go to the plains to cut additional hay. To manage the competition for the best hay lands, no cutting outside the river lots was allowed before July 20. This deadline also allowed those Metis returning from the summer hunt to take part. These hunters also returned in time to harvest the other crops of the settlement. Harvesting was usually complete before a smaller contingent of Metis hunters left for the second 'green meat' hunt, which lasted from mid-September to November. Those who stayed in the settlement during this second hunt harvested any remaining crops and took part in the autumn goose hunt. In late November, with both hunters and tripmen back in the settlement, the Metis began hauling their hay in from the plains and began to cut and haul firewood.

In November, the fall fisheries on Lakes Manitoba and Winnipeg also commenced. While the whitefish fishery customarily engaged few Metis, it did attract more attention whenever the hunt and farming produced less than expected.[75] Typically, the Metis living in the parishes along the Red River fished along the shores of Lake Winnipeg near Grand Marais, while those along the Assiniboine River fished at Oak Point on Lake Manitoba. They netted whitefish and hung them head down to dry. This technique kept them from spoiling before freeze-up. When snow and freezing temperatures did arrive, the Metis took their ox-drawn sledges to their caches and hauled frozen fish back to the settlement. This job was usually completed prior to the Christmas season.[76]

On the third Thursday in the months of February, May, August, and November, the colony's General Court provided a diversion as it tried cases that sometimes involved murder, abortion, and assault. More often, it dealt with liquor offences, unpaid debts, smuggling, and other petty crimes.[77] These proceedings, eagerly followed by all settlers, provided the grist for the colony's gossip mills.

In the 1830s, Red River represented an amalgam of small, largely Metis communities of varying ethnic and religious orientations. Daily social life in these communities turned almost exclusively on the parish and the neighbourhood: children grew up, went to school, courted, and married within the same parish. This notwithstanding, the Metis of all communities structured their lives according to a common economic pattern derived from a peasant subsistence economy based on river-front agriculture, the plains hunt, and tripping. While they lived in separate areas of the settlement during the rest of the year, and largely married within their own community, for a few months each year members of most communities lived in relative harmony while on the buffalo hunt. Thus, although the Red River parishes were unquestionably distinct entities, the English and French Metis followed a similar way of life throughout the 1830s. As late as 1845, in fact, Father Laflèche of St François Xavier noted that the colony was made up of French-Catholic and English-Protestant Metis sections, and that 'les deux sections de la population vivent en parfait union.'[78]

Social Structure and Conflict

In establishing the various parishes and settlements that made up the Red River Colony, both the Hudson's Bay Company and the churches attempted to recreate the social orders of the trading post and the European rural parish. The Anglican and Catholic clergy shared with the Hudson's Bay Company a common vision of the structure of Red River society in which the clergy, as well as the retired and active commissioned gentlemen of the company, formed the ruling elite in the colony.

At the top of this hierarchical social structure, defined by social standing and by material wealth, were the colony's 'principal settlers.' This small group consisted largely of British and a few Canadian-born officers of the former North-West Company and the Hudson's Bay Company who had retired with their Metis families to the Red River Settlement. They possessed not only the wealth but the habits (and, in some cases, the education) that qualified them to lead the settlement. As such, they were the social equals of senior officers in the Hudson's Bay Company service. In the English-speaking part of the settlement, these families included the Birds, Logans, Sutherlands, and Gunns.[79] Among the French-speaking settlers of St François Xavier, the principal settlers included the families of Angus McGillis, Cuthbert Grant, Pierre Falcon, and Alexander Breland. It is interesting to note that, among them, only Angus McGillis was Canadian-born. The others had been born in the settlement or in the Northwest, and headed second-generation Metis families. This pattern, unlike the one at St Andrew's, where most principal settlers were British-born, was a result of the tendency of Canadian-born officers of the fur trade to retire to Canada. Their Metis heritage reduced their standing with the company's officers and the British-born of the settlement.

Cuthbert Grant represented this squirearchy in St François Xavier, where his double river lot was the centre of the parish. In 1824 George Simpson had appointed Grant 'Warden of the Plains' to reward him for his role in settling the Pembina Metis in British territory. Not merely honorific, the title came with a salary of £200 a year, for which Grant was to act as representative of the Hudson's Bay Company. The Hudson's Bay Company was adamant about preventing the Metis from trading with anyone else; they were especially afraid that the Metis would set up their own posts in the west and take furs to American traders on the Missouri. Grant himself was allowed to trade, but in exchange he was expected to prevent his countrymen from doing the same. As chief of the plains Metis, Grant fulfilled this role effectively until the late 1840s. By 1835 he, along with his wife, Marie McGillis, and their six children, cultivated 20 acres and owned 24 cattle, 6 horses, and 10 carts, denoting Grant's dual involvement in agriculture and the hunt.[80]

James Sutherland, who occupied lots 96 and 97, was one of St Andrew's principal settlers. Originally from Ronaldshay in the Orkney Islands, Sutherland joined the Hudson's Bay Company in 1797 and was stationed at Cumberland House. From 1821 to 1827, when he retired to Red River with his family of seven children, he was chief factor in charge of Swan River District. He was married to Jane Flett, a native woman with whom he lived for many years. In 1835 Sutherland cultivated 25 acres, owned 18 cattle, 5 horses, and 3 carts, and lived in fine fashion.[81] Like other principal settlers, Sutherland was able to afford the accoutrements of life which constituted the 'correct' way. According to Sutherland, the Red River elite had 'introduced a system of extravagance in the place which is followed by all that can afford it, and to keep up in a little respectability have followed it in a small way.'[82] Sutherland noted that his own household expenses had doubled since he arrived in Red River.

The clergy, both Protestant and Catholic, were also part of the colony elite. Their social and spiritual leadership, along with their mutually supportive relationship with the Hudson's Bay Company, ensured this. There were, however, some important distinctions between the Protestant and Catholic clerics. The Catholic clergy, because of their religion, language, and Quebec origins, were somewhat more distant from the political leadership of the colony, which remained British-oriented and English-speaking. As a result, they were initially unaffected by the pursuit of status at Upper Fort Garry. The Anglican clergy, by contrast, had much greater pretensions to social leadership in the settlement. They regarded themselves as morally and racially superior to the Metis and the Indian, and considered it their duty to instil the values of civilization and Christianity among the native population. As Frits Pannekoek has pointed out, these beliefs and self-aggrandizement created social conflict among the Protestant elite 'since the fur trade officers were by no means willing to consider the clergy their equals, or their mixed-blood wives and children inferior.'[83]

Beneath the rank of principal settler and clergy was a small group consisting of private merchants and lay officials of the church (such as school teachers and catechists). This included a wide spectrum of individuals such as retired Hudson's Bay Company servants of senior rank and the Metis sons of retired officers who did not possess the same prestige as the principal settlers.[84] Below this were most of the Metis who worked small holdings, laboured on the boats, and hunted the buffalo.

This society offered little upward mobility. Between 1821 and 1826, the salaried workforce of the Hudson's Bay Company declined by 1,233 men, a reduction of 65 per cent that left little room for advancement. While Metis could and did become postmasters in the service of the company, few were promoted beyond this position. Whereas eighteenth-century Hudson's Bay Company apprentices and labourers could aspire to high position with some confidence, by the 1840s it was unheard of for any servant, white or native-born, to become a 'gentleman.'[85] James Sutherland was at a loss to ensure the social standing of his Metis children:

> I have now four sons at the house with me, the two oldest are now men fit for any duty in this part of the world [but] their [sic] is no opportunity for young people to push themselves forward in any way, better than labourers, either as farmers or Boatmen in the Cos service and either way they can barely make a living—my two youngest sons has got a better Education than I had when I came to this country yet it will be of no use to them ...[86]

The transition to a settled economy and a hierarchical social order that the majority of the Metis in the settlement had made by the 1830s was painful for many.[87] Having grown up near the trading posts in the Northwest, most were not only ill-prepared to become farmers, but found the labour of clearing land for cultivation unpleasant. This, combined with increasingly rigid social divisions and years of scarcity, led to a number of upheavals in the 1820s and 1830s. These uprisings and their quick collapse reinforce the view of Red River as a peasant society.

One of the first occurred during the winter and spring of 1825–6. The winter was very hard with deep snow. Buffalo ranged far from the colony, and cattle and horses found little fodder on the plains. By January of 1826, cattle were dying, the price of buffalo meat was exorbitant, and little grain was left. The destitute were forced to eat their dogs and horses.[88] As the Metis knew the Hudson's Bay Company had hay and grain stored up, they began demanding aid. Aware that governments in other countries afforded relief to people in hard times, they felt the company was morally obligated to provide for them in a time of scarcity.[89] The Hudson's Bay Company did step in and disperse food and grain to the settlers, but by April 1826 the company had only enough left for seed grain in spring.

Famine soon enveloped the colony. The poorer segments of the population, believing the Hudson's Bay Company and richer settlers still had food and grain, roamed the settlement in mobs and forcibly seized food when they found some.[90] This state of unrest grew worse as the cold weather continued. By April 8, the Hudson's Bay Company learned there were several conspiracies supported by the Metis, Canadiens, and De Meurons. These plots involved capturing and plundering Fort Garry and the colony's windmills, as well as robbing the richer Kildonan settlers. The only Metis who remained aloof were those under the influence of Cuthbert Grant at the White Horse Plain.[91]

With no police to protect their property, the officers of the Hudson's Bay Company tried to subvert these plots by a combination of conciliation and threat. To split up the conspirators, the officers promised seed grain to all Metis and Canadiens who remained peaceful. Donald Mackenzie, the officer in charge of Fort Garry, visited the Catholic priests at St Boniface and informed them of the threats to the company and the possible repercussions for the Catholic Church if an insurrection did break out. Bishop Provencher immediately understood Mackenzie's veiled threat and at High Mass exhorted the French Metis to refrain from further involvement. These actions left the De Meurons as the only committed insurrectionists, and they called off the planned attacks.[92] Any plans of insurrection were derisively drowned out when warmer weather finally arrived at the end of April and the Red River overflowed its banks. By 4 May 1826, the settlement was completely under water. When the flood waters receded, the disgruntled De Meurons and Swiss left the settlement for the United States and Canada.

The lack of markets, the low prices paid for pemmican, and hardening social lines produced another uprising in the 1830s. The Hudson's Bay Company's increased use after 1821 of seasonal labour weakened the bonds linking officers with servants, while the company's new practice of selecting its officers largely from Highland Scots in Great Britain severed the ties between the Metis and the officers active in the company's service.[93] Late in 1834, resentment escalated into an open rupture. Shortly before Christmas, a Metis tripman by the name of Antoine Larocque went to Upper Fort Garry, the administrative centre of the Hudson's Bay Company, to receive a second instalment of wages owed him for an upcoming trip.[94] According to surviving accounts, the Hudson's Bay

Company clerk used insulting language when addressing Larocque. The tripman returned the compliment. Thomas Simpson, the clerk in charge, became enraged at Larocque's insolence and struck him on the head with an iron poker. With blood streaming out of the wound, Larocque ran out of the fort to rouse other Metis to respond to this injustice. The entire Metis community in the settlement took up arms in Larocque's defence, demanding that if Simpson were not turned over to them for punishment they would demolish the fort.[95]

The English Metis might have remained aloof from this incident had they not also had standing grievances against the company and the social elite of the colony. They had been particularly insulted when, earlier in 1834, William Hallet, a Metis son of former officer, Henry Hallet, had been rejected as a suitor for the daughter of chief factor Allan McDonell in favour of the son of a Selkirk settler.[96] While the girl preferred Hallet, her guardian, the governor of Assiniboia, preferred the Scottish lad. The governor sent for Hallet and reprimanded him for aspiring to the hand of a lady accustomed 'to the first society.' As Hallet was a leader of the English Metis, this insult became a rallying point among them. According to Alexander Ross, they decided that if this was the way the Metis were to be treated they would henceforth band together against the leaders of the colony.[97] Thus, it was not surprising that when the French Metis approached them to join in their resistance following the Larocque incident, they readily joined the cause.[98]

Faced with a Metis mob insisting that Thomas Simpson be delivered up to them to be dealt with according to their law of retaliation, company officers immediately shut the gates of the fort and refused the demand. This only inflamed the growing mob, who threatened to scalp the governor and drive all the whites out of country.[99] In desperation, the governor of Assiniboia, Alexander Christie, turned to the Catholic clergy in hopes of pacifying the Metis. Father Belcourt was asked to talk with them. Belcourt, a favourite of the Metis, was able to sooth the assembled crowd. After hours of negotiation, he managed to convince them to disperse on the understanding that the governor would let Larocque draw his wages without performing his trip, and give the Metis a ten-gallon keg of rum and tobacco in proportion.[100] In St Andrew's, Cockran threatened his parishioners with perdition if they did not desist.[101]

Although stability quickly returned to the settlement, the uprising acted as a catalyst for change to the local government. Some Metis may have realized that if they stood united, the company would have to gain at least their tacit assent in order to govern the colony. For its part, the Hudson's Bay Company realized that it must distance itself, at least be seen to distance itself, from the government of the colony. As a result, in 1835 it expanded the membership of the Council of Assiniboia, made it more representative, and created new judicial machinery. It created four judicial districts, each with an appointed magistrate or justice of the peace who heard cases of petty offences, and a general court, held at the governor's residence the last Thursday of every quarter, which presided over more important cases.[102] To ensure the council also had some measure of authority, an armed police force of sixty officers and privates were proposed. This plan, however, was not put into practice. In 1835 Governor Simpson reported to the London governors of the Hudson's Bay Company that the settlement was more tranquil, and that the militia was no longer needed.[103] Government continued to rest on the consent of the Metis, who generally accepted the Council of Assiniboia.

This did not imply, however, docile acceptance of the situation. In 1835, following the transfer of the colony from the heirs of Selkirk to the Hudson's Bay Company, the Metis protested to the company about the cost of milling their wheat at the colony mills, and demanded more secure land titles, better prices for pemmican, and a market for their wheat. While Simpson and the company neither made concessions on land titles nor agreed to pay better prices for pemmican and wheat, they did agree to help construct new mill among the French Metis settlers in the upper sections of the settlement.[104] Similarly, when the council and judiciary acted in a manner contrary to accepted traditional practices, resistance could result. One example of this occurred in 1836, when the first petty jury in the settlement was empanelled to hear the case of Louis St Denis, who was accused of theft. While his conviction was accepted by the Metis community, his sentence of flogging created such a feeling of indignation that the man who administered the flogging had to flee for his life.[105] Thereafter, flogging was seldom used as a punishment.

The general characteristics of these protests are in keeping with what could be termed peasant revolts: spontaneous, unorganized political action based on little ideology, often appearing as short outbursts of accumulated frustration and rebellious feeling, but easily suppressed. Like peasant revolts around the world, these movements of protest frequently centred upon the myth of a social order more just and egalitarian than that of the existing hierarchy. They entailed a cry for vengeance on the oppressor, a righting of individual wrongs, and a desire for putting some curb on the powers of the rulers.[106] Social conflict mirrored the peasant economic organization and structure of the settlement. This relationship between economy and society can best be seen by examining the most basic building blocks of any society—its reproductive regime.

Notes

1. This conception of Metis society conforms very closely to A.V. Chayanov's concept of a peasant society. See A.V. Chayanov, *The Theory of Peasant Economy*, ed. Daniel Thorner, Basile Kerblay, and R.E.F. Smith (Madison 1986), 4–6.

2. Daniel Thorner, 'Peasant Economy as a Category in Economic History,' in *Peasants and Peasant Societies*, ed. Teodor Shanin (Harmondsworth 1971), 206–7.

3. Gerald Friesen, *The Canadian Prairies: A History* (Toronto 1984), 92.

4. See Richard Hodges, *Primitive and Peasant Markets* (London 1988) for a discussion of peasant markets.

5. John Foster, 'The Country-Born in the Red River Settlement, 1820–1850' (Ph.D. diss., University of Alberta, 1973), 219. This rapid population increase was largely the result of immigration.

6. Alexander Begg, *History of the North-West*, 3 vols (Toronto 1894), 1:232.

7. Marcel Giraud, *The Métis in the Canadian West*, 2 vols, trans. George Woodcock (Edmonton 1986), 2:128.

8. William H. Keating, *Narrative of an Expedition to the Source of St. Peter's River, Lake Winnepeck, Lake of the Woods, & c., Performed in the Year 1823*, 2 vols (London 1825), 2:42.

9. *Nor'Wester*, 28 December 1859.

10. John Morgan Gray, *Lord Selkirk of Red River* (Toronto 1964), 232–5.

11. Andrew McDermott, 'Peguis Refuted,' *Nor'Wester*, 28 February 1860. The Indians who did sign the treaty included Mochewheocab (Le Sonnant), Mechudewikonaie (La Robe Nolte), Pegowis, Ouckidoat (Premier, alias Grandes Oreilles), and Kayajieke-bienoa (L'Homme Noir).

12. Donald Gunn, 'Peguis Vindicated,' *Nor'Wester*, 28 April 1860.

13. Provincial Archives of Manitoba (PAM), MG 2, Al-9, copy of the Selkirk Treaty.

14. Andrew McDermott was born in 1789 in Ireland and was the son of Miles McDermott. He came to Red River Settlement with the second group of colonists in 1817 as a clerk with the Hudson's Bay Company. He severed his connections with the company in 1825 and became an independent trader based in Red River.

15. Andrew McDermott, 'The Peguis Land Controversy,' *Nor'Wester*, 14 May 1860.

16. Donald Gunn, 'The Land Controversy,' *Nor'Wester*, 28 June 1860.

17. Archer Martin, *The Hudson's Bay Company's Land Tenures and the Occupation of Assiniboia by Lord Selkirk's Settlers, with a List of Grantees under the Earl and the Company* (London 1898), 22–64; 'Memorandum for Captain R. Pelly respecting Red River Settlement, January 1823,' Selkirk Papers, reprinted in E.H. Oliver, ed., *The Canadian North-West: Its Early Development and Legislative Records*, 2 vols (Ottawa 1914), 250–1.

18. *Minutes of Council, Northern Department of Rupert Land, 1821–31*, ed. R. Harvey Fleming (London 1940), 37.

19. Church Missionary Society (CMS) Records, Incoming Correspondence (IC), Letter Book (LB) I, letter of Wm Cockran to the secretaries, 25 July 1833.

20. The price of land was initially set at 9 shillings an acre but reduced to 5 shillings in 1822 (Andrew Bulger to Bishop Juliopolis, 10 September 1822; reprinted in Oliver, ed. *The Canadian North-West*, 225).

21. See Hudson's Bay Company Archives (HBCA), E 6/10, 'Measurements of the Lands of Red River Colony, Survey'd in 1822 & 1823; HBCA, E 6/11, 'Index to the Plan of Red River Settlement .... '; PAM, MG 2, Al-13, typescript of a letter from George Simpson to Andrew Colvile, Red River Settlement, 15 May 1833 (the original letter is found in the Selkirk Papers, P-8500 to P-8505).

22. See H.Y. Hind, 'Papers Relative to the Exploration of the Country between Lake Superior and the Red River Settlement,' *British Parliamentary Papers: Papers*

Relating to Canada, 1859: Colonies 22, 562; and 'To Red River and Beyond,' *Harper's* 22, no. 129 (Feb. 1861), 317–18.

23. PAM, MG 2, Al-13, letter of George Simpson to Andrew Colvile, 15 May 1833, 2; testimony of George Simpson, *Report from the Select Committee on the Hudson's Bay Company* (London, 1857), 94; Hind, 'Papers Relative to the Exploration of the Country,' 563; 'To Red River and Beyond,' 318; Joseph James Hargrave, *Red River* (Montreal 1871), 309–10.

24. Margaret MacLeod and W.L. Morton, *Cuthbert Grant of Grantown* (Toronto 1963), 92–3.

25. PAM, MG 19, A4, W.D. Lane Papers, Correspondence Inward, letter of J. Clouston to Wm Lane, 9 October 1855.

26. HBCA, D4/102, 'Petition of Canadians and Halfbreeds,' 16 March 1835.

27. HBCA, D4/102, Simpson's reply to petition of 16 March 1835.

28. The debate can be followed in the pages of the *Nor'Wester*. See 'Native Title to Indian Land,' *Nor'Wester*, 14 February 1860; Andrew McDermott, 'Peguis Refuted,' *Nor'Wester*, 28 February 1860; Donald Gunn, 'Peguis Vindicated,' *Nor'Wester*,... 28 April 1860.

29. 'Indignation Meetings,' *Nor'Wester*, 15 June 1861.

30. See issues of the *Nor'Wester* in the spring and summer of 1869.

31. See Allan Greer, *Peasant, Lord, and Merchant: Rural Society in Three Quebec Parishes, 1740–1840* (Toronto 1985), xi. Greer defines the habitants of the pre-industrial Lower Richelieu as peasants.

32. Quoted in W.L. Morton, 'Introduction,' *London Correspondence Inward, Eden Colvile, 1849–1852*, ed. E.E. Rich (London 1956), xxiii-xxiv.

33. Ibid.

34. There was also the precedent of Metis river-lot settlements on the Great Lakes. At Green Bay, river lots were 1 to 5 arpents wide (1 arpent = 58 metres) running back from the river for 40 arpents. See the survey of Green Bay in *American State Papers: Public Lands*, vol. 5.

35. Morton, 'Introduction,' *London Correspondence Inward*, xxv.

36. PAM, MG 9 A4, manuscript of William Pearce's *The Three Prairie Provinces* (1925), 21.

37. Alexander Ross, *The Red River Settlement: Its Rise, Progress and Present State with Some Account of the Native Races, and Its General History to the Present Day*, (London 1856), 78.

38. Ibid., 110.

39. PAM, censuses of the Red River Settlement.

40. Archives de l'Archevêché de Saint-Boniface (AASB), Fonds Provencher, P0909-0999, letter of Father Laflèche, 1 June 1845.

41. Hind, 'Papers Relative to the Exploration of the Country,' 554–56; W.L. Morton, 'Agriculture in the Red River Colony,' in *Contexts of Canada's Past: Selected Essays of W.L. Morton*, ed. A.B. McKillop (Toronto 1980), 75–80.

42. This interpretation runs from Alexander Ross's *The Red River Settlement* (1856), through George F.G. Stanley's *The Birth of Western Canada* (1936), Marcel Giraud's *The Metis in the Canadian West* (1945), W.L. Morton's various works published in the 1940s and 1950s, to more recent studies such as W. Leland Clark, 'The Place of the Metis within the Agricultural Economy of the Red River during the 1840s and 1850s,' *Canadian Journal of Native Studies* 3, no. 1 (1983), 69–84.

43. *Nor'Wester*, 14 September 1860; see also Morton, 'Agriculture in the Red River Colony,' 74. The standard strain of wheat before 1850 was the 'Prairie du Chien' variety. Other wheat strains grown in the colony included 'Black Sea,' 'English,' 'Irish,' and 'Scotch' wheat.

44. Hind, 'Papers Relative to the Exploration of the Country,' 554; According to Hind, the wheat was ready for harvesting three months after sowing. A more careful calculation by W.L. Morton put the growing season at about 110 days. See Morton, 'Agriculture in the Red River Colony,' 71–3.

45. AASB, Fonds Provencher, P0909-0999, letter of Father Laflèche, 1 June 1845.

46. Morton, 'Introduction,' *London Correspondence Inward*, xxviii-xxix

47. Ross, *The Red River Settlement*, 121.

48. Hind, 'Papers Relative to the Exploration of the Country,' 555; Morton, 'Agriculture in the Red River Colony,' 75.

49. Barry Kaye, 'The Settlers' "Grand Difficulty": Haying in the Economy of the Red River Settlement,' *Prairie Forum* 9, no. 1 (Spring 1984), 3.

50. Morton, 'Introduction,' *London Correspondence Inward*, xxxi.

51. Using the technique of multiple regression on the various census variables, it was determined that the most important variable in predicting the number of cattle was cultivated acreage. Horses, according to this same statistical test, had a low correlation to cultivated acreage and apparently were not widely used for ploughing; however, they had a high correlation to the number of carts.

52. Morton, 'Agriculture in the Red River Colony,' 77.

53. F.G. Roe, *The North American Buffalo* (Toronto 1951), 368.

54. Ross, *The Red River Settlement*, 98.

55. Letter of Father Belcourt, 25 November 1845; reprinted in Executive Document no. 51, gist Congress, 1st Session.

56. Ross, *The Red River Settlement*, 244.

57. AASB, Fonds Provencher, Bishop Provencher to Bishop Panet, 1 July 1829; CMS Records, IC, LB II, William Cockran to the secretaries, 29 July 1830.

58. CMS Records, IC, LB II, Cockran journal, 12 June 1837.

59. The following description of the Red River buffalo hunt is summarized from the following sources: George Dugas, *Histoire de L'ouest canadien de 1822 á 1869* (Montreal, 1906), 107–14; F.G. Roe, 'The Red River Hunt,' *Transactions of the Royal Society of Canada*, Section II (1935), 171–218; Giraud, *The Metis in the Canadian West*, 1:140–52; Virginia M. Aldrich, 'Father George Antoine Belcourt, Red River Missionary,' *North Dakota Historical Quarterly* 2, no. 1 (Oct. 1927), 30–52; Ross,

The Red River Settlement, 242–74; MacLeod and Morton, *Cuthbert Grant of Grantown*, 108–19; and Various articles in the *Nor'Wester* in the 1860s.

60. 'Off to the Buffalo Hunt: Interviews with the Hunters and the Sioux,' *Nor'Wester*, 14 August 1860.

61. Ross, *The Red River Settlement*, 256–58; 'The Buffalo Hunt,' *Nor'Wester*, 28 August 1860.

62. 'The Summer Hunt,' *Nor'Wester*, 14 and 18 August 1860; *Nor'Wester*, 15 November 1861; 'Running the Buffalo,' *Nor'Wester*, 11 September 1862.

63. Aldrich, 'Father George Antoine Belcourt,' 40–1.

64. J.J. Gunn, *Echoes of the Red* (Toronto 1930), 24–9.

65. Ibid., 35.

66. Mgr-Taché, *Sketches of the North-West of America* (Montreal 1870), 102–3.

67. Margaret Arnett MacLeod, *Red River's Festive Season* (Winnipeg 1962), 6.

68. Ibid., 7; PAM, Peter Garrioch journal (typescript), Part V, 'the Home Journal 1845–7,' 25 December 1845.

69. MacLeod, *Red River's Festive Season*, 11–13; Mrs W. Cyprian Pinkham, 'Reminiscences of an Old Timer,' *Manitoba History* 20 (Autumn 1990), 20; PAM, parish registers of St Andrew's and St François Xavier.

70. PAM, Peter Garrioch journal, 3–18 January 1846, 284–7.

71. CMS Records, IC, LB IV, Smithurst journal, 1 February 1847.

72. CMS Records, IC, LB I, letter of William Cockran to the secretaries, 1 August 1827.

73. CMS Records, IC, LB IV, Smithurst journal, 8 February 1849.

74. PAM, Peter Garrioch journal, 1845–7; numerous references are made to these locations.

75. *Nor'Wester*, 24 October 1868; Morton, 'Introduction,' *London Correspondence Inward*, xi.

76. Ibid., xi; PAM, MG 2, C13, Samuel Taylor journal, 1843–67 (typescript), December 1864, 11–12, and October to December 1865, 18–20.

77. PAM, MG 2, BI, minutes of the Quarterly Court, District of Assiniboia

78. AASB, Fonds Provencher, P0932–3, Louis Laflèche to Quebec, 1 June 1845.

79. Elaine Allan Mitchell, 'Red River Gossip,' *Beaver* 291 (Spring 1961), 4–11 (this article consists of a number of letters of Robert Clouston, who was in the colony in the early 1840s and who commented on some of its leading personages); Foster, 'The Country-Born in the Red River Settlement,' 181–5; Robert Coutts, *St. Andrews Parish, 1829–1929, and the Church Missionary Society in Red River*, Parks Canada Manuscript Report (Ottawa 1986), 93–4; Morton, 'Introduction,' *London Correspondence Inward*, xviii-xx.

80. PAM, census of Red River, 1835.

81. Ibid.; Coutts, *St. Andrews Parish*, 93–4.

82. James Sutherland to John Sutherland, 10 August 1842, quoted in Foster, 'The Country-Born in the Red River Settlement,' 185.

83. Frits Pannekoek, *A Snug Little Flock* (Winnipeg 1991), 63.

84. Foster, 'The Country-Born in the Red River Settlement,' 186–9.

85. See Philip Goldring, *Papers on the Labour System of the Hudson's Bay Company, 1821–1900*, vol. 1, Parks Canada Manuscript Report, no. 362 (Ottawa 1979), 29–43, 206; and Jennifer S.H. Brown, *Strangers in Blood* (Vancouver 1980), 205–6.

86. James Sutherland to John Sutherland, 10 August 1842, quoted in Foster, 'The Country-Born in the Red River Settlement,' 185.

87. AASB, Fonds Provencher, P1855–8, J.B. Thibault (Red River) to Mgr L'Évêque de Quebec, 24 July 1836; CMS Records, IC, LB I,journal of Wm Cockran, 2 August 1832.

88. HBCA, B235/a/7,journal of Francis Heron, Fort Garry, 30 January 1826 and 1 February 1826, fos. 20–20d.

89. Ibid.; HBCA, D4/119, letter of D. McKenzie to G. Simpson, 4 May 1827, fos. 66–67d.

90. HBCA, B235/a/7,journal of Francis Heron, 5–19 April 1826, fos. 28–31d.

91. Ibid., 8 April 1826, fos. 29–29d.

92. HBCA, D4/119, letter of Donald Mckenzie to G. Simpson, 4 May 1827.

93. Foster, 'The Country-Born in the Red River Settlement,' 180; see also Goldring, *Papers on the Labour System of the Hudson's Bay Company, 1821–1900*. Goldring, in a study of Hudson's Bay Company recruitment practices, has since argued that the hiring procedures were not as biased as believed. However, he does acknowledge that many of more acculturated (to British norms) English Metis felt that the cards were stacked against them because of their race (Philip Goldring, 'Governor Simpson's Officers: Elite Recruitment in a British Overseas Enterprise, 1834–1870,' *Prairie Forum* 10, no. 2 ([Autumn 1985], 264–7).

94. Tripmen were paid in part before a trip was made, usually according to a fairly well established system: one instalment on the approach of winter, a second at Christmas or New Years, a third before leaving in summer, and the final payment after the voyage was made.

95. Accounts of this incident can be found in Ross, *The Red River Settlement*, 167–9; A.S. Morton, *History of the Canadian West to 1870–71*, 2nd ed. (Toronto 1973), 683–4; and Pannekoek, *A Snug Little Flock*, 90–1.

96. This Scotchman, who later married the girl, was John Livingston.

97. Ross, *The Red River Settlement*, 238.

98. CMS Records, lC, LB II, Wm Cockran to the secretaries, 20 October 1835.

99. A.G. Morice, *History of the Catholic Church in Canada* (Toronto 1910), 144–6; CMS Records, IC, LB II, Wm Cockran to the secretaries, 5 August 1835.

100. Morice, *History of the Catholic Church in Canada*, 146; PAM, Belleau Collection, letter of Belcourt to Bishop Singay, Quebec, 21 December 1847.

101. CMS Records, IC, I.B II, Wm Cockran to the secretaries, 5 August 1835.

102. Oliver, ed., *The Canadian North-West*, 1:86. The four districts were the following: (1) Image Plain to the Indian Settlement – James Bird; (2) Image Plain to the Forks – James Sutherland; (3) the Forks south – Robert Logan; (4) White Horse Plains – Cuthbert Grant.

103. HBCA, D4/102, Simpson's report of 10 June 1835.

104. HBCA, D4/102, 'Petition of Canadians and Halfbreeds,' 16 March 1835; and Simpson's reply.

105. Begg, *History of the North West*, 253.

106. Teodor Shanin, 'Peasants as a Political Factor,' in Shanin, ed., *Peasants and Peasant Societies*, 258; Eric R. Wolf, *Peasants* (Englewood Cliffs 1966), 106; E.J. Hobsbawm, *Primitive Rebels: Studies in Archaic Forms of Social Movement in the Nineteenth and Twentieth Centuries* (Manchester 1959), 5–24. On the relationship between the moral economy of plebian and peasant populations and rebellion, see Terrence Crowley, '"Thunder Gusts": Popular Disturbances in Early French Canada,' *CHA Historical Papers* (1979), 11–31: James C. Scott, *The Moral Economy of the Peasant: Rebellion and Subsistence in Southeast Asia* (New Haven 1976); and E.P. Thompson, *Customs in Common: Studies in Traditional Popular Culture* (New York 1991).

A LITTLE BRITAIN IN THE WILDERNESS

Frits Pannekoek

Although the efforts of the Protestant clergy in the 1830s to ensure the purity of the thoroughly British society they were attempting to create were often comical, their social and racial repercussions were serious. The Rev. William Cockran, a man of considerable influence, was firm in his belief that the European was superior to either the Indian or the halfbreed and that he who married an Indian or a halfbreed had debased his race, his culture and his religion. During the 1830s this belief found its way increasingly into the hearts of Red River Europeans and seriously affected the relations between them and the mixed-bloods. In order to re-establish their Christian respectability in the eyes of their peers, and of their clergyman who represented to so many the epitome of British civilization, a number of the most influential of the Company's retired gentlemen sought, whenever the opportunity presented itself, to replace their native wives with white ones. The clergy did little to make the transition an easy one. They and their wives found most of the new white women socially unacceptable. It will be seen that, conversely, some of the 'better' white women found the clerical establishment tainted with lower-class origins. A vicious and uncompromising war of gossip broke out among the new white women, the clergy's wives and the threatened native women, fracturing Protestant Red River into its Indian, Halfbreed, and European parts. The continual threat of insurrection by the Métis and some of the Halfbreeds during the 1830s and 1840s forced the retired officers and clergy to display a superficial

From *A Snug Little Flock: The Social Origins of the Riel Resistance, 1869–70* (Winnipeg: Watson and Dwyer Publishing, 1991). Reprinted by permission of Watson and Dwyer/J. Gordon Shillingford, Publisher.

unity, but the scandals of the early 1850s finally separated the clergy from both the mixed-bloods and European upper crust.

Since Catholic Red River was culturally and racially homogeneous except for the small group of French-Canadian settlers and priests, it avoided the racial conflicts that were to plague the Protestant half of the settlement with its Kildonans, fur trade patriarchs, and military. Furthermore, there was little social interaction between the clergy and the laity, in large part because the clergy had no wives to complicate their lives, but also because the Church failed, in spite of vigorous attempts, to recruit priests from among the Métis.

Not all of the Catholic clergy fell easily into the rhythmic life of Red River marked by the hunt, the trip, and the plough. There was a serious split between the sedentary and the nomadic clergy, specifically between Bishop Provencher and Father G.A. Belcourt. The split was not yet serious but dangers were evident in the late 1830s. By his silence the Catholic Bishop tended to support the Company in all its endeavours, while censuring the nomadic priests who tended to sympathize with the Métis. As a result the Métis, an increasingly religious people, in their fight against the Company and the Sioux sought direction from the nomadic priesthood, rather than the Bishop and his establishment at the Forks.

As Protestant Red River settled into a semi-isolated and rhythmic existence, in large part at the urging of the clergy, it attempted to become more sedentary and agricultural. The clergy saw themselves as warriors in a moral battle against the diabolical temptations and licentiousness inherent in the vast barbaric wilderness — to them the very antithesis of civilization. The Protestant missionary was convinced that the Indian, Métis, and Halfbreed were infected by the contagion of barbarism, and that they were lost to civilization. Cockran made it quite clear that 'the Dominant Race of this Continent are the English' and that the Indian and Halfbreed would always be immoral, capricious, intractable, indolent, callous, prideful, wayward, extravagant, ingracious, improvident and careless.[1] The clergy urged Red River to turn inward from the interior and outward to cultivate its European heritage and to resist the pull of the wild, in order to avoid the fate of the Halfbreed and the Indian.

Turn inward Red River did. Its imitation of European tradition and prejudices became more slavish, evidenced by the monogrammed silver service, the fine glass goblet, the expensive cariole, and the acquisition by several of the senior fur traders, both active and retired, of white wives. The ability to support a white woman reflected wealth and status, and was a sign of resistance to the degenerate barbarism of the wilderness. However genteel the moccasined Indian or Halfbreed wife might be, she had no place in the resurrected memories of Scotland, England, Canada, and the Orkney Islands that were evoked by the clergy. Of equal importance was the growing concern with social status in Europe. An Indian wife might well mean no promotion and a loss of position in the eyes of one's peers. The result was that some of the Halfbreed and Indian wives were 'turned off', that is, either abandoned or, more often, placed under the protection of another fur trader.[2] This is not to suggest that the clergy were the single cause of white marriages — only that their preachings and example were a critical factor.

Until the 1830s, Mrs Cockran, Mrs Jones, Mrs Pelly (Governor Pelly's ailing wife), along with the Selkirk women were the only white females. An influential minority of the fur traders took a succession of mixed-blood or Indian women, and actively attempted to ensure that the number of white marriages remained minimal. European women were considered fragile, demanding and, perhaps more important, useless in forming trade alliances. Chief Trader Donald Ross, Chief Trader McVicar and Chief Factor Clarke were at some point chided by the Company for their marriages to Selkirk and Swiss women. Even then, Hargrave thought Mrs Ross, a rough unrefined Selkirk, little better than an Indian woman in her habits. Simpson's desire to curb this trend meant that some of the commissioned gentlemen with racial and social sensibilities and concern for their future in the Company, such as James Hargrave at York Factory, would remain bachelors though certainly not monks until suitable white women were available, and not until they could afford to keep the fragile creatures in comfort.

The shift from native to European wives was made by small but influential numbers of the fur trade's élite in the early 1830s. The insistence of the clergy upon Church marriages caused, encouraged or gave excuses to a few well-placed commissioned gentlemen to reconsider their liaisons 'à la façon du pays' and to seize the opportunity to dispose of an 'old concern' and acquire a newer, younger and lighter-skinned wife. Simpson himself made the best known transition by 'turning-off' both Betsey Sinclair, a daughter of Chief Factor William Sinclair and Nahovway, an Indian woman, to Robert Miles, the clerk and later the Chief Factor at Moose Factory; and Margaret Taylor, the Halfbreed daughter of George Taylor, a former York sloop master, to Pierre Leblanc, the mason for the Lower Fort. The latter bargain required a £200 inducement. How many other Halfbreed or Indian wives were 'turned-off' in Rupert's Land is difficult to assess.[3] Yet, not all who now married white women 'turned-off' their wives. Some had never married, while others waited for their Halfbreed wives to die. But a noticeable number of new wives were white. The school mistresses were all that was available to those who did not relish wife-hunting in Europe or Canada, or could not persuade the Selkirk women to marry outside their community. After the death of his Indian wife, James Bird, the wealthiest of the retired Chief Factors, married the Widow Lowman, the school mistress who came out in 1835. Red River gossips had it that Bird, unkindly referred to as an 'old shrivelled bag of bones', had to purchase 'the fresh morsel of frail humanity, soul and body' for £3,000 made over to 'her and her heirs forever'. Miss Armstrong, Mrs Bird's successor at the school, married John Peter Pruden, a retired Chief Trader of crude habits but of kind heart and of generous pocketbook. Miss Allen, a fussy spinster who came out with James Hargrave's wife, Letitia, was on the verge of marrying James Sutherland, a retired Chief Factor of modest means. If Letitia is to be believed, Sutherland fortunately died of an overdose of calomel. These women, along with the wives of the clergy, formed Red River's new upper crust.[4]

With the new white wives came a new life style, approved by gentry and clergy alike. Simpson's new wife, his eighteen-year-old cousin, Frances, gave Red River 'an air of high life and gaiety' with a 'painted house of state, the Piano-forte, and the new fashioned Government Carriole.'[5] Even James Sutherland, by no means wealthy, felt that he had to keep up the pace and set about acquiring the symbols that signified membership in that very exclusive circle setting the conventions for Red River.

> We have now here some rich old fellows that have acquired large fortunes in the service, have got married to European females and cut a dash, have introduced a system of extravagance into the place that is followed by all that can afford it.[6]

The Halfbreed wife was too often oddly dressed, as was Mrs Gladman, the wife of the accountant at York Factory, who appeared 'in a Waterloo blue Merino, moccasins, and a straw bonnet lined with lilac satin, and was not considered sufficiently civilized to merit a place in this new society.'[7]

As wives of the retired and active commissioned officers, the new white women found themselves at the very pinnacle of Red River, presiding over the community's social life and being treated with deference and ceremony. For most, marriage had meant a considerable rise in status. Former farmers' wives, widows and teachers became the dictators of fashion and etiquette. The transition was a heady one. No native, irrespective of her position, and no clergyman's wife was allowed to compromise the newly found status. Yet the clergymen's wives felt themselves a cut above their Indian and Halfbreed friends, and would not tolerate the questioning of their status. The new white women resented, as did the native women, the parson's wife's role as watchdog over Red River's morals. The inability to accommodate one another's status led to exclusiveness and hostility.

George Simpson's attitudes were typical of those held by the élite towards the parson's wives and the natives. Only Mrs Jones, the wife of the sociable parson, was found 'possible'. Cockran's wife was rejected by both George Simpson and the 'blues' — the term frequently used by Red River to refer to the retired gentlemen and their families — because she had the misfortune to be 'a Dollymop or some such thing.' George Simpson further maintained rather viciously, although not without some truth as the scandals of 1851 would show, that Mrs Cockran's 'Puritanism...ill concealed the vixen', and that she only 'shined when talking of elbow grease and the scouring of pots and pans.[8] Frances Simpson would generally take communion in private with the parsons' wives,[9] and she was forbidden to favour the native ladies of Red River with her company. Simpson, for example, refused to allow Theresa Chalifoux, the wife of Chief

Factor Colin Robertson, the privilege of visiting Frances, possibly with some cause. Apparently only two Halfbreeds, both servants, were allowed in Mrs Simpson's presence and by 1833 all of Halfbreed Red River avoided her.

Mrs Simpson left in 1833, in ill health, destitute of company, never to return to the settlement she had grown to dislike. Yet she alone was regarded as a social equal by the parsons' wives. The white Mrs Bird, who attempted to replace her by holding sumptuous dinner parties and a variety of balls and dances, was only ridiculed. The vicious fur trade rumour-mill circulated the story that, contrary to Mrs Bird's firm insistence, her first husband might still be alive. Miss Armstrong, now Mrs Pruden, was put down by rumours that she had been in the 'habit of sleeping with Cap'n Graves on the voyage out.'[10]

The clergy were equally critical of the Halfbreeds that Mrs Cockran found 'indolent and licentious'. Their habit of going in all manner of 'detestable conversation' was condemned. They must be led out of their former ways and into the path of industry and discretion.[11] Although these comments were made specifically with regard to the poorer mixed-bloods, Mrs Cockran's attitudes to others of quality would have been similar, if perhaps kinder. The mixed-blood and Indian wives of the Red River 'blues' were aware of the disdain in which they were held. Mrs Alexander Ross and Mrs Robert Lane, the latter the wife of a respectable Red River merchant, seldom made their appearance except at church.[12] A new white society composed of the clergy and the commissioned gentlemen with white wives had displaced that of the Halfbreeds. They were now the indisputable leaders of society.

The outward sign of the tendency to exclusiveness was a significant increase in gossip. From 1830 to 1850, the period of the greatest changes in Red River society, the correspondence of the fur trade contained progressively more invective and gossip. Because gossip was informal and confidential, it was the best weapon for carrying out social warfare. Since everyone in Red River feared for his newly achieved position or was upset over his apparent decline in status, each combatant compiled an arsenal to be used both offensively and defensively against the most serious social rivals. A condescending superiority towards supposed social inferiors was the least harmful outcome; open social warfare was the worst and Red River was to experience both.[13] Up to 1850, however, no open social warfare was to break out, at least not seriously enough to cause violence. The threat of insurrection on the part of the Métis and Halfbreeds may have forced the 'blues', irrespective of race, and the clergy to unite. Equally important, the clerical establishment was still quite small, consisting of only Rev. W. Cockran and Rev. D. Jones and their wives. John Macallum, a graduate of King's College in Aberdeen, came out in 1833 after his graduation to assist Jones as schoolmaster, but he was not ordained until 1855. He was never a star in the clerical constellation. Open tensions, then, did not break out until 1850 after the clergy numbered half a dozen or more, and after the Church had glorified itself with a Bishop.

Gossip was especially used to minimize the threatening social influence and attempted dominance of the clergy. Cockran's decision to arrive, mounted atop a cow, at one of Mrs Simpson's dinner parties, Mrs Cockran's unfortunate social background, and Rev. Jones's misfortunes with the Presbyterians were discussed with relish. So was Cockran's all too evident lack of tact and education. Donald Ross unkindly informed Hargrave that Cockran had spun 'out his long yarns as usual, murdering the King's English most unmercifully in flights of pulpit eloquence and veiling [hinting] occasionally at the immoral habits of the fur trade.'[14] If such criticism was circumspect, it was only because the clergy were reckoned as powerful enemies. In discussing the general temperament of the missionaries one fur trader was convinced that they would 'pursue the object of their hatred...to the extremities of the earth, nay even to eternity if they could to obtain revenge.'[15] The private parlour and the pages of the confidential letter provided the best places for criticism of the clergy.

Despite Cockran's efforts, however, it was the moral deviations of the 'blues' and the mixed-bloods that served as the mainstay of gossip. While many of the cracks by the fur traders on each other were made with regard to alleged immorality — James Hargrave's romp in the bushes at York with Madame L'Esperance, the wife of the famous fur brigade leader had many aghast — the clergy seemed for the most part immune from sexual innuendo even when the opportunity presented itself.[16] When a commissioned officer's daughter, 'a poor half dead and alive stubborn silly thing' who went wrong with some of the young recruits from Canada in 1832, debauched an Indian boy who served in the kitchen at Jones's boarding school for young ladies, the parson got none of the blame. Instead he received a great deal of sympathy. Both Simpson and Hargrave were upset that Jones was in agony over the event, and indeed feared that this might mean the end of the boarding school. Hargrave put the blame squarely on the Halfbreeds. After all, 'everyone at all conversant with the morality of the half Caste Race at present must be persuaded that absolute purity cannot be attained in one generation.'[17]

It would seem that no one was willing to accept the social condescension of the clerical establishment; neither were the 'blues' willing to see the representatives of their highest goals morally criticized. The reasons for the failure to seize the opportunity for attack are by no means certain. Yet the mixed-bloods and the Whites did accept the brands of civilization and Christianity preached by the clergy, and scrambled to attain its perfection. Any moral shortcomings of the clergy would have illustrated that they had succumbed to the sensual evils of the wilderness. If the clergy were not immune from the contagion of barbarism, the fur trader would certainly be beyond redemption and forever doomed.

Since the clergy considered themselves equal, if not superior to the Red River élite, and since the clergy considered themselves the guiding light of civilization, they worked closely with the élite to ensure that the little Britain they were carefully building on the banks of the Red River would flourish. Their support of the private boarding school and their participation in the Council of Assiniboia reinforced the position of the élite, and tended to alienate further the majority of Protestant Red River already slighted by the marriages of the 1830s. The latter came to feel that the retired officers and the Company were the major concern of the clergy, and that they were of minor importance. There was sufficient evidence to support their fears.

In 1832, the Rev. David Jones, at the prompting of the fur trade's gentlemen, established a 'respectable seminary' on a large scale for the sons and daughters of Rupert's Land's gentlemen. The roster of surnames reads like a 'who was who' of the active and retired fur traders. John Stuart, John Lee Lewes, Francis Heron, Roderick McKenzie, J.D. Cameron, Allan McDonell, Donald Ross, Thomas McKay, F.N. Annance, William Todd, Donald Robertson, P.C. Pambrun, Thomas Thomas, Colin Robertson, Robert Miles, and Alexander Christie all sent their children. The fees were kept at a stiff £30 per annum (a Chief Factor realized about £500 per annum) to deter the socially unqualified, although it did not keep out those on the margin with money like Heron, McKay and Annance. 'A lady regularly bred up to the situation of Governess and qualified to instruct the children in the governmental branches of Education, in short an accomplished and well bred lady, capable of teaching music, drawing &c &c of conciliating disposition & mild temper' was to be brought over from England.[18] When Miss Armstrong was found to be unqualified to teach these subjects the Chief Factors threatened to withdraw their daughters. The boys and girls were separated from each other as well as from the native elements and their relatives in the settlement. They were to be English ladies and gentlemen. The two abandoned Halfbreed daughters of Kenneth McKenzie (since the 1820s, of the American Fur Company), Margaret and Isabella, for example, were forcibly kept from their Indian mother and whipped by John Macallum, the school master, when they attempted to give the poor ragged woman desperately needed clothing.[19]

The less fortunate mixed-bloods were taught by Peter Garrioch, educated by the Church Missionary Society; John Pritchard, a former Nor'Wester and principal settler, Donald Gunn, the Red River historian and correspondent for the Smithsonian Institution, and Rev. W. Cockran, at schools at the Upper Church, Frog Plain, Middle Church and Grand Rapids. The quality of education available to the run-of-the-mill mixed-blood was decidedly inferior to that offered the offspring of the Company's officers. They did not accept this situation without protest. In 1834 the Indian boys, who until this time had been educated by Jones and apparently associated with the boarding school, were transferred to Cockran at the Lower Church. The Chief Factors were fearful that they might corrupt their children, especially their daughters. The Halfbreeds of St. Andrew's, whose children were under Cockran's supervision, were not pleased. Cockran said that they argued that

> If these Indian boys are so bad as to corrupt and seduce the bastards of the Chief Factors, surely [they] will never [be] allow [ed] to enter the school where our children and daughters are educated. And again, we have married our wives and are endeavouring to train up our children according to christian principles, but still the bastards of the Chief Factors are more esteemed by our Ministers.[20]

The clergy also became tainted by their involvement in the Council of Assiniboia, the legislative body controlled by the Company, which regulated the day-to-day affairs of the Red River. The Minutes of the Council of May 4, 1834, concerning pigs and stallions roaming at large, fires, statute labour for the improvement of roads, public fairs, haying privileges, tariffs and the like, illustrate the scope of its influence. In 1835 the Hudson's Bay Company resumed possession of Red River from Lord Selkirk's heirs, and immediately set about to reform the Council by inviting the most influential of Red River's clergymen to become members, the intention being to make it more palatable to the mixed-bloods. Among the first new appointments of February 1834 were the Rev. David Jones and the Rev. William Cockran. The Catholic Bishop, Provencher, only attended as an observer and was not made a permanent member until 1837. This was probably due to his absence in Europe from 1835 to 1837, rather than discrimination.[21]

It is difficult to determine the role played by the clergy in the proceedings of the Council. Votes were not recorded until the 1850s and then only infrequently. It is equally impossible to determine the amount of legislation initiated by the clergy. All that can be ascertained is that Jones, Cockran, and the Bishop rarely missed meetings. They joined their old friends George Simpson, James Sutherland, John Pritchard, Alexander Christie, and W.H. Cook, and must have been in agreement over the regulations concerning the keeping of pigs, the hay privilege, and the occasional £50 given to the Roman Catholic and Protestant churches for educational purposes. Law and order and the state-supported church would never be opposed.

The widening of the membership of the Council could only be effective if the majority of Red River's inhabitants were willing to allow it control and had respect for the judgement of its members. The Selkirk and other principal settlers would accept, even if sometimes reluctantly, the usually mild dictates of the Council, especially since most of its regulations were for their benefit. The Halfbreeds, although accustomed at the interior fur posts to the military-like structure of the Company, required additional persuasion. This, Cockran provided as the leader of his halfbreed congregation in all matters temporal and spiritual. They allowed him 'to teach, admonish, exhort, reprove, warn, advise, console, with the greatest freedom.' That his influence was substantial can be seen by the fact that marriage and baptism were becoming increasingly common. In 1831 Cockran was ecstatic in his letter to the Church Missionary Society — there were only two recorded illegitimate births among a population of twelve hundred protestants, most recent converts to Christianity.[22] While Cockran's claim might be treated with scepticism, he wrote enough of his failures that the occasional triumph is credible.

By 1835 this optimism had begun to fade. Rev. David Jones could boast readily enough that the settlement was 'becoming a stronghold of Christianity in the centre of this vast wilderness.' He complained, however, that two clergymen were not sufficient to minister to the four Red River congregations. As a result they were losing 'the hold on the minds of the rising generation [they] once unquestionably possessed.' The situation had deteriorated even further by 1839. Jones again commented that while the native and 'half Castes' were becoming daily more enlightened, they were in equal measure becoming 'disaffected to the ruling power, [and] the general system of things at head quarters.'[23]

There seems to be no indication, however, that the brief bizarre flash of General James Dickson's Indian Liberating Army, made any impact in Red River itself. Dickson, possibly a mixed-blood son of a British trader and a leader in the War of 1812, sought to establish an Indian kingdom in California. Aware of Cuthbert Grant and the military prowess of the Red River Métis, Dickson intended to recruit them to this 'army'. From Red River he planned to march to Santa Fe, 'free' the Indians and establish his kingdom. On their way from Montreal, where Dickson had recruited some anti-Company Métis, he was shipwrecked. Some of his men were arrested. Finally in December 1836 with only eleven officers he arrived at the settlement. W.L. Morton, who provides a brief humorous account of the episode, noted Simpson's effective dealings with Dickson. He had Dickson's bank drafts refused, and he offered employment to his mixed-blood men. Dickson befriended Cuthbert Grant, but in the spring he left, his resources even scarcer than those with which he had arrived in the winter. The Métis considered him a heroic buffoon, if Pierre Falcon, the well-known Métis bard, is to be believed.[24]

The social exclusiveness of the clergy must have exacerbated the disaffection between the groups. The clergy were closely identified with the Hudson's Bay Company, its retired officers and its government. Fear that the clergy cared more for the Company and the 'blues' appeared justified by the events of 1834 and 1835. The Métis and Halfbreeds were threatening insurrection because of racial slights, inadequate prices for pemmican and agricultural produce, and the uncertainty of land tenure. A seriously provocative incident occurred when Antoine Larocque, a Métis, was struck by Thomas Simpson, the cousin of George Simpson. The Halfbreeds, connected to the Métis 'by a spirit of national sympathy' had cause to join the protest. One of their number, William Hallett, had recently been denied permission to marry the daughter of Chief Factor Allan McDonell by the Governor of Assiniboia, on racial and status grounds.[25] The situation was serious enough that many of the whites and 'blues' threatened to move to Canada or the United States. Drastic measures were needed. At the prompting of George Simpson, the clergy and élite of Red River on the Council of Assiniboia formed a volunteer corps, with Alexander Ross as Commander over a Sergeant Major, four Sergeants and fifty-four Privates. While nothing much came of the corps, the measure must have had an impact on the mixed-bloods. Here were the clergy and 'blues' making a concerted effort to suppress what they considered serious grievances. Fortunately exhortations by Cockran, Jones, and Belcourt and the success of the next summer's hunts saved Red River from insurrection.

By 1840, then, it appeared that the Protestant clergy had made common cause with the 'blues' of Red River. They attended their parties, they sat on their councils, they attempted to enforce their laws, and they gave special consideration to their children. This is not to say that the clergy were without criticism of the Company's policies. The criticism, however, concerned the problems of the missionaries more than the Halfbreeds. Cockran, for one, had many grievances against the Company, but he was warned by his superiors, the Secretaries of the Church Missionary Society, not to 'cast any reflection on any of the servants of the Company,' including Simpson.[26] Cockran was upset with Simpson's reluctance to allow an Indian settlement at Sugar Point near the outlet of the Red River. Indeed he more than once announced his doubts about the need for the fur monopoly. But he would oppose the intransigent Company, only peacefully, constitutionally, and circumspectly. The conclusion reached by his congregation, bred in the tradition of violence that characterized the relationship between the fur companies in the pre-1821 period, could only be that Cockran was under the Company's thumb. Of Jones, the jovial companion of the Company's officers, they would have no doubt. Reform therefore came to mean opposition to clergy as well as Company.

The Catholic clergy were relatively immune from developments on the other side of the river. They were as yet emphatically not listed among the élite of Protestant Red River, and did not expect to be.[27] An invitation to the occasional social gathering and representation on the Council of Assiniboia were all they merited. There was no comparable group to the Thomases, Simpsons, Birds and Bunns at Saint-Boniface, Pembina, or Saint-François-Xavier. Cuthbert Grant and Andrew McDermot, both prosperous traders, were the highest placed Catholics Red River could muster in the period before the free trade movement.[28] The extent of the Catholic exclusion is apparent upon analysis of Red River gossip. They never once provided the grist for the English or French Red River rumour mill, in spite of the fact that the Métis were as adept at gossip as their Protestant counterparts. When the clergy gossiped, it was to their superiors in Quebec about each other, not about Red River. The Catholic clergy were not linked by marriage to their congregations, despite the fact that they were an integral part of Métis society, and provided both spiritual and secular leadership. They had no blood connections with their charges, and made no progress in their efforts to change this situation by the recruitment of an indigenous clergy.

The composition of the Catholic clergy also changed little from the 1820s. Not only did Nicolet remain the principal training school for Red River's Roman Catholic clergy, but turnover continued at an alarming rate. Bishop Provencher, himself away in Canada or Europe in 1831 and from 1835 to 1837 was assisted by a succession of priests; Father Jean Harper, Charles Poiré, Jean Baptiste Thibault, and G.A. Belcourt. While Poiré, serving at Saint-François-Xavier from 1833 to 1839, was the chief cleric, Father Belcourt, arriving in 1831 and founder of the Saulteaux Indian mission at Baie Saint-Paul, managed to gain the greatest influence over the Métis at Saint-François-Xavier, six miles to the east of the Indian Mission.

Among these priests two distinct types can be discerned, the nomadic and the sedentary, the former having the greatest contact with the Métis. Among these can be included J.B. Harper, F. Boucher, Charles Poiré, G.A. Belcourt, and J.B. Thibault. In the period prior to the free trade troubles of the 1840s, Provencher himself was the most important sedentary priest. This had serious implications. Provencher was forced, largely by the nature of his position but also by his predilections, to an existence in his cathedral, to a seat on the Council of Assiniboia, and to reconciling policy with the Company. He would be considered unsympathetic, as indeed he was, to the cause of the Métis free traders.

Provencher refused to visit the remote parts of his diocese, failed to travel even to the Saint-François-Xavier mission, and completely avoided the hunt. If Pembina was visited, it was because it was en route to Canada. He spent the greatest part of his energies administering a diocese of from three to five priests, building an enormous and expensive cathedral, and assisting in the ecclesiastical squabbles of Canada. He had little patience or love for the great Northwest. His aim was to isolate himself from the surrounding barbarism, to create a civilized Catholicism at the Forks, letting it drift outwards from there. Until then, his clergy could care for the more nomadic parishioners.[29]

The Bishop could have brought the Cathedral establishment closer to the Métis, and avoided future difficulties by the establishment of an indigenous clergy. He failed, not because of a lack of effort but because of the refusal of the Church of Rome to relax the rigorous training required for ordination. There were four schools, by no means comparable to the Protestant academy under Jones and Macallum. One was located at Saint-François-Xavier with three others at Saint-Boniface, attended by approximately forty students at the first school and as many as eighty per school at Saint-Boniface, depending upon the time of year. From June to August when the hunt was on, and in the winter when food was scarce, attendance was negligible. Provencher had six Latin scholars under his care as early as 1834, but again success was not great. Few families devoted themselves to the service of the Church, with only the daughter of Augustin Nolin working for the clergy as a school teacher at Saint-François-Xavier and Baie Saint-Paul. This apparent lack of interest was more due to the lack of education than a lack of enthusiasm on the part of the Métis. The consequences, however, would be the same; clerical aloofness from the Métis, especially those at Saint-Boniface where most of the schools were located.[30]

Provencher's conflicts with *all* of his itinerant clergy, most of whom had close relations with the Métis, must have alienated some of the faithful. Neither Harper, Boucher, nor Poiré left Rupert's Land on good terms with the Bishop. Unfortunately those who were concerned refused to discuss specifics. Only Belcourt had the audacity to write his bishop, the Bishop of Quebec, about his problems, a privilege rarely exercised by the clergy of subordinate co-adjutor bishops like Provencher. Belcourt's problems with Provencher centred on principle as well as personality. The Bishop demanded an itinerant mission: Christ first, then settlement and the physical necessities like a chapel. A missionary, not a chapel, captured souls. Provencher found Belcourt's attempts at agricultural settlement a waste of time and an unnecessary drain on the funds of the diocese. Belcourt, conversely, complained that the Bishop failed to support the outlying missions as he should. The Bishop and his priest never became reconciled to their conflicting points of view. Provencher also became increasingly annoyed with what he believed were the priest's gross exaggerations of his success at Baie Saint-Paul, the Saulteaux mission six miles east of Saint-François Xavier on the left bank of the Assiniboine, and his continued delay completing his dictionary of the Cree language.[31]

But, if Belcourt's efforts at Baie Saint-Paul were a resounding failure, he did manage to cultivate the Métis. The extent of Belcourt's influence is, however, almost impossible to determine. He never fully discussed his role in the incidents of 1834 and 1836 with his friends and superiors in Eastern Canada. All conclusions must remain supposition. Although he never went on the buffalo hunt before 1838, he had adequate opportunity to cultivate contact with the Métis in his first year at Saint-Boniface. At Baie Saint-Paul he would have had less contact, except during frequent visits to Saint-François-Xavier. Perhaps his rather flamboyant personality and anti-Company stance won favour. Whatever the cause of his influence, he was definitely involved in quieting the December 1834 unrest over Thomas Simpson's striking of a drunken Métis, and the August 1836 York brigade rebellion, one of many about which little detail is known except that the Métis swore on a cask of sacramental wine to refuse to work for the Company.[32] Apparently neither Provencher nor Poiré, at Saint-Boniface during the 1834 incident, was involved. Why did Belcourt and not the Bishop quell the riot? Had the Bishop lost influence because he was identified with the Company? He had, after all, attempted to curry favour with constituted authority at every opportunity. Did the Métis follow Belcourt because he was known to be at odds with the Bishop and therefore presumably with the Company? One can only speculate, but given the events of 1846 and 1849, the above suppositions are not baseless.

Instead of a society delicately balanced between Protestant and Catholic, English and French, Métis and Halfbreed, Red River was exhibiting signs of fragmentation. Whites and mixed-bloods lacked internal consensus and there were serious incidents of conflict. Racial divergence became apparent as some native wives were discarded and others prevented from realizing a social position. Whites were opposed to mixed-bloods, Anglicans to Presbyterians, Catholics to Protestants, and Halfbreeds to Métis. It would take little to cause outright hostility. If Red River did not break out into open social war, it was because many of the tensions were still latent. It would be the free trade crisis of the 1840s, and the scandals of the 1850s that would cause an obvious divergence amongst the fragments that constituted Red River.

Notes

1. These were the most frequent descriptions employed by the missionaries, especially Cockran. For detailed citations see F. Pannekoek. 'The Churches and the Social Structure in the Pre-1870 West' (Queen's. 1974), 21–23. 55.

2. Excellent studies of the problem of the 'turning-off' process in the 1830s are Sylvia Van Kirk, 'Women in the Fur Trade', *The Beaver* Outfit 303, (Winter, 1972), 4–21 and *Many Tender Ties*, 50, 51, 88–89, 120–180.

3. The examples used by both Van Kirk *Many Tender Ties* and Brown *Strangers in Blood* tend to focus on the fur trade 'gentry'. It is difficult, as they both admit, to determine how frequently the practice was exercised by the vast majority, the illiterate. Given the nature of primary sources it is not possible to come up with quantifiable, definitive answers.

4. Letitia Hargrave, *The Letters of Letitia Hargrave*, ed. by M.A. Macleod, No. 28 (Toronto, 1947) 217–218, L. Hargrave to Mrs. D. Mactavish, 25 Feb. 1846; James Hargrave, *The Hargrave Correspondence* 1821–1843, ed. by G.P. de T. Glazebrook, No. 24 (Toronto 1947) 189, D. Ross to J. Hargrave, 13 March 1835.

5. Hargrave, *Correspondence*, 61, Alexander Ross to James Hargrave, 18 December 1830.

6. GA, Sutherland Papers, James Sutherland to John Sutherland, 7 August 1838. For similar comments see PAC, HP, 1177, Donald Ross to James Hargrave, 20 Feb. 1836.

7. L. Hargrave, *Letters* 73, L. Hargrave to Mary Mactavish, 1 Sept. 1840.

8. HBCA, B.135/c/2, fo. 54, G. Simpson to J.G. McTavish, 3 Jan. 1831; fo. 64d, G. Simpson to J.G. McTavish, 10 April 1831.

9. CMSA, D. Jones Journal, 24 May 1833.

10. L. Hargrave, *Letters*, 217–218, L. Hargrave to Mrs. Dugald Mactavish, 25 Feb. 1846.

11. CMSA, W. Cockran to the Secretaries, 3 Aug. 1831.

12. Elaine Allen Mitchell, 'A Red River Gossip.', *The Beaver*, Outfit 291 (Spring, 1961), 8.

13. An excellent study of status structure in small isolated resource communities is Rex A. Lucas, *Minetown Milltown Railtown* (Toronto, 1971). The sections on the function of gossip and rumour are particularly relevant. This invective, while most apparent in Letitia Hargrave's correspondence, is present in all of the informal missionary and Red River correspondence for the period. The Alexander Ross Papers in the Provincial Archives of Manitoba, and the Donald Ross Papers in the Provincial Archives of British Columbia exhibit marked tendencies to increased gossip. Of course, it is true as well that white women with leisure to write were introduced into fur trade society.

14. PAC, HP, 1002, Donald Ross to James Hargrave, 13 March 1835.

15. J. Hargrave, *Correspondence*, 18, Francis Heron to J. Hargrave, 1 Aug. 1826.

16. PAC, HP, 1717, Duncan Finlayson to J. Hargrave 12 Aug. 1839.

17. *Ibid.*, Letter book 8, 475, G. Simpson to J. Hargrave, 20 Dec. 1833 and J. Hargrave to G. Simpson, 20 Feb. 1833.

18. HBCA, D.5/4, fos. 370–371, D. Jones to G. Simpson, 8 May 1832; CMSA, D. Jones,

Journal, 14 July 1832.

19. L. Hargrave, *Letters*, 177–78, L. Hargrave to Mrs. D. Mactavish, 14–17 Sept. 1843.

20. CMSA, W. Cockran to D. Coates, 28 July 1834.

21. HBCA, A.6/24, fo. 137d, Committee to the Northern Department, 7 March 1838. See also E.16/2, fo. 3, 12 Feb. 1835, Proceedings of a Council of Assiniboia.

22. CMSA, W. Cockran to the Secretaries, 20 July 1831.

23. Ibid., D. Jones to Secretary, July 1833, 29 July 1837, 5 Jan. 1839.

24. Brown, *Strangers in Blood*, 190–193, W.L. Morton and M. A. Macleod, *Cuthbert Grant of Grantown* (Toronto, 1974), 117 - 119.

25. Foster, *Countryborn*, 236, Ross, *Red River*, 225–239.

26. CMSA, Secretary to Cockran, 20 March 1839.

27. CMSA, D. Jones, Journal, 28 Sept. 1832.

28. Robert Gosman, 'The Riel and Lagimodière Families in Métis Society, 1840–1860' (Manuscript Report Series 171, National Historic Sites, 1977), has an excellent account of social structure.

29. Read for example, 'Lettres de Monseigneur Provencher, Joseph Norbert Provencher, Premier Evêque de Saint-Boniface', *Bulletin de la Societé Historique de Saint-Boniface,* Vol. III (1913), Provencher's attitudes become apparent in these published letters.

30. Archives of the Sacred Congregation for the Propagation of the Faith, Rome, America, Incoming correspondence, Vol. III, 406, Provencher, 'Sur l'établissement de la mission de la Rivière Rouge et ses progrès dupuis 1818. '28 March, 1836. See also the Archives de la Propagation de la Fois, Paris, F. 193a, Provencher to the Secretary, 10 July 1833, and 1 February 1836. These letters contain an excellent account of the growth of the mission in the 1830s.

31. See for example, AAQ, RR I, 259, I. Bourget to Mgr. Turgeon, 12 Jan., 1839; RR IV, J.N. Provencher to M. Cazeau 29 Aug. 1832; RR II. 14, 15. G. Belcourt to J. Signay, 11 July 1834.

32. Alexander Simpson, *The Life and Travels of Thomas Simpson* (London, 1845), 100–102 discusses both incidents. See also G.A. Belcourt 'Autobiography of Father Belcourt', *Minnesota Historical Society Collection.* Vol. I (1850–1856), 194f.

CHAPTER

9

THE REBELLIONS OF 1837–1838 IN UPPER AND LOWER CANADA

Historian R.G. Collingwood's dictum that "every new generation must rewrite history in its own way" is well demonstrated by historical writings on the 1837–38 rebellions in Upper and Lower Canada. Successive waves of Canadian historians have both posed new questions about these events, and offered new answers to the old. As a consequence, historiographically the rebellions rank among the most complex issues in Canadian history, making it is impossible in a single chapter to do full justice to the subject. Questions which students should keep in mind while studying the rebellions include: were they isolated British North American events, or part of a larger, transatlantic revolutionary phenomenon? If the former, were they the consequence of long-term structural problems, or merely immediate responses to localized, short-term difficulties? Were they fundamentally political in nature? Economic? Social? Nationalist? Or some combination thereof? Were they generated by an élitist few, or did they have a much broader base of support within the various British North American populations? What were their short- and long-term consequences?

As Allan Greer notes in the most recent revisionist article on the subject and the first of those reprinted here, until well into the twentieth century the diverse and contradictory answers to these questions proffered by historians of all ideological stripes tended to share a common historical perspective: "...the rebels of 1837 were quite literally on the wrong track. They lost because they *had* to lose: they were not simply overwhelmed by superior force, they were justly chastised by the god of History." That, certainly, was the viewpoint of the early Whig historians such as J.C. Dent, for whom any resort to violence went be-

yond the bounds of legitimate political behaviour. But it was true of later
Canadian historians as well, for example, Donald Creighton, the acknowledged
English-Canadian authority on the nineteenth-century Empire of the St.
Lawrence, who argued that the rebellions represented inevitable economic conflict between backward-looking, rural agrarians, and progressive, urban-based
mercantile interests in the Canadas; and of Abbé Lionel Groulx whose Catholic
nationalistic perspective of the rebellion in Lower Canada was equally teleological. In "1837–38: Rebellion Reconsidered," Greer undertakes a major
reappraisal of the subject, claiming to eschew all such historical imperatives and
focusing on what he terms the "complexity and contingency" of these events.

A second important dimension of Greer's reconsideration is his examination of the interconnectedness of the rebellions in Upper and Lower Canada,
something that few of his contemporaries or immediate predecessors have attempted. Indeed, to find an approximate parallel to Greer's approach it is
necessary to jump back more than half a century to the relevant chapters of
Creighton's *The Empire of the St. Lawrence*. Perhaps because of the "Two
Solitudes" attitude that has tended to characterize the writing of Canadian history, historians of the generations between Creighton and Greer have, for the most
part, limited their scope to one or other of the Canadas. While the other two
readings in this chapter reflect this tendency, they are valuable because they
offer interpretive approaches that can readily and fruitfully be applied to the
'other' Canada. In "'Lawless Law,'" for example, Carol Wilton examines the use
of violence by the Conservative political élite in Upper Canada, undertaking in
effect a study of the political culture of the incumbents, a group often ignored in
a rebellious situation. Similarly, Bernier and Salée interpret "The Patriotes
Decade (1828–1838)" from a neo-Marxist perspective, and in the process challenge
both the most cherished tenets of the more traditional nationalist Québecois
historians, and aspects of the socio-economic perspective of Fernand Ouellet,
the acknowledged French Canadian *doyen* of Lower Canadian studies.

Suggestions for Further Reading

Bernard, Jean-Paul, "L'évolution de l'historiographie depuis les événements (1837–1982),"
in *Les Rébellions de 1837–1838: Les patriotes du Bas-Canada dans la mémoire collective et chez les historiens*. Montreal: Boréal, 1983, 17–61.

Bernard, Jean-Paul, *The Rebellions of 1837 and 1838 in Lower Canada*. Ottawa:
Canadian Historical Association Booklet No.55, 1996.

Bernard, Jean-Paul, "Vermonters and the Lower Canadian Rebellions of 1837–1838,"
Vermont History, 58, 4, 1990, 250–263.

Bernier, Gérald, "The Rebellions of 1837–38 in Lower Canada: A Theoretical Framework,"
Canadian Review of Studies in Nationalism, 18, 1–2, 1991, 131–143.

Blanchard, David, "Les Mohawks et les patriotes de 1837–38," *Récherches amerindi-
ennes au Québec*, 21, 1–2, 1991, 79–85.

Connor, Jennifer J., "Thomsonian Medical Books and the Culture of Dissent in Upper
Canada," *Canadian Bulletin of Medical History*, 12, 2, 1995, 289–311.

Craig, Gerald M., *Upper Canada: The Formative Years*. Toronto: McClelland & Stewart, 1963.

Creighton, D.G., *The Empire of the St. Lawrence*. Toronto: Macmillan of Canada, 1956.

Dominguez, Muriel Farley, "Politics and Poetics: A Study of Nineteenth-Century Nationalist Verse in French Canada," *Nineteenth Century French Studies*, 21, 1–2, 1992–93, 168–179.

Greer, Allan, *The Patriots and the People: The Rebellion of 1837 in Rural Lower Canada*. Toronto: University of Toronto Press, 1993.

Groulx, Abbé Lionel, *Histoire du Canada français depuis la découverte*. Montreal: Fides, 1960.

Kenny, Stephen, "The Canadian Rebellions and the Limits of Historical Perspective," *Vermont History*, LVIII, 3, 1990, 179–198.

Lamonde, Yvan, "Conscience coloniale et conscience internationale dans les écrits publics de Louis-Joseph Papineau (1815–1839)," *Revue d'histoire de l'Amérique française*, 51, 1, 1997, 3–37.

Lemire, Maurice, "Les Irlandais et la rebellion de 1837–1838," *British Journal of Canadian Studies*, 10, 1, 1995, 1–9.

McCulloch, Michael, "The Death of Whiggery: Lower Canadian British Constitutionalism and the 'Tentation de l'histoire parallel'," *Journal of the Canadian Historical Association*, 2, 1991, 195– 213.

Ouellet, Fernand, *Economic and Social History of Quebec 1760–1850 Structures and Conjunctures*. Ottawa: The Carleton Library, 1980.

Ouellet, Fernand, *Lower Canada, 1792–1841*. Toronto: McClelland & Stewart, 1980.

Read, Colin, *The Rising in Upper Canada, 1837–38: The Duncombe Revolt and After*. Toronto: University of Toronto Press, 1982.

Read, Colin, *The Rebellion of 1837 in Upper Canada*. Ottawa: The Canadian Historical Association Booklet No.46, 1988.

Read, Colin, and Ronald J. Stagg, eds., *The Rebellion of 1837 in Upper Canada: A Collection of Documents*. Ottawa: Carleton University Press, 1985

1837–38: REBELLION RECONSIDERED

Allan Greer

There was a time when historians thought they understood the events of 1837–38. They did not much *like* the Rebellion, and their accounts of the event itself were often sketchy in the extreme, but they knew where it belonged in the broad sweep of Canadian history; they could explain why it happened and what it meant. For the generation of academic historians writing before the deluge of the 1960s, the less said about the illegal machinations of Louis-Joseph Papineau, William Lyon Mackenzie, and their followers the better.[1] And yet, curiously, the Rebellion formed a major—I think it would be fair to say, *the* major—focal point

From *Canadian Historical Review*, Vol. LXXVI, no. 1, March 1995 (Toronto: University of Toronto Press, 1995), 1–18. Reprinted by permission of University of Toronto Press, Inc.

in their writings about the pre-Confederation century. Like the ghost of Hamlet's father, it brooded over a stage that historians proceeded to furnish with political backgrounds, social and economic causes, and imperial results. Developments converged on 1837, and then moved off in novel directions after 1838, but the tumultuous turning-point itself did not seem a worthy object of research once its essential character had been identified.

Donald Creighton saw the Rebellion as the climactic episode in the long-term struggle of "commerce and agriculture."[2] Reformers, rebels and *patriotes* represented a narrow-minded agrarianism opposed to the expansionist commercialism of the Montreal merchants and their Tory political allies. This second, capitalist/conservative camp was the one that grasped Canada's potential for greatness, promoted economic development, and, more or less unconsciously, laid the foundations of a transcontinental nation. Their conflict with the carping radicals came to a violent head in 1837, but, fortunately, things turned out for the best: rebellion was crushed and the empire of the St. Lawrence gained a new lease on life. The defeat of the rebels is hardly surprising, for, in Creighton's account, they had set their faces against the forward march of History itself.

Creighton's liberal-minded contemporaries had a somewhat different view of the subject.[3] Sympathetic to moderate reform and critical of the colonial oligarchy, they believed that a few extremists had temporarily hijacked a perfectly legitimate political movement. The ascendancy of Mackenzie and the radical *patriotes* had come about partly because of Tory intransigence, and the result was a revolt misguided in its principles and disastrous in its results. The liberal historians, too, had their view of the overarching thrust of Canadian history. It was a story of the gradual and peaceful development of British liberty within a framework of growing colonial autonomy. What was so deplorable about the rebels of 1837 was not only their violence but also their republicanism, their failure to appreciate the wonders of the British constitution. And yet, in the grand scheme of things, the role of the radicals and their revolt was ultimately positive, for, by their foolish actions, they unwittingly summoned up a saviour in the form of Lord Durham. Durham set in motion the liberalizing machinery that, in the fullness of time, brought forth Responsible Government, Confederation, and dominion autonomy. "The Rebellions," wrote A.R.M. Lower, "were blessings in disguise, the cornerstones of Canadian nationhood."[4]

While liberal and business/conservative interpretations held sway in English Canada, French-Canadian historiography was dominated by a Catholic nationalist school best represented by Abbé Lionel Groulx.[5] Papineau and the *patriotes* (like most Quebec historians then and now, Groulx had little to say about the Rebellion crisis outside the borders of Lower Canada) posed vexing problems for Groulx. Quite clearly, they were defenders of the nation, and that role gave them a major claim on the sympathies of a historian whose central preoccupation was the struggle of his people to maintain their ever-threatened cultural identity. But French Canada was, at its core, a Catholic and conservative society, as far as Groulx was concerned, and it was difficult to ignore the democratic, anti-clerical, and, in the end, revolutionary character of the *patriote* movement. To some extent, the historian contrived to reconcile his divided reactions by downplaying the *patriotes'* radicalism and by arguing that, strictly speaking, they were innocent of the crime of rebellion since it was the government that attacked them. Yet, insofar as the "mistakes" of the insurgents could not be ignored, Groulx was quite prepared to condemn them; consequently, his account featured a moral dissection whereby readers were advised to admire the *patriotes'* good points (their nationalism) and reject their bad points (their deism and republicanism). There are some striking affinities here with the liberal anglophone historians. Groulx's pulpit-style language may be more overtly judgmental than theirs, but in both the liberal and the Catholic versions of the Rebellion, resistance to constituted authority was seen as an understandable, though nonetheless egregious, error.

All these interpretive schemes that dominated Canadian historical writing through the middle decades of the twentieth century were built on the assumption that history had a discernible direction and flow. Canada was moving towards a goal in the nineteenth century; whether this end point was the construction of a transcontinental, commercial, and political union, the development of parliamentary government, or the preservation and resurrection of French Canada, it was certainly a Good Thing. Thus the rebels of 1837 were quite literally on the wrong track. They lost because they *had* to lose; they were not simply overwhelmed by superior force, they were justly chastised by the god of History. (The narrative structure in these older accounts resembles the revolutionary triumphalism then prevalent in American, French, and Soviet historiography, though, in the Canadian case, the form is inverted.) The Rebellion was the necessary anomaly in this providential account of the past, the sorry fate of the insurgents serving to validate the larger pattern, as well as providing Canadians with powerful moral and political lessons.

These teleological modes of explanation continue to resound down to the present day, even though historians long ago abandoned the confident overview genre favoured by Creighton, Groulx, and the rest. Original scholarship in the last few decades has veered in the opposite direction, away from overarching theses and towards specialized research on down-to-earth particulars. Moreover, since conflict and violence have ceased to be taboo subjects, empirical research on the Rebellion itself has made great strides since the 1960s. Military specialists have told us about troop movements and casualties;[6] imperial historians have shown us how Whitehall viewed the affair.[7] Meanwhile, research on the economy has revealed the financial and agrarian distress that helped to poison the atmosphere of the times.[8] A rich social-history literature has concentrated attention, as never before, on the ordinary people who formed the great majority of those caught up in the Rebellion;[9] even the religious background to

1837 has been explored.[10] The result has been a great advance in empirical knowledge: myths have been punctured, generalizations have been qualified, and a wealth of factual data has been accumulated.

However, reflection at the conceptual level has not kept pace with the progress of empirical and microscopic research. One can only pity the poor student or non-specialist reader who wanders into this historiographical terrain in search of answers to fairly basic questions about the Rebellion: what exactly was it? Was this a single phenomenon with various aspects and phases—the Rebellion—or were there two or more distinct rebellions? Why did it (they) occur and why did it turn out as it did? Was it a minor disturbance or an important event with lasting consequences? The student or reader will encounter a literature that seems more concerned with interpretive fine points than fundamental issues. Data abound on the rebels—the number who were Methodists, or the percentage who owned more than four cows—but what exactly makes someone a rebel? Books and articles enumerate the regiments involved in the battles of St. Denis and St. Eustache, but they say little about the effects of the British military presence on Lower Canadian politics.

This is not to say that the recent works lack conclusions, only that little thought seems to have gone into them. When it comes time to sum up, the discussion becomes crude and schematic; in many cases, historians fall back on the shopworn formulae of the traditional accounts. Even more pervasive is the "police officer's" conception of just what constitutes rebellion: it is essentially a crime, according to conservative historians, an illegal deed concerted in advance by ill-disposed traitors. More modern, liberal-minded writers try to avoid loaded vocabulary and strive to bring out the mitigating circumstances, but they still portray the revolt as a simple, unilateral *act*, something that rebels did—for whatever combination of social, economic, and political reasons. The behaviour of the government and of other actors is, in most accounts (though not those of the French-Canadian nationalists), merely reactive: normal, unremarkable, unproblematic.

This police officer's view of the subject underlies many of the implicit definitions of rebellion currently favoured in the literature. For many historians, particularly those who concentrate on Upper Canada and on Mackenzie, a rebellion seems to be a sudden and forcible attempt to unseat a government, something virtually indistinguishable from a *coup d'état*. But if Mackenzie's attack on Toronto is the Rebellion, what term do we apply to the all-important *context* of that exploit, a situation in which Upper Canadian radicals believed legitimate government had already ceased to exist? Violence seems to be a defining feature of rebellion in many accounts, and it is usually associated with the rebels, even though the violence of the government and its supporters was far more extensive and deadly. There is even a tendency to assimilate the fighting of 1837–38 with the various riots and brawls that punctuated the history of pre-Confederation Canada. Conservative commentators thus find confirmation of their view that the Rebellion was simply the most dramatic of many cases of lower class hell-raising, while writers on the left, seduced by a vision of the toiling masses in arms, find this a cheering instance of popular resistance. (Resistance to what? To whom?) Missing again is an appreciation of context, of the exceptional political circumstances which brought conflict to a bloody climax, and which gave the fighting an importance quite different from that of a canal workers' riot or an Orange-Green brawl.

The time has come, I believe, for some basic rethinking about the Rebellion of 1837–38, and I will suggest lines on which such a reconsideration might proceed. In my view, we should pause in the search for causes and effects and concentrate first on identifying more clearly the phenomenon that is to be explained. Surely the "what" question is prior to the "why" question. We can best approach this definitional problem, I would argue, by looking more closely at the crisis of 1837–38 as a complex series of events, one involving the actions and interactions of several parties, not just those identified as rebels. Rather than focusing on a one-dimensional act of revolt, we should recognize the contingency of events. Choices were made, actions taken, not as the inevitable result of metaphysical forces or of rigidly determining structures, but in response to rapidly changing circumstances. Placing the accent on complexity and contingency may seem a recipe for chaos rather than definitional clarity; nevertheless, as I hope to show, this is the only way to achieve an integrated view of the Rebellion and to grasp its essential nature.

Two major obstacles stand in the way of any synthetic initiatives of the sort outlined above: the comparative isolation of Canadian historiography from larger international currents, and the yawning chasm separating studies of Lower Canada and works on Upper Canada. The historiography of this country, strong in many other areas, lacks precisely the language and conceptual tools needed to make sense of revolutionary matters. Given Canada's history, as well as the historiographic traditions mentioned earlier, this is hardly a cause for wonder; what is surprising is the failure of Rebellion specialists to make fuller use of the enormous literature, empirical and theoretical, on revolutionary episodes in Europe and the Americas in the late eighteenth and early nineteenth centuries.[11] Not that the Canadas had the same experience as Belgium and Poland in 1830, or as Argentina and Venezuela in 1808. Naturally, there were numerous points of contrast, as well as similarities, but we cannot even begin to identify elements that are peculiarly and specifically Canadian in the absence of a comparative framework. Indeed, we can hardly find the words to describe the events of 1837–38 without drawing on the histories of other revolutionary outbreaks.

While a broader international view might provide useful concepts and points of comparison, any attempt to construct an integrated account of the Canadian Rebellion is still bedevilled by a particularly advanced case of historiographical apartheid. Creighton was quite prepared to encompass Upper and

Lower Canada in his classic work, but since his time, researchers on the two sides of the Ottawa River have been pursuing different issues using different methods and, on the whole, ignoring one another.[12] The Canadian Historical Association, following the prevailing trends but also awarding them a sort of official stamp of approval, commissioned two Historical Booklets on the Rebellion: one devoted to Upper Canada, the other to Lower Canada. This gap, mirroring the separation of French- and English-Canadian historiographies, greatly magnifies the effects of fragmented views and specialized research—a situation prevailing in almost all fields of history—and makes consideration of larger questions particularly difficult. Above all, it tends to obscure the links connecting developments in the two provinces.

These days, it appears that only the authors of textbook syntheses are forced to examine both rebellions. Drawing of necessity on a bifurcated monographic literature, these writers often seem, quite understandably, at a loss as to how to integrate the diverse materials on the two provinces. Those writing in French tend to solve the problem by simply ignoring Upper Canada altogether and concentrating on the historical ancestor of the province of Quebec.[13] English textbook writers do their best to present a pan-Canadian view of the Rebellion, but the results are still disjointed—in most instances the two rebellions are covered in separate chapters—and rather cockeyed owing to the effects of an anglophone and Ontario bias. In four recently published histories of Canada, I found roughly equal space allotted to the Upper and Lower Canadian phases of the Rebellion, in spite of the fact that the crisis in Lower Canada was far deeper and, by any standard, much more significant. Three of the books placed the Upper Canadian rising *before* the Lower Canadian, even though the chronological and logical order of events was just the opposite.[14] The remaining work gets the sequence right, but recognizes no connection between the two rebellions, as if it were pure coincidence that Mackenzie attacked Toronto just after fighting broke out in the Montreal region.[15]

My own view, as should be apparent by now, is that events in the two provinces were indeed connected; in fact, I believe they can best be understood as various elements of a single phenomenon. It is quite true that conflict took different forms in Upper Canada and Lower Canada, and that the populations involved came from dissimilar backgrounds, but the Canadas are not the only British possession where revolts occurred in dispersed locations and involved people of different religions and languages. The Irish Rebellion of 1798 saw risings in various areas of the north and the south; Protestants and Catholics, English-speakers and Irish-speakers, all clashed with the existing order (and with one another as well) in a complicated eruption of violence.[16] The Indian Rebellion of 1857 (formerly known as the Mutiny) was just as multidimensional: there were agrarian insurrections as well as military revolts; various provinces, ethnic groups, religions, and castes were involved.[17] And yet, in both the Irish and the Indian cases, historians seem to have no difficulty applying the singular term "rebellion" to events that were actually far more plural than the Canadian crisis.[18] In other words, there is no reason to consider dispersal over space and diversity in form to be, in themselves, grounds for denying the basic unity of a revolt.

Although my point is mainly about the integrity of the events of 1837–38, I might also observe that the structural antecedents of revolt in the two Canadas were not as dissimilar as has often been supposed. Both provinces had essentially pre-industrial economies and a preponderance of independent farming families. Everywhere there was widespread anxiety about procuring new lands to settle the rising generation, and so government policies that threatened to restrict access to wilderness lands were naturally a matter of grave concern in these settlements. Tensions between town and country were as much apparent in the Toronto region as in Montreal's hinterland, and, as a consequence, conflict tended to follow a rural-urban pattern when fighting broke out in 1837. Seigneurial tenure, on the other hand, was unique to Lower Canada, and with it went landlord–*habitant* friction, a dynamic of rebellion in that colony. Lower Canada was, in general, an older settlement with a larger population that was in majority French-Canadian; in contrast, its neighbour was expanding rapidly, thanks to the effects of agricultural prosperity and massive immigration from the British Isles. Some immigrants also settled in Lower Canada, with the result that a linguistic minority of British origin shared the province with the old-stock *canadiens*.

According to Lord Durham and a long succession of historians after him, tensions between English and French in Lower Canada lay at the root of the civil strife of 1837–38. The Rebellion in Lower Canada, we are often told, was "racial" and, as a consequence, it was sharper than—indeed fundamentally different from—the milder strife that disturbed "English" Upper Canada. But, in fact, Upper Canada was also a divided society with friction between British immigrants and older settlers of Canadian and American origin, as anyone who has read Susanna Moodie can attest. Furthermore, research by Ronald Stagg and Colin Read reveals that the North American-born and the recent immigrants tended to gravitate to opposing camps when civil strife broke out in this "racially" homogeneous colony.[19] The language of race suits the purposes of those wishing to emphasize distinctions between the Upper and the Lower Canadian rebellions and to denigrate the latter (a matter of prejudices rather than principles), but it does so by concealing an important similarity. The civil strife of 1837–38 saw an ethnocultural polarization on both sides of the Ottawa River— long-established settlers tending to come to blows with unassimilated newcomers. The fact that immigrants were, in relative terms, so much more numerous in Upper Canada goes a long way to explaining the weaker showing of insurrection in that province.

The constitutions of the two provinces were identical, though politics had developed along somewhat different lines. Without delving into the complex particulars of ideologies, grievances, and programs, we might simply note the existence in both Canadas of polarizing tendencies that produced, by the mid-1830s, two basic political camps: on one side, office-holding oligarchies loosely affiliated to more broadly-based "Tory parties," composed mainly of British immigrants, and, on the other, a "Reform" opposition, critical of existing power structures. Because of the larger proportion of immigrants in the Upper Canadian population, Tories in that province, and not Lower Canada, enjoyed considerable electoral strength. The *patriote* opposition in Lower Canada was marked by its origins as a French-Canadian ethnic movement, though its nationalism was far less narrow by 1837 than it had been earlier. An outlook that might, for shorthand purposes, be labelled masculine-democratic-republican predominated among *patriotes*, their rhetoric dwelling on the rights of the people (read propertied men), the dangers of corruption, and the need to defend the independence and prerogatives of the colonial Assembly.[20] Mackenzie spoke for those who took a similar radical line in Upper Canada, though most Reform politicians in that province favoured a more moderate approach.

This, very roughly, was the situation in the Canadas on the eve of the Rebellion. I am quite aware that this compressed sketch of the social and political background could be debated in almost every one of its particulars. Indeed, my hope is that brave souls will someday come forward to examine these issues in some depth and from an integrated point of view encompassing both Canadas. Meanwhile, I am anxious to get on to the events of 1837–38. The potted history that follows pays particular attention to the linkages connecting developments in Upper Canada and Lower Canada in an attempt to gain a better grasp of the essential nature of the Rebellion crisis as a whole.

If we place ourselves at the beginning of 1837, almost a year before armed struggle erupted, we find the Canadas already embroiled in a serious political crisis. The legislative business of Lower Canada had by then ground to a complete halt, owing to acute conflict between the elected and the appointed elements of the legislature. City councils and school boards no longer existed because the statutes creating them had expired and could not be renewed. No budgets were approved, and funds for routine state operations had to be raised by extraordinary means. In Upper Canada, the situation was superficially normal; harmony reigned between the executive and a Tory-dominated Assembly. However, the legitimacy of that Assembly was by no means universally accepted; it was a matter of notoriety that the 1836 election had been marked by poll violence, fraud, and gubernatorial interference, and, whether or not these factors had truly determined the defeat of Reform, many Upper Canadians certainly thought they had. The Tories clearly had doubts about their popularity for, knowing that the king did not have long to live and that consequently a new election would have to be called soon, they passed a bill extending the life of the Assembly in disregard to the established practice of dissolving the House upon the death of a monarch. Reform politicians concluded that traditional parliamentary politics were at an end; the moderates among them retired from public life, while Mackenzie used his newspaper to propound the view that the current Assembly was not simply of the wrong political complexion, but was illegal and illegitimate.

Many *patriotes* and radical Reformers seem to have looked forward to the day when Canada would be free of the "baneful domination" of Great Britain. However, this was a blessing they expected in the distant future; meanwhile, the threat of secession could be employed to extract concessions from the Colonial Office. Historians are quick to warn us that, at this stage, and even later when the crisis deepened, most Upper Canadians did not want a revolution. Insofar as revolution was associated with lawlessness and bloodshed, this observation is of course perfectly correct, and it applies to Lower Canadians as well. But they did not want tyranny, oppression, and injustice either. The fact that most Canadians lacked what might be called a revolutionary consciousness in 1837 is quite unremarkable; it simply puts them in the same category as most French people in the spring of 1789, most Russians in early 1917, and most Europeans at the beginning of 1848. Revolutions are almost never launched in consequence of some prior shift of public opinion in favour of revolt. Of course, the development of widespread alienation from the existing order does frequently play a role in precipitating a crisis of government, but the populace need not have insurrection on its mind at the outset. It is when the authorities are unable to co-opt, channel, or crush opposition, or when they are overwhelmed by financial collapse (France, 1788) or military failure (Russia, 1905 and 1917), that the situation becomes explosive. In other words, revolutions occur when governments find themselves unable to govern, and this was just the situation facing the colonial administration of the Canadas as the spring of 1837 approached.

Dangerous political gridlock could not be allowed to endure indefinitely; His Majesty's government, claiming ultimate authority over British North America, therefore had to find a way out of the impasse. After years of vacillation and repeated attempts to conciliate irreconcilable colonial parties, the cabinet now opted for a crackdown on the Lower Canadian *patriotes*. Lord John Russell's Ten Resolutions were not exactly draconian in their specific provisions, but they did constitute a clear rejection of *patriote* demands for democratic constitutional reform. Furthermore, they allowed the colonial Governor power to spend funds without the approval of the Assembly, and this violated the sacred principle of "no taxation without representation" proclaimed since the time of the American Revolution. In the strained atmosphere of the day, these measures were bound to provoke angry reactions; the Colonial Office understood this clearly and immediately ordered additional troops to Lower Canada. Sure enough, as soon as news of the provocative Russell Resolutions reached Quebec, radical newspapers began howling with indignation about "despotism" and "robbery" of the public purse.

Only the lower province was directly implicated in these developments, but Upper Canadians of all political stripes followed them with the closest attention. In Lower Canada's ongoing crisis, they not only saw a more vivid and starkly drawn coercion of their own debates and conflicts, but they discerned unmistakable portents for the future of their corner of British North America. Thus, in the furore over the Russell Resolutions, Upper Canadian Tories fulminated against "treason" and "French republicanism," while an increasingly anti-British Mackenzie sounded more and more like the leader of a Lower Canada solidarity campaign. Paranoid Tory fantasies notwithstanding, this was not the product of any interprovincial revolutionary conspiracy. Indeed, communications with the *patriotes* were limited, and personal relations between Mackenzie and Papineau were less than cordial, but when the British moved to provoke a confrontation with their neighbours, Upper Canadian radicals knew that their own future was hanging in the balance. The famous declaration (28 July) of the Toronto Friends of Reform put it this way: "The Reformers of Upper Canada are called upon by every tie of feeling, interest, and duty, to make common cause with their fellow citizens of Lower Canada, whose successful coercion would doubtless be in time visited upon us."[21]

Meanwhile the *patriotes* were mobilizing a wider public for a massive campaign of protest. Local committees were established and, between May and September, rallies were held in towns and villages across Lower Canada. Upper Canada followed suit beginning in July. Mackenzie was the driving force, using the pages of his newspaper to urge the creation of local "political unions" and touring the outlying settlements to rouse audiences with his fiery oratory. The speeches and the resolutions passed at these Upper Canadian meetings naturally dwelt on the familiar litany of Family Compact abuses and other grievances of strictly local interest. The occasion of the campaign, unprecedented in its intensity, was nevertheless the confrontation between the Lower Canadian *patriote* movement and the government of British Empire. "We earnestly recommend every township to form political unions," editorialized the St. Thomas *Liberal*, "to hold meetings and to express boldly and above board their determination to rise or fall with their brethren in Lower Canada."[22]

Through the summer and fall, conflict in Lower Canada only intensified. The Governor, in a vain attempt to stem the agitation, had outlawed "seditious assemblies" in June; they continued unabated, in spite of government efforts to get local officials to enforce the ban. The administration's next recourse was to dismiss "disloyal" militia officers and Justices of the Peace, but this action politicized local government and precipitated *patriote* countermoves against "loyal" magistrates and officers. The upshot was that, by late October, early November, large sections of the rural District of Montreal had set up their own revolutionized local regimes.[23] Such a state of affairs constituted a clear challenge to the sovereignty of the British Empire and so, with ever larger numbers of soldiers arriving in Montreal, it became increasingly apparent that armed force would soon be used against the *patriotes*.

These new and graver developments had a double impact on Upper Canada. First of all, they provided an opportunity for action by stripping the province of

British troops. The military build-up in the District of Montreal took place at the expense of other colonial garrisons with the effect that, by early November, not a single soldier remained in Upper Canada. Power relations accordingly tilted in favour of the anti-government forces, though not to the degree that Mackenzie, greatly underestimating the loyalist militia, thought. The Lower Canadian drift towards war provided an impulse, as well as an opportunity, to Upper Canadian radicals. Facing a major military onslaught, the *patriotes* stood in obvious need of support: not just support in the customary form of speeches and encouraging resolutions, but substantial diversionary action. "Let me advise every friend of the people," Mackenzie wrote on the eve of the Battle of St. Denis, "to provide himself with a rifle, or a musket or gun... *keep your eyes on Lower Canada.*"[24] In early December, shortly after news would have reached Upper Canada of the outbreak of armed conflict in the District of Montreal, insurgents marched down Yonge Street in their ill-fated attempt to capture Toronto. Word quickly spread westward to the London District and there, in a tertiary reaction, radical forces assembled in support of their colleagues but dispersed without firing a shot when it became clear that the game was up and that resistance was futile. The fighting in 1837 had been far more extensive and intense in Lower than in Upper Canada; the casualty figures reflect the disparity: about 250 men killed in battle in the former, four in the latter.[25] Yet it was only a matter of weeks from the time the bullets began to fly until the government and its supporters had triumphed decisively in both provinces.

The crisis was by no means at an end, however. Hundreds, perhaps thousands, of refugees fled to the United States in the wake of the first round of fighting and, in the process, they helped to keep the revolution alive while widening its geographic scope. There was tremendous public support for the Canadian rebels, especially in the borderlands of northern Vermont, New York, Ohio, and Michigan. However, the United States government, a major actor in the crisis of 1837–38, decided to preserve peace with Great Britain at the expense of revolution in the Canadas, and this decision eventually sealed the fate of the latter. Yet, for a time, the federal government had difficulty imposing its will on the turbulent northern frontier. "Patriots," American as well as French- and English-Canadian, launched a series of border raids in 1838; these culminated in November of that year in a comparatively large-scale invasion of Lower Canada, coupled with a rising of Lower Canadian rebels. Cross-border actions against Upper Canada tended increasingly to be the work of U.S. citizens, locked now in conflict not only with the British colonial regime but also with their own government, which quickly expanded its army by about 50 per cent in order to take active measures to preserve American neutrality and bring northern Patriots to heel.[26]

By the end of 1838, the colonial regime had completely mastered the situation from a military point of view; politically, far-reaching changes were under way, all designed to consolidate the victory and strengthen government. For the Rebellion was not exclusively—or even primarily—a military affair, nor was it only the work of "rebels." The seriousness of the crisis can be gauged not only in the far-reaching challenges to the existing order, but also in the extraordinary measures taken to preserve British rule. In addition to mounting military assaults against its Lower Canadian foes, the government also effected an unprecedented juridical revolution to guarantee its victory. Martial law was imposed, *habeas corpus* suspended, and arrests were carried out on a massive scale and largely without charges being laid. Legal surgery was less radical in Upper Canada where the revolutionary threat was less serious, but even here the right of *habeas corpus* was abridged: an unorthodox system was established of summary conviction and attainder of prisoners who petitioned for pardons. Finally, legislation passed in March 1838 gave immunity from prosecution to loyalists who may have broken the law in apprehending rebels.[27] This last provision points us in the direction of the unofficial but very real actions taken against opponents of government in the Rebellion years. Both Canadian provinces provide dozens of instances of assault, theft and destruction of property, and arbitrary arrest committed by loyalist forces. Of course, such irregularities are almost inevitable in times of civil strife, but they do constitute an additional dimension to the abandonment of the rule of law.

In the years following the fighting, the British colonial regime was not so much restored as reconstituted. The state, in its administrative and executive aspects, grew enormously in size, scope, and power. In the short run, soldiers and police proliferated, but, before long, more peaceful agencies of regulation came to predominate: schools, prisons, asylums, and above all, bureaucracies. (By the end of the 1840s an arrangement known as Responsible Government had been worked out to help coordinate executive, legislature, and electorate.) The provincial Assembly of Lower Canada was gone for good; in its place, an appointed Special Council (1838–41) was free to pass unpopular measures in fields such as the law, property, and municipal government.[28] The two Canadas were united, as is well known, in order to allow the resumption of the parliamentary system without letting the French Canadians have the degree of power their numbers would otherwise entitle them to. A punitive forced marriage, the Act of Union attempted to solve the "French-Canadian problem" through repression, and, as such, it represented the negation of the insurgent spirit of 1837–38 with its implicit commitment to self-determination and mutual support. (Successor regimes would be paying the price for that authoritarian solution for many years to come!) All in all, the decisive defeat of republican opposition in the Canadas paved the way for a major transformation of imperial rule.

No matter how paltry the military contests of the Rebellion may seem, this had been a political turning-point of the first magnitude. From the summer of 1837 until the end of 1838, the central part of British North America underwent a thoroughgoing crisis of sovereignty, one in which the very framework of state power was in danger of collapse. Fundamental questions came to the fore, not as abstract debating points but as real problems requiring immediate answers: who would rule the Canadas? How would that rule be carried out? Its legitimacy contested in theory and challenged in practice, the state could hardly carry out its normal function as ultimate arbiter; instead of containing and channelling political contention, it was now the actual object of conflict. Wherever there are parties and factions one finds competition for power and influence, and, in parliamentary systems, for the right to form a government; but, in 1837–38, the actual framework of politics was at stake: that is what made this a revolutionary crisis.

Much has of necessity been left out of the compressed account of the crisis of 1837–38. However, I hope that its inadequacies can be overlooked in keeping with the spirit of the exercise. I have tried to bring out the contingency of events and to dispense with the metaphysical forces of Fate, Destiny, and capital-h History; also absent are master-plotters scripting their revolutionary scenarios in advance of events. Almost every action, whether by rebels, loyalists, or government, was also a reaction: developments were interconnected and reciprocal, repression and resistance provoking one another in dialectical fashion. A spatial dynamic is also apparent, with the effects of conflict radiating outward from an epicentre in the District of Montreal. Each succeeding political or military explosion there sent out shockwaves that detonated secondary upheavals, first in the Toronto area, then around London, and finally across adjacent regions of the United States. Clashes took different forms in each of the widely dispersed areas affected; moreover, the people involved in the two Canadas and in the United States spoke different languages, partook of different political cultures, and cherished a variety of aspirations. Yet, for all its internal diversity, this was a single historical phenomenon, and no phase of it can be fully understood in isolation from the whole.[29]

Notes

1. For the sake of brevity, I am confining my attention here to influential works belonging to what might be called the academic mainstream. Dissenting interpretations that never received the attention they deserved include S.D. Clark, *Movements of Political Protest in Canada, 1640–1840* (Toronto: University of Toronto Press 1959), and Stanley B. Ryerson, *Unequal Union: Confederation and the Roots of Conflict in the Canadas, 1815–1873* (Toronto: Progress Books 1973). My own approach owes much to these writers, particularly Clark.

2. Donald Creighton, *The Empire of the St. Lawrence* (Toronto: Macmillan 1956), 255–320.

3. See, for example, A.R.M. Lower, *Colony to Nation: A History of Canada* (Toronto: Longmans, Green 1946), 213–56; J.M.S. Careless, *Canada: A Story of Challenge* (Toronto: Macmillan 1963), 164–87; Kenneth McNaught, *The Pelican History of Canada* (Harmondsworth: Penguin 1969), 85–89.

4. Lower, *Colony to Nation*, 256.

5. Lionel Groulx, *Histoire du Canada français depuis la découverte*, 2nd ed., 2 vols. (Montreal: Fides 1960), 2; 162–77. For an excellent overview of the historiography of the Rebellion in Lower Canada, see Jean-Paul Bernard, "L'évolution de l'historiographie depuis les événements (1837–1982)," in *Les Rébellions de 1837–1838: Les patriotes du Bas-Canada dans la mémoire collective et chez les historiens* (Montreal: Boréal 1983), 17–61.

6. Elinor Kyte Senior, *Redcoats and Patriotes: The Rebellions in Lower Canada, 1837–38* (Ottawa: Canada's Wings 1985); Mary Beacock Fryer, *Volunteers and Redcoats, Rebels and Raiders* (Toronto: Dundurn 1987). Please note that, in this note, and in those which follow, only a few of the more significant recently published books are included. This is not a comprehensive bibliographic essay.

7. Peter Burroughs, *The Canadian Crisis and British Colonial Policy, 1828–1841* (Toronto: Macmillan 1972); Phillip A. Buckner, *The Transition to Responsible Government: British Policy in British North America, 1815–1850* (Westport, Conn.: Greenwood 1985), 205–49. Imperial history of a different sort can be found in George Rudé, *Protest and Punishment: The Story of the Social and Political Protesters Transported to Australia, 1788–1868* (Oxford: Clarendon Press 1978).

8. The relevant literature is vast, but the works of Fernand Ouellet are particularly noteworthy: *Economic and Social History of Quebec, 1760–1850: Structures and Conjunctures* (Toronto: Macmillan 1980), and *Lower Canada 1791–1840: Social Change and Nationalism*, translated by Patricia Claxton (Toronto: McClelland & Stewart 1980). See also the highly perceptive discussion by Douglas McCalla in *Planting the Province: The Economic History of Upper Canada, 1784–1870* (Toronto: University of Toronto Press 1993), 187–93.

9. In addition to the works by Ouellet cited above, see Leo A. Johnson, *History of the County of Ontario, 1615–1875* (Whitby: County of Ontario 1973), 95–127; Colin Read, *The Rising in Western Upper Canada, 1837–87: The Duncombe Revolt and After* (Toronto: University of Toronto Press 1982); Bryan Palmer, *Working-Class Experience: Rethinking the History of Canadian Labour, 1800–1991* (Toronto: McClelland & Stewart 1992), 69–75; Allan Greer, *The Patriots and the People: The Rebellion of 1837 in Rural Lower Canada* (Toronto: University of Toronto Press 1993).

10. Richard Chabot, *Le curé de campagne et la contestation locale au Québec de 1791 aux troubles de 1837–38* (Montreal: Hurtubise 1975); Gilles Chaussé, *Jean-Jacques Lartigue, premier évêque de Montréal* (Montreal: Fides 1980); Albert Schrauwers, *Awaiting the Millennium: The Children of Peace and the Village of Hope, 1812–1889* (Toronto: University of Toronto Press 1993).

11. A qualification is in order: on particular themes, Rebellion specialists have indeed drawn on a comparative literature covering such matters as riots in eighteenth-century Britain or the agrarian economy on the eve of the French Revolution, but they have shown hardly any interest in revolutionary episodes *per se* and in their integrity.

12. *Mea culpa!*

13. An exception is Denis Vaugeois and Jacques Lacoursière, eds., *Canada-Québec: synthèse historique* (Montreal: Éditions du Renouveau pédagogique 1976), 306–18, which integrates a good, though very brief, account of Upper Canadian events into a chapter devoted primarily to the Rebellion in Lower Canada.

14. R. Douglas Francis and Donald B. Smith, *Origins: Canadian History to Confederation* (Toronto: Holt, Rinehart and Winston 1988), 227–31, 249–53; David J. Bercuson et al., *Colonies: Canada to 1867* (Toronto: McGraw-Hill Ryerson 1992), 219–24, 236–39; J.M. Bumsted, *The Peoples of Canada: A Pre-Confederation History* (Toronto: Oxford University Press 1992), 248–57.

15. Margaret Conrad, Alvin Finkel, and Cornelius Jaenen, *History of the Canadian Peoples*, vol. 1: *Beginnings to 1867* (Toronto: Copp Clark Pitman 1993), 412–24.

16. Gearoid O'Tuathaigh, *Ireland before the Famine, 1798–1848* (Dublin: Gill and Macmillan 1972); Thomas Pakenham, *The Year of Liberty: The Story of the Great Irish Rebellion of 1798* (London: Hodder and Stoughton 1969).

17. Christopher Hibbert, *The Great Mutiny: India 1857* (London: Penguin 1978); Eric Stokes, *The Peasant Armed: The Indian Rebellion of 1857* (Oxford: Clarendon 1986).

18. I am on record as favouring the term revolutionary crisis rather than rebellion (Greer, *Patriots and the People*, 4). I still think the former phrase applies, but consideration of the Irish and Indian cases makes me more inclined to go along with the prevailing usage which prescribes the word "rebellion" for colonial revolts that do not culminate in the overthrow of the imperial regime.

19. Ronald J. Stagg, "The Yonge Street Rebellion of 1837: An Examination of the Social Background and a Reassessment of the Events" (Ph.D. thesis, University of Toronto 1976), chaps 6 and 8; Read, *The Rising in Western Upper Canada, 164–204*.

20. Affinities in the rhetoric, tactics, and political styles between the colonial radicals and analogous elements in Britain have yet to be explored in depth. The term "reform" had rich and varied connotations in the early 1830s, and Mackenzie's use of the term "political unions" would have had powerful Old-Country resonances. See John Belcham, "Republicanism, Popular Constitutionalism and the Radical Platform in Early Nineteenth-Century England," *Social History* 6 (Jan. 1981): 1–32.

21. Colin Read and Ronald J. Stagg, eds., *The Rebellion of 1837 in Upper Canada: A Collection of Documents* (Ottawa: Carleton University Press 1985), 54. Compare 62, 70, 77, 87, 104, 105, 107, 316.

22. Read and Stagg, eds., *1837 in Upper Canada*, 65. Mackenzie even announced his initial plans to organize an extra-parliamentary network halfway through an article describing the progress of the anti-government campaign in Lower Canada. Clark, *Movements of Political Protest*, 375.

23. For further details see Greer, *The Patriots and the People*, 219–26.

24. *The Constitution*, 22 Nov. 1837, quoted in Anthony W. Rasporich, ed., *William Lyon Mackenzie* (Toronto: Holt, Rinehart and Winston 1972), 69 (emphasis in original).

25. Senior, *Redcoats and Patriotes*, 213; G.M. Craig, *Upper Canada: The Formative Years, 1784–1841* (Toronto: McClelland & Stewart 1963), 247–48. Note that these figures apply to the first phase of the Rebellion crisis only. My thanks to Colin Read for guidance on this subject.

26. See especially Albert B. Corey, *The Crisis of 1830–1842 in Canadian-American Relations* (New Haven: Yale University Press 1941), 44–69, but also Oscar A. Kinchen, *The Rise and Fall of the Patriot Hunters* (New York: Bookman 1956); Orrin Edward Tiffany, *The Relations of the United States to the Canadian Rebellion of 1837–1838* (Buffalo 1905); Edwin C. Guillet, *The Lives and Times of the Patriots* (Toronto: University of Toronto Press 1968); John Duffy and H. Nicholas Muller, "The Great Wolf Hunt: The Popular Response in Vermont to the *Patriote* Uprising of 1837," *Journal of American Studies* 8 (Aug. 1974): 153–69.

27. Read and Stagg, *The Rebellion of 1837 in Upper Canada*, lxxxvii–viii.

28. Brian Young, "Positive Law, Positive State: Class Realignment and the Transformation of Lower Canada, 1815–1866," in Allan Greer and Ian Radforth, eds., *Colonial Leviathan: State Formation in Mid-Nineteenth Century Canada* (Toronto: University of Toronto Press 1992), 50–63.

29. Certainly the Rebellion was multifaceted and, as a consequence, historians of ethnicity or of class struggle, gender formation or popular violence, can find ample material in 1837–38 for research and reflection. I hope it is understood that, far from disparaging inquiries of this sort, I welcome them. Similarly, there is no reason to object to the study of the Rebellion in the context of Ontario history or Quebec history, as long as neither province is treated as a completely self-contained entity.

The author wishes to thank an anonymous *Canadian Historical Review* assessor for helpful comments, and the Social Science and Humanities Research Council of Canada for research funding.

"LAWLESS LAW": CONSERVATIVE POLITICAL VIOLENCE IN UPPER CANADA, 1818–41

Carol Wilton

The Types Riot of June 8, 1826, is the most celebrated episode of conservative political violence in Upper Canada.[1] It was directed against William Lyon Mackenzie, an immigrant from Scotland and a newspaper editor in York (Toronto) who had perfected a style of journalism characterized by scathing personal abuse of the colony's leaders.[2] About a dozen well-connected individuals, most of them lawyers or law students, broke into the offices of Mackenzie's *Colonial Advocate* newspaper in its owner's absence. Terrorizing Mackenzie's mother, son, and assistants, the rioters wrecked the press and scattered the types, throwing some of them into the bay nearby. In a harbinger of what was to come, more than one magistrate looked on without interfering. The attorney general, John Beverley Robinson,[3] neither disciplined the lawyers and law students among the rioters nor prosecuted them in the criminal courts. Nor did he discourage the collection of a subscription to assist them in paying the damages of £625 that a civil jury determined they owed Mackenzie. In the longer term, although one of the guilty parties was dismissed as the lieutenant governor's confidential secretary, the rioters all went on to enjoy distinguished careers, many of them in the provincial administration.

The Types Riot and its aftermath are the focal point of the most important debate in Upper Canadian legal history, one with significant implications for our

From *Law and History Review* 13:1, Spring, 1995, 111–136. Copyright © 1995 by the Board of Trustees of the University of Illinois. Used with the permission of the University of Illinois Press.

understanding of both the legal culture and the political system of the province.[4] The discussion, whose leading proponents include law professor Blaine Baker and historian Paul Romney, has raised numerous significant questions about the place occupied by the rule of law in Upper Canadian legal thought and practice. Baker has cogently argued that the types rioters had no real conception of the rule of law and were not even operating on the basis of a worldview that was noticeably shaped by legal concepts. Rather, as members of a self-conscious aristocratic caste in the process of professional formation, they were acting in defense of a particular colonial ordering of society, one which was theistic, monarchical, and hierarchical.[5] It was this social ordering of society that Mackenzie's newspaper had by implication assaulted in criticizing members of the elite, a situation that the young Tory patricians believed cried out for reprisal. Romney has sharply challenged this perspective, arguing in his work on the office of Ontario's attorney general and elsewhere with equal vigor and considerable insight that the rule of law was only too well understood in Upper Canada. Romney would have it that the types rioters and other figures associated with the judicial system persistently and cynically violated the rule of law, part of a pattern of maladministration. This pattern extended throughout the system of government and created widespread dissatisfaction, which in 1837 culminated in—if it did not provoke—armed rebellion.

There are serious deficiencies in these interpretations. The Types Riot together with a few similar occurrences offer much too narrow a basis for large generalizations about the legal culture of Upper Canada; what is required is a more wide-ranging examination of patterns of conservative political violence through the critical colonial period.[6] The Types Riot was part of a far larger structure of political violence, a kind of "lawless law" executed by those in power. By the 1830s, Reform political meetings and elections were being ruthlessly targeted, the violence constituting a dangerous threat in many areas to opposition activities.

Another deficiency of the debate as defined by Baker and Romney is that neither has offered any constitutional or legal doctrine that may have been used by the Tories themselves to justify or explain conservative political violence. It is hard to accept Baker's notion that the worldview of lawyers and their students (to the extent that they engaged in these activities) was not in any fundamental way shaped and ordered by legal concepts. At the same time, Romney's rule-of-law interpretation leaves little room for the possibility of varying modes of legal discourse in Upper Canada or of alternative values held by the governing elite.

In this context a comparative approach is helpful. British legal historians have offered a sophisticated interpretation of the significance of the rule of law in British society; they have additionally examined the behavior of English political elites in periods of political tension comparable to the late Upper Canadian period. The legal history of Lower Canada also provides a useful point of comparison, particularly Murray Greenwood's work. Greenwood emphasizes the pervasiveness of Baconianism—the practice by which a loyal judge's first duty was to support the government rather than to strive for impartiality—in Lower Canada's judicial system.[7] An examination of Upper Canada's judicial/political system from this perspective is helpful in explaining the existence and timing of conservative political violence in Upper Canada, and in assessing its significance to Canadian history generally.

To put the matter crudely but directly, let us suppose that Chief Justice John Beverley Robinson came home early one day from court to find his dear wife Emma in bed with the gardener—not an entirely unusual episode in Upper Canadian history. Outraged, Robinson pulled out a pistol and shot the gardener. Baker would say: "Look at how Robinson treats his social inferiors!" Romney would say: "Robinson has violated the rule of law!" I suggest that we must find an explanation consistent with Robinson's understanding of the law and to do so, it becomes essential to offer a wider context by examining other incidents of the same character that could enlarge our understanding of the legal institutions of the time.

In general, conservative political violence between 1818 and 1841 falls within the category of what Lawrence Friedman has recently termed "lawless law," episodes of lawlessness that "take place 'inside' the legal system itself, or are aspects of that system."[8] Friedman offers police brutality as an example of lawless law, a situation in which "lawlessness masquerades as law, or acts as a secret supplement to law, or replaces law."[9] Lawless law is characterized by the complicity of law enforcement or judicial officials in activities that would normally be considered illegal, and is thus to be distinguished from other "private" forms of lawlessness such as urban riots, lynchings, and vigilante movements.

The lawless law of Upper Canadian conservatives was in part a response to challenges to the ideology of the colony's pre-industrial elites—the professional, commercial, and administrative elements that governed this rapidly expanding population of agriculturists engaged in mixed farming and forestry.[10] The political ideology of that elite, best characterized as "adherence to loyalty,"[11] was fully supported by the institutional framework of the colony. Governmental structures established under the Constitutional Act of 1791 gave institutional expression to elite devotion to the monarchy and the "balanced constitution" of Britain, as opposed to the republicanism and democracy of revolutionary America and France. The only concession to popular sentiments in the constitution was a relatively powerless assembly elected by the forty percent of the adult males who could meet the property qualification.[12] Otherwise, the appointive principle was supreme: Virtually every official from the (British) lieutenant governor through the executive and legislative councilors to the justices of the peace and other officers of the local government and the militia was appointed.[13] Naturally, this included judicial officials such as judges and sheriffs.

This political structure facilitated the suppression of challenges to the status quo, a task also undertaken by the Church of England. The church represented a minority of the colony's population but derived an artificial pre-eminence by virtue of its many privileges. The process of state formation was, however, incomplete in Upper Canada. The bureaucracy was tiny, the educational system rudimentary, the penal system embryonic, and the financial structure of the state precarious.[14]

To add to the insecurities of the elites, their efforts to keep the colony British seemed perpetually under siege from within and without. According to S. F. Wise, "the attempt to maintain a counterrevolutionary society on the borders of a revolutionary state" produced "a Vesuvian mentality" among Upper Canadian elites, who were all too aware of the dangers of another eruption.[15] The American Revolution, which contributed the colony's first sizable influx of non-native inhabitants (the "Loyalists" or "Tories" in American parlance), was followed by British wars against revolutionary and later Napoleonic France. A byproduct of the latter conflict, the War of 1812, brought waves of American invaders to the colony, and conquest was narrowly averted. Moreover, as J. K. Johnson has pointed out, "The possibility that the War of 1812 might be the last to be fought on Upper Canadian soil does not appear to have occurred to prominent Upper Canadians at all ....Upper Canadians lived with war, or the rumour of war, or the expectation of war."[16]

Domestic turmoil was no less anxiety-provoking. The presence of large numbers of post-Loyalist Americans on Upper Canadian soil enhanced fears of domestic disaffection and betrayal during the War of 1812;[17] thereafter, the battleground became a domestic one as the government attempted to disfranchise the American-born. By the time this "Alien Question" was resolved in the immigrants' favor in 1827, members of the elite were accustomed to equating domestic opposition with rebellion and revolution, a habit that also died hard in the mother country.[18]

Challenges to the elite were also launched by those of British origin. Robert Gourlay, a Scottish agrarian radical, provoked the full fury of the provincial establishment in 1818 when he attempted to organize a provincial convention to make recommendations for constitutional changes.[19] His fellow Scot, William Lyon Mackenzie, took up the torch of reform in 1824 with the founding of the *Colonial Advocate* newspaper. Not content with the role of commentator, however, Mackenzie soon began organizing petition campaigns aimed at achieving political reforms.[20] In 1828, he successfully sought election to the Provincial Assembly, where he sometimes cooperated with other reformers, including John Rolph and W. W. Baldwin.[21] His career as a legislator was a stormy one, featuring no less than five expulsions from the Tory-dominated Assembly in 1831–34. By 1837, Mackenzie had given up hope of peaceful reform and turned to armed resistance. He led the abortive and short-lived rebellion of 1837 in Toronto, companion (along with another small revolt in the southwestern part of the province) to the much more widespread rebellions of 1837–38 in Lower Canada.[22]

In Upper Canada, the ideologically based concerns of the elite, apparently confirmed by the dramatic events of 1837 and 1838, produced lawless law in two senses: the original offense, and the lack of legal sanctions against the offenders.

The thirty cases of conservative political violence in Upper Canada between 1818 and 1841 considered in this article (see Table 1), fall broadly into five categories: First, there were physical attacks on opposition leaders. In a notorious incident of the 1820s, for example, George Rolph, the brother of reformer John Rolph, was tarred and feathered in Ancaster near Hamilton at the western tip of Lake Ontario in June 1826 by a group of men with blackened faces dressed in sheets. Criminal indictments were returned by the grand jury of the Gore District quarter sessions in April 1828 against ten men, including the deputy clerk of the crown for the Gore district, a district magistrate, the district sheriff (also a magistrate), and two attorneys (one a future prime minister).[23]

Reform leader William Lyon Mackenzie, in addition to being the victim of the types riote in 1826, was personally attacked in York (Toronto) in 1832 when he became the target of stones and brickbats as he attempted to address a public meeting. The wagon from which he was speaking was then mobbed by a group of Irishmen armed with clubs, but Mackenzie escaped while the wagon was hijacked and some of his supporters were brutally beaten. "During all these shamefull proceedings" observed Mackenzie sympathizer James Lesslie, "the Authorities were among the disturbers of the peace and if they did not aid them they did at least give countenance—but some say they were among the aggressors themselves."[24]

TABLE 1 Examples of Conservative Political Violence. 1818–41[a]

Date	Location	Description
June 1818b	Cornwall (Eastern dist.)	attack on Robert Gourlay
June 1818b	Kingston (Midland dist.)	Christopher Hagerman (lawyer, future solicitor general, attorney general, and judge) horsewhips Robert Gourlay
1826c	Ancaster (Gore dist.)	Mackenzie hanged in effigy G. Rolph tarred and feathered
June 8, 1826d	York (Toronto)	Types Riot
Feb. 4, 1832e	Amherst (Newcastle dist.)	attack on Mackenzie supporters at public meeting
Mar. 19, 1832f	Hamilton (Gore dist.)	attack on Mackenzie supporters at public meeting
Mar. 19, 1832f	Hamilton	attempt to murder Mackenzie by Kerr and others
Mar. 23, 1832g	York (Toronto)	attack on Mackenzie supporters & Mackenzie's effigy burnt
July 4, 1832h	St. Thomas (London dist.)	attack on July 4 celebrations
Aug. 18, 1832i	Port Hope (Newcastle dist.)	rowdyism directed against opponents of magistrate
Jan. 1833h	St. Thomas	attack on founders of St. Thomas political union

TABLE 1   cont'd

Date	Location	Description
1833h	St. Thomas	attack on Liberal office & presses thrown down hill
Mar. 9, 1833h	Farmersville (Leeds county)	Orange attack on reform meeting
Apr. 1, 1833h	Brockville (Leeds county)	Brockville police board elections— Orangemen attack reformers
Oct. 6, 1834j	Beverly (Leeds county)	Orange disruption of poll
Mar. 1835j	Beverly	Orange electoral & post-electoral violence
Mar. 1835j	Leeds	other electoral riots
June 1836k	London (London dist.)	Orange electoral violence
June 1836h	St. Thomas (London dist.)	attack on reform election agents
June 1836h	Beverly	Orange electoral violence
June 1836h	Brockville	electoral violence
June 1836l	Prescott (Johnstown dist.)	Orange electoral violence
Aug. 1837m	Albion (Home dist.)	Orange attack on reformers
Aug. 1837m	Churchville (Home dist.)	attempt on Mackenzie at reform meeting
Apr. 1839n	Whitby (Home dist.)	reform candidate James Small attacked
July 8, 1839o	Cobourg (Newcastle dist.)	attack on reform (Durham) meeting
July 27, 1839p	Hamilton	attack on reform (Durham) meeting
Oct. 15, 1839q	Richmond Hill (Home dist.)	attack on reform (Durham) meeting
Apr. 1840q	Toronto	Orange attack on Examiner office

a This list is not exhaustive. It does not, for example, contain references to incidents of magistrates' abuse of power in Upper Canada in the immediate aftermath of the rebellion of 1837.

b Lois Darrocch Milani, *Robert Gourlay, Gadfly: Forerunner of the Rebellion in Upper Canada 1837* (n.p.: Ampersand Press, 1971), 153, 155.

c Chris Raible, *Muddy York Mud*, 91.

d Paul Romney, *Mr. Attorney*, 109–14, 130ff.

e *Colonial Advocate*, Mar. 8 and 22, 1832; *Brockville Recorder*, Mar. 8, 1832.

f *Colonial Advocate*, Mar. 28, 1832; Donald R. Beer, *Sir Allan Napier MacNab* (Hamilton: Dictionary of Hamilton Biography, 1984), 47–48.

g Armstrong. "The York Riots of March 23, 1832," 61–72.

h Patterson, "Elections and Public Opinion," 110, 126–27, 238–40, 280, 282.

i L. Soper to Lord Goderich, Jan. 28, 1833, Ontario Archives, MS. 38 (49), Reel 3-680. C.O. 42/416, 507–13; *Cobourg Star*, Aug. 29, 1832, quoted in Edwin C. Gulllet, ed., *The Valley of the Trent* (Toronto: University of Toronto Press, 1957), 295–96.

j Patterson, "Elections and Public Opinion," 254–56, 267–68; Akenson, *The Irish in Ontario*, 183, 186ff.

k Brian Dawe, *Old Oxford is Wide Awake!: Pioneer Settlers and Politicians in Oxford County 1793–1833* (n.p., 1980), 54; Landon, *Western Ontario*, 152.

l Patterson, "Elections and Public Opinion," 282; *Constitution*, Nov. 23, 1836.

m *Constitution*, Aug. 16, 1837.

n *Brockville Recorder*, Apr. 25, 1839.

o *Kingston Chronicle*, July 13, 1839; *St. Catharines Journal*, July 11, 1839; *Brockville Recorder*, July 18. 1839.

p *British Colonist*, July 24, 31, and Aug. 7, 1839; *St. Catharines Journal*, Aug. 7, Sept. 5, 1839; *Brockville Recorder*, Aug. 8, 1839.

q Kealey, "Orangemen and the Corporation," 44.

Even more threatening was a nearly successful attempt on Mackenzie's life in Hamilton in March 1832 on the day of a well-attended political meeting. Colonel W. J. Kerr, magistrate, superintendent of the Burlington Bay canal, and son-in-law of Mohawk Chief Joseph Brant,[25] appeared at Mackenzie's door that night and lured him outside on the pretext of doing private business. A number of men lying in wait set on him and beat him badly. Many Upper Canadians, including the editor of the London (Upper Canada) *Sun* found the involvement of Colonel Kerr, a pillar of the local establishment, to be disgraceful.[26] When Kerr was ultimately brought to trial at the Grand Assizes in August 1832 by a friend of Mackenzie, he was fined an amount that Mackenzie for one thought far too small. His co-conspirators remained unindicted.[27]

A second category of conservative political violence was the crime of effigy-burning, an offense against public order that, like the assaults mentioned above, was highly personal in its targets. William Lyon Mackenzie was burned in effigy while visiting Ancaster shortly after the Types Riot in 1826, and again in York following the public meeting of March 23, 1832.[28] On the latter occasion, the effigy was carried around York on a high pole, a gingerbread cake suspended from its neck by a yellow ribbon, and evidently dressed in some cast-off clothes of the grandson of the chief justice.[29] The effigy was burned outside the *Colonial Advocate* office, which was then subjected to a barrage of missiles and other forms of abuse. Like other supporters of the administration who specialized in arresting the victims of attack rather than the perpetrators, magistrate Captain James FitzGibbon attempted to restore order by arresting first an apprentice of Mackenzie's and then Mackenzie himself.[30] Although the authorities ultimately did act to protect Mackenzie through the night, Lesslie concluded that "the whole proceedings of this day have done more to... bring the Authorities into merited unpopularity than any of their previous acts.[31]

A third category of political violence involved assaults on the opposition's presses. Although the Types Riot was unique in the attention it received, the *Colonial Advocate* was attacked on at least one other occasion, in March 1832. In western Upper Canada the following year, the St. Thomas *Liberal* office was the target of an attack, which saw the presses thrown down a hill, allegedly by the "hot-headed sons of the local gentry," who were also responsible for a number of other assaults on oppositionists in the neighborhood.[32] The owner of the press was shortly beyond the possibility of obtaining redress from the legal system: "rising from a sick-bed to view the damage, [he] suffered a relapse and died" at the age of twenty-eight.[33]

The remaining instances of conservative political violence involved physical threats and abuse at opposition meetings and the systematic deployment of electoral violence. By 1832, the focus of lawless law appears to have shifted somewhat from individual targets like Rolph and Mackenzie to institutions prominent in opposing the established political order. Attacks on political meetings were becoming common in 1832 as conservatives mobilized against

Mackenzie's dramatically successful petition campaign. This campaign, undertaken the previous year, had resulted in ten thousand Upper Canadian signatures on a petition to the king asking for political reforms.[34] As a consequence, Mackenzie's supporters, sometimes along with Mackenzie himself, became accustomed to being roughed up at public meetings and clubbed on occasion. Personal assault, it seems, was the method of choice. These attacks frequently took place in the presence of one or more magistrates, who typically made no effort to intervene. Although these tactics soon burned themselves out, they had a considerable impact in the critical 1836 election. They also served as a dress rehearsal for the aftermath of the rebellion of 1837, when more than eight hundred suspected Reform sympathizers were rounded up and jailed, and many others, innocent of any involvement in the rebellion, were forced to flee for their lives.[35]

The disruption of opposition meetings became common again in 1839, when reformers organized a series of "Durham meetings" throughout Upper Canada to demonstrate public support for Lord Durham's report and its recommendation of responsible government.[36] The most celebrated of the meetings occurred at Richmond Hill north of Toronto on October 15. Since the sheriff refused to call a meeting, the reformers did so themselves. A large party of anti-Durhamites, identified by colored armbands and ribbons and carrying clubs concealed up their sleeves, attended from Toronto. The Tory shock troops were under the leadership of no less a personage than Sheriff William Botsford Jarvis, a former conservative representative in the Assembly, who took personal charge of a spirited attack on the reformers. Other participants on Jarvis's side, according to the *Toronto Examiner,* included the mayor of the city, several aldermen, and several justices of the peace and their subordinate officers.[37] Here, it seemed, was Toryism in official panoply determined to exercise yet one more time its divine right of violence.

The official reaction to these events conformed to the earlier patterns of assumed indifference or tacit approval. In reply to a memorandum from the organizers of the meeting, lieutenant governor Arthur did suggest "recourse... to the legal tribunals of the country," but seems to have done nothing to expedite this.[38] The *Toronto Examiner* suggested that the government could not follow the proper course and conduct its own investigation because of the wrongful involvement of so many grand jurors in the incident.[39] There is no record that any legal actions were undertaken against any of the aggressors at this meeting, though there had actually been a fatality among the reformers. Ultimately, however, the reform view of the meeting was vindicated in a 1841 Assembly inquiry into the "Yonge Street riot."[40]

Conservative electoral violence in the 1830s was particularly blatant and dangerous in the county of Leeds, a rural constituency in the Johnstown district on the St. Lawrence River in the eastern part of the colony. Significantly, the county had experienced an influx of Irish immigration after the end of the

Napoleonic wars, and by 1830 the Irish formed a majority in at least some of its townships.[41] These immigrants, and their compatriots elsewhere in Upper Canada, provided promising soil for the transplant and growth of the Orange Order, an Anglo-Irish institution founded in 1795 and associated with the Protestant ascendancy in Ireland. Not surprisingly, the order was comfortably at home with violence.[42]

It was in Leeds that Ogle Gowan, the Grand Master of the Orange Order in British North America, made his Upper Canadian headquarters and was determined to make his mark. Gowan, who was quite successful in becoming a force in Upper Canadian politics, harnessed the Orange potential for violence in his bids for election in Leeds in 1834 and 1835.[43] The results of both were voided because of the extent of undisguised Orange violence that the authorities were unwilling or unable to control.[44]

By 1836, as the political temperature of Upper Canada rose, Orange violence was condoned in official circles and in spite of government efforts to suppress the order in Britain. As Donald Akenson has pointed out, Gowan, his violent tactics notwithstanding, was always considered loyal to the British constitution, as the reformers were not.[45] Numerous Orange-inspired electoral disturbances arose from the general election of 1836, in the village of London in the southwestern part of the colony, for example, one observer reported:

> if you had been in London at the last election, you would have seen a set of government tools called Orange men, running up and down the streets crying five pounds for a liberal; and if a man said a word contrary to their opinion he was knocked down. Many were knocked down in this way and others threatened; and all this in the presence of magistrates, Church of England ministers and judges, who made use of no means to prevent such outrages.[46]

In London, as elsewhere in the province, the Orangemen were establishing a reputation as the political shock-troops of the conservative party, which they would further consolidate during the 1840s and after.[47]

Reformers did not let the incidents pass without complaint. Reform politician Dr. Charles Duncombe, who represented the county of Oxford in the southwest not far from London, eventually secured the appointment of a select committee of the Upper Canadian Assembly to investigate abuses during the election of 1836. Since the Assembly was dominated by government supporters, it came as no surprise to the reformers that many of Duncombe's complaints were dismissed as groundless.[48]

Conservative political violence, then, manifested itself in a remarkable number of incidents in the period 1818–41 and assumed several forms: personal assaults, effigy-burning, attacks on the press, disruption of political meetings, and electoral violence. These incidents were not confined to one part of the province, but occurred over a wide area from St. Thomas in the west to Cornwall in the east. The areas most prone were Brockville/Leeds county (seven incidents), [York]/Toronto/ Home District (seven), St. Thomas (four),

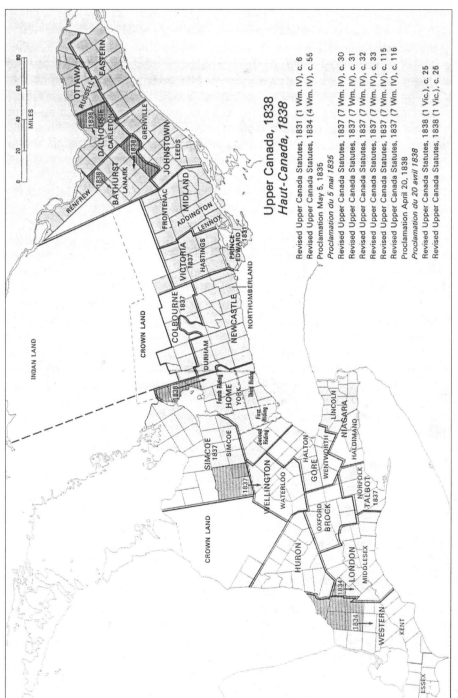

Upper Canada, 1838
Haut-Canada, 1838

Revised Upper Canada Statutes, 1831 (1 Wm. IV), c. 6
Revised Upper Canada Statutes, 1834 (4 Wm. IV), c. 55
Proclamation May 5, 1835
Proclamation du 5 mai 1835

Revised Upper Canada Statutes, 1837 (7 Wm. IV), c. 30
Revised Upper Canada Statutes, 1837 (7 Wm. IV), c. 31
Revised Upper Canada Statutes, 1837 (7 Wm. IV), c. 32
Revised Upper Canada Statutes, 1837 (7 Wm. IV), c. 33
Revised Upper Canada Statutes, 1837 (7 Wm. IV), c. 115
Revised Upper Canada Statutes, 1837 (7 Wm. IV), c. 116

Proclamation April 20, 1838
Proclamation du 20 avril 1838

Revised Upper Canada Statutes, 1838 (1 Vic.), c. 25
Revised Upper Canada Statutes, 1838 (1 Vic.), c. 26

Source: *Economic Atlas of Ontario*, Government of Ontario. © Queen's Printer for Ontario, 1969. Reproduced with permission.

Hamilton/Ancaster (five), Cobourg/Amherst (two), followed by Cornwall, Prescott, Kingston, Port Hope, and London with one each.

The number of incidents escalated considerably over the three decades: there were two in 1818, three in the following decade, and twenty-five between 1831 and 1840 as the oppositionists developed their political organization. Clearly the political atmosphere became more menacing for reformers over time. Moreover, the threat of violence was often present, even if no incident occurred. For example, the night after the York riot of March 1832, death threats against William Lyon Mackenzie prompted friends to mount a guard over his premises for the night.[49] Mackenzie went into hiding in the countryside for some weeks thereafter.

Mackenzie was by no means the only victim of conservative efforts at intimidation. At the Simcoe county election in 1834, the conservative cause was strengthened by the presence of the "Toronto Volunteers" under George Duggan, a lawyer, future mayoral candidate, and judge.[50] This force apparently "struck terror into the enemies [sic] ranks" making a signal contribution to the conservative electoral victory.[51] Another incident occurred at the Gore District Durham meeting in July 1839. During the meeting at the Court House Square, the 1st Gore regiment marched past with music playing and bayonets fixed. Few believed Sir Allan MacNab, the colonel of the regiment, when he said that he had told the militia to stay away from the meeting. Not accidentally, the pace of the meeting was speeded up immediately thereafter in the interests of avoiding violence.[52] The threat of conservative political violence was more pervasive than the actual number of violent incidents would suggest.

The evidence clearly demonstrates that the reformers were much less violence-prone than the conservatives. The major exception is the rebellions of 1837. Rebellion, however, was uncharacteristic of reform activities both before and after 1837, and did not represent the general drift of reform politics. Certainly reformers turned to violence themselves on occasion, but such outbreaks were vehemently discouraged by reform leaders, who understood that they must provide no pretext for the further use of force against themselves. On the whole, then, partly because of their own vulnerability, the reformers were not prone to use political violence to nearly the same extent as their opponents.

The foregoing analysis provides some basis for evaluating the arguments of Baker and Romney and the significance generally of the rule-of-law debate. Baker's position relies on an argument that might be described as "the divine right of violence." The types rioters, he argues, had been educated through the Juvenile Advocates' Society, an organization designed to inculcate gentlemanly values in young lawyers, to conceive of the Upper Canadian bar "as a guardian of the theistic, closely knit, ordered, content, and secure community" of Upper Canada; Mackenzie's newspaper attack on members of the governing elite "challeng[ed] nothing less than providence, a divinely inspired theory of government, the gentle code, the provincial constitution, and the predestined existence of

Upper Canada itself."[53] Violence in defense of these sacred values, presumably, was no offense, in their own minds at least.

Baker's argument may help explain the behavior of the types rioters, but it has limitations in illuminating political violence more generally in Upper Canada. First, in its narrow sense, it is limited in its application to lawyers and law students.[54] It cannot explain the behavior of sheriffs, magistrates, and other government officers. These worthies were rarely lawyers and consequently had not been subjected to the process of socialization that Baker argues was crucial in developing the rioters' worldview.

Nonetheless, enthusiasm for "the divine right of violence" was not an attitude fully shared by leaders of the judiciary. When the assailants of George Rolph attempted to justify their attack on him with reference to his supposed adultery, the presiding judge, James B. Macaulay, reported that "I did not think such conduct—however immoral or reprehensible if true—could either justify or mitigate so gross a violation of his person." Consequently, Macaulay would not allow evidence on the point to be admitted at the trial.[55] Macaulay was clearly unsympathetic to the articulation of alternative codes of behavior through the courts.

Similarly, when Macaulay sentenced W.J. Kerr for his attack on Mackenzie, he expressed outrage at Kerr's actions, which he deemed no common assault, and commented that he had assessed a heavier penalty than usual because the attack was politically inspired.[56]

John Beverley Robinson, who was long the acknowledged leader of provincial Toryism,[57] offers another example of judicial attitude from his lofty perch as chief justice of the court of King's Bench from 1829–62. In the 1830s, when conservative political violence was at its height, his grand jury charges stressed the impartiality of the law, the duty of magistrates to be fair and objective, and the necessity for strict neutrality in assessing legal disputes.[58] When an effigy-burning case finally came before his court in 1849, Robinson roundly denounced the practice as libelous and illegal even in the absence of a riot.[59] Robinson's official pronouncements, then, offer cold comfort to those who believe the Upper Canadian elite entirely subscribed to the "divine right of violence." On the contrary, the colony's highest judicial officers, at least on a number of occasions, deplored the wanton violence of some Tory supporters and acted to discourage it.

These views may have sometimes been in evidence at the highest reaches of official Toryism, but Paul Romney insists that Robinson, his judicial colleagues, and many other Tories ignored the rule of law when it conflicted with their political interests and their political prejudices. Romney argues that the essence of the British constitution was the rule of law, a concept comprising "equality before the law, due process, and an independent judiciary."[60] The concept of the rule of law was deeply familiar to Upper Canadian lawyers, resonating as it did throughout the judgments of Robinson and his colleagues. But it extended beyond the bench to the very heart of the Law Society. As Romney points out, it was a reform leader, the Law Society Treasurer W. W. Baldwin, who wrote Robinson a letter criticizing his conduct as attorney general on rule of law grounds.[61] In this view, Robinson did wrong and he had every reason to understand the significance of his failure to uphold the duties of his position as attorney general. The lawyers and officials of Upper Canada who disregarded the rule of law, then, engaged in intentional wrongdoing according to Romney, demonstrating remarkable hypocrisy in the process.

The concepts of equality before the law and due process were certainly familiar to Upper Canadians, as Robinson's grand jury charges confirm.[62] Romney's argument, however, is not entirely convincing, in theoretical terms. E. P. Thompson, whom Romney cited as an authority for his argument,[63] has demonstrated from a Marxist perspective how slippery a concept the rule of law actually was in the fullness of British history. In his study of the notorious Black Act of 1723, Thompson subscribed to the idea that the concept of the rule of law was imbricated in the fabric of eighteenth-century society, but nowhere did he argue that adherence to the rule of law was a constant and operative principle of eighteenth-century government. On the contrary, he observed:

> I have shown in this study a political oligarchy inventing callous and oppressive laws to serve its own interests. I have shown judges who... were subject to political influence, whose sense of justice was humbug, and whose interpretation of the law served only to enlarge their inherent class bias. Indeed .... this study has shown that for many of England's governing elite the rules of law were a nuisance, to be manipulated and bent in what ways they could .... [64]

In Canada, no less than in Britain, the rule of law was sometimes honored more in the breach than in the observance, and the frequently lawless behavior of the local elites still remained recognizably within the British tradition as described by Thompson.

The same point is true of the behavior of British elites during and shortly after the French Revolution, when the British people were subjected to a period of repression and official violence. Thompson describes "church and king mobs," often incited by the authorities themselves, attacking the property of those suspected of republican and democratic sympathies during the last years of the eighteenth century. Some local authorities encouraged "paint-burnings," where effigies of the radical dissident Thomas Paine were burnt and/or otherwise symbolically punished. These ritualized forms of demonstrating disrespect were seen by the authorities in Britain essentially as a form of public education.[65] Again, in the five years or so following the Napoleonic wars, the British government resorted to massive domestic repression that seemed to fly directly in the face of rule of law ideology. The massacre at Peterloo in 1819 is the most famous example.[66] These events, which occurred within the memories of many Upper Canadians, provided an unmistakable imperial example for the behavior of violence-prone conservatives in the outposts of empire. Both in theory and in practice, the British experience offered living alternatives to the rule of law as a mode of governing in times of crisis and exemplified the Tory belief that "extremism in the defense of liberty is no vice. And ... moderation in the pursuit of justice is no virtue."[67]

There was another doctrine, well known in British constitutional thought, which is relevant to the situation in Upper Canada: the Baconian interpretation of the constitution. This interpretation traced its name to Sir Francis Bacon, the attorney general of James I, who claimed that judges were "'lions under the throne, being circumspect that they do not check or oppose any points of sovereignty.'"[68] According to Murray Greenwood, Bacon insisted that a loyal judge's duty was less to manifest impartiality and more to support the government.[69] Though Bacon's rival, Sir Edward Coke, who championed standards of judicial impartiality, commanded widespread support in Britain, Lower Canadian judges in the era of the French Revolution were, according to Greenwood, "thoroughly Baconian." In a large measure, this was because colonial judges were far more involved in partisan politics than their British counterparts, sitting for example in the executive council, which was the equivalent of a cabinet position or even a prime ministership.[70] The judges' identification with the interests of Great Britain (and the government to which they owed their appointments), including an acceptance of the colonial relationship, was reflected in their interpretation of their judicial role. Their partisanship manifested itself in security questions; Greenwood argues that "all judicial decisions and reasoning on security matters from 1794 to 1810... were highly favourable to the crown."[71] Baconianism characterized the Lower Canadian judiciary until the late 1830s.

Judicial independence in Upper Canada was undermined by some of the same government structures and political fears as in Lower Canada. The chief justice sat on the executive council until the early 1830s and was *ex officio* speaker of the legislative council.[72] Until 1834, judicial offices were held at pleasure rather than on good behavior, as in England.[73] The impartiality of the legal process was also compromised in the view of some observers because, as Barry Wright has pointed out, legal procedures in Upper Canada gave more power to the authorities than was the case in England. The power of the executive over the judicial process was thereby increased, with obvious potential for abuse.[74] Judges also might work closely with members of the executive in matters related to sedition. The Seditious Meetings Act of 1818 was drafted in concert with the justices of the Court of King's Bench, a move that ensured there would be no subsequent successful legal challenge, in addition, in 1818 Robinson as attorney general strongly supported the decision to submit suspected subversive Robert Gourlay's situation to the rome justices to determine whether Gourlay could be tried under the Sedition Act of 1804.[75] Like the Lower Canadian justices, moreover, those in Upper Canada were extremely sensitive to any movement that appeared to threaten the imperial tie.[76] The result was a series of thirty-four prosecutions for sedition before 1830, many of them under the Sedition Act of 1804, which was in force until 1829.[77] Without a doubt, the criminal law was one of the most important means of controlling domestic dissent in Upper Canada.

This discussion suggests two points that are relevant to the explanation of conservative political violence. First, the biases of the Upper Canadian political/judicial system must have been evident even to the most dull-witted magistrate in the most remote township. For those who were reading the lips of administration figures, it would have been clear that both the executive and the judiciary would take a tolerant view of conservative political violence, as they had in the Types Riot case. Moreover, local officials had a wide measure of discretion in dealing with offenses in their own bailiwicks, and could, within limits, turn a blind eye to offenses that targeted the politically incorrect of that society.[78]

The second point is that conservative political violence in the 1830s was taking place in a context in which the state had been forced to withdraw from certain accustomed forms of repression. The Seditious Meetings Act of 1818 had been repealed in 1820, and events of the 1820s had established the right of public assembly in Upper Canada.[79] The Sedition Act of 1804 was finally repealed in 1829. By the late 1820s, too, the attorney general was extremely reluctant to use libel laws to suppress opposition presses, because he "'feared to call the Papers into Notoriety, and to protract their Existence, by the political Excitements which Prosecutions for Libel usually occasion.'"[80] The difficulties encountered in managing criminal prosecutions under the eyes of watchful oppositionists further discouraged the use of the criminal courts for political purposes. As Barry Wright has noted, "the exercise of the crown's prosecutorial authority was in public disrepute and there was little confidence in obtaining compliant regular juries."[81] By the 1830s, then, officials of the central administration were hamstrung in dealing with political dissent short of treason.[82] Officials at the lower levels of the administration filled the vacuum with political violence.

The lawless law of Upper Canadian conservatives in the 1820s and 1830s was an indication of the weakening of conservative hegemony in the province, notwithstanding the apparent strengths of the regime.[83] Paradoxically, the appearance of order could only be maintained through the resort to violence. Ultimately, however, this was a losing game, for political violence brought a further loss of legitimacy for the regime. Reformers, unwilling and essentially unable to use the same devices, routinely denounced such episodes, which in fact became an integral part of a reform mythology of Upper Canadian history, and which they spread about at every opportunity. Reform handbills denounced the extent to which reformers were "slandered, persecuted, insulted, and degraded; their feelings wounded and their usefulness impaired." Public opinion, they claimed, was "set at defiance, and fundamental principles of the constitution openly violated."[84] Newspapers unfavorable to the regime were founded as a result,[85] and private citizens penned fervent letters to the editor proclaiming that conservative political violence had politicized them in favor of the opposition.[86] Thousands signed petitions critical of the regime in the late 1820s and early 1830s, and oppositionist political organizations proliferated.[87] It has been argued, indeed, that conservative political violence went far to legitimize violence against the regime itself, and even served to provoke the rebellion.[88] The widespread use of conservative political violence was a sign that the days of the old regime were numbered; a different kind of hegemony would be established with the union of the Canadas and responsible government in the 1840s.

Conservative political violence continued into the 1840s, but its frequency diminished, and by the 1850s it seems largely to have disappeared. A major reason for this was the acceptance of political opposition during the 1840s, after the British government endorsed the reform program of responsible government, thereby removing a major source of discord between the conservatives and their chief political opponents.[89] Significantly, the last major outbursts of conservative political violence in Toronto occurred as a result of the passage of the Rebellion Losses Bill in 1849.[90] Acceptance of this bill by the British government suggested that responsible government was here to stay, and that opposition to it, violent or otherwise, was not productive.

Beyond the legitimization of the concept and practice of political opposition, a number of influences discouraged conservative political violence from the late 1830s on. The British government, trying to suppress Orangeism at home, embarked after 1836 on a campaign to discourage it in Upper Canada as well, initially with mixed results.[91] At another level, both the authorities and members of the middle class more generally became increasingly concerned about threats to public order. Toronto newspapers, for example, showed great concern about the perceived increase in rowdyism during the 1850s, and the police force of the city expanded by a factor of seven between 1847 and 1856;[92] it grew even more dramatically thereafter. Gregory Kealey has argued that by the 1850s the bourgeois elements of Toronto society had rethought their attitude to political violence in response to the threat to public order posed by the rise of an indigenous working class.[93] Even in areas considerably less industrialized than Toronto, the threat of rowdyism was an omnipresent concern for society's respectable elements in the 1860s and 1870s.[94] The decline of conservative political violence must also be related to a long-term decline in violence in Toronto and elsewhere between the mid- and the late nineteenth century, measured by the rate of offenses against the person, a phenomenon that was part of a much larger, long-run decline it violence in western society more generally.[95]

The era of lawless law in Upper Canada lasted for a generation and more. Initially it was provoked by and then it contributed to the loss of conservative moral authority in the 1820s and 1830s. Much later, by the 1850s, with the emergence of political consensus on a different basis, built on moderation and brokerage politics, it had outlived any residual usefulness. The Baconian constitutional views that it partly expressed lived on, however, and would reappear after Confederation (1867) at such times of acute political stress as the Winnipeg General Strike of 1919,[96] and the rise of separatism in Quebec in the late 1960s and early 1970s.[97] Therein lies the continuing relevance of Upper Canadian political violence; therein too lies the ambiguous heritage of Upper Canadian legal culture. In the peaceable kingdom, many Canadians, steeped perhaps unwittingly in ancestral acceptance of lawless law, have remained far too accepting of raw incursions of state power in situations of perceived emergency. Canadians, it would seem, have paid a steep price for this particular Tory legal doctrine and political practice.

Notes

1. Several terms in this article need to be defined: First, the use of the term "conservative" here is anachronistic; it did not come into widespread use until the 1850s. The term "government supporter" would be more accurate, but it is both unwieldy and unfamiliar to the modern reader. Contemporaries referred to government supporters as "tories," members of the "family compact party," and Orangemen, but all of these have a somewhat narrow partisan focus; second, by "conservative political violence" I mean some form of assault, property damage, or offense against public order, directed against those opposed to the existing political order by its self-proclaimed supporters; third, from 1791 to 1841, 'Ontario' and 'Quebec' were called Upper Canada and Lower Canada respectively; from 1841 to Confederation (1867) they were called Canada West and Canada East, and were referred to as the 'United Canadas' or 'the Province of Canada.'

2. Frederick H. Armstrong and Ronald J. Stagg, "Mackenzie, William Lyon," [1795–1861] *Dictionary of Canadian Biography* 9:496–510.

3. John Beverley Robinson (1791–1863) was one of the colony's outstanding political and legal personalities. His abilities had been recognized when he was made acting provincial attorney general at the age of twenty-one. After a fuller legal education in England, he returned to Upper Canada, where he acted as attorney general and led government forces in the Assembly for much of the 1820s. In 1829 he became chief justice of the Court of King's Bench, a position he held until 1862. See Robert E. Saunders, "Robinson, Sir John Beverley," *Dictionary of Canadian Biography* 9:668–79.

4. Paul Romney, *Mr Attorney: The Attorney General for Ontario in Court, Cabinet, and Legislature 1791–1899* (Toronto: The Osgoode Society, 1986); Paul Romney, "From the Types Riot to the Rebellion: Elite Ideology, Anti-legal Sentiment, Political Violence, and the Rule of Law in Upper Canada," *Ontario History* 79 (1987): 113–44; Paul Romney, "Very Late Loyalist Fantasies: Nostalgic Tory History and the Rule of Law in Upper Canada," in *Canadian Perspectives on Law & Society: Issues in Legal History*, ed. W. Wesley Pue and Barry Wright (Ottawa: Carleton University Press, 1988), 119–47; G. B. Baker, "'So Elegant a Web': Providential Order and the Rule of Secular Law in Early Nineteenth-Century Upper Canada," *University of Toronto Law Journal* 38 (1988): 184–205.

5. Baker, "'So Elegant a Web.'"

6. Romney's *Mr Attorney* briefly considers the Upper Canadian judicial system in a general way in the context of "verbal, constitutional, and physical violence against the reformers on the part of the provincial administration and its supporters." *Mr. Attorney*, 153–57.

7. F. Murray Greenwood, *Legacies of Fear: Law and Politics in Quebec in the Era of the French Revolution* (Toronto: The Osgoode Society, 1993).

8. Lawrence M. Friedman, *Crime and Punishment in American History* (New York: BasicBooks, 1993), 172.

9. Ibid.

10. By 1840, Upper Canada's population was approaching four hundred thousand. See Douglas McCalla, *Planting the Province: The Economic History of Upper Canada 1784–1870* (Toronto: University of Toronto Press, 1993), 8, 45–91.

11. S. F. Wise has argued that loyalty went beyond "adherence to the Crown and the Empire" to mean "adherence to those beliefs and institutions the conservative considered essential in the preservation of a form of life different from, and superior to, the manners, politics and social arrangements of the United States." See "Upper Canada and the Conservative Tradition," in *Profiles of a Province: Studies in the History of Ontario*, ed. Edith G. Firth (Toronto: Ontario Historical Society, 1967), 31; and David Mills, *The Idea of Loyalty in Upper Canada 1784–1850* (Kingston and Montreal: McGill-Queen's University Press, 1988).

12. See Elwood Jones, "The Franchise in Upper Canada, 1792–1867," paper presented at the Annual Meeting of the Canadian Historical Association, Winnipeg, June 7–9, 1986.

13. The executive council was a kind of cabinet made up of elite advisers to the lieutenant governor; the legislative council was a powerful appointed body like a senate. Membership on the two councils often overlapped. See Frederick H. Armstrong, *Handbook of Upper Canadian Chronology*, rev. ed. (Toronto and London: Dundurn Press, 1985), 38–39, 55–57. The system of appointment in Upper Canada has been scathingly summarized as involving "an entrenched, irremovable group of powerful administrators decided, using criteria of their own, who was to receive or to be denied status and favour." See J. K. Johnson, *Becoming Prominent: Regional Leadership in Upper Canada, 1701–1841* (Kingston and Montreal: McGill-Queen's University Press, 1989), 166.

14. See Allan Greer and Ian Radforth, eds., *Colonial Leviathan: State Formation in Mid-Nineteenth-Century Canada* (Toronto: University of Toronto Press, 1992).

15. S. E Wise, "The Family Compact: A Negative Oligarchy," in *The Family Compact: Aristocracy or Oligarchy?* ed. David W. L. Earl (Toronto: Copp Clark, 1967), 142–43.

16. Johnson, *Becoming Prominent*, 77, 79.

17. The aboriginal inhabitants of the province (seven to ten thousand) along with six thousand or so Loyalists who had settled in Upper Canada by 1785, were swamped by post-Loyalist migrants from the United States; by 1811, the province contained sixty to seventy thousand settlers, most of them of post-Loyalist American origin. The character of the population was substantially altered by British migration to Upper Canada during 1815–25, which is estimated to have totalled 129,000. McCalla, *Planting the Province*, Table 1.1, p. 249; Table 3.6, p. 256.

18. See Mills, *Idea of Loyalty.* Compare Richard Hofstadter, *The Idea or a Party System: The Rise of Legitimate Opposition in the United States, 1780–1840* (Berkeley: University of California Press, 1969), and John Stevenson, *Popular Disturbances in England 1700–1832,* 2d ed. (London and New York: Longmans, 1992), 244.

19. Gourlay's initiative met with charges of seditious libel, imprisonment, and a sentence of banishment. See S. F. Wise, "Gourlay, Robert Fleming," *Dictionary of Canadian Biography* 9:330–36.

20. Carol Wilton, "'A Firebrand amongst the People': The Durham Meetings and Popular Politics in Upper Canada," *Canadian Historical Review* 75 (September 1994): 348–49.

21. Dr. John Rolph (1793–1870), an Englishman who migrated permanently to Upper Canada in 1821, was both a doctor and a lawyer. He was one of the most prominent reformers in the parliamentary sessions of 1824–8 and 1828–30. See G. M. Craig, "Rolph, John," *Dictionary of Canadian Biography* 9:683–90.

    Dr. William Warren Baldwin of Toronto (1775–1844), an immigrant from Ireland, was also a doctor and a lawyer. He is best known as the father of both politician Robert Baldwin and the doctrine of responsible government. (See below, note 36). See Robert L. Fraser, "Baldwin, William Warren," *Dictionary of Canadian Biography* 7:35–44.

22. See Colin Read and Ronald J. Stagg, eds., *The Rebellion of 1837 in Upper Canada: A Collection of Documents* ([Ottawa]: Carleton University Press, 1985); and Colin Read, *The Rising in Western Upper Canada 1837–8: The Duncombe Revolt and After* (Toronto: University of Toronto Press, 1982).

23. Rolph decided against prosecuting the accused, perhaps because he feared the assize grand jury would be biassed against him. Rolph had previously launched a civil action that resulted in very light damages; the Court of King's Bench refused to hear an appeal. Romney, *Mr. Attorney,* 109–14.

24. E H. Armstrong, "The York Riots of March 23. 1832," *Ontario History* 55 (1963): 61–72; James Lesslie, "Diary of James Lesslie, March 22–24, 1832," in *Change and Continuity: A Reader on Pre-Confederation Canada*, ed. Carol Wilton (Toronto: McGraw-Hill Ryerson, 1992), 194.

25. See "Kerr, William Johnson," *Dictionary of Canadian Biography* 7:466–67.

26. Excerpt from London [Upper Canada] *Sun*, Ontario Archives, MS. 38 (49). Reel 3-680, C.O. 42/417: 51.

27. Ibid., 55–56. Mackenzie complained bitterly that in Kerr's trial, "the person who tried the case [Judge James Buchanan Macaulay] and the person who conducted the case for the crown [solicitor general Christopher Hagerman] were the two counsel for the parties who destroyed my types in 1826!" Mackenzie's son-in-law noted, however, that Macaulay "showed the greatest impartiality on the trial." Charles Lindsey, *William Lyon Mackenzie* (Toronto, 1909), 220.

28. Chris Raible, *Muddy York Mud: Scandal & Scurrility in Upper Canada* (Creemore, Ont.: Curiosity House, 1992), 91.

29. Armstrong, "York Riots," 69.

30. The apprentice had fired a gun into the crowd. Accounts differed as to whether it was

loaded with type or whether it merely contained powder intended to frighten the crowd. According to Armstrong, FitzGibbon tried to arrest Mackenzie "for his own protection," but ultimately entrusted the editor to the care of some of his friends and in fact conducted Mackenzie home. Armstrong, "York Riots," 70.

31. In the interests of keeping order, FitzGibbon reportedly threatened to call out the troops. The *Colonial Advocate* reported that "Magistrates sat up all night in the police office; Special Constables were sworn in. A voluntary guard of the towns-people watched at the Advocate Office and Mr. Mackenzie's house." Quoted in Armstrong, "York Riots," 71; Leslie, "Diary," 195.

32. Graeme H. Patterson, "Studies in Elections and Public Opinion in Upper Canada" (Ph.D. diss., University of Toronto, 1969), 111.

33. Ibid., 110–11.

34. See Carol Wilton, "'The People Shall have Their Associations Also': William Lyon Mackenzie and the Upper Canadian Petitioning Movement of 1831–32," (forth-coming).

35. Barry Wright, "The Ideological Dimensions of Law: The Treason Proceedings of 1838," *Criminal Justice History: An International Annual* 10 (1989): 131–78, is the best source on this subject. Compare Allan Greet, *The Patriots and the People: The Rebellion of 1817 in Rural Lower Canada* (Toronto: University of Toronto Press, 1993), chap. 11.

36. The earl of Durham, a major British politician, was appointed governor general of British North America by the British government in the wake of the 1837 rebellions. Charged with the task of advising on needed political changes, Lord Durham in his report of January 1839 recommended the implementation of responsible government, which implied party government, cabinet government, and a measure of local autonomy within the British empire. See Gerald M. Craig, *Upper Canada 1784–1841: The Formative Years* (Toronto: McClelland and Stewart, 1963), 257–70. On the Durham meetings, see Wilton, "'Firebrand,'" 346–75.

37. *Toronto Examiner*, Oct. 23, 1839; Ontario Archives, Mackenzie-Lindsey Clippings, no. 448. On Jarvis, see Robert J. Burns, "Jarvis, William Botsford," *Dictionary of Canadian Biography* 9:411–12.

38. *Toronto Examiner*, Oct. 30. 1839; Ontario Archives, Mackenzie-Lindsey Clippings, no. 448.

39. Ibid.

40. *Toronto Examiner*, Oct. 27, 1841.

41. See Donald Harman Akenson, *The Irish in Ontario: A Study in Rural History* (Kingston and Montreal: McGill-Queen's University Press, 1984), 166–68.

42. Its lodges also served its members as social centers. Cecil J. Houston and William J. Smyth, *The Sash Canada Wore: A Historical Geography of the Orange Order in Canada* (Toronto: University of Toronto Press, 1980), 8–14.

43. Gowan initiated his leadership of the Irish of Leeds by launching an attack on the magistrates of the district and on "native Canadians" (non-immigrants), according to articles in the *Brockville Recorder*, Jan. 17 and May 23, 1833. The authorities, who

might have been expected to be hostile as a result, were nevertheless remarkably tolerant of Gowan's disruptive activities in the period 1834–36. See Akenson, *Irish in Ontario*, 176ff.; Patterson, "Elections and Public Opinion," 266–68. See also Hereward Senior, "Gowan, Ogle Robert," *Dictionary of Canadian Biography* 10:309–14. Compare with Scott W. See, *Riots in New Brunswick: Orange Nativism and Social Violence in the 1840s* (Toronto: University of Toronto Press, 1993).

44. When Orange violence broke out at the 1834 poll for Leeds, the returning officer, Sheriff Adiel Sherwood, refused to intervene on the bizarre grounds that his authority did not extend beyond the hustings. At the new elections in March 1835, the returning officer declared Gowan and his running mate elected on the first day of a poll that was supposed to go on for six days; Orange violence had made further polling impossible. Akenson, *Irish in Ontario*, 183–87.

45. Sean Gerard Conway, "Upper Canadian Orangeism in the Nineteenth Century: Aspects or a Pattern of Disruption" (M.A. thesis, Queen's University, 1977), 47; Akenson, *Irish in Ontario,* 176.

46. Robert Davis, *The Canadian Farmer's Travels,* 14. Quoted in Fred Landon, *Eastern Ontario and the American Frontier* (1941: reprint Toronto: McClelland and Stewart, 1967), 152.

47. See W. James S. Mood. "The Orange Order in Canadian Politics 1841–1867" (M.A. thesis, University of Toronto, 1950), 31; by 1843, a reform organizer in Belleville (Victoria district) was reporting that "our opponents ... have resorted to the orange system for organization." John Ross to Robert Baldwin, Metropolitan Toronto Central Library, Baldwin Room, Robert Baldwin Papers, A68#37.

48. Conway, "Upper Canadian Orangeism," 51. Duncombe was a leader of the rebellion in the southwest of Upper Canada in 1837; see Michael S. Cross, "Duncombe, Charles," *Dictionary of Canadian Biography* 9:228–32.

49. Lesslie, "Diary," 195.

50. On Duggan, see Barrie Dyster, "Duggan, George," *Dictionary of Canadian Biography* 10:262–63.

51. *Toronto Patriot,* Oct. 31, 1834.

52. *Brockville Recorder*, Aug. 8, 1839; *British Colonist,* July 24, 31, and Aug. 7, 1839; *St. Catharines Journal*, Aug. 7 and Sept. 5, 1830; *Bytown Gazette,* Sept. 11, 1839.

53. Baker, "'So Elegant a Web," 190, 197–98.

54. Baker sometimes implies that the beliefs of the types rioters were a specialized subset of those held by members of the colony's elite more generally. The point of this article, however, is to explore the worldview of the legal elite specifically.

55. Quoted in Romney, *Mr. Attorney,* 110.

56. Ontario Archives, R.G. 5. A1, Upper Canada Sundries, Circuit Report, J. B. Macaulay, York, Oct. I, 1832. I am indebted to Peter Oliver of Toronto's York University for this reference.

57. Patrick Brode, *Sir John Beverley Robinson: Bone and Sinew of the Compact* (Toronto: The Osgoode Society, 1984).

58. Donald J. McMahon, "Law and Public Authority: Sir John Beverley Robinson and

the Purposes of Criminal Law," *University of Toronto Faculty Law Review* 46 (Spring 1988): 410–11, 414–15.

59. Quoted in Gregory S. Kealey, "Orangemen and the Corporation:' in *Forging a Consensus: Historical Essays on Toronto*, ed. Victor L. Russell (City of Toronto Sesquicentennial Board, 1984), 59.

60. Romney, "Types Riot," 135; See also Romney, "Very Late Loyalist Fantasies."

61. Romney, *Mr. Attorney,* 133–39.

62. The independence of the judiciary will be considered later.

63. Romney, "Very Late Loyalist Fantasies," 124.

64. E. P. Thompson, *Whigs and Hunters: The Origin of the Black Act* (New York: Pantheon Books, 1975), 265.

65. Idem, *The Making of the English Working Class* (1963; reprint Harmondsworth. Middlesex, England: Penguin Books, 1968), 121–23, 126–27; Alan Booth, "Popular loyalism and public violence in the north-west of England 1790–1800," *Social History* 8 (1983): 295–313. Also of interest is Clive Elmsley, "Repression, 'terror' and the rule of law in England during the decade of The French Revolution," *English Historical Review* 100 (1985): 801–25.

66. Thompson, *Working Class,* 746–65.

67. Barry Goldwater, acceptance speech, Republican presidential nomination, July 16, 1964.

68. Quoted in Greenwood, *Legacies of Fear,* 27.

69. Ibid., 27–28.

70. Ibid., 29.

71. Ibid., 257.

72. Romney, *Mr. Attorney*, 151.

73. Greenwood, *Legacies of Fear,* 28; Romney, *Mr. Attorney,* 151.

74. Wright, "Sedition in Upper Canada: Contested Legality," *Labour/Le Travail* 29 (1992): 17–18.

75. Ibid., 32–38.

76. See J. B. Robinson. *Canada and the Canada Bill* (London. 1840; Johnson Reprint 1967).

77. Wright, "Sedition in Upper Canada," 23.

78. Susan Lewthwaite, "Keepers of the Peace: The Magistrates of Georgina Township, 1830–1850" (unpublished paper, University of Toronto, 1987) 61–68.

79. Hartwell Bowsfield, "Upper Canada in the 1820s: The Development of a Political Consciousness" (Ph.D. diss., University of Toronto, 1976), 281.

80. John Beverley Robinson to Lieutenant Governor Maitland, May 10, 1828, quoted in Wright, "Sedition in Upper Canada," 45.

81. Ibid., 48.

82. For the treatment of treason, see Wright. "Ideological Dimensions of Law," 131–77.

83. In his recent study of members of the Assembly, J. K. Johnson has stressed the strengths of the old regime in the 1830s: "dominance by established groups and families... continued or increasing militarism... and adherence to Conservative political principles," *Becoming Prominent,* 143. Others have emphasized the degree to which the old system was changing. David Mills, for example, highlighted the emergence of moderate Toryism in the 1930s. *Idea of Loyalty,* 92. The extraordinary methods resorted to by the Tories to win the 1836 election, including political campaigning by the lieutenant governor, the manufacture of votes, and electoral violence, cast some on the extent to which the composition of the 1836 assembly genuinely reflected the strength of conservatism. See Lillian E Gates, *Land Policies of Upper Canada* (Toronto: University of Toronto Press, 1968), 186–88.

84. *Colonial Advocate*, Jan. 19. 1832; *Brockville Recorder*, Jan. 19, 1832; see also handbill in Colborne to Goderich, Jan. 31, 1832, in Ontario Archives, MS. 38 (45), Reel 3–676, C.C. 42/411: 15.

85. *Cobourg Reformer*, quoted in *Brockville Recorder*, June 7, 1832.

86. G. M. Boswell to the editor of the *Cobourg Star,* Mar. 2, 1831, reprinted in the *Colonial Advocate*, Apr. 12, 1832.

87. Wilton, "'Firebrand," 348–49; Eric Jackson, "The Organization of Upper Canadian Reformers, 1818–1867," in *Historical Essays on Upper Canada*, ed. J. K. Johnson (Toronto: McClelland and Stewart, 1975), 96–121.

88. Romney, "Types Riot," 139.

89. See generally Carol Wilton [Siegel], "The Transformation of Upper Canadian Politics in the 1840s" (Ph.D. diss., University of Toronto, 1985), and Mills, *The Idea of Loyalty.*

90. Kealey, "Orangemen," 41 passim, The Rebellion Losses Bill was passed in the Assembly of the United Canadas in Montreal in 1849. Intended to meet the claims of those who had suffered losses during the 1837 rebellion in Lower Canada, it aroused the fury of conservatives who believed that its effect would be to "compensate" many rebels. When governor general Lord Elgin accepted the bill on April 25. 1849, his carriage was stoned. That night, an angry mob burned the parliament buildings in Montreal. In Toronto in 1849, there were several outbursts of conservative disorder occasioned by the passage of the Rebellion Losses Bill, including effigy burnings of William Lyon Mackenzie and Lord Elgin, and a riot.

91. Conway, "Orange Order," 47–51.

92. Carol Wilton, "Crime in Mid-Nineteenth Century Toronto" (unpublished paper, University of Toronto, 1977), 26, 34–35.

93. Kealey. "Orangemen," 69.

94. See Richard B. Anderson, "Respectability vs. Rowdyism: Non-Material Culture, Ideology, and Geography in Victoria County Ontario 1860–1880" (M.A. thesis, York University, 1984).

95. See Wilton, "Crime Rates," 32; W. A. Richardson, "Crime and the Labouring Community in Toronto, 1870–1891" (research paper, University of Toronto. 1976), 31; V. A. C. Gattrell and T. B. Hadden, "Criminal Statistics and Their Interpretation" in *Nineteenth-Century Society: Essays in the Use of Quantitative Methods for the Study of Social Data,* ed. E. A. Wrigley (Cambridge. England: Cambridge University Press, 1972). 336–94; Lawrence Stone, "Interpersonal Violence in English Society

1300–1980," *Past and Present* (1983): 22–33; J. A. Sharpe, "Debate: The History of Violence in England: Some Observations," *Past and Present* (1985): 206–15.

96. The Winnipeg General Strike of 1919, the most impressive display of labor unrest in Canadian history, essentially closed down the city from May 15 to June 21, 1919. In an effort to break the strike, ten of its leaders were arrested on June 16. The arrests, undertaken without proper authority, were actually illegal, as federal minister of justice Arthur Meighen acknowledged. Meighen wrote the agent of the ministry in Winnipeg: "Notwithstanding any doubt I have as to the technical legality of the arrest and the detention at Stony Mountain [penitentiary], I feel that rapid deportation is the best course now that the arrests are made, and later we can consider ratification." Quoted in Norman Penner, ed., *Winnipeg 1919: The strikers' own history of the Winnipeg General Strike* (Toronto: James Lewis & Samuel, 1973), 235–36.

97. The most notorious episode was the burning or a barn near Montreal in 1972 by the Royal Canadian Mounted Police (federal security force), an action directed against the separatists. See John Sawatsky, *Men in the Shadows: The RCMP Security Service* (Toronto: Doubleday Canada, 1980), 282. For routine police violence in an earlier era, see Greg Marquis, "'A Machine of Oppression Under the Guise of the Law': The Saint John [New Brunswick] Police Establishment." *Acadiensis* 16 (Autumn 1986): 63.

A DISCOURSE OF PROTEST: THE PATRIOTES DECADE (1828–1838)

Gérald Bernier and Daniel Salée

So far, our presentation has made it appear as if there was no resistance to the hegemony of the landowning class. It might also seem that the totality of social relations encompassed those between the peasantry, be they *censitaires* or residents of the townships, and landowners. In a sense, this comes as no surprise in that throughout previous chapters, emphasis has been on the fact that precapitalist relations of production were dominant and that the fundamental classes of the social formation were the various strata of the peasantry and the landowning class. As the period is one of transition to capitalism, other social groups or class segments were found, such as a small number of capitalist entrepreneurs and a working class in the making. Also present were artisans, various categories of merchants, storekeepers, maid servants, servants, and so on. Not much resistance emanated from these quarters, except the peasantry and, at times, the working class (Palmer, 1987).

The pervasiveness of the *ancien régime* character of Lower Canadian society did not go unchallenged. During the early 1820s, a new discourse emerged

From *The Shaping of Quebec Politics and Society: Colonialism, Power, and the Transition to Capitalism in the 19th Century* (Washington: Crane Russak, 1992), 99–123. Reprinted by permission.

among elements of the petite bourgeoisie, namely, members of the liberal professions, and to a lesser degree, storekeepers, retail merchants, small entrepreneurs, and artisans. They were regrouped in what first came to be known as the Patriote movement and, as of 1827, the Patriote party. Their ideological discourse has varied according to conjuncture, but in essence at one moment or another, it called for an alternative project of society resting on absolute political sovereignty, the abolition of *ancien régime* social, economic, and political structures, and the establishment of a liberal democracy.

This Patriote resistance found its expression in the House of Assembly, which was controlled by those elements belonging to the petite bourgeoisie. This institutional resistance took on many forms over the years, with gradual radicalization taking place, as follows: (a) opposition to measures taken by the Governor and his Executive Council; (b) opposition to the dictates of the Colonial Office; (c) introduction of bills aimed at reforming various aspects of colonial administration, most notably in the fields of landownership and land management practices; (d) attempts at decentralizing political authority by the creation of elective local institutions; and (e) paralysis of the colonial government through refusal to vote appropriations necessary to pay the civil servants and the government's daily operations. This last action brought dissolution of the House of Assembly by the Governor in 1836. The House was never to sit again because the Rebellions put an end to the institutional régime introduced by the Constitutional Act of 1791. Even more radical actions were taken during the years 1837—1838 as the Patriote party transformed itself into a revolutionary movement and engaged in direct confrontation with British authorities.

The question of Patriotes being at the forefront of resistance brings to light an interesting analytical point to be explained by the colonial status of the Lower Canadian social formation. As events unfolded, leading to the armed confrontations of 1837 and 1838, it would become apparent that in Lower Canada an attempted bourgeois revolution was waged without the presence of a true bourgeoisie in its midst. As previously discussed, one of the distortive effects of colonial rule was the absence in the colony of an emerging industrial bourgeoisie that in self-sustaining developed societies was the spearhead of challenges to the landed aristocracy's economic hegemony and its sociopolitical order. Consequently, in the absence of such an industrial bourgeoisie, the torch of liberalism was borne by the petite bourgeoisie. But what about the merchants, a social group more commonly associated by the historiography with the advent of capitalism in Canada? Representatives of commercial interests—the so-called commercial or merchant "bourgeoisie," according to numerous authors—were completely pledged to the large landowners and partook in their socioeconomic order and worldview. They had subsumed themselves to landed interests. No challenge of the existing facets of the *ancien régime* order was to be expected from them. Their entrenchment in support of the established order was in total conformity with their economic class interests and position within the dominant relations of production. Their livelihood depended on the maintenance of the colonial link. As such, they had no interest whatsoever in severing colonial ties.

In such a context, it is hardly surprising that themes, which in European social formations had been formulated and espoused by the nascent industrial bourgeoisie, were professed in Lower Canada by elements of the petite bourgeoisie. This somehow poses a challenge to historians because they must search for the intelligibility of the revolutionary movement beyond the perception its participants had of it. The logic of a revolution is not to be found in the actions of a class or an élite, whatever its role may be. Rather, the meaning of historical reality must be looked for in the social processes, in the existing structures, and other objective conditions that trigger action.

In terms of analytical perspective, there are four ways to apprehend the period. The 1830s and, more specifically, the rebellions of 1837 and 1838 can be seen as (1) an expression of the national questions, that is, an ethnic conflict between French- and English-speaking Canadians; (2) a struggle for national liberations, that is, liberating Lower Canada from its colonial status and gaining full economic and political independence from Britain; (3) a manifestation of the transition to capitalism and to a liberal democratic polity; (4) and a frontal assault on the institutions, social relations, political structures, power relationships, and practices of social control of an *ancien régime* that had previously and continued to dominate Lower Canadian society. Our position rests on a combination of the latter three categories of factors.

Following this composite perspective, we interpret actions of the petite bourgeoisie as a function of a societal environment governed by a colonial and imperialistic frame of economic exploitation and the presence of authoritarian structures and practices of power. Indeed, the functions and mechanisms of the Lower Canadian state were geared toward the redeployment of the social hegemony of the large landowners. As seen in Chapter 3, the Legislative and Executive Councils as well as important sections of the judiciary and public service were the almost exclusive preserve of large landowners or of their representatives; they unequivocally operated on the basis of *ancien régime* principles. Similarly, the more informal means of social control (such as the moral authority of the parish priest) or the untold pressure to comply with certain accepted social behavior—always very strong in small rural communities (Chabot, 1975; Gagnon and Hardy, 1979)—also reinforced social relations that characterized an *ancien régime* civil society.

This *ancien régime* societal environment should be at the core of any explanation of events taking place during the 1830s. It is more appropriate to assess these events as attempts to overthrow a precapitalist economic régime and social order and to instigate the development of capitalism and liberal democracy. The Rebellions and the preceding period called into question all of the societal structures and practices.

The British authorities' reaction to the Rebellions must be interpreted along similar lines. Military retaliation and the crushing of the Rebellions were not only reactive measures to a challenge of colonial rule but an action to ensure the re-production of the social hegemony exercised by the agents of landed property. Through its military arm, the state intervened to preserve, against increasingly pressing attacks by antifeudal social agents, the types of social relations essential to the reproduction of a feudal/mercantile socioeconomic order.

The analysis of the Rebellions' gains if the events are understood as part and manifestation of the transition process taking place during the period under study. It also sheds light on some of the complexities and contradictions occurring during such a period. Finally, it puts to rest any claim as to the progressive character—in the Creightonian sense—of the so-called merchant bourgeoisie. It can no longer be argued that this social group existed independently from its landowning allies as a duly formed bourgeois class. Nor can it be claimed that because of the "nationalist" character of the Patriotes' action, and as a show of loyalty to the British Crown, merchants were somehow "forced" to entrench themselves in a position of support for the régime and its established order. The mask falls and they are shown for what they were: part and parcel of that order.

We favor such an analytical path and contend that it offers more explanatory power than the one resting on the national question concept, which has been dominant, as readers will later see, in the historiography of the Rebellions. The transition to capitalism from a precapitalist or feudal mode of productions has not really been fully exploited in relation to the Rebellions of 1837–1838. Only Stanley B. Ryerson (1968) alludes to it, but without systematic recourse, in order to characterize the period during which the revolutionary process takes place. Yet the very idea of transition is pertinent because it corresponds to a vivid socioeconomic reality in Lower Canada.

A glance at the material conditions of the period enables one to actually determine that the insurrections and other forms of agitation took place at the moment when the transition to industrial capitalism was gaining in intensity. The progressive advance of petty commodity production toward the manufacturing stage, and the gradual proletarianization of certain strata of the rural population (expropriated peasants unable to meet their debts, or sons of peasants denied access to small landed property) and of urban dwellers (small artisans reduced to the ranks of employees), all pointed to the emergence of relations of production portending industrial capitalism. But what was more significant still, was that those phenomena attested to the existence of social relations whose logic was in complete opposition to Lower Canada's dominant merchant/feudalistic societal structures; an antagonism present not only in the economic sphere but also in social, political, and ideological practices and relations.

It is because this antagonism expressed a global social process that the notion of transition is so fruitful; it points to a moment of reversal or substantial transformation of the dominance exercised by a given socioeconomic order. Inasmuch as it relates to a sizable portion of nineteenth-century Lower Canadian historical reality, the notion of transition stresses the existence of a complex and conflictual sociopolitical conjuncture that is not foreign to the turmoil of the 1830s and its final outcome in 1837–1838. Again, the insurrections indicate that Lower Canada was pervaded by a profound, highly contradictory societal dynamic, too complex to be limited analytically to the narrow confines of politics or a nationalist struggle between French and English. The Patriotes were not to be happy with a simple refurbishing of the colonial edifice; theirs was a frontal attack on the global societal foundations and configuration of power on which Lower Canadian society rested. At its radical apex, the insurrectionary project produced an intensely political determination to topple the traditional *ancien régime* structures of domination and objurgated all the elements constituting the dominant mode of social interrelationship. With its denunciations of the prevalent systems of landownership, the 1838 Declaration of Independence signified in no uncertain terms that the Patriotes wanted to build a new kind of society in which social relations would be completely redefined along levelling principles.

As we deal with further when we analyze the Patriotes' discourse, degradation of relations with Britain eventually led to a call for severance of the colonial tie. Some analysts have confused, when not completed ignored, this form of nationalism with an internal conflict opposing the two founding ethnic groups; we prefer referring to it as a struggle for national liberation. The national question as an analytical tool for the apprehension of nineteenth-century Québec political dynamics has been dealt with at length in our introductory chapter. Here, we need to address briefly only those direct contributions to the discussion of the limits of such an approach.

The National Question Approach, or Putting One's Foot into the Wrong Shoe

Without making it a blanket statement, one must acknowledge that Canadian Francophone and Anglophone historians have tended to represent the Rebellions of 1837–1838 in terms of an ethnic conflict between the French and the English of Lower Canada. For the most part, this approach appears to be an anachronistic view. Good literature surveys can be found in Bernard (1983, pp. 17–62), Ouellet (1984), and Salée (1980, pp. 11–48).

The "national question" interpretation leaves little room for socioeconomic considerations, much less for the overall societal context in which the Rebellions occurred. Interpretations stressing the ethnic factor overstate this dimension and dilute the genuine meaning of the Rebellions.

The traditional historiographical imagination has generally tended to depict the events leading to the civil outbreak of 1837 in narrow institutional terms as though they were the unhappy conclusion of a straightforward struggle for political power turned sour. In a sense, this intellectual bias is understandable: The events concluded a series of political confrontations that almost always remained on the institutional terrain. Until the fateful Russell resolutions of March 1837, the Patriotes had consistently vented their claims and demands within the parliamentary arena and other legal channels (often, much to their own frustration). Yet, the meaning of the insurrections must be sought outside strict institutional parameters. These events require a broader interpretative analytical framework, one that considers other societal dimensions, such as the economic sphere, dominant social relations of production, the nature of the state, and the features of the exercise of state power. As such, the national question approach has little value in explaining the 1837–1838 Rebellions in Lower Canada. Thus, we prefer an analytical model that focuses on the assault by the Patriotes on the *ancien régime* order during the transition to capitalism and democratic government.

The Anglophone presence within the Patriotes ranks is a theme that received little attention in the historiography of the Rebellions. Although the great majority of members of the Patriote party were French-speaking, there was nonetheless a significant Anglophone representation, especially in the leadership of the party. Without making much of this phenomenon, Bernard (1983, p.323) estimates Anglophone representation at 7.8 percent for the whole of Lower Canada, and at about 25 percent and 7 percent for the cities of Montréal and Québec, respectively.

The Anglophone endorsement of the Patriote cause rested on the sharing of an ideology and, more particularly, on the convergence of class interests. The prominent Anglophone members (John Neilson, the Nelson brothers, Edmund O'Callaghan, T. S. Brown, Daniel Tracey, W. H. Scott, etc.) were recruited among the same social strata as their French counterparts, namely, the various elements of the petite bourgeoisie. In this sense, the ethnic factor was not strong enough to mask the sharing of common interests and to prevent a social bond from emerging (Bernier, 1982, pp. 214–215). Anglophones were not merely confined to leadership positions within the party; they also were part of the Patriote electorate, with intense support stemming from the Irish segment of the Anglophone community, especially in urban settings (Galarneau, 1979). Among French Canadians, peasants were very prone to support the party, whereas among other occupational categories, support was less massive, thereby indicating that socioeconomic factors took precedence over the ethnic dimension.

In view of the contours of current historiography, Bernard's figures regarding Anglophone representation in the party are astonishing. One would imagine that both the nationalist and antinationalist schools of interpretation need explaining. For the nationalists, the Patriote episode was essentially limited to the confines of the French community, whereas for the antinationalists no Englishman in his right mind would have joined the movement. As for Marxists, they are still looking for the constitutive elements of a working class to confirm that the Rebellions were the result of an aborted capitalist bourgeois revolution. Inasmuch as a bourgeoisie existed, there also had to be a working class or proletariat (Ryerson, 1968; Vance, 1964–1965).

Dominant historiography of the Rebellions of 1837–1838 in Lower Canada has tended to view the events as an expression of conflict between the forces of progress (i.e., English Canadians) and those opposed to progress and nostalgic for the French *ancien régime* (i.e., French Canadians (Creighton, 1970; Ouellet, 1968,

1971). As expressed by Ouellet, "their real objective was to restore, despite their rationalizations borrowed from liberal and democratic ideologies, an *ancien régime* society on the banks of the St. Lawrence" (Ouellet, 1971, p. 434). Ouellet is also too quick in equating nationalism and conservatism. The Patriote nationalism cannot be taken to connote any xenophobic meaning. The general Patriote discourse was undeniably couched in nationalistic overtones but these reflected an anticolonialist discourse that ultimately voiced the interests of all the Lower Canadian people, and not exclusively the French Canadian nationality. It may be that the situation was more complex than appeared at first glance and that the liberalism professed by the Patriotes was sincere and less manipulative than Ouellet would wished it to be. It may also be that socioeconomic stakes transcended the national questions. There is no denial that antagonisms between the French and English communities occurred at times, but to predicate the whole decade on such a conflict is a different matter altogether. The national questions, as understood in present-day terms, had little to do with the Patriote cause of the 1830s. At stake, in nationalistic terms, was an expression of the will to break with colonial ties. A number of Anglophones could and did subscribe to this goal. On numerous occasions the French Canadian press made it clear that actions undertaken during the 1830s were directed at British colonial rule and their local representatives rather than against their fellow countrymen of British origin. An article in *La Minerve* makes a clear point of it:

> There are in this country a great number of respectable Englishmen that the country acknowledges because of community of interests; the country finds among those honest citizens a large number of defenders of its rights, and is most grateful to them. French Canadians do not want an exclusive control of power; they have no national hatred against the English, and as soon as a countryman of English origin shows that is a truly inhabitant of this country, there is no longer any difference. (*La Minerve*, April 2, 1835; our translation)

If, as additional proof of the nonsectarian nature of the Patriotes' struggle against imperial authorities, parts of two resolutions voted in electoral district meetings held in the spring of 1837 are reproduced, as well as an account of a public gathering of British and Irish reformists in Québec City:

> [W]e are calling for unity between the inhabitants of this Province regardless of creed, language, and origin.... We have never supported and have, on the contrary, always disapproved of those unfortunate national distinctions that our common enemies have sought and maliciously seek to stir up among us. We openly claim that the fact put forth in reports transmitted to Her Majesty's government according to which the struggle here was between citizens of British origin and those of Canadian [i.e., French Canadian] origin, is a malicious information denied by the well-known disposition of Canadian inhabitants.... (Bernard 1988: 52–53)

> Resolved that the opposition of the people of this province is based solely on principles of equity and good government. We refute the charge laid against

us by members of the Royal Commission stating that the struggle in which the inhabitants of this country are engaged is due to national prejudices.... Far from nurturing prejudices against our co-subjects of foreign origin, we are, on the contrary, (as has been demonstrated in many elections) always willing to lend our support and confidence to those among them who fight for the people's cause. (Bernard, 1988, p.58)

Almost every public meeting voted a resolution along the lines of the preceding ones. When the national question construed in its narrow sense was raised, it was most often at gatherings held by supporters of the administration (known as loyalists). Bernard's book (1988) is replete with statements raising the national question issue in those loyalist rallies.

The Vindicator reports on a meeting held in Québec City on May 15, 1837, attended by Irish and British reformists. It notes:

The meeting was confined, with a few, worthy, and honorable exceptions. to the mechanic and operative class. We are informed by our correspondent that some little noise took place at the opening of the meeting, in consequence of the presence of one of the proprietors of the *Little Herald*, well known for his unfriendly disposition, and the hostility which already characterises this journal, against reformers, particularly the British and Irish portion, who identify themselves with the Canadian people....(Bernard, 1988, pp. 42–43)

There is enough evidence to be found in the Patriote press to repudiate interpretations of the Patriote ideology and movement as (a) the expression of a wish to return to an *ancien régime* (Ouellet, 1971)—as if the *ancien régime* features of Lower Canada had vanished with the conquest; (b) the advocating of revenge (Séguin, 1968); or (c) an ultranationalist clash between two ethnic communities who share, against their will, the same territory (Filteau, 1975).

The Patriotes: From Social Movement to Political Party and Revolutionary Movement

The social forces that developed in resistance to the dominant class and its feudalistic socioeconomic order were organized and had institutions for expressing this resistance. Seldom was discontent and resistance expressed through spontaneous outbursts of mob violence in the form of riots or *jacqueries* (peasant revolts).

The creation of a House of Assembly in 1791 had quickly given rise to the formation of parliamentary groups with a rather consistent voting discipline as required under a full-fledged British parliamentary system (Hare, 1973). In this instance, such discipline was rather astonishing because responsible government had not yet been established and therefore there were no links between the government and its parliamentary wing in the Legislature, as is the case under British parliamentarism. In other words, voting discipline was not yet called for, yet it existed anyway. This points to conflictual relations between the elective branch of the Legislature and local representatives of the imperial authorities.

The French Canadian parliamentary group exhibited such cohesive voting behavior that, at the beginning of the nineteenth century, the press started referring to it as le Parti Canadien, and to the less-organized English Canadian representatives as the Bureaucrat party (Ouellet, 1971, pp. 226 et seq.). In the first case, this was clearly premature because, according to the canons of literature on the sociology of political parties they were still a parliamentary group: le Parti Canadien had no permanent structures, no membership outside the House, nor any identifiable stable leadership.

After 1827, however, this group came to be known as the Patriote party, this time with full-bloom characteristics of a modern party: permanent structures, complex organization, action directed at gaining a majority of seats, and formulation of a program with definite and coherent ideological contours (Bernier, 1982). The early appearance of a modern political party in Québec (before most other western democracies) had a lot to do with the very liberal electoral franchise contained in the Constitutional Act of 1791. The existence of the House of Assembly elected on the basis of almost universal suffrage meant that candidates had to canvass for the electorate's vote by holding meetings, printing a program or declaration of intention in the press, and so on. All of these campaign activities favored the early development of political parties.

In comparison with western European societies, in which extension of suffrage to the working class was resisted by the dominant class and was finally obtained as a result of conflicts that favored the formation of class solidarity and consciousness, liberal suffrage in Canada had different consequences. It was obtained before the formation of the working class and had undeniable effects on Canadian and Québec political culture. Some differences were the absence of a strong, working-class oriented party (especially in Québec), lack of a radical political tradition carried over into the twentieth century, and lack of political parties with strong ideological bent.

The Patriote party had all the features of a mass party with its various specialized units in which to regroup its members. The party had committees in most parishes and electoral districts. Those committees sent representatives to the Permanent Central Committee, located in Montréal. This Central Committee was divided into subcommittees, each assigned a specific mission: correspondence, information, propaganda, consultation, data gathering, and so on (Filteau, 1975, pp. 207 et seq.). Given the limited means of communication in those days, it is astounding that within two weeks the party was able to gather eighty thousand signatures in support of the Ninety-Two Resolutions expressing Patriotes' grievances in 1834 (Filteau, 1975, pp. 269 et seq.). The party had other specialized units, such as a youth wing, at least a few women's committees, control over an extensive network of newspapers covering most of the province, and such rallying symbols as a flag, banners, and various other means of identification (Filteau, 1975, p. 106).

The party functioned as such until the spring of 1837, when it became more and more apparent that what so far had been expressed without success through parliamentary means would eventually have to be resolved through an armed confrontation with British forces. Desertions abounded. Yet, by the middle of the 1830s, virtually everyone who had felt some form of dissatisfaction with the colonial régime, its economic and social policies, or with the general orientation of Lower Canadian society was a member or a sympathizer of the Patriote party. At the 1834 general election, nine out of ten voters had voted for a Patriote candidate; 77 out of the 88 seats at stake in the House of Assembly were filled by Patriotes. Because the electoral campaign had been fought on the issue of the Ninety-Two Resolutions, the outcome of the election was probably the most eloquent testimonial to the pervasiveness of the Patriote sociopolitical influence in Lower Canada. Three years later, a mere handful would embark on the insurrectionary adventure. Had the Patriotes lost their momentum? Admittedly, there is a boundary between electoral support and revolutionary action that most people would never cross under any circumstances. But the support in favor of the Patriotes remained unflagging after 1834; they maintained a well-tuned and extensive political organization in most regions. In the next chapter, we attempt an explanation as to why support foundered when the Patriotes made the move from what, so far, had been a political party and transformed themselves into a revolutionary movement.

The Course of Events and the Patriote Party's Political Discourse: From Politics to Armed Confrontation

Documents to reconstruct the Patriote discourse have been gathered from various sources: accounts of public meetings and resolutions in electoral district protest meetings (Bernard, 1988), speeches printed in newspapers, texts of bills submitted in the House of Assembly, the famous Ninety-Two Resolutions, manifestos and declarations, countless newspaper articles, and letters to the editor. Reconstruction is made somewhat difficult because as events progressed toward the insurrections of 1837–1838, the party split into ideological factions. This has enabled historians to vindicate their own views and prejudices because they were at liberty to concentrate on any given faction; thus resulted a historiography as complex and divided as the phenomenon under study.

The content of the discourse evolved during the period 1827 to 1838 and tended toward radicalization in direct proportion to the intransigence shown by British authorities in the face of expressed claims and grievances. Three factions and tones of discourse can be distinguished during this period. Between 1827 and 1834 the party was controlled by moderates and the tone of discourse reflected this. Their most important document was the Ninety-Two Resolutions, in the spring of 1834. This document contained a catalogue of grievances and proposed a series of constitutional and political reforms to be submitted to imperial authorities. Only Resolutions 52 to 62, pertaining to The Tenure Act, had an economic connotation. The debates held in the House of Assembly on the content and working of the resolutions had given rise to tensions in the party, and some prominent members walked out, among them, John Neilson, the principal party spokesman in Québec City. From then to the early fall of 1837, while they awaited a response to the Resolutions, tensions intensified and a reformist faction emerged and took control of the party. The discourse had become more extreme during this waiting period. Finally, in the fall of 1837, as armed confrontation appeared to be the most likely outcome of the Patriotes' ten-year political struggle with local administrators and British authorities, the party was taken over by a radical faction. Also, a distinction must be made between the 1837 and 1838 outbursts of violence. Though mostly made up of individuals who had taken part in the crushed rebellion of 1837, the 1838 faction of revolutionary leaders was more radical than those who had led the 1837 episode, as their Declaration of Independence attests. In addition, popular support for the 1838 rebellion was much weaker.

In the rest of the chapter, we review those three periods in more detail and pay attention to constitutional and political grievances that came to be embodied in the party platform. In a separate section, we look at the Patriotes' economic discourse through an analysis of documents found in newspapers sympathetic to the Patriote cause (Bernier, 1991a) and resolutions voted in public meetings (Bernard, 1988; Blanchette-Lessard and Daigneault-Saint Denis, 1975).

The Moderate Period: 1827 to Spring 1834

This was a time when grievances and expressions of discontent were mostly channelled through the House of Assembly. Only toward the end of that period did the debate begin to gain resonance outside of the House through holding of meetings in public places and electoral districts. On the agenda were measures designed to remedy the ills of the existing institutional system and its related practices of exercise of state power.

The Ninety-Two Resolutions of 1834 can be seen as part of this process. The Resolutions were considered as moderate inasmuch as they called for redress of perceived abuses caused by the institutional system and the practices that followed from it. In other words, the Patriotes were asking that the British authorities acknowledge some sort of social contract in recognition of the colony's attitude of neutrality during the Wars of 1775 and 1812 between Britain and the United States. Among other parliamentary institutional reforms sought by the Patriotes was the election of Members of the Legislative Council. The Patriote party also wanted to introduce reform of the legislative process whereby House Members would have more input into law making and greater control over daily administration of the colony. On this issue, their main demand was in the field of financial control. The Patriotes wanted greater control over expenditures incurred for the administrative services of the colony because those were discretionary expenses reserved for the Governor's approval and the focus of much favoritism, discrimination, and patronage (Creighton, 1931; Taft-Manning, 1943). They also sought more equitable French representation in the Executive Council, the civil service, and the magistracy. As observed in our study of political personnel, these three loci of power were the main preserve of English representatives of the colonial administration. Moreover, these were quarters in which patronage, favoritism, and corruption were particularly prominent. The Patriotes' demands were founded on the principle of equity in representation. No specific reference to the practices to which those institutions gave rise was made.

The Patriotes brought up the question of ministerial responsibility (or responsible government) a few times during this period, but not forcefully, because they were more inclined to look to a republican institutional set-up as a model for any future reform. The American model had great appeal for the Patriotes (Greenwood, 1979). This virtual indifference with regard to ministerial responsibility is somewhat puzzling, because it meant that the Governor and his Executive Council would have been held responsible and accountable before the elective branch of the Legislature.

The Reformist Period: Spring 1834 to Early Fall 1837

As the Patriotes awaited an answer to the Ninety-Two Resolutions, tensions mounted within the party and among the population. In the House, during the fall of 1836, the Patriotes introduced all sorts of reform bills and launched the equivalent of a parliamentary strike by refusing to vote the necessary appropriations for the functioning of the administration. The Governor had no choice but to call for adjournment of the session. The consequences of such an action were serious because the struggle would no longer be contained mostly in the House of Assembly but was forced out into the streets.

The British response came in the spring of 1837 in a document that came to be known as the Russell Resolutions. These resolutions were sent to the Governor and made public. All of the Patriotes' demands met with an emphatic "No." Based on the report of the Commission sent to investigate the claims of the Ninety-Two Resolutions, the Russell Resolutions: (a) declared the creation of an elective Legislative Council inopportune; (b) rejected the proposal of a responsible Executive Council; (c) maintained the British American Land Company; (d) authorized the Governor to take funds that the Assembly had refused to grant from revenues in the Receiver-General's hands; (e) provided for the cession of the Crown revenues to the Assembly if the latter granted the civil list; and (f) urged the Legislatures of Upper and Lower Canada to settle their common interests (Wade, 1968, p. 157).

Reaction in the colony was sharp and unequivocal. For instance, Edmund Bailey O'Callaghan, an Irish-born supporter of Louis-Joseph Papineau—the leader of the Patriote party—and editor of Montréal's The Vindicator, wrote in no uncertain terms in his newspaper:

A combined and dishonorably junction of Whigs and Tories, in a House of Commons 'reformed' but in name, may pass Resolutions to annihilate the last remnant of Liberty left in the colonial Legislatures. A House of Lords, the fundamental principle of whose Constitution is inimical to human freedom, may endorse the determination of the combined enemies of freedom in the Lower House, but neither the Resolutions, their authors, nor their supporters, can change the nature of things. *Robbery will be robbery still....* Our rights must not be violated with impunity. A howl of indignation must be raised from one extremity of the Province to the other, against the robbers, and against all who partake of the plunder. Henceforth, there must be no peace in the Province—*no quarter for the plunderers.* Agitate! Agitate!! Agitate!!! Destroy the Revenue; denounce the oppressors. Everything is lawful when the fundamental liberties are in danger. The guards die—they never surrender. (Wade, 1968, p. 158; original emphasis)

O'Callaghan had always been one to favor resorting to violence in order to bring the colonial government to its knees. His passionate appeal was finally to be heeded when a few weeks later, a round of protest meetings was inaugurated in the Richelieu Valley village of Saint-Ours. Between the months of May and October 1837 countless meetings were held in numerous parishes all over the province. They were the preamble to the violent outburst of the fall of 1837 and winter of 1838.

The resolutions passed at those meetings unequivocally challenged the legitimacy of the government and the colonial tie. Although an extension of the claims and demands was already contained in the Ninety-Two Resolutions of 1834, the tone of these new resolutions, however, was much more radical and translated a deeply felt frustration at the manner in which the Lower Canadian polity had been administered. On several occasions, some of the speakers invited to address the meetings would openly call for armed action. Weeks before the first armed confrontations, the speeches at protest rallies had become more vindictive and more virulent. Violent action seemed the only way out. A few leaders would claim that "Time has come to melt our pewter pots and spoons in order to make bullets out of them" or again, "The time for speeches has passed, now we must send lead to our enemies" (Filteau, 1975, p. 275).

The Saint-Ours resolutions were to serve as a model for the following meetings. Dubbed the *Déclaration de Saint-Ours*, they were, according to one historian, as significant in the context of 1837 Québec as the Declaration of the Continental Congress was in the American colonies of 1774, or the *Déclaration des droits de l'Homme et du citoyen* in 1789 France (Filteau, 1975, p. 213). Most of the Saint-Ours and other resolutions passed in the ensuing months at other meetings echoed Rousseauian notions of liberty and several paragraphs of the French *Déclaration des droits de l'Homme.* Constant references to the social contract and to the imperatives of the sovereignty of the people (as opposed to the rule of one individual) ran through the pre-insurrectionary discourse.

The *Déclaration de Saint-Ours* expressed a certain defiance toward Britain but, at the same time, it left the door open to some form of compromise as both tone and words were cautious. They conveyed the impression that the slightest gesture of goodwill on the part of London would result in a conciliatory stance from the Patriotes and in the stoppage of various measures of civil disobedience that had begun to take place as a result of resolutions adopted at public meetings. Among those measures was a boycott of British products and the nonconsumption of imported products from other British colonies; and the intensification of the smuggling trade with the United States. Maintenance of these measures was reiterated in the *Déclaration de Saint-Ours*. Otherwise, the Declaration contained all the ingredients for assertion of colonial autonomy but stopped just short of taking that ultimate step. Its authors knew full well that they could not win an armed confrontation with British forces. The Declaration stated:

> We deny the British Parliament's right to legislate on internal matters regarding this colony without our consent and participation.... We now consider ourselves being linked to the British government by force alone and as such we will submit to it, *expecting from God, our own rights and circumstances a better fate, freedom and a fairer government.... It is our duty and honor to resist* by every means at our disposal a tyrannical power in order for us to reduce as much as possible those means of oppression. (Latouche, 1977, pp. 71–72; our emphasis)

Portions of the Declaration convey that if the Patriotes' demands were to be dealt with by a more liberal and conciliatory government that should come to power in Britain, some sort of agreement could be reached. For instance:

> In these circumstances [following the Russell Resolutions] we cannot regard a government which would have recourse to injustice, to force, and to a violation of the social contract, as but an oppressive power, a government by force, for which the measure of our submission should from now on solely be determined by our numerical force, to which could be added the support we will find elsewhere [i.e., the United States].... The high esteem in which we held the British people for their sense of justice and honor made us hope that the parliament which represents it would positively remedy our grievances. (Latouche, 1977, pp. 71–72)

Throughout the late spring, summer, and early fall of 1837, Patriotes rallies were being regularly held, more or less hammering out the same themes. At times, matters not previously discussed would arise, such as (a) the creation of local institutions either through election of parish councils or the setting up of municipal governments; (b) provisions for secret ballot for electing members of the House of Assembly; and (c) easier access to primary education.

This period ends with the advance to the forefront of the most radical elements of the party, as the Manifesto, put out by the youth wing known as *Les Fils de la Liberté*, demonstrates, in a similar fashion to their counterpart during the American Revolution. Their manifesto calls for the severance of the colonial tie with Britain and the establishment of independent rule in Lower Canada. The newly created State would be free to choose its political institutional régime. It then states:

> The authority of a mother-country over its colony can exist as long as it enjoys the consent of the colonists, for having been established and populated by these colonists, their country is theirs by right and consequently may be severed from all external connection whenever inconveniences, resulting from an executive power located thousands of miles away which ceases to be in harmony with the local legislature, render such an outcome necessary for its inhabitants in order to protect their lives, their liberties or to acquire prosperity.... A separation has now begun between colonists and the mother-country. It will never be possible to cement that union once again. This separation will only accelerate until unexpected and unforeseen events such as occur occasionally in these times, offer us a favorable opportunity to take our place in the ranks of the sovereign countries of the Americas. (Latouche, 1977, pp. 76–77)

The responsibility for this outcome—should it occur—rests on the shoulders of imperial authorities.

> Our connection with Britain has been betrayed by British authorities, and for us it would be criminal and a show of our dispositions towards servitude if our resistance was to be limited to petitions.... It is our task to pursue our forefathers' projects and to immediately liberate our dear country from all human authority other than a sound democracy installed in its midst. (Latouche, 1977, p. 77)

Again, as these elements of the Patriotes' discourse demonstrate, this is far from the narrow interpretation of those events in terms of an ethnic conflict between French and English residents of Lower Canada. Much more is at stake.

The Radical Period: From Early Fall 1837 to Winter 1838

A few weeks after publication of *Les Fils de la Liberté's* manifesto, the party took on the traits of a revolutionary national liberation movement. As each day went by and the likelihood of recourse to violence grew stronger, defections were numerous among moderates and reformists. In the late fall of 1837, ten years of political struggle with the imperial authorities and their local representatives found their inevitable conclusion in numerous armed confrontations between a disorganized Patriote revolutionary movement and British forces that had been reinforced by a new contingent during the summer. The Patriotes were trounced; the leadership was on the run and those eventually caught were condemned to capital punishment or to exile for high treason. In 1838, a small group of rebels who had taken refuge in the United States attempted a second rebellion with no more success than the previous year. Led by Robert Nelson, this group was marginal (when looked at in the general context of the party's eleven-year existence) and professed the most radical ideas and propositions formulated during the decade. They established a provisional government under Robert Nelson and issued a *Déclaration d'independance*. At this point, the Patriote discourse transcended its traditionally political content to encompass a more global societal perspective. While bringing the resolutions of the 1837 protest meetings a step further and announcing the termination of Lower Canada's allegiance to the British Crown, the *Déclaration d'independance* addressed more social and, in many respects, larger issues. The document decreed the separation of Church and State, with the consequent suppression of the tithe and the creation of state-run schools; and the abolition of the seigneurial system, the death penalty (except for murder), and imprisonment for debt. It proclaimed freedom of the press, universal manhood suffrage (including the Indians, who were given all the rights of citizenship), and the secret ballot. It ordered the nationalization of the Crown lands and those of the British American Land Company. A Constitution was to be drafted and subject to popular ratification. Both the French and the English languages were to be used for all public affairs. The Declaration stated that Lower Canada was to become a republic and take on the republican form of government, and that this government would be responsible to the people (Latouche, 1977, pp. 79–80). Article 1 of the Declaration was unequivocal:

> In the name of the people of Lower Canada... we solemnly declare that as of this day, the People of Lower Canada is relieved from any allegiance to Great Britain and that all political connection between it and Lower Canada Ceases this day. (Latouche, 1977, p. 79; emphasis in the original)

Our analysis of the Patriote party's political discourse shows that it fluctuated according to power relations within the party. Overall, it tended to be a moderate project aimed at reforming existing structures. When those reforms failed to meet the approval of imperial authorities, some elements in the party became more receptive to the thought of severing the colonial link. Yet, this step was not taken until the radical faction took over the party and transformed it into a revolutionary movement. The 1837 insurrection was conducted under the banner of national liberation, whereas that of 1838, still espousing that cause, had a definite social dimension. It was an attempt at bringing down the existing socioeconomic order.

Before attempting an explanation as to why the insurrections did not succeed, a topic to be taken up in the next chapter, it is important to take a look at what the Patriotes stood for in terms of economic policy.

The Patriotes' Economic Discourse

This is a lesser known aspect of the Patriotes' discourse. Historiography of the rebellions is divided on this issue, if and when it is considered. The nationalists have paid very little attention to this facet of the Patriotes' ideology, concentrating solely on the political dimension of their struggle apprehended in its institutional aspect and often reduced to a long parliamentary quarrel. When taken into consideration by antinationalist historians, the Patriotes' economic discourse and their developmental project have been caricatured as either nostalgic of French régime feudal institutions (Ouellet, 1971) or as opposed to progress

(Creighton, 1931, 1970). The progress Creighton refers to is of a precapitalist nature because it basically alludes to trade with Britain rather than aspiring to the development of an industrial base within the confines of Lower Canada. Such views lead one to believe that the Patriotes had nothing to say about the economy, which testifies to total ignorance of their economic project. This lack of interest for their economic discourse communicates a sense that they were completely ignorant about economic thought and the laws of economic development. Marxists and neo-Marxists (Bourque, 1970; Ryerson, 1968; Vance, 1964–1965) have been more sensitive to this aspect of the Patriotes' ideological discourse. Their hypotheses are interesting but their demonstrations often rest on tenuous ground.

To remedy the gap encountered in the existing literature we have investigated *in extenso* the Patriote press of that period (Bernier, 1991a). It has enabled us to trace the outlines of an economic project far different than what traditional historiography has to offer has to offer on this question. especially the antinationalist school of interpretation. Trade, industry, banking, and agricultural development are among the themes reviewed.

Trade

There are two basic issues on this question. On the one hand, the Patriotes wanted an end to Britain's monopoly on trade, especially with foreign countries, and more particularly with the United States. So they called for liberalization of international trade and abolition of the various Navigation Laws and Canada Trade Acts. Liberalization would favor the development of a commercial agriculture, for the United States might want some products that were of no interest to Britain. On the other hand, the Patriotes sought to promote greater French Canadian representation among wholesalers. To this end, *La Minerve* ran an extensive campaign in favor of the creation and support of a Canadian House of Commerce to be established in the import-export sphere with offices overseas, particularly in Britain. Maintenance of the colonial link was often mentioned as an obstacle to trade expansion and general economic prosperity of the colony.

An anonymous writer made a connection between French Canadian weakness in wholesale import and export trade and their internal political weakness. As he explained:

> It is only too notorious a fact that up until now foreign trade, in this province, has been in the hands of men for whom the metropolitan interest is everything, and the colonial interest is nothing. They represent a small clique in which even the lowest of clerks aspire at fortune-making in order to return to their country of origin and enjoy their fortune, or to make use of it here with the objective of politically dominating the Legislative Council.... When the permanent inhabitants of Canada [i.e., French Canadians] will have managed to control a significant share of foreign trade, they will be more inclined to sustain social and political relations in Britain with independent and enlightened men, a prospect that is current circumstances preclude.... Nominations to the Legislative Council,

and to power positions in general, will no longer be the preserve of the minority, owing to the pretext of the importance of trade. The injustice would be too obvious if Canadian commerce [i.e., French Canadian] was not also to be represented [in those circles of powers]. (*La Minerve*, June 10, 1833, p. 10)

On the importance of French Canadian ties overseas in the field of wholesale trade and the political consequences resulting from such a venture, someone writes:

It is natural to infer that in a colony the influx of metropolitan capital results in giving control of external trade to its nationals, inasmuch as laws favor trade monopolies. This is what happened in this country. Following the dictate to import all goods from Britain, merchants who came from that country and who had a monopoly of links with the manufacturing sources, and enjoyed a common language and culture with the producers, have up until now controlled the import side of trade. In contrast, Canadian [i.e., French Canadian] [retail] merchants have a similar edge over them, namely their direct contacts with consumers, and this is what has generally been responsible for their control of retail trade.

Would it be possible for those merchants who know particularly well the needs and tastes of consumers to establish links in Britain and elsewhere abroad in order to finally share with their counterpart of British origins the import-export trade of this country?...

It is not only the material gain aspect of this venture that must guide [French] Canadian interests in this project; profits of another kind, yet not less advantageous, will result. Out of this enterprise, we will gain moral and political strength.

If [French] Canadians were to share international trade with their British counterpart...they would, in difficult times, have the ear of imperial authorities, or be able to support institutions and projects useful to the well-being of our people. Our adversaries are not acting in good faith when they take exception to our poverty and whenever their unjust claims call for more public contributions [i.e., taxes] on our part. We do not stand on equal ground, and we have no connexion outside this country. We do not use [as they do] foreign capital to create our own. (*La Minerve*, March 5, 1832)

On April 25, 1837, *The Vindicator* published an article signed "An Irish Radical" that takes to task the colonial link and the unequal exchange to which it gives rise. Illustration is based on the lumber trade.

But we get more than this; we get the boasted Lumber Trade. Well, now for the Lumber Trade. Let us see what we gain by the Lumber Trade. In my opinion we would be infinitely better without it. It is true the Lumber Trade employs a large number of our people, but what do we gain by that? The able bodied spend their youth year after year hewing, preparing, and bringing lumber to the British Merchant at Québec; and what do we or they get in return for it? Rum, Brandy and Gin.... If there be any profit attached to the trade, it does not come into the hands of the people of this country; it remains with the British Merchant at Québec, who when he realizes a sufficiency, will pick up his crumbs and take flight off to spend it in England or some other country....

Now let us examine what we lose by our connexion with England. In the first place, they confine the trade and commerce of this province exclusively to themselves, and exclude all other nations from trading with our people, from which we could obtain the necessaries we require much cheaper than from them. In this [illegible] place, we lose every probable chance of establishing manufactures in this country.... We lose free trade with all other nations, and more particularly with the United States, the single trade of which would be of more real value to the people of this country in one year, than all their boasted connexion would be in ten. (*The Vindicator*, April 25, 1837)

Manufacturing and Industry

The discourse on industry and manufacturing establishments inevitably calls into question the colonial link and the dependency generated by it: dependency with respect to consumption of British manufactured products, and in the sense that the colony's economic development is constrained by all sorts of laws and regulations, especially with regard to the development of an industrial sector. The discourse clearly identifies obstacles to the colony's developmental potential within the field of manufacturing. Evolution of the Patriotes' discourse on the economic question reveals a more focused consciousness of the weight of colonial dependency regarding the possibilities of achieving economic diversification in the colony. The colonial link and its so-called benefits for Lower Canada were being questioned by the Patriotes. In so doing, their discourse elaborated an alternative scenario about what a Lower Canada freed from British tutelage might look like.

Our investigation of the Patriote press begins with an acknowledgement of French Canadian economic inferiority. With no bitterness or envy toward their English Canadian compatriots, the Patriotes sought to identify causes and remedies regarding that situation. Two excerpts attest to the frame of mind informing the Patriotes' queries.

With the Conquest [French] Canadians found themselves in the presence of actors more familiar with the roles about to be played. Furthermore, they were lacking in capital, an essential ingredient for the development of large-scale enterprises. (*La Minerve*, December 19, 1831)

[French] Canadians are accused of lacking entrepreneurship. This indictment when not an insult, is a blunder.... It is the means, or in other words the instruments, namely capital, which until now, have been lacking and have precluded [French] Canadians from entering the world of big business. (*La Minerve*, February 13, 1834)

Britain's colonial policies regarding the development of a domestic industrial sector drew scalding remarks in the Patriote press. The metropolis was accused of having held up industrial development in Lower Canada. Comparative reference was often made with the advanced state of industrial development in the American New England states.

Why are we poor? Why is the country without resources? Who must be blamed for the state of shortage and destitution in which the country finds itself? The government, yes, the government, which not only refuses to encourage the development of manufactures, but prohibits their establishment. A man who spends more than his revenues is bound to be poor. A country without manufactures that cannot produce enough goods in proportion to what is owed for its imports will soon be ruined. Commerce is most certainly a good thing, but before buying we must first make sure that we can pay. It is a given fact that the expenses of the country well exceed its revenues. We do not have enough goods to offer in exchange for those articles we import annually. If at least we limited our imports to articles of absolute necessity, we could make do with this situation for a little while, but luxury is at its peak. (*La Minerve*, July 18, 1836)

And what is the key to wealth? Industry. If we want to acquire national wealth, we must create a national industry. This is the road to follow. All that does not tend towards achieving that goal is all but secondary, and often dangerous by giving a false impulsion to our energy. (*La Minerve*, March 20, 1837)

The same writer expressed the view that economics should take precedence over politics and that French Canadians had paid too much attention to politics and not enough to their economic well-being.

To make the grade we must cling to industry and science; the hands of our people must be tied to those two sources of power. What we need is industrial restlessness instead of political restlessness whose violence only dizzies the people. (*La Minerve*, March 20, 1837)

Another writer linked economic and political power:

Industry first; it is for us [i.e., French Canadians] a necessary and urgent task. By what means does the foreign population [i.e., of British origin] surpass and dominate us? By its wealth derived from commercial and industrial enterprises. We must challenge them by the same means. Otherwise, let us resign ourselves to a state of poverty, of misery, and subsequently to political nullity, and thereafter to serfdom. (*La Minerve*, April 10, 1837)

Banking

Banks were perceived as institutions par excellence to allow French Canadians to exercise greater control over the destiny of Lower Canada's economy. The Patriotes favored banks instituted under the limited partnership principle rather than the existing chartered banks controlled by English Canadian interests, the risk for depositors being less in the limited partnership system. The Patriotes wanted easier access to credit. To this end, they tried to create during the 1830s a network of banking and financial institutions. In the end, one institution had been created. Called *Banque du Peuple* (People's Bank), its main objective was to provide small French Canadian commercial and industrial entrepreneurs with easier access to credit than was the case within the larger

English Canadian system that had began to develop in 1817 (Rudin, 1985). In this sense, the *Banque du Peuple* might be considered a development bank.

The overall discourse regarding the banking system was cautious. It foretold Francophone preference for the cooperative (or credit union) formula. Although recognizing the social and collective function of banks for the development of French-controlled businesses, there was nonetheless a preoccupation with minimizing individual risk.

Part of a public notice appearing regularly in the newspapers on behalf of Patriote sympathizers Viger, DeWitt and Company (which was to become *La Banque du Peuple* in Montréal) read:

> Our only goal is to be useful to the country, to develop its resources and promote its well-being by circulating capital which is not presently profitable to society, by favoring the development and protection of existing industries in general, and mostly by fostering and sustaining agriculture, commerce, and manufactures who beneficial actions extend to all social classes. (*La Minerve*, February 18, 1835)

The discourse on banking frequently dwelt on the difficulty of the French Canadian business community in securing credit from existing banking institutions controlled by the English merchant group who had, in some instances, started to diversify its economic activities by making, among others, an incursion into finance capital.

> We need today more than ever the establishment of a financial institutions, entirely distinct from the existing one [The Bank of Montréal, created in 1817]. This institution should be created by capitalist reformists whose mother-tongue is that of the majority.... What has precluded and will continue to preclude [French] Canadians from gaining preponderance in terms of numbers and capital in wholesale trade, is monetary favoritism. Should a bank offer them the means, to be sure many businesses would immediately emerge in all sectors of the economy. Those businesses already in existence could more securely expand their facilities and gain in size....
>
> In almost every branch of industry, [French] Canadians are but hired hands. By means of a bank created by people who would know them—and don't we all know one another—they would succeed in honorably competing with foreigners [i.e., English Canadians]. (*La Minerve*, December 11, 1834)

Agricultural Development and the Land Question

The agrarian question was very prominent in the Patriotes' discourse. However, it was also very complex, especially in regard to the seigneurial tenure. Three themes dominated in the press and in the various resolutions voted at public rallies during the summer and fall of 1837.

First and foremost was the question of the seigneurial tenure. Three options were considered: abolition, reform, or status quo. Reformists were mainly interested in redressing what they saw as abuses and undue exploitation on the part of seigneurs who had taken liberties with the provisions of the Coutume du Paris which was supposed to govern relationships between seigneurs and censitaires. Those abuses had taken on many forms over the years, as seen in Chapter 2. Reformists sought to return to administrative practices that prevailed under the French régime, especially those spelled out in the Edits de Marly of 1711.

Abolitionists mainly saw the seigneurial system as an obstacle to the commercial and industrial development of the colony because under this tenure system one never had absolute ownership of his piece of land—a necessary requisite for capitalist development. At stake were the famous *lods et ventes* or mutation fees. This question was raised at public rallies, among the Patriotes' parliamentary wing, and fiercely evoked by the nascent industrial bourgeoisie. *Lods et ventes*, it will be recalled, entitled a seigneur to keep one-twelfth of the amount of the sale price of any transaction taking place on the censitaire's land. He could also collect a tax on improvements made to the various constructions erected on the premises or to the land itself.

Stopping short of calling for total abolition of the system, one writer warned that changes ought to be made with regards to *lods et ventes*:

> I have already expressed my views on that odious tax [the mutation fine], which by being perpetual and unlimited deprives the censitaire of the profit which is there to enjoy for the peasant under the freehold tenure. This tax is responsible for the state of backwardness in which we find ourselves. To this tax we owe the absence of capital in this country, and as a consequence, land desertion, inadequate cultivation of the soil, the impossibility to develop a respectable school system, the ignorance of our civil and political rights, and all the ills that derive from poverty....
>
> The time is not far when what is left of partisans of the feudal tenure will join us in maintaining that it is a nuisance
>
> 1. To agriculture, because it burdens—without benefit to the state—landowners with taxes and charges.
>
> 2. To the establishment of manufactures, because should the industrial capitalist want to sell his business erected on seigneurial territory, he would have to remit the seigneur one-twelfth of the sale price.
>
> 3. To commerce, because the right of lender attributed to the seigneur, deprives the censitaire from the possibility of obtaining more credit than freehold property would bring him as he can only give a feeble guarantee to his creditors based on the mortgage of his belongings [but not his land]. (*Le Canadien*, March 22, 1837)

The seigneurial tenure was the area where the Patriotes' discourse was most ambivalent and ambiguous. This is not surprising when at different moments of its existence, the party had seigneurs within its ranks and, up to the very end was led by a seigneur, Louis-Joseph Papineau, considered by all to be the head of the party and of the revolutionary movement of 1837.

Denouncing the abuses to which this tenure system had given rise over the years was not tantamount to calling for its abolition. Reforms voted in the House of Assembly to put an end to some of these practices could suffice. In the same vein, to raise the issue of some of the hindrances the system posed to the development of capitalism did not, of necessity, mean that it should be abolished or than the freehold tenure (free and common soccage) should be generalized. Some of the problems raised by the system as the economy was progressing toward capitalism might be solved through legislative intervention.

It seems that the party's rural militants were very much interested in these questions. A content analysis of resolutions adopted in thirty six public meetings in 1837 found that out of 56 economic grievances expressed, 8 made reference to land monopolization, whereas 13 questioned the pertinence of maintaining the seigneurial system (Blanchette-Lessard and Daigneault-Saint-Denis, 1975).

A second question raised throughout the period was the problem of land monopolization and speculation. These lands were located in townships under freehold tenure. Often owned by absentee landlords or local speculators, they were not put to use, were not for sale, or if so, were at prohibitive prices. This at a time when demographic pressures on seigneurial territory made it very difficult for peasants' sons to establish themselves on a farm. Some solutions had to be found to put an end to these unproductive practices. Two came up regularly, with the second one finding more favor with the press and militants attending protest meetings. The first one was to have the government reclaim those unexploited lands, revoke ownership, and return the lands to the Crown's territories. The second solution put forth was based on the same principles but would have put the reclaimed lands under the stewardship of the House of Assembly. The House could establish more equitable and less onerous modes of distribution.

> The Legislature could facilitate the establishment of these lands and lay them open to the youth of the country who know not already where to settle themselves. This would be an excellent means of preventing monopoly and the money thus employed would return to the advantage of the country. (*The Vindicator*, April 10, 1832)

Another writer expressed similar views in more detailed fashion:

> Everyone must see the necessity for the provincial legislature's limited intervention in the management of wastelands [i.e., nonexploited but valuable lands]. Enough at least to insure that peasants' sons will be able to earn a living and take root in a land conquered and brought to civilization by their forefathers. The only way they can obtain those means is from a legislature aware of their needs and situation. Thus the absolute necessity that their legislative representatives enact the system of land distribution under which they will acquire land....
>
> It is only with regard to wastelands that the people need solace and protection. For there are many seigneurs who inhumanly take advantage of the peasants' needs and require from them excessive feudal burdens and impose them with costly charges in contempt of the laws of the land and causing great harm to individu-

als. It has been said that there are seigneurs who refuse to grant land at whatever price is offered. It is of absolute necessity for the legislature to review the old laws and enact new ones to insure that farmers get the protection they need in an agricultural country such as ours. (*Le Canadien*, October 12, 1832)

Finally, there was the question of the land companies. To insure a revenue for the government that would escape the scrutiny of the House of Assembly, they had been granted huge tracts of land by the colonial government under the freehold tenure at ridiculous prices. They sought to make substantial profits by selling plots to peasants' sons or immigrants from Britain. However, this system could not solve the problem of overpopulation on seigneurial territory because peasants' sons could not gain access to those lands for lack of the necessary funds for the down payment, let alone paying a lump sum for their plot. This again was seen as a case of insensitivity on the part of the colonial government whose allies has some shares in the British American Land Company (Little, 1989). For Patriotes sympathizers, this whole matter should also be referred to the House of Assembly.

> We cannot conceal the fact that the company in question will have its principal aim to become possessed of all the finest properties to put their own creatures and by that means to acquire in the country a dangerous influence. It will also have for its object to make immense profit on lands which it will dispose of; and also, on other sources of revenue which it will have in its power to create. (*The Vindicator*, April 10, 1832)

As previously mentioned, there was a lack of consensus regarding maintaining the seigneurial tenure. As the years went by, there was a great deal of soul-searching on the matter. As means of communications improved, travellers and observers of the foreign press could see some of the benefits of private ownership. One writer emphasized those benefits. His contribution took the form of a plea in favor of private property as opposed to working for someone else.

> The power of a State is a function of its population; the population is a function of abundance; abundance is a function of cultivating the soil, and cultivating the soil is a function of personal and direct interest, that is to say, of the pride derived from ownership. It therefore follows that the more a farmer moves closer to the passive state of a mercenary, the less industrious and active he is. On the other hand, the closer he gets to full ownership of his land, the more he cares and produces thereby contributing to the development of the general wealth of the State. Thus the greater the number of people who own property, the stronger the State....
>
> To favor the development of agriculture, it should be an absolute prerogative of our provincial parliament to dispose of our forests in favor of [French] Canadians and of the working-classes from overseas that come to us as a result of persecution and famine.... Ownership doubles a man's force. He works for himself and his family with more intensity and pleasure than he would for a master.... [As private ownership is the key to prosperity], the age of liberty will become for

our country the age of prosperity. Our country will then reach in commerce the rank and role that belong to it. (*Le Canadien*, August 19, 1835)

Our study of the Patriote press reveals a coherent discourse on the relationships between agriculture, commerce, and industry, assuming knowledge of the fundamental complex features and linkages in the functioning of a capitalist society. The discourse offered a clear project in overall development of the Lower Canadian economy on a capitalist path: Development should revolve around the three fundamental pillars of agriculture, commerce, and industry, and Francophone representation among those three sectors should be maximized.

Contrary to the dominant views expressed in the historiography of the rebellions (Creighton, 1931; Filteau, 1975; Ouellet, 1971; Séguin, 1968), the discourse was progressive, open on the world, and conciliatory toward fellow compatriots of British origin. It was a discourse of a nation held under trusteeship but searching for its political and economical emancipation.

Deviations did exist, and narrow and petty nationalism was evident at times. However, to us, the dominant discourse was different and the quotations from the press used in this chapter attest to this eloquently.

If the Patriotes had such a coherent and articulated program tantamount to a blueprint for socioeconomic development as an independent country, and massive popular support as expressed in election results, why is it that the rebellions failed so miserably? The answer to this question is the subject matter of the next chapter, as we attempt an explanation of the rebellions' failure and the consequences entailed for the formation of the Canadian State and on Québec and Canada's political culture.

Note

Throughout this chapter we incorporate into the text liberal translations of nineteenth-century French-language documents. Attempts at literal translations would be painstaking because the French punctuation, syntax, and orthography have greatly evolved since then. Nonetheless, we offer the original text in the form of endnotes.

[The French text has been omitted from this volume. —Ed.]

CHAPTER
10 TRAVELLERS, INNS AND FEASTING

Canadian lodgings and victuals were belittled more often than praised by travellers in the nineteenth century. The inns and hotels deserved their reputations, yet the food available to most British North Americans was substantial and nutritious if, at times, bizarre. Consider this dinner served to Charles Frederic Morrison on British Columbia's Stikine River in 1868: "Our Christmas dinner, I remembered, consisted of a young beaver stuffed like a suckling pig, which proved delicious. Lynx also makes a good stew if you do not think of cats, and squirrels make *un grand ragout*."[1] The more typical meal in Canada consisted of potatoes, beans and salt pork. While cod and salmon were consumed on the coasts and bison was the staple on the prairies, the pig, with a carcass so versatile that "everything is used but the squeal," was almost ubiquitous. It was the rare traveller indeed who did not have something to say about Canadian pork. Some, like Morrison, may have invented as much as they recalled, for they were of the British élite, for whom they wrote. Keep this in mind as you read "The Roads to the Bay: Tavern Food" from *Tavern in the Town: Early Inns and Taverns of Ontario* by Margaret McBurney and Mary Byers. They offer an affectionate, anecdotal description of the food and the changing roles of the taverns with their "crackling fire of pine logs . . . festoons of sliced apples for winter pies, hung round it to dry . . . hot steaks, fried bacon and potatoes . . . tea and toast."

If McBurney and Byers use dining to encapsulate the ambience of the era, Bonnie Huskins uses food merely as an apparatus that reveals the hierarchical nature of society in "From *Haute Cuisine* to Ox Roasts: Public Feasting and the Negotiation of Class in Mid-19th-Century Saint John and Halifax." Though also dependant on anecdotal evidence, Huskins's analytical study exposes the structured inequality of the society. "Public feasts," she writes, "not only served to differentiate working-class recipients from respectable artisans and middle-class providers and participants, but also to distinguish the "deserving" from the "undeserving" poor."

Note

1. Quoted in *British Columbia: A Centenial Anthology* (Toronto: McClelland and Stewart, 1958), edited by Reginald Eyre, p.18.

Suggestions For Further Reading

Abrahamson, Una, *Domestic Life in Nineteenth Century Canada*. Toronto: Burns & MacEachern, 1966.

Barss, Beulah M., *The Pioneer Cook: A Historical View of Canadian Prairie Food*. Calgary: Detsleig Enterprises Ltd., 1980

Eddington, Bryan, "A Fine Table: Feasting with the North Westers at Old Fort William," *Beaver*, 73:6, November 1993, 37–44.

Fingard, Judith, "'A Great Big Rum Shop': The Drink Trade in Victorian Halifax," in James H. Morrison and James Moreira, eds., *Tempered by Rum: Rum in the History of the Maritime Provinces*. Porters Lake: 1988.

Guillet, Edwin C., *Pioneer Inns and Taverns*, 5 vols., Toronto: University of Toronto Press, 1954–1962.

Hoffman, Frances and Ryan Taylor, "Cooking," in *Much To Be Done: Private Life in Ontario from Victorian Diaries*. Winnipeg: Natural Heritage/Natural History Inc., 1996, 92–108.

Russell, Loris, *Everyday Life in Colonial Canada*. Toronto: Copp Clark, 1973.

Tannahill, Ray, *Food in History*. New York: Stein and Day, 1973.

Visser, Margaret, *The Rituals of Dinner: The Origins, Evolution, Eccentricities and Meaning of Table Manners*. New York: Harper Collins, 1991.

Warsh, Cheryl Krasnick, ed., *Drink in Canada: Historical Essays*. Montreal and Kingston: McGill-Queen's Press, 1993.

THE ROADS TO THE BAY: TAVERN FOOD

Margaret McBurney and Mary Byers

'... the proverb of "God sending meat and the devil cooks" never was so fully illustrated as in this country; for, with a superabundance of the raw material, the manufactured article of a good dinner is hardly to be found in a public-house in the province.'

William 'Tiger' Dunlop, *Statistical Sketches of Upper Canada*, 1832

Pioneer A.M. Stephens was one of a party of men cutting a trail through dense bush from Mount Forest to Owen Sound in the winter of 1842. Their meals,

From *Tavern in the Town: Early Inns and Taverns in Ontario* (Toronto: University of Toronto Press, 1987). Reprinted by permission of the authors and University of Toronto Press Incorporated. © University of Toronto Press Incorporated.

prepared by the camp cook, consisted of bread and salt pork—and usually all of it was frozen before it reached them. Ten days and forty miles after they began, they found themselves lost—in the middle of nowhere, knee-deep in snow, and nearly out of food. After a cold and hungry night they sent their foreman to try for a sighting of Georgian Bay. A welcome gunshot soon announced that they had reached the bay and civilization in the form of three log buildings. Closer scrutiny revealed that they had found the rainbow's end—and a pot of gold—for one of the three log buildings was an inn.

Stephens and his men undoubtedly found whisky to warm them when they reached that welcome inn, but finding a good meal may well have been a different matter. Meals in those early backwoods hostelries ranged from adequate to abysmal. Travellers suggested that it was necessary to be ravenous in order to appreciate the food placed in front of them. Such was the case at Hall's Tavern, between Horning Mills and Mono Mills, an establishment known as 'Starvation Hall' to at least one disgusted patron, George Snider. An agent for the Toronto-Sydenham Road, Snider wrote that he preferred living alone in the bush to enduring the vermin at Hall's and the scanty food served there.

Country inns such as Hall's were typical of many throughout the province and often induced culture shock in travellers accustomed to a refined table. Thomas Need, travelling in the Cobourg area in 1838, described in *Six Years in the Bush* a scene faced by many an unwary visitor when a meal was announced. After a general rush to the table,

> the work of destruction commenced—plates rattled, cups and saucers flew about, and knives and forks found their way indifferently into their owners' mouths or the various dishes on the table... The company was of a motley description, Yankees and emigrants, washed and unwashed... At the top of the table, enveloped in sundry great coats, sat a large unshaved backwoods settler, just dismounted from his waggon: —opposite to him, with his hat on, an amusing contrast—a little, prim, puritanical store-keeper, with well-brushed clothes, sleek countenance, and straight greasy hair... The post of honour at this meal was occupied by our despotic host in person, who dealt out a 'Benjamin's mess' to each hungry expectant:—puddings and creams succeeded the substantials, which were conveyed to the mouths of the different guests with frightful rapidity, on the blades of sharp dirty knives. I ventured to ask for a spoon, a request which only drew from 'Miss' a disdainful toss of the head, accompanied by the exclamation of 'my? if the man be'ent wanting a spoon now?'

Yet the difficulties faced by innkeepers were many. The arrival of the stagecoach often brought surprises, not all of them pleasant. Seldom did the woman of the house know how many people she would have to feed and at what meal. Edward Talbot, travelling in the London District in 1824, recalled with wry humour that, after obtaining lodging and requesting a meal, the ingredients of that meal were

> still in a very awkward state for mastication. The bread, for instance, was yet in the flour bag, the chickens were feeding at the barn door; the tea was in the

grocer's canister, and the cream in the cow's udder...but...before the lapse of an hour all were smoking on the table in prime condition.

Improvisation was the order of the day. One traveller overheard an exasperated wife demanding of her husband just what he expected her to feed their nine unexpected breakfast guests. 'Eggs and ham, summat of that dried venison and pumpkin pie,' he suggested. And there was always the staple 'salt pork fried, hot potatoes, doughnuts made of strips of dough twisted into corkscrew forms and fried in fat ...' Whatever was served, there was a strong possibility that it would emerge swimming in a pool of grease.

At Fergus, where the Garafraxa Road began, Hugh Black's tavern offered food for both soul and body. Church services were held there on occasion, with worshippers and patrons seated uncomfortably on the floor, since innkeeper Black had little in the way of furniture. But because a few of the floor boards were missing, diners could sit with their legs dangling through the holes. The floor in front of them served as a table.

From Fergus, the Garafraxa Road (now Highway 6) led north to Georgian Bay, and before long the communities of Arthur, Mount Forest, and Durham, grew up along its length, with numerous taverns interspersed between them. At the village of Chatsworth, the Garafraxa Road joined the Toronto—Sydenham Road, the terminus for both roads being the burgeoning community of Sydenham, a few miles to the north. (Later Sydenham was renamed Owen Sound after Sir Edward Campbell Rich Owen, who had charted Georgian Bay in 1815.)

Built in fits and starts during the early 1840s as an inducement to settlement, the Garafraxa Road was soon handling an ever-increasing influx of optimistic pioneers taking advantage of free fifty-acre land grants in the Queen's Bush. By mid-century the wife of an innkeeper on the Garafraxa claimed that within one week she had served meals to two thousand of these hardy souls. A missionary travelling the road at the time mentioned that he had passed eighteen or twenty log taverns, one every two or three miles. Certainly pioneer James Cochrane of Derby Township had no complaints on that score. He fondly recalled that the proprietors were, as a rule

> the most generous and good-hearted men that I have ever met. As to numbers, after one hour's drive, on a cold winter's day, you did not think that one [tavern] every 3 or 4 miles was too many.

By 1853 all the lots in the remote village of Sydenham had been sold, and its future looked promising. Even Toronto's *Daily Leader* grudgingly allowed on 14 September 1853 that although there were twenty-five acres of marsh on the south of the bay, Sydenham boasted 'one of the best harbours in America. In point of capacity, it might contain the fleets of the world.'

A scant ten years passed between the welcome discovery of the lone log tavern at Sydenham and the construction nearby of the Jones Falls Tavern. Samuel Ayres Jones bought his land and considerable adjacent acreage near the falls of the Pottawahamie from surveyor Charles Rankin in 1849. Jones built a mill and, when it was working to capacity, looked to the next order of business: he built a tavern. The two-storey frame inn, which was completed in the mid-1850s, is located west of Owen Sound on the road that runs west from Meaford on Georgian Bay across the base of the Bruce Peninsula to Southampton on Lake Huron. Then known as the Southampton Road, it is now Highway 21. The community too changed its name, from Jones Falls to Springmount, and so the inn followed suit and became the Springmount Inn.

For many years the Springmount Inn was popular with people from Owen Sound, for it was an easy drive from town, and William Brown, for many years the proprietor, kept a good house. The old inn made headlines in the Owen Sound *Advertiser* of 26 March 1971 when the widow of innkeeper Brown was found

> dead in her room in the old Springmount Inn under circumstances that would seem to point to foul play... When found Mrs Brown was half kneeling against the bed in her room with her face upon the edge of the mattress... Blood was sprinkled over the bed clothing and the furniture was upset and the general appearance of the room would indicate that there had been a scuffle... The widow had lived alone for many years in one end of the old inn, the other end being occupied until recently by a horse trader who has moved to town... Mrs Brown was known in the neighbourhood as 'Beauty Brown'... At one time she was proprietor of the old Springmount Inn.

A coroner's jury determined that Mrs Brown (who had outlived her husband by thirty-eight years) had not been the victim of foul play but had died of a stroke. The following year a local farmer purchased the inn and moved it across the road to use as a barn. It stands there today perched on a high stone foundation.

An eccentric Yankee named Nathaniel Harriman was one of the first innkeepers on the Garafraxa Road. He settled in the area in 1839. After living for sixteen years in a small log house, he built a splendid stone building, which he operated as an inn, calling it Rockford Castle. A night's lodging cost twenty-five cents, and breakfast, typical of that served in most good inns, consisted of beef steaks, cold meats, potatoes, bread, eggs, tea, and coffee. Harriman reputedly built himself a coffin, which he kept on the premises and used for his afternoon nap. Eccentricity, of course, was often good for business.

The village of Hepworth owes its existence to an innkeeper. Located south of Wiarton on the Bruce Peninsula, this remote community developed on land ceded to the government by the Saugeen Indian Council of 1854. Two years later lots were put up for sale but, as most were sold to speculators, development was slow. In 1862, William Spencer, a young Englishman living in Oshawa, saw an ad for bush land near Owen Sound, purchased two hundred acres in Amabel Township, Grey County, and set off with his wife, his two children, and his brother-in-law on a journey of more than two hundred miles. Three years later, having established a successful farm, Spencer was elected as a councillor from his municipality. Walking the twelve miles home from a meeting in Wiarton, he passed the present site of Hepworth, decided that the dearth of inns was insupportable and, since the spot on which he stood seemed as good a place as any for a halfway house, he built one. The community grew up around it.

As William Spencer prospered, he was able to build and move into a bigger inn nearby. By 1889 the population of Hepworth had soared to 310, at which time, not surprisingly, the only hotel was Spencer's. Five years later business warranted another addition; the present Victorian building at 513 Spencer Street is that expanded hostelry. It is now used as a store.

Of Spencer House and its proprietor a publication of the day boasted that:

> The dining room is always supplied with the best that can be procured, the bed rooms are large, airy and well furnished, and commodious sample rooms are at the disposal of commercial men. First-class stable accommodation is available for horses, and nothing is omitted that is necessary to give the best of accommodation to the travelling public. As a citizen Mr Spencer is one of the most enterprising, ever in the front rank with those who assist any legitimate business enterprise that is likely to result in benefit to the community, and never behind in the cause of charity.

William Spencer, it seems certain, was a paid-up subscriber to the publication.

Spencer House may indeed have provided 'the best that can be procured' in its dining-room, but such was not the case in all such establishments; certainly not half a century earlier when the irrepressible William 'Tiger' Dunlop felt compelled to warn those who would venture on a tour of the colonies just what they might encounter in the way of food. In *Statistical Sketches of Upper Canada: by a Backwoodsman*, Dunlop obligingly provided 'recipes':

To Dress a Beef Steak

Cut the steak about a quarter of an inch thick, wash it well in a tub of water, wringing it from time to time after the manner of a dish-clout; put a pound of fresh butter in a frying-pan (hog's-lard will do, but butter is more esteemed) and when it boils, put in the steak, turning and peppering it for about a quarter of an hour; then put it in a deep dish, and pour the oil over it; till it floats, and so serve it.

To Boil Green Peas

Put them in a large pot full of water, boil them till they burst. Pour off one half of the water, leaving about as much as will cover them; then add about the size of your two fists of butter, and stir the whole round with a handful of black pepper. Serve in a wash-hand basin.

To Pickle Cucumbers

Select, for this purpose, cucumbers the size of a man's foot, —if beginning to grow yellow, so much the better; split them in four, and put them into an earthen vessel—then cover them with whiskey. The juices of the cucumber, mixing with the alcohol, will run into the acetous fermentation, so you make vinegar and pickles both at once; and the pickles will have that bilious, Calcutta-looking complexion, and slobbery, slimy consistence, so much admired...

To Make Butter Toast

Soak the toasted bread in warm milk and water; get ready a quantity of melted butter and dip the bread in it; then place the slices stratum super stratum in a deep dish, and pour the remainder of the melted butter over them.

How poultry is dressed, so as to deprive it of all taste and flavour, and give it much the appearance of an Egyptian mummy, I am not sufficiently skilled in Transatlantic cookery to determine; unless it be, by first boiling it to rags and then baking it to a chip in the oven.

Anna Jameson was inclined to agree with Dunlop's assessment of the food: 'Pork—morning, noon and night—swimming in its own grease,' she wailed. 'No wonder I am thin; I have been starved—starved upon pritters [potatoes] and pork, and that disgusting specimen of unleavened bread...cakes in the pan.'

The ever-present salt pork was a staple in virtually every tavern in the province. As for the rest of the meal, clearly the offerings of the landlord's table varied between succulent and inedible with a leaning in the latter direction. A low point was reached for William Lewis Baby and a friend named Felin, travellers on the road near Chatham in the 1830s, when they stopped for a meal that became an unforgettable experience. the fare was pancakes, and

the fragrant odor arising from the hot iron, as it permeated the surrounding atmosphere of this rural retreat, acted like a charm, for in an instant a bevy of young urchins, followed by a half-starved cat and cur, came rushing in seeking what they could devour. The youngest, a yearling I should judge, was clad in nature's garb (with the exception that a cloth was substituted in place of a fig leaf) and clung tightly to its mother's skirts...I expected that some mishap would befall the little scamp and my expectations were shortly afterwards fully realized. Felin's sudden appearance at the door caused the good lady to quickly turn around, in doing which she switched the little brat plump into the batter. You are mistaken if you think this untoward event disconcerted her in the least. She simply seized the imp by the nape of the neck and swashed the batter from its naked limbs into the trough whence it came, and proceeded with her culinary art as if nothing had happened. There was a grave consultation held outside of the hut immediately after that between Felin and myself. He was for total abstinence, and so was I if I could, but couldn't. It proved that hunger was an uncompromising foe, and proved the victor. (*Sic semper Tyrannus.*)

But John Howison of Edinburgh, in *Sketches of Upper Canada*, took a less jaundiced view of the fare when he wrote in 1821 of a visit to a log tavern:

This tavern...had a sign swinging before the door, so covered with gilt and emblematic paintings, that it probably cost more than the house itself...there we found a table amply furnished with tea, beef-steaks, cucumbers, potatoes, honey, onions, eggs etc. During this delectable repast, we were attended by the hostess, who poured out the tea as often as we required it, and having done so, seated herself in the door-way, and read a book (which I afterwards found to be *Miss Edgeworth's Tales of Fashionable Life*).

That same year, John Duncan was writing *Travels through Parts of the United States and Canada*, in which he related surprisingly pleasant memories of Canadian food and

> a crackling fire of pine logs...festoons of sliced apples for winter pies, hung round it to dry...hot steaks, fried bacon and potatoes...tea and toast.

Tavern food, in spite of the fact that it was most often served floating in grease, could look particularly appealing after a hard night in a coach. A glass of gin and bitters helped to whet the appetite. Thomas Fowler, a Britisher writing in 1832, described a journey by stage in which the stop for breakfast was the only good thing to be said for the trip:

> the gentlemen went to the bar and had a glass of bitters to cheer their drooping spirits after the fatigue of so unpleasant a night. In the course of an hour we were shown into a large room where the breakfast was set...tea and coffee, cold beef, pork ham and potatoes, with plenty of bread, butter, crackers and eggs.

Even Anna Jameson, who was revolted by the grease, on another occasion and in a better frame of mind identified the 'travellers' fare in Canada—venison steaks and fried fish, coffee, hot cakes, cheese and whiskey punch.'

In spite of the sometimes indifferent quality of the food served, early inns and taverns continued to be well patronized. Some patrons, of course, were singularly uninterested in the food. The *Huron Signal* of 11 February 1848 cautioned that

> numbers of persons instead of meeting to discuss the business of the township came there apparently with no other aim than that of getting drunk...

One tavern frequently used for such township meetings was in Chepstow, a quiet village north of the Durham Road—an east-west artery that bisected both the Garafraxa and Sydenham roads. Chepstow was first called Phelan's Dam after Irish immigrants John and Bridget Phelan, but the loyal Phelan, his heart still in Ireland, wanted the village called Emmett, to honour an Irish patriot. He petitioned the government requesting a change of name, but before the application could be approved bureaucracy intervened in the form of an English clerk who chose the name Chepstow, after the home of Earl Strongbow, an Englishman who had invaded Ireland.

Irish quarrels, however, would have held little interest for Chepstow innkeeper Lawrence Hartleib, owner of Hartleib's Hotel, a thriving establishment and the location for many years of various community meetings. Hartlieb purchased the property in 1871, and by 1885 the tavern was regularly being used for Court of Revision meetings. County council meetings also took place there, and in 1890 the hotel served as a polling place during elections.

Minutes of the Court of Revision held at Hartleib's indicate that social assistance was an interest of the county councillors. On 28 May 1899 they granted $5 to James McNeil for keeping an indigent girl for a month. Later that same court granted 'That Mary Taylor who had lost her husband by death should be granted a rebate of $13.10 as she was in straightened circumstances.'

Today, Hartleib's, now called the King Edward Hotel, is still drawing appreciative customers from miles around. Its exterior appearance has changed little since Lawrence Hartleib's day, but the brew dispenses inside is no longer a local product, as it once was. The *Bruce Herald* of 8 January 1891 raised this sensitive topic in its Chepstow news with a searching question: 'our genial hotel keeper has been required by his numerous customers to secure the celebrated Formosa beer. What's the matter with Chepstow beer?'

The people responsible for Formosa's competing brew were virtually all German or Alsatian immigrants. Naturally, they knew about beer and breweries for, as historian Norman Robertson remarked in his *History of the County of Bruce*:

> A German settlement without a brewery would be incomplete. This need was supplied to Formosa in 1869... In a purely German settlement lager beer is partaken of as one of the ordinary and necessary things of life...every Sunday morning after hearing mass the hotels were filled by the churchgoers having a quiet mug before starting the drive back to the farm; and, strange as it may seem, the license operators did not think it advisable to enforce the law there in regard to prohibited hours.

Formosa's beer did not have a monopoly in the neighbourhood. Chepstow obviously made its own and, at nearby Neustadt, an industrious Henry Heuther was busily brewing beer and hauling it by wagon to appreciative customers throughout the district.

Neustadt ('new town' in German) was an exclusively German settlement. Immigration from Germany to this area of Grey County began in the mid-1850s, and soon these settlers had chosen the rich lands in the south-western part of Normandy Township. An 1865 directory described Neustadt as having 'a Flouring Mill, Sawmill, Flax-Mill, Brewery, Tannery, Post Office, 3 stores, 3 Hotels, 2 blacksmith shops...' The population was three hundred and growing. The brewery 'was built in 1859, a stone building—Heuther, Henry, Proprietor; who reports his operations extending every year.'

Heuther's Crystal Spring Brewery was housed in a long, low stone structure with, at one end of the building, a sizeable inn, the Royal Hotel, run independently from the brewery. Damaged by fire in 1869, the brewery was rebuilt with stone brought to the site by local farmers. It was built on a natural rock foundation, its vaults, hewn out of rock, serving as cooling rooms for the beer. Underground pipes brought spring water from across the road. Horses, stabled in Heuther's barns behind the brewery, were used to haul the beer to local inns.

Henry Heuther died at age sixty-seven, his passing noted by the *Bruce Herald* on 30 January 1896: 'Though lacking the ruggedness of the typical German he considered the Fatherland set the model for everything.' Heuther left an estate of $15,800, a healthy amount for the day. His brewery and hotel were valued at $10,000.

Irish innkeeper Hugh Bell was only thirty-eight years old when he died, yet he was able to leave his second wife, Catherine, a comfortable seven thousand dollars. Included in the estate was the fine two-storey stone structure he had built in the village of Dunkeld in 1868. It served as an inn, post office, and store, It still stands at the north-west corner of concession 4 and Bruce County road 3.

On 19 February 1874, the Orangeville *Sun* announced Bell's untimely death:

> Mr Hugh Bell, a prominent citizen of Dunkeld, County Bruce, and well known in Brampton and Orangeville died on the 2nd inst. By his enterprise and energy he had accumulated considerable property, and was yet in the prime of his life when his sudden death occurred.

Bell was survived by his widow, aged twenty-seven, and two children, Jane and James, products of his first marriage. Several children born to Catherine had all died young.

From the brewing communities of Formosa, Chepstow, and Neustadt near Walkerton, the Durham Road led west to Lake Huron and east to Barrie on Lake Simcoe. It was one of a network of secondary roads crossing the Garafraxa Road at Durham and the Sydenham Road at Flesherton. Between these communities was the quiet village of Priceville, in Artemesia Township, Grey County, a convenient halfway stop for stage-coaches travelling between these two points.

Though quiet, the village supported six inns with no difficulty. One of these hostelries was built by Alexander Brown, a man who had a curious set of standards. He disapproved of the serving of spiritous liquors so he rented the inn to a proprietor who had no such qualms, thereby pacifying his conscience and deriving some income at the same time.

Across the road from the site of Brown's inn stands the Commercial, a building constructed of local white brick with red-brick trim, an attractive combination of materials seen in most of the other buildings on the old main street (which curves off from and runs parallel to the present Highway 4). The property was part of a block of one thousand acres held by the government and gradually put on the market when the Durham Road was built. The patent for the site of the Commercial was granted to Archibald McArthur in 1862. McArthur is listed as proprietor of the Wellington Hotel in 1865. That same year McArthur sold the land for $299. Three years later the same plot sold for $1,300. This sizeable jump in purchase price would indicate that the inn was probably built during those three years. In 1879 Thomas Atkinson became the owners, paying $2,300.

Atkinson ran the inn with this wife, Sarah. He died intestate in 1888, and the letters of administration contained the following statement by his widow, Sarah Ruth Atkinson:

> All the household furniture and effects in the Hotel of which the said Thomas Atkinson was proprietor at the time of his death, were and are my own property and did not belong in any way to the deceased.

Sarah later married Archie Butter. The hotel remained in her name until 1910.

The Sydenham Road led north-west from Toronto (following the present Highway 10) through Caledon, Orangeville, Jelly's Corners (Shelburne), Flesherton, and on to where it joined the Garafraxa Road at Chatsworth. In the Caledon Hills, scene of a brief and disappointing gold rush in 1818, Richard Church, a hotel-keeper from Cooksville, discovered a ghost town called Gleniffer where, thirty years earlier, eager fortune hunters had flocked in search of gold near the Credit River. A new village grew up there called Church's Falls and, later, Cataract.

By 1866, Cataract was home to a grand total of seventy-five people, thirty-seven of whom petitioned that year 'Praying for a licence to be granted to John Hawkins to keep a hotel in the township, known as the Cataract House.' Hawkins was granted his licence and opened his doors to a thirsty public. He wouldn't have wanted it any other way—penalties in Peel County for selling without a licence ranged from, for the first offence, '$20–$50 plus costs. Second offence hard labour in the county jail for three months. Third offence hard labour in the county jail for six months.' The county councillors meant business.

In 1871 Joseph Silk followed Hawkins as proprietor of Cataract House. He was succeeded in the 1880s by a Mrs Glen, who renamed it, unfortunately, the Dewdrop Inn. Today it is proudly called the Horseshoe Inn, and is still popular and well known for the hospitality to be found there.

From Caledon, the Sydenham Road led through Mono Mills, where innkeeper John Kidd's bid for immortality was carried out after his death in 1892. His teenage wife (she was about eighty years younger than he) followed his instructions to the letter and had his body placed in a glass-topped coffin, which was then interred in a tomb near the old road into the village.

After Mono Mills the Sydenham Road continued to Orangeville, a town laid out in 1843 by Orange Lawrence. What Lawrence didn't own in Orangeville, Jesse Ketchum did. A son of the Toronto educator and philanthropist of the same name, Jesse had inherited a great deal of Orangeville property from his uncle, the bristly, devout, and eccentric Seneca Ketchum, who died in 1850. Orange Lawrence owned most of the land south of Broadway, while the land to the north was owned and laid out by Jesse Ketchum. The fine stone inn at the corner of East Broadway and Second Street, now a restaurant called Greystones, was owned by Ketchum and run for many years by an Irishman, James Graham. On 10 December 1874, the Orangeville *Sun* reported that Graham, although he had been an innkeeper there for many years, was fined twenty dollars and costs for operating without a licence, the rules in Dufferin County being similar to those in neighbouring Peel.

Jesse Ketchum never ran the inn himself. No doubt he was fully occupied administering his holdings and managing a family that consisted of fifteen children—five by his first wife, Elizabeth Wilson, and then by his second wife, Mary Colvin. He died at the age of fifty-four in Michigan, where, according to the *Elora Observer* of 16 October 1874, 'he was taking mineral waters for his health.'

From Orangeville the Sydenham Road, important both to the military and to the settlers, led through Shelburne and Dundalk to Flesherton. The road had just been surveyed when, in 1849, Aaron Munshaw decided to move from Thornhill to Flesherton, where fifty-acre lots were available for the taking, just as long as settlement duties were met. Munshaw was then in his early fifties. His wife, Mary, was not much younger, and the youngest of their six children was only five, so their journey up the newly opened Sydenham Road was a difficult one. It was little more than a trail then; but, fifteen years later, the Sydenham had been gravelled, and thus in 1865 Smith's *Gazeteer and Directory of the County of Grey* could extol its virtues: the road was 'cleared out to a great breadth, and as straight as an arrow; a splendid drive in sleighing, or in good weather anytime.'

The Munshaws settled at Artemesia Corners (later named Flesherton after W.K. Flesher, a county warden). It was an inspired choice. Not only could they cater to travellers along the Sydenham Road but, in due course, the Durham Road also went by their door, and so the Munshaws, happily situated at the crossroads, drew customers from all directions.

For a few years the Munshaws lived in a one-storey log house, but by 1864 they were able to build a larger building. The substantial two-storey brick structure was called Flesherton House or Munshaw House. It had two large dormitory-style rooms for sleeping and, at the north end of the building, two rooms for use as sample rooms by travelling salesmen. Here the salesmen could display their goods to the residents of Flesherton while at the same time providing the local citizens with a welcome diversion. Innkeepers willingly offered space to salesmen, who in the course of selling their wares also attracted customers to the bar.

These itinerant vendors of everything from shoes to fancy goods travelled many roads and paddled many streams in search of customers. Their place of work and their home were the same—one of the province's welcoming hostelries. One mobile merchant, calling himself 'a guerilla,' wrote of his life as a travelling salesman, calling his treatise *Notes on the Road*. This work was an attempt, he said, to 'record the sober realities of a commercial traveller's every day life.' To anyone contemplating this line of work he offered, in a 'sadder but wiser' vein, a few words of advice:

> How many scores of times I have heard a novice express his admiration of a guerilla's life, and paint with his own imaginative fancy the jolly times he would have, the sights he would see and the tales he would hear. Verily, young man, thy dreams of the same are pleasant. Continue to indulge in the soothing delusion; but for the sake of romance, never undertake the sober reality.

He then obligingly proceeded to paint the reality as he saw it:

—Tough customers and still tougher grub.

—Fried pork for breakfast, boiled pork to dinner, and pork cold for supper... Pork! pork! universal pork! thy fragrance seems to linger around the dining-room of every country tavern.

—Feather beds made of straw, crowned with an almost invisible pillow (called by such courtesy) and lined with two sheets; the dampness of which gave me a nightly attack of ague.

Even worse was a mattress stuffed with corn-leaves:

...if one's body was moved ever so fractional a part of an inch, the rustling sound that proceeded from this novel stuffing would have awoke the Seven Sleepers.

And, of course, there was the ever-present insect population:

...there was...before morning a bug stained floor and a blood marked wall. The sacrifice of insect life was immense. The piled up carcasses of the slain attested the vigilant night watch of the unfortunate.

Finally, for washing, 'a lump of that useful compound called yellow soap,' was accompanied by 'a towel...this eight by six inch rag...and that unique object tacked to the wall which does service for a looking-glass.'

But the life of a commercial traveller was not all fleas and pork. There were adventures for the taking. On one occasion, a number of salesmen were

splashing through the mud and mire on the road between Arthur and Mount Forest. The inclemency of the weather was a sufficient excuse for the speed with which the party were hurrying onward independent of visions of a good hot supper and cosy rooms at friend Wilson's. Nothing unusual occurred till they arrived on the toll-gate near their destination, and through which the first team dashed at full speed, the other three following suit.

The toll-gate keeper, deprived of his fare, followed the guerillas to their inn. They managed to induce him to partake of the wares of the host until he fell to the floor. They said he 'took his tippling well.'

In spite of his denials, the 'guerilla's' memoirs showed that he had, for the most part, enjoyed his travels through the bush. It was a way of life chosen he admitted, because, 'I like elbow room.'

The host behind the bar of a nineteenth-century inn was, with few exceptions, an Irishman or a Yankee. In each case the atmosphere was the same—democratic. Such must have been the situation at the Exchange Hotel in the village of Singhampton. It had been built by a man named Josiah Sing, the son of an Irish father and an American mother, so it seems likely that the establishment would be operated along egalitarian lines.

In Ireland, Cyrus Richmond Sing's ancestors spelled their name Synge, as did Irish playwright J.M. Synge, but in Upper Canada the spelling became Sing, probably because so much Canadian spelling was phonetic. Edward and Elizabeth Synge, grandparents of Cyrus, were linen weavers, a family tradition that their descendants continued in Upper Canada. Edward and Elizabeth eventually came to Ontario, but they were preceded by their eldest son, Joseph, who made the crossing in 1816. He settled in Bloomfield, Prince Edward County, and combined teaching with preaching and travelling the saddle-bag circuit.

Joseph married Sarah, daughter of Cyrus Richmond, a United Empire Loyalist from New York State. According to her descendants, Sarah was 'fair and good to look upon,' and her friends persuaded her that the young, serious Quaker with a gift for oratory 'was a fine young man with no bad habits and she would have a home of her own.' After their marriage the couple moved to Pickering Township just east of York, where Joseph took up his two-hundred-acre farm.

Sarah Sing produced children, while Joseph produced debts. According to family tradition, 'he traded 100 of his 200 acres... When Joseph sold the remaining acres she refused to sign away her dowerage.' By this time, Sarah had lost twin daughters, another daughter, and Gersham, one of twin sons. She took her remaining children—son Cyrus and two daughters—and moved to the village of Duffin's Creek (now Pickering), where she supported them all by her weaving. Another son, seven-year-old Joseph, went with his father to live on fifty acres of bush land in Brock Township, where Joseph, Senior, intended to teach and preach. Later, undernourished from a diet of salt pork and potatoes, young Joseph was taken in by relatives, who raised him and called him Josiah.

In 1848 Cyrus Sing, then in his middle twenties, settled in Osprey Township at a point between the Saugeen, Beaver, and Nottawasaga rivers where the potential for mills was excellent. He wrote to his brother, Josiah, urging him to come, and so Josiah, by then seventeen, trekked up Yonge street from Newmarket, with his small white dog for company. Within a year or two the two young men were able to send for their mother and sisters, who joined them at the site of Meaford. The brothers bought a carding machine and moved it overland in winter to the Nottawasaga River and then by schooner to Meaford. Later, as business expanded, the Sings added a fulling mill and a sawmill.

In 1852 the Sings moved to Mad River Mills, where they ran mills, a store, and the post office. The postal station took their name—Singhampton. They laid out the townsite and, in the mid-1860s, built the spacious Exchange House to serve passengers and merchants on the Collingwood run.

Cyrus returned to Meaford in 1857 and became the town's first mayor and warden of Grey County. Josiah and Cyrus brought their parents to Singhampton, but the couple who had separated back in Pickering were not about to change the situation at that late date. Crotchety old Joseph lived, hermit-like, in a small log house by a swamp. Later he moved to a house in town provided for him by the loyal Josiah. Sarah lived with the family and was later remembered as a short lady of five-foot-two inches and weighing 210 pounds.

A stage line was operating between Singhampton and Jelly's Corners (Shelburne) by the mid-1860s when the Exchange House was built. After stopping at one of the five taverns in Jelly's Corners a passenger could connect with the line east to Cookstown operated by Dan McCallum, a man famous for his small but carefully trimmed white beard. At Rosemont, a convenient halfway point between the two towns, the coach was sure to stop at Thomas Henderson's two-storey frame Globe Hotel.

The 1866 directory for Simcoe County, with the usual enthusiasm shown by such journals, called Rosemont a 'post village rapidly increasing in importance...in the midst of one of the finest agricultural districts of the County.' The population then was 140. Irishman Thomas Henderson of the Globe Hotel had paid Alfred Coulson of Toronto $1,300 for the property in 1859, a sizeable amount of money for one acre, so the hotel may already have been on the site. Business was so good that competition, in the form of two new inns, soon developed. By 1886 the population had reached 275, and Thomas Henderson was forced to contend with rival innkeepers George McCarthy and William Reid. By 9 April 1891, the Shelburne *Economist* noted sardonically: 'We are blessed (?) with what few places of the same size as Rosemont can boast of—three licensed hotels.'

Rivalry was fierce. According to local legend, the Globe possessed the only water pump in the village, so when a fire broke out at a tavern across the road, the proprietor's wife made the most of the opportunity. She chose to protect her water supply and sat by her pump, shot-gun at the ready, to ensure that the competition did indeed burn to the ground.

It is unlikely that the aggressive spouse was Thomas Henderson's wife, Elizabeth, for that couple seemed to be community-minded, though perhaps inclined to nepotism. The Orangeville *Sun* of 3 March 1870 suggested something of the sort when it reported the following local event:

Shooting Match

Company met at the Drill Shed on Feb 18 to compete for a valuable silver cup presented by Mr T Henderson of the Globe Hotel and a number of other prizes. Although the day was stormy, quite a number of Volunteers turned out, and competition was keen. The cup, however, was finally carried off by Mr R. Henderson and Mr. W. Henderson of Stanton obtained second prize.

After presenting his trophy, Henderson no doubt took advantage of the day of the competition to sell some of his wares. Perhaps he took similar advantage of the famous Fenian scare in 1866. A local Paul Revere rode through town shouting that the Catholics of Adjala Township were about to attack. The turn-out was swift. Protestants hastily congregated at Rosemont ready to meet the attack in the name of King Billy. But nothing happened. The rumour was unfounded, and the stalwart Protestants, undoubtedly disappointed, headed for home.

Perhaps three inns were too many for the small community. Liquor, the panacea of the hard-working settler, created problems here as elsewhere. Rosemont's reporter in the *Economist* of 18 September 1890 described the situation:

We would like to know where our once quiet little village is drifting. The air is full of wars and rumours of wars, and if such conduct continues we shall have to organize a corps of police to maintain law and order... Friday night of last week was one of the wildest nights that has ever been experienced here. All through the night could be heard the sounds of brawling and fighting.

Thomas Henderson died in 1891 at the age of seventy. He was in business to the end, having been granted a renewal of his tavern licence five months before his death. As the *Economist's* faithful reporter noted, 'A large concourse of people followed his remains to their last resting place at St Luke's... The bereaved family have our deepest sympathy.'

The road from Shelburne through Rosemont led to Cookstown, where it met another north-south artery, now Highway 27. Not far to the north was the village of Thornton, where passengers were welcomed by an innkeeper who, in spite of a Scottish-sounding name, had come from Ireland. Andrew Stewart was the proprietor of the Bee Hive Hotel (now the Village Inn), an impressive brick structure built in 1858. Thornton's population of one hundred—and the travelling public, as well—beat a path to his door.

Within eight years, however, Stewart decided to sell. The *Examiner and County of Simcoe Advocate* of 4 January 1866 announced that the Bee Hive was up for sale: 'part of the north half of lot 1 in the 7th concession of the township of Innisfil [the poetic name for Ireland, presumably the choice of many Irish residents of the township]...on which property there is erected a dwelling house and driving shed, now used as a tavern by Andrew Stewart of Thornton which property will be sold at auction at the town of Barrie on 30 December 1865.' The notice was quickly followed by a postponement to 13 January 1866. Apparently further postponements came into play, for Andrew Stewart was still listed as a hotel-keeper in the 1871 census. He was then sixty and assisted by his wife, Annabella, and his children, Alexander, John Andrew, and Mary. Elsewhere Stewart was identified as a carpenter, and his son Alexander as a farrier (a blacksmith and horse doctor). In Thornton, as elsewhere, innkeepers were men of many talents.

Whether a jack-of-all-trades or a will-o'-the-wisp, the average innkeeper had a hand in a multitude of activities. This was one reason why succulent meals might be low on his list of priorities. Good cooks were scarce, supplies were limited, and refrigeration was, particularly in the summer months, virtually non-existent. The frustrated traveller penning a nightly journal while trying to digest yet another meal of greasy salt pork might have felt fortunate that at least the host had not put tainted meat on the table. It is to be hoped that few innkeepers felt it necessary to follow the instructions that appeared in the Niagara *Gleaner* on 31 December 1825:

> Meat tainted to an extreme degree may be speedily restored by washing it in cold water and afterwards in strong cammomile tea; after which it may be sprinkled with salt and used the following day; or if steeped and well washed in beer, it will make a pure and sweet soup, even after being fly blown.

FROM *HAUTE CUISINE* TO OX ROASTS: PUBLIC FEASTING AND THE NEGOTIATION OF CLASS IN MID-19TH-CENTURY SAINT JOHN AND HALIFAX

Bonnie Huskins

> We ought to have had our guns charged—Ay, and our glasses too, in readiness—so that the moment of the joyful event should reach the city—we would have nothing to do but 'let go and haul.'

Saint John *Morning News* 3 April 1840

Introduction

One of the most popular and universal forms of celebration is feasting and drinking. Despite its popularity and universality, the public feast has not received sufficient scholarly attention from historians. Most of the historical studies on feasting focus on the role of the feast in medieval or early modern Europe.[1] The literature on the Victorian era tends to chronicle changing manners and eating habits in a rather antiquarian fashion.[2] An exception is Harvey Levenstein's *Revolution at the Table: The Transformation of the American Diet*, which examines "why and how [people in the 19th and early 20th centuries] change or do not change their food habits."[3] In the Canadian historiography, much of the recent literature centres on drink and responses to drinking, in the form of the temperance and prohibition movements.[4] While the experience of drinking in the Victorian era is currently being dissected by scholars such as Judith Fingard, who graphically portrays the consequences of alcoholism on recidivists in *The Dark Side of Life in Victorian Halifax*, James Sturgis, who describes the Rennie family's battle with alcohol in 19th-century Canada, and Cheryl Krasnick Warsh, who examines the "drinking woman" at the turn of the century,[5] more emphasis needs to be placed on "what lay behind...the fervid advocacy of temperance" and moral reform.[6] We also need more analyses of the experience of eating (as well as drinking) in 19th-century Canada. Thus, the primary objective of this paper is to delineate a typology or hierarchy of public feasts in mid 19th-century Saint John and Halifax, which will provide us with an alternate lens through which to view class and culture. Joseph Busfield has commented that "what is eaten and how it is eaten constitute a mode of communication and can be read as a cultural object, embodying the attributes of social organization or general culture."[7] In the popular bestseller, *Much Depends on Dinner*, Margaret Visser similarly notes: "Food—what is chosen from the pos-

Reprinted with the permission of the editor from *Labour/Le Travaille*, 37 (Spring 1996), pp.9–32. © Canadian Committee on Labour History.

sibilities available, how it is presented, how it is eaten, with whom and when, and how much time is allotted to cooking and eating it—is one of the means by which a society creates itself and acts out its aims and fantasies."[8] While an analysis of feasting and drinking can provide many insights into the nature of society, this paper will focus on how we can use food and drink as markers of class and as instruments in the process of class formation. This emphasis on food, drink, and social relations is borrowed from structuralists like anthropologist Mary Douglas and sociologist Pierre Bourdieu, who argue that "food categories encode social events, as...they express hierarchy, inclusion and exclusion, boundaries and transactions across boundaries."[9] Mary Douglas has noted that "...we need to stop thinking of food as something that people desire and use apart from social relations... It is disingenuous to pretend that food is not one of the media of social exclusion."[10] Did feasting and drinking in mid 19th-century Saint John and Halifax help to define the boundaries of inclusion and exclusion, as suggested by these social scientists?

In order to answer this question, it will be necessary to explore the various meanings and uses of public feasts. Why did people in different classes partake of "victuals" and "spirits"? How does this reflect their different priorities and social practises at mid century? Mary Douglas argues that "...the ordinary consuming public in modern industrial society works hard to invest its food with moral, social, and aesthetic meanings." If we do not seek out these meanings, "festivities [will be] treated as illegitimate demands on the world's productive system, the source of social inequalities and ultimately responsible for the maldistribution of food," clearly an incomplete and misleading understanding of such events.[11] In this paper I will systematically explore the meanings of the public feast for the middle-class and working-class inhabitants of mid-Victorian Saint John and Halifax. Emphasis will be placed on public secular feasts—that is, the banquet, ox roast, institutional repast, and tea and coffee soirée—which were held to commemorate royal and patriotic anniversaries. The most notable celebrations in this analysis include the observance of Queen Victoria's coronation in 1838 and her marriage in 1840, the birth of the Prince of Wales in 1841, and the celebration of his visit in 1860 and his marriage in 1863. This is by no means meant to be a comprehensive analysis of feasts or celebrations. The focus here is on public secular feasting—I will not be dealing with religious feasting or the private dinner. It is only through these local micro-studies that we can effectively "get at" the meanings associated with food and drink. As Mary Douglas notes: "The meanings of food need to be studied in small-scale exemplars."[12]

Context

Saint John and Halifax were both commercial entrepôts in the 19th century. Saint John processed timber from its hinterland—the Saint John River Valley—and competed in an international timber trade and ship-building industry.[13]

Halifax relied on a salt fish trade, particularly with the West Indies, and a general import trade.

By mid-century, urbanization had created rather complex urban landscapes in Saint John and Halifax. Initially the ward had been the basis of civic government, with the alderman functioning as a *paterfamilias*, creating an intricate network of relationship operating on the foundation of blood, service, and patronage, By mid century, however, ward politics was being supplanted by a professionalized civic administration, which was "more comprehensive, less personal, better organized, less arbitrary but more capable of imposing its will on a broader front."[14]

Increasing class differentiation also accompanied the growth of these urban centres. Irish Roman Catholic immigrants swelled the ranks of the working class in the 1840s. Poverty was further accentuated by the susceptibility of the colonial economy to the vagaries of external and internal trends and erratic business depressions.[15] Many "respectable" middle-class citizens distanced themselves as much as possible from the working-class poor in order to avoid the social problems associated with poverty, such as the outbreaks of cholera which infested the cities at mid century.[16] This desire for social distance is most effectively illustrated by the residential make up of the two cities. In Halifax, suburbanization of the rural Northwest Arm began when middle-class businessmen, politicians, and lawyers moved there and built lavish estates in the 1840s and 1850s. By the 1860s, the south end of the city had become known as the "court end of town," because of the existence of the residences of major merchants and government officials. A black community called Africville established itself by 1850 on the shores of the Bedford Basin and the Harbour, and the presence of the railway in the north end of the city encouraged the creation of a working-class community called Richmond. Halifax's major British garrison and naval station also reinforced residential segregation as a sailortown emerged along the waterfront and a soldiertown around the base of Citadel Hill.[17] In Saint John, the southernmost ward of Sydney was comprised largely of working-class inhabitants who provided services for the resident garrison. The adjacent Dukes ward boasted a mixed neighbourhood of "artisans, merchants, and mechanics." Queens ward, a little further north, housed the largest proportion of merchants and other "businesspeople." A "Protestant" artisanal population resided in the eastern part of Kings ward, and an Irish Roman-Catholic neighbourhood in the western end, called York Point. By the early 19th century, African-New Brunswick residents had settled in a segregated community in the vicinity of Loch Lomand.[18]

The garrisons in both cities reinforced the distinction between "rough" and "respectable" in more ways than one. Rank and file soldiers supported networks of taverns, brothels, and similar industries, while the officers entered the ranks of the local elite. This effect was particularly magnified in Halifax due to the larger size of the garrison. Regular soldiers, numbering between

2,000–4,000, comprised close to 25 percent of the resident male population of Halifax in the 19th century.[19]

What role did drinking and feasting play in the creation and dramatization of class distinctions in mid-Victorian Saint John and Halifax? All classes dined and imbibed at mid century; it was a "heavy-eating, hard-drinking age."[20] Residents could choose from a wide variety of taverns and saloons. In 1830, Saint John issued 206 tavern licenses and 29 retail licenses, which meant that 1 citizen in 50 held a liquor seller's license. Halifax contained between 200–300 drinking houses and shops by the 1860s, approximately 1 drinking establishment for every 100 inhabitants, including women and children.[21] Many working-class recreations "centred on the tavern," and liquor had also become an "integral part of the work culture." Respectable men and women largely confined their drinking to the home or to more exclusive venues. Eliza Donkin, a young Victorian woman from Saint John, noted the "habitual use of liquor in the family circles."[22] National societies often celebrated their anniversaries with annual banquets.[23] Celebrants also dined in observance of certain *rites de passage*, Christmas, and other high days and holy days, as well as during commemorative celebrations. Although all classes drank and feasted, did they do so in the same way and for the same purpose? Indeed, it is the argument of this paper that different forms of feasting reflected and reinforced contemporary class divisions. Middle-class and elite residents, for example, drew their social circles tighter by partaking of exclusive indoor banquets.

Banquet

The banquet, a frequent accompaniment to the grand ball, was one of the most long standing and popular elite entertainments. Judith Fingard mentions the ball (and banquet) as one of the leisure activities which united the "well-to-do" in the winter months in pre-industrial Canada.[24] Private citizens, provincial and civic officials, and voluntary organizations usually orchestrated the entertainments. Saint John's common council hosted a "corporation dinner" in honour of Queen Victoria's coronation in 1838.[25] Two years later, the lieutenant governor of Nova Scotia marked Queen Victoria's marriage by holding a ball and banquet, as did members of the North British Society, Highland Society, and the St. George's Society.[26] In Saint John, similar entertainments were given by the "Victoria Club," a volunteer company, and the Freemasons.[27] A committee of private citizens and government officials organized the dinner and dance held in honour of the visit of the Prince of Wales in 1860.

Balls and banquets promoted exclusivity by restricting attendance to a clique of local, provincial, imperial, and military dignitaries, and by charging a relatively high subscription or admission price for everyone else. A perusal of the guest list for Saint John's "corporation" banquet in 1838 shows that it mainly consisted of civic and provincial officials, military and militia officers, and commercial and mercantile elites. One local correspondent complained:

a dinner to fifty persons, including the corporate body is not in form or intent a public festival, but merely a private concern apparently to answer some party, and to gratify a few persons at the expense of the public.[28]

"A Bluenose" requested that the idea of an exclusive ball and banquet be abandoned for Halifax's coronation celebration, and that the day be

spent in a manner in which all could enjoy themselves; —the halls of our Provincial Building have been desecrated enough already. This cannot be the case with a public ball [and banquet], which make it as public as you please, will not be attended by the generality of the community. It would be more highly prized, (as doubt not they will also think), if His Excellency, the Army, the Navy, and those in high rank among our civilians, would for this occasion, unbend as much of their exclusiveness as would be proper, and encourage and patronise such amusements as all without exception, high and low, rich and poor, may participate in with exultant satisfaction.[29]

Organizers of the ball and banquet held for the Prince of Wales in Halifax in 1860 restricted admission to 250 invitations and 1000 tickets, priced at a restrictive two sovereigns for a man and one sovereign for a woman. According to the *Evening Express*, these prices kept the attraction "a rather more aristocratic affair than it otherwise would have been."[30]

Such events provided an opportunity for the display of respectability, breeding, and refinement. Thorstein Veblen has remarked that "conspicuous consumption" is *primae facie* evidence of one's "pecuniary success" and "social worth."[31] "A Bluenose" described the typical ball and banquet as an event at which

Tom, Dick, and Harry, tag, rag, and bobtail, might have an opportunity of displaying their breeding before the wives and daughters of the big wigs; and the wives and daughters of the little wigs an opportunity of being laughed at by Tom, Dick, and Harry, by Lord Somebody, and the honble [sic]. Mr. Nobody, or the red-coat and blue-coat schools. No such thing Mr. Editor—by the powers!— this is not the way the Coronation of Her Majesty should be observed in any of her dominions—at home or beyond the seas.[32]

The dinners served at these events were notable for the "strict rules" governing the "presentation of food, the varieties permitted at a given occasion, and rules of precedence and combination."[33] The menu for the Prince of Wales' marriage feast at the Halifax Hotel in 1863 is an example of 19th-century *haute cuisine*. Many of the dishes features in the bill of fare are French in origin. Indeed, culinary respectability has been associated with French (and Italian) cooking since the exchange of cooks and recipes among the "courtly strata" in the Middle Ages.[34] However, the 19th century witnessed the "full establishment of a French international culinary hegemony," not only in Europe, but in North America as well, as the great French chefs fled from their aristocratic employers after the Revolution, and set up their own restaurants, and wrote cooking manuals, which disseminated their culinary arts.[35] Most of these French dishes were rather "fussy" items, noted for their sauces. Some of the simpler English dishes did survive the French culinary onslaught, particularly the basic meat items. The caterer of the Halifax banquet undoubtedly consulted one of the cooking manuals written by these French chefs, for many chefs like Alexis Soyer specialized in organizing and catering grand banquets, like the one in Halifax.[36]

The courses served at the Prince of Wales' marriage feast resemble those associated with "service à la française." "Service à la française" was a tradition of serving dinner dating back to the Middle Ages, and was characterized by three set courses and dessert. Soup and/or fish comprised the first course. The second course consisted of the meat dishes, divided into "entrées" (fancy side dishes, usually of French origin) and "relevés" (larger and plainer items, usually English in origin). The third course was usually game and/or shellfish, followed by desert (sometimes divided between "relevés" and "entremets"). Proponents of "service à la française," as evident in this menu, also offered a number of options in each course, and served them all simultaneously, like a modern buffet.[37]

In the 1860s, "service à la russe" made its appearance in England and France, although it was not universally followed until the 1870s-1890s. The main difference between "service à la française" and "service à la russe" was that, in the latter, the servants carved and portioned the meal, and served the dishes in pairs or sets of alternatives. Dishes were passed around and not laid on the table; also, menus were distributed.[38] This gave the hosts more time to entertain their guests and "drew attention to the quality and sophistication of individual dishes."[39] The Prince of Wales' marriage feast in Halifax reflects "service à la russe" in that menus were evidently printed, and courses listed as sets of alternatives in the bill of fare. However, it is not known whether or not the dishes were served this way by the servants; also, the courses themselves still reflect "service à la française." Regardless, Haligonians evidently found it important to structure their banquets according to typical middle-class rules of etiquette. This structure undoubtedly helped to define the banquet as "one of the weapons in the social armory" of respectability and exclusivity.[40]

The nature of the wines served at such events also expressed class identity. Mary Douglas reminds us: "We must take note of the exclusionary potential represented by the serried ranks of vintage and lesser wines...."[41] For the banquet held in Halifax in 1860 in celebration of the visit of the Prince of Wales, the organizing committee selected 12 dozen sherries, 31 dozen high quality champagnes, including 23 dozen of "Mumm's," and 28 dozen of the cheaper wines.[42]

Banquets also reinforced middle-class masculinity. Although the ball was one of the only celebratory activities in the mid-Victorian period in which middle-class women could actively participate,[43] they usually retired from the banquet table before the toasts began because public drinking was primarily a male ritual. The men often raised their glasses in honour of the women, but such "accolades" were only "minor and perfunctory exercises."[44] According to Levenstein, women were also expected to show greater "gastronomic restraint."[45]

The list of toasts at such affairs acknowledged the hierarchy of colonial society. Royal occasions particularly paid tribute to the lieutenant governor, as the

Queen's representative. At Saint John's corporation dinner in 1838, those present acknowledged Lieutenant-Governor Sir John Harvey and his actions in the recent border war with the United States.[46] Toasts were also customarily extended to Queen Victoria and the royal family, the colonial secretary, the governor general, the British officers and the army and navy, the provincial administration, the sister colonies, the lieutenant governor's wife and the "fair daughters" of the colonies, and other special guests.[47]

Thus, the balls and banquets held during public celebrations in the early-to-mid 19th century promoted exclusivity and respectability by restricting attendance, encouraging displays of opulence and finery, serving *haute cuisine* and fine wines, and toasting and thereby reinforcing the *status quo*, including the inequalities of class and gender.

Ox Roast

Celebratory regalement was not confined to the middle and upper classes. The general public also partook of "great outdoor feasts where massive quantities of meat, game, and liquor were consumed."[48] The Nova Scotia Philanthropic Society inaugurated the custom of having an annual picnic to celebrate the founding of Halifax.[49] The first natal day picnic at the Prince's Lodge in 1839 consisted of an "abundance of viands and lots of good liquor to moisten them." Similarly, approximately 300 people enjoyed a feast of "fish, flesh, and fowl" during the 1845 picnic.[50]

Larger outdoor feasts were also held in the public squares and commons. It is significant that the feasts provided for the general public and the poor took place out of doors. One reason was pure logistics. Organizers did not have the facilities sufficient to accommodate large crowds. But the "out of doors" also conveyed images of democracy and freedom which suited the mass demonstration. In a letter to the editor of the *Morning Journal*, a Haligonian admitted that the "Codfish Aristocracy" had every right to hold a ball and banquet for the Prince's visit in 1860, and to set the admission so high that "plebians" could not attend, but it was not so with outdoor demonstrations, which "ought to be every person's business, and every person's privilege to share in."[51] The *Acadian Recorder* also described the out of doors as "the proper field for a full and unrestrained feast of enjoyment."[52]

In 18th and early 19th-century England, public outdoor feasts functioned as instruments of paternalism organized by the British gentry, well-to-farmers, and members of the local government, on such occasions as the completion of the harvest, and historical and patriotic anniversaries.[53] In mid-Victorian New Brunswick, ruling merchants in single industry towns provided similar feasts, as in Chatham, where Joseph Cunard provided free food and drink for the working-class inhabitants dependent on his sawmills and mercantile enterprises.[54]

Providers of outdoor feasts in the more complex urban centres of Saint John and Halifax also wished to gratify the masses and ensure their own popularity.

In Saint John, the onus for such meals lay primarily with the mayor, aldermen, and assistants who were primarily artisinal in makeup.[55] Most of the common council's appropriation for Queen Victoria's coronation and marriage festivities in 1838 and 1840 went toward the provision of outdoor feasts for the public. In 1838, the council allocated £332/16s/3d for the public "repast" (compared to only £115 for the corporation banquet and £7/10s for a supper in the city jail).[56] Of the £250 earmarked for the marriage celebration in 1840, £210 was expended on outdoor feasts, £30 for dinners in the charitable and penal institutions, and £10 for gun powder for the militia.[57] During the coronation festivities, two aldermen and assistant aldermen cut up and distributed the food in their constituency on the west side (Carleton), symbolizing the central role of the common council in providing "victuals."[58] Since Halifax was not incorporated until 1841, private citizens and provincial and imperial officials organized and financed the events in 1838 and 1840. In addition, the Nova Scotia Philanthropic Society sponsored outdoor feasts for the Mi'kmaqs in 1840 and during the Halifax centenary in 1849. During its first year, the new Halifax city council conformed to the Saint John practice by superintending a spread for the poor.[59]

The provision of these feasts was based on the premise that a full stomach ensured favourable and loyal sentiments. "A Looker On" observed that Carleton's coronation feast in 1838 produced "an effect on the people, calculated to call forth the best feelings toward the parent state and our youthful and maiden Queen." By the same token, the lieutenant governor of New Brunswick thought that the Queen's marriage celebration in Saint John should involve the poor, and thus "...promote a happy spirit of social union, harmony, and loyalty among them."[60]

Gratuitous feasts can also be understood as an expression of philanthropy. The well-to-do were "goaded by tender consciences and insistent churches" to provide for the poor as a "christian duty". Many believed the maxim that the rich man's "wealth is a talent, for the employment of which he must hereafter render an account."[61] Providers also responded to popular demand; the public expected good deeds during such occasions, just at the English gentry were "obliged by custom to make disbursements for recreations."[62] The *Acadian Recorder* saw the voluntary offerings of the elite during Halifax's coronation celebration in 1838 as

> the contribution of all, whom fortune has blessed, with the means of bestowing happiness to others, and testify to the whole world how highly Nova Scotians value the privilege and honour of belonging to the British empire, having a direct interest and concern in the grand constitutional ceremony which consecrates Victoria our Queen.[63]

The public feast also had great ritual significance, the selection of the ox as the favoured entrée for these public feasts can partially be explained by its capacity to feed a large number of people, but also by its symbolism. Feasts were based on "mythical or historical events" which were "re-enacted...through symbols and allegories."[64] According to Hugh Cunningham, roast beef, plum pudding, and ale revived images of John Bull and Merrie England, and were considered part of the English "birthright." In the latter half of the 19th century, Victorians adopted these staples as "sacraments" in a "continuing mythology of national superiority and class identity."[65] Ritual significance also accompanied the practice of roasting the ox. In proposing an ox roast for the poor on the Grand Parade in Halifax in 1838, a correspondent referred to it as "an imitation of good old English hospitality."[66] The ox roast also had pagan roots and, as such, exhibited ritualistic behaviours and traits developed through custom and precedents.[67] Before the barbecue, participants adorned the ox with ribbons in imitation of "sacrificial garlands," and processed with the animal as during pagan sacrificial rituals.[68] In Saint John in 1838, the ox was led on its cortege by a black man named Jim Brown, probably a butcher, for later he carved the ox after it had been slaughtered and roasted. Butchers often marched with oxen during trades processions, afterwards slaughtering them and distributing the meat as alms.[69]

The class makeup of those who attended these events is difficult to determine. It is clear that the providers were primarily artisanal (in the case of Saint John), and middle class (in the case of Halifax). It is also clear that these providers intended the repasts primarily for the working class and the poor. While the "rich" could "partake [of public feasts] if they pleased," Alderman John Porter of Saint John contended, the "poor should be especially invited."[70] Some middle-class feasters did attend, often distancing themselves from the crowds in private marquees and tents. During the Halifax coronation celebration, an exclusive clientele patronized a private marquee on the common, where "Her Majesty's health was drunk with the utmost possible enthusiasm." The Charitable Irish Society of Halifax erected a "hospitality tent" during the coronation celebration and the centenary in 1849 where "members could refresh themselves...and dance."[71] It is probable, however, that most of the people who attended ox roasts were working-class in origin, given the increasingly non-respectable image and reputation of such events.

What did outdoor repasts mean to the working-class participants who partook of them? First and foremost, the public feast was a source of free food and drink. As in 18th-century America, ceremonial occasions and holidays determined the type of meal to be eaten by the "lower orders."[72] Not only did the public dine on ox meat, but other foodstuffs as well. In 1838, Saint John's common council provided barrels of bread baked into small half-pound loaves, plum pudding, and two hogsheads of ale. During the Queen's marriage celebration in Saint John in 1840, the people on Saint John's east side consumed 36 hams, 35 rounds of boiled corn beef, and a large quantity of cheese, as well as 8 roasted sirloins, 1250 pounds of bread, and 120 gallons of wine and ale. In King Square, servers also cut up and distributed a large wedding cake.[73] The prevalence of large fatty joints and sweets, and the paucity of vegetables and fruits, reflects the general nature of the working-class diet in 19th-century America.[74]

Although a Saint John newspaper congratulated the citizens in 1840 for "not having outraged *all* decency," a little "irregularity" was observed, which suggests that some tried to commandeer more than their fair share, a reflection of the tendency of the poor in pre-industrial Canada to "feast and be merry" during seasons of plenty.[75] Saint John's *Morning News* satirized the public's perception of the Queen's marriage feast as an opportunity for gluttony, in the form of a "letter" written by a "servant" named "Dorothy Prim":

> Tables are to be spread in King and Queen square for the poor people to stuff themselves at; and Sam says I shall have a cut of roast beef, and whatever else is goin. I do hate this livin on Gaspereau all one's life.[76]

Although this letter was undoubtedly a satirical creation of the editor, it still reflects actual sentiments among the working-class inhabitants of Saint John and Halifax, for they did complain about having to rely on fish.[77] Thus, in this context, the ox roast can be seen as a diversification of the regional working-class diet.

Homeless children also enjoyed the feast organized in honour of Queen Victoria's marriage in 1840:

> Ragged urchins about the streets, were upon the alert much earlier than usual, and strained their treble pipes more outrageously than ever to testify their joyful anticipation of roast beef and cake.[78]

Roast beef and cake were also anticipated by those who found themselves in poor houses and public carceral facilities during public celebrations.

Institutional Repast

> —let the poor in the jails forget their sorrows in rejoicing over the entertainment we prepare for them, and let the poor in the poor-house dance for joy and gladness on that day (Cheers).[79]

Michael Tobin, Halifax, 1838

Public feasts not only served to differentiate working-class recipients from respectable artisans and middle-class providers and participants, but also to distinguish the "deserving" from the "undeserving" poor. Victorian middle-class philanthropists portrayed the "deserving" poor as honest and enterprising citizens victimized by illness or misfortune, while the "undeserving" poor were characterized as lazy, profligate, and even criminal.[80] Organizers of public feasts wished to ensure that only the "deserving" poor received victuals, but at public distributions it was difficult to identify the deserving recipients.[81] During a public meeting to consider the celebration of the birth of the Prince of Wales in Halifax in 1841, Samuel G.W. Archibald, the attorney general of Nova Scotia, referred to the disorder of the coronation feast in 1838 which interfered with the orderly distribution of the food.[82] A correspondent of the *New Brunswick Courier* believed that very few poor deserved a feast in honour of the Queen's marriage in 1840 because in Saint John he perceived "very little suffering from poverty, unless it be where poverty and vice are united."[83]

The distribution of food could be more readily monitored by institutionalizing the public feast. The fragmentation of public feasts into individual dinners for the poor in penal and charitable institutions made them much easier to control than outdoor ox roasts.[84] Thus, provisions for the poor and unfortunate during special occasions frequently took the form of "repasts" in the poor asylums and public carceral facilities. Halifax's committee for the celebration of Queen Victoria's coronation in 1838 organized special dinners for inmates of the poor house, the city jail, and the Bridewell. Similarly, the Saint John common council organized a dinner in the gaol and, in 1840, distributed provisions to the almshouse, hospital, asylum, gaol, and workhouse in commemoration of Victoria's marriage. In Halifax during the nuptial celebration, Nova Scotia's lieutenant governor, Sir Colin Campbell, donated a supply of beef, bread, and beer to the inmates of the poor asylum and the prisoners in the gaol, and the Charitable Irish Society raised subscriptions for dinners in the poor asylum, the gaol, and the Bridewell. When the Charitable Irish Society entered the poor asylum, they found the "old ranged around the room, children in the centre, and tables 'literally groaning' under a profusion of substantial fare."[85]

Poor houses and penal institutions also marked the prince of Wales' *rites de passage* with special feasts and entertainments. The inmates of the asylum, gaol, and Bridewell in Halifax enjoyed special dinners as part of the celebration of the birth of the Prince of Wales in 1841. The Prince of Wales' visit nineteen years later was observed with a gaol dinner in Saint John and an entertainment in Halifax's poor asylum. The lieutenant governor of New Brunswick donated provisions to several poor asylums in the province in honour of the Prince's wedding in 1863, and the Nova Scotia treasury also paid for a dinner at the poor asylum.[86]

Who attended the feasts in these institutions and what functions did they play? The institutions catered to a wide spectrum of working-class inhabitants, ranging from the "under-class" recidivists described by Judith Fingard, to the elderly poor, homeless children, and otherwise well-established artisans who had fallen on hard times. Indeed, poor asylums have been described as "catch-all" institutions.[87] A reporter described the different categories of recipients who sat down to a repast in the Saint John asylum in 1863:

> ...such inmates as were able to move sat down to the sumptuous repast provided for them. The sight was truly interesting. At one table might be seen the poor, decrepid old man, at another the child of misfortune; at one table the emaciated youth, at another, the enfeebled woman.[88]

Judith Fingard has discovered that some poor inhabitants arranged to enter the poor house and the prison in order to take advantage of special dinners, as well as for protection and security.[89] The poor debtors in the gaols who did not have the resources to buy bread, and had to rely on rations from other prisoners, undoubtedly welcomed these celebratory meals.[90] Institutional feasts were also significant for those who were used to a more substantial diet. An

inmate of the Saint John poor house, who had recently fallen from relative respectability as an artisan, commented that "the victuals here is bad and the
allowance not half enough for anyone in health."[91]

Regardless of need, inmates expected to be treated "properly" during these
dinners in the institutions.[92] The gaol commissioners in Saint John prepared a
special meal for the prisoners during the Prince of Wales' visit in 1860, consisting of salmon, roast beef, vegetables, plum pudding, and a keg of ale.
However, two or three "turbulent spirits" led by an elderly debtor named Barney
O'Brien, managed to convince the other prisoners in the upper hall *not* to attend
the dinner because they were not be treated like *gentlemen*. They contended
that it would not be "dignified" to sit down to a feast unless one of the gaol
committee or at least the high sheriff presided at the table as chairman.
Participation would also be considered if they were provided with the "proper
appendage" —a gallon of whiskey. Unfortunately, their protest came to naught,
and the next day their share was fed to the prisoners in the lower hall.[93]

Thus, the organization of special feasts for the inmates of the poor relief
and penal institutions can be understood as a more rational and controlled
means of providing for the poor during public celebrations. Inmates utilized
these feasts as sources of much-needed "victuals," and Barney O'Brien and his
conspirators even attempted to use the repast as a vehicle for the attainment of
working-class respectability.

Tea and Coffee Soirée

For another segment of the population, none of these forms of feasting sufficed.
They provided an alternative—the tea and coffee soirée.

Why would people turn away from the customary feast and search for an alternative? Changing palates may have led to a gradual shift in eating patterns
and preferences. Among the articulate, the popularity of roast beef and plum
pudding waned by the late 1840s. One commentator commented in 1849 that
"John Bull...has taken uncommonly to eating turkey and potatoes [two American
dishes] for his Christmas dinner, although he continues to swear by roast beef
and plum pudding before strangers." He went on to suggest that

> we Nova Scotians should adopt the fare so liberally awarded to us for our na-
> tional dish, and serve it up as a *pièce de résistance* for the benefit of those who
> may drop in upon us with the laudable desire to write a book about 'the man-
> ners and customs of the Nova Scotians.'[94]

The changing palates of the residents was accompanied by a growing concern over the manner in which the ox was cooked, primarily the waste involved
in roasting the whole animal, and the aesthetics of the practice.[95] In 1838, the
Novascotian thought that the "days of ox-roasting may as well go after the days
of chivalry."[96] As ox roasts become more sporadic, the knowledge of how to cook
the animals properly gradually disappeared. The Charitable Irish Society tried

to roast an ox in Halifax during the coronation in 1838, but it was eventually disposed of, probably due to over-cooking.[97]

The effects of urbanization also help to explain the erosion of public feasts. Ox roasts were initially a product of pre-Victorian times, when Saint John (and Halifax) resembled a "collection of small market villages."[98] But the "village atmosphere" which had generated communal feasts was changing in the 19th century. One of the most obvious victims of urban growth was the ward system of civic government and, by extension, many of the ox roasts which had been organized by the common council and held in the individual wards. In 1863, the Saint John common council declined the suggestion made by Alderman Robinson to provide each ward with a grant toward "furnishing the poor of the ward with dinner at public expense" in celebration of the Prince of Wales' nuptials. Instead, Alderman Robinson personally provided food and drink for the poor of his Sydney ward and other wards as well.[99] Despite this isolated display of paternalism, communal ward activities like ox roasts were being superseded by city-wide spectacles organized by a more impersonal civic administration.

Public feasting also suffered from the effects of 19th-century moral reformism. Beginning in the 1820s, Halifax and Saint John experienced the emergence of evangelical, temperance, and rational recreation movements. While these causes found support at all social levels, abstinence and prohibition were taken up in force by the evangelical elements of the lower middle and respectable working classes. Besides an array of temperance organizations, a reformist clique called the "puritan liberals" emerged on the Saint John common council who were committed to temperance and purity in public life. The Halifax city council also demonstrated a growing commitment to the bourgeois ideals of efficiency and progress.[100]

Reformers displayed a variety of responses to public feasting and drinking. Some reformers had no use at all for public festivities, particularly when they functioned as gratuitous charities. The emerging bourgeoisie in Victorian England experienced considerable tension between work and leisure, accentuated for those with the evangelical convictions of the "Protestant work ethic." Public entertainments such as feasts were considered to be frivolous and irreconcilable with the "dignity of labour." Indeed, a familiar maxim advised that the "truest charity is to find employment that will give food; and not food without employment." The feast tended to induce idleness, drinking, and other slothful qualities.[101]

Some reformers reconciled the tension between this demoralizing frivolity and the sanctity of work by either attempting to modify or change existing celebrations, or by providing alternative rational recreations. Temperance and abstinence reformers centred on drink as the primary concern. Some moderates advocated a simple reduction in the amount of liquor consumed, while other "distinguished patricians" of the temperance cause in Saint John, such as Charles Simonds and John Gray, moved for a restriction of the type of alcohol served, finding nothing wrong with ale and wine, but drawing the line at hard liquors.[102]

The arrival in the 1840s of the American fraternal temperance organization called the Sons of Temperance facilitated the movement toward abstinence as a form of social control. These abstainers thought that public celebrations should be changed into more rational and orderly events by prohibiting the use of alcohol. The *Morning Sun* spoke of the influence of temperance on public relations:

> The general effect which 'Temperance principles' have on some of these occasions, and perhaps on all of them to some extent, go far to remove old objections to such modes of recreation. The great blame of festive occasions, was that of the miserable cup of intoxication; —prohibit that, and many enjoys himself, generally as a respectable creature.[103]

Alderman Salter, a puritan liberal on Saint John's common council, objected to the availability of intoxicating beverages at the marriage celebration in Saint John in 1840. He believed that the common council would not be setting a good example for their constituents by encouraging intemperance in this way. He saw drunkenness at the ox roast in Carleton in 1838 and had no doubt that again many would go away "gloriously drunk." He advocated a more "rational and consistent" celebration which avoided unnecessary noise, confusion, and intemperance: "Englishmen might not get drunk on ale, because they were accustomed to it; but Bluenoses might, and the temptation might be very dangerous." He did not approve of the loyalty of the bottle, but preferred "sober, honest" loyalty.[104] However, fellow puritan liberals Aldermen Porter and John Humbert, and "populist conservatives" such as Gregory Vanhorne, Thomas Harding, and Assistant Aldermen William Hagarty and Ewan Cameron spoke out in favour of the feast.[105] Alderman Porter saw little drunkenness at the coronation. He "would let the poor have a good glass of ale if they wished it," and did not think it would do them any harm. Indeed, the majority of the aldermen voted in favour of a conventional feast for the celebration of Queen Victoria's marriage in 1840.[106]

Other proponents of temperance and abstinence suggested offering more rational alternative events, such as temperance soirées. These attractions did not merely offer free food and entertainment, but also instruction and thereby respectability.[107] Offended by the drunkenness during public celebrations, the St. John Temperance Society organized a tea and coffee soirée during Queen Victoria's coronation celebration in Saint John in 1838, as did the Provincial Temperance Society and the St. John Auxiliary to the New Brunswick Foreign Temperance Society in 1840 to celebrate the Queen's nuptials.[108] The programs were pseudo- religious and instructive, incorporating hymns, band music, and discourses on themes ranging from temperance to "Our Laws" and the "British Constitution." The messages of many of these speeches reinforced middle-class family values and separate spheres ideology. During the soirée in celebration of the Queen's marriage, Captain O'Halloran delivered an oration on "Matrimony" in which he urged those who had not yet been "tyed by Hymen" to follow the illustrious example of their Queen and Prince Consort.[109] These temperance entertainments were attended by a number of women, who also joined the ranks of the temperance organizations. In 1840, Sir John Harvey congratulated the tea and coffee meeting for the large proportion of women present. He echoed the sentiments of the "cult of true womanhood," referring to women as "the good angels of the other sex sent to win them back to the ways of Purity and Peace."[110]

The food served at the temperance soirées was of a lighter fare than that associated with ox roasts, banquets, and institutional repasts, with tea and coffee as the only liquid refreshments, perhaps reflecting the influence of American food reformers as well as temperance advocates.[111] Although organized by temperance societies, the events were probably attended by abstainers as well, for temperance supporters had no qualms about using ale.[112] One guest contended that the atmosphere did not suffer because of the lack of alcohol: "we may safely defy Port or Madeira to impart to their votaries more genuine hilarity and social feelings than were inspired by these fragrant productions of the East." Instead of a drunken display, the coronation meeting was a source of "rational intercourse" and a "feast of reason for the soul." The guest concluded: "long live Victoria to share the affections of such a loyal people, and long liver the Temperance Cause to suggest so rational a mode of expressing those feelings." The success of the temperance soirées in 1838 and 1840 ensured its continuation as a "regular feature of temperance life" in Saint John.[113]

Moral reformers in the temperance and abstinence camps were not entirely successful in regulating popular behaviour during celebrations. The inherent class bias of their organizations posed one of the most serious problems. While reformers condemned the nature of public feasts and tried to change them in an effort to contribute to the improvement and elevation of the general public, their efforts at individual reformation, and the provision of alternative forms of celebrating, catered more to people of their "own kind," that is, the middle class and particularly the respectable working class. William Baird contended that the "more important work for the members of the Division [Sons of Temperance] seemed to be the reformation of talented and influential men, whose example was producing a most damaging effect."[114] The restriction of attendance at the soirées reflected this class bias, as tickets were first offered to members of the temperance societies and then to the general public.[115] An "insistence upon certain prerequisites of conduct and appearance" at the events further excluded "the unscrubbed." At a time of heightened social extremes, attempts to ameliorate and elevate the lower orders were jeopardised by many middle-class citizens who were more concerned with reinforcing not reducing social distance.[116]

Conclusion

Public feasting and drinking in Saint John and Halifax obviously reflected and reinforced the more general pattern of mid-Victorian diversity and class differentiation. In the first place, each type of feasting supported a very different class of recipient: the banquet was attended largely by the middle class, the ox roast by the general public (particularly the working class), the institutional repast by the "institutionalized poor" (representing a wide spectrum of working-class citizens), and the temperance soirée by the lower middle and upper working classes.

The food, drink, and attendant ritualism of these different types of public feasts also expressed hierarchy and defined the boundaries of inclusion and exclusion. The structure and content of French *haute cuisine* and the drinking and toasting rituals at middle-class banquets symbolized the respectability and exclusivity of the dinners. The ox roast, on the other hand, revived images of Merrie England and John Bull paternalism. There is evidence, however, that the working-class recipients interpreted the ox roast in a more pragmatic utilitarian fashion: as a source of free food and drink, and as a vehicle of respectability. Finally, the soirée's juxtaposition of tea, coffee, and instruction against the alcohol, heavier fare, and drunkenness of the banquet, ox roast, and institutional repast permitted respectable working-class temperance advocates to separate themselves from the gluttony of the "gentry" and the vulgarity of the "masses."

Social distance was also reinforced by accessibility; middle-class participants could attend just about any form of festivity they wished (indeed, they organized most of the ox roasts and institutional repasts). The lower classes, however, were blocked from attending the balls and banquets, the temperance soirées, and institutional repasts, as organizers instituted various forms of "screening," such as high ticket prices and availability, codes of dress and etiquette, and evidence of deservedness.

This desire for social distance intensified by the 1860s, as middle-class and respectable working-class organizers began appropriating more of the celebration budgets for their own exclusive banquets. In other words, they transformed "feasts of participation" into "feasts of representation."[117] You will recall that £210 of a total £250 appropriated for the celebration of the Queen's marriage celebration in Saint John in 1840 was expended on outdoor feasts for the poor; however, by 1860, the organizing committee for the Prince of Wales' visit to Halifax spent over half of their £4579/13s/1d on the grand ball and banquet.[118] The *St. John Globe* of 1863 commented on the changing priorities of celebration committees:

> A provision to give a good dinner to the poor was voted down, that two or three hundred of the elite, including the Common Council, may be able to enjoy a dance. Was there ever anything more heartless or cruel?[119]

The end result of this "gentrification" of public celebrations was that, by the late 19th century, few alternatives save private picnics and treats remained for the general public and poor who "measured improvement" by the "bellyful."[120]

Notes

1. Bridget Ann Henisch, *Fast and Feast Food in Medieval Society* (University Park and London 1976). Feasting and drinking were some of the primary functions of festivals in the early modern period (*Carnaval* in Southern Europe and autumn feast days in Britain), Peter Burke, *Popular Culture in Early Modern Europe* (London

1978), 178, 183, 186, 193, 195, 195. "Sustenance" as well as "sociability" were important components of public celebrations in 18th-century America, Barbara Karsky, "Sustenance and sociability: eating habits in eighteenth-century America," *Annales*, 40 (September-October 1985), 51–2. By the time of King George III's jubilee in 1809, the British expected a "free meal" during celebrations. See Linda Colley, "The Apotheosis of George III: Loyalty, Royalty, and the British Nation, 1760–1820," *Past and Present*, 102 (February 1984), 199.

2. Sarah Freeman, *Mutton and Oysters. The Victorians and their Food* (London 1989); Jean Latham, *The Pleasure of Your Company. A History of Manners and Meals* (London 1972); Gerard Brett, *Dinner is Served: A History of Dining in England, 1400–1900* (London 1968).

3. Harvey A. Levenstein, *Revolution at the Table. The Transformation of the American Diet* (New York 1988). For the subsequent volume, see Levenstein, *Paradox of Plenty. A Social History of Eating in Modern America* (New York 1993).

4. For a by no means complete list of studies on the 19th century temperance movement, see: Ernest J. Dick, "From Temperance to Prohibition in 19th Century Nova Scotia," *Dalhousie Review*, 61 (Autumn 1981), 530–52; J.K. Chapman, "The-Mid-Nineteenth-Century Temperance Movements in New Brunswick and Maine," *Canadian Historical Review*, 35 (1954), 43–60; T.W. Acheson, *Saint John. The Making of a Colonial Urban Community* (Toronto 1985), ch. 7; Gail G. Campbell, "Disfranchised but not Quiescent: Women Petitioners in New Brunswick in the mid-19th Century," *Acadiensis*, 18 (Spring 1989), 22–54; Gary Hartlen, "'From a Torrent to a Trickle': A Case Study of Rum Imports and the Temperance Movement in Liverpool, Nova Scotia," in James H. Morrison and James Moreira, eds., *Tempered by Rum. Rum in the History of the Maritime Provinces* (Porters Lake 1988), 62–75; Cheryl Krasnick Warsh, "'John Barleycorn Must Die': An Introduction to the Social History of Alcohol," in Cheryl Krasnick Warsh, ed., *Drink in Canada* (Montréal 1993), 3–26; Jan Noel, "Dry Patriotism: the Chiniquy Crusade," in Warsh, *Drink in Canada*, 27–42; Glenn J. Lockwood, "Temperance in Upper Canada as Ethnic Subterfuge," in Warsh, *Drink in Canada*, 43–69; Jacques Paul Courturier, "Prohibition or Regulation? The Enforcement of the Canada Temperance Act in Moncton, 1881–1896," in Warsh, *Drink in Canada*, 144–65.

5. James L. Sturgis, "'The spectre of a drunkard's grave': One Family's Battle With Alcohol in Late Nineteenth-Century Canada," in Warsh, *Drink in Canada*, 115–43; Cheryl Krasnick Warsh, "'Oh, Lord, pour a cordial in her wounded heart': The Drinking Woman in Victorian and Edwardian Canada," in Warsh, *Drink in Canada*, 70–91.

6. Sturgis, "The spectre of a drunkard's grave," 115.

7. Joseph Gusfield, "Passage to play: rituals of drinking time in American society," in Mary Douglas, ed., *Constructive Drinking: Perspectives on Drink from Anthropology* (Cambridge 1987), 76. This comment is an explanation of the structuralist perspective.

8. Margaret Visser, *Much Depends on Dinner* (Toronto, 1986), 12.

9. Stephen Mennell, *All Manners of Food* (Oxford 1985), 11. Mennell is discussing the contributions of the structuralists; Mary Douglas, "A distinctive anthropological perspective," in Douglas, *Constructive Drinking*, 8.

10. Mary Douglas, "Standard Social Uses of Food: Introduction," in Mary Douglas, ed., *Food in the Social Order. Studies of Food and Festivities in Three American Communities* (New York 1984), 36.

11. Douglas, "Standard Social Uses of Food," 5–6.

12. *Ibid.*, 8.

13. Acheson, *Saint John*, ch. 1; Graeme Wynn, *Timber Colony, A historical geography of early nineteenth-century New Brunswick* (Toronto 1981).

14. Acheson, *Saint John*, 195.

15. Judith Fingard, "The Relief of the Unemployed Poor in Saint John, Halifax, and St. John's, 1815–1860," *Acadiensis* 5 (Autumn 1972), 60.

16. Geoffrey Bilson, "The Cholera Epidemic in St. John, New Brunswick, 1854," *Acadiensis*, 4 (Autumn 1974), 85–99.

17. Description based on Janet Buildford, "Halifax, 1850–1870," unpublished paper, 18–23; Susan Buggey, "Building Halifax, 1841–1871," *Acadiensis*, 10 (Autumn 1980), 90–112. For discussions of sailortown and soldiertown, see Judith Fingard, *The Dark Side of Life in Victorian Halifax* (Porters Lake 1989) and Fingard, *Jack in Port. Sailortowns of Eastern Canada* (Toronto 1982).

18. Scott W. See, *Riots in New Brunswick: Orange Nativism and Social Violence in the 1840s* (Toronto 1993), 26–27; Acheson, *Saint John*, ch. 1.

19. Fingard, *The Dark Side of Life*, 15; Judith Fingard, "Beyond the Halifax Barracks: the Social Context of Late Victorian Army Life," the MacNutt Memorial Lecture, University of New Brunswick, 1983–84, 3.

20. J. Murray Beck, "James Boyle Uniacke," *Dictionary of Canadian Biography*, VIII, 903.

21. Acheson, *Saint John*, 140; Judith Fingard, "'A Great Big Rum Shop': The Drink Trade in Victorian Halifax," in Morrison and Moreira, *Tempered by Rum*, 90.

22. Acheson, *Saint John*, 142; Reminiscences of Eliza Donkin, collected and compiled by Morley, Scott, 33, New Brunswick Museum (NBM).

23. I. Allen Jack, *History of St. Andrew's Society of St. John New Brunswick, 1798–1903* (Saint John 1903); D.C. Harvey. "N.S. Philanthropic Society," *Dalhousie Review*, 19 (October 1939), 287– 95; Robert P. Harvey, "Black Beans, Banners and Banquets: The Charitable Irish Society of Halifax at Two Hundred," *Nova Scotia Historical Review*, 6 (1986), 16–35.

24. Judith Fingard, "The Poor in Winter: Seasonality and Society and Pre-Industrial Canada," in Michael S. Cross and Gregory S. Kealey, eds., *Pre-Industrial Canada, 1760–1849* (Toronto 1985), 63–4.

25. D., "Corporation Dinner, alias Humbug!" in Saint John *Weekly Chronicle*, 22 June 1838, also 29 June 1838.

26. Halifax *Acadian Recorder*, 11 April 1840; Halifax *Times*, 14 April 1840.

27. "An Infant," Saint John *Commercial News and General Advertiser*, 27 March 1840 (shortly after renamed *Morning News*); Saint John *Morning News*, 29 May 1840; *New Brunswick Courier*, 28 March 1840, 4 April 1840, 30 May 1840.

28. "Corporation Dinner, alias Humbug!" Saint John *Weekly Chronicle*, 22 June 1838. An old man in Thomas Hardy, *The Mayor of Casterbridge*, (London 1962), 39, describes a similar corporation dinner: "'tis a great public dinner of the gentle-people and such like leading volk—wi' the Mayor in the chair. As we plainer fellows bain't invited, they leave the winder-shutters open that we may get jist a sense o't out here."

29. "A Bluenose," Halifax *Times*, 22 May 1838.

30. Meeting of the Acting Committee, 21 June 1860, in Minutes of the Meetings of the committee for the Reception of H.R.H. the Prince of Wales, 1860, MG1, 312A, Public Archives of Nova Scotia (PANS); Halifax *Evening Express*, 3 August 1860.

31. Thorstein Veblen, *The Theory of the Leisure Class* (New York 1934), 127.

32. "A Bluenose," Halifax *Times*, 22 May 1838.

33. Douglas, "Standard Social Uses of Food," 15.

34. Mennell, *All Manners of Food*, 60, 102.

35. *Ibid.*, 135, 136.

36. *Ibid.*, 102, 147, 150–1.

37. Freeman, *Mutton and Oysters*, 184–91; Mennell, *All Manners of Food*, 79, 150.

38. Mennell, *All Manners of Food*, 150; Freeman, *Mutton and Oysters*, 184–91.

39. Levenstein, *Revolution at the Table*, 16.

40. *Ibid.*, *Revolution at the Table*, 14.

41. Douglas, "A distinctive and anthropological perspective," 9.

42. Meeting of the Acting Committee, 10 July 1860, in Minutes of the Meetings of the Committee for the Reception of H.R.H. the Prince of Wales, 1860, MG1, 312A, PANS.

43. Halifax *Morning Sun*, 27 July 1860.

44. Halifax *Sun*, 11 June 1845; Halifax *Novascotian*, 20 August 1860. In San Francisco in 1855, women were invited to observe the elaborate preparations for a banquet, but were then expected to leave "demurely." See, Mary P. Ryan, *Women in Public: Between Banners and Ballots, 1825–1880* (Baltimore 1990), 18; men raising their glasses, see Ryan, *Women in Public*, 135. In court circles, Queen Victoria tried to avert excessive drunkenness by insisting that gentlemen not be left on their own for too long, see Alan Delago, *Victorian Entertainments* (London 1971), 12. Cheryl Krasnick Warsh notes that the drinking woman in Victorian Canada was viewed as a form of "bastardized masculinity," see Warsh, "'Oh lord, pour a cordial in her wounded heart'," 89.

45. Levenstein, *Revolution at the Table*, 12.

46. *New Brunswick Courier*, 30 June 1838.

47. For a customary list of toasts, see Halifax *Times*, 3 July 1838, 28 April 1840.

48. Karsky, "Sustenance and sociability," 61.

49. Harvey, "N.S. Philanthropic Society," 292. The Charitable Irish Society had their first picnic in 1846, see Harvey, "Black Beans, Banners, and Banquets," 22–3.

50. *Nova Scotian*, 12 June 1839; *Halifax Sun*, 6 and 11 June 1845.

51. "A Right Loyal Citizen," Halifax *Morning Journal*, 30 May 1860.

52. Halifax *Acadian Recorder*, 18 April 1863.

53. Robert W. Malcolmson, *Popular Recreations in English Society*, 1700–1850 (Cambridge 1973), 59–65; G.S. Metraux, "Of Feasts and Carnivals," *Cultures*, 3 (1976), 8. For a description of a harvest supper in rural England in the early 19th century, see Thomas Hardy, *Far From the Madding Crowd* (London 1967), 240–6.

54. Wynn, *Timber Colony*, 135–7, 167.

55. Acheson, *Saint John*, ch. 2.

56. Saint John Common Council Minutes, 7, 15 June 1838, 5 July 1838, 12 March 1840, microfilm NBM; excerpt in the Saint John *Daily Sun*, 12 April 1887.

57. Saint John Common Council Minutes, 13 May 1840, 19 March 1842, NBM; *New Brunswick Courier*, 16 May 1840; excerpt in Saint John *Daily Sun*, 12 April 1887. The corporation was congratulated in 1840 for their "liberality." See Saint John *Morning News*, 25 May 1840.

58. "A Looker On," *New Brunswick Courier*, 7 July 1838: Saint John *Daily Sun*, 18 June 1887.

59. Halifax *Acadian Recorder*, 25 April 1840, 2 May 1840; Halifax *Times*, 5 May 1840; Halifax *Times and Courier*, 7 June 1849; Halifax *Times*, 21 December 1841.

60. "A Looker On," *New Brunswick Courier*, 7 July 1838; *New Brunswick Courier*, 9 May 1840.

61. Fingard, "The Relief of the Unemployed Poor"; Judith Fingard "Attitudes towards the Education of the Poor in Colonial Halifax," *Acadiensis*, 2 (Spring 1973), 19; Gwenyth Andrews, "The Establishment of Institutional Care in the Mid-Nineteenth Century," Honours essay, Dalhousie University, 1974, 2.

62. Malcolmson, *Popular Recreations*, 56, 66.

63. Halifax *Acadian Recorder*, 2 June 1838.

64. Metraux, "Of Feasts and Carnivals," 7.

65. Hugh Cunningham, "The Language of Patriotism, 1750–1914," *History Workshop*, 11 (1981), 11, 18, 21; for images of John Bull, see Patrick Joyce, *Culture, Society, and Politics* (London 1981), 286–7, 295; Peter Bailey, *Leisure and Class in Victorian England: Rational Recreation and the Contest for Control, 1830–1885* (Toronto 1978), 89.

66. Halifax *Times*, 29 May 1838. The Halifax *Times*, 28 April 1840 commented re: a dinner and dance given by the St. George's Society: "For once John Bull forgot to grumble, and did his best to honour his Patron by proving the strength and tension of his digestive faculties, qualities in the composition of Englishmen, which, were roast beef and plum pudding are concerned, are said to be of no mean order."

67. Metraux, "Of Feasts and Carnivals," 8.

68. Saint John *Daily Telegraph*, 21 April 1883.

69. Saint John *Daily Telegraph*, 21 April 1883; excerpt in Satin John *Daily Sun*, 18 June 1887; Susan G. Davis, *Parades and Power: Street Theatre in Nineteenth Century Philadelphia* (Philadelphia 1986), 121. I am unsure whether or not the meat was distributed cooked or uncooked.

70. *New Brunswick Courier*, 23 May 1840.

71. Excerpt in Halifax *Acadian Recorder*, 30 June 1887; Charitable Irish Society Minute Book, 25 May 1849; 8 June 1849, PANS; Harvey, "Black Beans, Banner, and Banquets," 21, 23. for description of such a tent, see Hardy, *The Mayor of Casterbridge*, 109–11.

72. Karsky, "Sustenance and sociability," 59.

73. *New Brunswick Courier*, 30 June 1838; Saint John *Weekly Chronicle*, 29 June 1838; Saint John Common Council Minutes, 7, 15 June 1838, NBM; reminiscence in Saint John *Daily Sun*, 18 June 1887; Saint john *Morning News*, 25 May 1840; *New Brunswick Courier*, 30 May 1840. In Carleton, a great deal of food was also eaten.

74. Levenstein, *Revolution at the Table*. 4–5.

75. Saint John *Morning News*, 25 May 1840. (Emphasis is mine); Fingard, "The Poor in Winter," 76.

76. "Dorothy Prim," Satin John *Morning News*, 22 May 1840.

77. See Rev. Dr. Cochran in W.M. Brown, "Recollections of Old Halifax," Nova Scotia Historical Society *Collections*, 13 (1908), 89.

78. Saint John *Morning News*, 25 May 1840.

79. Extract in Halifax *Acadian Recorder*, 10 June 1887.

80. Fingard, "The Relief of the Unemployed Poor," 38–9.

81. Andrews, "The Establishment," 4.

82. *Novascotian*, 16 December 1841. Also recall the "irregularities" during the marriage feast in Saint John. See Saint John *Morning News*, 25 May 1840. In 1897 the Halifax *Herald* described a feast for the poor as an "indiscriminate and unintelligent" form of almsgiving. See *Herald*, 5 July 1897.

83. Letter to editor in *New Brunswick Courier*, 18 April 1840.

84. Institutional repasts were also a function of the "discovery of the asylum" as an accepted mode of dealing with poverty and other social problems. See Andrews, "The Establishment," 2, 89; Whalen, "Social Welfare," 55–6. However, Francis does not think that the Lunatic Asylum was a humane method. See Daniel Francis, "The Development of the Lunatic Asylum in the Maritime Provinces," *Acadiensis*, 6 (Spring 1977), 23–38.

85. For the Halifax coronation, see Halifax *Acadian Recorder*, 11 August 1838; for Saint John coronation, see excerpt in Saint John *Daily Sun*, 12 April 1887; for Saint John marriage, see Saint John Common Council Minutes, 14 May 1840, NBM; *New Brunswick Courier*, 16 May 1840; Saint John *Weekly Chronicle*, 29 May 1840; for Halifax marriage, see Halifax *Acadian Recorder*, 11 April 1840; for Charitable Irish Society, see *Novascotian*, 23 April 1840; Halifax *Times*, 21 April 1840; Halifax *Acadian Recorder*, 25 April 1840; Charitable Irish Society Minutes, 9, 27 April 1840, 18 May 1840, PANS.

86. For birth see *Novascotian*, 16 and 30 December 1841; Halifax *Acadian Recorder*, 25 December 1841; for visit, see Saint John *Morning Sun*, 23 July 1860. Also see entry for a dinner in the poor asylum on the occasion of the Prince's visit to Nova Scotia in 1860 in Halifax's Poor Asylum Account Book, August 1860, RG 35–102, 33

B.1, PANS; for wedding, see *St. John Globe*, 11 March 1863; Saint John *Morning News*, 18 March 1863; Halifax's Poor Asylum Account Book, May 1863. Inmates of the charitable and penal institutions continued to receive special meals during the celebrations of Queen Victoria's jubilees in the late Victorian era. See Halifax *Acadian Recorder*, 20 June 1887; Saint John *Daily Echo*, 14 May 1897; Halifax *Herald*, 25 June 1897.

87. Whalen, "Social Welfare," 60; Judith Fingard defends her use of the term "under class" in the introduction to *The Dark Side of Life*.

88. *New Brunswick Courier*, 14 March 1863.

89. Fingard, *The Dark Side of Life*, 52, 54–5, 57.

90. John Smith to Mayor Robert Hazen, 17 april 1838, in Robert F. Hazen papers, Box 1, Shelf 36, Packet 2, #15, NBM.

91. James Thompson to the North British Society, 16 November 1838, in Records of the North British Society, MG 20, vol. 253, no. 185A, PANS.

92. Fingard, *The Dark Side of Life*, 51.

93. Report of Justice Balloch to a meeting of the sessions in Saint John *Morning News*, 5 September 1860; Saint John *Freeman*, 6 September, 1860.

94. "Ventriloquus," Halifax *British Colonist*, 24 May 1849. Similarly, another Haligonian contended that the "youngsters" of the late Victorian age would "turn their noses up" at the barrels of gingerbread (plum pudding) which were served during the coronation celebration in 1838. See "Doesticks," Halifax *Acadian Recorder*, 10 July 1897.

95. See the mayor's comments in *New Brunswick Courier*, 28 March 1840, and Alderman Porter's remarks in 23 May 1840. There was also concern about the waste and excess of festivals in early modern Europe. See Burke, *Popular Culture*, 213.

96. *Novascotian*, 5 July 1838.

97. Halifax *Times*, 3 July 1838.

98. Acheson, *Saint John*, 5. An ox was roasted in many pre-Victorian celebrations in Saint John, included the defeat of Napoleon in May 1814, the coronation of George IV in October 1821, and the ascension of William IV. See J.V. Saunders, "Early New Brunswick Celebrations," *New Brunswick Historical Society Newsletter*, 24 (November 1987), 3–4; *New Brunswick Courier*, 13 October 1821. In this sense they resembled the roasts held during village fairs and festivals. See Malcolmson, *Popular Recreations*, 59–64.

99. Saint John Common Council Minutes, 7 March 1863, NBM; compare this to the 50th anniversary of the landing of the loyalists in Saint John in 1833, when the mayor provided a special feast for the poor at his own expense. See Saint John *City Gazette*, 16 and 23 May 1833; For Alderman Porter, see *St. John Globe*, 11 March 1863; *New Brunswick Courier*, 14 March 1863.

100. For puritan liberals, see Acheson, *Saint John*, 181–2; for Halifax city council, see Janet Guildford, "Public School Reform and the Halifax Middle Class, 1850–1870," PhD thesis, Dalhousie University, 1990.

101. For Protestant work ethic, see Bailey, *Leisure and Class*, 5; Fingard, "The Relief of the Unemployed Poor," 36. A correspondent of the Halifax *Herald* opposed holding

a feast for the poor during Queen Victoria's diamond jubilee celebration in 1897 because it undermined the "pride and spirit of self-reliance" of the deserving poor. See *Herald*, 5 July 1897.

102. The *Novascotian*, 10 December 1840, commented regarding the reduction of whiskey consumed at a fair in Ireland: "How much of confusion, and quarrelling, of profane swearing, and loss of time, and of evils, was avoided by leaving the difference between 8 gallons and 8 puncheons unswallowed"; for selective policy, see Acheson, *Saint John*, 146.

103. Halifax *Morning Sun*, 20 July 1846, as quoted in David Francis Howell, "A History of Horse Racing in Halifax, N.S., 1749–1867," MSc thesis, Dalhousie University, 1972, 44.

104. This connection between drunkenness and loyalty can be traced back to at least 1809, when the press commented regarding King George III's jubilee: "It is not amidst intoxication...that we are to look for that steady or enthusiastic loyalty which is at once the pledge and test of popular allegiance." See Colley, "The Apotheosis of George III," 117.

105. For a discussion of these aldermen, see Acheson, *Saint John*, 181–2.

106. For debate, see *New Brunswick Courier*, 23 May 1840.

107. Bailey, *Leisure and Class*, 39, 42; Acheson, *Saint John*, 159.

108. Although there were no soirées in Halifax for the public celebrations in question, they were becoming popular events that as well. The *Novascotian*, 9 December 1841, recommended a soirée as an event for the celebration of the birth of the Prince of Wales.

109. Saint John *Morning News*, 27 May 1840.

110. In Saint John, women served as members of the "Saint John Total Abstinence Society." They composed 40 per cent of the organisation before 1835, less than 25 per cent after that date, and edged up to 30 per cent in 1840. See Acheson, *Saint John*, 144. Women also formed their own "Ladies' Total Abstinence Society for the City and County of Saint John," which submitted a temperance petition to the legislature in 1847. See Campbell, "Disenfranchised but not Quiescent," 37; *New Brunswick Courier*, 30 May 1840.

111. Levenstein, *The Revolution at the Table*, ch. 4.

112. Acheson, *Saint John*, 145.

113. "A Guest," *New Brunswick Courier*, 30 June 1838; for temperance life, see Acheson, *Saint John*, 146.

114. William I. Baird, *Seventy Years of New Brunswick Life* (Saint John 1890), 162, Saint John Regional Library (SJRL); Reminiscence of Eliza Donkin, NBM.

115. *New Brunswick Courier*, 23 June 1838, 18 April 1840, 22 and 25 May 1840.

116. For prerequisites, See Bailey, *Leisure and Class*, 105; Because of "mischievous conduct," no youths were permitted at the temperance meetings in Halifax in 1843 unless accompanied by a parent or guardian, or signed in by a member. See Halifax *Morning Herald*, 31 May 1843; for social distance, see Malcolmson, *Popular Recreations*, 164.

117. Metraux, "Of Feasts and Carnivals," 8–9.

118. A sum of £2530/17s/9d was expended on the ball and banquet—Financial account at the end of the Minutes of the Meetings of the Committee for the Reception of H.R.H. the Prince of Wales, 1860, MG1, 312A, PANS.

119. *St. John Globe*, 7 March 1863. In the column "Things Talked of in Halifax," the *Halifax Reporter*, 11 April 1863, had a similar "beef":

> The provincial funds, the peoples' money, the public chest must be freely bled to give a few (who least deserve it) a luncheon, a jollification, a swig at a champagne glass, while the same amount spent in providing comforts for the many needy and poor persons in the city, would be the means of bringing gladness and joy to the hearts of those who are in want.

120. Bailey, *Leisure and Class*, 89.

This paper has been a long time in coming and has undergone many changes and revisions. I would like to thank Dr. Judith Fingard for her untiring efforts to help me with several versions of an earlier paper, and Dr. Scott See, whose encouraging remarks, as a CHA commentator, gave me the confidence to submit this article for publication.

CHAPTER

11 THE IRISH COME TO CANADA

The Irish immigrants who came to British North America in the decades before Confederation not only altered the composition of the population and its religious make-up, but also served as a catalyst for innumerable other changes. The absorptive capacity of Canadian society was severely tested by that unprecedented inundation of Irish who were attempting to escape from the economic devastation wrought in their homeland by the potato famine of the 1840s. Since then there has been sharp disagreement over the nature of the Irish experience. The early literature, which dominated for almost one hundred years, exaggerated the "paddy" stereotype. In the 1960s, however, the "Irish" in Canada were reinvented by a growing army of academics. It is usually the Catholic Irish who are studied, for it was they who shattered the Protestant monopolies in the Maritimes and Canada West. The impact of that sudden and massive influx of largely destitute souls affected both the society and those who wrote about it. The "Irish" riots, strikes and parades jump out of the pages of the newspapers of the 1840s and 1850s, and while the stereotypes of the early writers have been rejected by all but the most determined, there is no consensus on the "new Canadian Irish."

There are professional Irish apologists, and they have their critics. To a certain extent, this was influenced by modern multiculturalism and the desire to recapture the fading of the green. There are ideological splits over class, religion, contribution, and politics. The most significant disagreement centres on the rural/urban roles and occupations of the Irish. For some years, the question which seemed to require an answer was why the Irish, deriving as they did from a rural, peasant culture, evolved into an urban proletariat ghetto in Canada. The debate over the nature of the urban proletariat and rural yeomanry became as rancorous as it was indecisive, and some might add tedious.

410

The two readings selected here concentrate on the dramatic, the riot and the parade, but in each case the events merely provide the backdrop for an analysis on the nature of the whole society. The first reading is by Scott W. See on "The Orange Order and Social Violence in Mid Nineteenth-Century Saint John." The centrepiece of this article is the Saint John riot of 12 July 1849, one of the most violent in Canadian history, but one that See finally explains. See does not pretend to be a detached observer, however, and students should speculate on the implications of that. A later article by See on "Mickeys and Demons *vs.* Bigots and Boobies: The Woodstock Riot of 1847" in the autumn *Acadiensis* of 1991 extends his argument on Protestant bigotry beyond Saint John.

If the See article is characterized by an undercurrent of rage, then a very different spirit prevails in Michael Cottrell's "St. Patrick's Day Parades in Nineteenth-Century Toronto: A Study of Immigrant Adjustment and Élite Control." Like the parades of July 12, those of March 17 frequently ended in violence, yet as Cottrell shows it is a mistake to dismiss them as unimportant. The hierarchy of the Roman Catholic Church certainly did not dismiss them, and instead manoeuvred to exploit and control them. Cottrell demonstrates the complexity and ameliorativeness of the St. Patrick's Day Parades. He also shows, as See does not, the change that comes with the passage of time.

Suggestions for Further Reading

Akenson, Donald, "Ontario: Whatever Happened to the Irish?," in *Canadian Papers in Rural History*, vol. III, 1982, pp. 204–205, 217–56.

Elliot, Bruce S., *Irish Migrants in the Canadas: A New Approach*. Kingston and Montreal: McGill-Queen's University Press, 1988.

Darrock, Gordon, "Half Empty or Half Full? Images and Interpretations in the Historical Analysis of the Catholic Irish in Nineteenth-Century Canada," *Canadian Ethnic Studies*, 25, 1, 1993, 1–8.

Duncan, Kenneth, "Irish Famine Immigration and the Social Structure of Canada West," *Canadian Review of Anthropology and Sociology*, February 1965, pp. 19–40.

Houston, Cecil J. and William J. Smyth, *The Sash Canada Wore: A Historical Geography of the Orange Order in Canada*. Toronto: University of Toronto Press, 1980.

Kealey, Greg, "The Orange Order in Toronto: Religious Riots and the Working Class," in Greg Kealey and Peter Warrian, eds., *Essays in Canadian Working Class History*, Toronto: McClelland and Stewart, 1976.

Lockwood, Glen J., "Irish Immigrants and the 'Critical Years' in Eastern Ontario: The Case of Montague Township, 1821–1881," *Canadian Papers in Rural History*, IV, 1984.

Nicolson, Murray, "The Irish Experience in Ontario: Rural or Urban?," *Urban History Review*, 14, 1, June 1985, pp. 37–46.

Senior, Hereward, *Orangism: The Canadian Phase*. Toronto: McGraw-Hill Ryerson, 1972.

THE ORANGE ORDER AND SOCIAL VIOLENCE IN MID NINETEENTH-CENTURY SAINT JOHN

Scott W. See

In March 1839, the St. Patrick's, St. George's and St. Andrew's societies held a joint meeting in Saint John, New Brunswick. Delegates noted and condemned the Protestant-Catholic confrontations that appeared to be endemic in Boston and other unfortunate American cities. In a spirit of congeniality, they applauded themselves on the good fortune of living in a British colony free of such acrimonious religious strife. Generous toasts were proposed to young Queen Victoria, Lieutenant-Governor Sir John Harvey and, most effusively, to each other.[1] A short eight years later, after Saint John and neighbouring Portland had experienced a series of bloody riots involving Protestant Orangemen and Irish Catholics, those sentiments would be recalled with bitter irony. Sarcastic comparisons would then be drawn between Saint John and New Orleans, a tumultuous city with a reputation for collective violence.[2]

What happened to shatter the calm, and why would the toasts of 1839 turn out to be so farcical in the light of events during the 1840s? Why would Saint John and Portland, relatively stable communities that escaped major incidents of social violence prior to the 1840s, become ethno-religious battlegrounds involving natives and immigrants?[3] The growth of Irish Catholic immigration to Saint John and Portland before mid-century was accompanied by the expansion of the Orange Order as an institutionalized nativist response to those unwelcome settlers. Confrontations between the two groups began with relatively mild clashes in the late 1830s and culminated in the great riots of 1847 and 1849. The Ireland-based Orange Order, fuelled originally by British garrison troops and Irish Protestant immigrants, attracted significant numbers of native New Brunswickers and non-Irish immigrants because of its anti-Catholic and racist appeal. By mid-century it functioned as a nativist organization whose purpose was to defend Protestantism and British institutions against Irish Catholic encroachment. The clashes in Saint John and Portland were not primarily the result of transplanted rivalries between Protestant and Catholic Irish immigrants, as was commonly believed by contemporaries and historians.[4] Rather they represented both a vehement rejection of certain immigrants because of cultural and religious differences, as well as a symbolic struggle to protect Protestant jobs against competitive Irish Catholic famine victims during a decade of severe economic hardship. Thus as Irish Catholic immigration burgeoned, so did the nativist Orange Order.

From *Acadiensis*, Vol. XIII, no. 1 (Autumn 1983), 68–92. Reprinted by permission.

Saint John was New Brunswick's most populous city in the nineteenth century.[5] Settled by Loyalists in 1783 and incorporated two years later, it rapidly developed into the province's primary port for the export of staple timber goods and the import of manufactured products and foodstuffs. Lying in its northern shadow was the shipbuilding and mill town of Portland, now annexed into greater Saint John. The localities were connected by several roads, the busiest thoroughfare being a dilapidated bridge spanning an inlet on the harbour's northern extremity.[6] Both communities bustled in mid-century; along the narrow streets and wharves sailors rubbed shoulders with tradesmen, merchants, lawyers, mill workers and itinerant labourers. Moreover, both gained their economic focus almost entirely from New Brunswick's timber staple. Sawn lumber and deals were shipped to the British Isles from their wharves, while numerous sawmills and shipyards dotted their skylines. In turn, the two communities received the bulk of New Brunswick's imports, inducing immigrants.[7]

Despite their industriousness, Saint John and Portland had fallen on hard times in the 1840s. Indeed all of New Brunswick suffered from the worst sustained downturn since the colony's inception.[8] Several factors accounted for this. First, the colony had enjoyed decades of timber trading privileges with Great Britain due to a combination of preference subsidies and high tariffs for foreign imports. But starting in 1842, England began to shift toward a policy of free trade in an attempt to curtail its soaring deficits. Subsequently it lowered or dropped its foreign tariffs and increased colonial duties. News of England's policy change created chaos in New Brunswick. Fears of the ramifications of such a move led to a decade of lost confidence among investors and merchants. Although New Brunswick would experience a slight recovery in 1844, due primarily to speculation that Great Britain's railroad fever would stimulate timber trade, the decade would be marked by high unemployment, rising commodity prices, commercial bankruptcies and legislative indebtedness.[9] Second, a worldwide glut of lumber and the over-exploitation of New Brunswick's forests caused a severe export slump.[10] Later in the decade, moreover, hundreds of workers were displaced as the province's sawmills abandoned labour-intensive operations in favour of steam-driven machinery.[11] These factors combined to create a decade of commercial distress that crippled Saint John and Portland, especially in the years 1842–43 and 1845–49.

During this decade of financial hardship, these communities experienced dramatic changes in immigrant patterns. Prior to the 1840s, both were relatively homogeneous. Indeed New Brunswick in general consisted primarily of the descendants of Loyalists and pre-Revolutionary War New England settlers, plus a moderate number of immigrants from England, Scotland and Ireland. The only significant non-Protestants were the Acadians, who populated the northern and eastern shores and the north-western interior. Moreover, the immigrant flow throughout the 1830s was strikingly consistent: for example, 1832 and 1841 differed in raw totals by only twelve.[12] This fairly uniform influx brought an increasingly large proportion of Irish, a trend that would continue to mid-century.[13]

Prior to the 1840s the majority of these Irishmen came from the Protestant northern counties. Most were of Scots or English ancestry, reflecting the British colonization of Ireland. They were artisans and tenant farmers with modest savings who sought a better life within the British colonial system. Most importantly, they shared cultural and ideological views with the native New Brunswickers and other British emigrants they encountered. They adhered to Protestantism and supported the English constitutional and political domination of Ireland. Thus they made a relatively smooth transition to their new lives in New Brunswick.[14]

During the 1830s, however, emigrant patterns within Ireland shifted and thereby profoundly altered the demographic face of New Brunswick. The more skilled, financially-solvent Protestant Irishmen from northern counties began to be replaced by more destitute Catholics from Ireland's poorer southern and western regions. The percentage of Irish Catholics who emigrated to New Brunswick before 1840 was small, yet ever-increasing. The trickle became a flood as a tragic potato famine decimated Ireland's staple crop from 1845 to 1848.[15] New Brunswick's immigration rate would increase yearly by at least 150 per cent from 1843 until 1847, when the Irish famine tide finally crested. For the mid-1840s, the province would receive virtually all of its immigrants from the Catholic districts of Ireland. For example, of the 9,765 immigrants arriving in 1846, 99.4 per cent were from Ireland. Of these, 87 per cent landed in Saint John, clearly underscoring the city's role as the province's chief immigration port. The overwhelming majority were poor Catholic agricultural labourers.[16] New Brunswick in the 1840s, and particularly Saint John, was bombarded with thousands of non-Anglo-Saxon Protestants.

The influx of Irish Catholics dramatically altered the ethno-religious faces of Saint John and Portland. Although perhaps half of the incoming Irish used the ports as temporary shelters, earning enough at manual labour along the docks for the fare on a coastal vessel heading for the United States, thousands of the poor agrarian peasants remained.[17] By mid-century, more than one-third of the residents of Saint John and Portland were born in Ireland. More profoundly, Catholicism mushroomed. Roman Catholics were as large as any Protestant sect in Saint John by the mid-1840s; when the 1861 census appeared, the first to include religious data, both localities had populations almost 40 per cent Catholic. Since the Acadians, who were New Brunswick's only other substantial Catholic population, were practically nonexistent in the Saint John region during mid-century, Irishmen accounted almost entirely for the high Catholic population.[18]

The Irish Catholics settled primarily in two sections of Saint John and Portland. They clustered in overcrowded squalour in York Point, a district of north-western Saint John bounded roughly by Union Street to the south, George's Street to the east, Portland Parish to the north and the bay to the west.[19] In Portland, they huddled in the busy wharf area on the harbour's northern shore. The two districts, connected by the "Portland Bridge," grew into twin ethno-religious ghettos during the 1840s.[20] They were so strongly identified with Irish Catholics that they would play host to virtually all of the major episodes of social violence between Orangemen and Irishmen during the decade.

The influx of thousands of Celtic Catholics into the Protestant Anglo-Saxon bastions of Saint John and Portland triggered a nativist response among the more entrenched residents. A useful paradigm for interpreting nativism was pioneered by John Higham, and while his model concerned American movements, it applies equally well for any nativist response. Higham's nativism was the "intense opposition to an internal minority on the ground of its foreign... connections," or a "defensive type of nationalism." Though Higham cautioned that the word "nativism," of nineteenth-century derivation, has become pejorative, his definition provides a valuable intellectual foundation for analysing people's reaction to immigrants.[21] In the context of the British colonial experience, nativists tended less to focus on place of birth than to draw inspiration from the virtues of Protestantism and British institutions.[22] From this perspective, the local response to incoming Irish Catholics may clearly be considered as a nativist response. Protestants who wanted to discourage Catholic settlement and block further immigration began to channel their energies into an institutionalized counter-offensive during the 1840s. As Saint John's *Loyalist and Conservative Advocate* explained:

> The necessity... for Protestant organization in this Province, arose not more from the many murderous attacks committed upon quiet and unoffending Protestants, by Catholic ruffians, than from the dreary prospect which the future presented. The facts were these: several thousands of immigrants were annually landing upon our shores: they were nearly all Catholics, nearly all ignorant and bigotted, nearly all paupers, many of them depraved... What have we to expect but murder, rapine, and anarchy? Let us ask, then, should not Protestants unite? Should they not organize?[23]

The call to battle was dutifully answered by an organization with a history of responding to similar entreaties in Ireland and England—the Loyal Orange Order.

The Orange Order became the vanguard of nativism in mid nineteenth-century New Brunswick, yet the organization was neither new nor unique to the province. After a violent birth in Loughgall, Ireland in 1795, Orangeism quickly spread throughout Northern Ireland and England. As a fraternal body tracing its roots to a feuding tradition between Protestant and Catholic weavers and farmers, the Orange Order paid ideological homage to the British Crown and Protestantism. Group cohesion was provided by a system of secret rituals, an internal hierarchy of five "degrees" and the public celebration of symbolic holidays such as July 12, the anniversary of the victory of the Prince of Orange (King William III) over Catholic King James II at the Battle of the Boyne in 1690. In the early nineteenth century the Orange Order was firmly entrenched in the British Isles, where its members fervently combated the growth of Jacobinism and Roman Catholicism.[24]

Given the ideological foundations of the Orange Order, it transferred well within the British Empire. British garrison troops who joined the organization while stationed in Ireland carried warrants for new lodges when they transferred to new posts. Irish Protestant immigrants who settled in England and British North America also brought Orange warrants as part of their "cultural baggage." By the early nineteenth century, British regulars in Halifax and Montreal were holding formal Orange meetings. Lodges mushroomed as they found support among Loyalists and the swelling ranks of Irish Protestant immigrants. In 1830 a Grand Orange Lodge, headquartered in Upper Canada, obtained permission from Ireland to issue lodge warrants for all of British North America except New Brunswick.[25]

New Brunswick's organized lodges, dating from the turn of the century, clearly reflected a similar pattern of garrison troop and Irish immigrant conveyance. The earliest known lodge, formed among soldiers of the 74th Regiment in Saint John, met regularly by 1818. Six years later they obtained an official Irish warrant.[26] After several abortive efforts to establish civilian lodges in the mid-1820s, Orangeism became rooted among Saint John's Irish Protestants in 1831. Initial growth was sluggish. Fifteen local, or "primary" lodges existed by 1838, representing ten in Saint John and Portland. Membership tended to be small, with some lodges having only a handful of regular participants. Even the establishment of a provincial Grand Orange Lodge in 1837–8, under the mastership of James McNichol, failed to generate widespread growth and attract significant numbers. With the advent of the 1840s New Brunswick's Orange Lodges, particularly in Saint John and Portland, were staffed primarily by small numbers of recent Irish Protestant immigrants and British troops.[27]

A catalyst appeared in the 1840s to spur growth in the fledgling organization. The rising tide of famine immigration brought concerned Protestants to the organization's doorstep, seeking action and viable solutions to the Irish Catholic "menace." By the close of 1844, when the transition from Protestant to Catholic emigrant was well under way in Ireland, New Brunswick had twenty-seven lodges. Of these, ten were less than a year old. As Irish Catholics arrived and filtered throughout the province, Orange Lodges burgeoned to lead the counter-offensive. Buttressed by a network of primary, county, district and provincial lodges, Orangeism swept up the St. John River Valley hard on the heels of the Catholic immigrants. Mid-century found 123 primary lodges across the province, representing a five-year growth of 455 per cent.[28] Together with its smaller Nova Scotia affiliates, New Brunswick's Orange Order boasted an estimated 10,000 members. Yet despite its impressive expansion, the Orange Order's seat of power and membership base remained firmly rooted in Saint John and Portland.[29]

The traditional membership pools did not account for the explosive growth of Orangeism. Irish Protestant immigration dropped dramatically during the 1840s, becoming negligible by mid-century. Moreover, Britain reduced its garrison troops because of budgetary constraints. What, then, explained the Orange Order's meteoric rise? How did the organization broaden its attraction to ensure its survival? The answers were to be found in the Order's ideological appeal to native New Brunswickers and non-Irish Protestant immigrants.

Evidence of Orange membership in the 1840s clearly proved that initiates came from various cultural groups and classes. While the organization may have been rooted among British garrison troops and Irish Protestant settlers, it succeeded only because it found a willing supply of Loyalist and New England descendants and non-Irish immigrants who shared its philosophical tenets. In other words, to tell the story of Orangeism in mid nineteenth-century New Brunswick is to trace the growth of an indigenous social movement. At least half of all identified Orangemen in mid-century were born in New Brunswick. They came from all walks of life, including legislators, barristers, magistrates, doctors, ministers, farmers, artisans and unskilled labourers. Motivated primarily by locally-defined problems and prejudices, many New Brunswick natives and immigrants found the Orange Order both philosophically and socially attractive.[30]

In the Saint John region, some natives participated in Orange activities when lodges first appeared in the early nineteenth century. Indeed, several of the nascent city lodges drew their membership exclusively from transplanted New Englanders and Loyalists from America's mid-Atlantic and southern regions.[31] When the provincial Grand Orange Lodge organized in 1844, prestigious native Saint John residents were there. They included W.H. Needham, a Justice of the Peace, H. Boyd Kinnear, a lawyer, and Thomas W. Peters, Jr., a city official. Each would assume an Orange leadership role at some point in his career.[32] During the period of intensified social violence, from 1845–49, Saint John and Portland residents embraced the Orange Order because of its campaign to protect Protestantism and British hegemony against the bewildering and oftentimes frightening effects of Irish Catholic immigration.[33] For example, Portland's Wellington Lodge welcomed its largest initiate group since its inception in the meeting following the great Orange-Catholic riot of 12 July 1849.[34]

Membership lists also illuminated the Orange Order's effective appeal to native-born in Saint John and Portland. Data gleaned from official lodge returns, trial transcripts, Orange histories and newspapers yielded the names of eighty-four active Orange members in the late 1840s. When matched against the available 1851 manuscript census returns from Saint John County, they showed significant native involvement in Orangeism: 56 per cent were not Irish-born, including 43 per cent native and 13 per cent other Protestant immigrants.[35] Moreover, the entrenchment of Irish Protestants in the Orange Order was evident because 80 per cent of them had emigrated to New Brunswick prior to 1840. The occupational range already noted for provincial Orangemen was corroborated by the Saint John evidence, though a higher proportion of members could be classified as skilled or unskilled labourers. Finally, the portrait of Saint John Orangemen revealed a youthful organization: almost three-quarters of those traced were less than forty years old in 1851.[36] Clearly, the Orange Order in Saint John and Portland in mid-century represented a mixture of native-born and Protestant immigrants.

The essential ideological glue of the Orange Order was unquestioning loyalty to the Crown and an emphatic rejection of Roman Catholicism. With these concepts codified in the initiation oaths, Orangeism guaranteed itself a philosophical continuum that transcended the divergent social appeals and emphases of individual primary lodges.[37] In New Brunswick, lodges exercised a great deal of independence. Several accepted only temperate men; others attracted members by offering burial insurance plans; still more touted their commitment to charitable endeavours.[38] New Brunswick's Orange Lodges had disparate social and functional appeals, and many men gathered under the symbolic Orange banner. Except in the rare case where evidence exists, individual motives for joining the organization are a matter for speculation. Nevertheless, the philosophies and goals of Orangemen may be justifiably construed from organizational rhetoric and collective behaviour.

Orange rhetoric in the 1840s strikingly resembled the propaganda campaigns carried out by American and British nativists during the same period. New Brunswick Orangemen charged an elaborate counter-offensive to combat Irish Catholic immigration and permanent settlement. The organization's views were stated succinctly in two documents from the late 1840s. In a welcoming address to Lieutenant-Governor Edmund Head, Orangemen explained:

> Our chief objects are the union of Protestants of the several denominations, to counteract the encroachments of all men, sects or parties, who may at any time attempt the subversion of the Constitution, or the severance of these Colonies from the British Empire; to bind Protestants to the strict observance of the Laws, and to strengthen the bonds of the local authorities, by the knowledge that there is ever a band of loyal men ready in case of emergency, to obey their commands, and assist them in the maintenance of order.[39]

Thomas Hill, the zealous Orange editor of the *Loyalist and Conservative Advocate*, was more direct in his appraisal of the fraternity:

> Orangeism had its origins in the *necessity* of the case; it has spread in this Province, also from *necessity*, for had not the country been infested with gangs of lawless ruffians, whose numerous riots, and murderous deeds compelled Protestants to organize for mutual defence, Orangeism would have been scarcely known. And whenever the *Cause* shall disappear, Orangeism may retrograde.[40]

Underscored in the above quotations was the unique philosophical framework which Orangemen operated within: unquestioning loyalty, exclusive Protestantism and the threat to carry out their policies with vigilante force.

New Brunswick's Orangemen, in an effort to check the Irish Catholic invasion, fought a rhetorical battle on several fronts. The overarching goal was to maintain the colony as a Protestant and British bulwark against Catholicism. The Orange Order directly appealed to all Protestants who feared that the ethno-religious supremacy enjoyed by Anglo-Saxons would be permanently undermined or destroyed by the swelling numbers of Celtic Irishmen. Orangemen even advocated the repeal of legislation giving Catholics the franchise and the right to serve in the Legislature.[41]

Anti-Catholic diatribes grew in part from a Papal conspiracy myth that enjoyed a North American vogue in the mid nineteenth century.[42] New Brunswick's Orangemen claimed the famine immigration was but a skirmish in a global battle, masterminded in the Vatican, to expunge Protestantism from the earth. A Saint John editor who supported Orangeism warned that "A great, perhaps a final, conflict is at hand between Protestant Truth and Popery leagued with Infidelity."[43] Orangemen embarked on a propaganda campaign to educate Protestants about the Pope's despotic control over Catholics—in church, the home, the workplace and on the hustings. Only by removing the insidious network of priests, Orangemen argued, could papal control over the "uncivilized minds" of the Irish Catholics in New Brunswick be broken.[44]

Another vital weapon in the Orangemen's arsenal rested upon the assumption that the Celtic Irish were inherently an unruly and violent race. The stereotype had a measure of truth. As a subjugated people under English rule, Irish Catholics often resorted to disruptive tactics to achieve their goals.[45] As poor Irish Catholics crowded into squalid quarters in York Point and Portland, Orangemen bandied stereotypes of the Celtic propensity for strong drink and villainy. After all, they argued, "no one can deny that the lower orders of the Roman Catholic Irish are a quarrelsome, headstrong, turbulent, fierce, vindictive people."[46] Petty crime did increase dramatically as Saint John and Portland absorbed thousands of the famine immigrants, but it is more plausible to suggest that factors such as overcrowding, poverty and hunger were more responsible for creating a crucible for crime than were cultural idiosyncrasies.[47] Tragically, Orangemen painted all Catholics with the same nativist brush. Though even the most scurrilous propagandists recognized that not all immigrants participated in this orgy of crime, they nevertheless called for Orange vigilantism in York Point and Portland. Moreover, they suggested dispersing the immigrants among loyal Protestants. The theory was that such a dilution would facilitate social control and the assimilation of those immigrants who chose to remain. For the Orangemen of mid nineteenth-century Saint John, every Celtic Irishman was a potential criminal.[48]

New Brunswick's Orange rhetoric was also laced with racism, mirroring the contemporary British philosophy of Anglo-Saxon superiority.[49] Ethnicity was mingled with class as Orangemen railed against the "ignorant Mickie" hordes who formed a substandard "class of people." The destitution of famine immigrants as they disembarked in Saint John, and the squalour of their ghettos in York Point and Portland, appeared to corroborate Orange assertions of Celtic inferiority. Here was positive proof that the Protestant Anglo-Saxon must remain firmly in legislative and judicial control in order to assure the colony's peaceful survival.[50] The more zealous Orange propagandists, believing that assimilation was a bankrupt concept, called for the deportation of all Celtic Catholics.

One might as well, they argued, "attempt to change the colour of the Leopard's spots, or to 'wash the Ethiope white,' as to attempt to tame and civilize the wild, turbulent, irritable, savage, treacherous and hardened natives of the Cities and Mountains of Connaught and Munster."[51] The editors of the *Loyalist and Conservative Advocate*, the *Weekly Chronicle* and the *Christian Visitor*, all either Orange members or openly sympathetic to the organization's policies, regularly exposed their readers to racist editorials, Irish jokes, and vignettes pointing out the sub-human proclivities of the Celtic immigrant. Through their efforts, the argument of Anglo-Saxon racial superiority fell convincingly upon the ears of native Protestants who feared the demise of peace, order and good government in New Brunswick.[52]

Yet another focal point for Orange propagandists was the tangible threat that the poor Irish Catholic immigrants represented a formidable and willing pool of cheap labourers.[53] The famine victims, thrust into the severely depressed economy of the 1840s, were greeted as pariahs by Saint John's working classes. The destitute Irish Catholics eagerly accepted the most demanding and lowest-paying jobs, which in a healthy economic environment would be vacant. But during the "hungry forties," unemployed native labourers were forced to compete with the immigrants for these undesirable jobs.[54] In an attempt to combat the debilitating effects of immigrant competition, such as a general lowering of wage scales, Orangemen sounded the call for economic segregation. They suggested that Protestant merchants and employers should hire and do business only with co-religionists. By ostracizing Roman Catholic labourers, Orangemen hoped to persuade entrenched immigrants to leave and to discourage incoming Catholics from settling in the community.[55]

While Saint John's Orangemen fought a rigorous rhetorical battle, perhaps their most effective campaigns involved physical engagements with Irish Catholics. Indeed, collective social violence grew in direct proportion to the rising levels of famine immigration and Orange membership during the 1840s. In the aftermath of each confrontation, Orangemen enjoyed even greater Protestant support from natives and immigrants alike. The number of local lodges and engorged memberships at mid-century were tributes to the Orange Order's successful appeal. The persuasive rhetorical campaigns may have won converts, but the bloody riots gave concerned Protestants tangible "proof" of the Irish Catholics' uncivilized behaviour.

The first clearly identifiable incident of collective violence between Orangemen and Catholics in Saint John occurred on 12 July 1837. Small Catholic crowds forced entry into two merchants' stores and attempted to burn them.[56] In later years such incendiarism was eclipsed by more traditional rioting. The spring of 1841 found Irish Catholics clashing with Orangemen in the streets of Saint John. At issue was an Orange commemorative arch erected to celebrate the visit of a dignitary.[57] Catholics reacted similarly the following year on 12 July, when a crowd of several hundred gathered outside a Saint John home flying the Union Jack festooned with orange ribbons. Their jeers and taunts brought Orange reinforcements from across the city; by evening a general riot prompted Major William Black to swear in 150 special constables. The all-Protestant volunteer squad arrested several Irish Catholics, most of whom were ultimately found guilty of rioting.[58] Although these early disturbances paled when compared to subsequent riots, they established important patterns that would be repeated throughout the decade. While Irish Catholics would be deservedly or incorrectly labelled the aggressors, the Orangemen would invariably be perceived as the defenders of Saint John's Protestant and Loyalist traditions. Moreover, an exclusively Protestant constabulary and judiciary would consistently arrest and convict only Irish Catholics for disturbing the peace.

The next three years, coinciding with the first substantial waves of Irish Catholic immigrants and the attendant surge of Orangeism, brought several important episodes of social violence. The Twelfth of July in 1843 witnessed clashes between religious crowds in Saint John and Portland, though an official Orange procession was not held.[59] A more serious incident occurred in March of the following year. Squire Manks, Worshipful Master of the recently-established Wellington Orange Lodge, shot and mortally wounded a Catholic Irishman during a dispute at York Point. Angry residents poured into the streets and demanded revenge. Rather than being arrested, however, Manks was placed into protective custody and expeditiously exonerated by an examining board of city magistrates. The verdict was self-defence.[60] The year closed with sporadic riots from Christmas until after New Year's. Crowds of up to 300 Irish Catholics roamed throughout York Point and Portland's wharf district, attacking Orangemen and their property. The Orangemen enthusiastically reciprocated. Two companies of British regulars finally succeeded in quashing the disturbances, but not before one Catholic had died and dozens more from both sides had received serious injuries. Although uninvolved residents bemoaned the apparent state of anarchy, the rioting was neither indiscriminate nor uncontrolled. Catholics and Orangemen carefully picked fights only with "certain... obnoxious individuals."[61]

The tensions of the winter of 1844–45 culminated in a St. Patrick's Day riot that eclipsed all earlier Orange-Catholic conflicts in its violence. On 17 March 1845, Portland Orangemen fired without provocation upon a group of Catholic revellers. The incident touched off a wave of reprisals. By nightfall general rioting between Orangemen and Irish Catholics had spread throughout the wharf district and York Point. The fighting was most intense at the foot of Fort Howe Hill in Portland.[62] The rioters dispersed when British troops positioned an artillery piece near Portland's wharves. The ploy was at best symbolic, for the concentrated fighting abated in the evening when the well-armed Orangemen gained a measure of control over the streets. The riot killed at least one Catholic, although several bodies were probably secreted away for private burials. The tally of wounded was correspondingly high, with dozens of combatants being hurt seriously enough to warrant medical attention.[63] The examinations and trials in the riot's aftermath followed the patterns established in 1842. Although authorities arrested several Orangemen, including two suspected of murder, Saint John's all-Protestant Grand Jury pre-emptively threw out their bills before the cases could be brought to trial. Instead the jury returned bills for several Irish Catholic rioters, two of whom were ultimately found guilty and sentenced. The swift vindication of Orangemen by the Grand Jury, despite an abundance of damaging testimony, illustrated the reluctance of Protestant authorities to condemn Orange violence and their continuing propensity to convict only Irish Catholics.[64]

Saint John and Portland escaped collective social violence for the next two years, but the hiatus did nothing to diminish enmity or foster peaceful linkages between Orangemen and Irish Catholics. The latter abstained from public displays on the St. Patrick's Days of 1846 and 1847. Orangemen quietly observed July 12 in their lodges in 1845; the following year they took a steamer to Gagetown for a procession with their brethren from Queens, Kings and York Counties.[65] For 1847's Twelfth of July, when famine immigration was reaching its zenith, city Orangemen invited neighbouring brethren and staged the largest procession since the organization's inception. On 14 July a Saint John newspaper trumpeted the now-familiar requiem for the Orange holiday: "Dreadful Riot! The Disaffected District [York Point] Again in Arms—Shots Fired—Several Persons Dreadfully Wounded—the Military Called Out."[66] The two-year truce had yielded only larger numbers of Catholic immigrants and nativist Orangemen, and a more sophisticated network for the combatants in both groups to utilize in battle.

July 12 started quietly enough in 1847, but as Saint John's and Portland's Orangemen began to make their way to their lodges, crowds of wary Irish Catholics spilled into the streets. One of the larger Portland lodges, probably Wellington, entertained the amateur band from the local Mechanic's Institute. All of the band members were Orangemen. In the early evening, the group led a procession of Orangemen and onlookers through the streets of Portland, across the bridge, and into the heart of the Roman Catholic ghetto at York Point.[67] The tunes they played, like most Orange favourites, were clearly offensive to Irish Catholics.[68] At the foot of Dock Street, the crowd attacked the procession with sticks and bricks, smashing many of the band's instruments and forcing the revellers to flee back across the Portland Bridge. Gathering reinforcements and firearms from their lodges and homes, the undaunted Orangemen quickly returned to their enemy's stronghold.[69]

The Irish Catholic crowd, which by now had grown to several hundred, also made use of the respite and collected weapons in the event of a reappearance of the humiliated band members and Orangemen. The buttressed Orange legions did attempt to revive the procession and music when they reached York Point. A battle was inevitable. Volleys of shots from both parties shattered the summer air, leaving scores of wounded lying in the streets along the procession route. The melee continued throughout the evening, with most of the bloodshed occurring along Dock and Mill Streets and the bridge. At midnight detachments of the 33rd Regiment, dispatched at the mayor's request, converged upon York Point only to find the streets deserted. Rather than chance an engagement with the military, both sides ceased hostilities.[70] Aided by the darkness, the Irish Catholics escaped capture and returned to their homes. The constabulary failed to make any arrests after the riot, and the grand jury issued no warrants.[71]

Assessment of the riot's severity is hampered due to the secretive removal of the dead and wounded by both parties, particularly the Irish Catholics. Official tallies included only one Catholic killed and several seriously wounded, but everyone involved knew that many had died during the encounter.[72] The significance of the conflict, however, emerged unclouded in the following months. Both sides were organized, well-stocked with weapons and clearly prepared to kill for their beliefs. Catholics had gathered hours before the Orange procession had entered York Point; they were motivated by a desire to "defend" their "territory." Orangemen consciously provoked the enemy by twice marching in procession and playing obnoxious songs through the most Catholic district of Saint John. An undeniable linkage also emerged between the Orange Order and the Mechanic's Institute, which was symbolic of the nativist attraction that Orangeism had to the economically beleaguered Protestant workers facing stiff competition from famine immigrants. Finally, the riot underscored the Orange belief in vigilante justice. The procession's return to York Point represented a "heroic" action to remove a dangerous Catholic "mob" from Saint John's thoroughfares. According to Orange sympathizers, the anaemic state of the city's constabulary justified the vigilantism.[73] In retrospect, the riot of 1847 illuminated the entrenchment of social violence as a perennial method of interaction between Orangemen and Catholics.[74]

A year of bloody skirmishes was the riot's true legacy, for neither side had emerged with a clearcut victory on the Twelfth. A wave of assaults and murders swept Saint John and Portland during the weeks that followed; Orange and Catholic vengeance was the motive for all of them.[75] A sensational series of witness examinations after the murder of a suspected Orangeman in September brought religious antipathy to a fever pitch. Dozens of testimonials exposed paramilitary networks operated by militant Orangemen and Catholics. Personal revenge on a small scale appeared to be the favourite tactic of the weaker and outnumbered Catholics. Orangemen, enjoying the support of a Protestant majority, preferred a collective vigilantism whereby they dispensed extralegal justice while acting as an unofficial watchdog of the Irish lower orders.[76] By the year's end, it was apparent that the Orange-Catholic struggle had not diminished. Both sides habitually armed themselves if they ventured into unfriendly districts; each tried desperately to identify its most virulent enemies, and in many cases, both were prepared to kill for their causes.

The religious conflict of the 1840s peaked two years later in Saint John's worst riot of the nineteenth century. The city was quiet in 1848, much as it had been in 1846, because local Orangemen travelled to Fredericton to participate in a massive demonstration.[77] But as the Twelfth approached in 1849, Saint John's Orangemen advertised for the first time their plans for hosting provincial brethren and sponsoring an elaborate procession.[78] Motivated by vivid memories of the inconclusive 1847 conflict, Orangemen and Irish Catholics grimly prepared themselves for battle. On the eve of the holiday, Mayor Robert D. Wilmot met with local Orange officials and asked them to voluntarily abandon their plans to march. But the Orangemen, well-versed on their rights, rejected the suggestion because no provincial statute gave civilian officials the authority to ban public processions.[79] The march, they insisted, would proceed as planned.

With a measure of fatalism, Saint John prepared for the occasion. While Orangemen from Carleton, York, Kings and Queens Counties were boarding steamers and carriages for Saint John, Irish Catholics were buying arms and ammunition. Shopkeepers along Prince William Street, King Street and Market Square boarded their windows and decided to declare the day a business holiday.[80] Early on the morning of the Twelfth, hundreds of Orangemen from Saint John and Portland collected at Nethery's Hotel on Church Street and marched to a nearby wharf to greet the Carleton ferry. Among the disembarking brethren was Joseph Corum, the Senior Deputy Grand Master of the New Brunswick Grand Lodge. As the procession leader, Corum would have the honour of representing King William by riding a white horse. The Orangemen came heavily armed with pistols, muskets and sabres. After assuming a military file, they began the march to the Portland suburb of Indiantown where they would meet the steamer bringing reinforcements from the northern counties. Their planned route would take them through both Irish Catholic bastions—York Point and Portland's wharf district.[81]

Upon reaching York Point they encountered a large pine arch, symbolically green, which spanned the foot of Mill Street. Several hundred jeering Irish Catholics clustered near the arch's supporting poles; they implored the Orangemen to continue. Outnumbered for the moment, the Orangemen accepted the humiliation and dipped their banners as they passed under the arch. While a few stones were hurled at the Orangemen, and they responded with warning shots, no fighting broke out.[82] Without further incident, the procession reached Indiantown where it gratefully welcomed scores of reinforcements. Among the newcomers was another pivotal Orange leader. George Anderson, a Presbyterian grocer and primary lodge master, was a veteran of several disturbances in his home town of Fredericton. Anderson, bedecked with a sword that indicated his rank, assumed a position next to Corum at the column's head. The procession now numbered approximately 600 people. The men were heavily armed, the majority carrying muskets on shoulder straps. A few clutched axes that would be used to destroy the green bough when they returned to York

Point. Finally, a wagon filled with weapons and supplies took up a station at the rear of the procession. As the Orangemen made their way back to York Point, Portland inhabitants observed that the procession resembled a confident army about to engage in battle.[83]

In the meantime, authorities attempted to alleviate the growing tensions with three separate plans, all of which would ultimately fail to prevent a conflict. Mayor Wilmot's first scheme was to defuse the powder keg by removing the pine arch and dispersing the Catholic crowd in York Point. Wilmot, accompanied by a magistrate and a constable, was physically rebuffed in this endeavour by a cohesive, territorially-minded crowd that chanted "Stay off our ground!" He then dispatched Jacob Allan, the Portland police magistrate, to intercept the Orangemen before they reached York Point.[84] Allan asked Corum and Anderson to bypass the Catholic district by using the longer Valley Road on their approach to Saint John. After conferring with their followers, the leaders rejected Allan's suggestion. Their men had suffered humiliation during the morning's passage under the Catholic arch; now they insisted on "Death or Victory."[85] Wilmot borrowed the third and final plan from Saint John's history of dealing with riots. At his request, sixty British soldiers stationed themselves in Market Square to prevent general rioting. While the choice of location would do nothing to prevent a conflict, for Market Square lay to the south of York Point and the Orangemen would enter from the north over the Portland Bridge, it would serve to contain the battle to the Catholic ghetto. The detachment's failure to position itself between the advancing Orangemen and the offensive arch, when it had ample time to do so, raised questions about the sincerity of the authorities' attempts to prevent bloodshed.[86]

General rioting broke out along Mill Street before the procession arrived at the bough. The Catholic crowd now numbered approximately 500, and like the Orangemen, many had armed themselves with muskets. Reports of who fired the first shots varied, but roofers working on a Mill Street building agreed that Orangemen opened fire after being met with a volley of stones and brickbats.[87] Several Catholics lay wounded or dying after the barrage, and then their guns answered the Orangemen's. A heated battle ensued. Men and women along Mill Street threw anything they could at the better-armed Orange contingent. Some engaged in fistfights with individuals that they were able to pull from the Orange ranks. Corum struggled to free himself after a handful of Irishmen grabbed his horse's tether. A dozen Catholics captured the wagon filled with arms and gave its driver a sound thrashing. Hundreds of shots were fired, and at least twelve combatants lost their lives. The Irish Catholics suffered most of the casualties. After several minutes of furious fighting, the Orangemen emerged from York Point. As they headed for the safety of the troops, their procession was still intact.[88]

The British garrison, after remaining stationary in Market Square throughout the heat of the battle, went into action as soon as the Orangemen left the Irish Catholic ghetto. Without firing a shot, the soldiers marched past the procession and positioned themselves on Dock Street to seal off the Catholic district. This manoeuvre effectively doused what remained of the conflict.[89] It also gave the Orangemen the opportunity to continue their procession unmolested, for any Catholics wishing to leave York Point in pursuit would have to contend first with the soldiers. The Orangemen, heady with their successful assault on the enemy's territory, proceeded through Market and King Squares and made a circle through the city's centre. Only when they entered Market Square again, with the intention of parading through York Point for the third time, were the troops commanded to impede their progress. Being satisfied with their efforts, the Orangemen agreed to disband. With the Orange threat finally removed, the Irish Catholics waiting in York Point also dispersed. The great Saint John riot of 1849 was over.[90]

The riot's judicial aftermath followed patterns well-established by 1849, although there was one notable exception. At Lieutenant-Governor Edmund Head's insistence, the Saint John Grand Jury served warrants on Orange participants as well as the Catholics. This attempt at impartiality was severely undermined, however, by a prejudiced investigative team that included the prominent Orangeman W.H. Needham.[91] Ultimately, all but five of the bills against Orangemen, including those for Corum, Anderson and eighteen others, were dropped before the defendants reached trial. The five Orangemen who actually stood in the dock were swiftly declared innocent by a jury that remained seated. Much to the prosecution's dismay, the jury ignored recent provincial legislation that clearly outlawed armed public processions.[92] For the Irish Catholics, on the other hand, the judicial pattern of the 1840s remained intact. Of the twenty-four implicated, six were tried on assault charges, one for attempted murder and four for unlawful assembly. Two were eventually found guilty, including the alleged "ringleader" who led the defence of the green arch. John Haggerty, immigrant labourer and father of three, would spend his sixty-third birthday in the provincial penitentiary while serving his one-year sentence for assault.[93]

The 1849 riot signalled an end to collective social conflict between Orangemen and Catholics, although small skirmishes would continue for years.[94] Various factors brought about this extended truce, the most important being the hegemony established by Orangemen in Saint John and Portland. In a sense, Orangemen had won the battle of the 1840s. The Irish Catholics' attempts to check the growth of Orangeism with counter-demonstrations had failed. They undeniably suffered the most casualties in the course of the riots. Moreover, a fusion between all levels of authority and the Orange Order had taken place. Orangemen, constables and British soldiers had combined to contain every major disturbance within the Irish Catholic ghettos of York Point and Portland. The Orange Order became an acceptable accomplice for the maintenance of social control. A double standard had clearly emerged: authorities found Orange vigilantism preferable to "mob rule" by the Irish Catholic "lower order."[95] During the 1840s Orangemen served as constables, magistrates and legislative representatives.

Excepting one active magistrate in Saint John, the Irish Catholics were excluded from power. This inequity profoundly shaped law enforcement during the riots and trials. No Catholic would be allowed to sit on juries; moreover, only Irish Catholics would be found guilty of rioting offences. Even when Orangemen stood in the dock, such as after the York Point riot of 1849, they were expeditiously exonerated.[96] Ethnicity and religion targeted the Irish Catholics for suppression during the 1840s; meanwhile Orangeism developed into an unofficial arm of social control to protect the Protestant majority.

New Brunswick's improved economic environment after mid-century contributed to the demise of collective conflict by alleviating some of the fierce competition between immigrants and natives. The "Hungry Forties" had indeed been more than a historical cliché to many colonists. A sustained depression had brought scarcities of goods, food and services. Natives had competed with Irish Catholic immigrants for limited jobs, a factor that had contributed to the rapid growth of Orangeism. Economic variables alone did not cause the Orange-Green riots, but they certainly helped to account for a foundation of social tension.[97] As the province successfully weathered the English transition to free trade in the 1850s, investment capital increased and jobs became more available.[98] Thus Orangemen found one of the key elements of their rhetorical campaign against Irish Catholics undermined. Ultimately, fuller employment fostered better relations between Protestant and Catholic workers.

Another factor in the disappearance of perennial disturbances between Protestants and Catholics was the Orange Order's discontinuance of July 12 processions while it fought for provincial incorporation. Saint John and Portland Orangemen wisely decided not to risk any negative publicity that might accompany collective violence with Irish Catholics while the bill was being debated in the New Brunswick legislature. The process lasted 25 years, but eventually the trade-off of abstention for legitimacy proved fruitful.[99] Not until after the bill finally passed in 1875, in the midst of the emotional separate schools issue, would Orangemen again take to Saint John's streets to display their fervent brand of loyalty and Protestantism.[100]

Finally, a drastic reduction in the number of Irish Catholic immigrants after 1848 helped to subdue the nativist impulse. The tide of famine immigrants had dropped as precipitously as it had risen. Improving conditions in Ireland accounted for a general reduction in emigrants, especially from the poorer Catholic counties. In addition a discriminatory immigration policy, instituted at the behest of Lieutenant-Governors Sir William Colebrooke and Sir Edmund Head, curtailed Catholic immigration while it increased the number of more desirable Protestant settlers from the British Isles.[101] The results were striking: between 1851 and 1861 the percentages of Irish compared to the total immigrant population dropped dramatically in both Saint John and Portland. This decrease also reflected the continuing out-migration of transient Catholics to the "Boston States" and to other British North American provinces.[102] Finally, it indicated the beginnings of a process of acculturation; the sons and daughters of Catholic and Protestant immigrants would be listed as New Brunswickers in the 1861 census. The "soldiers" of the 1840s—both Orange and Green—would be supplanted by generations to whom the violent experiences of the "Hungry Forties" would be historical anecdotes.

The Orange Order was New Brunswick's institutionalized nativist response to Irish Catholic immigration during the 1840s. Prior to this decade, the organization was a small and mostly invisible fraternal order dominated by Irish Protestant immigrants and British garrison troops. As Irish Catholic famine victims poured into Saint John and Portland during the 1840s, however, Protestant natives and non-Irish-born immigrants joined the Orange Order. Orangemen spearheaded a rhetorical campaign to combat the famine immigration, using anti-Catholic and racist propaganda to discourage the Irish from settling permanently in the city. Additionally, the Orange Order increasingly acted as a paramilitary vigilante group that freely engaged in riots with bellicose Irish Catholics. The combination of nativist rhetoric and a mutual willingness to engage in armed conflict provided a decade of collective social violence that culminated in the tragic riot of 12 July 1849. Thus Saint John and Portland, like several eastern seaboard cities in the United States, experienced a strong nativist impulse and several destructive episodes of social violence.

Notes

1. *Weekly Chronicle* (Saint John), 22 March 1839.

2. *Morning News* (Saint John), 24 September 1847.

3. For this study, social violence is defined as "assault upon an individual or his property solely or primarily because of his membership in a social category." See Allen D. Grimshaw, "Interpreting Collective Violence: An Argument for the Importance of Social Structure," in James F. Short, Jr. and Marvin E. Wolfgang, eds., *Collective Violence* (Chicago, 1972), pp. 12, 18–20.

4　Sir Edmund Head to Lord Grey, 15 July 1849, Colonial Office Series [CO] 188, Public Record Office [PRO], London: *Royal Gazette* (Fredericton), 19 September 1849; D.R. Jack, *Centennial Prize Essay on the History of the City and County of St. John* (Saint John, 1883), pp. 136–37; Reverend J.W. Millidge. "Reminiscences of St. John from 1849 to 1860," *New Brunswick Historical Society Collections*, Vol. IV (1919), pp. 8, 127.

5. Its mid-century population stood at 23,000, making one in every 8.5 New Brunswickers a Saint John resident. Portland, with 8,500 inhabitants, was roughly one-third the size of Saint John. See New Brunswick Census, 1851, Provincial Archives of New Brunswick [PANB].

6. Presentment of the Saint John Grand Jury, 27 October 1847, Minutes, Saint John General Sessions, PANB.

7. *Morning News*, 8, 11 September 1843; Abraham Gesner, *New Brunswick: With Notes for Emigrants* (London, 1847), pp. 122–24: Reverend W.C. Atkinson, *A Historical and Statistical Account of New Brunswick, B.N.A. with Advice to Emigrants* (Edinburgh, 1844), pp. 28–29, 36–37.

8. The 1840s was a particularly depressed decade, but as Graeme Wynn eloquently pointed out, the colony was already a veteran of the nineteenth-century boom and bust "bandalore"; in 1819, 1825 and 1837, New Brunswick suffered trade depressions due to financial downturns and the erosion of speculation capital in Great Britain: *Timber Colony: A Historical Geography of Early Nineteenth Century New Brunswick* (Toronto, 1981), pp. 3–33, 43–53. See also P.D. McClelland, "The New Brunswick Economy in the Nineteenth Century," *Journal of Economic History, XXV* (December, 1965), pp. 686–90.

9. W.S. MacNutt, *New Brunswick, a History, 1784–1867* (Toronto, 1963), pp. 283–84, 296: MacNutt, "New Brunswick's Age of Harmony: The Administration of Sir John Harvey," *Canadian Historical Review, XXXII* (June 1951), pp. 123–24; D.G.G. Kerr, *Sir Edmund Head: The Scholarly Governor* (Toronto, 1954), pp. 39–54; Wynn, *Timber Colony*, pp. 43–44, 51–53.

10. *Colonial Advocate* (Saint John), 14 July 1845; MacNutt, *New Brunswick*, p. 285; Wynn, *Timber Colony*, pp. 51–53.

11. *New Brunswick Reporter* (Fredericton), 13 October 1848, 24 August 1849; *Morning News*, 28 May 1849; Wynn, *Timber Colony*, pp. 150–55; MacNutt, *New Brunswick*, p. 320.

12. Immigration Returns, New Brunswick Blue Books, 1832–50. Public Archives of Canada [PAC]: "Report on Trade and Navigation." *Journal of the House of Assembly of New Brunswick*, 1866.

13. Only in 1853, after the famine abated in Ireland, would English immigrants once again become the largest group. See New Brunswick Census, 1851: "Report on Trade and Navigation," *Journal of the House of Assembly of New Brunswick*, 1866; William F. Ganong, *A Monograph of the Origins of Settlements in the Province of New Brunswick* (Ottawa, 1904), pp. 90–120.

14. Cecil Woodham-Smith, *The Great Hunger: Ireland 1845–9* (London, 1962), pp. 206–9; Lawrence J. McCaffrey, *The Irish Diaspora in America* (Bloomington, Ind., 1976), pp. 59–62; William Forbes Adams, *Ireland and Irish Emigration to the New World* (New York, 1932); Donald Akenson, ed., *Canadian Papers in Rural History*, Vol. III (Gananoque, Ont., 1981), pp. 219–21.

15. Woodham-Smith, *Great Hunger*, pp. 29, 206–13; John I. Cooper, "Irish Immigration and the Canadian Church Before the Middle of the Nineteenth Century." *Journal of the Canadian Church Historical Society*, II (May 1955), pp. 13–14; Adams, *Ireland and Irish Emigration*; McCaffrey, *Irish Diaspora*, pp. 59–62; Oliver MacDonagh, "Irish Emigration to the United States of America and the British Colonies During the Famine," in R. Dudley Edwards and T. Desmond Williams, eds., *The Great Famine: Studies in Irish History 1845–52* (Dublin, 1956), pp. 332–39.

16. Immigration Returns, New Brunswick Blue Books, PAC; M.H. Perley's Report on 1846 Emigration, in William Colebrooke to Grey, 29 December 1846, CO 188.

17. *Ibid.: Royal Gazette*, 17 March, 7 July 1847; *Saint John Herald*, 12 November 1845; James Hannay, *History of New Brunswick* (Saint John, 1909), Vol. II, p. 70; MacDonagh, "Irish Emigration," pp. 368–73; Adams, *Ireland and Irish Emigration*, p. 234; Woodham-Smith, *Great Hunger*, pp. 209–10.

18. New Brunswick Census, 1851, 1861; *Morning News*, 8, 11 September 1843; Alexander Monro, *New Brunswick: With a Brief Outline of Nova Scotia, and Prince Edward Island* (Halifax, 1855), p. 125; James S. Buckingham, *Canada, Nova Scotia, New Brunswick, and the Other British Provinces in North America* (London, 1843), pp. 409–10.

19. Kings Ward, which included all of York Point and was roughly equal in size to the other Saint John wards, had twice the population of any ward in the 1851 New Brunswick Census. For descriptions of York Point, see Grand Jury Reports, 16 December 1848. Minutes, Saint John General Sessions, PANB, and D.H. Waterbury, "Retrospective Ramble Over Historic St. John," *New Brunswick Historical Society Collections*, Vol. IV (1919), pp. 86–88.

20. Colebrooke to Grey, 28 January 1848, CO 188; Gesner, *New Brunswick*, p. 124.

21. John Higham, *Strangers in the Land: Patterns of American Nativism 1860–1925* (New Brunswick, N.J., 1955), pp. 3–4; Higham, "Another Look at Nativism," *Catholic Historical Review*, XLIV (July 1958), pp. 148–50.

22. For examples of Canadian nativist studies, see Howard Palmer, *Land of the Second Chance: A History of Ethnic Groups in Southern Alberta* (Lethbridge, 1972); Palmer, "Nativism and Ethnic Tolerance in Alberta: 1920–1972," Ph.D. thesis, York University, 1974; Simon Evans, "Spatial Bias in the Incidence of Nativism: Opposition to Hutterite Expansion in Alberta," *Canadian Ethnic Studies*, Vol. VI, Nos. 1–2 (1974), pp. 1–16.

23. *Loyalist and Conservative Advocate* (Saint John), 13 August 1847. See also issues from 20, 27 August 1847.

24. For histories of the Orange Order, see Hereward Senior, *Orangeism in Ireland and Britain 1765–1836* (London, 1966), especially pp. 4–21, 194–206; Senior, "The Early Orange Order 1795–1870," in T. Desmond Williams, ed., *Secret Societies in Ireland* (Dublin, 1973); Peter Gibbon, "The Origins of the Orange Order and the United Irishmen," *Economy and Society*, I (1972), pp. 134–63.

25. Canadian Orange Order histories include Cecil Houston and W.J. Smyth, *The Sash Canada Wore: A Historical Geography of the Orange Order in Canada* (Toronto, 1980); Hereward Senior, *Orangeism: The Canadian Phase* (Toronto, 1972); Senior, "The Genesis of Canadian Orangeism," *Ontario History*, LX (June 1968), pp. 13–29.

26. James McNichol's report, *Loyal Orange Association Report, 1886* (Toronto, 1886), *Sentinel*, 3 July 1930; J. Edward Steele, comp., *History and Directory of the Provincial Grand Orange Lodge and Primary Lodges of New Brunswick* (Saint John, 1934), p. 11.

27. Miscellaneous Orange documents, courtesy of Professor Peter Toner, University of New Brunswick at Saint John; James McNichol's report, *Loyal Orange Association Report*, 1886; Steele, *History of the Orange Lodges of New Brunswick*, pp. 11, 17–21; Houston and Smyth, *The Sash Canada Wore*, pp. 69–70.

28. Lodge returns, in *Minutes of the Grand Orange Lodge of New Brunswick* (various publishers, 1846–53); *Annual Reports of the Grand Orange Lodge of the Loyal Orange Association of B.N.A.* [various publishers, 1846–50]; *New Brunswick Reporter*, 10 May 1850; *Loyalist*, 8 June 1848; *Carleton Sentinel* (Woodstock), 15 July 1854; *Sentinel*, 3 July 1930; Steele, *History of the Orange Lodges of New Brunswick*, pp. 11–13, 37–39, 53–55, 59.

29. Because Nova Scotia's lodges, who received their warrants directly from New Brunswick, were only two years old in mid-century, the vast majority of the 10,000

members resided in New Brunswick. See "Minutes of the Grand Orange Lodge of New Brunswick and Nova Scotia," in *Weekly Chronicle*, 6 July 1849; Orange Order documents, Peter Toner; *Minutes of the Grand Orange Lodge of New Brunswick, 1846–50; Sentinel*, 3 July 1930.

30. Correspondence from John Earle in *Annual Report of the Grand Orange Lodge of the Loyal Orange Association of B.N.A.*, 1851; *New Brunswick Reporter*, 26 April 1850; Head to Grey, 7 September 1847, CO 188; *New Brunswick Courier* (Saint John), 25 July 1840; Steele, *History of the Orange Lodge of New Brunswick*, p. 11.

31. Houston and Smyth, *The Sash Canada Wore*, pp. 70–72; Steele, *History of the Orange Lodges of New Brunswick*, pp. 115–18.

32. "Minutes of the Organizational Meeting of the Grand Orange Lodge of New Brunswick, 1844," in Steele, *History of the Orange Lodges of New Brunswick*, p. 11; New Brunswick Census, 1851.

33. James Brown letters to *New Brunswick Reporter*, 28 April, 5, 12 May 1848; *Morning News*, 18 July 1849; John Earle's correspondence in *Annual Report of the Grand Orange Lodge of the Loyal Orange Association of B.N.A.*, 1851.

34. Minute book, Wellington Orange Lodge, Portland. New Brunswick Museum (NBM), Saint John.

35. 1851 manuscript census returns from Saint John County are incomplete. Returns from only four of the city's wards are extant: Kings, Dukes, Sydney and Queens. Records from Portland Parish and Carleton are missing.

36. Returns for Saint John County, New Brunswick Manuscript Census, 1851, PANB; Orange documents, including dispensations and lodge returns, Peter Toner; *Minutes of the Grand Orange Lodge of New Brunswick*, 1846–55; Evidence, Saint John Riot Trials, Documents, New Brunswick Executive Council Records, PANB; New Brunswick Supreme Court Documents, PANB. The newspapers consulted were the *Loyalist, Weekly Chronicle* and *Morning News* for the 1840s, as well as the *Daily Sun* (Saint John), 13 July 1897, and Steele, *History of the Orange Lodges of New Brunswick*.

37. *Laws and Ordinances of the Orange Association of British North America* (Toronto, 1840), p. 11; *The Orange Question Treated by Sir Francis Hincks and the London "Times"* (Montreal, 1877).

38. For example, Portland's Wellington Lodge attempted to combat negative publicity after a decade of social violence by declaring itself a "benefit" organization in 1851. See Minute Book, Wellington Orange Lodge, NBM. See also *Rules and Regulations of the Orange Institution of British North America* (Toronto, 1838), p. 5; Steele, *History of the Orange Lodges of New Brunswick*.

39. *Morning News*, 24 January 1849; *Headquarters* (Fredericton), 24 January 1849.

40. *Loyalist*, 1 October 1847.

41. *Minutes of the Grand Orange Lodge of New Brunswick*, 1852; Rev. Gilbert Spurr's address to Orangemen, in *Loyalist*, 15 October 1847; Head to Grey, 26 July 1848, CO 188; *New Brunswick Reporter*, 26 October 1849; *Carleton Sentinel*, 2 July 1850; *Weekly Chronicle*, 15 July 1842, 4 February 1848; *Christian Visitor* (Saint John), 8 March 1848; Steele, *History of the Orange Lodges of New Brunswick*, pp. 13–15, 21.

42. For discussions of the papal conspiracy theory in North America, see S.M. Lipset and Earl Raab, *The Politics of Unreason* (New York, 1970), pp. 47–59. David B. Davis,

"Some Themes of Counter-Subversion: An Analysis of Anti-Masonic, Anti-Catholic, and Anti-Mormon Literature," *Mississippi Valley Historical Review*, XLVII (September, 1960), pp. 205–7, Higham, *Strangers in the Land*, pp. 5–6.

43. *Church Witness* (Saint John), 21 September 1853.

44. *Minutes of the Grand Orange Lodge of New Brunswick*, 1846–55, particularly S.H. Gilbert's sermon in 1854; Grand Orange Lodge of New Brunswick's address to Queen Victoria, in Head to Grey, 28 April 1851, CO 188; *New Brunswick Reporter*, 9 April 1850; *Carleton Sentinel*, 16 July 1850; *New Brunswick Reporter*, 1 October 1847; *Weekly Chronicle*, 31 August 1849, 18 July 1851; *Loyalist*, 24 September 1847; *Church Witness*, 16 July, 13 August 1851, 6 July 1853.

45. Adams, *Ireland and Irish Emigration*, pp. 363–64; Carl Wittke, *The Irish in America* (Baton Rouge, La., 1956), pp. 46–47; Kenneth Duncan, "Irish Famine Immigration and the Social Structure of Canada West," *Canadian Review of Sociology and Anthropology*, II (February, 1965), pp. 33, 39.

46. *Loyalist*, 6 April 1848.

47. Alexander McHarg Diary, NBM; *Morning News*, 8 January, 8 December 1841, 6 January, 14 June 1843, 5 January 1848; *Weekly Chronicle*, 5 January, 28 June 1844, 26 November 1847; Queen vs. David Nice, New Brunswick Supreme Court Documents, PANB.

48. *Loyalist*, 30 March 1848; *New Brunswick Reporter*, 20 April 1850; *New Brunswick Assembly Debates*, 8 March 1850, PANB; *Morning News*, 24 January 1849; *Loyalist*, 16 July, 15, 28 October, 4 November 1847; *New Brunswick Reporter*, 19 November 1847, 15 March 1850; *Morning News*, 11 August 1847.

49. For excellent studies of racism in the British Isles, see L.P. Curtis, Jr., *Anglo-Saxons and Celts: A Study of Anti-Irish Prejudice in Victorian England* (Bridgeport, Conn., 1968), pp. 8–9, 24–26, and *Apes and Angels: The Irishman in Victorian Caricature* (Devon, England, 1971), *passim*.

50. *Weekly Chronicle*, 31 August, 28 September 1849; *Loyalist*, 24 September 1847.

51. *Loyalist*, 1 October, 11 November 1847.

52. *New Brunswick Reporter*, 10 May 1850; *Loyalist*, 16 July, 17 September, 15 October 1847; *Weekly Chronicle*, 29 July 1842.

53. The theme of competition between immigrant labourers and nativists in North America is explored in Oscar Handlin, *Boston's Immigrants* (Cambridge, Mass., 1959), pp. 180–87. Higham, *Strangers in the Land*, p. 57. Adams, *Ireland and Irish Emigration*, p. 353.

54. M.H. Perley's Report on 1846 Emigration, in Colebrooke to Grey, 29 December 1846, CO 188; *Royal Gazette*, 17 March, 7 July 1847; Wynn, *Timber Colony*, pp. 155–56; Kathryn Johnston, "The History of St. John, 1837–1867: Civic and Economic," Honours thesis, Mount Allison University, 1953, pp. 24–28.

55. *Loyalist*, 24 March 1845, 17 September, 28 October, 4 November, 9, 23 December 1847; *New Brunswick Reporter*, 10 September 1847; *New Brunswick Reporter*, 19 November 1847.

56. Joseph Brown to R.F. Hazen, 11 July 1837. R.F. Hazen Papers, NBM: *Weekly Chronicle*, 14 July, 1837.

57. *New Brunswick Reporter*, 26 April, 10 May 1850.

58. *Morning News*, 13 July, 5 August 1842; *Weekly Chronicle*, 15 July, 12 August 1842; *New Brunswick Courier*, 16 July, 13, 27 August 1842; Minutes, Saint John General Sessions, 9, 10, 17 December 1842, 25 March 1843, PANB; *Sentinel*, 29 October 1891.

59. *New Brunswick Reporter*, 26 April 1850.

60. Mayor Lauchlan Donaldson to Alfred Reade, 8 March 1844, New Brunswick Supreme Court Documents, PANB; McHarg Diary; *Morning News*, 5 April 1844.

61. *Weekly Chronicle*, 3 January 1845; *Morning News*, 3 January 1845; *Headquarters*, 8 January 1845; McHarg Diary.

62. Donaldson to Reade, 29 March 1845, Saint John Grand Jury to Colebrooke, 27 March 1845, "Riots and Disasters." New Brunswick Executive Council Records [Executive Council Records], PANB; *Loyalist*, 24 March 1845; *Weekly Chronicle*, 21 March 1845.

63. Minutes, New Brunswick Executive Council, 7 April 1845, PANB; Report of Doctors Robert and William Bayard, 17 March 1845. "Riots and Disasters." Executive Council Records: McHarg Diary; *Weekly Chronicle*, 21 March 1845; *Morning News*, 19 March 1845; *Observer* (Saint John), 18 March 1845; *New Brunswick Reporter*, 21 March 1845; *New Brunswick Courier*, 22 March 1845; *Loyalist*, 24 March 1845.

64. Minutes, Saint John General Sessions, 20, 22, 26 March, 14 June 1845; Donaldson to Reade, 22 March 1845. "Riots and Disasters." Executive Council Records: *New Brunswick Courier*, 5 July 1845; *Saint John Herald*, 2 July 1845.

65. *Minutes of the Grand Orange Lodge of New Brunswick*, 1847; *Weekly Chronicle*, 17 July 1846.

66. *Morning News*, 14 July 1847.

67. Orange supporters tried to disassociate the Orange Order, the Mechanic's Institute Band and the crowd that followed the procession. *The Loyalist*, 16 July 1847, claimed that the band had nothing to do with the Orange procession, while Clarence Ward made the dubious assertion that the Orange entourage consisted of "children." See "Old Times in St. John—1847." *Saint John Globe*, 1 April 1911, p. 8. Yet an article in the *Orange Sentinel*, 29 October 1891, proudly revealed that all the band members were Orangemen.

68. For examples of these songs, see *The Sentinel Orange and Patriotic Song Book* (Toronto, 1930?) and R. McBride, ed., *The Canadian Orange Minstrel for 1860. Contains Nine New and Original Songs, Mostly All of Them Showing Some Wrong that Affects the Order or the True Course of Protestant Loyalty to the British Crown* (London, 1860). Note particularly "Croppies Lie Down," a nineteenth century favourite of Orangemen in Europe and North America.

69. *New Brunswick Courier*, 17 July 1847; *Morning News*, 14 July 1847; *Loyalist*, 16 July 1847; *Sentinel*, October 1891; McHarg Diary.

70. *Morning News*, 14 July 1847; Colebrooke to Grey, 30 July 1847, Documents, Executive Council Records, PANB; McHarg Diary *New Brunswick Courier*, 17 July 1847; *Loyalist*, 16 July 1847; Ward, "Old Times in St. John—1847."

71. *New Brunswick Courier*, 7 August 1847.

72. Colebrooke to Grey, 30 July 1847, CO 188; *Morning News*, 14 July 1847.

73. *Loyalist*, 16 July 1847; Ward, "Old Times in St. John—1847."

74. One newspaper referred to it as a "civil war," *Morning News*, 14 July 1847.

75. *New Brunswick Courier*, 24 July 1847; *Morning News*, 14, 21, 23, 28 July 1847; *Loyalist*, 23 July 1847; *Weekly Chronicle*, 30 July 1847.

76. Queen vs. Dennis McGovern, 7–17 September 1847. New Brunswick Supreme Court Documents, PANB. Note especially the testimonies of Thomas Clark, James Clark, Ezekiel Downey and Edward McDermott. See also *Morning News*, 24 January 1848, *Weekly Chronicle*, 10 September 1847, *New Brunswick Courier*, 11 September 1847; *Loyalist*, 10 September 1847; *Morning News*, 8 September 1847.

77. *Weekly Chronicle*, 14 July 1848. Fredericton's Orangemen invited provincial brethren to celebrate the anniversary of their successful 1847 battle with Irish Catholics: *New Brunswick Reporter*, 10 May 1850.

78. *Weekly Chronicle*, 6 July 1849.

79. Head to Grey, 15 July 1849, CO 188. The question of the legality of public processions, especially armed ones, would become a hotly debated topic in the House of Assembly after the riot, yet no restrictive legislation would emerge from the debate.

80. Testimonies of Thomas Paddock and Francis Jones, "Riots and Disasters," Executive Council Records; *New Brunswick Reporter*, 13 July 1849; Head to Grey, 15 July 1849, CO 188.

81. *Morning News*, 13 July 1849; *New-Brunswicker* (Saint John), 14 July 1849; *New Brunswick Courier*, 14 July 1849; Testimonies of Francis Jones, George Noble, Jacob Allan, Charles Boyd, Squire Manks and George McKelvey. "Riots and Disasters," Executive Council Records; Head to Grey, 15 July 1849, CO 188.

82. Testimonies of Josiah Wetmore, Jeremiah McCarthy, George Nobel and Jacob Allan. "Riots and Disasters." Executive Council Records; Head to Grey, 15 July 1849. CO 188; *Sentinel*, 3 July 1930.

83. Testimonies of Jacob Allan, George Mason, Samuel Dalton, Samuel Gordon and Francis Jones. "Riots and Disasters," Executive Council Records; Head to Grey, 15 July 1849, CO 188; *Weekly Chronicle*, 13 July 1849; *New Brunswicker*, 14 July 1849; *Sentinel*, 3 July 1930.

84. Head to Grey, 15 July 1849. CO 188; Testimonies of James Gilbert, Henry Gilbert, John Nixon, John Fitzpatrick, Joseph Wetmore and James Clark. "Riots and Disasters," Executive Council Records.

85. Testimonies of Jacob Allan, Francis Jones and Squire Manks, "Riots and Disasters," Executive Council Records; Head to Grey, 15 July 1849, CO 188; *Sentinel*, 29 October 1891, 3 July 1930.

86. Head to Grey, 15 July 1849, CO 188; Jacob Allan testimony, "Riots and Disasters," Executive Council Records; *Morning News*, 13 July 1849; *Temperance Telegraph* (Saint John), 19 July 1849.

87. Testimonies of James McKenzie, William Smith, Francis Wilson and Francis Jones, "Riots and Disasters," Executive Council Records; *Temperance Telegraph*, 19 July 1849; *Weekly Chronicle*, 13 July 1849; *Morning News*, 13 July 1849.

88. Testimonies of Squire Manks, James McKenzie, William Smith, Francis Wilson and Jeremiah Smith, "Riots and Disasters," Executive Council Records; *Morning News*, 13 July 1849; *Christian Visitor*, 14 July 1849; *Weekly Chronicle*, 13 July 1849.

89. Head to Grey, 15 July 1849, CO 188; Charles Boyd testimony, "Riots and Disasters," Executive Council Records; *Morning News*, 13 July 1849; *New-Brunswicker*, 14 July 1849; *Weekly Chronicle*, 13 July 1849.

90. Testimonies of Charles Boyd and Jacob Allan, "Riots and Disasters," Executive Council Records; *Morning News*, 13 July 1849; Head to Grey, 15 July 1849, CO 188.

91. Head to Grey, 15 July 1849, CO 188; *Morning News*, 23 July 1849; *New Brunswick Courier*, 21 July 1849.

92. William B. Kinnear to Head, extract, 6 September 1849, in Head to Grey, 7 September 1849, CO 188; Recognizances, July-September 1849. "Riots and Disasters," Executive Council Records; Documents, Saint John Justice Court, 1849, PANB; Inquests, 1849, New Brunswick Supreme Court Documents, PANB; 12 Victoria, c. 29, 1849, *New Brunswick Statutes*, 1849; *Morning News*, 30 July 1849; *New Brunswick Courier*, 21, 28 July 1849; *Temperance Telegraph*, 23 August 1849.

93. Documents, Saint John Justice Court, 1849; Kinnear to Head, extract, 6 September 1849, in Head to Grey, 7 September 1849, CO 188; John Haggerty petition to Head, September 1849, in Judicial Documents, Executive Council Records; *Weekly Chronicle*, 24 August 1849; *New Brunswick Courier*, 18, 25 August 1849.

94. *New Brunswick Courier*, 19 July 1851, 16, 23, 30 July 6, 13 August 1853; *Weekly Chronicle*, 18 July 1851; *Morning News*, 15, 20 July 1853; *New Brunswick Reporter*, 15, 22 July 1853; *Freeman* (Saint John), 14 July 1855; McHarg Diary.

95. *Loyalist*, 30 March 1848; *New Brunswick Reporter*, 20 April 1850. Irish immigrants in the United States experienced a similar double standard: see Theodore M. Hammett, "Two Mobs of Jacksonian Boston: Ideology and Interest," *Journal of American History*, LXII (March 1976), pp. 866–67.

96. Documents, Saint John Justice Court, 1849: "Riots and Disasters," Executive Council Records.

97. W.W. Rostow explored the linkages between social unrest and economic downturns in *British Economy of the Nineteenth Century* (Oxford, 1948) pp. 123–25.

98. Wynn, *Timber Colony*, pp. 84–86, 166–67; MacNutt, *New Brunswick*, p. 329; James R. Rice, "A History of Organized Labour in Saint John, New Brunswick, 1813–1890," M.A. thesis, University of New Brunswick, 1968, pp. 33–34.

99. *Journal of the House of Assembly of New Brunswick*, 1850–51, 1853–54, 1857–60, 1867, 1872–75; 38 Victoria, c. 54, 1875, *Statutes of New Brunswick*, 1875.

100. Saint John's Orangemen sponsored a massive procession on the first Twelfth of July following the bill's assent. See *Freeman*, 13, 15, 18 July 1876; *Morning News*, 14, 17 July 1876.

101. Colebrooke to Grey, 30 July 1847, Head to Grey, 15 July 1849, CO 188; Colebrooke Correspondence, 1847. Head Correspondence, 1849. PANB.

102. New Brunswick Census, 1851, 1861; Immigration Returns, New Brunswick Blue Books, 1850–55, PAC: "Report on Trade and Navigation," in *Journal of the House of Assembly of New Brunswick*, 1866.

ST. PATRICK'S DAY PARADES IN NINETEENTH-CENTURY TORONTO: A STUDY OF IMMIGRANT ADJUSTMENT AND ÉLITE CONTROL

*Michael Cottrell**

Irish immigrants brought to nineteenth-century British North America a rich and diverse cultural heritage which continued to flourish in the areas they settled. A particular fondness for parades and processions was part of this inheritance, and annual demonstrations commemorating the Battle of the Boyne and the feast of St. Patrick were soon commonplace throughout the colonies. In the charged sectarian climate of Ireland, however, "parades were at the very centre of the territorial...political and economic struggle" and these connotations were also transplanted.[1] Especially in Toronto, where Catholic and Protestant Irish congregated in large numbers, parades frequently became the occasion of violent confrontation between Orange and Green.[2] But while the July 12 activities of the Orange figure prominently in Canadian historiography, little attention has been paid to St. Patrick's Day celebrations or their significance for Irish Catholic immigrants. This study seeks to redress this imbalance by tracing the evolution of St. Patrick's Day parades in nineteenth-century Toronto, beginning with a close examination of the 1863 celebration which was one of the largest and most impressive on record.

The tone was set the previous evening by the garrison drums beating "St. Patrick's Day in the Morning" and this was followed by the Hibernian Benevolent Society band's late-night promenade, "discoursing some of the choicest [Irish] national airs." Crowds began to gather at St. Paul's Church on King Street early the next morning and at ten o'clock, the procession began marching towards St. Michael's Cathedral. About 2,000 strong, the assemblage was drawn largely from the "humbler elements," some of whom had reportedly journeyed to the city from surrounding districts. The Cathedral was "filled to its utmost capacity" for the mass which was celebrated by Bishop John Joseph Lynch, assisted by over a dozen other Irish priests from the Toronto diocese. The high point of the service was undoubtedly the sermon delivered by the Bishop on the exploits of the "glorious saint," concluding with an exposition on the providential mission of the Irish diaspora to spread Catholicism to the four corners of the world.[3]

Religious obligations having been fulfilled, the procession then reformed and paraded through the principal streets of the city. Led by the Hibernian band, whose repertoire seemed to consist of nostalgic and militant tunes in equal measure, the procession swelled even further as it slowly returned to

From *Histoire sociale / Social History*, Vol. xxv, no. 49 (May 1992), 57–73. Reprinted by permission.

*Michael Cottrell is professor of history at the University of Saskatchewan in Saskatoon.

St. Paul's Church. Here, a platform had been erected for the occasion and various notables, including the Bishop, members of the clergy, prominent Catholics and officers of various Irish organizations addressed the crowd. The obvious favourite, however, was Michael Murphy, president of the Hibernian Benevolent Society. Murphy's oration was received with "loud cheers and applause," especially when he denounced British government in Ireland as "radically wrong" and compared it to the suffering of the Polish people under a "powerful military despotism." But he prophesied that Irish deliverance was at hand from an organization rapidly growing among her exiles. In Canada alone, he claimed, there were 20,000 Irishmen ready to rally to the cause:

> ...three-fourths of the Catholic Irish of this country would offer themselves as an offering on the altar of freedom, to elevate their country and raise her again to her position in the list of nations. Nothing could resist the Irish pike when grasped by the sinewy arm of the Celt.[4]

Murphy then commended the Hibernians for keeping the spirit of Irish nationality alive in Canada, despite the opposition and hostility which this evoked from the host society. But he ended in a more conciliatory tone by expressing "perfect satisfaction" with the laws of Canada because, here, the people "were their own law-makers."[5] When the speeches were over, the procession broke up into smaller parties and soirées which lasted late into the night. And "thus passed away one of the most pleasant St. Patrick's Days we have ever spent in Toronto."[6]

For those who participated, almost exclusively Catholic Irish immigrants, the St. Patrick's Day celebration was obviously an extremely important event. On a social level, it provided a holiday from work and an occasion to parade about the city dressed in their Sunday best. Those who lived outside the city could visit friends and relatives, shop at the large stores and partake of the excitement of city life for a day. This influx undoubtedly provided a welcomed boost for the many Irish cabmen, storekeepers and tavernkeepers who lived a normally precarious existence. For the pious, it was an occasion to worship, for the notables an opportunity to speechify and revel in a stature which rarely extended beyond that day. But the event also had a deeper significance, for it was, in essence, a communal demonstration, an annual and very public assertion of Irish Catholic presence and solidarity in Toronto. It was perhaps the one day in the year on which Irish Catholics could claim the city as their own and proudly publicize their distinctiveness on the main streets. The ritualistic nature of the celebrations—with parades, masses and speeches being constants—obviously played a vital role in rekindling tribal memories and inculcating the collective consciousness necessary for reforging a group identity in a new environment. St. Patrick's Day parades were therefore central both to the emergence of Irish Catholic ethnicity in Toronto and to the communication of identity to the host society.[7]

The celebrations also reflected the interests and aspirations of those who assumed direct responsibility for organizing them. Since high visibility and prestige were the rewards, control of the event allowed different elements to establish supremacy within the Irish Catholic community, to impose their stamp on the group's corporate image and thereby to decisively influence its relations with the larger society. Thus, the intermittent struggle both for control of the celebrations and over the form which they should take revealed a great deal about the experience of Irish Catholic immigrants as they adjusted to an unfamiliar and often hostile environment. Like most ethnic groups, the Irish oscillated between the extremes of separation and integration, persistence and assimilation; and the celebration of the feast of St. Patrick was central to the resolution of these internal tensions for Irish immigrants in Toronto.[8]

Yet, to the host society comprising largely Loyalist and British settlers, the event had a very different significance. An annual reminder of the existence of a substantial alien Irish presence, it also demonstrated the determination of these immigrants, once settled into the country, to preserve aspects of their traditional culture. More ominously, speeches such as that delivered by Michael Murphy in 1863 evidenced a continued Irish obsession with the problems of their homeland, and the frequent violence which accompanied the parades demonstrated that the importation of these problems to British North America could prove extremely disruptive. Hence, the Canadian press was less than enthusiastic in its coverage of the event, expressing the wish that such celebrations, and the Old World orientation which they represented, would shortly be abandoned.[9]

The establishment of the Toronto St. Patrick's Society in 1832 attested to the growing Irish presence in the city and by 1861, Irish Catholics constituted over one-quarter of the population. However, a sharp increase in immigration and steady out-migration contributed to their decline as a percentage of the population thereafter.[10] Early St. Patrick's Day celebrations were usually low-key affairs—concerts, balls and soirées—which brought together the Irish élite to honour their patron saint and indulge their penchant for sentimental and self-congratulatory speeches.[11] Largely free from the sectarian biases so evident in the 1860s, they suggested a cordiality between early Catholic and Protestant immigrants. But while the St. Patrick's Society survived into the 1850s, the inclusive definition of Irish ethnicity which sustained it was undermined by the Famine immigration of the late 1840s. Since Catholics predominated among those who settled in Toronto, this influx shattered the virtual Protestant consensus which had previously existed, and the destitution of many of these Famine victims further contributed to a nativistic backlash from the host society.[12] This prejudice prompted Irish Protestants to dissociate themselves from their unpopular Catholic counterparts and instead to look to the Protestant, loyalist values of the Orange Order as the focus of their identity.[13] But since Catholics found themselves largely consigned to the lowest ranks of the occupational hierarchy and excluded from the emerging British Protestant colonial consensus, their response was to withdraw into an exclusive and essentially defensive form of ethnicity.[14] By the 1860s, the polarization of Irish immigrants along religious and cultural lines was complete and observers noted that the "Irish constitute in some sort two peoples: the line of division being one of religion and...one of race."[15]

These changes were reflected in the way in which St. Patrick's Day was celebrated, as the seventeenth of March became increasingly identified with Irish Catholicism. Partly a response to rejection by the host society and dissociation of the Protestant Irish, this development was also encouraged by elements within the Irish Catholic community. After the Famine, the Roman Catholic Church created a network of social and religious institutions to assist the adjustment of Irish immigrants and re-establish clerical control over their lives.[16] After a few small-scale and generally disorganized parades in the late 1840s, the clergy soon enlisted St. Patrick in their campaign and by the early 1850s, the annual celebration revolved primarily around the Catholic Church. Organized and led by Church-sponsored societies, processions to the Cathedral

TABLE 1   Population of Toronto, 1848–1881

Date	Irish	Catholic	Total
1848	1,695	5,903	25,503
1851	11,305	7,940	30,775
1861	12,441	12,125	44,821
1871	10,336	11,881	56,092
1881	10,781	15,716	86,415

Source: Census of Canada, 1848–1881.

TABLE 2   Irish Catholic Occupational Profile, 1860

Unskilled	45.0%
Semi-skilled	13.5%
Skilled	12.1%
Clerical	2.8%
Business	16.7%
Professional	3.3%
Private means	6.6%

Source: B. Clarke, "Piety, Nationalism and Fraternity: The Rise of Irish Catholic Voluntary Associations in Toronto, 1850–1895" (Ph.D. dissertation, University of Chicago, 1986), 33.

now became a regular feature and the clergy assumed a prominent role through-out.[17] But though the celebrations became larger and more public, the mass was clearly the focus of the event, and the sermons preached on these occasions had the effect both of strengthening the association between Irishness and Catholicism and of fostering a sense of ethno-religious particularism among Irish Catholic immigrants. The heroic figure of St. Patrick provided an easy continuity between the Irish history of persecution and their current experience as unwelcomed exiles in a strange land, and served as a rallying symbol for Irish Catholics in the New World, as Father Synnott's exhortation of 1855 indicates:

> Go on then, faithful, noble and generous children of St. Patrick, in your glorious career...keep your eyes ever fixed on the faith of St. Patrick which shall ever be for you a fixed star by night and a pillar of light by day—forget not the examples and memorable deeds of your fathers—be faithful to the doctrines of your apostle. A voice that speaks on the leaf of the shamrock—that speaks in the dismantled and ruined abbeys of lovely Erin—yea a voice that still speaks on the tombstones of your martyred fathers and in the homes of your exiled country-men—be faithful to the glorious legacy he has bequeathed to you.[18]

In the early 1850s, then, the Roman Catholic Church was instrumental in transforming St. Patrick's Day into an essentially religious event, to establish Catholicism as the primary identity of Irish immigrants and thereby strengthen clerical authority. For by encouraging Irish immigrants to see themselves first as Catholics and to hold themselves aloof from the Protestant majority, the clergy reinforced their claim to leadership and control. But the Catholic Church was unable to satisfy all the needs of Irish immigrants. Under the French-born Bishop Armand de Charbonnel, it was unable to express the cultural or political nationalism which these immigrants transported as baggage.[19] Moreover, the group's organizational infrastructure was so tightly controlled by the clergy that it frustrated the desire for leadership and initiative among the Irish Catholic laity, especially the small but ambitious middle class which began to emerge in the mid-1850s.[20]

Irish nationalism provided one of the few rationales for lay initiative independent of the clergy, and it also served both as a catalyst and a vehicle for expressing the growing ethnic consciousness among Irish Catholics in Toronto.[21] Indicative of this was the establishment, in 1855, of the exclusively Catholic Young Men's St. Patrick's Association, an ethnic organization which sought to provide a social life for Irish immigrants, based on their traditional culture, and to secure their collective advancement in Toronto.[22] Animated by the Irish Catholic middle class, it quickly moved to put its stamp on what had become the group's leading communal event, and in the late 1850s, the new lay élite assumed responsibility for organizing the St. Patrick's Day celebrations.

Under their auspices, the event changed dramatically. Parades, which had previously been merely a prelude to the mass, now increased in size and colour to become major public demonstrations. In 1857, over 1,000 people, their faces animated by "a sacred patriotic fire," marched behind 400 members of the Young Men's St. Patrick's Association.[23] Religious hymns were replaced by popular tunes and secular emblems such as shamrocks, harps and wolfhounds were now more prominent than Catholic icons. As the clergy lost their previous stature in the extra-Cathedral festivities, the whole tone of these events also changed. Clerically-induced temperance gave way to alcoholic good cheer, and instead of the expressions of loyalty and three cheers for the Queen, which had previously characterized the proceedings, mildly anglophobic speeches were now heard.[24]

Alienated from the larger society by a growing "No Popery" crusade which was expressed through the mainstream press and the hostile activities of the Orange Order, Irish Catholics in the late 1850s used St. Patrick's Day parades to assert their ethno-religious distinctiveness and protest their marginalized position within the city. But changes in the parade also reflected a shift in the internal dynamics of the group, as a struggle was clearly developing between the clergy and members of the laity for leadership and control of the Irish Catholic community. While the latter agreed that Catholicism defined the parameters of Irish ethnicity, they emphasized a secular and cultural dimension to this identity which went beyond the clergy's narrowly religious vision. These tensions were demonstrated by Bishop de Charbonnel's refusal, in 1856, to hold mass to coincide with the parade, but the events of St. Patrick's Day 1858 healed this rift, at least temporarily.[25]

The growth of the Catholic population in the city, its increasing visibility and public assertiveness on occasions such as St. Patrick's Day were all seen as evidence of a growing menace by Upper Canadian Protestants already inflamed by the British Papal aggression crisis and the American Know-Nothing movement.[26] The parades, especially, were seen as unduly provocative by the Orange Order which had become the most popular vehicle for expressing militant Protestantism in Upper Canada.[27] This tension boiled over in 1858 when Orange attempts to disrupt the parade resulted in widespread violence during which one Catholic was fatally stabbed with a pitchfork.[28]

Coming at a time of growing self-confidence and rising expectations among the Catholic Irish population, this debacle was a sobering experience, for it demonstrated both the continued hostility of their traditional Orange enemies and the vulnerability which Catholics faced as a consequence of their minority position in Toronto. Moreover, the blatant partisanship of the police and judiciary indicated where the sympathies of the authorities lay, and served notice that the triumphalist behaviour involved in the parades was out of place in a community subscribing to a British and Protestant consensus.[29] As a result, both lay and clerical Irish leaders concluded that a lower public profile would have to be adopted if the acceptance, recognition and prosperity which they desired were to be achieved. This new spirit of conciliation and moderation was expressed most clearly by the decision to forego public processions on St. Patrick's Day for an indefinite period. The suspension of the parades for the next three years followed a conscious decision of the Irish élite to relinquish their right to the streets in the interests of public harmony. Yet, while this moderation forwarded the desires of the clergy and middle class for an accommodation with the Canadian establishment, it did not meet acquiescence from all elements within the Irish Catholic community, and it was soon challenged by rumblings from below.

The murder of Matthew Sheedy by Orangemen on St. Patrick's Day 1858 was symptomatic of the growing hostility experienced by Irish Catholics in Toronto. Prejudice, harassment and attacks on Catholic priests and Church property all contributed to the growth of a siege mentality among Catholics. While this beleaguerment produced the above-mentioned conciliatory stance from the Irish élite, it also generated a more militant response in the form of the Hibernian Benevolent Society. Established after the 1858 debacle to protect Catholics from Orange aggression, the Hibernians invoked the traditional Irish peasant prerogative of self-defence in the face of the failure of the authorities to secure their rights or redress their grievances. But they soon rose above these Ribbonite roots and by the early 1860s, had evolved into a full-fledged ethnic voluntary organization.[30] As well as rendering Toronto safer for Catholics, the Hibernians took over, from the Young Men's St. Patrick's Association, the tasks of generating an extensive social life and material benefits for its largely working-class male members. In keeping with the values of the latter, the organization also sought to inject a more aggressively nationalistic spirit into the Irish community to engender pride and self-confidence, thereby strengthening the demand for recognition and respect for the Irish in Toronto.[31]

One of their first steps in this direction was to reassert the Irish Catholic right to the streets of the city by resuming parades on St. Patrick's Day. Unlike the Young Men's St. Patrick's Association which had openly flouted the authority of the clergy, however, the Hibernians showed great deference to the new Bishop of Toronto, John Joseph Lynch. When the Hibernians sought clerical permission to revive the parades, in 1862, Lynch supported their decision despite strong opposition from "the most respectable Catholic inhabitants of the city." Led by members of the now-defunct Young Men's St. Patrick's Association, they argued that a resumption of public processions would inevitably provoke a confrontation with the Orangemen, and since Catholics would automatically be depicted as the aggressors, the good feelings which developed from their suspension would be lost. Lynch was thus implored to ban the parade or at the very least to "hold mass at such an hour as not to suit the procession."[32] But the Bishop chose to ignore their warnings and not only granted his approval, but addressed the parade from the steps of the cathedral and commended the Hibernians for their "noble efforts on behalf of faith and fatherland."[33]

This dispute over the resumption of the parades suggested an ongoing conflict within the Irish Catholic community about the appropriate response to their countries of origin and of adoption, and acute divisions on the strategy which would best secure them a comfortable niche in the latter. Upwardly-mobile middle class immigrants argued that the best route to success lay in winning the confidence of the host society by quietly discarding those aspects of their traditional culture which were found objectionable and by working through the political system to redress outstanding grievances. But the organized Irish working class, in the form of the Hibernians, rejected the timidity and abandonment of cultural distinctiveness which this policy entailed, and instead demanded a more vigorous assertion of the Irish Catholic presence in the city.[34] For symbolic effect, the St. Patrick's Day parade surpassed all else, since it represented both a commitment to the preservation of Irish culture and an insistence on the right to advertise this distinctiveness on the streets of Toronto.[35]

This conflict between strategies of accommodation and protest constitutes the typical dilemma faced by ethnic groups in a new environment and is frequently related to economic adjustment. Ironically, it was the Irish middle class which had first resorted to protest in the mid-1850s, only to retreat from ethnic militancy once it became obvious that this jeopardized its attainment of social acceptance and economic prosperity. Control of the parades had now changed hands and since this event provided one of the major opportunities for lay initiative, it seems that leadership of Irish-Catholic ethnicity in Toronto was passing from the moderate and accommodationist middle class to the militantly separatist lower class. The power and prestige of the Roman Catholic clergy were also demonstrated by this embroglio, however, for Bishop Lynch's moral role as adjudicator between the warring lay factions was clearly recognized. On this occasion, he sided with the Hibernians, primarily because their uncompromising nationalism reinforced the Church's attempt to foster religious particularism and strengthened the hierarchy's claim to communal leadership.[36] But the limits of this control would soon be tested and the alliance between clergy and nationalists severely strained in the process.

Unknown to Bishop Lynch, the Hibernians established contact with the revolutionary American Fenian Brotherhood in 1859, and the Hibernian president, Michael Murphy, became head-centre of the Fenian organization in the Toronto area. Although sworn Fenians were always a minority of the Hibernians' membership, the organization became more militant under their influence. The establishment in January 1863 of the weekly ethnic newspaper, the *Irish Canadian*, further evidenced their increasing sophistication, for this mouthpiece augmented their influence within the Irish-Catholic community and enabled the Fenians to articulate their concerns to the larger society. Under the editorship of Patrick Boyle, the *Irish Canadian* sought to "link the past with the present, the old country with the new," and propagated the simple message that religion, patriotism and support for the liberation of Ireland were all inseparably linked with the demand for Irish recognition and the achievement of prosperity, success and respect in their new environment.[37]

The prominence which the Hibernians established within the Irish Catholic community was demonstrated by their complete control of St. Patrick's Day celebrations in the early 1860s. As statements of Irish protest and radicalism, they surpassed all previous efforts. The years 1863 and 1864 saw the largest parades on record and in keeping with Hibernian membership, those who led and those who followed were increasingly drawn from the Irish Catholic lower class. A new militancy was apparent in the playing of martial tunes such as "The Croppy Boy," "God Save Ireland" and "The Rising of the Moon," and changes in the route of the parade also suggested a spirit of confrontation previously lacking. These two parades covered a wider territory than ever before and while this was obviously designed to assert their right to the entire city, the provocation involved in marching past so many Orange lodges could not have been lost on the organizers. Even more ominous was the proliferation of Fenian sunburst banners among the crowd and the open expressions of support for Fenianism which concluded both of these parades.[38]

Bordering on treason, Murphy's speeches incurred the wrath of the host society and also alienated many Irish Catholics who feared the new radicalism he represented. Led by Thomas D'Arcy McGee, moderates argued that the Fenian-sympathizing Hibernians would confirm the stereotype of Irish disloyalty held by the host society, inevitably prompting a violent reaction from the Orange Order. Even sympathetic Protestants would be alienated by this extremism, he suggested, and the resulting backlash would obliterate all of the tangible gains made by Irish Catholics since the bitter era of sectarian warfare in the 1850s.[39] The situation was particularly embarrassing for the Catholic Church since Lynch's presence alongside Murphy on the podium on both occasions gave rise to allegations that the clergy sanctioned these treasonous sentiments. As rumours of a Fenian invasion mounted, Bishop Lynch came under increasing pressure to denounce the Hibernians and he finally bowed to internal and external pressure. In August of 1865, he condemned the Hibernians and called on all Catholics to quit the organization since they had "fallen away from Catholic principles."[40]

Once again, a struggle for leadership and control of the Irish community was apparent, but the internal alliances had shifted since the early 1860s. Now the clergy were supported by the middle class élite, as moderate Irish Catholics sought to rein in a working-class organization whose radicalism threatened their interests. This clash, essentially one between strategies of protest and accommodation, came to a head in March 1866 amid rumours that the long-anticipated Fenian invasion was to coincide with a huge St. Patrick's Day parade organized by the Hibernians.[41] As tension within the city mounted in the preceding weeks, Irish moderates sought to distance themselves from the Hibernians to reassure the Protestant majority that the latter's extremism was not shared by all. Having supported and even encouraged the extremists, Bishop Lynch found himself at the centre of the storm, as moderates appealed to him to control the Hibernians. "Everything depends on Your Lordship," D'Arcy McGee warned the Bishop, and he insisted that the future of the entire Irish

Catholic community in Canada was at stake: "The position of our Church and race in Canada for the next twenty-five years, will be determined by the stand taken, during these next six weeks."[42]

In this situation, Lynch clearly had no choice but to ban the parade, which he did shortly thereafter by advising all Catholics to spend the day either in Church or at home. By this point, however, the Hibernians had moved beyond the control of the clergy. Having foregone the procession at the Bishop's insistence the previous year, they were less amenable on this occasion, and insisted on their right to take to the streets regardless of the consequences. Clearly, the Hibernians were determined to push the strategy of protest and their strident assertion of ethnic persistence to its extreme. But they had by now left the bulk of Irish Catholics behind in this respect. While a great many supported their call for Irish liberation and fervently resented the domestic prejudice which the Hibernians sought to counter, very few were willing to provoke the wrath of the host society or flout the authority of their bishop to express these sentiments. Thus, only the die-hard Hibernians turned out to march in the smallest parade in years, and the anti-climax was completed by the failure of the Fenian invasion to materialize.[43]

This caution was even more forcibly demonstrated when the Fenian raids finally occurred in June of 1866. For despite a widespread expression of sullen resentment, an overwhelming majority of Irish Canadians were induced to hold themselves aloof from the Irish American "liberators" by a combination of clerical and lay pressure, instincts of self-preservation and the desire for acceptance in their new homeland.[44] The Fenian raids, nevertheless, cast a shadow of suspicion over the entire Irish community in Canada. The inevitable Protestant backlash produced what one individual described as a "reign of terror," confirming McGee's dire predictions of the consequences of flirting with treason.[45] In this hostile climate, Catholics naturally reverted to a low profile and there was no suggestion of holding a public celebration on St. Patrick's Day 1867.

Once boisterous and triumphant, the Hibernians found their influence and prestige within the Toronto Irish community greatly undermined, and the round-up of suspected Fenian sympathizers further decimated the radical leadership. Control of the organization now reverted to relative moderates, such as Patrick Boyle, editor of the *Irish Canadian*; and while he followed Murphy's old lead in some respects, marked changes soon became apparent. Nationalism had proven its effectiveness as a vehicle for mobilizing the ethnic consciousness of Irish Catholic immigrants and focusing their resentment against the marginalization they experienced in their new home. But unlike the American situation, where republican nationalism placed Irish immigrants within the ideological mainstream, in Canada these sentiments clearly isolated them from the larger British population.[46] As well as separating the Irish from their neighbours, it also had the effect of alienating Catholics from their Church, which was the only institution in Canada the Irish could claim as their own. To rehabilitate themselves, therefore, nationalist leaders had to reforge the link between nationalism and Catholicism; develop a variation of nationalism which integrated rather than isolated Irish Catholics from Canadian society; and make their message more relevant by addressing the material needs of Irish Catholic immigrants in Toronto and Ontario. As with many other shifts within the Irish community, these developments would be reflected in the way St. Patrick's Day was celebrated.

After the Fenian fiasco, the Hibernians reverted to their former deference towards the Catholic Church and the first public sign of this rapprochement came in 1868 when Bishop Lynch approved a resumption of the St. Patrick's Day parades. Although 400 Hibernians turned out to lead the procession, both the attendance and the tone were far cries from the massive demonstrations of the early 1860s. A subdued atmosphere pervaded the celebrations and this was clearly reflected in the speech delivered by Patrick Boyle which focused on the plight of Fenian prisoners in Canadian jails, but avoided more contentious issues.[47] This uncharacteristic moderation of the Hibernians stood in sharp contrast to the obsession which the nationalist press began to exhibit in provincial and federal politics. Obviously a more practical and effective means of improving the position of the Irish than the Utopian promises of the Fenians, this new focus also facilitated a growing cordiality between nationalists and members of the middle class who were determined to transform Irish Catholics into an influential political pressure group in Ontario.[48] The politicization of Irish nationalism received public expression on St. Patrick's Day 1869 when John O'Donohoe, a former member of the Toronto corporation and veteran political activist, was invited to deliver the keynote speech to the procession from the steps of St. Michael's Cathedral.[49] Although he paid lip-service to the traditional nationalist shibboleths, O'Donohoe focused primarily on the political situation and the social inferiority suffered by Irish Catholics because of their lack of political influence. In the Legislature of Ontario, he lamented, "we find our body as completely excluded as if we formed no portion of the body politic," and he insisted that the only means of improving their standing within the province was by putting aside their internal differences and demanding their rightful share of power and the spoils of office: "Let us practice unanimity and in cordial cooperation form a united phalanx, determined to live in harmony with all men—but determined for our right."[50]

A consensus clearly existed within the Irish community concerning its subordinate status in Ontario and on the efficacy of political activity as a means of overcoming it. With the new moderation of the nationalists paving the way for closer cooperation with the clergy and the lay élite, all were soon working together within the Catholic League, a political pressure group established in 1870 to forward the political interests of the province's Catholics.[51] The League soon became the focus of Irish organizational activities and this new concern with politics was reflected in the prominence which these matters received in subsequent St.

Patrick's Day celebrations. Long an occasion for reaffirming religious or nationalist solidarity, the parades in the early 1870s also became a vehicle for disseminating political propaganda—indicating once again the flexibility of Irish immigrants to adapt traditional cultural practices to the needs of a new environment.[52]

This concern with politics reflected a very important change in the celebration of St. Patrick's Day, a change which manifested a wider shift within the Irish Catholic community in Toronto. Rather than emphasizing religious or ethnic exclusivity and separatism as had been the practice in the past, both the sermons and the outdoor speeches now focused on the need to carve out for Irish Catholics an acceptable place in Ontario society.[53] These new integrationist tendencies may be seen as by-products of the growing adjustment of Irish immigrants to Ontario and the increasing acceptance and respect which they were receiving from the host society.[54] Moreover, the success of the Catholic League in attracting attention to Irish grievances and securing the election of an increasing number of Irish candidates suggested that they were gradually coming to wield the power and influence they felt they deserved within the political structures of their adopted home.[55]

By the mid-1870s, therefore, the collective fortunes of Irish Catholics in Toronto had improved considerably, and these changes were reflected in the celebration of St. Patrick's Day. While it was still felt necessary to advertise their presence and distinctiveness by taking to the streets on the feast of their patron saint, the event differed radically from the boisterous nationalist demonstrations of the early 1860s. The Hibernians were still present, but they attracted nowhere near the numbers they previously commanded. Their once splendid banners were now dilapidated and the speeches in support of Home Rule and constitutional solutions to the Irish problem, while compatible with their presence in a self-governing colony, were a far cry from Michael Murphy's fiery harangues of an earlier time.[56] Increasingly anachronistic, the Hibernians no longer exercised a stranglehold over the celebrations and they were forced to share the podium with organizations such as the Father Matthew Temperance Society, the Emerald Benevolent Association and the Sons of St. Patrick.[57] The values which the latter sought to impress both on their audience and on the host society—sobriety, temperance, self-help and thrift—in short mid-Victorian respectability—represented the new collective identity of the Irish Catholic community.[58] Indeed, the primary function of St. Patrick's Day celebrations now seemed to be to put lingering stereotypes to rest by demonstrating that Irish Catholics were worthy of full citizenship and total acceptance from a host society that had once expressed reservations about their fitness.[59]

Distance and time were gradually weakening the attachment of Irish immigrants to the Old Country and militant nationalism was giving way to nostalgic sentimentality. Increasingly prosperous and secure both economically and socially, and with a new generation growing up for whom Ireland had very little relevance, Irish Torontonians were in fact becoming Canadianized.[60] On a personal level, it was no longer necessary to rely on the ethnic support group for survival, and collective self-respect no longer depended upon a constant assertion of distinctiveness. Their efforts, instead, were directed towards downplaying the differences between themselves and their neighbours and, in this, the St. Patrick's Day celebration was an obstacle rather than an asset. Commenting on the extremely poor turnout at the 1876 parade, Patrick Boyle suggested that the time had come to re-evaluate the annual celebrations. These demonstrations perpetuated the isolation of Irish Catholics, he concluded, for of all the ethnic groups in Canada, they alone insisted on "placing before the public their persons and sentiments in a more or less ridiculous drapery."[61] More important than the ridicule of their neighbours, however, was the fact that such displays were increasingly incompatible with their higher duty as citizens of Canada:

> Their abandonment is demanded by many considerations of good citizenship. They serve to maintain in this land, to which we have all come for quiet rather than broil, the miserable dissension and violence of a past which the present generation has outlived and outgrown. As a duty to the concord of society, to peace and order, to industry and steadiness, to that perfect unity which proves strength to the State, those processions which were instances of bad citizenship in this country...ought to be abandoned.[62]

With even the remnants of radical nationalism losing interest, the future of the event was obviously in doubt, and it came as no surprise that 1877 saw the last public St. Patrick's Day celebration in Toronto for over a century.[63]

While it lasted, the event was the most visible demonstration of Irishness in the city and, as such, provided an important continuity between the Old World and the New for Irish immigrants. The parades, however, can only be understood in the context of the needs of the Irish Catholic community in their new environment. The unfurling of the green banners on St. Patrick's Day asserted the Irish Catholic right to the streets and constituted both a "ritualized demand for recognition and an affirmation of ethnic solidarity in a predominantly Protestant city."[64] The parades thus allowed Irish immigrants to define their collective identity, to advertise their distinctiveness and, in the process, to demand corporate recognition for their presence. The two decades after the Famine were crucial to the first of these goals, as Catholicism and nationalism were established as the parameters of Irish ethnicity and served as the focus of the celebrations until the 1870s. Resolving the appropriate response to the host society was much more contentious, however, as evidenced by the struggle for control of the celebrations by different elements within the Irish community. Protest and accommodation were ultimately the alternatives offered by those vying for ethnic leadership, and by the mid-1870s, the issue had been resolved in favour of the latter. Thus, nationalism was largely discarded because of its fundamental incompatibility with the prevailing English-Canadian ideology, and religion became the primary identity for a group who increasingly defined themselves as English-speaking Catholic Canadians.

The abandonment of the parades in the mid-1870s may therefore be seen as a crucial indice of Irish assimilation, but also points to an important relationship between ethnic persistence and structural integration. For as long as Irish Catholics found themselves outside the Canadian mainstream, elements within the group insisted on preserving and advertising their distinctiveness, especially on St. Patrick's Day. When the political and economic structures began to embrace them, and Irish Catholics were afforded the same social acceptance as other groups, however, the need for displaying such distinctiveness was no longer perceived to exist. Thus, public celebrations of St. Patrick's Day, which had once served the interests of Irish immigrants recently arrived in a strange environment, were abandoned when they became an impediment to the group's subsequent and natural desire to become Canadian.

Notes

1. S.E. Baker, "Orange and Green: Belfast, 1832–1912," in H.J. Dyos and M. Wolff, eds., *The Victorian City: Images and Realities*, Vol. II (London and Boston: Routledge and Keegan Paul, 1973), 790; D.W. Miller, "The Armagh Troubles, 1784–87," in S. Clark and J.S. Donnelly, Jr., eds., *Irish Peasants: Violence and Political Unrest, 1780–1914* (Madison: University of Wisconsin Press, 1983), 174–76.

2. G.S. Kealey, "The Orange Order in Toronto: Religious Riot and the Working Class," in R. O'Driscoll and C. Reynolds, eds., *The Untold Story: The Irish in Canada* (Toronto: Celtic Arts of Canada, 1988), 841–47.

3. This report was taken from the *Irish Canadian*, 18 March 1863; the *Canadian Freeman*, 19 March 1863; and the *Globe*, 18 March 1863.

4. *Irish Canadian*, 18 March 1863.

5. *Ibid.*

6. *Canadian Freeman*, 19 March 1863.

7. St. Patrick's Day celebrations as an institution within the Irish diaspora have received surprisingly little attention. *See* C.J. Fahey, "Reflections on the St. Patrick's Day Orations of John Ireland," *Ethnicity*, Vol. II (1975), 244–57; O. MacDonagh, "Irish Culture and Nationalism Translated: St. Patrick's Day, 1888 in Australia," in O. MacDonagh, W.F. Mandle and P. Travers, eds., *Irish Culture and Nationalism, 1750–1950* (London: Macmillan, 1983), 69–82.

8. J. Higham, ed., *Ethnic Leadership in America* (Baltimore and London: The Johns Hopkins University Press, 1978), 1–18.

9. *Leader*, 18 March 1863; and *Globe*, 18 March 1863.

10. For a demographic profile of Irish Catholics in Toronto, *see* Table 1.

11. *Mirror*, 19 March 1841, and 24 March 1843.

12. G.J. Parr, "The Welcome and the Wake: Attitudes in Canada West Toward the Irish Famine Migration," *Ontario History*, Vol. LXVI (1974), 101–13; K. Duncan, "Irish Famine Immigration and the Social Structure of Canada West," *Canadian Review*

of Sociology and Anthropology, Vol. II (1965), 19–40; D. Connor, "The Irish Canadians: Image and Self-Image" (M.A. thesis, University of British Columbia, 1976), 50–92.

13. D.S. Shea, "The Irish Immigrant Adjustment to Toronto: 1840–1860," *Canadian Catholic Historical Association. Study Sessions* (1972), 55–56; C. Houston and W.J. Smyth, "Transferred Loyalties: Orangeism in the United States and Canada," *American Review of Canadian Studies*, Vol. XIV (1984), 193–211; G.S. Kealey and P. Warrian, eds., *Essays in Canadian Working Class History* (Toronto: McClelland and Stewart, 1976), 13–34.

14. For an occupational profile of Irish Catholics in Toronto, *see* Table 2.

15. *Leader*, 25 January 1862.

16. M.W. Nicolson, "The Catholic Church and the Irish in Victorian Toronto" (Ph.D. dissertation, University of Guelph, 1981); *idem*, "Irish Tridentine Catholicism in Victorian Toronto: Vessel for Ethno-Religious Persistence," *Canadian Catholic Historical Association, Study Sessions*, Vol. L (1983), 415–36; B.P. Clarke, "Piety, Nationalism and Fraternity: The Rise of Irish Catholic Voluntary Associations in Toronto, 1850–1895" (Ph.D. dissertation, University of Chicago, 1986), Vol. I.

17. *Mirror*, 7 March 1851; 14 March 1852; and 11 March 1853.

18. *Mirror*, 23 March 1855.

19. For the complex relationship between Catholicism and nationalism in Irish culture, *see* L.J. McCaffrey, "Irish Catholicism and Irish Nationalism: A Study in Cultural Identity," *Church History*, Vol. XLII (1973), 524–34.

20. The best evidence for the existence of this middle class was the proliferation of advertisements for wholesale establishments and professional services in the Irish ethnic press. *See* the *Mirror* or *Canadian Freeman*, 1850s.

21. The emergence of lay voluntary organizations revolving around Irish nationalism is explored in detail in Clarke, "Irish Voluntary Associations, Vol. II."

22. *Mirror*, 30 November, and 21 December 1855.

23. *Mirror*, 20 March 1857.

24. *Ibid.*

25. *Mirror*, 28 March 1856.

26. J.R. Miller, "Bigotry in the North Atlantic Triangle: Irish, British and American Influences on Canadian Anti-Catholicism, 1850–1900," *Studies in Religion*, Vol. XVI (1987), 289–301.

27. The power of the Order was perhaps best demonstrated by its virtual stranglehold on municipal politics for much of the nineteenth century. *See* G.S. Kealey, "The Union of the Canadas," in V.L. Russell, ed., *Forging a Consensus: Historic Essays on Toronto* (Toronto: University of Toronto Press, 1984), 41–86.

28. P. Toner, "The Rise of Irish Nationalism in Canada" (Ph.D. dissertation, National University of Ireland, 1974), 27–35; Clarke, "Irish Voluntary Associations," 305–7.

29. *Globe*, 18 and 19 March 1858; *Leader*, 18 and 19 March 1858.

30. For an introduction to the Ribbonite tradition, *see* T. Garvin, "Defenders, Ribbonmen and Others: Underground Political Networks in Pre-Famine Ireland," *Past and Present*, Vol. LXXXXVI (1982), 133–55; and J. Lee, "The Ribbonmen," in T.D. Williams, ed., *Secret Societies in Ireland* (Dublin: Gill and Macmillan, 1973), 26–35.

31. Clarke, "Irish Voluntary Associations," esp. 289–329; G. Sheppard, "God Save the Green: Fenianism and Fellowship in Victorian Ontario," *Histoire Sociale / Social History*, Vol. XX (1987), 129–44.

32. Archives of the Archdiocese of Toronto (henceforth A.A.T.), Archbishop Lynch Papers, Rev. G.R. Northgraves to Lynch, 4 March 1865.

33. *Leader*, 18 March 1862, and *Canadian Freeman*, 20 March 1862.

34. Occupational profiles of Hibernian membership demonstrate it was "predominantly a working-class organization." Clarke, "Irish Voluntary Associations," 365–66.

35. *Canadian Freeman*, 20 March 1862; *Irish Canadian*, 18 March 1863 and 23 March 1864.

36. A.A.T., Lynch Papers, Bishop Lynch to Bishop Farrell, 12 August 1865 and Bishop Lynch to Archbishop T. Connolly, 1 February 1866.

37. *Irish Canadian*, 7 January 1863.

38. *Irish Canadian*, 18 March, 25 March 1863 and 23 March 1864; *Canadian Freeman*, 19 March 1863, 24 March and 31 March 1864; *Leader*, 18 March 1864.

39. *Canadian Freeman*, 31 March, 14 April and 21 April 1864.

40. A.A.T., Archbishop Lynch Papers, Bishop Lynch to Bishop Farrell, 12 August 1865; *Canadian Freeman*, 17 August 1865.

41. *Globe*, 9 March 1866.

42. A.A.T., Archbishop Lynch Papers, T.D. McGee to Bishop Lynch, 7 March 1866.

43. *Globe*, 18 March 1866; *Irish Canadian*, 21 March 1866.

44. W.S. Neidhardt, *Fenianism in North America* (Pennsylvania: Pennsylvania State University Press, 1975), 50–80.

45. National Archives of Canada, J.L.P. O'Hanley Papers, Vol. 1, J.L.P. O'Hanley to J. Hearn, 4 May 1868.

46. For the role of Irish nationalism in the integration of Irish immigrants into American society, *see* T.N. Brown, *Irish-American Nationalism, 1870–1890* (New York: J.P. Lippincott, 1966.)

47. *Leader*, 18 March 1868 and *Irish Canadian*, 18 March 1868.

48. M. Cottrell, "Irish Catholic Political Leadership in Toronto, 1855–1882: A Study of Ethnic Politics" (Ph.D. dissertation, University of Saskatchewan, 1988), 225–312.

49. For O'Donohoe's career, *see* M. Cottrell, "John O'Donohoe and the Politics of Ethnicity in Ontario," *Canadian Catholic Historical Association, Historical Papers*, forthcoming.

50. *Irish Canadian*, 24 March 1869.

51. M. Cottrell, "Irish Political Leadership," 225–312.

52. *Irish Canadian*, 23 March 1870, 20 March 1872, 19 March 1873 and 22 March 1876; *Canadian Freeman*, 23 March 1871.

53. *Irish Canadian*, 22 March 1871 and 18 March 1874.

54. M. McGowan, "We Endure What We Cannot Cure: J.J. Lynch and Roman Catholic-Protestant in Toronto, 1864–75. Frustrated Attempts at Peaceful Co-Existence," *Canadian Society of Church History Papers*, Vol. XV (1984), 16–17.

55. M. Cottrell, "Irish Political Leadership," 313–454; D. Swainson, "James O'Reilly and Catholic Politics," *Historic Kingston*, Vol. XXI (1973), 11–21.

56. *Irish Canadian*, 20 March 1872 and 18 March 1874.

57. *Ibid.*, 22 March 1876.

58. Clarke, "Irish Voluntary Associations," 433–38.

59. *Irish Canadian*, 22 March 1876 and 21 March 1877.

60. For the transformation of Toronto's Irish Catholics into an English-speaking Canadian Catholic community, *see* M. McGowan, "We Are All Canadians: A Social, Religious and Cultural Portrait of Toronto's English-Speaking Roman Catholics, 1890–1920" (Ph.D. dissertation, University of Toronto, 1988).

61. *Irish Canadian*, 5 April 1876.

62. *Ibid.*, 5 April 1876.

63. *Ibid.*, 20 March 1878.

64. Clarke, "Irish Voluntary Association," 460.

CHAPTER
12 THE SOCIAL CONTEXTS OF RESPONSIBLE GOVERNMENT

For more than a century after the event, the acquisition of responsible government in the 1840s was considered one of the most important developments in Canadian history. The reason is not difficult to discern. So long as Canadian historians, in the grand teleological Whig tradition that dominated the profession in the latter part of the nineteenth and the first decades of the twentieth centuries, perceived it their primary function to trace Canada's political evolution from colony to nation within the framework of the British Empire-Commonwealth, the achievement of responsible government was pivotal, a turning point of perhaps even greater significance than Confederation itself. For according to that long-held historical wisdom, not only did responsible government represent a new departure in the relationship between the Mother Country and her British North American colonies, but Lord Durham's ground-breaking 1839 *Report*, with its suggestion of colonial self-government, provided a blueprint for the later restructuring of ties between Great Britain and her other Dominions as well.

In Canada, as well as in Great Britain, therefore, the myth of responsible government served several generations of politicians and historians well, providing an essential link in the Whig-Liberal interpretation of a past divided into forces of light and forces of darkness. Robert Baldwin and Louis Hippolyte Lafontaine and their 1848 triumph over the philistine, reactionary Tories were but the first of a series of 'Great [Liberal] Men' that progressed through George Brown, Edward Blake and Wilfrid Laurier to, poetically, William Lyon Mackenzie King, the grandson of the Upper Canadian leader of the 1837 Rebellion which precipitated both Lord Durham's *Report* and responsible government. From a Whig perspective, the Canadian political universe unfolded as it should, at least until the 1920s.

In the 1930s the Whig approach to Canada's past came increasingly under attack, particularly from historians such as Donald Creighton whose understanding of British North America in the 1830s and 1840s reflected a very different hue, ideologically and historiographically. Shifting the emphasis from political to economic factors, implicitly disputing the 'Great Man' approach to the subject, and turning conventional partisan bias on its head, Creighton's iconoclastic reconsideration of the rebellions and responsible government, while in the short run substituting one orthodoxy for another, in the longer term opened the way for new interpretations of the events. One revisionist work, for example, that of British imperial historian Ged Martin, even raised serious doubts about the influence of the Durham *Report*, either in British North America or elsewhere in the British Empire.

With the rise in the 1970s of the new social history, and its attendant subthemes of regionalism, class, gender and ethnicity, to name only a few, the study of national, political history fell into disfavour among Canadian historians, and the subject of responsible government temporarily lay fallow. In the past decade or so, however, Canadian social historians have turned their attention to the era of responsible government, and in the process have brought new life to an old, sometimes tired, topic. Two such studies are presented here. In "'The Tombstone Affair,' 1845," Christopher Anstead and Nancy Bouchier analyse the social transformation of Woodstock, a small Upper Canadian town, in the 1840s by focusing on a very specific but telling local conflict. David Sutherland takes quite a different tack with respect to the development of voluntary associations in early Victorian Halifax, Nova Scotia, but arrives at surprisingly similar conclusions. Interestingly, neither article deliberately sets out to examine the concept of responsible government itself, but each adds considerable depth to our understanding of the subject by providing the local, social context of its implementation.

Suggestions for Further Reading

Ajzenstat, Janet, *The Political Thought of Lord Durham*. Montreal and Kingston: McGill-Queen's Press, 1988.

Buckner, Phillip A., *The Transition to Responsible Government: British Policy in British North America, 1815–1850*. Westport, Conn.: Greenwood Press, 1985.

Campbell, Gail C., "Disfranchised But Not Quiescent: Women Petitioners in New Brunswick in the Mid-Nineteenth Century," in Janet Guildford and Suzanne Morton, eds., *Separate Spheres: Women's Worlds in the Nineteenth Century Maritimes*. Fredericton: Acadiensis Press, 1994, 39–66.

Careless, J.M.S., ed. *The Pre-Confederation Premiers: Ontario Government Leaders, 1841–1867*. Toronto: University of Toronto Press, 1980.

Careless, J.M.S., *The Union of the Canadas: The Growth of Canadian Institutions, 1841–1857*. Toronto: McClelland & Stewart, 1972.

Courville, Serge, J.-C. Robert and Norman Seguin, "The Spread of Rural Industry in Lower Canada, 1831–1851," *Journal of the Canadian Historical Association*, 2, 1991, 43–70.

MacNutt, W.S., *The Atlantic Provinces: The Emergence of Colonial Society, 1712–1857*. Toronto: McClelland & Stewart, 1965.

Martin, Ged, "The Influence of the Durham Report," in Ronald Hyam and Ged Martin, eds., *Reappraisals in British Imperial History*. Toronto: Macmillan, 1975, 75–87.

Mills, David, *The Idea of Loyalty in Upper Canada*, Montreal and Kingston, McGill-Queen's Press, 1988.

Monet, Jacques, *The Last Cannon Shot*. Toronto: University of Toronto Press, 1969.

Noel, S.J.R., *Patrons, Clients, Brokers: Ontario Society and Politics, 1791–1896*. Toronto: University of Toronto Press, 1990.

Piva, Michael J., "Financing the Union: The Upper Canadian Debt and Financial Administration in the Canadas, 1837–1845," *Journal of Canadian Studies*, 25, 4, 1990–1991.

See, Scott W., "'Mickeys and Demons' vs 'Bigots and Boobies': The Woodstock Riot of 1847," *Acadiensis*, 21, 1, 1991, 110–131.

Young, Brian, "Positive Law, Positive State: Class Realignment and the Transformation of Lower Canada, 1815–1866," in Allan Greer and Ian Radforth, eds., *Colonial Leviathan State Formation in Mid-Nineteenth Century Canada*. Toronto: University of Toronto Press, 1992, 50–63.

Way, Peter, "Street Politics: Orangemen, Tories and the 1841 Election Riot in Toronto," *British Journal of Canadian Studies*, 6, 2, 1991, 275–303.

Wilton, Carol, "'A Firebrand Amongst the People': The Durham Meetings and Popular Politics in Upper Canada," *Canadian Historical Review*, 75, 3, 1994, 346–375.

THE "TOMBSTONE AFFAIR," 1845: WOODSTOCK TORIES AND CULTURAL CHANGE

Christopher J. Anstead and Nancy B. Bouchier

Nineteenth-century Ontario witnessed the transition of hegemonic dominance away from an established elite group (sometimes identified as the "Family Compact" or "Tories"), toward a social group typically denoted the "Victorian middle class"; the early history of the small southwestern Ontario town of Woodstock provides an ideal window into the mechanics of this transformation. In the 1830s Woodstock originated as a planned village, dominated by a group of transplanted British military officers. The "gentry's" position in town and county suddenly declined in the late 1840s and early 1850s, while professionals and businessmen took over the reigns of political and cultural power. One

---

From *Ontario History*, 86, 4, 1994, 363–381. Reprinted by permission.

of the milestones on this route came with the "tombstone affair" of 1845. A dispute over the wording of an epitaph exploded into a fracas involving charges of legal tyranny and political corruption, as well as the violation of a grave. The involvement of archetypical figures—almost caricatures—on each side added to the drama. This incident both exemplified and broadened the split between the old and new social orders: the hegemony of Tory paternalism bowed in the face of the rise of middle-class respectability.

One particular set of social and cultural power structures characterized the fifty-year period of Upper Canada's constitutional existence: the hegemony of paternalism. Within this complex system, the dominant social group comprised a relatively small number of males, interconnected through ties of marriage, kinship, and patronage, generally with a British or Loyalist background, wealth derived from both land and mercantile interests, commissions in the magistracy or militia, and, often, government positions.[1] Deference, order, loyalty, stability, and Britishness were key values in this cultural mix.[2] The structures of local government enabled the consolidation of political power. The justice of the peace system, for example, acted as both an instrument of, and an arena for, power. Its form, negotiated at the local level, commanded the confidence of local elites as well as lesser members of society. At the same time it linked local hegemonies to central, colonial, sites of cultural dominance, such as York.[3]

The hegemony of paternalism was an uneven one, where the dominant values often failed to penetrate. In part, this derived from the nature of pioneer settlement: before the coming of the railways, Upper Canada consisted of little more than a set of isolated communities. Counter hegemonies frequently erupted, often drawing upon narrowly political symbols and language. The result could be coercion, rather than consensus. Structural weakness was compounded through time by struggles over language and meaning which arose within the ruling hegemonic group, as an assimilative definition of loyalty—associated with moderate Reformers in politics—replaced the older Tory exclusivity. At this point, the newer members of the dominant group found their wealth in new ways—in law and business careers—challenging the nature of the hegemonic fraction.[4]

The cultural hegemony of Tory paternalism thrived in the village of Woodstock, situated on the upper branch of the Thames River, on the Governor's Road roughly seventy miles southwest of York. Imperial militarism, a potent arm of this hegemony, influenced Woodstock's earliest history. In 1793 John Graves Simcoe deemed the site ideal for his scheme of provincial settlement; its inland location was at a safe distance from the border between Upper Canada and the newly formed American states. Like many other places in the province, the area was initially settled by Americans who arrived some while after the Revolutionary War. At first these settlers made up part of the hinterland of what is now known as Beachville, but during the decade after the War of 1812, a small community formed. Their school and Baptist church shared a building, but their tavern stood on its own.[5]

The plans for the type of town first envisioned by Simcoe lay dormant until the politically turbulent 1830s. At that time acute concern about the Reform politics of non-Loyalist settlers—particularly in the Norwich Quaker settlement and in the Brantford and London areas—prompted a form of government intervention which completely altered Woodstock's economy and culture. Lieutenant-Governor Sir John Colborne consciously adopted a strategy of "combating the influence of settlers from the United States" through inducing British immigrants loyal to the crown and supporters of the provincial Tory elite to settle politically troubled regions of the province.[6] In doing so, the authorities sought to create a network of communities of cooperative men who could exert considerable influence in local and regional affairs, while forestalling the spread of Reform ideas.

In 1832 Andrew Drew, an English half-pay naval captain, arrived in Upper Canada. While keeping an eye on his own interests, Drew also acted as the agent of Henry Vansittart, a vice admiral from Bishum Abbey, Berkshire, and the fifth son of a long-serving parliamentarian. Vansittart wished to secure for his younger sons a landed estate in Upper Canada.[7] Excited by the prospect of the admiral heading a quasi-military settlement of half-pay officers in the troubled London District, the colonial authorities successfully courted Vansittart through Drew. They offered substantial incentives for the two men and their families to join two other officers already settled in Blandford Township.

With this group in place, immigrants of similar persuasion moved to join the quasi-aristocratic society of this backwoods settlement. The heart of the Woodstock oligarchy soon comprised roughly a dozen former military officers. A mixture of naval and army veterans, most had advanced to at least the rank of captain (in the army) or (if in the navy) to the command of a ship. Near the pinnacle were a pair of colonels, while Admiral Vansittart held the position of greatest honour. A few men without military careers, but tied to military or aristocratic families and linked to the provincial elite, added to the group. These men, their wives and adult children, formed Woodstock's cultural elite.[8]

Many of the retired officers listed among their assets family ties to English gentry, impressive letters of introduction from the Colonial Office, university educations, and the right social connections in Upper Canada.[9] Some used their access to colonial political and social networks to give them short cuts through an otherwise inflexible bureaucracy and, more important in an age of unreformed politics, to gain plum appointments like the local magistracy (which a handful of men dominated within months of their arrival in 1833).[10] This meant immediate access to the strongest mechanism of local consensual control. As one of the officers recalled a few years later,

> When I first came to Woodstock, any trifling dispute among the people, was always settled by a blow or a kick...'till a magistracy were appt., who lost not time to enforce the Summary Punishment Act, and this or firm examples of inflicted fines, completely restored order, and now we very seldom hear of any assaults; civility and good manners [having replaced] ruffianism.[11]

In 1839 the colonial government made Woodstock the District Town for Brock, which gave the officers control of the district's political organization, administration, and justice.

Woodstock's atypical society contributed to unusual economic development. The combined capital of the officers and their friends stimulated the local market, and created a demand for workers, including skilled artisans, who "gathered the shekels that they scattered."[12] Thus Woodstock's economy did not depend completely on agricultural connections. At the same time, artisan or labourer families resisted complete integration into a labour market relationship by growing vegetables for their own tables or for trade to Native hunters for venison, and by brewing their own beer.[13]

The settlement of the officers in Woodstock also gave the community an unusual social situation. Most of these families disdained business and manufacturing enterprises (though a few individuals from this circle did speculate on land and mortgages), and chose to invest their money "freely in the improvement of their estates and in the enjoyments of life."[14] The half-pay officers' British reference group might call themselves middle class, referring to eighteenth-century notions of such things, but clearly the officers and their families did not fit the emerging North American definition of that term, since local people referred to them as "aristocrats," "gentry," or even "noblemen." Yet, like members of the provincial elite, Woodstock's Tories used their own understanding of their English counterparts to fashion their society and leisure, and, in doing so, reinforced their own local elite status.[15] They expressed what they believed to be their own superiority in a natural social hierarchy.

Their social traditions reveal non-utilitarian attitudes toward life and leisure. They participated in lavish and conspicuous leisure consumption and in the formation of a local estate culture in the backwoods of Upper Canada. Their society quickly featured large country estates, great mansions, splendid libraries, large retinues of servants, carriages emblazoned with heraldic shields, and impressive stables.[16] Few entered their small yet powerful social enclave strengthened by intermarriage, Anglo-ethnic bonding, and a common Church of England affiliation.

Their sporting pursuits—riding to hounds, steeplechasing, hunting parties, and cricket—reaffirmed their ties to the mother country and asserted their social presence in Oxford County. Their derbies "were gala days of the year [for which] crowds flocked in from all parts."[17] Shortly after they settled in the Woodstock area they formed one of the earliest and most noted cricket clubs in the colony. The economic costs and social assumptions of this pastime restricted it to this elite circle, while fences around the grounds prevented any intrusion by outsiders. The sport's social atmosphere, social propriety, and convention, particularly regarding "gentlemanly" behaviour, permeated club affairs.[18]

Other social institutions, especially St. Paul's Anglican Church, also solidified elite group identity. Drew had started the church, and another former military officer, the Reverend William Bettridge, occupied its pulpit. Even the building's seating pattern marked social rank in the community in a hierarchical fashion. Parishioners paid premium pew rents for the choice seats located closest to the altar. When Governor Sir Edmund Head visited his friend and former classmate Edmund Deedes, he could be found during Sunday service in the conspicuously located Deedes family pew.[19] The rebellion of 1837 threw this connection into stark relief, when the church served as a jail for captured rebels.

In fact, Mackenzie's rebellion, and the local version led by Charles Duncombe, marked a watershed in the power of Woodstock's Tory elite. During the revolt at least three of the half-pay officers headed locally-raised militia contingents, while Andrew Drew led the expedition which cut out and burnt the rebel supply ship *Caroline* at Niagara Falls.[20] For the next few years the gentry sought to use their military successes to ensure their dominance in the Brock District. Despite being a numerical minority in the electoral rolls of the county, they saw their candidate for MLA returned for Oxford in two of the next three elections.[21] This political situation, however, was to prove short-lived.

During the 1840s Woodstock's social and economic matrix changed and the village became linked more firmly to the developing provincial economy, mainly through the production activities of area settlers of more humble social origins. In 1846, when the village's population reached just over one thousand, Woodstock had two grist mills, a sawmill and a carding and fulling mill, along with other establishments and workshops.[22] The village also had some service agencies, including a bank. To accommodate an integration into the evolving provincial exchange economy, inhabitants convinced the government to connect the main east-west road to Dundas Street at Woodstock. This improvement facilitated daily connections to London and Hamilton via stagecoach.[23] A few years later the town became part of a new network of toll roads being constructed in the county.[24]

The tombstone affair affords a window into many of the implications of these changes. At the centre of this controversy stood the Reverend William Bettridge, the Cambridge-educated rector of Woodstock's St. Paul's Church. This high Tory's connections allowed him direct entry into the local elite circle. A career officer before taking his holy vows, Bettridge had served under Wellington, and had obtained a staff appointment by the end of his career. His personal appeal to his former commandant, Sir John Colborne, ensured that St. Paul's was included among the last group of churches endowed in the province. It is perhaps not surprising, then, that he conducted his services with an air of militarism. Known for his profound religious intolerance, he considered members of the Church of Scotland to be heretics not worthy of the Clergy Reserves. He regarded the outlawing of that church (as well as others) to be a viable proposition.[25]

The tombstone affair began with Bettridge's insistence that he have final approval of all inscriptions on monuments placed in his church's graveyard.[26] In an advertisement dated 10 April 1845, but first published some twelve days later, Bettridge declared: "In order to prevent unnecessary expense, or disappointment to the parties concerned, I hereby give notice that all proposed monumental inscriptions to be placed in any of the churches, or churchyards, of this Rectory, must be first submitted to me for approval."[27] Within the month, Bettridge's attempt to enforce this policy opened a public controversy which would have major consequences in Woodstock.

The affair began (the exact day is uncertain) when Bettridge, waiting in the graveyard for an out-of-town funeral procession to arrive, strolled over to examine the work of a local stonemason preparing a tombstone. The monument was intended to mark the grave of Jane Rowley Wilson, an Anglican who had died in childbirth at the age of twenty-four on 5 October, 1843. The widower, local cordwainer William Wilson, had requested that the epitaph read,

> In death she is from care and trouble free
> In life she was all that a wife should be.

This inscription, which had been chalked onto the stone, but not yet carved, outraged Bettridge, who immediately ordered the mason to cease his work. Apparently Bettridge found the epitaph to be contrary to truth, in an abstract sense: no woman, and here Bettridge cited his own wife as an example, could be "all that a wife should be." Revealing his own rigid adherence to biblical interpretation and socially sanctioned gender prescriptions for females, he deemed marriage to be a woman's highest calling. That the deceased had met some ultimate standard was, to Bettridge, only her husband's view.

While Bettridge remonstrated with the mason, a friend of Wilson's, a local painter and grocer James Kintrea, intervened. Kintrea defended Wilson's choice of language, but did suggest a compromise wording. Bettridge, however, argued that Wilson should obtain a whole new inscription, and suggested he consult a "village poet." When Wilson heard of the events surrounding his late wife's memorial he was furious. Neither an Anglican nor a Tory himself, Wilson refused to bow to Bettridge's authority, insisting that the epitaph's wording remain the same.

Bettridge called on Wilson in the company of a churchwarden (William Lapenotiere, another member of the elite circle, with connections to the highest levels of the British military and the colonial office)[28] on the following day, but they were unable to sway him. After the mason had finished his work the stone was left in the graveyard, but not on top of Jane Wilson's grave. Wilson planned to remove both the stone and his wife's body and place them together at some other place. The rector, however, refused permission for the body's removal, and ordered that the stone be taken away. After two more weeks of bickering, Wilson backed down with a veiled threat: he agreed to take the stone, but threatened to set it up in a public place, with an additional inscription describing Bettridge's actions. The following night, before Wilson could act, some unknown parties stole the stone and smashed it to bits in a nearby quarry.

The vandalism sparked a fierce, though short-lived, debate between Tory and Reform factions in the provincial press.

The Montreal *Pilot*, edited by Reformer Francis Hincks, lambasted Bettridge and Woodstock's Anglicans, for their "Clerical Intolerance." In defence, Woodstock's *Monarch*, a Tory paper formerly edited by Bettridge—now succeeded by Major Beale, another British half-pay officer, and proud member of both the Church of England and the Orange Order—printed editorials in support of the presumed Tory action:

> ...it cannot be considered unimportant to guard even the memorials of the dead from everything that may infringe upon Scriptural truth, or offend the sober judgement of the discriminating and pious. It is, it must be admitted, quite possible to affirm some very serious error of doctrine, even upon a tombstone; while it is certainly not at all uncommon to transgress the rules of Scriptural teaching, by unauthorized eulogy and reckless adulation.[29]

Other letters from the principal participants in the debate reveal many dimensions of the conflict. Wilson personalized his attack, describing Bettridge's actions as the result of his dissatisfaction with his own wife. Bettridge countered that his wife was an example of the closest thing to perfection, while nevertheless arguing ultimate perfection to be impossible for any human being. Wilson also claimed offence in that Bettridge's proposal of a "village poet" had referred to none other than his Tory ally, Major Beale. Bettridge countered, claiming that he had made the suggestion of Beale's name as one among many poets in the village "playfully." Presumably Bettridge wished to goad the bereaved widower.[30]

Indeed, Bettridge's letters resound with the agony of one who has benefited from the existing cultural structure, yet who suspects that he is witnessing the passing of, or at least the questioning of, his essential world-view. He felt betrayed that many of the local people arrayed against him had at one time bought town lots from him. To him this smacked of an unspeakable disloyalty. Claiming that he always was generous in his dealings with them, volunteering to take the purchase price in goods and services, rather than demanding outright cash, he lamented the end of the era of client-patron relations. He viewed Wilson's use of the word "Clergyman" to describe ministers of other denominations as another attack, for it watered down his high office, an important local symbol of cultural hegemony.

Wilson's subsequent threat to remove his wife's body without permission only reinforced this undermining of authority. Bettridge wrote that "two men, Shenstone, [*sic*], a harness maker, and the aforesaid Kintrea, a painter, both intimates of Mr. Wilson, declared in the hearing of two Tory churchmen, that they would be first and second to disinter the body of Mrs. Wilson, in defiance of the Rector or any one else."[31] That T.S. Shenston, a "Hincksite...of the rabid kind,"[32] supported Wilson is hardly surprising considering his Reform politics. In a letter to the *Pilot*, Kintrea and Shenston confirmed their willingness to aid Wilson in disinterring the body, "in the presence of churchmen," if need be.[33]

When, sometime in the night of 27 June, someone did remove Jane Wilson's remains from the graveyard, local Tory opinion immediately blamed Wilson, Kintrea, and Shenston. Despite his lacking any evidence other than the above-mentioned threat, Bettridge swore an oath before Tory magistrate Philip Graham that

> the body of Jane, the late wife of Wm. Wilson, of Woodstock, boot and shoe maker, was feloniously and surreptitiously stolen, taken and carried away from the church yard of St. Paul's Church at Woodstock aforesaid, and that this complainant hath reason to believe, and doth believe that W. Wilson aforesaid, James Kintrea, painter, and T.S. Shenston, saddler, did aid and assist or were principals in the said stealing and carrying away of the said body by disinterring the same.[34]

The three were arrested on Sunday, 29 June, denied bail, and tossed into jail. The manner of their arrest, and their treatment by Captain Philip Graham, caused another debate to erupt.

Graham made no bones about his allegiance in the matter. First appointed a justice of the peace in 1833, just one year after his arrival in Woodstock, he was a pillar of the Tory elite community and the master of the local Orange Lodge.[35] His ordering of a house-to-house search for the three accused men on a Sunday, despite the fact that they were respected freeholders, drew the headline "Magisterial Tyranny at Woodstock" in the *Pilot*. According to the paper, Graham acted upon Bettridge's urging, since "Mr. Bettridge could not conceal his impatience to get them off to gaol." Graham charged the men with theft of the coffin and grave clothes. Although such charges were normally bailable, Graham refused to release the men, despite offers by them and their friends to pay as high a bond as necessary.[36] Instead he ordered them confined in jail, so the three were marched down the main street in Woodstock under guard, past a crowd of spectators and two church congregations (including that of Shenston's own Baptist church). When James Laycock, a merchant, argued with the magistrate about the mistreatment of his friends outside the court, Graham ordered him to put up "sureties" to keep the peace, or go to jail.

Because Graham had stipulated that they not be held together, each arrested man ended upon in a cell with "a condemned felon" or a person "subject to mental derangement." Just before midnight two other JPs, storekeeper Archibald Burtch and gentleman-farmer John Hatch, both neither Tory nor Anglican, managed to arrange bail. A two-day inquiry followed, after which the local judge dismissed the charges, pointing out that no felony had been committed (after all, if anyone owned the coffin and grave clothes, it was Wilson) and that trespass could only be charged if the church wardens agreed (they did not). Jane Wilson's earthly remains were reinterred on 19 July, three weeks after their midnight removal.[37]

Upset and angry at their treatment, Kintrea, Shenston, and Laycock petitioned the governor general for redress; before the issue was decided, Graham and Bettridge visited their government friends in Montreal. The executive council decided that Graham's actions were wrong, but not carried out in a partial manner, or for political reasons. They ruled that Graham erred in calling for a vigorous search on the Sabbath, when he could easily have waited until Monday. He also erred in refusing to grant bail, since the only information he had was indirect, and the men were prosperous freeholders. The council agreed with Judge McQueen that no felony had taken place, and further mentioned that Bettridges's charge did not refer to the coffin or grave clothes. Finally, Graham's act in demanding a bond from Laycock was described as an unwitting mistake: "The propriety of a Justice binding a person over to keep the peace towards himself is open to question." Despite their litany of condemnation, the government left Graham seemingly unscathed. It refused to requests to remove him from office, simply suggesting that his errors in judgment must have resulted from his being too easily influenced by the feelings of others—apparently an excusable flaw in a Tory magistrate.[38]

At one level, the tombstone affair can be explained in terms of personal and political vendettas. Graham, Bettridge, Kintrea, Shenston, and Wilson had all been active in the controversial election of October 1844 in Oxford. Francis Hincks stood as the incumbent candidate in Oxford, having won election as an extreme Reformer in 1841, and as a more moderate Reformer in the by-election of 1842 (brought about by his appointment to the executive council). In the 1844 election, local Tories portrayed Hincks as a turncoat, because his acceptance of a seat on the executive council contradicted a strong stand he had taken in 1841. The presence of a third candidate, an "anti-Hincks Reformer" who did not show up on election day, generated enough feeling against Hincks to swing the vote to the extreme Tory candidate, Robert Riddell, son-in-law of Admiral Vansittart.[39]

Hinck's forces felt that other factors were involved in the narrow (742 to 722) decision, and called for an inquiry into disreputable electioneering tactics. The campaign to unseat Riddell was led by William Wilson, among others. On the days of the election, Wilson had served as Hinck's scrutineer at the Woodstock polls. At the same time Bettridge was functioning as a Riddell campaign worker, bringing in friendly voters, and exhorting the reluctant to do their duty. Several times Wilson and Bettridge quarrelled over the eligibility of certain voters, with Wilson accusing Bettridge of knowingly lying about the qualifications of Riddell voters. During the provincial inquiry into the election, Kintrea brought forward evidence to show that Bettridge had falsified deeds in order to make certain people eligible. Bettridge, for his part, defended his political actions: "I am aware that in years gone by, many of the Clergy at home were afraid of the epithet 'political parsons' and consequently hid their 'talent' of influence: that time is passed. Can any reason be assigned why, as a Clergyman, I should not be allowed to exercise my influence over those of my 'cure' to do that which I am satisfied is right [?]"[40] Bettridge then protrayed himself as a victim of Wilson's overzealous enforcement of the rules.

In addition, Shenston and Graham were involved in a bitter personal feud. Shenston had tried to get Graham removed from office because he no longer held the property necessary for his appointment, and because Graham refused to honour a two-year-old debt, despite a legal judgment in Shenston's favour. The previous May, when a group of soldiers stayed overnight in Woodstock, Graham had used his authority to billet some thirty men in Shenston's small house, far more than any other householder had to accommodate, with many avoiding any billeting at all.[41]

When the tombstone affair first erupted, these political entanglements ensured that it became a cause célèbre. All of the charges against Bettridge first raised in the provincial inquiry were brought up again. The *Pilot* accused Bettridge of refusing the tombstone for political reasons and personal revenge.[42] The *Monarch* tried to turn a similar attack against Wilson:

> It is very obvious, too, that the conduct of the aggrieved party, judging from his published letter, savours more of the disappointment of the partizan than the heartfelt grief of a Christian mourner. It is impossible, indeed, to peruse his letter without perceiving how much its tone and language are at variance with that subdued and quiet feeling which the chastenings of the Lord should produce in the breast of the humble and really afflicted believer.[43]

The paper also followed Bettridge's convoluted rules of religious bigotry to "prove" that "*Mr. Hincks is not a Christian.*"[44]

Ultimately, the graveyard affair boosted the Reform cause in Woodstock and Oxford, by driving moderates away from the extreme Tories.[45] Many other factors also worked to this end. The Baldwin Act of 1849, which heralded responsible government at the local level, a long-standing platform of the province's political reformers, further undermined the power of the old elite and lessened their single-handed domination of local politics. Death and out-migration also weakened Woodstock's Tory elite. After pension cuts, initiated by the British government, began to affect them, some of the retired officers abandoned their lifestyle and the town. Others, old men by the late 1840s, died. Among the five councillors elected in Woodstock's first municipal election in 1851, members of the elite's social and political circle were completely absent.[46] A new group, made up of middle-class men, had started to challenge the older group for local leadership.

The public careers of the men jailed in the graveyard affair symbolize the success of Woodstock's middle-class Reformers. William Wilson and Thomas Shenston were both appointed magistrate in 1849—the first time since 1833 that Philip Graham, dead for some three months, did not appear on the commission of the peace. At the first municipal elections in Woodstock in 1851 (supervised by Shenston as returning officer), the people elected Wilson as one of five councillors. At the first meeting the council elected Kintrea as city clerk; he became a councillor the following year. Both Wilson and Kintrea later served terms as mayor of the town.[47] Between 1850 and 1852 Shenston sat in a number of offices, such as county clerk and county census commissioner. He also served on the Board of Public Instruction, the Board of School Trustees, and the board of a local road company. After that Shenston moved to Brantford, serving as county registrar from 1853 until his death in 1895.[48] For the remainder of the century, Woodstock's leaders continued to come from the middle class; mayors made their living as bank officers, lawyers, factory owners, merchants, or publishers, as did the local members of Parliament.

The effects of the tombstone affair were more than just political; by bringing the system of government by magistracy into local disrepute, and undermining the authority of the Anglican rector, the affair both served notice of, and contributed to, the crumbling of the old hegemony of paternalism. This phenomenon has to be seen in the context of a broad change taking place throughout the colony as Ontario's economy was transformed into one based on import substitution through industrial production. More and more people increased the level of their personal integration with the marketplace, or came to be dependent on a capitalist industrial economy for the first time. These changes also altered the competing cultural interpretations of the world. The new Victorian middle class, which had emerged in the 1830s and 1840s, had a chance to form alliances and claim to speak for all.[49]

The world-view which would come to dominate Ontario society started out as a minority position brought into the region before mid-century. It was linked to the growing power of the new social group, which called itself the "middle class."[50] Part of the reason for the success of the middle-class hegemony derived from the growing importance of occupation as a way of identifying and defining individuals. Industrialization and the associated division of labour created a much more specialized occupational pattern. An individual's identification with a specific full-time occupation became more permanent. At the same time an increased dependence on the capitalist economy made regular employment very important in the lives of individuals and their families. As a result, people thought of themselves more and more in terms of their vocational role, and society became increasingly organized in terms of occupational groupings, though the nature of these groupings underwent continual fluctuations.[51] The broad pattern of occupational change in the Victorian period involved large increased in the proportion of non-manual and skilled manual workers in the province.

When Bettridge referred to "a person of the name of Kintrea, a painter,"[52] offence was taken by Wilson. He retorted in a letter: "From the very uncourteous manner in which you notice Messrs. Shenstone [*sic*] and Kintrea no one unacquainted with them would suppose that they were two of the most *respectable* tradesmen in the place, one of them is Secretary to the Temperance and to the Tract Societies."[53]

The emphasis on the "respectable" description is telling; in fact, the cultural forces moving into a position of dominance in Upper Canada took this word as their central defining image. Although the precise definition of respectability changed through time, its essence proved durable: a respectable male individual had to be industrious, sober, religious, compassionate, morally upright, and responsible for his own welfare and that of his family. The Victorian middle class sought to define respectability in ways which brought order to a world shaken by new types of disruption arising from the very same economic processes which had made the middle class itself a powerful social force.

The most clear expression of the world-view associated with this new social group came in the first temperance campaigns, which defined respectability in a manner which differentiated the middle class from those above and below. Thus the connection of Shenston to the Temperance Society places him squarely in the emerging hegemonic faction—in shorthand, the "Victorian middle class."[54] (Eventually this group dropped the loud concern with total abstinence as a fundamental part of their world-view; while sobriety remained important, pledging total abstinence did not appeal to potential allies or consenting subordinates.)[55]

In the late 1840s and early 1850s the coming of the railway age completed the process of change in Woodstock's leadership group. The town experienced wholesale economic change, particularly after 1853 when the Great Western Railway connected Woodstock to the dominant Toronto-Hamilton-London-Windsor corridor. This brought the dawn of a new era of urban and industrial expansion through access to distant markets. The attraction of this transport link, and the construction of a number of gravel roads in the county over the next few years, soon resulted in the expected industrial activity.[56]

Most of the remaining gentry joined middle-class businessmen in one particular railway scheme, looking to join Woodstock to Lake Erie at Port Dover.[57] In this pursuit they allied with former political foes, notably reformer Francis Hincks, the premier of Canada in 1852 and perhaps the province's greatest railway promoter of the day. In pursuing outright commercialism they stepped outside their squire and parson concept of society and stimulated a loose rapprochement between themselves and the province's rising group of urban mercantile men.

At the same time, a flock of new institutions offering employment opportunities for the middle class appeared in town, and provided services for the community and its rural hinterland. Insurance companies appointed several local agents, working on a part-time basis, in the 1850s.[58] Local building societies—another institution influenced by the middle class—appeared in Woodstock in 1847, 1851, and 1865; James Laycock was a key figure in the first two.[59]

By 1870 Woodstock's population had reached almost four thousand, and the town's industrial workforce stood twenty-first amongst those of urban Ontario;[60] Woodstock's leaders nevertheless sought to improve the town's economic position in any way that they could. With the aid of the town council, the Board of Trade used its sizable cash bonuses and tax incentives to protect and stimulate local industrial development.[61] In addition, civic leaders used social and voluntary agencies, urban reform, and organized sport to boost their town.[62] They supported gazetteers and newspaper special editions to work to this end, painting rosy-coloured portraits by focusing upon select town features—industry, business and consumer interest, neighbourhood, and upstanding local morals. The marked interest in securing and sustaining industrial manufacturing firms was symptomatic of middle-class perceptions connecting industrial prosperity to generalized local prosperity.

As the dominant leadership group changed, Woodstock's social sphere also changed substantially. Although the Cricket Club and Constitutional Society reflected aristocratic ideals in the 1840s, fledgling middle-class social institutions also existed at that time: for example, Woodstock boasted a Mechanics' Institute, a St. George's Society, two other Scottish social societies, and a Volunteer Fire Company.[63] Each organization, based upon meritocratic principles, enabled members to construct their own social milieu and to present their own vision of the world. In the 1850s and 1860s other voluntary social agencies for this constituency emerged. Among them were a local Horticultural Society, the Oxford Literary Society (which merged with the Mechanics' Institute in 1869), and a voluntary militia regiment which was officered by middle-class townspeople.[64]

As the old Tory elite declined, the associated social institutions found their dominance challenged. A symbol of the switch in influence from the "established" Protestant churches to the "dissenting" ones appeared in Woodstock in 1860 when the Canadian Literary Institute, a prestigious Baptist college and forerunner to McMaster University, opened. The cricket club too had had its day and "dwindled into obscurity." In 1858 the *Canadian Cricketer's Guide* noticed the move: "It pains us deeply," it wrote. "It seems strange that cricket [in Woodstock] should be entirely abandoned to the more absorbing claims of railways and politics."[65]

Woodstock's tombstone affair—at first glance a comic opera episode in a backwater community—represents a rare chance to observe clearly the process of hegemonic change. In Ontario a cultural world-view associated with the Victorian middle class became dominant after mid-century, and reached its peak of power in the 1870s and 1880s. In contrast to the fading world of paternalism, this hegemony centred on the notion of respectability achieved through meritocratic means. The issues which set Graham and Bettridge against Wilson, Kintrea, and Shenston all resonated with the wisespread cultural alterations of the time. The role and status of the magistracy and the Anglican church, the fading of client-patron relations, the rising importance of respectability, the campaign for temperance—all of these areas appeared in broad strokes on Woodstock's social canvas of 1845.

In the decades following the tombstone affair, the industrial development of Woodstock took place under the leadership of a middle-class elite whose value structure had solidified and become institutionalized by the 1870s. As a Toronto newspaper commented at the time, "race of thrifty, industrious money-getting men, with ideas more in unison with the place and the time" now ran the town's affairs.[66] The gentry, their fate sealed by a process of which the debacle of 1845 was emblematic, had disappeared.

Notes

1. J.K. Johnson, *Becoming Prominent*: *Regional Leadership in Upper Canada, 1791–1841* (Kingston and Montreal 1989); F.H. Armstrong, "The Oligarchy of the Western District of Upper Canada, 1788–1841," Canadian Historical Association *Annual Report* (1977); F.H. Armstrong, *Handbook of Upper Canadian Chronology*, rev. ed., (Toronto 1985); D.H. Akenson, *The Irish in Ontario*: *A Study in Rural History* (Kingston and Montreal 1984), pp. 68–78.

2. On these values, see S.F. Wise, "Upper Canada and the Conservative Tradition," in E. Firth, ed., *Profiles of a Province* (Toronto 1967); S.F. Wise, "Liberal Consensus or Ideological Battleground: Some Reflections on the Hartz Thesis," *Canadian Historical Association Historical Papers* (1974); David Mills, *The Idea of Loyalty in Upper Canada*, 1784–1850 (Kingston and Montreal 1988); Jane Errington, *The Lion, the Eagle and Upper Canada*: *A Developing Colonial Ideology* (Kingston and Montreal 1987).

3. Akenson, *The Irish in Ontario*, pp. 89–98; Armstrong, "Oligarchy."

4. Mills, *The Idea of Loyalty*; Johnson, *Becoming Prominent*, p. 166.

5. G.S. Patterson, *Land Settlement in Upper Canada, 1783–1840* (Toronto 1921); Art Williams and Edward Baker, *Bits and Pieces* (Woodstock 1967), pp. 9–16; R.W. Sawtell, "The Woodstock of the Days that are Gone" (newspaper clipping, C. 1906), R.W. Sawtell Collection, Scrapbook no. 1 (Woodstock Public Library).

6. Gerald M. Craig, *Upper Canada*: *The Formative Years 1784–1841* (Toronto 1979), pp. 226 ff.

7. For Vansittart's background, see *Concise Dictionary of National Biography* (London, England, 1965), p. 133; Ethel Canfield, *Vice Admiral Henry Vansittart* (Woodstock 1934); on Drew, see "Andrew Drew," *Dictionary of Canadian Biography* 10, pp. 259–60; John Ireland (pseud.) "Andrew Drew, the Man Who Burned the Caroline," *Ontario History* (1967), pp. 137–56; idem., "Andrew Drew and the Founding of Woodstock," *Ontario History* 60 (1968).

8. On the officers see: W. Bettridge papers, Ontario Archives, MU 131; Alfred Dommett, *Canadian Journal* (1833–35) E.A. Horsman and Lillian Rea Benson, eds., (London 1955); "Statement of Pewholders and Pew Rentals Due St. Paul's Church, Woodstock, 1848," (Woodstock Public Library); W.E. Elliott, "The Parish of Woodstock," *Ontario Historical Society Papers and Records* 30 (1934), pp. 83–95; Ireland, "Andrew Drew," pp. 230–31; Ethel Canfield, "Early Parishioners of Old St. Paul's" (Woodstock Public Library 1934); Thomas S. Shenston, *The Oxford Gazetteer* (1852: reprint Woodstock, 1968); and Arthur Sweatman, *A Sketch of the History of the Parish of Woodstock* (1902?).

9. On military rank and land grants, see Lillian Gates, *Land Policies in Upper Canada* (Toronto 1968).

10. On local commissions, see Shenston, *The Oxford Gazetteer*, pp. 86–88.

11. "Sidney" to W. Bettridge, 8 May 1838, Bettridge Papers.

12. Blunderbus (pseud.), *A History of Brighton* (1901; reprinted Woodstock n.d.), p. 14.

13. Ibid., pp. 3–13.

14. "That Aristocratic Neighbourhood of Woodstock," *Globe*, 24 May 1878.

15. Richard Gruneau, *Class, Sports, and Social Development* (Amherst 1983), pp. 95 ff.

16. See "That Aristocratic Neighbourhood of Woodstock,"; A.R. McCleneghan, "Woodstock was the Scene of a Gay Social Life in the Old Days" (1909), and "Our Pioneer Noblemen" (1901), both are reprinted in *Aristocratic Woodstock* (Woodstock 1987); Elliott, "Parish of Woodstock," p. 89.

17. Blunderbus, *History of Brighton*, p. 14; Nancy B. Bouchier, "'Strictly Honourable Races': Woodstock's Driving Park Association and Nineteenth Century Small Town Civic Holidays," *Canadian Journal of the History of Sport* 24, no. 1 (May 1993), pp. 29–51.

18. Nancy B. Bouchier, "'Aristocrats' and their 'Noble Sport': Woodstock Officers and Cricket during the Rebellion Era," *Canadian Journal of the History of Sport* 20, no. 1 (May 1989), pp. 16–31; St. Catharines' Cricket Club, *The Canadian Cricketer's Guide and Review of the Past Season* (St. Catharines, Ontario, 1858). A full description of the building of the Woodstock pitch is found in "A Cricket Sheaf" (Oxford County Library, uncatalogued material in storage room). See also R.W. Sawtell, "The Thames Valley" (Sawtell Scrapbook no 2, Woodstock Public Library) for a description of the pitch and his recollections of playing in 1845. On the social atmosphere of pre-confederation cricket, see Peter L. Lindsay, "A History of Sport in Canada, 1807–1867" (Ph.D. dissertation, University of Alberta 1969) pp. 98 ff; and Bernard F. Booth and John S. Batts, "The Political Significance of Organized Sport in Upper Canada, 1825–1867," *Proceedings of the VII HISPA International Congress* (Paris 1978), pp. 399–416; S.F. Wise, "Sport and Class Values in Old Ontario and Quebec," in *His Own Man. Essays in Honour of Arthur Reginald Marsden Lower*, eds. W.H. Heick and Roger Graham (Montreal 1974), pp. 93–117; and Charles Anthony Joyce, "At Close of Play: The Evolution of Cricket in London, Ontario 1836–1902" (MA thesis, University of Western Ontario 1988). The journal of Alfred Dommett reveals that the Woodstock elite also appreciated blood sports. He writes on 4 December 1833 that he observed a "splendid fight between Deedes' scotch terrier and four young boars."

19. "Statement of Pewholders and Pew Rentals Due St.Paul's Church, Woodstock 1848" (Woodstock Public Library); R.W. Sawtell, "Regal and Vice Regal Visits to Oxford County" (Sawtell Scrapbook, no. 2, (Woodstock Public Library).

20. See Colin Read, *The Rising in Western Upper Canada 1837–1838. The Duncombe Revolt and After* (Toronto 1982); Irene Crawford, *Captain Andrew Drew* (Woodstock 1981); Ireland, "Andrew Drew, the Man who Burned the Caroline." Fifteen months before the Duncombe revolt over three hundred concerned Woodstonians had sent the lieutenant-governor a loyal address. They pledged to "make any sacrifice should the urgency of the case demand it, to preserve inviolate the Constitution." *Upper Canada Sundries*, "Loyal Address From Woodstock," 14 May 1836, v. 167, 91098.

21. Brian Dawe, *'Old Oxford is Wide Awake!' Pioneer Settlers and Politics in Oxford County 1793–1855* (Woodstock 1980), pp. 63–74.

22. Smith, *Canadian Gazetteer*, p. 223.

23. The situation did not last; by about 1847 the condition of the Governor's Road portion had deteriorated so much that most east-west traffic returned to the old stage road.

24. W.B. Hobson, "Old Stage Coach Days in Oxford County" *Ontario Historical Society Papers and Records* (1919), p. 34:, Dawe, *'Old Oxford'*, p. 89.

25. On Bettridge, see Ethel Canfield, "Canon Bettridge" (Woodstock Public Library, n.d.) On the church itself, see A. Sweatman, *A Sketch of the History of the Parish of Woodstock*; Maurice S. Baldwin, *Old St. Paul's Church Ninetieth Anniversary, 1834–1924* (Woodstock 1924); Elliott, "The Parish of Woodstock."

26. Dawe offers a brief treatment of this affair (pp. 77–78); however, the following description of the events of 1845 is based primarily on the letters, editorials, and extracts from other papers published in the Montreal *Pilot* and Woodstock *Monarch* between April and December 1845.

27. *Monarch*, 22 April 1845.

28. Lapenotiere, the lawyer son of a post captain who had served under Lord Nelson at Trafalgar and a key member of the local cricket club, had letters of reference from Lord Glenelg, Sir John Colborne, and Sir George Arthur. Dawe. *'Old Oxford'*, p. 76.

29. *Monarch*, 20 May 1845.

30. Letters from William Wilson, published in *Pilot*, 3 May 1845, and from William Bettridge, published in *Pilot*, 17 May 1845, also published in *Monarch*, 27 May 1845.

31. Bettridge letter, *Pilot*, 17 May 1845.

32. From Revell, *History of Brant*, as cited in *Mrs. Canfield's People* (Woodstock 1986), p. 67.

33. Kintrea and Shenston letter, *Pilot*, 10 June 1845.

34. *Pilot*, 16 December 1845.

35. Shenston, *Oxford Gazetteer*, p. 87. Graham's obituary was published on 30 June 1849 in the *British American*. On the connection between Graham, the Tory elite, and the Orange Order in Woodstock, see Christopher J. Anstead, "Fraternalism in Victorian Ontario: Secret Societies and Cultural Hegemony" (Ph.D dissertation, University of Western Ontario 1992), pp. 314–23.

36. Simon Fraser Robertson, local barrister, for example, was refused the opportunity to secure bail for them.

37. Burial Register, St. Paul's Anglican Church (Woodstock Public Library).

38. *Pilot*, 16 December 1845.

39. Dawe, *'Old Oxford'*, pp. 72–74; Francis Hincks, *Reminiscences of His Public Life* (Montreal 1884), pp. 136–47; see also Shenston Papers (Woodstock Public Library).

40. Bettridge letter, *Monarch*, 27 May 1845.

41. D. Daly to T. Shenston, 23 September 1845, Shenston Papers; *Pilot*, 16 December 1845.

42. *Pilot*, 3 May 1845.

43. *Monarch*, 20 May 1845.

44. Ibid., 10 June 1845 (original emphasis).

45. Dawes (p. 78) has asserted, "If those who suffered at Graham's hands had not been all solid Reformers before, they certainly were after the graveyard affair."

46. Shenston, *Oxford Gazetteer*, p. 124.

47. Ibid., pp. 88, 124, 215; Dawe, 'Old Oxford', pp. 78–79.

48. Shenston, *Oxford Gazetteer*, pp. 86–97; *Brantford Courier*, 16 March 1895.

49. For a similar interpretation of Victorian America, see Carroll Smith-Rosenberg, *Disorderly Conduct* (Oxford 1985), especially pp. 50, 79–88, 167–73.

50. P.E. Johnson, *A Shopkeepers' Millennium* (New York 1978); Sean Wilentz, *Chants Democratic* (New York 1984), pp. 4–15; John S. Gilkeson, *Middle-Class Providence, 1820–1940* (Princeton, 1986), pp. 9–95.

51. See, for example, B. Palmer, *A Culture in Conflict* (Montreal 1979); G. Kealey, *Toronto Workers Respond To Industrial Capitalism* (Toronto 1980); M. Katz, *The People of Hamilton, Canada West* (Cambridge, Mass: 1975); and Michael Bliss, *A Living Profit* (Toronto, 1978).

52. Bettridge letter, *Pilot*, 17 May 1845.

53. Wilson letter, *Pilot*, 10 June 1845 (emphasis added).

54. Shenston Papers; see also J.M. Clemens, "Taste Not; Touch Not; Handle Not; A Study of the Social Assumptions of the Temperance Literature and Temperance Supporters in Canada West between 1839 and 1859," *Ontario History* 64, no. 3 (1972), pp. 143–60.

55. Christopher Anstead, "The Limits of Hegemony: Orange Lodges, Temperance Lodges and Respectability in Victorian Ontario," Paper presented to the International Congress on the Social History of Alcohol, London, May, 1993.

56. Williams and Baker, *Bits and Pieces*, p. 81; J. Sutherland, *County of Oxford Gazetteer and General Business Directory for 1862-3* (Ingersoll 1862), p. 205.

57. Public Archives of Canada, MG 24, Buchanan Papers, D. 16, vol. 99, The Woodstock and Lake Erie Railway and Harbour Company, *Minute Book*.

58. *British-American* (Woodstock), 24 September 1852, Shenston, *Oxford Gazetteer*, pp. 217–18; D. Bonk, "Businessmen in the 1857 Woodstock Directory" (unpublished paper), Woodstock Public Library.

59. Shenston, *Oxford Gazetteer*, pp. 104–5; Williams and Baker, *Bits and Pieces*, p. 81.

60. Elizabeth Bloomfield, "Industry in Ontario Urban Centres, 1870," *Urban History Review* 15, no. 3 (February 1987), pp. 279– 83.

61. *Consolidated Bylaws of the Town of Woodstock* (Woodstock 1896).

62. Nancy B. Bouchier, "'For the Love of the Game and the Honour of the Town': Organized Sport, Local Culture and Middle Class Hegemony in Two Ontario Towns, 1838–1895" (Ph.D. dissertation, University of Western Ontario 1990).

63. *Monarch*, 1 December 1842, 7 January 1845, 18 April 1848; *British-American*, 30 September and 2 December 1848; Smith, *Canadian Gazetteer*, p. 223.

64. *County of Oxford Gazetteer*, 1862–3, pp. 205–14; *Sentinel Review*, "Inaugural Edition," 1–2 July 1901.

65. *Canadian Cricketer's Guide*, p. 71.

66. *Globe*, "That Aristocratic Neighbourhood."

VOLUNTARY SOCIETIES AND THE PROCESS OF MIDDLE-CLASS FORMATION IN EARLY-VICTORIAN HALIFAX, NOVA SCOTIA

David A. Sutherland

This inquiry begins with a story, set in Halifax, Nova Scotia, in the summer of 1848. At dawn, on the morning of August 8th, a steamship named the *Unicorn* came puffing down the harbour. Packed with some 400 men and women, it was headed for Lunenburg, on Nova Scotia's south shore. The passengers on board were members and guests of the Union Engine company, the key component of Halifax's volunteer fire-fighting establishment. Following custom, the firemen were out for a day of recreation and frivolity. When the *Unicorn* reached open water it began to pitch and toss with sufficient vigour to render many seasick. As the suffering became ever more widespread rumours spread that nausea could best be remedied with a large dose of brandy. Accordingly, at eight in the morning the steward obliged by opening the bar. Several of the passengers, along with a number of crew, drank steadily until the vessel reached Lunenburg, at about noon.

Tumbling ashore amidst considerable mirth, the company spent the next couple of hours delighting in the hospitality offered them by residents of that friendly little outport. Then everyone trooped on board to pay a call at the neighbouring community of Chester. En route liquor was sold "as freely as at a race course," including to those in charge of navigation with the result that the *Unicorn* grounded on her way into harbour. She broke free, however, and made it to port. There more good times were had until about dusk when the *Unicorn's* captain summoned all for the return journey to Halifax. On the way "drinking and drunkenness" increased such that the vessel narrowly avoided colliding with George's Island, at the centre of Halifax harbour. Tie-up occurred up at midnight but festivities continued until two in the morning, when passengers finally gave a last salute and found their way home.

One of the first to leave was a lawyer by the name of Alexander James. At age 32, an officer in both the Mechanics Institute and the Sons of Temperance, as well as a prominent supporter of the newly ascendant Liberal party, James was appalled by what had taken place on board the *Unicorn*. Such was his fury that on reaching home he sat up all night writing a letter of protest aimed primarily at Archibald Scott, who had kept bar on board the pleasure craft. Scott, an insurance broker, also worked for Samuel Cunard, proprietor of the *Unicorn*, as agent in charge of arranging excursion parties. In return for relatively low

From *Journal of the Canadian Historical Association*, vol. 5, 1994, 237–263. Reprinted by permission.

charter fees Scott obtained monopoly rights to sell food and drink while the vessel was on hire.

All this was perfectly legal but James, in his letter of denunciation, which appeared anonymously in Halifax's *Morning Chronicle*, insisted that Scott's behaviour violated prevailing standards of propriety. First of all, it was said that male consumption of alcohol should not have been permitted in the presence of the ladies. Secondly, when drinking turned into intoxication, the bar should have been shut. Finally Scott, an elder in St. Matthew's Presbyterian church, should not have been so flagrantly involved in such a display of gross debauchery.

Scott, aged 44, was a prominent Haligonian, sufficiently well-respected by his peers to have secured office in both the genteel Halifax Horticultural Society and the Lay Association in Support of the Church of Scotland. He also ranked as a militant supporter of the Conservatives, a party now mourning its loss in the general election of 1847 which carried Nova Scotia into the era of "responsible government." Outraged by what he saw as a slur on his character Scott demanded, through his attorney, that the *Morning Chronicle* reveal who had written about events on board the *Unicorn*. The paper complied and when James refused to retract what he had written, Scott sued for libel. The case came to court in August, 1849, A series of witnesses appeared, essentially to establish whether Scott had used undue influence to persuade men to drink. In the end it was decided that he had not. But while finding for the plaintiff the jury gave him damages of only one penny, thereby providing Alexander James with a redeeming moral victory.[1]

The firemen's excursion and the controversy it provoked occurred against a background of massive dislocation in the Nova Scotian capital. After 1815 protracted war had given way to sustained peace, forcing Halifax to look beyond its imperial military garrison to trade as the mainstay of future economic activity. But commerce proved to be a fickle friend, exposing this east coast port to a pattern of boom and bust that persisted into the 1850s. At the same time locals experienced a dizzying population upheaval, involving both large-scale growth and relatively novel ethnic and sectarian diversity, in particular that associated with a mass influx by Irish Roman Catholics. New wealth flourished alongside unprecedented concentrations of mass poverty. Technological innovation ranging from gas street lamps and harbour steamers coexisted with the dire threat of "modern" diseases such as cholera. Out of it all came an effort to transform Halifax from an eighteenth-century town to a nineteenth-century city, an effort which involved a host of reform enthusiasms ranging from evangelical religion to political liberalism. The struggle to extract progress from flux spawned a contradictory blend of ambition and anxiety among Haligonians. Their mood vacillated between boosterish claims of possessing a destiny for greatness and complaint that Halifax would forever be doomed to a "dull, stupid, phlegmatic" existence.[2]

Most outspoken of in expressing both hope and fear about the future were those who belonged to what contemporaries referred to as the "middling element" of the community. Primarily made up of professionals, tradesmen, artisans and clerks, they were prime beneficiaries of Halifax's development through the second quarter of the nineteenth century. Growing in absolute numbers, increasingly literate, with ever more disposable income and leisure time, members of this strata tended to become, over time, increasingly self-conscious and ambitious. The local press, itself the creation of those with middling rank, helped foster what by the 1830s can begin to be referred to as a middle-class identity. Discussion in print of scandals involving the exercise of power by their supposed betters, along with censure of riot and arson committed by the "lower orders," transformed individual dissatisfaction into alienated public opinion. That in turn prompted bold insistence that community affairs should now be entrusted to the "self-made" men who had emerged as the true "bone and sinew" of Halifax society. Out of this potent blend of pride and prejudice came political agitation that led, in 1841, to Halifax's incorporation as a city, complete with a major and council elected to office by those whose success had made them ratepayers. Coinciding with and complementing that achievement was a surge of institutional activity outside the realm of government, activity which ultimately came to pay a central role in the process of middle class formation.[3]

Here the focus is on what has come to be known as "voluntary societies," formally structured private-sector organizations with a membership recruited through free choice. A few such societies had always existed in Halifax, but in the early-Victorian era their numbers grew dramatically, reaching a total of over sixty by mid-century. Simultaneously, voluntary societies became increasingly diversified in the range of their activities, moving into virtually every sector of human endeavour, from philanthropy to recreation. As well, they acquired an ever higher profile, to the point that their activities came to dominate press coverage of local news. In all of this Halifax was simply emulating a situation found elsewhere in the cities of Britain and the United States.[4]

Urbanization and the pursuit of modernization rather than the relatively narrow dynamics of industrialization seem to have provided the basic stimulus for the surge in voluntary society activity. Rapid growth, especially when associated with mass immigration, meant that many city residents found themselves isolated in a sea of strangers. For such people voluntary societies could function as a substitute for lost kinship connections. Similarly the sense of being caught up in a breakdown of traditional patterns of deference drew people to associations that promised to function as instruments of social control. Again idealism, rooted in such things as religious commitment or enthusiasms for science and technology, prompted like-minded people to set up organizations devoted to the pursuit of virtue and enlightenment. Finally, there were those who saw in associational life an opportunity to assert that there community was no longer a provincial or colonial backwater but instead had come to embrace the prevailing "spirit of the age."[5]

Analysis of the membership lists that have survived for voluntary associations in Halifax suggests that they did not attract a cross-section of the urban population.[6] Journeymen workers, unskilled labourers and common servants failed to join up, most likely because of poverty and lack of leisure time. Members of Halifax's traditional ruling elite, what might be called the "gentry," appeared relatively infrequently, probably because their privileged status meant they already possessed both self-assurance and what was needed for effective self-assertion. In contrast lawyers, doctors, clerics, manufacturers, retail shopkeepers, master craftsmen, manufacturers, and clerks—those occupations generally seen as being the core of the nineteenth century middle class—demonstrated an avid enthusiasm for society life. As a result, they dominated the mainstream of associational life in Halifax, at least at the level of the general membership.[7]

In an attempt to discern more precisely why those of middle rank were drawn to voluntary societies in early Victorian Halifax a detailed inquiry has been conducted into their activity, using both organizational records and reports in the press. Rather than look at every society, emphasis has been placed on those which placed a high value on active participation. Thus the Halifax Bible Society, which met only once a year and where most members did little more than pay subscriptions, has been neglected in favour of entities which strove to promote strong brotherhood bonds among their rank and file.[8]

Substantial information is available for several fraternal-style organizations which flourished in Halifax through the 1840s, an era of seminal importance for associational life in the Nova Scotian capital. These were the Union Engine and Axe Companies, the Freemasons, the Mechanics' Institute, the Charitable Irish Society, the North British Society, the St. George's Society and the Nova Scotia Philanthropic Society. Other organizations existed where membership brought extensive involvement but with respect to size, durability and prominence, these seven tended to prevail.[9]

Entry into the Charitable Irish Society, for example, involved far more than offering an annual donation. Attendance at both annual and quarterly meetings was compulsory. Absenteeism, regardless of cause, rendered members vulnerable to a fine and persistent non-attendance led to expulsion. The Mechanics' Institute did not go so far as to insist on attendance at its weekly lectures, but members were pressured through press announcements to turn out on a regular basis. As for the firemen, a portion of them got together every time flames threatened the community, a phenomenon which occurred as often as forty times a year. In addition to the foregoing, all these societies sponsored an elaborate round of social gatherings. Banquets, balls, picnics, soirees, and excursions became an ever larger part of the fraternal experience through the 1840s. Members were not obliged to attend these special occasions but a majority appear to have done so, perhaps because of peer pressure, but more likely in order to enjoy themselves.[10]

Individual identification with the group was further encouraged by means of welfare schemes. For example, the Union Engine Company collected $7^{1}/_{2}$d. per quarter to maintain a fund "for relief of Members who may be injured at the time of duty."[11] The Nova Scotian Philanthropic Society provided members with sick benefits of up to 10s. per week. In the event of death application could be made for help in meeting funeral costs and the society would consider offering assistance to widows and orphans. The Freemasons went one step further by insisting that all members turn out in full regalia for the funeral of one of their "brethren."[12]

Rules and conventions existed within all these organizations for the purpose of stimulating friendship and co-operation among the membership. For example, the Mechanics Institute banned discussion "on party or domestic politics, or on controverted religious topics." Moreover, the executive vigorously expressed its disapproval of the "injudicious habit," especially among young members, "of making numerous expressions of applause," lest speakers not so flattered take offence. Similarly the Freemasons of St. Andrew's Lodge insisted that "no private disputes or altercations shall be permitted during Lodge hours on any subject." Putting things somewhat more positively, the Charitable Irish Society told its rank and file they had an obligation "to conduct themselves with kindness and affection," to "promote friendship and harmony," and to "aid and assist a member when in adversity or trouble;" and if a member seemed likely to suffer from "imprudent conduct," they were to intervene or seek assistance from the Society. The quest for "brotherhood" often fell short of complete attainment. Problems persistently arose over delinquency with respect to attendance at meetings and payment of dues, and on occasion meetings fell prey to what one veteran member described as "miserable political jealousy and intrigue." Periodically, executive authority had to be invoked to curb "bad language" and "disparaging remarks" among the membership.[13]

Each organization professed to have a relatively open admissions policy. Most liberal of all was the Mechanics Institute, which welcomed anyone, male or female, who could pay an annual membership fee of 10s. All other societies excluded women from their ranks. They also insisted that applicants be at least nineteen years old and have risen beyond the rank of apprentice. Freemasons further required members to be self-employed. In order to join one of the four ethnic societies one had to have been born either in the British Isles or Nova Scotia, or be descended from someone born in those places. While religion was never formally mentioned as a criterion for admission to any of these seven organizations, the Union Engine Company had a reputation for discriminating against Roman Catholics. All societies appear to have granted their members an unrestricted right to join other organizations.[14]

Prospective members invariably had to meet formal minimum requirements with respect to affluence and popularity. Initiation fees of either 10s. or 20s. were the norm, except for the Freemasons who charged £5 just for the privilege of applying to enter. Normally one had to be nominated by an existing member in good standing. Applications were then reviewed either by a special committee or by those attending one of the quarterly meetings. Veto power over candidates for membership varied by organization. For example, the Charitable Irish Society required approval by two-thirds of those present and voting, while at St. Andrew's Freemasons Lodge three negative ballots translated into rejection. Only the Freemasons combined admission with formal ritual, and that organization also was unique in providing for promotion through a series of ranks. Every step up the ladder cost members 40s. At each quarterly meeting those in attendance had to pay an instalment on their annual dues, along with a charge for refreshments. The cost ranged from a low of 1s.3d at one of the Masonic lodges to a high of 4s.3d at gatherings of the North British Society. Additional fees were charged for regalia and the various special events mounted by each society.[15]

Every year a few members resigned or had to be struck off the records. But these losses were more than compensated for by success in finding new recruits. For example, through the nine years after its founding in 1834, the Nova Scotian Philanthropic Society took in 398 members while losing, through death, resignation and departure from Halifax, only 71. Among the seven organizations under review individual membership, at any one time, ranged from a low of approximately 100 to a high of about 300. By mid-century they collectively held the allegiance of approximately 1300 individuals. In other words, mainstream fraternalism, as represented by these seven societies, accounted for perhaps six per cent of Halifax's overall population.[16] Scholars now suggest that those with taxable amounts of property made up no more than one fifth of the total population. Accordingly it would appear that the fraternal portion of voluntary society activity in Halifax had come to embrace half or more of those situated between the gentry and the poor.[17]

Just because entities such as the Charitable Irish Society drew most of their rank and file from the middle ranks of urban society did not mean that their leaders also came from that strata. Studies of voluntary societies in other cities suggest that organizational leaders tended to be superior to the rank and file with respect to income and status. To some extent that was also true in Halifax, facilitated by the fact that nominations to high office tended to be controlled by committees of insiders. Moreover, some societies preferred to have the same incumbents in office year after year, especially when those officers were recruited from among Halifax's gentry. On the other hand, significant numbers of men with occupations traditionally defined as non-genteel (brewer, for example) and without kinship ties to established "old families" rose to positions of leadership in Halifax's fraternal organizations.[18]

Complete identification of those who joined up is impossible given gaps in available data, but it appears that membership began when men were in their early thirties, a time when most would be consolidating their position in terms of both career and family life. Voluntary societies proved especially attractive to those who had been born outside Halifax and who thus most likely lacked strong kinship networks within their adopted home. Protestant Dissenters and Roman Catholics as well as those of Scottish and Irish background, all of whom were deemed to be somewhat disreputable according to oligarchic convention in

Halifax, flocked into fraternal organizations. In other words, entities such as the Freemasons flourished essentially because of their ability to draw in young, assertive, and upwardly mobile elements of the community. Recruits were attracted by what these voluntary societies had to offer concerning conviviality, mutual support, and an opportunity to develop the skills and reputation needed for advancement into the leadership ranks of Halifax society.[19]

Most of those drawn into Halifax's fraternal world led lives of quiet obscurity. But a few of their "brothers" did much better, often in ways which suggested that their success derived substantially from voluntary society activity. Consider, for example, the case of James R. DeWolf. The son of a Methodist outport merchant, DeWolf trained in Scotland for a career in medicine and then moved to Halifax in 1844, at age 26. Setting up in what had become a highly competitive profession, DeWolf sought security and connections, both through marriage and membership in various of Halifax's voluntary societies. In particular he threw himself into the Nova Scotia Philanthropic Society with such energy that he became its president in 1848, a post which allowed him, despite being a relative newcomer, to preside a year later over Halifax's centennial celebrations. Other honours followed, climaxing in 1857 with DeWolf's appointment as Superintendent of Nova Scotia's Hospital for the Insane.[20]

Another who rose to prominence largely through voluntary society activity was Lawrence O'Connor Doyle. Although born in Halifax and the son of a leading local merchant, Doyle suffered the twin disadvantage of being Irish and Roman Catholic. Opting for a career in law and politics, Doyle inserted himself into virtually every organization set up to promote the interests of Halifax's expanding Irish Roman Catholic community. In 1843 the city's Charitable Irish Society, long under the control of Protestant notables such as the Uniacke family, elected Doyle as its president at age 39. Thereafter the Charitable Irish featured the struggle to end Protestant ascendancy in Halifax's public affairs, a struggle which in 1848 carried Doyle into the first provincial executive to function under the rules of "responsible government."[21]

Accompanying Doyle into office on that occasion was William Young, who had come from Scotland to Halifax as a youth during the war of 1812. After failure of the family business amidst Nova Scotia's postwar economic slump Young, a Presbyterian, turned to law and then entered politics. He, too, saw fraternal activity as a means of buttressing his career. In his case it involved membership in Halifax's prestigious North British Society, an organization which by the 1840s was also in the process of being taken over by relative newcomers. In 1848, at age 49, Young ascended to its presidency, and such was his gratitude for what this organization had done to foster his career that, years later, he left it a bequest of $100,000.[22]

Another who fostered the notion that success lay through participation in voluntary societies was William Caldwell. The son of an Irish Methodist immigrant who settled in Nova Scotia's rural interior, Caldwell moved to Halifax toward the end of the 1820s. Setting up as a master blacksmith Caldwell quickly joined the Union Engine Company. A decade later, at age 46, he became Captain of the Company. The prestige of that office, as well as the network of connections it brought, proved crucial in allowing Caldwell to be elected mayor of Halifax in 1850.[23] Much the same path was followed by Andrew Mackinlay, who came to Halifax from Scotland in the mid 1820s. Going into business as a bookseller, Mackinlay, a Presbyterian, prided himself on being an exponent of intellectual enlightenment. As such he developed an enthusiasm for the Mechanics' Institute and rose to serve as its president from 1838 to 1849. Success in discharging that office, combined with a strong enthusiasm for public service, propelled Mackinlay into politics and led to his election as mayor of Halifax in 1845 when in his mid 40s.[24]

A final example of how leadership could be forged within the fraternal world is provided by the career of Alexander Keith. Born in Scotland, and a Presbyterian by faith, Keith came to Halifax in 1817 at age 22 where he went into business as a brewer. Having joined the Freemasons prior to emigration, Keith transferred his membership to a local lodge immediately on arrival in Halifax. That affiliation proved extremely valuable as Keith struggled to develop his brewery into what eventually became one of the most successful manufactures on Halifax's waterfront. His dedication to the Freemasons, an organization then suffering considerable disarray, brought promotion, climaxing in 1840 when Keith was selected Grand Master of the Nova Scotian order. The new leader moved aggressively over the next decade to expand membership and end quarrelling among the various Masonic lodges. Successful both as a capitalist and as a lodgeman, Keith found himself co-opted into politics. After winning election as mayor of Halifax in 1843, he secured appointment to Nova Scotia's prestigious Legislative Council.[25]

The extent to which Keith or any of the others owed their advancement to voluntary society activity cannot be established with precision. It is clear, however, that fraternal leaders were in the public eye. By the 1840s local news in the Halifax press was dominated by society activities. Typical of the era was what the triweekly *Morning Post* had to say in April 1845 about a banquet put on by an elite group of Freemasons. Readers learned that some sixty gentlemen had dined starting at 7 p.m. Those at the head table appeared in regalia, and the walls of the hotel room were adorned with a host of banners and insignia. A military band played lively airs and mid-way through the proceedings a touring company of singers performed for the crowd. At 9 p.m. toasts began to be delivered, interspersed with songs and speeches. Twenty times in succession members raised their glasses in honour of everything from the spirit of Freemasonry to the fair daughters of Nova Scotia. At one in the morning the entire company proceeded out into the street "two-and-two, arm in arm, after the band, which struck up the Freemason's march." They then accompanied Grand Master Alexander Keith to his residence. Amidst deafening cheers, participants saluted their leader, first with "auld land syne," followed by the national anthem. As the bandsmen proceeded back to barracks, playing as they went, Halifax Freemasons staggered on home, as the reporter put it, "to forget even convivial scenes in the balmy luxury of sleep."[26]

Similar festivities were put on at least once a year by most Halifax voluntary societies. Invariably held at a hotel, so as to have access to first-class catering service, attendance (male only) usually ran in the 50 to 150 range. Members came, along with invited guests, who usually included the presidents of other fraternal organizations, officers from the garrison, and leading public officials, such as the mayor. Special delight was taken when organizers managed to secure the presence of and a speech by Nova Scotia's lieutenant-governor. Typically, "mirth, fellowship, and conviviality prevailed." It was an occasion, a reported noted, when "sectional distinctions and local prejudices are forgotten, and countrymen meet as friends." The *Morning Herald* , commenting on the combination of speeches, songs, and twenty-six toasts featured in 1843, when the Charitable Irish Society met on St. Patrick's Day, observed that "a more jovial party never sat around the festive board." Protracted large-scale consumption of alcohol took its toll, however, prompting a participant in a similar affair to observe that "a few...yesterday morning were complaining of headaches and nausea."[27]

The street processions which often accompanied these festive occasions heightened public awareness of voluntary society activity. For example, in June 1843 Halifax's six Masonic lodges celebrated the feast day of their patron saint beginning at 10 a.m. with a rally at city centre. The members paraded through the streets to St. Paul's Anglican cathedral church for a special service. Next came a parade to Alexander Keith's home for a salute to their leader. Attracted by colourful banners and regalia, as well as music provided by a regimental band, "thousands" of Haligonians thronged the downtown to get a glimpse of the spectacle.[28] A similar pattern of events took place at the annual meeting of the St. George's Society in 1849. Accompanied by a military band, wearing insignia, and waving banners, the members marched through town at mid-day to pay respects to their patron, the lieutenant-governor. Observed by "vast crowds," made up of both men and women, the members then proceeded back to the centre of the city to give three cheers for the Queen.[29] Much the same happened when Halifax's Charitable Irish Society celebrated St. Patrick's day in 1850. The affair began with morning high mass presided over by the archbishop. Marching out of church in the wake of a military band, members saluted the residences of three of their leading figures and then called on the lieutenant-governor. Having affirmed their allegiance by singing "God Save the Queen," the host strolled back through town, cheering in front of the Roman Catholic cathedral before dispersing in preparation for the evening's festivities.[30]

A final example of how public display could be used both to enhance a society's morale and also make a statement to the public at large was provided by

Halifax's African Abolition Society. One of three friendly societies established during the 1840s to serve the small and acutely marginalized Black population resident in the Nova Scotian capital, this organization rallied in August 1850 to commemorate the abolition of slavery throughout the British empire. After a meeting which featured such toasts as one to "Africa, the land of our Forefathers, may she...at last vanquish her foes," the members marched through town escorted by "half the population of the city." Preceded by a military band they made their way to Government House, there to cheer the lieutenant-governor, a gesture deliberately designed to make the point that Blacks should be recognised as full subjects of the crown.[31]

Even more effective in giving voluntary societies a high public profile were the summer excursions which, through the 1840s, became a highlight of Halifax's social season. The custom apparently began in June 1839 when the Philanthropic Society organized a picnic to commemorate Halifax's founding, ninety years earlier. Having rented one of the cross-harbour ferries, members of the Society proceeded into Bedford Basin to land at Prince's Lodge, the site of what in the 1790s had been the estate of Queen Victoria's father, the Duke of Kent. There, an "abundance of substantial viands, and lots of good liquor to moisten them" had been laid on. After lunch participants played games, walked in the woods, enjoyed a bottle of wine or listened to music provided by a military band. At dusk they came back to town, proceeded to the Grand Parade, and ended by singing a song especially written for the occasion by Joseph Howe, publisher of Halifax's leading newspaper.[32]

The success of this venture proved infectious. Soon every Halifax voluntary society was holding some form of summer outing. Most popular were picnics, with the preferred site being Prince's Lodge, thanks to its bucolic charm and aristocratic connections. Over time the ceremony became ever more elaborate. For example, in 1847 when the St. George's Society held its first picnic, the affair began with a morning march through the downtown streets. Once on board their steamer, members and guests progressed around the harbour, saluting various warships with cheers and patriotic songs such as "Rule Britannia." They then moved on to the shores of Halifax's North-West Arm for an afternoon of games and dancing. Dinner was served under a massive tent pavilion while an orchestra played in the background. At dusk the whole company strolled back to town, their way lit by torches. Preceded by a military band they made their way to Masons Hall for refreshments and then danced until midnight. All this came immediately in the wake of equally extravagant outings by the Charitable Irish and North British societies. Well over one thousand people had participated in these events, many of them consisting, as one contemporary put it, of "intelligent, well dressed persons of the middling class of life."[33]

All the foregoing activity took place in the near-total absence of factional strive. The only occasion on which violence threatened to mar proceedings occurred in August, 1848. Roused to bitter suspicion by news of the failure of the rebellion in famine-ridden Ireland, a group of Irish "Repealers" attempted to disrupt a street parade by Halifax's North British Society to seize what they mistakenly believed to be an Orange banner. Significantly, the incident received hardly a mention in the local press, presumably because local editors feared provoking violence.[34] With this exception, private and public ceremonies put on by Halifax's voluntary societies demonstrated their growing ability to forge a sense of unity that went beyond the boundaries of a single organization. Instead of accentuating ethnic, sectarian and political fragmentation, fraternalism actually bridged those gaps, especially within the middle rank sections of Halifax society.

At the same time, however, an undercurrent of dissatisfaction developed among certain Haligonians over the extent to which the ceremonials of fraternal life were in conflict with what they wanted as the standards of public morality. More than anything else this concern focused on prominent and heavy use of liquor to promote the bonds of brotherhood. Debate over consumption of alcohol persisted through the 1830s at a low level, but burst forth a decade later into a powerful campaign seeking not just moderation, but total abstinence and even prohibition. One consequence was a dramatic upheaval in the character of voluntary society activity in Nova Scotia's capital.[35]

Seeking both to heighten their public profile and build internal morale, temperance leaders emulated the behaviour of other voluntary organizations. For example, in June 1842 the new St. Mary's Temperance Society, led by Lawrence O'C. Doyle, marched 1200 strong through downtown Halifax to pay their respects to the lieutenant-governor. After being received "graciously" members resumed their procession, which features "medals, sashes, rosets, and other badges, and several splendid flags," two military bands and a troop of horsemen, A core group of 400 then went by steamer to McNab's Island, at the mouth of the Halifax harbour, for a picnic complete with sports and dancing. Returning to Halifax they marched in style to St. Mary's Cathedral for a salute to the Roman Catholic clergy. It all came off, one newspaper commented, with "order, comfort, and respectability."[36]

Organizations set up on such a vast scale quickly failed. They were too large to offer intimacy and also suffered from collapses in revenue when hard times prevented the poor they sought as recruits from mustering fees. Far more durable were the Sons of Temperance, which arrived from the United States in 1847 to set up a proliferation of small, highly motivated "divisions". Their weekly (later monthly) meetings gave members a chance to dress up in formal regalia, drink tea, listen to lively music, and be addressed by impassioned speakers, several of whom were professional orators brought in from the American lecture circuit. In July of that year the Sons hosted a mass picnic, where participants engaged in "dancing, and singing, playing at ball, pitching quoits, and other enjoyments," all without a drop of rum, beer or wine.[37]

Exactly who joined the Sons of Temperance is difficult to establish since membership lists have not survived. But those who served as officers are known and they tended to have a lot in common with those entering non-temperance fraternal organizations. For example, the young lawyer Alexander James, who caused such a ruckus over the fireman's excursion to Lunenburg, combined membership in the Mechanics' Institute with executive office in the "Mechanics' Division" of the Sons of Temperance.

Alongside the Sons were two parallel organizations set up to cater to the special interests of two special constituencies which by the 1840s had begun to assert themselves. The first involved male youth, meaning those old enough to have joined the work force but who had not yet stepped into marriage. In 1847 activists founded the Young Man's Total Abstinence Society and within a year it boasted a membership of some two hundred. The organizations's appeal derived largely from its entertainment programme. Meetings occurred monthly and through the winter featured speeches, debates and choral music. Members of the general public could attend most proceedings, on payment of a small entrance fee. Young ladies received a particular welcome and for them special events were arranged, including picnics in summer and dances in winter. Such mixed gatherings, at least one of which lasted until 3 a.m., generated complaints. But the society also won widespread approval. As a supporter observed, "we like to see the young fellows enjoy themselves, and we think those special parties, where the inebriating cup is discarded do good."[38]

Women did more than simply add life to male-organized events. As early as 1844 they had established a Female Temperance and Benevolent Society which quickly grew to over one hundred members. Lieutenant-Governor Harvey agreed to serve as their patron and in 1849, when the women convened a public meeting at Masons Hall, they had enough influence to secure the presence of a military band. Moreover the mayor attended, along with a gender-mixed audience described as "representing the wealth, intelligence and beauty of the city."[39]

Members of the Young Men's and the Ladies Benevolent societies maintained a close working relationship. For example, in 1848 the women organized a fund-raising soiree to help the men in their effort to establish new meeting facilities. In return the men "rapturously passed" a vote of thanks to their sisters in the cause. Co-operation extended to include the new Sons of Temperance. Speakers were mutually shared, picnics were opened to one another, and on one celebrated occasion a committee of women appeared before a mass rally of "Sons" to present them with a new banner. In a gesture daring by the standards of the day. Mrs. Crane, president of the Ladies Society, addressed the crowd, in as the reporter conspicuously noted, "an audible voice." In reply her committee received and oration which stressed the extent to which women had become essential for the achievement of public virtue.[40]

Temperance agitation and self-assertion by both young men and women gradually began to transform the mainstream of fraternal life in Halifax. In 1841, for example, the Charitable Irish Society inaugurated the tradition of allowing toasts at its annual banquet to be drunk using water. Five years later the

Charitable Irish barred alcohol from its summer picnic, a move anticipated in 1842 by the Philanthropic Society. Similarly, organizers of the June 1847 outing put on by Dartmouth's Mechanics Institute stressed that in order to promote "healthful and rational amusements," they would impose "the most stringent regulations...to prevent the sale of intoxicating liquors."[41]

As for young men, at the beginning of the 1840s both the Charitable Irish and the Philanthropic Societies established youth auxiliaries. Immediately those auxiliaries began agitating for inclusion of women as guests at their public outings. After some chauvinistic grumbling about how the presence of women could compromise the spirit of true brotherhood, the elders gave in. By the end of the decade it had become an accepted custom to invite females to society outings in order to impart to the occasion "a higher tone."[42] Nevertheless, membership was not an option offered to women. They were accepted only as guests and even then as the firemen's controversial outing of 1848 demonstrated, their presence did not necessarily mean abandonment of "rough" forms of male celebration.

Despite lack of consensus as to how to define "respectability," especially as it pertained to alcohol, Halifax's voluntary societies became ever more confident of their ability to shape not just their own affairs and also the affairs of the larger community. This self-confidence led to increasing experimentation with events open to the general public. For example, in August 1846 the Mechanics Institute hosted a festival on McNab's Island where people could come to see such wonders of the age as steam engines and hot air balloons. The mayor declared a holiday from business to assure a mass turnout. It was a bold move, since early-Victorian crowds had a tendency to turn rowdy, but on this occasion decorum prevailed. Emboldened by other successes fraternal leaders began to plan for the celebration of Halifax's centennial, seeing it as an ideal opportunity to present themselves as central to what it meant to be a Haligonian.[43]

Preparation for this, the largest public ceremony in the pre-Confederation history of Halifax, began in April 1849 when the Philanthropic Society sent a circular to its peer organizations asking for co-operation in staging the centennial. Next, some thirty society leaders met and decided to hand matters over to a small executive committee headed by J.R. DeWolf, president of the Philanthropic Society. Almost immediately controversy erupted, fed in large measure by the stress of hard times and political uncertainty associated with the transition to Responsible Government. One disgruntled Tory newspaper asked, "with one half the population starving and the other half running away, with bankruptcy, famine, and disease rife among us, is it time to rejoice?" Nevertheless, planning went ahead, helped by the fact that DeWolf, the chief organizer, was a high profile Conservative and thus could appeal for support from those who otherwise might have seen the centennial as a partisan event put on by the new Liberal government.[44]

Festivities were scheduled for June 8th, to commemorate the entrance into Chebucto harbour of the city's founder, Lt.Col. Edward Cornwallis.[45] It would be a public holiday, with all offices and businesses closed so that citizens could become involved, either as spectators or participants. The morning dawned with sunshine. Citizens woke up to a 100-gun salute fired by Halifax's Volunteer Artillery company. Then came a "merry peel" of bells from various churches as well as the tower of the town clock. From nine a.m. until noon soldiers of the garrison conducted military manoeuvres, climaxing in a mock attack on Citadel Hill. Meanwhile, something like five thousand celebrants, all male, were forming up at the Grand Parade. At mid-day they moved out into the streets. In the words of the *Acadian Recorder*:

> the procession was upwards of a mile long, and it took nearly half an hour, from the time the van went by until the rear came up... It was the most imposing spectacle of the kind that was ever seen in Halifax. The City Council and Magistrates, mounted, preceded; then followed a Printing Press, and the Fire Engines, elaborately ornamented, drawn by splendid horses, and two carriages, one carrying Micmac chiefs and a moose calf, the other, a number of the oldest men in the country.... After these came the Volunteer Artillery, N. S. Philanthropic Society, Temperance, African, St. George's, Charitable Irish, North British, and Highland Societies, Free Mason, and Truckmen mounted.[46]

Downtown Halifax was packed with both residents and visitors from the interior. Despite the numbers, decorum prevailed. According to the *British Colonist*, "the most extreme courtesy marked the crowd...and the most refined lady might have passed to and fro without her ear being in the slightest degree offended." Women of respectable status did appear but mostly in upper story windows, from where they could cheer on the marchers with "bright eyes and healthful cheeks, and welcome smiles."[47]

As the parade moved out onto the Commons it encountered "such a vast concourse of people as was never before witnessed in Halifax." Women turned out either on horseback, in carriages or within the security of a square formed by the marchers. At 2 p.m. the Volunteer Artillery company hailed the arrival of the lieutenant-governor by firing a 21-gun salute. After Sir John Harvey had reviewed the procession a series of speeches were given, the main one by Beamish Murdoch, long-time president of the Halifax Temperance Society. He was followed by Provincial Secretary (and former president of the Charitable Irish Society) Joseph Howe who read a poem composed specifically for the occasion. Both speakers stressed the theme of how "mother" Halifax deserved the affection of her residents. In Murdoch's words, "other lands may boast greater wealth, other cities a more numerous population; but where can you find a city or a province whose sons and daughters love her and cling to her, as fondly, as proudly, as exclusively, as we do to Halifax, to Nova Scotia." It was Murdoch's way of telling the assembled throng that they owed a fundamental allegiance to one another as residents of a new community, one that could thrive through mobilization of a common sense of unit.[48]

That evening revolving gas lights on public buildings gave Halifax's downtown core a "mid-day splendor." Illuminated signs spelled out such patriotic words as "1749" and "VR." A shower of fireworks erupted from Citadel Hill, to be matched by half an hour of salvoes fired from a warship anchored in the harbour. Several private parties had been organized, including one by the firemen, who turned their Engine House into a ballroom and there "passed the evening right merrily." Most lively of all was the dinner/dance put on at Masons Hall by a combination of the North British and Highland Societies. Attracting a numerous array of men and women drawn from "the middle classes and *élite* of the city and garrison," this affair went roaring on until 3:30 in the morning. Despite such *joie de vivre*, the city avoided disorder. Next morning one local editor summed up the event by saying that "the occasion passed off as peacefully, soberly, and happily as a 'small tea party'."[49]

Civic pride prompted talk of the need for an enduring symbol of Halifax's having come of age. Discussion quickly came to focus on the building of a public hospital. As a last gesture before disbanding, the centenary committee endorsed the project. Moreover Dr. DeWolf and several other fraternal leaders who had been active in the centennial formed themselves into a lobby designed to convince government that it should fund the enterprise. The press immediately rallied in support of the idea. In the words of one editor, "something was needed to denote to posterity that so much philanthropy existed in the breasts of the generation of 1849."[50] A decade would pass before enthusiasm had been converted into institutional achievement but the hospital issue illustrated a major shift in contemporary thinking and behaviour. By mid-century Halifax voluntary societies had begun to assume responsibility for setting the agenda for employment of the power of the state.[51]

Of course it would be an exaggeration to suggest that Halifax had experienced an entire change of personality. Visitors to mid-Victorian Halifax repeatedly commented on what they saw as the dirt, disorder, and relative stagnation of Nova Scotia's capital. For example, in 1850 a Boston editor complained that Halifax displayed "a sad want of the freshness, liveliness and cheerfulness which marks a New England town."[52] However, such acerbic observations overlooked fundamental elements of change that had taken place through the second quarter of the nineteenth century. One of the most significant of these changes involved emergence of a Halifax middle class.

At the beginning of this era Halifax society possessed a "middling element" but it was one which lacked organizational capacity and could muster only the rudiments of collective consciousness. By the mid 1830s people in this category had begun to come together, in terms of both structure and mentality, but their actions and statements tended to be more negative than positive. Basically they had a better idea of what they were against than what they were for. Driven by a sense of victimization and vulnerability, those of modest means turned to political protest in the hope that liberal/democratic reform might improve their lot. But often that proved divisive, opening up ethnic, sectarian, and party divisions among those manoeuvring across the middle of Halifax's social hierarchy. At the same time however, these people acquired an enthusiasm for voluntary societies, seeing them as both a shelter from adversity and an opportunity for advancement. Over time fraternalism evolved from the pursuit of individual self-help to a campaign for collective self-assertion. Societies and their members made a strategic transition from the private to the public sector. New notions of both respectability and citizenship began to be articulated, notions infused with bourgeois assumptions about the importance of work, thrift, sobriety and stewardship. In other words by 1850 middle class formation, as regards both structure and idealogy, was well under way in Halifax.

Tables *(Pages 488–91)*

The following abbreviations apply throughout: CIS = Charitable Irish Society; GEO = St. George's Society; MAS = Freemasons; MI = Mechanics Institute; NBS = North British Society; PHIL = Nova Scotia Philanthropic Society; UE/A = United Engine Company and Axe Fire Company

Occupational categories have been constructed as follows: (included here are those job descriptions which appear frequently)

Artisans (ART): baker, blacksmith, block maker, butcher, carpenter; cabinet maker, carriage maker, cooper, hatter, mason, moulder, painter, plumber, printer, ropemaker, saddler, sailmaker, shipwright, shoemaker, tailor, tanner, tinsmith, watchmaker, wheelwright

Retailers (RET): bookseller, confectioner, dealers, druggist, grocer, shopkeeper, tobacconist

Merchants / Professionals (M/P): architect, auctioneer, brewer, cleric, distiller, doctor, engineer, founder, lawyer, notary public, publisher, wholesaler

Other / high (O/H): bank officer, broker, gentleman, government officer (imperial or provincial), military officer

Other / low (O/L): boarding house keeper, clerk, farmer, foreman, innkeeper, librarian, policemen, sea captain, soldier, surveyor, teacher, truckman

Unknown (U.)

Table One: Occupational distribution by voluntary society for all members (percentages exclude the unknowns)

	CIS		GEO		MAS		MI	
	No.	*%*	*No.*	*%*	*No.*	*%*	*No.*	*%*
ART.	78	30	25	20	35	27	22	25
RET.	73	28	17	14	18	14	15	17
M/P.	49	19	58	46	38	29	38	44
O/H.	41	16	19	15	17	13	10	13
O/L.	17	7	6	5	23	17	2	1
U.	192		27		115		17	
Total	450		152		246		104	

	NBS		PHIL		UE/A	
	No.	*%*	*No.*	*%*	*No.*	*%*
ART.	70	37	129	42	137	77
RET.	38	20	34	11	25	14
M/P.	58	31	85	28	5	3
O/H.	17	9	15	5	2	1
O/L.	6	3	42	14	8	5
U.	96		104		60	
Total	285		409		237	

Overall distribution of the general membership by occupational grouping:

	No.	*%*
ART.	496	39
RET.	220	17
M/P.	331	26
O/H.	121	10
O/L.	104	8
U.	611	
Total	1883	

Table Two: Occupational distribution by voluntary society for those serving as officers.

No.	CIS		GEO		MAS		MI	
	No.	*%*	*No.*	*%*	*No.*	*%*	*No.*	*%*
ART.	1	7	0	0	7	24	0	0
RET.	4	27	2	15	4	14	2	25
M/P.	9	60	8	62	10	35	4	50
O/H.	1	7	3	23	6	21	2	25
O/L.	0		0		2	7	0	
U.	1		0		11		2	
Total	16		13		40		10	

	NBS		PHIL		UE/A	
	No.	*%*	*No.*	*%*	*No.*	*%*
ART.	1	6	8	50	20	83
RET.	8	47	1	6	2	8
M/P.	7	41	6	38	0	0
O/H.	1	6	1	6	1	4
O/L.	0	0	0		1	4
U.	1		0		4	
Total	18		16		28	

Overall distribution of officers by occupational grouping:

	No.	%
ART.	37	30
RET.	23	19
M/P.	44	36
O/H.	15	12
O/L.	3	3
U.	19	
Total	141	

Table Three: Distribution of voluntary society officers according to whether they possessed kinship and/or business connections with the inner circle of oligarchy.

	Insiders		Outsiders	
	No.	*%*	*No.*	*%*
CIS	5	31	11	69
GEO	12	83	2	17
MAS	11	30	26	70
MI	3	33	6	67
NBS	8	44	10	56
PHIL	6	38	10	62
UE/A	2	8	24	92

Appendix: Voluntary societies found in Halifax, Nova Scotia during the 1840s as listed by Belcher's Farmer's Almanack and/or The Nova Scotian Almanack. Coding: > > = lasted beyond 1850

Name	*Founded*	*Terminated*
African Abolition Society	1843?	> >
African Friendly Society	1830s	> >
African Union Society	1849	> >
Athenaeum Society	1850	> >
Auxiliary Colonial Society	1830s?	1843
Auxiliary Naval & Military Bible Society	1845	> >
Axe Fire Company	1760s	> >
Baptist Board, Foreign & Dom. Missions	1830s	> >
Baptist Education Society	1820s	> >
Barristers Society	1820s	> >
Benefit Building Society	1850	> >
Bible Society	1820s	> >
Carpenters Society	1790	> >
Catholic Literary Institute	1848	> >
Chamber of Commerce	1822	1842
Charitable Irish Society	1786	> >
Christian Doctrine Society	1840	1844
Colonial Church Society	1830s	> >
Diocesan Church Society	1830s	> >

Female Temperance Society	1848	1850
Freemasons	1750s, etc.	> >
Halifax Agricultural Society	1820s	> >
Halifax Bethel Union	1846	1846
Halifax Literary & Scientific Ass'n	1840?	1845
Halifax Mariner's Society	1830s?	1841
Halifax Temperance Society	1831	> >
Hand-in-Hand Fire Company	1790s	> >
Harmonic Society	1842	1846
Heart and Hand Fire Company	1820s?	1841?
Highland Society	1838	> >
Horticultural Society	1830s?	> >
Irish Education Society	1845	1845
Ladies Temperance & Benevolent Society	1844	> >
Lay Ass'n...Church of Scot'ld	1845	> >
Mechanics Institute	1831	> >
Micmac Missionary Society	1849	> >
North British Society	1768	> >
Nova Scotia Philanthropic Society	1834	> >
Sabbath Alliance	1850	> >
Sabbath School Union	1841	1846
Seaman's Friend Society	1847	1849
Society...Encouragement of Trade	1841	1842
Sons of Temperance	1847	> >
St. George's Society	1838	> >
St. John's Young Men's Association	1845	> >
St. Mary's Total Abstinence Society	1841	> >
St. Mary's/St. Patrick's Temperance Society	1844	> >
Star Fire Company	1810s?	> >
Sun Fire Company	1790s	> >
Union Engine Company	1768	> >
Volunteer Artillery Company	1830s?	> >
Wesleyan Auxiliary Missionary Society	1820s	> >
Wesleyan Female Benevolent Society	1828	> >
Young Charitable Irish Society	1845	> >
Young Men's Debating Club	1847	> >
Young Men's Enterprising Association	1850	> >
Young Men's Temperance Association	1847	> >
Young Men's Presbyterian Association	1842	1845
Youth Philanthropic Society	1841	> >

Note: the foregoing does not include voluntary societies established to serve the cross-harbour village of Dartmouth.

Notes

1. A detailed report of the trial is found in Halifax *Novascotian*, 13 August 1849. See also Halifax Sun, 11 August 1848.

2. Halifax *Acadian Recorder*, 12 January 1850. Contemporary attitudes are explored in D.A. Sutherland, "Joseph Howe and the boosting of Halifax," in Wayne A. Hunt (ed.), *The Proceedings of the Joseph Howe Symposium* (Sackville, New Brunswick, 1984): 71–86. An overview of Halifax and the Maritime region during the second quarter of the nineteenth century is provided by P.A. Buckner and J.G. Reid (eds.), *The Atlantic Region to Confederation: a History* (Toronto and Fredericton, 1994), chs. 12–14. Also invaluable for establishing context is T.W. Acheson, *Saint John: the Making of a Colonial Urban Community* (Toronto, 1985).

3. The reform impulse in early nineteenth Halifax and the extent to which it involved use of the press is discussed by J.M. Beck, *Joseph Howe: Conservative Reformer, 1804–1848* (Montreal and Kingston, 1982). For shopkeeper agitation on behalf of municipal reform in Halifax, see D.A. Sutherland, "Thomas Forrester," *Dictionary of Canadian Biography* (hereafter *DCB*), VII: 307–309.

4. Developments in the United States and Britain are examined by Mary Ann Clawson, *Constructing Brotherhood: Class, Gender, and Fraternalism* (Princeton, 1989) and R.J. Morris, "Voluntary societies and British urban elites, 1780–1850: an analysis", *The Historical Journal* 26: 1 (1983): 95–118. See also Mark C. Carnes, *Secret ritual and manhood in Victorian America* (New Haven, 1989).

5. The linkage between urbanization and class formation is explored by Stuart M. Blumin, *The Emergence of the Middle Class: Social Experience in the American City, 1760–1900* (Cambridge, MA., 1989); Stuart M. Blumin, *The Urban Threshold: Growth and Change in a Nineteenth Century American Community* (Chicago, 1976); Mary Ryan, *Cradle of the Middle Class: the Family in Oneida County, New York, 1790–1865* (Cambridge, 1981); Paul E. Johnston, *A Shopkeepers Millennium: Society and Revivals in Rochester, New York, 1815–1837* (New York, 1978); R.J. Morris, *Class, sect and party: the making of the British Middle Class, Leeds, 1820–1850* (Manchester and New York, 1990), as well as Leonore Davidoff and Catherine Hall, *Family Fortunes: men and women of the English middle class, 1780–1850* (Chicago, 1987).

6. The following sources have provided the backbone of the information on society membership in Halifax: Charitable Irish Society (Halifax), minute books, 1834–1850, Public Archives of Nova Scotia (hereafter PANS), MG20, vol. 67; St. George's Society (Halifax), membership and dues book, 1838–1867, PANS, MG20, vol. 338; North British Society (Halifax), minute books, 1768–1886, PANS, MG20–, vol. 231–232; Mechanics Institute (Halifax), minute books, 1831–1845, PANS, MG20, vol. 222(a); *Rules and Constitution of the Charitable Irish Society* (Halifax, 1840 & 1854); *Rules of the St. George's Society* (Halifax, 1852); *Bye-laws of Saint Andrew's Lodge no. 137 of Free and Accepted Masons* (Halifax, 1862); *Rules and Bye-laws of the Royal Union Chapter no. 137* (Halifax, 1863); *Rules and Bye laws of Royal Sussex Lodge no. 704* (Halifax, 1851); *Byelaws of St. John Lodge no. 161* (Halifax, 1863); *Rules of the Halifax Mechanics Institute* (Halifax, 1832); *The Constitution, Fundamental Rules and Bye laws of the Nova Scotia Philanthropic Society* (Halifax, 1843).

7. See Table One.

8. *Nova Scotia Bible Society, Annual Report* (Halifax, 1847). See also *British Colonist*, 14 April 1849, 2 February 1850.

9. R.P. Harvey, "Black Beans, Banners and Banquets: the Charitable Irish Society at two hundred," *Nova Scotia Historical Review* 6 (1986); 16–35; T.M. Punch, *Irish Halifax: the Immigrant Generation* (Halifax, 1981); J.S. Macdonald, *Annals of the North British Society* (Halifax, 1868 and 1905); R.S. Longley and R.V. Harris, *A Short History of Freemasonry in Nova Scotia, 1738–1966* (Halifax, 1966); E.T. Bliss, *Masonic Grand Masters of the Jurisdiction of Nova Scotia, 1738–1965* (Halifax, 1965); C.B. Fergusson, *Mechanics Institutes in Nova Scotia* (Halifax, 1960); D.C. Harvey, "Nova Scotia Philanthropic Society," *Dalhousie Review* 19: 3 (October 1939); 287–295; B.E.S. Rudachyk, "The Most Tyrannous of Masters: Fire in Halifax, Nova Scotia, 1830–1850" (M.A. thesis, Dalhousie University, 1984).

10. In 1840 the Charitable Irish Society met as follows: 17 February (quarterly meeting, 125 present: 17 March (annual dinner, 106 members and guests present); 20 April (banquet to celebrate the Queen's marriage, 137 members and guests present); 18 May (quarterly meeting, 75 present); 17 August (quarterly meeting, 96 present); 2 October (special meeting to pass a motion of congratulations to the Queen for having escaped an assassination attempt, 90 present); 17 November (quarterly meeting, 114 present), Charitable Irish Society minutes, 1840, PANS MG20, vo. 67. In 1847 the following round of activity was reported in the Halifax press: January (sleighing party by the Union Engine Company); February (ball by the same); March (St. Patrick's Day banquet by the Charitable Irish Society); April (St. George's Day banquet by the St. George' Society); June (picnic by the Philanthropic Society); August (picnic by the Charitable Irish and North British societies); September (picnic by the St. George's Society); October (opening of the Mechanics Institute's autumn/winter lecture series); December (St. John's Day banquet by the Freemasons), as noted by the following Halifax newspapers: *Acadian Recorder, Morning Post, Sun,* and *Times.*

11. Rudachyk, "Fire in Halifax," 125.

12. The Philanthropic Society declared that is members were "unwilling to have, their indigent brethren subsisting solely on the bounty of benevolent strangers," *Constitution*, 1. During the 1840s Alexander Keith, head of the Freemasons, gave high priority to establishment of a benevolent fund; see Longley/Harris, *Short History*, 58. Attendance at funerals by Freemasons and later others is noted by Halifax *Morning Herald*, 8 September 1843; Halifax *Sun*, 26 October 1847; Halifax *British Colonist*, 26 October 1848; Halifax, *Times*, 15 December 1848.

13. Mechanics Institute, *Rules*; Mechanics Institute minutes, 7 April and 10 May 1840, PANS, MG20, vo. 222(a); Saint Andrew's *Bye-laws*, 10; Charitable Irish, *Rules*, 11; Macdonald, *Annals* (1905), 233.

14. After considerable debate over membership policy the Mechanics Institute opted to grant admission to anyone buying an annual admission ticket. The growing presence of women at lectures was described as a "cause for congratulations" since the "ladies" would "powerfully enforce...the importance and delights of intellectual pursuits." See Mechanics Institute minutes, 6 May 1840, 5 October 1841, 2 May 1842, PANS, MG20, vol. 222(A). Allegations that the firemen practised discrimination

are to be found in Halifax *Sun*, 24 April, 13 November 1846; *Sun*, 5/10 March 1847.

15. At mid-century common labourers in Nova Scotia earned a daily wage of 2 to 3 shillings; skilled workers made 4 shillings. See Lt. Gov. Harvey to Col. Sect. Grey, 8 May 1848, PANS, RG 1, vol. 120, f. 129. The seasonality of employment and high cost of living in the colony likely meant that none but master craftsmen (what contemporaries referred to as "mechanics") could participate in fraternal life. This theme is explored by Julian Gwyn, "A little province like this": the economy of Nova Scotia under stress, 1812–1853," in D.H. Akenson, ed., *Canadian Papers in Rural History*, vol. 6 (Gananoque, 1988): 192–225; see also Judith Fingard, "The winter's tale: the seasonal contours of pre-industrial poverty in British North American, 1815–1860," Canadian Historical Society, *Historical Papers* (1974): 65–94.

16. Philanthropic Society, *Constitution*. While data are incomplete, membership at mid-century probably stood approximately as follows: Union Engine Company and Axe Fire Company (124), Mechanics Institute (100), Freemasons (300), St. George's Society (140), North British Society (200), Charitable Irish Society (230), Philanthropic Society (250). In 1851 Halifax had a population just over 20,000.

17. See not only the research of Blumin and Morris cited above but also Edward Pessen (ed.), *The Many-Faceted Jacksonian era: new interpretations* (Westport, CT., 1977).

18. Morris, *Class, sect and party*, 161–203. The Halifax situation is detailed in Tables Two and Three.

19. Biographical information on voluntary society members has been gleaned from the following: *Cunnabell's City Almanack and General Business Directory* (Halifax, 1842); *Nugent's Business Directory of the City of Halifax* (Halifax, 1858); Nova Scotia census, 1838, PANS, RG1, vol. 448; Camp Hill Cemetery burial books, PANS, MG5, microfilm; Halifax County Registry of Deeds. In addition invaluable assistance in identifying obscure people has been provided by Halifax genealogist, Terrence M. Punch.

20. Colin D. Howell, "James R. DeWolf," *DCB*, XIII: 272–3.

21. C.B. Fergusson, "Lawrence O'C. Doyle," *DCB*, IX: 224–227.

22. J.M. Beck, "William Young," *DCB*, XI: 943–949.

23. When Caldwell first entered municipal politics, he was assailed by Liberal opponents for being "merely a blacksmith: see Halifax *Morning Post*. 1/4 October 1840. For the later phase of his career see Halifax *Sun*, 21 May 1847; Halifax *British Colonist*, 3 October 1850; Halifax *Novascotian*, 7 October 1850. Mention of Caldwell's family background appears in A.W.H. Eaton, *The History of Kings County* (Salem, MA, 1910), 594–595.

24. L.K. Kernaghan, "Andrew Mackinlay," *DCB*, IX: 510.

25. K.G. Pryke, "Alexander Keith," *DCB*, X: 395–396.

26. Halifax *Morning Post*, 26 April 1845. The paper's publisher/reporter was J.H. Crosskill, a Freemason who delighted in providing his readers with local colour. Thanks to his own drinking, brawling and womanizing, Crosskill personally generated a large share of news about town. See, for example, Halifax *Acadian Recorder*, 22 February 1840, 24 July 1841, 25 June 1842, 6 February 1847 and Halifax *Morning Herald*, 26 July 1841.

27. Halifax *Morning Herald*, 20 March 1843. See also ibid., 26 April 1843 and Halifax *Morning Post*, 3 December 1844.

28. Halifax *Morning Post*, 28 June 1843.

29. Halifax *Times & Courier*, 26 April 1849.

30. Halifax *Acadian Recorder*, 23 March 1850.

31. Interracial harmony on this occasion was marred by partisan political controversy over whether Joseph Howe, now the Provincial Secretary, had compromised the dignity of his office by being overly-familiar with Halifax Blacks. See Halifax *British Colonist*, 3/6 August 1850; Halifax *Novascotian*, 5/12 August 1850. Black demands for civil rights is explored by Judith Fingard, "Race and respectability in Victorian Halifax," *Journal of Imperial and Commonwealth History* 20: 2 (May, 1992): 169–195.

32. Halifax *Novascotian*, 12 June 1839.

33. Halifax *Times*, 14 September 1847; Halifax *Acadian Recorder*, 21 August, 4 September 1847; Halifax *Sun*, 3 September 1847.

34. Macdonald, *Annals* (1905), 264–265; Halifax *British Colonist*, 17/19 August 1848. Contemporaries would have been aware of the ethnic/sectarian violence then building in neighbouring New Brunswick. Analysis of that situation is provided by Scott W. See, *Riots in New Brunswick: Orange Nativism and Social Violence in the 1840s* (Toronto, 1993).

35. For the surge of temperance activity across America see Ian R. Tyrrell *Sobering Up: from Temperance to Prohibition in Antebellum America, 1800–1860* (Westport, CT, 1979); W.J. Rorabaugh, *The Alcoholic Republic: an American Tradition* (New York, 1979.) See also Sandra Barry, "Shades of vice and moral glory: the temperance movement in Nova Scotia, 1828–1848" (M.A. thesis, Acadia, 1986).

36. Halifax *Novascotian*, 23 June 1842; Halifax *Morning Post*, 23 June 1842.

37. Sons of Temperance activity is reported in the Halifax *Sun*, 7/11/28 February, 12 April, 28 July, 21 August, 6 October, 22/24 November 1848; Halifax *Presbyterian Witness*, 26 August 1848.

38. Items on the Young Men's Temperance Society appear in the Halifax *Morning Post*, 23 October, 31 December 1847; Halifax *Sun*, 15 September, 11 October 1847, 17 November 1848; Halifax *Presbyterian Witness*, 18 March 1848; Halifax *Novascotian*, 21 August 1848.

39. Halifax Female Temperance and Benevolent Society (Halifax, 1844); Halifax Morning Chronicle, 13 March, 20 August 1844; Halifax *Novascotian*, 19 March 1849.

40. Halifax Presbyterian Witness, 29 January, 8 July 1848; Halifax *Novascotian*, 10 July 1848.

41. Halifax *Acadian Recorder*, 20 March 1841; Halifax *Morning Post*, 9 June 1842; Charitable Irish Society minutes, 17 August 1846, PANS, MG20, vol. 67; Halifax *Acadian Recorder*, 12 June 1847.

42. Halifax *Morning Post*, 9/11 June 1842, 10 June, 3 August 1843, 18 August 1845, 9 June 1846; Halifax *Morning Herald*, 9 June 1843; Halifax Morning Chronicle, 4 June 1844; Halifax *Sun*, 11 June, 11 July 1845; Halifax *Acadian Recorder*, 21 August, 4 September, 1847.

43. Halifax *Sun*, 5/10 August 1846; Halifax *Morning Post*, 4 August 1846; Halifax *Times*, 11 August 1846; Halifax *Acadian Recorder*, 7 October 1848; Halifax *British Colonist*, 3 October 1848; Halifax New *Times*, 2 October 1848; Halifax, *Novascotian*, 2 October 1848.

44. Halifax *Times & Courier*, 9/17 April, 12/26 May 1849; Halifax *British Colonist*, 15 May, 2 June 1849. For context see Bonnie L. Huskings, "Public celebration in Victorian Saint John and Halifax" (Ph.d thesis, Dalhousie, 1991).

45. Cornwallis actually arrived on June 21st. But in 1839, when celebrations of the founding began, it was apparently thought that the event had occurred some two weeks earlier. See Halifax *Novascotian*, 6/12 June 1839; Halifax *Church Times*, 8 June 1849, Thomas H. Raddall, *Halifax, Warden of the North* (Toronto, 1971), 22.

46. Halifax *Acadian Recorder*, 9 June 1849.

47. Halifax *British Colonist*, 12 June 1849. On the present of women at urban festivities see Mary Ryan, *Women in Public: Between Banners and Ballots, 1825–1880* (Baltimore, 1980).

48. Halifax *Times & Courier*, 9 June 1849. Murdoch's career is explored by K.G. Pryke, "Beamish Murdoch", *DCB*, X: 539–540. Overlooked in that account is the fact that Murdoch died an alcoholic. See PANS, MG100, vol. 74, #29.

49. Halifax *Sun*, 13 June 1849; Halifax *Novascotian*, 18 June 1849.

50. Halifax *British Colonist*, 12/21 June 1849; Halifax *Novascotian*, 25 June 1849; *Presbyterian Witness*, 7 July 1849.

51. The transition from voluntaryism to advocacy of state intervention is discussed by R.J. Morris, "Voluntary Societies," 116–118.

52. Halifax, *Novascotian*, 29 July 1850. See also Isabella Lucy Bird. *The Englishwoman in America* (London, 1856), 21–23.

Initial research for this project was supported by a grant from the Social Sciences and Humanities Research Council of Canada. Special appreciation is owed to Sue Brown, Larry Stokes, and others of the Friday seminar group at Dalhousie, who commented on an earlier version of this paper.

CHAPTER

13 GROWING UP IN PRE-INDUSTRIAL CANADA

Glimpses of the family and children growing up rarely emerge from the pages of Canadian history. Stereotypes do exist such as the *habitant* flock on the seigneury or the street urchins in the industrial cities. Yet even if these glimpses are rare and atypical, the most characteristic of Canadian institutions was the family unit, either nuclear or extended, and the majority of Canadians for much of the past were children and teenagers. The preoccupation of Canadian historians with political developments largely explains their aloofness from numerous topics. With the broadening of content areas in the 1960s, the family and childhood were discovered. Sources, unfortunately, are always problematic and the concept of family itself has divergent meanings at various times and places. Insights have been borrowed from sociologists, psychologists, educationalists and demographers. Approaches to the subject have been diversified as well, ranging from the traditional impressionistic study to advanced statistical analyses.

In the summer of 1995 Statistics Canada released a study called *Family Over the Life Course* which concluded that the "typical" family no longer existed because of the dramatic changes in modern society. It was apparently assumed that the "typical" family had been universal. In her introduction to *Childhood and Family in Canadian History* in 1982 Joy Parr stressed the changing nature of concepts such as childhood and family, which are formed by historical rather than biological phenomena. She also saw them as social rather than natural associations, being moulded by economic and cultural forces. The readings included here confirm her observations, and make the observations of Statistics Canada less startling than readers might think. For Canada during the pre-industrial era the nature of the family and ideas about children were fluid. Whether it was on the farm, in the fur trade, in urban shops, or in the family mansion, children were essential participants.

In this unit three strands of the study of growing up in Canada are presented. The first by John F. Bosher on "The Family in New France" is a thoughtful reappraisal of an aspect of the Canadian past where history is presumed but obviously misunderstood. The second selection, by anthropologist Jennifer S.H. Brown on "Children of the Early Fur Trades," clearly demonstrates the fluid nature of "family" over the long and unstable history of the fur trade. She recreates those atypical families over time, especially for the children of the Northwesters who "experienced some shocks, cultural, psychic, and even physiological" when about age six they left one or both parents and moved to strange cultures. According to Brown that between-culture crisis was stressful indeed.

The third reading by Chad Gaffield is less specific than either Bosher or Brown in that his concern is with the impact of industrialization on the nature of the family. Gaffield resists the traditional view that industrialization shattered the extended family, seeing the changes as more complex. Industrialization, he writes, "affected the roles of men, women, children, and thereby transformed social organizations. The factors of age, gender, and social class have contributed to a diverse range of individual experiences during this transformation."

Suggestions For Further Reading

Bradbury, Bettina, ed., *Canadian Family History: Selected Readings*.Toronto: Copp Clark Pitman Ltd., 1992.

Brown, Jennifer S.H., *Strangers in Blood: Fur Trade Families in Indian Country*. Vancouver: University of British Columbia Press, 1980.

Condon, Ann Gorman, "The Family in Exile: Loyalist Social Values After the Revolution," in Margaret Conrad, ed., *Intimate Relations: Family and Community in Planter Nova Scotia, 1759–1800*. Fredericton: Acadiensis Press, 1995, 42–53.

Gaffield, Chad, "Children, Schooling, and Family Reproduction in Nineteenth-Century Ontario," *Canadian Historical Review*, LXXII, No. 2, (June 1991), 157–191.

Graff, Harvey J., "Remaking Growing Up: Nineteenth-Century America," *Histoire Sociale / Social History*, XXIV, 47, (May 1991).

Houston, Susan E., "The Role of Criminal Law in Defining 'Youth' in Mid-Nineteenth Century Upper Canada," *Historical Studies in Education*, 6, 3, (1994), 39–55.

Houston, Susan E. and Alison Prentice, *Schooling and Scholars in Nineteenth-Century Ontario*. Toronto: University of Toronto Press, 1988.

Mattingly, Paul H. and Michael B. Katz, eds., *Education And Social Change: Themes From Ontario's Past*. New York: New York University Press, 1975.

Mays, Herbert J., "'A Place to Stand': Families, Land and Permanence in Toronto Gore Township, 1820–1890," CHA *Historical Papers*, (1980), 185–211.

Medjuck, Sheva, "Family and Household Composition in the Nineteenth Century Case of Moncton, N.B. 1851–1871," *Canadian Journal of Sociology*, (Summer 1979), 275–286.

Parr, Joy, ed., *Childhood And Family In Canadian History*. Toronto: McClelland and Stewart, 1982.

Rooke, Patricia T. and R.L. Schnell, eds., *Studies in Childhood History: A Canadian Perspective*. Calgary: Detselig, 1982.

"Special Issue on Childhood and Family in the Twentieth Century," *Canadian Historical Review*, Vol. 78, No. 3, (September), 1997.

THE FAMILY IN NEW FRANCE

John F. Bosher

One of the fundamental changes in Quebec since the 1940s is a marked decline in the birth rate which has lately become the lowest in Canada.[1] The large family is quickly disappearing, but until recently it was, as is well known, characteristic of French-Canadian society. Furthermore, if we go back to the history of that century-and-a-half before 1763, when Quebec was a French colony, we find that the family, large or small, was a stronger and more prominent group than it is now. It was, indeed, one of the main institutions in New France. The study of it may help to explain how early Canadian civilization is so different from our own.

The typical family of New France may be described in figures drawn from statistical histories, making a sort of statistical portrait.[2] In the early eighteenth century, families had an average of five or six children, but this average includes families in which one of the parents had died and so stopped its growth. Those "arrested" families had, on the average, four or five children, whereas the complete family, in which neither parent had died, had eight or nine. These averages conceal the variety, of course: some 16 percent of all families had from ten to fourteen children and 2.8 percent had no less than fifteen children. Death among the children also kept numbers down, and to a degree staggering in comparison with our present-day infant mortality. We now lose twenty or twenty-one babies out of every thousand; but in New France 246 out of every thousand died during the first year of life, and that was normal in the eighteenth century. What the figures suggest is that the small families at the bottom of the statistical scale were made so by the hazards of death, not by the habits or wishes of the parents. If no parents or children had died, most families would have numbered a dozen or more children. These figures are for the early eighteenth century, it should be added, after the immigration from France had fallen off; and an analysis of the population in 1663 shows it at an earlier stage when four-fifths of all families had no more than from one to six children. But at every stage the family was enormous compared to the average Quebec family in 1951 which had only 2.2 children.

From *In Search of the Visible Past*, Barry M. Gough, ed. (Waterloo: Wilfrid Laurier University Press, 1975), 1–11. Reprinted by permission.

Taken by themselves, the statistical facts for New France may seem to confirm two common traditions about the family habits of all our ancestors: first, that women married very young; and second, that they tended to be eternally pregnant thereafter and to have a baby every year. Yet the facts for New France—as for Old France and England also—contradict both those traditions. The average age of women at their first marriage was nearly twenty-two in New France and about twenty-five in Old France. There are, of course, some well-known cases of girls being married at twelve, which was the youngest a girl might legally marry in New France. In 1637, the explorer, Jean Nicollet, set an extreme example by marrying an eleven-year-old girl, Marguerite Couillard, who was Champlain's god-daughter. Not many girls followed that example, it appears, because on 12 April 1670 the royal government ordered the Intendant to pay a premium—or a bounty, perhaps—to every girl under sixteen who found a husband, and to every man who married under twenty. The Crown thought it necessary to encourage people to marry younger. For the same purpose, the Crown also decided to help poor families with the dowries for their girls, and this brings to our notice one of the impediments to an early marriage: the dowry, often a struggle for a father to find for a numerous family of girls. For this and other reasons, too, no doubt, some 18 percent of women did not marry until they were thirty or more; 10 percent waited until they were thirty-five or over; and 6 percent until they were over forty. Women married later than tradition and a few famous examples have led us to believe. Men, too, married older—on the average at nearly twenty-seven.

As for the frequency of births in a family, we learn that in New France women tended to have babies about every two years, not every year as legend has held. The demographic effects of such a difference were, of course, enormous; and one historian has concluded that the reason for this pause between babies, a pause of some twenty-three months from birth to birth or fourteen months plus nine months of pregnancy, was that women tended to remain temporarily sterile during the period of breast-feeding.[3]

To sum up, a typical "complete" family, which had not lost a parent, might consist of a father just over forty, a mother in her middle thirties and about eight children ranging from fourteen years of age down to a few weeks old. This may seem to be a very simple conclusion, disappointingly obvious, but it has the great merit of some basis in historical fact.

It leaves us wondering how to account for the phenomenal rate of the population's growth. In 1663, there were just over 3,000 people in New France, and a century later there were perhaps 70,000.[4] The population had multiplied by more than twenty-three. During that century, it appears that less than 10,000 immigrants came from the mother country. The remaining 57,000 people had all been born to the 3,000 Canadian families or to immigrant families as they came in, in less than five generations. If the French population had multiplied at that rate during the same century there might have been some 400 million Frenchmen by 1763, whereas there were, in fact, only 22 or 23 million. Lest we should be tempted to dismiss the figures for New France as improbable, we should glance at the increase during the two centuries after 1763 which amounts to an even more staggering rise of from 70,000 to 5.5 million, or an eighty-fold increase. If the French had multiplied as quickly as the French Canadians since 1763 there would be nearly 2 billion Frenchmen by now, or more than half the population of the entire world. In this context, the figures for the twenty-three-fold increase in New France during the century before 1763 do not seem improbable. But they are nevertheless in need of explanation.

Leaving the mathematics of the problem to the demographers, we may sum up in general terms as follows: if women did not marry so young as we thought; if they had babies half as often as we thought; if nearly one-quarter of those babies died before they were a year old and nearly another fifth of them died before the age of ten; and if the annual crude death-rate for the country was somewhere between twenty and forty per thousand; then why did the population increase so quickly? Why was the crude birth-rate so much higher than the crude death-rate or from forty-eight to sixty-five per thousand? The answer (and the missing fact in the problem as I have posed it) is that the people of New France had a high propensity to marry. They were exceptionally fond of the married state.

People in Quebec today marry at an annual rate of about seven or eight per thousand, which is below our national average. The French during the eighteenth century used to marry at the rate of about 16.5 per thousand. But in the colony of New France, the marriage rate was between 17.5 and 23.5 per thousand. The result of this high marriage rate was that from 30 percent to 40 percent of the total population were married or widowed, and this proportion seemed to be increasing in the first half of the eighteenth century.[5]

In addition to this, we find a marked tendency to remarry. Nearly one-fifth of married men married twice, and nearly one-fifth of families had fathers who had been married before. Widows were not snapped up quite so quickly as Peter Kalm and other travellers like to think, but the average widow remarried after three years of widowhood. One way or another very few women reached the age of forty without having married and even remarried. The remarriage rate was 16.3 per thousand or nearly twice as high as in 1948.

Another figure that may reflect the strong propensity to marry is the low rate of illegitimacy: it seems to have been not more than ten or twelve per thousand whereas in 1969 the average in Quebec was seventy-six per thousand. We are, I think, obliged to conclude from all the evidence that Canadians were fond of the married state and that this is one reason for the high birth rate. For all that the frontier, like any frontier, had large numbers of single young men, and for all that many Canadians were attracted by the adventurous life of the *coureur de bois*, the society as a whole consisted mainly of married people with families. After all, the *coureurs de bois* were not very numerous and not many girls went into religious orders. There were forty-one women in religious orders in 1663 and in 1763 all seven of the orders of nuns numbered only 190 women altogether, a large number of them from France.

The marriage ceremony which these early Canadians went through in such large numbers left people in no doubt about what their main duty was as a couple. Immediately after the couple had been blessed by the officiating priest, the marriage bed was blessed with the sprinkling of holy water, prayers, and exorcisms. The exorcisms were intended to ward off the evil effects of an especially dangerous curse which some enemy of the couple might put on the marriage to make it barren. This curse was known as the *nouage de l'aiguillette*, and on occasion the Church would dissolve a marriage which produced no children on the grounds that this evil magic had made it barren, so important was the procreation of children in that society. And yet the bed in which children were to be conceived and born was not supposed to be a place for pleasure, as the official ceremony for Quebec, *Le Rituel du diocèse de Québec*, made very clear. The priest was to say to the newlyweds,

> Remember that your wedding bed will some day be your death bed, from whence your souls will be taken to be sent before God's Tribunal....[6]

When we come to consider why the people of New France married so willingly and in such large numbers we may at first be tempted to think that the Church forced them into it. Marriage was, after all, a Christian institution, one of the seven sacraments of the Church. There was no civil marriage, nor any civil status at all, in New France. All marriages had to be Catholic marriages and priests were forbidden to marry anyone who was not a Catholic. Very few Canadians married Indians, baptized or not, and very few married Protestants. Priests had to make sure that people who wanted to marry were satisfied that God had called them to marriage; that they had been instructed of the duties and religious principles of marriage (for instance, that it was for having children and for no other purpose); that they had made a full and true confession and communion in their parishes; and that they intended to appear and to behave decently on their wedding day, not to give way to the Devil's temptation to dress vainly or to eat and drink too much. In 1682, Bishop Laval spoke out against women coming to church "in scandalous nakedness of the arms, of the shoulders and the throat or being satisfied to cover them with transparent cloth which often serves only to give more lustre to these shameful nudities."[7] We might be inclined to conclude that it was as good and faithful Catholics in a theocracy that the people of New France were drawn to marriage.

However, we do not have to look very far to see that marriage in that society was not only a religious sacrament, but much else besides. For one thing, weddings were one of the main social events, famous for celebrations lasting several days or even weeks together. That was why most marriages were held in November, January or February, the idle months of the year between the labours of autumn and the labours of spring. Marriage was also set about with pagan customs like the *charivari*, a ritual gathering of young people who made a disturbance outside the house of a widow who had just been married soon after being widowed, or of people of very unequal ages who had married. The crowd shouted until the newlyweds came out and either explained their actions or else paid a fine.[8] Another folk custom, brought from France, like nearly all Quebec customs, was for young people who wished to marry without their parents' consent, or without a proper wedding, to attend a regular church service and announce at the end of it that they regarded themselves as married. This was called *mariage à la gaumine* and was based on a strict and (said the clergy) illegitimate interpretation of the Papal ruling that marriage required the Church's blessing. Although it died out in the eighteenth century, this custom showed that some people viewed the Church's rules as hindrances to marriage. But all these things are only small clues to the irreligious side of marriage. Much more importantly marriage was an act of the family as a business and social enterprise. It was only rarely an act of two free individuals.

In New France, and in Europe at the time, the family was truly the fundamental unit of society and not the frail and limited group we know today. But in New France, the family was particularly important because some of the other French social groups had not taken root here. The typical French peasant lived in a close-knit village with common lands, common taxes, and a collective or communal life reflected in the word "commune" still used in France more or less as a synonym for "village."[9] However, the *habitants* of New France were not peasants, for the most part, and they lived dispersed across the countryside without common lands or duties in a pattern of rural settlement known as *le rang*.[10] Again, tradesmen in France were organized in guilds or *corporations* which governed most aspects of their working lives, but in New France they worked in a much freer and more independent way. The family was therefore a relatively more important social unit.

In both France and New France, however, as Guy Fregault writes, "The ties of family relationship had extraordinary strength at that time."[11] Four of its basic features will show what I mean. First, the family tended to be a business or agricultural unit with every member expecting to live on the family wealth and in turn expected to take part in the family enterprise. It was also a social enterprise in which every member tried to assist in the advancement of the whole. Families climbed socially like ivy up a wall. The mentality of social advancement at the time may be glimpsed in, for instance, some statements by an eighteenth-century Governor whose attitudes may be taken as exemplary in the colony. This is Vaudreuil, who wrote to the minister at Versailles on 15 November 1703: "We have chosen the Honourable Chevalier de Courcy to carry these letters ... to you because he is the nephew of Monsieur de Callieres. We have been pleased to give him this honour to let him know the respect we have for the memory of his late uncle." A year later, Vaudreuil wrote to the Minister on behalf of his own children: "I have eight boys and a girl who need the honour of your protection. Three of them are ready for service. I entered the musketeers when I was as young as my oldest. I hope you will have the goodness to grant me for him the company of the Sieur de Maricourt who has died." He then discusses his wife's relations and concludes, "On my side [of the family] I have only one relation, to whom the late Sieur Chevalier de Callieres gave a small office as ensign. I beg you to grant him a lieutenancy...."[12]

Of course patronage extended beyond the family, but the strongest claims were on blood relations and for them. We cannot read very far in any official correspondence of the time without encountering such claims, for there was almost no other way of getting ahead in life. The system of patronage is revealed in a vocabulary all its own, peculiar to the *ancien regime* whether in France or in Canada: *protection* meant patronage; *grâce* referred to a post, a promotion, a pension or a title conferred by a patron or at his request; *estime* was the attitude of the patron towards his *créature* and it was the reason they both alleged for the *grâce*. And *crédit* was the power a friend or relation had to obtain a *grâce* from someone else; whereas *faveur* expressed the power he had to obtain something for himself.

A second feature of the family is that the act of marriage was in part a business event. In particular, the family had to find a dowry for a girl or else she would probably never find a husband. Trying to marry a girl off without a dowry would have been like fishing without bait on the hook. To use another image, the dowry was a sort of marriage "scholarship," and this metaphor seems all the more true when we remember that Talon gave the *filles du Roi* dowries of fifty *livres* in linen and other goods, and that in 1711 the government of New France set aside the sum of 3,000 *livres* to be distributed as dowries among sixty girls. In New France, dowries varied a good deal and they reflect roughly the social level of the family. Here is an example of a modest dowry which Magdeleine Boucher brought to her husband, Urbain Baudry Lamarche:

> Two hundred *livres* in silver; four sheets; two table-cloths; six cloth and hemp napkins; a mattress and a blanket; two plates; six pewter spoons and six pewter plates; a pot and a cauldron; a table and two benches; a flour bin; a chest with a lock and key; one cow; two pigs, male and female. The parents gave the bride a suit of clothes and as much underwear as she wanted.[13]

This was an *habitant* family affair, of course. A rich shipping merchant's daughter, at the other end of the scale of commoners, might bring thousands of *livres* to her marriage. Denis Goguet, who retired to La Rochelle after making his fortune in Canada, put up dowries of 50,000 *livres* for his daughters.[14]

The main point about such dowries is that they were family property transferred by legal contract. At the time of the marriage a contract was drawn up before a notary stating this transfer of property and other business terms pertaining to the marriage. Marriage thus had a business side to it and the business negotiations were usually between the families rather than the betrothed couple. As a rule, the families signed these contracts in large numbers; we find the signatures of uncles, aunts, cousins and so on scrawled on the last page. One of the interesting effects of this system is that the wife, represented by her family and bringing considerable property to the marriage, tended to have a greater material equality with her husband than most wives in our time.

Needless to say, therefore, both families were very much interested in arranging the marriage in the first place, and this brings up my third point about the family as enterprise: marriage was a major theatre of the family struggle for social advancement or for security. To marry above the family station was a triumph, a step upward for the entire family. The new link with a grander or more noble family was a source of benefit through the influence it afforded. If the daughter of a successful merchant married a government official or his son, the assumption was likely to be that henceforth they were allies in a common struggle for advancement.

Why, we may wonder, would a family ever allow a marriage with a lesser family? The answer is that wealth attracted the poor but respectable; and respectability attracted the rich but low-born. Or else a powerful merchant or clerical family might be glad to marry into a large family of military officers with strong connections in the army. The benefit would still be mutual. Professor Cameron Nish has shown with many examples how the various social spheres intermarried in New France, there being only one ruling class and no such thing as purely military, purely seigneurial or purely administrative families.[15]

The fourth feature of the family was its hierarchy with the father in command, captain of the family enterprise. It is all too easy these days to imagine that paternal authority was merely a rank injustice or a quaint superstition. Far from it. Every enterprise in a competitive world must be under the command of someone or some group with authority to make decisions: a manager, a president, a ship's captain, a general in the army, a board in a company, and so on. The family enterprise in New France and Old France was nearly always under the father, though there were no impediments to a widow taking over her husband's family firm. In France, especially, there were many firms with "widow" in their titles: *La Veuve Charly* of La Rochelle, *La Veuve Augier et fils aîné* of Tonnay-Charente; *La Veuve Courrejolles et fils* of Bayonne, and so on.

It has been said that circumstances in Canada tended to put women and children much higher in the social scheme of things than French women and children and to make them more equal with the husband and father.[16] Yet such a difference was not sanctioned either by custom or by law, and normally the father's authority extended to most things, unless he died in which case his widow might assume some, though by no means all, of his authority. Parental authority over children may be seen very clearly in the field of marriage. No child could marry without his father's or widowed mother's consent until the age of twenty-five for girls and thirty for men. Until those ages, the children were considered minors. And in a world where life was shorter than it is now, we must add several years to those ages in order to appreciate the significance of that law. Marriage was primarily the family's business and by law as well as by custom the children were expected to make their marriages according to the best interests of the family.

French law provided that if a son, for example, wanted to marry a girl of whom his father did not approve, he might draw up three "respectful applications" (*sommations respectueuses*) at a notary's office, one after the other at a few weeks' intervals. Let me read to you the first respectful application that a certain Jean-Claude Louet made to his father in January 1733. He was then thirty years old and wanted to marry a shoemaker's daughter, but the father did not approve of the marriage.[17]

> My Very Dear Father,
>
> I am in the throes of misery at finding myself deprived of the kindnesses that I was used to receiving from you. I am extremely pained that your tender impulses which have moved me so often and so deeply are entirely extinct. However, dear father, if I withdraw the obedience and submission that I owe you it is out of an indispensable obligation to restore the reputation of the one whom I have lost, without which there is no salvation for me.
>
> Finally, dear father, I entreat you in your paternal love, and by all that is dearest to you of your own blood, to let yourself be touched and persuaded by the pitiable fate of the poor girl and the lamentable state to which I have been reduced for so long. You have spoken; I have obeyed. You have sent me away to a place where I have nothing but tears and sighs to console me and keep me company.
>
> I believe, however, that today you will be moved by my woes and will grant me the favour I am asking of you.
>
> From he who is,
My Dear Father,
Your most humble and submissive son,

C. Louet

After the third such letter, the son was then legally entitled to marry because he was thirty years old. Under thirty, if his father still refused to consent the son would have had to wait.

We see in all this that the family was engaged in a collective struggle for survival or advancement, and children could not usually please themselves as individuals but had to act as members of the family team. This state of affairs was not merely a quaint custom, but enforced by the law of the kingdom. The law in New France, as in Old France, was prepared to punish children who disobeyed and defied their fathers; for the government, the Church and the society saw the family in that age as though it were itself a tiny kingdom in which the father, like a king, had almost total authority to rule, reward and punish. In other words, in that society the family appeared as the smallest political cell in the kingdom, modelled on the kingdom itself.

This metaphor is, however, reversible, and if we reverse it we find that the family in that eighteenth-century society served as a general pattern of organization and authority. The Church, for example, appeared to the people as a sort of family because God was presented as a father to be obeyed as one obeyed one's own father. The letter of Claude Louet above reads a little like a prayer. And not only was God a father-like figure, but beneath him there was a whole hierarchy of fathers in authority: the archbishops, the bishops and the priests. Catholic priests were addressed as "father" while the lay brothers were "brothers." The head of an order of nuns was, of course, a "mother superior," and the nuns were either "mother" or "sister." Girls first entering religious orders were expected to bring dowries as though they were being married, and a nun's dowry was not merely a symbol but a substantial sum of money, a piece of land or a parcel of goods. Records of dowries brought to Quebec orders are a useful guide to the wealth of the girls' families: some brought several thousand *livres* in cash, others came with a dowry of annuities or planks, barrels of wine, linen, furniture, wheat and so on.[18] When a Canadian girl chose to go into a monastery, she and her family prepared for the event in somewhat the same way as if she were going to be married, for they saw her as marrying into the Church. She joined the Church just as she might have joined a husband's family. Of course there were differences, but the similarities are striking.

Listen to the following ecstasies of love written by a woman who spent most of her life in New France: "Oh, beloved of my soul! Where are you and when shall I possess you? When shall I have you for myself and entirely for myself? Ah, I want you, but I do not want only half of you. I want all of you, my Love and my Life.... Come, then, come Oh my Love! The door of my heart is open to you ..." and so on. Now who was this passionate woman? And who was the fortunate man to whom she was so passionately drawn? She was none other than Marie de l'Incarnation, a nun in the seventeenth century and now a saint in the Canadian Catholic calendar, and all these emotional outpourings were addressed to God. She was expressing her vocation, her call to a life in New France in God's service to which she devoted herself passionately. The point is that as these and other such passages show she saw herself as in some sense married to God or to Jesus and in her writings often referred to him as "my dear Husband."[19]

The image of the family was also present in the army. When a soldier wanted to marry, he needed the consent of his captain or other senior officer and of the Governor of New France. These two consents, which were not merely perfunctory, were duly registered by the officiating clergy. Military authority was thus in some measure paternal authority. But all authority which is not defined by clear regulations must inevitably appear as paternal in the sense that it has no limits and may extend, like a father's authority, into personal and family matters.

The political hierarchy, too, was organized on the family plan. What was the King in the Bourbon kingdom but a great father with paternal care for his subjects and paternal authority over them? Under him, the Governor and Intendant were also father figures expected to enforce not the law, but the King's paternal will. They themselves had paternal rights and duties; and this explains why they used their authority in many matters great and small which astonish us. Paternal authority had very different limits from those of men in authority in our world. "You must maintain good order and peace in families," the minister at Versailles wrote to one Canadian Governor, "refrain from joining in private discussions except to bring them to an end and not join in them if you cannot settle them, never listen to women's talk, never allow anyone to speak ill of someone else in front of you and never do so yourself.... " As the Intendant Raudot said, the colony was supposed to be managed "as a good father of a family would manage his estate."[20] When, for instance, the Minister happened to hear of an officer who was not supporting his impoverished mother, he arranged to have the officer punished and part of his pay withheld for the mother.[21]

There were, then, a number of hierarchies of authority in Canada all patterned on the family and all helping to reinforce one another in the Canadian mind. To introduce the rule of law into such a society, as the British tried to do after 1763, was a difficult task. How could it be introduced in a society where all authority was regarded as personal and paternal? Still, under British rule, the change began in New France a quarter of a century before it began in Old France during the French Revolution. Since then the French have reverted frequently to the paternal authority of a father figure such as the Bonaparte emperors and General de Gaulle, not to mention Maréchal Pétain whose regime used the motto, *Famille, Patrie, Travail.* Let us hope that in Quebec the rule of law has taken a firmer hold on the minds of the people during the past two hundred years, and that the ancient vision of the polity as a family has faded away.

Notes

1. *The Canda Yearbook for 1972*, 241–42.

2. Jacques Henripin, *La Population canadienne au début du XVIIIe siècle* (Paris, 1954); Henripin, "From Acceptance of Nature to Control: The Demography of the French Canadians since the Seventeenth Century," in M. Rioux and Y. Martin, *French-Canadian Society*, vol. 1 (Toronto, 1964), 204–216; Marcel Trudel, *La Population du Canada en 1663* (Montreal, 1973); J.N. Biraben, "Le Peuplement du Canada français," *Annales de démographie historiques* (Paris, 1966), 104–139.

3. Jacques Henripin, "La Fécondité des ménages canadiens au début du XVIIIe siècle," *Population*, vol. 9 (Paris, 1954), 74–84.

4. Trudel, 11. Professor Trudel lists 3,035 people, but admits that he is not sure of 221 of them. On immigrants, see Biraben, and Henripin, *La Population canadienne*, chap. II, quoting Georges Langlois, *Histoire de la population canadienne française de Montréal* (1934).

5. Trudel finds that in 1663, the proportion was nearly 50 percent (p. 74).

6. Robert-Lionel Seguin, *La Vie libertine en Nouvelle-France au XVIIe siècle*, vol. 2 (Ottawa, 1972), 365–66.

7. Paul-Andre Leclerc, "Le Mariage sous le régime français," *Revue d'histoire de l'Amérique française*, 13 (1959): 525.

8. *Ibid.*, 229ff. On "mariage à la gaumine," see *Le Rapport de l'Archiviste de la Province de Quebec* (henceforth cited as R.A.P.Q.), 1920–21, 366–407.

9. Marc Bloch, *Les Caractères originaux de l'Histoire rurale française* (Paris, 1952) [first published in 1931], chap. V.

10. Pierre Deffontaines, "The Rang—Pattern of Rural Settlement in French Canada," in Rioux and Martin, *French-Canadian Society*, 3–18.

11. Guy Fregault, *Le XVIIIe siècle canadien* (Montreal, 1968), 179.

12. *R.A.P.Q.*, 1938–39, 21–22 and 49–50.

13. Leclerc, 59.

14. Archives départementales de la Charente maritime (La Rochelle), minutes of the notary Delavergne, 10 December 1760 and 4 June 1770.

15. Cameron Nish, *Les Bourgeois-Gentilshommes de la Nouvell-France, 1729–1748* (Montreal and Paris, 1968), chap. X, "La Bourgeoisie et le mariage."

16. Philippe Garigue, *La Vie familiale des canadiens français* (Montreal and Paris, 1962), 16–17.

17. *R.A.P.Q.*, 1921–22, 60–63.

18. Micheline d'Allaire, "L'Origine sociale des religieuses de l'Hôpital-général de Québec," *Revue d'Histoire de l'Amérique française* 23 (March 1970): 559–83.

19. Dom Albert Jamet, ed., *Le Témoignage de Marie de l'Incarnation, Ursuline de Tours et de Québec* (Paris, 1932), 70–72.

20. Guy Fregault, *Le XVIIIe siècle canadien*, 162–63.

21. *Ibid.*, pp. 163–64.

CHILDREN OF THE FUR TRADES

Jennifer S.H. Brown

Many thousands of people in North America can trace their ancestry to the French and British fur traders of the seventeenth to nineteenth centuries and the Indian women who befriended, tolerated, or endured these European strangers. The descendants of fur trade alliances have followed many different paths, sometimes remembering and emphasizing their distinctive parentage, and sometimes establishing white or Indian identities that minimize their bi-racial origins.[1]

Such identity-building begins in the small and circumscribed context of an individual's immediate family and community. Children born in the fur trade

From *Childhood and Family in Canadian History*, Joy Parr, ed. (Toronto: McClelland and Stewart, 1982), 44–68. Reprinted by permission.

country experienced family and community relationships that varied considerably according to the time, place, and company setting in which they matured, and depending on the social standing and ethnic identity of their parents.

These patterns reflected the history of the fur trade itself and its complexities. Socially and organizationally, it was not one monolithic entity, although its European participants all pursued the same or similar resources with similar motives. The northern fur trade was dominated early by the French, and later by English and Highland Scottish entrepreneurs who drew on French expertise and labour to build the businesses that eventually coalesced into the North West Company. The Hudson's Bay Company began with English employees and later took on large numbers of Lowland and Orkney Scots; its servants' social origins and home affiliations thus contrasted with those of the Scots of the North West Company, although both were British and anglophone.[2] European traders' relationships with their native-born children, and the mothers of those children, were correspondingly diverse.

The early days of both the French and the British fur trades were characterized by trader bachelorhood. New France in its first decades contained a preponderance of young males, many of whom engaged in the fur trade. Much to colonial administrators' concern, traders were slow to establish stable family units. White women and potential wives were few. Indian women were not, and many from among the Huron and other tribes became involved in alliances with French traders.[3]

Such unions, usually temporary and unsanctioned by European norms, were not acceptable within New France. There, marriage was a Roman Catholic ritual that required a commitment for life. The traders who turned to Indian women, then, sought short-term personal gratification and trade advantages and did not expect their familial obligations to be permanent. In so doing, they did not necessarily violate Indian values. Missionaries who accompanied traders inland found to their dismay that the relatives of Indian women usually encouraged these relationships.

The Huron perceived ties between Frenchmen and Huron women as bases for personal kinship alliances that converted trader strangers into relatives and led to mutual trust and goodwill. Thus French priests as well as traders were offered Huron wives from motives of hospitality and trade-related friendship. The possibility that such unions might not be permanent did not surprise the Huron, for in their own society divorce was an accepted occurrence. Huron courtship customs, too, were relaxed. Young men and women accepted premarital sexual relations as normal, and marriages were stabilized as such only when children were born.[4] As long as they accepted Huron codes of politeness and proper behaviour among kin, French traders could ally themselves with Huron women without causing offence to any but their own churchmen.

The paths of such unions were probably smoothed by the fact that the French traders' occupational roles approximated those of Huron husbands in certain respects. Huron males, like their French allies, were absent from their homes for considerable periods, to pursue trading, provisioning, and political activities. The women remained at home, tending their crops and maintaining their matrilineal and familial ties and traditions. The children born to them, whether to Huron or French husbands, were readily absorbed into the female-centred extended families that resided in the large longhouses of Huron villages.[5] Half-French children became Huron, members of their mother's matrilineage. If orphaned, they still had a broad network of relatives who accepted them as kin, without raising the questions of legitimacy and morality that troubled the French authorities and clergy. The Huron themselves would doubtless have resisted yielding orphaned youngsters to French care if that option arose. Maternal descent placed them in the mother's line, not the father's. And children, in the Huron view, were happier and better-treated in their society than among the French. Huron children never suffered corporal punishment as discipline, and the Huron were shocked by the French advocacy and use of that method, just as the French were perturbed at its absence among the Huron.[6]

The destruction of the Huron confederacy and its dispersal in 1649 disrupted the formation of new kinship ties between French and Huron. But traders' own inclinations, in combination with widespread Indian interests in alliance through kinship, continued to foster trader-Indian intermarriage. In later periods, unknown numbers of fur trade children continued to be assimilated as members of northern Algonkian and other Indian groups, as long as their maternal relatives' communities were able and willing to absorb them.

After 1650, as the French trade reached farther inland, some of its participants loosened their ties with New France and formed more lasting bonds with each other and with their Indian associates, at a distance from the restricted and regulated life of their home colony. Officials wrote with concern about how attracted these young men were to "this Indian way of life" and how increasing numbers were living in the Indian country for years at a time.[7]

A major base for these men's activities was Michilimackinac at the junction of Lakes Huron and Michigan. It served as a depot for supplies from Montreal and a departure point for establishing outposts that eventually spread from the Ohio River to Lake Winnipeg and the Hudson Bay drainage. Clergy saw Michilimackinac as a den of sin, where informal and unsanctified liaisons flourished between French and Canadian-born white men and Algonkian women. Traders, however, welcomed Indian women as companions and helpmates on inland expeditions, as well as at remote winter outposts and at the major posts. Fur trade families arose as domestic units in which children matured, at least for a time, with both parents present. By 1695, sixty or so bark-covered dwellings were said to be housing such families in the vicinity of Michilimackinac.[8]

The continuing campaigns of the clergy against such relationships probably encouraged many traders to separate themselves still further from New France and its moral and legal strictures. The Jesuits, who urged that traders and Indians be kept as separate as possible, and the Governor-General of New France, who forbade mixed marriages at the post of Detroit in 1709, had few means to enforce compliance from people who by choice had removed themselves from respectable colonial society. The Detroit prohibition gave Governor-General Vaudreuil occasion to note the distinctiveness of these traders and to generalize about their offspring: the former were *"libertins fenéans, et d'une independence insuportable,"* ("lazy libertines and insufferably independent,") and the latter, *"d'une fenéantise aussy grande que les sauvages mesmes* ("as bone-lazy as the Indians themselves.")[9]

Details about these men's family lives and their children are hard to come by. But we can infer certain things about the fur trade parents and children of the late 1600s and early 1700s. From the numbers of their descendants and the diversity of their French names, we may conclude that a substantial proportion of early traders around Mackinac and elsewhere had such families and that many fathers were remaining sufficiently in touch to transmit their surnames to their offspring.

The mission registers of later years are also informative. From 1670 until the end of the French regime a mission priest was resident at Mackinac, and the registers of that place, which are relatively intact after the 1720s, preserve details on numbers of families who, sooner or later in their domestic cycles, accepted marriage or baptismal sacraments, in some instances while visiting Mackinac from outlying points such as Green Bay, Chequamegon, and Prairie du Chien, Wisconsin. On 22 July 1747, for example, the priest married Jean Baptiste Tellier de la Fortune and Marie Josephe, a Nipissing woman baptized that morning, and thereby legitimized their children, aged nineteen, fourteen, ten, six, three and six months. On 4 February 1748, "former *voyageur*" Charles Hamelin married Marie Athanasie, "a Sauteux [northern Ojibwa] woman Savage recently baptized." The marriage of Jean Manion l'Esperance to his Sauteux wife on 30 August 1749 legitimized their three children, aged about eight, six and three. Numerous other entries are similar in content.[10]

These registers are only a partial record but, in combination with other data on later fur trade families, they suggest the development of certain demographic patterns. Indian families, according to historical descriptions, were usually small, and children were commonly born three, four, or more years apart, owing to long periods of nursing that reduced the mothers' fecundity and sometimes to post-partum taboos on sexual relations. In times of hardship, infanticide and starvation might take their toll on newborns. Indian women's alliances with whites, however, tended to produce more children, more closely spaced, if the couple lived together fairly constantly. Children's survival chances were perhaps enhanced by access to fur trade centres and supplies, and European males were probably intolerant of long nursing and post-partum sexual restrictions. Whatever the importance of these various factors, fur trade families, once established as ongoing units, grew at rapid rates equalling those of New France and other expanding European colonies in North America.[11]

As the numbers and sizes of these families grew, they formed their own communities around the Great Lakes and westward in the direction of Red River. Mothers and children who became separated from their trader husband-fathers continued to rejoin their Indian relatives, but local Indian bands, by the mid-1700s, had difficulty absorbing all their progeny. Fathers who continued to reside in the Indian country retained their native kin around them. They supported themselves and their families by continuing in the direct employ of the fur trade, or by becoming *coureurs de bois*—outlaw traders, or *gens libres*—freemen who made an independent living by supplying the trade and subsisting on country resources, eventually to retire and die in the North-west.

Their early unplanned communities lacked visibility as recognized political entities, and their land titles were problematic. Owing to environmental and subsistence limitations the communities of the Great Lakes *métis* remained small, usually consisting of no more than a few hundred persons. Dependent mainly on local furs, game, and other resources shared cooperatively with Indian kinsmen nearby, *métis* populations were obliged to disperse into scattered nuclei. But unlike the Indians' more seasonal and temporary shelters, their clusters of upright-log, bark-covered cabins with high-pitched roofs might last many years. Several became the foci of later towns. Reflecting the importance of water transport, their homes were strung out along a lake or river with small, narrow, fenced gardens cut into the woods behind.

Children grew up with a mixed Indian-French heritage—a blending of languages, customs, and foods, for example, crêpes and maple sugar. They matured to wear distinctive apparel combining moccasins, leggings, pantaloons, ruffled shirts, and decorative feathers. Neither Indian nor French, yet both, some moved into major broker roles between New France to the east and Algonkian and Siouan groups to the west. Interpreting, guiding, transporting goods, messages, and people, they learned to function "not only as human carriers linking Indians and Europeans, but as buffers behind which the ethnic boundaries of antagonistic cultures remained relatively secure."[12]

Some of the sons became well-known personages, and yet they charted an independent course with respect to both their parental cultures. Charles Langlade was the son of a French trader and officer and of the sister of an Ottawa chief. Charles alternated in youth between wintering with his maternal kin and being tutored by Jesuits at Michilimackinac where his father was commandant. Believed by the Ottawa to possess a powerful manito, he might have become prominent among them but instead became a trader and military leader. Married first to an Ottawa Indian woman and later to a Detroit trader's daughter, he had his son schooled in Montreal and his daughters tutored at home. His children's marriages repeated the pattern of his own—Indian-*métis* alliances and *métis* endogamy, reinforcing Indian-*métis* ties around the western Great Lakes and swelling the ranks of the *métis* themselves.[13] With the rise and spread of the Langlades and countless other similar families, a new ethnically and culturally distinctive population had become an established presence around the Great Lakes by the end of the French regime.

The British conquest of New France in 1763 opened a new chapter in the Canadian fur trade and in fur trade family history. In the next years, political and economic control of the colony passed to anglophone leaders, among whom Highland Scots were conspicuous.

The mainly Scottish takeover of the higher echelons of the French fur trade and its related Montreal businesses in this period has been well-documented.[14] The process was accelerated by the Highlanders' tendency to reinforce and expand their commercial partnerships by recruiting Scottish kinsmen and friends from home or from among those who had migrated to New York and New England. Partners first formed strong competing networks in the fur business and later tended to combine forces as costs of rivalry grew and as the networks themselves spread and intersected. The North West Company was a group of partnerships that joined forces in 1784 and expanded rapidly thereafter. In 1804, it combined with its major remaining rival, the New North West or XY Company, to gain an effective monopoly of the Montreal fur trade.[15]

The North Westers formed a unified superstructure built on a foundation of French trade expertise, labour, and organization. Its winterers followed the old French trade routes, using Canadians and *métis* of French descent as guides, interpreters, and *voyageurs*. A two-tiered social system developed. French fur trade society had been truncated by the conquest, and its leadership had been removed or demoted. Its upper levels were taken over by newcomers who assumed prominent roles not only as winterers in the fur trade country but also in the higher social ranks of the growing business centre of Montreal. Even after long absences inland, these partners had incentives to return to Montreal where they could rejoin their kin and consolidate their fur trade gains and their social standing. Remaining active in the business, they also participated in the Beaver Club, their own society of former winterers, and in churches and other organizations.

As partners and company directors, the British North Westers also had opportunities to recruit and train their own successors. The young men whom they chose as clerks and possible future partners were, like themselves, predominantly British, usually being kinsmen or personal acquaintances. Collateral relationships extending among active and prospective colleagues were significant links for this purpose. Thus, for example, Simon McTavish, one of the leading merchant partners in Montreal, brought three of his sister's sons, William, Simon, and Duncan McGillivray, from Scotland and also introduced John George McTavish, the son of his clan chief, into the business; all four became important figures in the fur trade.[16]

The emphasis that the North Westers placed on these wider kin ties sometimes detracted from their marriages and immediate families. Simon McTavish married the daughter of a distinguished old French fur trading family, Marie

Marguerite Chaboillez—an alliance that fostered good relations with those few French Canadians who still maintained standing in the fur business. But this late marriage, contracted when he was forty-three, did not become the sole focus of his life. Before his death in 1804, he made a will whose provisions paid as much attention to his Scottish kin as to his wife and four children. And he made it clear that Marie Marguerite and her relatives were not to have the management of the children; rather, they were to be given a proper British education.[17] Their deaths at early ages left unanswered the question of how their own ties and allegiances might have developed.

When the British North Westers travelled into the Indian country, they carried their loyalties, mutual connections, and familial attitudes with them. Like the French before, and like the Indians with whom they traded, they were receptive to unions with women who would cement alliances with native trading partners. Yet, unlike many French, most British North Westers were too well-placed in their home society to develop permanent attachments in the Indian country.

Additionally, unlike the French traders among the Huron and westward, they lacked the constraint of being observed and reported upon by the churchmen resident in the Indian country; after the British conquest of Canada, the clergy rarely made visits even as far as Mackinac, and mission activity in the North-west practically ceased until the 1820s.[18] The private partnerships whose interests these Britishers served were not concerned to convert or civilize the fur trade country; nor did they undertake to build up governmental or legal structures beyond those supervisory functions required by the trade.

The result was that formal European legal and moral constraints in the Montrealers' North-west were weaker than they had been in the areas penetrated by the French. Among North Westers and their Canadian and *métis* employees as they extended their activities to the Athabasca country and beyond, codes of conduct with regard to native families varied depending on local circumstances and the individuals concerned. Most became involved, sooner or later, in what were known as marriages "according to the custom of the country" (*en façon du pays*). But "marriage" could mean several different things. It was sometimes a transitory union, lasting only while a man was engaged in local trade with the woman's relatives. It might be longer-term like William Connolly's, with the woman and her children accompanying a trader to different posts, perhaps far away from her Indian kin. Or it might prove to be lifelong, as did some—notably the well-recorded marriages of Daniel Williams Harmon and John Macdonell.[19] But alongside these relationships were others that were more exploitative and abusive, involving seizures of women or their sale among traders. Fur trade marriages could be matters of "custom and ceremony" or alternatively involve few or no ritual or social sanctions. One woman from the fur trade country testified in the Connolly court case in Montreal that she knew nothing of marriage rituals in such unions: "The custom is that one sleeps with men."[20]

The children of these alliances had diverse experiences. Those who, like the early French *métis*, were absorbed into Indian societies, generally left little trace in the historical record. We know more about the offspring of men whose long attachment to their native families drew their children away from their maternal relatives. A number of their histories have been published elsewhere.[21] One useful source concerning some of them has not been systematically investigated before, however, and makes an interesting focus for discussion here.

Some North Westers were Roman Catholics and Anglicans; but others were Presbyterians who by the 1790s were actively supporting their own church in Montreal, the St. Gabriel Street Presbyterian Church. The registers of this church for the years from 1796 to 1821, when the North West Company and the Hudson's Bay Company merged, list the baptisms of seventy-five children born of alliances between North Westers and women of the Indian country.[22] The entries are revealing and yet also curiously elliptical about the familial relationships behind them.

A North Wester who sent his native children back to Montreal for baptism assumed certain paternal obligations and expenses. He did not necessarily thereby establish an ongoing "nuclear family" of co-residing parents and children. With occasional exceptions, the mothers of children listed in the St. Gabriel Street records were absent from the ceremony and left unnamed; the standard description included the child's name and age, and then read "son" (or "daughter") of, for example, "Roderick McKenzie of the North West Company Esquire by a woman of the Indian Country." The mother's invisibility in this context was no proof that she was unknown or that her alliance with the child's father had terminated: some, such as Roderick McKenzie's with Angelique,[23] became lifelong; some had ended; some would end later as North Westers set aside old liaisons for respectable white marriages. But plainly at that time such relationships were rarely accepted or made permanent in Montreal. The clergy were willing to baptize the native children of North West Company gentlemen, but most mothers, unbaptized and unmarried by Christian rite, remained unacknowledged.

Of fifty-seven baptismal entries listing parentage, seven did name mothers, and these families have some special interest. On 25 July 1796, Charles Phillips, "Indian Trader," presented two sons and a daughter for baptism. Their mother was "Jenny the Red Bird of the tribe of the Hurons," whom he married that day. Phillips had been a North Wester, for many years in charge of Rivière Dumoine (Quebec). But by the time of his marriage he had left the company, under criticism for mismanagement of his charge, and was trading independently at Point St. Claire.[24] He was evidently a marginal figure both among company colleagues and in his decision to marry Jenny the Red Bird in Montreal.

The noted explorer David Thompson and his family are another exception. Thompson entries account for three of the seven in which mothers are named. On 30 September 1812, Thompson and his country wife, Charlotte, daughter of North Wester Patrick Small and a Cree woman, presented three sons and a daughter for baptism; on 30 October, the parents were married by minister James Somerville. Later entries record part of the history of this large family: in 1813, a son was baptized at the age of one month; in early 1814, two of the children baptized earlier were buried; and in 1815, a daughter, aged eight weeks, was baptized. During this period, the family was living at Terrebonne, where several other old North Westers, notably Roderick McKenzie, may have offered congenial company. Yet Thompson, like Phillips, was in some respects a marginal North Wester. A product of the charitable Grey Coat School in England, he had been apprenticed in 1784 to the Hudson's Bay Company, which he served until 1797 when he joined the North West Company. Certainly he lacked, both in England and Canada, the broad kinship and friendship networks in which so many North Westers were intertwined. This absence of competing ties and his strong sense of morality constrained him from setting aside his native wife and children for other allegiances. Unrecognized for his great fur trade explorations once he left the North West Company, he and his family lived a penurious and obscure existence for many years thereafter, in Terrebonne and later in Williamstown (Ontario), another centre of retired traders.[25]

Two other North Westers named lifelong companions as the mothers of their children, although they did not marry them in the St. Gabriel Street Church. John Thomson and Frances Boucher presented a son and two daughters, aged nine, eleven, and two, for baptism in May of 1811; the mother, aged about twenty-five, was also baptized. The family was long-lasting. Françoise Boucher and John Thomson "cohabited together for many years in the Indian Territory, by which they had a family of six children and on their arrival in Lower Canada, married, having previously executed before Seguin and his confrere Notaries a contract of Marriage bearing date 8 March 1822 at Terrebonne in the District of Montreal." A seventh child was born after Thomson's death in 1828 causing the estate to be divided into eight equal shares.[26]

In 1812, the same year that David Thompson married Charlotte Small, John McDonald of Garth brought her sister, Nancy (seemingly misnamed Catharine in the register), and two children to the St. Gabriel Street minister for baptism; an older daughter had been baptized in 1810. Their familial ties also were lifelong. Possibly McDonald's attachment to Nancy was reinforced by the fact that his mother was a relative of her father, Patrick Small, through family connections going some distance back in Britain.[27]

The final mother named in the register is most notable for her description; nothing more is known of her or her son. Whether by disguise or by some arrangement, she became the only woman known to have served as an employee of the North West Company. Her son's entry, dated 13 December 1818, reads, "Charles Grant, Esqr., North West Company, and Lizette or Elizabeth Landry, an Engage formerly in the service of the North West Company had a son born at Athabaska, about five years ago." Neither parent signed the register; the boy was presented by two members of other families active in the fur business.

Slightly more often than not, twenty-eight instances of a possible fifty-four, the fathers of children baptized were not present at the ceremony (two fathers were deceased). Absences of fathers, like non-naming of mothers, held varying significance. Some fathers were able to coordinate their Montreal leaves from the Indian country with their children's journeys east; others could not manage to do so and entrusted to eastern relatives or friends the baptisms and perhaps also the care and schooling of their offspring.

Children experienced some shocks, cultural, psychic, and even physiological, as at an average age of six[28] they left one or both parents and the informal, isolated life of the North-west to face uncertain welcome among the strangers who were their father's city kinsmen and friends. The strain of the transition told on some. Eight of the seventy-five children surveyed here died within a few days to a few years after their baptisms. Another five native-born children were buried from the church without having been baptized there.

The St. Gabriel Street Church baptismal entries yield other information about familial relations among the North Westers. The father's surname was invariably conferred, affirming paternity in cases in which traders might have ignored or denied it. North Westers baptizing their children thus made explicit an immediate personal commitment whatever their subsequent actions.

The North Westers' children presented for baptism were, however, a selected group. Two-thirds of the St. Gabriel's fur trade children (fifty-one of seventy-five) were boys. Given the costs involved, North Westers usually sent east sons who could be educated and carry on their father's name in some suitable occupation, usually assumed to be the fur trade. Daughters more often remained in the fur trade country, marrying Indians, traders, or native-born sons of traders, often at early ages. Some found homes in the *métis* communities around and beyond the Great Lakes. But a North West Company ruling of 1806, one of few dealing with social and moral matters, suggests that a high proportion of traders' daughters remained around the posts and required some consideration; it dictated that North Westers henceforth were to choose their fur trade mates only from among the daughters of white men.[29]

Not much is known about the life histories of most of the North Westers' children baptized on St. Gabriel Street. Some, such as Alexander William McKay (b. 1802) and Benjamin McKenzie (b. 1805), matured to take company positions. But there was little prospect of advancement for "half-breeds" once the North West and Hudson's Bay Companies merged in 1821 and the labour retrenchments of the 1820s and 1830s set in. Cuthbert Grant (b. 1793), being found politically useful in Red River Settlement, was better rewarded than some.[30]

The case of George, son of Duncan McDougall, reveals persisting childhood ties with a father, although the son's later life is obscure. During 1803–06, Duncan McDougall and a party of North Westers were established on James Bay to compete with the Hudson's Bay Company. They were assisted by one Jack

Hester, "Indian," probably a son or grandson of HBC officer James Hester who had retired from Albany in 1767. Jack's sister or daughter, Nancy, became McDougall's companion during that time. A few years after McDougall had left the area, George Gladman, officer at Eastmain, baptized George and Anne, children of "Duncan McDougall and Nancy Hester"; presumably they and their mother were dependents of that post.

The father, in this period, left the North West Company, joined the Pacific Fur Company in 1810, helped to found Fort Astoria on the Columbia River in 1811, and rejoined the North West Company when it took over Astoria in 1813. He was known particularly for contracting a temporary but helpful fur trade alliance with the daughter of the Chinook chief Concomly, who acquired in exchange for "this precious lady" fifteen guns and fifteen blankets, "besides a great deal of other property." Yet his Hudson Bay children, or at least the son, were not completely forgotten. George, aged eight, was brought to Montreal by an unknown party by the fall of 1812 and baptized there on 26 October, with Alexander McDougall and Mary Anne McDougall as sponsors. Doubtless he remained with his Montreal relatives while his father (who died in the Northwest in 1818) continued in the company. His sister Anne evidently stayed with her maternal relatives around Eastmain.[31]

This evidence sustains some general observations about the children of the British North Westers. Montreal or Scottish and company attachments loomed large in their fathers' lives, and allegiances to native wives and children could be correspondingly weak. Alternatively, fathers might draw on their kinsmen and friends in the fur business to care for those children, usually sons, whom they particularly favoured but with whom they were unable to remain. This pattern is traceable both in eastern Canadian records and in the fur trade country, for example, when Daniel W. Harmon became temporary tutor to the son of Archibald Norman McLeod and an Indian woman in 1801.[32]

Daughters were more likely to remain with their maternal relatives in the Indian country. There they raised families of mixed ancestry, some of whom came to assert the importance of their maternal heritage and later expressed pride in their Indian ancestry by supporting Louis Riel's *nation métisse*. Those women who separated from their trader fathers or husbands and rejoined subarctic Indian societies may have found themselves especially in harmony with and may also have reinforced the "matri-organizational" emphasis of some of these societies.[33]

Most British North Westers did not form permanent nuclear families with their native mates; decisions to retire, to go on leave, or to change location severed bonds with some or all of their children and with their children's mothers. Such familial ties and responsibilities were individual affairs, individually interpreted. Although some social pressures existed to maintain country wives, to look after native families, or to place them in another's care, these were private matters in which the company hardly interfered, except for the regulation of 1806. If the North Westers had not merged with the Hudson's Bay Company in 1821, they probably would have begun to provide more regularized care and formal education for their native children; in 1820 partners and clerks in both the Indian country and Canada were said to have subscribed "several thousand dollars toward the establishment of a school, either at the Rainy Lake, or at Fort William, for the instruction of the children, connected with their establishments."[34] But this plan emerged relatively late, more than a decade after similar projects had been advanced for the native children of Hudson's Bay. Hudson's Bay children were not necessarily possessed of more supportive fathers than their North West counterparts. But their formative social and company context was different.

To compare the Hudson's Bay Company posts and personnel with those of the Montreal fur trade is a little like comparing greenhouse vegetation with what develops in the garden outside it. Both were subject to regulation and supervision—but to very different degrees and in different ways. The Hudson's Bay Company was founded by a royal charter that granted power and ownership to a London-based committee of shareholders or "Adventurers" who typically never travelled to Hudson Bay. Their concerns were to maintain their monopoly against French interlopers, to control their employees, and to establish cordial diplomatic ties with Indian groups who were expected, unrealistically, to share European understandings about such formalities. The posts on the Bay were fortified residential enclaves organized in accord with military and rather monastic ideals. Disciplined, celibate men, serving the company for years at a time, were to conduct its business in orderly fashion and protect its interests, by force if needed.

This rational model for behaviour proved unrealistic. HBC traders were not skilled or successful as military men or builders of fortifications. The occasional French attacks on their posts were usually successful. Still more problematic was the company effort to maintain discipline and chastity among its men. The distance between London and the Bay was great, and the periods of isolation endured by the Bayside employees were long. Most early recruits were bachelors, many being young apprentices who signed for seven-year terms. Older men who had families were after one unsuccessful experiment in 1683, forbidden to bring them to the Bay. Having few social ties at home and scant opportunity to reinforce those that they had, the lives of Bay men, which initially centred on their posts and colleagues, later came to include Indians as trading partners, familiar acquaintances, and kin.[35]

Company rules forbade the free admission of Indians, especially women, into the posts, and urged formal circumspection in interactions with them. But the Cree along the Bay, like their earlier counterparts among the French to the south, saw kin ties as a natural basis of friendly trading partnerships. HBC traders were often subject and frequently susceptible to offers of female companionship. The chief officers of the posts, being recognized by the Indians as men of power and privilege, were most frequently approached. Some took advantage of their high standing to claim Indian wives while enforcing the company's rules against women upon sometimes resentful subordinates.

These women were sometimes abused; and in at least one instance, the attack on Henley House in 1755, the Indians vigorously retaliated.[36] But more often HBC traders formed relatively stable familial relationships. Despite the old restrictions, these attachments were less covert after the 1740s and were receiving considerable company attention by the 1790s.

Fathers were concerned for their country wives and children in the event of their own deaths, dismissals, or retirements from the Bay. Unlike its Montreal counterparts, the HBC forbade former employees to remain in the country either as pensioners or free traders who could become burdens or rivals to its own commerce. Nor would it normally allow native dependents a passage in its ships to England. For many decades, then, the families of HBC men were left behind, typically to rejoin their maternal relatives, usually Cree "Home" or "Homeguard" Indians, around the posts. Increasingly, traders provided families with legacies and annuities to be dispensed by the local HBC factors. Distinct mixed-descent communities could not develop freely and maintain themselves as they had around the Great Lakes; children of Hudson's Bay families remained or once again became Indian, though they might bear a former trader's name or visit a post regularly to trade and claim an annuity.

Some men, admitting that their native dependents would face severe adjustment problems in Britain, left their families behind as a matter of practical kindness. Others sought a middle ground, bringing one or two male children to England if the company could be persuaded to grant them passage and returning their wife and perhaps daughters to Indian relatives. Several such daughters, for example those of Matthew Cocking, William Pink, Isaac Batt, and Humphrey Marten, became the country wives of traders. A few sons, after visiting England or receiving some education there, returned to the Bay as company employees. Early classed as English (for example, James Isham's son, Charles), they later became numerous enough to acquire their own label in the books as "natives of Hudson Bay." The families of George Atkinson and William Richards were known in this way.[37]

As the numbers of these mixed-blood offspring grew, the daughters among them matured to found new fur trade alliances whose progeny were tied more closely to company than to Indian life. Neither the company nor its traders wished an ungoverned, dependent, and possibly troublesome mixed-blood population to develop around the posts; nor did many fathers wish their family ties severed. For these dilemmas, diverse solutions arose between 1790 and 1810. Some officers began systematic efforts to train and educate "factory boys," including their own sons, as a "colony of very useful hands" for permanent company service. They pressed for local education of both sons and daughters with some modest success; company schools were founded at several bayside posts in 1807–10. Finally, in Lord Selkirk's colony at Red River, the company provided a place where former employees and their native families might remain together and find new livelihoods in the North-west while still under company monopoly and governance.[38]

The rising aspirations and growing attachment of many HBC men for their families are especially clear in the Moose Factory register of families. Chief officer John Thomas began the register in 1808, following the company request for records of the names and ages of employees' children at the post. Thomas took the duty as a personal opportunity to note far more data about his nine children than the company required to plan its school for Moose. His entries give an unusually full picture of a family that spanned three decades and had become closely interconnected with other James Bay traders and their offspring. Most of the children had not been baptized, but spaces were left for christening dates to be entered, in the event that the rite became available. The Thomas entries are worth quoting as a sample of these early records and their format:

John Thomas Sen[r] declares that he has the following children:

Eleanor Thomas born Old Brunswick House the 22[d] Nov.[r] 1780 Christened the _____ now Married to William Richards of this Factory.

John Thomas born at this Factory 25th Sept.[r] 1784 Christened _____ now resident at Kenogumesee House.

Margaret Thomas born at this Factory 25th Sept.[r] 1784 Christened _____ in England she is now resident.

Elizabeth Thomas born at this Factory July _____ 1785 (relict of the late Richard Story Robins) now married to Jas. Russell of this Factory, Christened the _____.

Charlotte Thomas born June 2[d] 1788 at this Factory Christened the _____ now married to Peter Spence of this Factory.

Charles Thomas born at this Factory 9th Sept.[r] 1793 Baptized in St. Benedicts Church, Fenchurch Street 11th Dec.[r] 1800, his Father John Thomas & Alex[r] Lean [HBC Secretary] Godfathers Mrs. Lean Godmother, now resident at this Factory.

Ann Thomas born at this Factory the 29th Dec.[r] 1795 Christened the _____ now married to Thomas Hodgson of Albany Factor.

Frances Thomas born at this Factory 17th Dec.[r] 1798 Christened the _____.

Henry Thomas born at this Factory 20th June 1807 Christened the 5th July 1807.

Several details of these entries are of interest. The baptism of Charles was sponsored by his father and an important company official in London. The entry for Henry Thomas, and many thereafter, indicates that the traders themselves began to conduct lay baptisms at Moose Factory, clergymen being absent; compare the baptisms of the Hester-McDougall children at Eastmain, noted earlier. Margaret's residence in England, evidently permanent (she was still there when her mother died at Moose in 1813), was unusual for a daughter of the time. The absence of reference to the children's mother is at first glance reminiscent of the North Westers' St. Gabriel Street baptisms. But when Thomas, as a "disconsolate Husband," recorded her death in the register on 31 December 1813, he left no doubt about her name and standing as "Mrs. Margaret Thomas." Similarly, although no clergy were present to sanctify their unions in Christian terms, he described his daughters as married.[39] In this he followed an increasingly visible Hudson's Bay convention that was reflected in the register after 1814; baptismal entries after that year almost invariably named both parents.

Of eighty offspring whose sex was indicated (it is undetermined for two), forty-six were girls and thirty-four were boys, a proportion of 57.5 per cent to 42.5 per cent, which suggests that the selectivity evident in the St. Gabriel Street entries was not operative here. This bias toward girls, not extreme for a sample of this size, may, however, have reflected two factors: the general tendency of more females than males to survive birth, and the possibility that some traders' sons were not mentioned because they had been sent to Britain.

Numbers of the people mentioned between 1808 and 1821 were members of families that had been linked with Moose and other James Bay posts for two or more decades previously—the Thomases, the Richardses (later Rickard?), the Turnors (later Turner), the Moores, the Gills, and Sarah Good, the daughter of eighteenth-century officer Humphrey Marten. Some branches of these families have continued to live in the Moose area until the present day.[40]

Other company families from HBC posts began in the early 1800s to move southwards as families when their husband-fathers retired or were dismissed, rather than face separation or the strain of making new homes in Britain. Some moved to Red River, particularly after 1820 when the settlement seemed safely established. Others, beginning in about 1810, went to eastern Canada, and some traces of them are found in their company rivals' territory—along the Ottawa River and in the Montreal area. When John Hodgson was dismissed for mismanagement of Albany in 1810, he and his family travelled south to Lac des Chats where they took up land and lived for a number of years, quite inelegantly, according to some later Ottawa River travellers who visited them.[41]

In the same year, a company family from farther inland made a similar journey, to settle at Vaudreuil by the mouth of the Ottawa River. Robert Longmoor, who had entered the company as a labourer in 1771, retired "to enjoy the fruits of his labours; he is now worth about £1,800," as a contemporary reported. Thanks to the St. Gabriel Street Church registers in Montreal, we know that about eight family members were with him. On 29 March 1813, Jane Longmoor, aged about twelve, "daughter of Robert Longmoor of Vaudreuil by a woman of the Indian country," was baptized, with Robert and Andrew Longmoor as witnesses. On 11 June 1813, daughters Catharine, aged about twenty-five, and Phoebe, aged about seven, were baptized, as were Catharine's four young children, "born to James Halcro of Vaudreuil farmer (formerly of the Northwest)," with Halcro as witness. Halcro, an Orkneyman, had joined the Hudson's Bay Company in 1789 and served on inland rivers as Longmoor's pilot. By this date, Longmoor had died; Catharine and Phoebe were identified as "daughters of the late Robert Longmoor ... and Sally Pink spinster."

Sally was doubtless the native-born daughter of William Pink, inland explorer from York Fort in the 1760s and 1770s. Now a widow in Hudson's Bay if not in Montreal church terms, she was baptized on 1 July 1813 as Sally Pink, with James Halcro as witness. And on that day, minister James Somerville married Halcro and Catharine Longmoor.[42] Their success as a farming family in Vaudreuil is not known, but their familial ties, stretching back many years in the Hudson's Bay territories, were evidently strongly maintained in their new setting.

Another contingent of Hudson's Bay families, whose names already appear in this text, travelled to Vaudreuil the next year. The Moose Factory journal of 24 June 1814 recorded that John Thomas, who had just resigned his position there, departed that day for Canada, accompanied by his son Charles with wife and child, his daughter Charlotte and her husband (Peter Spence) and their three children, and three other grandchildren, Henry and Richard Thomas and Richard Robins. Three children of Thomas Knight, a surgeon at Eastmain who had died there in 1797, travelled with the party. The beginnings of their new life were evidently shaky; in November, 1815, John Thomas asked the company if he might return to Moose. This request was rejected, but the London committee offered Thomas land at Red River and his sons employment at Moose. Charles Thomas returned north and served the company for some years. But the other Thomases remained at Vaudreuil for at least some time and were joined by more kin. On 23 February 1819, Elizabeth, daughter of John Thomas, was formally married in the St. Gabriel Street Church to "James Russell of Vaudreuil merchant," her husband at Moose Factory since 1808. On the same day, she and her son Richard, "by the late Richard Story Robins of Hudson's Bay," were baptized. On 4 March, Catherine, aged eighteen, daughter of HBC surgeon Thomas Thomas, was baptized with James Russell as witness. Plainly these Hudson's Bay families remained together after leaving their company posts and supported relatives and other HBC offspring in their new environment.[43]

The St. Gabriel Street Church and Moose Factory registers overlap closely in time, and record a similar number of fur trade children from two different contexts—seventy-five from the North Westers' "Indian Country" and eighty-two from Hudson's Bay. These two sources are unique to their respective companies. No document comparable to the Moose Factory register survives from a North West Company post. No Canadian and probably no British church served so conspicuously as a centre for Hudson's Bay men as St. Gabriel Street did for the North Westers (although more records of Hudson's Bay offspring doubtless await discovery in various churches in London and elsewhere). The two registers reveal the differing family and company settings which affected the fur trade children before 1821. Plainly the policies and attitudes of the two companies regarding fur trade dependents differed widely, and fur trader fathers were constrained by different company and home settings as they made decisions about their native offspring.

The North Westers relied in both their occupational and personal lives upon networks linking kinsmen and friends sometimes over broad distances—from

Scotland to Montreal and western Canada. These ties seemed to compete with nuclear family bonds, particularly where native families of unproven legitimacy and doubtful standing were involved. White relatives were unwilling to concede inheritance rights to these families and some North Westers' estates, most notably William Connolly's, were subject to intense court disputes. Connolly made specific testamentary provisions for his mixed-blood children after he set aside his Cree wife of many years to marry a Montreal cousin, but these provisions faced stiff resistance from other claimants.[44] Thus Montreal and Scots networks often posed strong challenges to the position and welfare of fur trade families.

Yet eastern connections also helped traders with their country families. A father seeking to secure the future of particular children, most usually males, might place them with colleagues in eastern Canada. Old mutual ties gave some assurance that these guardians would carry out their duties with care, although some fathers found their confidence misplaced.[45]

From the children's viewpoint, these placements posed graver problems. The children faced a traumatic move away from both parents into a foreign setting where adults' interest might be diffuse and shallow. Certainly some children proved unable to meet their fathers' aspirations. The involvement of some North Westers' sons in a short-lived native independence movement, the Indian Liberating Army on the Great Lakes in 1836, reflected their sense of rootlessness in eastern Canada and their persisting attachment to the Indian country.[46]

Most HBC traders did not have the extensive interlocking social ties of the North Westers. Their legacies to native dependents were not challenged in courts. But their children were not easily brought to Britain for care and education. Even if the company were persuaded to give passage, many traders had no English kin who could take their children. The result was that, especially before Red River was established, many HBC offspring were assimilated by the Indians. As an alternative, their fathers by the late 1700s pressed the company to provide education, training, and employment for their children at the main posts, allowing the formation of distinct company communities.

When such families ended their post life—when a husband-father retired or was dismissed—they increasingly relocated as families, as did the Hodgsons on the Ottawa River, the Longmoors and Thomases at Vaudreuil, and others at later dates at Red River. The persistence of these Hudson's Bay Company families as integral units, even in eastern Canada (a persistence mirrored also in the family of former HBC man David Thompson), reflects the distinctiveness of their company origins and suggests that their familial attitudes, priorities, and decision-making patterns differed in important ways from the North Westers' more open, diffuse, and far-reaching kin relationships.

The 1820s brought drastic changes to the lives of fur traders' offspring in the North-west—the Great Lakes *métis*, the "half-breed" descendants of the British North Westers, and the "Indian" or "Hudson's Bay native" offspring of the Hudson's Bay Company. Around the southern and western Great Lakes,

American government and courts sought to organize and civilize the mixed communities whose antecedents lay in the old French fur trade. In a one-week court session in 1824 in La Baye (Green Bay), Michigan Territory (now Wisconsin), a newly-arrived judge declared that the long-standing customary marriages of most of that community's principal inhabitants were invalid. To avoid penalties, most couples agreed to be (re)married by a Justice of the Peace, although a few defended the *de facto* legitimacy of their unions as being based on "the customs of the Indians."[47] The incident was a token of impending developments—the incursions of officialdom, new legal standards, and settlers and missionaries who would overshadow and eventually submerge the small *métis* fur trade settlements they encountered.

To the north, parallel developments modified the old ways of traders and their families. The Hudson's Bay and North West Companies merged in 1821, bringing a unified governance and control to the North-west. The first Anglican and Roman Catholic clergy reached Red River by 1820 and attempted to enforce Christian marriage as a necessary rite to legitimize customary alliances and their progeny. Traders found themselves obliged to make conscious decisions about their commitments. Some yielded to clerical pressure and married in church. A few, like the die-hards of Green Bay, asserted that local custom, long-term co-residence, and mutual affection had already validated their marriages and that the Christian ritual was superfluous. And some, notably former North Westers, saw in clerical non-recognition of customary marriages an excuse not to recognize their own. Leaving behind old country entanglements, they found white brides in their home social circles, following the example of their new company Governor, George Simpson, whose fur trade liaisons were not permitted to interfere with his marriage to his cousin Frances in 1830.[48]

These developments, along with post-merger reductions in fur trade employment opportunities, meant that fathers, more than before, had to assume an active role if their children's futures were to be secured. Many men took their children from the growing social and economic strains of the fur trade country to secure them gentlemanly eastern livelihoods. As means of communication and transport improved, more Hudson's Bay and old North West Company families found new homes in eastern Canada or Britain, hoping to ease their offspring into white society, toward what one father aptly called "ultimate respectability."[49]

Many fur trade children had more difficulty finding work and a secure identity. Few could find success within the new monopoly, and the prejudices of Governor Simpson against "half-breeds," particularly evident in his personnel records of the early 1830s, dimmed the prospects of those sons who did maintain company positions. The political agitations that surfaced among some fur trade sons in the Guillaume Sayer free-trade trial of 1849 and again in the Louis Riel risings of 1869 and 1885 were understandable responses to hardships imposed by economic monopoly and lack of opportunity. They were also reactions to the incursions of new governmental structures and controls and new settlers into a country the *métis* viewed as their inheritance through both their fathers and their mothers.

These movements came mainly from native sons of North West Company origin who developed a distinctive sense of identity in Red River and beyond—in lands which most of their fathers had been quite willing to leave behind when they retired. Old Hudson's Bay families, in contrast, seemed more content to settle together in Red River and, later, in other western communities where their descendants retained identities as members of company families or "Rupertslanders" and showed little affinity for *métis* causes.[50]

Farther east, in the original heartland of the Hudson's Bay Company territories, the term *métis* as an ethnic category appeared relatively late. Many company descendants of mixed ancestry continued living as Indians through the nineteenth century and into the twentieth and were officially classed as Indian, for example by the Treaty No. 9 commissioners who visited James Bay in 1905. But that year several families at Moose Factory "were refused treaty by the Commissioners on the grounds that they were not living the Indian mode of life," and some, describing themselves as half-breeds, petitioned the government of Ontario for attention, noting that "scrip has been granted to the Halfbreeds of the North West Territory." The Ontario government, however, had no provisions for issuing scrip to half-breeds; and a government proposal to issue 160-acre land patents instead was never acted upon.[51] Some descendants of the people thus left in limbo, without distinctive rights or recognition, have in recent years become active in local *métis* associations or in the Ontario *Métis* and Non-Status Indian Association.

Choices of career paths and ethnic identities remain problematic for many descendants of the fur trade who still reside in the North-west. Their distinctive fur trade contexts—French, British North Wester, and Hudson's Bay—have been blurred by a century and a half of radical social, economic, and government pressures that have changed and challenged older ways of life. Current generations seek to reconcile their distinctive pasts with the overbearing demands of the present. At the same time, numerous descendants of families who early left the fur trade are reclaiming that portion of their heritage, discovering the ways that their own family histories and Canadian history have intersected in the last two to four centuries.

Notes

1. Fur trade social historians are often reminded that identity-building is a dynamic process continued from generation to generation, as they try to answer the genealogical queries of traders' descendants pursuing and rediscovering their origins. Some descendants have themselves contributed actively to fur trade scholarship—for example, Elaine Allan Mitchell, *Fort Timiskaming and the Fur Trade* (Toronto: University of Toronto Press, 1977); Jean Murray Cole, *Exile in the Wilderness: The Life of Chief Factor Archibald McDonald, 1790–1853,* (Seattle: University of Washington Press, 1979).

2. For a detailed discussion of these differences and their implications, see Jennifer S.H. Brown, *Strangers in Blood: Fur Trade Company Families in Indian Country* (Vancouver: University of British Columbia Press, 1980), Chapters 1 and 2.

3. On demographic patterns in early New France, see Marcel Trudel, *The Beginnings of New France, 1524–1663* (Toronto: McClelland and Stewart, 1973), 260–61.

4. Bruce Trigger, *The Children of Aataentsic: A History of the Huron People to 1660* (Montreal: McGill-Queen's University Press, 1976), vol. 1, 365, 49–50.

5. *Ibid.*, 40–41, 45.

6. *Ibid.*, 47, 263; vol. 2, 762.

7. W.J. Eccles, *The Canadian Frontier 1534–1760* (New York: Holt, Rinehart and Winston, 1969), 90, quoting the Marquis de Denonville (1685) and Intendant Jean Bochart de Champigny (1691).

8. *Ibid.*, 109–10, 90–91; Jacqueline Peterson, "Prelude to Red River: A Social Portrait of the Great Lakes *Métis*," *Ethnohistory*, 25, 1 (1978), 47–48.

9. Eccles, *The Canadian Frontier*, 91, 199, n. 11.

10. Reuben G. Thwaites (ed.), *Collections of the State Historical Society of Wisconsin*, vol. 18, 1908 (Mackinac Register of Marriages—1725–1821); vol. 19, 1910 (Mackinac Register of Baptisms and Interments—1695–1821).

11. On later fur trade demography, with special reference to the higher ranks of traders, see Jennifer S.H. Brown, "A Demographic Transition in the Fur Trade Country: Family Sizes and Fertility of Company Officers and Country Wives, ca. 1751–1850," *Western Canadian Journal of Anthropology*, 6, 1 (1976), 61–71. On birth rates in New France, see Jacques Henripin, *La population canadienne au debut du XVIIIe Siècle: Nuptialité, Fécondité, Mortalité infantile* (Paris: Presses Universitaires de France, 1954). In 1828, Major Anderson, Indian agent, "computed the number of Canadians and mixed breed married to Indian women, and residing on the north shores of Lake Huron, and in the neighbourhood of Michilimackinac, at nine hundred. This he called the *lowest* estimate." Anna Jameson, *Winter Studies and Summer Rambles in Canada* (New York, 1839), vol. 2, 141n.

12. Peterson, "Prelude to Red River," 55.

13. *Ibid.*, 57–58.

14. For extensive biographical data on the British North Westers, see the appendix to W.S. Wallace (ed.), *Documents relating to the North West Company* (Toronto: Champlain Society, vol. 22, 1934).

15. See Marjorie Wilkins Campbell, *The North West Company* (New York: St. Martin's Press, 1957).

16. Brown, *Strangers in Blood*, 40.

17. Wallace, *Documents*, 134–43.

18. Thwaites (ed.), *Collections of the Wisconsin State Historical Society*, vol. 18, xiii. The founding of Red River Colony brought both Roman Catholic and Anglican clergy into that area by 1821.

19. Brown, *Strangers in Blood*, 100–7.

20. Johnstone *et al.* v. Connolly, Court of Appeal, 7 September 1869, *La Revue legale*, 1, p. 287.

21. For some examples, see Brown, *Strangers in Blood*, 171–72.

22. St. Gabriel Street Presbyterian Church registers, 1796–1821, Provincial Archives of Ontario, Toronto, microfilm.

23. M. Elizabeth Arthur, "Angelique and her Children," *Thunder Bay Historical Museum Society Papers and Records*, 6 (1978), 30–40.

24. Mitchell, *Fort Timiskaming and the Fur Trade*, 38, 62.

25. James K. Smith, *David Thompson, Fur Trader, Explorer, Geographer* (Toronto: Oxford University Press, 1971), 105–6.

26. Hudson's Bay Company Archives (hereafter HBCA), A. 36/13, fo. 192.

27. Brown, *Strangers in Blood*, 98–99.

28. Baptismal ages ranged from under one year to thirteen for the seventy-one children whose ages were given.

29. Wallace, *Documents*, 211.

30. Glyndwr Williams (ed.), *Hudson's Bay Miscellany 1670–1870* (Winnipeg: Hudson's Bay Record Society, 1975), 219 (McKay), 233 (McKenzie), 209–11 (Grant).

31. K.G. Davies (ed.), *Northern Quebec and Labrador Journals and Correspondence 1819–35* (London: Hudson's Bay Record Society, 1963), 263–64, 281. HBCA, A. 1/43, fo. 156, on James Hester. HBCA, B. 59/Z/1, fo. 92, baptisms of George and Anne McDougall. Elliott Coues, *New Light on the History of the Greater Northwest. The Manuscript Journal of Alexander Henry ... and of David Thompson* (New York, 1897), vol. 2, 901. The diary of George Nelson from Tete au Brochet in 1818–19 (Provincial Archives of Ontario) for 16 December 1818 records that McDougall's death occurred at Fort Alexander on 25 October 1818.

32. W. Kaye Lamb, *Sixteen Years in the Indian Country, the Journal of Daniel Williams Harmon 1800–1816* (Toronto: Macmillan, 1957), 50.

33. Charles A. Bishop and Shepard Krech III, "Matriorganization: The Basis of Aboriginal Social Organization," *Arctic Anthropology*, 17, 2 (1980).

34. Lamb, *Sixteen Years in the Indian Country*, 6 (Rev. Daniel Haskel's preface to Harmon's edited journal).

35. Brown, *Strangers in Blood*, 6–22, discusses the social organization of the early Hudson's Bay Company.

36. Charles A. Bishop, "The Henley House Massacres," *The Beaver* (Autumn, 1976), 36–41.

37. *Dictionary of Canadian Biography* (Toronto: University of Toronto Press, vols. 4 [1981] and 5 [forthcoming]) contains biographical information on most of the families named. On William Pink's daughter, see the discussion of the Longmoor family later in this text.

38. Brown, *Strangers in Blood* , 162–69.

39. Moose Factory register of baptisms, marriages, and burials, Provincial Archives of Ontario, microfilm.

40. Data from cemetery records and Moose Factory residents, 1980.

41. For example, the accounts of Colin Robertson in E.E. Rich (ed.), *Colin Robertson's Letters, 1817–1822* (Toronto: Champlain Society for the Hudson's Bay Record Society, 1939), 52, 220.

42. See Coues, *New Light*, vol. 2, 599, for Alexander Henry the Younger's description of Longmoor. On James Halcro, see Alice M. Johnson (ed.), *Saskatchewan Journals and Correspondence 1795–1802* (London: Hudson's Bay Record Society, 1967), xlvii, n; 189. On William Pink, see E.E. Rich, *History of the Hudson's Bay Company 1670–1870* (New York: Macmillan, 1961), vol. 2, 17, 19, 22, 32.

43. E.E. Rich and A.M. Johnson (eds.), *Moose Fort Journals, 1783–1785* (London: Hudson's Bay Record Society, 1954), 370; St. Gabriel Street Church registers.

44. The court case of William Connolly and that of his colleague, Alexander Fraser, are discussed in some detail in Brown, *Strangers in Blood*, 90–95.

45. For examples, see letters of John McDonald le Borgne and Donald McIntosh quoted in *ibid.*, 180–82.

46. *Ibid.*, 190–92.

47. Peterson, "Prelude to Red River," 41–42.

48. Sylvia Van Kirk, "Women and the Fur Trade," *The Beaver* (Winter, 1972), 11–21.

49. Brown, *Strangers in Blood*, 181.

50. *Ibid.*, 218–19.

51. John S. Long, *Treaty No. 9: The Half-Breed Question, 1902–1910* (Cobalt, Ont.: Highway Book Shop, 1978), 7–8.

WAGE LABOUR, INDUSTRIALIZATION, AND THE ORIGINS OF THE MODERN FAMILY

Chad Gaffield

Canada's industrial revolution had a dramatic impact on the character and structure of the family. Urbanization and the replacement of handicraft production by machine production in factories altered considerably the family's position in society. In the preindustrial setting, the Canadian economy was in many ways the sum of family economies in which men, women, and children all played productive roles. With industrialization, Canada's economy became increasingly a collection of factories and agricultural businesses staffed by men whose wives were at home and whose children were at school. This development represented a profound reorganization of society affecting both private experience and public policy. The industrial revolution contributed to new ide-

From *The Family: Changing Trends in Canada*, (Toronto: McGraw-Hill Ryerson, 1984), 21–33. Reprinted by permission.

als, new legislation, and new institutions, all of which related to the place of the family in society.

This chapter examines the relationship between industrialization and the history of the family, especially during the nineteenth century. The basis of this examination is recent research which has substantially revised many accepted views about the extent to which modern families differ from those of the preindustrial period. For example, contemporary discussion often assumes that families have traditionally been stable units, pillars in a society otherwise undergoing constant transformation. In this view, the family has been until recently an important element of continuity within larger social changes. Similarly, observers usually juxtapose the wide variety of contemporary family patterns with an historical image of a single family form. Current diversity in marriage forms, child-bearing decisions, and living arrangements is judged with reference to an imagined time of conformity and standard behaviour. In both myths contemporary families are seen as radically different from those of former times, and critics often interpret this difference as evidence of unprecedented crisis.

Such assumptions about the history of the family are accurate to a certain degree. However, recent research indicates that images of stability and conformity cannot be fully applied to Canadian families of the past, especially during the period of industrialization. This research has shown that current instability and diversity in family patterns are not simply modern phenomena and that the suggestion of crisis in the family has a long tradition which was particularly important in the nineteenth century. Similarly, families have historically been nuclear, fragmented, or single parent in various times and places. The implications of these findings extend to the major themes of Canada's social, economic, and intellectual history, and they suggest quite different ways of assessing the family patterns of contemporary society (Anderson, 1980; Soliday, 1980; Light and Strong-Boag, 1980; Parr, 1982; Larose, 1977 to present).

The following discussion begins with a description of the ways in which changes in modes of production affected the economic position of men, women, and children. The changing productive roles of family members provide the key to examination of the structural alterations and new ideals for the family which characterized the late nineteenth century. In turn, the new ideals and structure of the family were related to a social reorganization most dramatically represented by the expansion of formal education. Taken together, these developments are central themes in the history of the modern family.

From Domestic to Factory Production

The process of industrialization is often described as a revolution, since an urban industrial society differs so markedly from a rural preindustrial community. However, the term revolution implies a sudden event and, in this sense, it is misleading, since industrialization occurred over many decades and involved several transitional stages. In the same way, the impact of industrialization on the family cannot be understood in "before and after" terms; rather, family alterations paralleled each stage of the transition to urban industrial society. An appreciation of the complexity of these developments is the first step toward understanding the origins of the modern family.

In the *preindustrial economy*, which predominated in Canada until the nineteenth century, almost all productive activity took place in individual households. Homes were both places of residence and places of work. Production was very small scale and exceedingly labour intensive. The vast majority of the population lived on farms and engaged in some-combination of agriculture, fishing, lumbering, and the fur trade, according to the seasons of the year and the region in which they lived. In addition, these settlers had to produce their own clothing, and thus, most households included a spinning wheel and a loom. Cities such as Montreal and Quebec were primarily commercial and administrative centres, although they did include craftsmen such as blacksmiths and coopers. These craftsmen set up shops in their own households and worked by hand with very basic tools to produce their goods. The preindustrial economy was, therefore, relatively small scale, labour intensive, and domestically focused (Dechêne, 1974).

The first stage of industrialization is termed the *manufactory stage*, in which handicraft production still predominated but manufactories increasingly brought together various craftsmen into one operation. Carriage-makers joined wheelwrights, blacksmiths, carpenters, and other skilled workers. At the same time, these new establishments also increased the trend toward specialization. Shoemaking, for example, now involved cutters, fitters, and other more specialized occupations (Kealey, 1980). In certain economic sectors, this division of labour also involved *proto-industrialization*, in which traditional domestic work patterns combined with new forms of labour in manufactories. In the proto-industrial system, domestic activity was responsible for part rather than all of the production process. In the case of textiles, for example, households began producing cloth for sale to dressmakers and yarn for sale to weavers. As a result, households became less self-reliant and more integrated into an emerging cash economy. The overall scale of production increased, although the manufactories were still small operations. This system thus reflected the past and anticipated the future of the production process. Domestic activity continued to be important but production outside the home was increasingly significant (Medick, 1976).

The emergence of manufactories and proto-industrial activity affected only a minority of the Canadian population for most of the nineteenth century. A large export market and the availability of land, especially in the territory which became Ontario, encouraged settlers to concentrate on agriculture and lumbering. Gristmills and sawmills were established on waterways throughout the countryside, especially during the 1830s and 1840s. One crucial change, however, was the spread of wage labour which accompanied the expansion of wheat and lumber production. Shantymen and millhands worked in the lumber industry, agricultural labourers toiled for established landowners, and navvies built the canals and railroads which facilitated commercial activity. These workers were often young men who hoped to accumulate enough capital to settle on a farm of their own. However, restrictive land policies, the activity of speculators, and the irregular nature of employment worked against fulfillment of this aspiration. As time passed, wage labour became a way of life for an increasing proportion of the population. The shift from farmers and craftsmen in the preindustrial economy to propertyless wage labourers in the emerging industrial economy is termed *proletarianization*. This process combined with the spread of manufactories and, to a lesser extent, with proto-industrialization to provide the context for rapid urban and industrial growth (Gagan, 1981).

The proliferation of machines and steam engines during the 1850s and 1860s heralded the beginning of a full *industrial economy* in Canada. The introduction of sewing machines in the early 1850s transformed the shoe industry, while hydraulic presses allowed the Canadian tobacco industry to prosper during the Civil War in the United States. Such industrial growth was certainly not reflected in all types of production, but the trend toward mechanization is evident in the rapid growth of large factories. In Hamilton, Ontario, for example, in 1851, only 24 percent of the labour force worked in establishments employing ten or more individuals. Just twenty years later, a full 83 percent of all employees in Hamilton worked in such establishments.

Moreover, just over one-half of workers in manufacturing held positions in firms with fifty or more employees. Hamilton's industrial development at this time was unusual for Canadian cities, but the pattern was certainly not unique. In Toronto, slightly more than two-thirds of the city's factory workers in 1871 were employed in establishments with thirty or more workers (Katz, 1975; Kealey, 1980).

Mechanization and the centralization of production affected various economic sectors at different times and in different ways. The general transition from production at home to workshops and factories was uneven, with some industries continuing to rely on household activity even as machines were proliferating. In the clothing trade, for example, work in factories and work at home expanded together during the nineteenth century, with each activity representing a different phase of the production process. Factory machines made and cut cloth from which women and older daughters then made garments in their own households as employees of the clothier. This example illustrates that the impact of industrialization on the production process was not always abrupt or complete but rather took place gradually over many decades (Bradbury, 1979).

The transition from preindustrial to industrial modes of production redefined the economic role of the family. In the preindustrial economy, families operated as economic units in which individual members performed tasks associated with age and gender. Women and children were active producers within family economies, and material security could only be achieved through collective labour. The contributions of all able-bodied family members were necessary in the labour-intensive rural economy of the time. As a result, the European traditions of apprenticeship for boys and work as domestic servants for girls were not fully maintained in Canada, where economic opportunity meant that children could often be most useful to parents by working at home. From an early age, children would be integrated into productive activity by learning to help with land clearing, seeding, and domestic work such as spinning. Similarly, women were responsible for cooking, making clothes, and farm work such as vegetable gardening. The preindustrial setting was composed, therefore, of *family economies* in which family members laboured in the context of household production (Gaffield, 1979; Gagan, 1981).

The manufactory stage signalled the beginning of the separation of production from the household. The growth of manufactories, an increased division of labour, and the trend toward centralized production made household production an increasingly supplementary aspect of the economy. Moreover, these developments encouraged the spread of wage labour, which was already occurring during the 1830s and 1840s in activities such as lumbering and canal building. Employment outside the home redefined the extent to which productive activity characterized family life, and consequently, this alteration transformed family economies into *family wage economies*. Centralized production and wage labour meant that certain families began pooling the wages rather than the actual labour of various family members. The key to material security for families in this new situation involved employment outside the home for as many family members as possible, especially older children. A single wage was rarely sufficient to provide for a family, and the general irregularity of employment maintained the traditional interdependency of family members. Therefore, families continued to be economic units, although the appearance of the family wage economy represented an important departure from the traditional character of family activity and organization (Tilly and Scott, 1978).

The replacement of collective household labour by individual wage earning did not always have a simple or immediate effect on the family. In the early phases of industrialization, there was a considerable number of job opportunities for youth, especially teenage boys, and in certain cases family members continued to work together through collective employment in mills and factories. In fact, some employers advertised to attract families, recognizing both the profitability of cheap child labour and the value of having parents to supervise young workers. Employers would sometimes provide dwellings for families working at their establishments. The quality of such accommodation was generally very poor, but the provision of dwellings did reflect the fact that the family could still function as an economic unit despite the new modes of production (Bradbury, 1979; Katz, Doucet, and Stern, 1982; Gaffield, 1982).

Recent studies have also found that while many families needed more than one income, they also wanted to maintain contact among family members. The employment of children was consistent with the tradition of families working together, and thus parents did not hesitate to seek work for their children. Established workers pressured employers to hire younger family members, sometimes by threatening to quit if additional employment was not provided. Of course, such threats were only effective in times of severe labour shortages, but the attempt of family members to work together shows that the traditional concept of collective family labour still operated during the process of industrialization (Kealey, 1973; Harvey, 1979).

The emergence of a wage-labour economy and the growth of manufactories are often described as the beginning of the separation of home and work. However, this description implies significant narrowing of the definition of work to mean wage labour only. In earlier times the contributions of all family members were considered work, and cooking and cleaning were recognized to be an important part of the family economy. However, the wage-labour economy expropriated the concept of work for paid employment. Thus the "separation of home and work" must be understood to mean the "separation of home and place of wage labour."

While early industrial expansion included employment for women and older children, the number of job opportunities for these family members did not match the number of available workers, and, in fact, these opportunities decreased rapidly over time. In Toronto, for example, the 1880s were a decisive decade in the dislocation of young teenagers from the labour force. Industrialization in the boot and shoe, printing, and tobacco sectors encouraged a sharp decline in the proportion of workers who were under the age of sixteen; this proportion fell from 11 percent in 1881 to 5 percent in 1891 (Kealey, 1980). Economic change especially transformed the position of young women, for whom there were fewer and fewer employment opportunities in cities and no jobs which paid a wage sufficient for material independence. Women continued to gain positions as factory workers or elementary school teachers in the nineteenth century and as nurses and secretaries in later decades. But married women were often excluded from these jobs, and their wages were substantially less than those offered to their male counterparts. In the late nineteenth century, a female teacher received about one-half of the average salary of a male teacher (Acton, Goldsmith, and Shepard, 1974; Danylewycz, Light, and Prentice, 1983). In this context, the economic role of women within families became increasingly confined to domestic chores that were not considered "productive" in the new sense of the word. This new definition of work trivialized both implicitly and explicitly the important activity which continued in the home and which made possible employment outside the home. Moreover, the value judgments which distinguished between home and work must be recognized as contributing factors in the development of contemporary attitudes toward domestic activity.

In stylized terms, the separation of productive activity from the home and the economic dislocation of women and children changed the family from a unit of production to a unit of consumption. In the new *family consumer economy*, family life involved decisions and activity related to the purchase and use of goods produced in specialized workplaces. The roles of various family members became much more sharply differentiated, with men as producers, women as homemakers, and children as dependents. This differentiation became increasingly evident among Canadian families as higher wages in the late nineteenth and early twentieth centuries made single-income families a viable possibility. In this way, the family consumer economy became characteristic of urban, industrial society in Canada. The implications of this development extended beyond economic changes to include important changes in the size and structure of families. An examination of these changes provides the next link in understanding the historical development of the modern family.

Family Structure and Kinship

Recent studies have re-examined the ways in which the changing economic role of the family altered the size and structure of households. The traditional version of the transition describes a radical shift during the period of industrialization from large extended households to small nuclear units. This shift is said to involve not only a decline in fertility but also a decrease in kinship attachment beyond parents and children. However, research in different settings suggests that this traditional interpretation of the impact of industrialization needs to be reconsidered, both with respect to structural changes in the family and the importance of kinship.

Throughout Canada the size of families steadily declined after the mid-nineteenth century. Until this time a marriage was soon followed by the birth of the first child, and children continued to be born every two or three years, with the gap between each birth increasing as the parents aged. By the mid-1800s, however, this natural fertility began to be inhibited by the attempt to limit further pregnancies after a certain family size was achieved. The trend continued to grow in the late nineteenth and early twentieth centuries before reaching a plateau at the modern average of about two children per family (Henripin, 1968; McLaren, 1971; Gagan, 1981; Katz, Doucet, and Stern, 1982). Many factors contributed to this development, including the production of better contraceptives and, more significantly, the gradual redefinition of children as consumers rather than producers. This redefinition first became apparent in more privileged families who were not dependent on their children's labour. Their fertility rates decreased more quickly than did those of rural and urban working-class families. Over time, however, the increasing dislocation of children from productive activity, both in agricultural settings and in the urban working class, encouraged these parents to similarly limit family size in order to minimize expenses. A study of the 1931 census showed that the families of wage-earners had, in fact, become on average considerably smaller than those of employers or those who were self-employed. The authors of this study suggested that "limitation in family size for many people is the only alternative to poverty and misery" (Pelletier, Thompson, and Rochon, 1938:19). Thus, the dominant trend has been toward smaller and smaller families throughout the social structure.

Declining family size did not mean, however, that families became isolated nuclear units. Families continued to function within kinship networks throughout the transition from the family economy to the family wage economy and to the family consumer economy. The continuing importance of kinship is related to the fact that the stability of families has never been absolute at any point in the past. While contemporary instability due to the high incidence of separation and divorce is unprecedented, families have always faced uncertainty, especially with respect to health and material welfare. In the past, traditionally high rates of mortality meant that the disruption of marriage by the death of a spouse was not uncommon. Partial evidence from France and England in the seventeenth and eighteenth centuries suggests that about one-third of all children younger than age fourteen had lost one or both of their parents. One study in England indicates that one out of every five children was an orphan during these centuries (Tilly and Scott, 1978:28–29). While mortality rates declined in the New World as a result of better nutrition and lower population density, the stability of family units was constantly undermined by warfare and natural disasters. The important productive roles of both men and women made remarriage both common and necessary in preindustrial Canadian society, but new unions could only follow an inevitable period of family disruption. Thus, the history of orphans and single-parent families in Canada begins at the time of first settlement and not in recent years (Dechêne, 1974:107–09; Charbonneau, 1975:183–88).

Wage labour and industrialization ensured that families would face even more serious challenges to their stability, and they relied on kin to help in the search for employment and housing and to support them in times of need. Kin could be instrumental in securing employment for relatives at the same mill or factory where a family member already worked. Relatives could facilitate the migration of a family to a new area by providing temporary accommodation or information about available dwellings. The insecurity of employment and the need of many families for more than one income meant that kinship networks also represented a welfare system in which the hardships of certain families might be somewhat balanced by the relative well-being of others. This type of support was especially crucial in industrializing cities, where there was little formal assistance in the struggle to survive (Hareven and Langenbach, 1978).

The growing cities developed major sanitary problems, urban housing was very inadequate, and the new workplaces had inadequate ventilation and dangerous machinery. Illness, accidents, irregular employment, and low wages placed families in precarious positions if kin were unable to lend support. Even two-parent families were sometimes unable to care for their children. In nineteenth century Montreal, for example, some working-class parents dealt with family crises by temporarily placing their children in orphanages, where they could at least have some food and shelter. When and if the situation of the parents improved, the children would be brought home again, perhaps to contribute to the family's survival by seeking employment themselves (Bradbury, 1982; Snell, 1983).

In the modern industrial economy, the responsibility of the family for the material welfare of its members declined with the professionalization of health care and the slow emergence of state aid for those in need. The traditional pattern of home births, home remedies, and informal kinship support systems has been replaced to a great extent by hospitals, clinics, and publicly funded welfare offices. The general direction of the twentieth century has been toward the building of public institutions to support individual existence (Strong-Boag, 1979; Struthers, 1983). Nonetheless, these institutions do not fully respond to individual needs, and families have maintained an important support role for family members as well as for kin. The process of industrialization may have encouraged some sense of individualism, but family and kin still provide an important framework for personal welfare.

The increased instability of the family during the urban growth and industrial development of the mid-nineteenth century caused considerable concern among politicians and other public leaders, who feared that widespread social disorder would result from the rapid pace of social change. These leaders believed that the family was in peril as a social institution, and so they promoted new ideals for family members, especially for women and children, who were most affected by the new modes of production. The major development for children was the establishment of schooling as a dominant experience in growing up. For women, the result was a definition of their responsibilities which limited them to the home and to the roles of wives and mothers.

The Establishment of Compulsory Schooling

The redefinition of the family as a unit of consumption rather than one of production paralleled the development of formal education as a major social institution. Over time, childhood and youth became an extended period of dependency when schooling was a characteristic experience. From the time of early settlement, schoolhouses appeared throughout Canada, but the need for children within family economies meant that formal education was limited to certain periods of the year, to certain age groups, and, generally, to a small elite. In the preindustrial economy, families were the dominant institutions for education, transmitting habits and values as well as vocational training. Childhood involved productive activity rather than reading and writing, and children learned practical skills from parents, older siblings, and relatives. In this context, age groups intermingled in both work and play. The children of the elite were an exception to this pattern, and among them both boys and girls received some training by religious orders. However, most children learned at home within the framework of the family unit (Gaffield, 1981; Moogk, 1982).

The pattern of learning at home continued during the early nineteenth century, when schooling was still limited to children from families with both the interest and the affluence to arrange privately for individual or small group instruction. However, attitudes toward formal education changed rapidly, especially during the 1840s and 1850s, when public concern mounted about the present and future behaviour of unoccupied children. The increasing removal of productive activity from the home left many children without time-consuming responsibilities within the family. Public leaders believed that the phenomenon of "idle youth" boded ill for the maintenance of social order in the major cities. This belief encouraged them to promote the building of schools where children could not only be supervised but also taught the values and habits considered essential in the new social context (Houston, 1972; Prentice, 1977).

The promotion of schooling by educators and politicians was facilitated by the construction of better roads and the growing population density, both of which made attendance much easier than in the scattered rural settlements of earlier times. Similarly, many parents came to see formal education as a necessary condition for successful participation in the new technological era. Literacy and arithmetical skills, for example, seemed to be high priorities in an increasingly complex society. As a result, general support for schooling emerged rapidly during the mid-nineteenth century, and within several decades all the Canadian provinces had comprehensive education systems (Katz, 1972).

The pattern of increased school attendance occurred throughout the social structure, although it was less pronounced among materially disadvantaged social groups, where youth remained associated with the search for productive opportunities. The continued need for some families to rely on child labour was actually reflected in the Ontario compulsory school attendance legislation of the early twentieth century, which stipulated that the officially accepted age of school leaving could be reduced by two years to age twelve if parents were able to demonstrate a need for income from their children. The 1911 census showed that children in Hamilton, for example, did in fact contribute substantially to the survival of working-class families. Employed children from the families of general labourers contributed just over 44 percent of total family income. This proportion varied among different working-class families, but the trend was consistent (Synge, 1979). The ideal of children as students was simply inappropriate for materially insecure families. Overall, however, children have spent a greater number of years in school and have been dependent on their parents for longer periods since the mid-nineteenth century.

The New Ideal of Womanhood

The redefinition of children as students was part of a new ideal for families which included a considerable narrowing of the female role in society. Separation of production from the home encouraged what historians have called the *cult of true womanhood*, which defined women primarily as reproducers and creators of havens from the hustle and bustle of the productive world. The ideal woman was pure, pious, and submissive but also capable of effective nurturing and efficient household management. Despite the transformation of the family's economic role in society, the woman's place was still in the home. New attitudes to cleanliness, child rearing, and marriage led to a complex array of prescribed female duties to replace women's traditional participation in a family economy. The goal of these duties was to counterbalance the negative aspects of urban industrial development, which had moral and spiritual flaws since it was created by men, who were believed to be naturally less sensitive to the nonmaterial aspects of life. The role of women was to raise children and support husbands in ways which would offset the heartless nature of the marketplace. By the late nineteenth century the ways to create a proper family environment were specified in an extensive prescriptive literature which included books, pamphlets, and magazines describing the path to "true womanhood." This view was also institutionalized in the development of domestic science as part of the public school curriculum and as the accepted course of advanced study for women (Welter, 1966; Rowles, 1966; Morrison, 1976; Cook and Mitchinson, 1976; Stamp, 1977).

The most vigorous challenge to the exclusive definition of women as mothers and wives came from certain middle-class women who decided that the new ideal of womanhood could be effectively extended beyond the family and into the larger society. These women agreed with the basic concept of natural female virtue but argued that these "feminine" qualities had to be exercised not only in private but also in public spheres. And so middle-class women formed groups to speak out on temperance, child welfare, sanitation, and similar social issues which attracted concern in the late nineteenth century. The same beliefs motivated the "maternal feminism" of the suffrage movement which helped women gain the vote at most levels of government by the 1920s. By modern standards these early challenges to the cult of true womanhood may not seem very radical, since they operated within a framework of accepted gender distinctions. However, the activities of these reform groups demonstrate that women continued to be active agents in the historical process, despite their image of passivity and their restriction to the home.

Conclusion

The extent to which the economic changes associated with the emergence of modern society altered the family varied with social class. In general, the alterations were less extensive for working-class families than for middle-class families during the formative decades of the nineteenth and early twentieth centuries. Despite the ideal family pattern of husbands as sole breadwinners, wives as mothers, and children as students, the concept of a family wage economy remained important as a result of insecure employment and low wages. The economic growth of Canadian society from the late nineteenth century made the ideal of single breadwinners increasingly realistic, but many families still had to rely on supplementary income. The strong stigma against married women in the paid labour force placed a large economic burden on other family members, even young teenagers. In comparison to the general trend, a large proportion of working-class children continued to pursue job opportunities, and many of them did not attend school on a regular basis. At the beginning of the twentieth century, the majority of working-class children in Hamilton, Ontario, for example, were already wage-earners by the age of fourteen. Some children from single-parent families worked full-time in local mills and factories (Synge, 1979; Brandt, 1981; Coulter, 1982).

Similarly, the concept of women as domestic nurturers has never been applied equally by all social groups at all times. In the twentieth century married women became a reserve labour force to be called upon when the supply of male workers did not match the number of job opportunities. During both world wars, married women worked in munitions factories, textile mills, and other establishments considered vital to the war effort. In these years the prejudice against employed wives was suppressed out of concern about the war effort (Pierson, 1977).

The role of women as a reserve labour force was extended after World War II to include employment to supplement family income during periods of high expenses, such as when older children were in university. More recently, our society has accepted in principle the idea that women should share equally with men in opportunities for vocational training and financial independence. However, many aspects of the nineteenth century ideals of womanhood continue to characterize the reality of contemporary family life. Employed women are still paid less than their male counterparts, and they remain fully responsible for most duties within the home (Luxton, 1980). The current position of women must therefore be evaluated with an understanding of the past, which reminds us that social ideals and social realities have only converged at particular points in time and among specific groups in society.

The evidence examined in this chapter emphasizes that an historical perspective should inform discussion of the current state of the family and of its future. The history of the family reveals the ways in which the development of a wage-labour economy and the process of industrialization affected the roles of men, women, and children, and thereby transformed social organization. The factors of age, gender, and social class have contributed to a diverse range of individual experience during this transformation. Within the general trends, family patterns have included elements of both change and continuity, stability and instability, cohesiveness and fragmentation.

It is not obvious that the historical trends describe either a prelude to the final crisis of the family or proof that the family is a truly resilient and permanent social institution. Serious research on the history of the family has only been undertaken during the past two decades, and many basic questions have yet to be explored (Shorter, 1975; Stone, 1977; Lasch, 1977; Flandrin, 1979; Anderson, 1980; Parr, 1980; Rooke and Schnell, 1983). Moreover, the variety and amount of evidence available for research is limited, since all societies view routine family experience as unexceptional and thus not worthy of documentation. One inescapable conclusion, however, is that the family must be analysed within a larger social and economic context. The character and structure of families relate directly to the pressures and possibilities of the external material environment. In this sense, questions about the future of the family actually represent questions about the future of modern society.

References

Acton, Janice; Goldsmith, Penny; and Shepard, Bonnie, eds. 1974. *Women at Work: Ontario, 1850–1930*. Toronto: Canadian Women's Educational Press.

Anderson, Michael. 1980. *Approaches to the History of the Western Family*. London: Macmillan.

Bradbury, Bettina. 1979. "The Family Economy and Work in an Industrializing City: Montreal in the 1870s." In Canadian Historical Association *Historical Papers*.

———. 1982. "The Fragmented Family: Family Strategies in the Face of Death, Illness and Poverty, Montreal, 1860–1885." In Joy Parr, ed. *Childhood and Family in Canadian History*. Toronto: McClelland and Stewart.

Brandt, Gail Cuthbert. 1981. "'Weaving It Together': Life Cycle and Industrial Experience of Female Cotton Workers in Quebec, 1910–1950." *Labour/Le Travailleur*, Spring.

Charbonneau, Hubert. 1975. *Vie et mort de nos ancêtres: Etude démographique*, pp. 183–88. Montreal: University of Montreal.

Cook, Ramsay and Mitchinson, Wendy, eds. 1976. *The Proper Sphere: Women's Place in Canadian Society*. Toronto: Oxford University Press.

Coulter, Rebecca. 1982. "The Working Young of Edmonton, 1927–1931." In Joy Parr, ed. *Childhood and Family in Canadian History*. Toronto: McClelland and Stewart.

Danylewycz, Marta; Light, Beth; and Prentice, Alison. 1983. "The Evolution of the Sexual Division of Labour in Teaching: A Nineteenth-Century Ontario and Quebec Case Study." *Histoire sociale/Social History*, May.

Dechêne, Louise. 1974. *Habitants et Marchands de Montréal au XVIIe Siécle*, pp. 107–109. Montreal: Plon.

Flandrin, Jean-Louis. 1979. *Families in Former Times: Kinship, Household and Sexuality in Early Modern France*, trans, by Richard Southern. Cambridge: Cambridge University Press.

Gaffield, Chad. 1979. "Canadian Families in Cultural Context: Hypotheses from the Mid-Nineteenth Century." Canadian Historical Association *Historical Papers*.

———. 1981. "Demography, Social Structure and the History of Schooling." In David C. Jones, Nancy M. Sheehan, Robert M. Stamp, and Nell G. McDonald, eds. *Approaches to Educational History*. Winnipeg: University of Manitoba Press.

————. 1982. "Boom and Bust: The Demography and Economy of the Lower Ottawa Valley in the Nineteenth Century." CHA *Historical Papers*.

Gagan, David. 1981. *Hopeful Travellers: Families, Land and Social Change in Mid-Victorian Peel County, Canada West*. Toronto: University of Toronto Press.

———— and Mays, Herbert. 1974. "Historical Demography and Canadian Social History: Families and Land in Peel County, Ontario." In M. Horn and R. Sabourin, eds. *Studies in Canadian Social History*, pp. 96–122. Toronto: McClelland and Stewart.

Hareven, Tamara K. and Langenbach, Randolph, eds. 1978. *Amoskeag: Life and Work in an American Factory City*, Part Five, "Families." New York: Pantheon Books.

Harvey, Fernand. 1979. "Children of the Industrial Revolution in Quebec," trans, by Robert Russell. In J. Dufresne et al., eds. *The Professions: Their Growth or Declines?* Montreal: Société de publication critère.

Henripin, Jacques. 1968. *Tendances et facteurs de la fécondité au Canada*. Ottawa: Queen's Printer.

Houston, Susan. 1972. "Politics, Schools, and Social Change in Upper Canada." *Canadian Historical Review*, September.

Katz, Michael. 1972. "Who Went to School." *History of Education Quarterly* XII.

————. 1975. *The People of Hamilton, Canada West: Family and Class in a Mid-Nineteenth-Century City*. Cambridge, Mass. Harvard University Press.

———— and Davey, Ian E. 1978. "Youth and Early Industrialization in a Canadian City." In John Demos and Sarane Spence Boocock, eds. *Turning Points: Historical and Sociological Essays on the Family*, pp. S81–S119. Chicago: University of Chicago Press.

————; Doucet, Michael J.; and Stern, Mark J. 1982. *The Social Organization of Early Industrial Capitalism*. Cambridge, Mass.: Harvard University Press.

Kealey, Gregory S., ed. 1973. *Canada Investigates Industrialism*. Toronto: University of Toronto Press.

————. 1980. *Toronto Workers Respond to Industrial Capitalism 1867–1892*. Toronto: University of Toronto Press·

Larose, André. *Histoire sociale / Social History* (annual bibliographies on historical demography).

Lasch, Christopher. 1977. *Haven in a Heartless World: The Family Besieged*. New York: Basic Books.

Light, Beth and Strong-Boag, Veronica, eds. 1980. *True Daughters of the North: Canadian Women's History, An Annotated Bibliography*. Toronto: OISE.

Luxton, Meg. 1980. *More Than a Labour of Love: Three Generations of Women's Work in the Home*. Toronto: Women's Educational Press.

McLaren, Angus. 1978. "Birth Control and Abortion in Canada, 1870–1920." *Canadian Historical Review*, September.

Medick, Hans. 1976. "The Proto-Industrial Family Economy: The Structural Function of Household and Family During the Transition from Peasant Society to Industrial Capitalism." *Social History*, October.

Moogk, Peter N. 1982. "Les 'Petits Sauvages: The Children of Eighteenth-Century New France." In Joy Parr. ed. *Childhood and Family m Canadian History,* pp. 17–43. Toronto: McClelland and Stewart.

Morrison, T.R. 1976. "'Their Proper Sphere': Feminism, the Family and Child-Centered School Reform in Ontario 1875–1900." *Ontario History,* March.

Parr, Joy. 1980. *Labouring Children: British Immigrant Apprentices to Canada, 1869–1924.* Montreal: McGill-Queen's University Press.

_____. 1982. *Childhood and Family in Canadian History.* Toronto: McClelland and Stewart.

Pelletier, A.J.; Thompson, F.D.; and Rochon, A. 1938. *The Canadian Family,* Census Monograph No. 7, p. 19. Ottawa: J.O. Patenaude.

Pierson, Ruth. 1977. "Woman's Emancipation and the Recruitment of Women into the Labour Force in World War II." In Susan Mann Trofimenkoff and Alison Prentice, eds. *The Neglected Majority: Essays in Canadian Women's History.* Toronto: McClelland and Stewart.

Prentice, Alison. 1977. *The School Promoters: Education and Social Class m Mid-Nineteenth Century Upper Canada.* Toronto: McClelland and Stewart.

Rooke, Patricia T. and Schnell, R.L. 1983. *Discarding the Asylum: From Child Rescue to the Welfare State in English-Canada (1800–1950).* Lanham, Maryland: University Press of America.

Rowles, Edith Child. 1966. *Home Economics in Canada: The Early History of Six College Programmes.* Saskatoon: Modern Press.

Shorter, Edward. 1975. *The Making of the Modern Family.* New York: Basic Books.

Soliday, Gerald L., ed. 1980. *History of the Family and Kinship: A Select International Bibliography.* Millwood, N.Y.: Kraus.

Snell, James G. 1983. "The White Life for Two: The Defence of Marriage and Morality in Canada, 1890–1914." *Histoire sociale / Social History,* May.

Stamp, Robert M. 1977. "Teaching Girls Their 'God Given Place in Life': The Introduction of Home Economics in the Schools." *Atlantis,* Spring.

Stone, Lawrence. 1977. *Family, Sex and Marriage in England, 1500–1800.* New York: Harper and Row.

Strong-Boag, Veronica. 1979. "Wages for Housework: Mothers' Allowances and the Beginnings of Social Security in Canada." *Journal of Canadian Studies* XIV (1).

Struthers, James. 1983. *No Fault of Their Own: Unemployment and the Canadian Welfare State 1914–1941.* Toronto: University of Toronto Press.

Synge, Jane. 1979. "The Transition from School to Work: Growing Up Working Class in Early 20th Century Hamilton, Ontario." In K. Ishwaran, ed. *Childhood and Adolescence in Canada.* Toronto: McGraw-Hill Ryerson.

Tilly, Louise and Scott, Joan. 1978. *Women, Work and the Family.* New York: Holt, Rinehart and Winston.

Welter, Barbara. 1966. "The Cult of True Womanhood: 1820–1860." *American Quarterly,* Summer.

CHAPTER

14 CONFEDERATION

Confederation solved a variety of political, economic, diplomatic and ethnic difficulties that jeopardized British North America's future in the 1860s. Despite early discontent the union was not seriously threatened in its first century. Not surprisingly, historians have generally treated Confederation as the inevitable unfolding of a scenario stretching back to the American Revolution. The leading Fathers such as Sir John A. Macdonald, Sir George-Etienne Cartier, George Brown and Sir Charles Tupper were ascribed heroic qualities in the numerous studies that preceded the Centennial in 1967. Donald Creighton's *Road to Confederation: The Emergence of Canada, 1863–1867* (1964) was the preeminent narrative depiction of heroes and villains in a drama that ended with a rising sun on shining faces. His study and others surveyed every conceivable aspect of the happy story. English Canada paid scant attention to naysayers in Quebec such as Abbé Lionel Groulx and Maurice Séguin, whose disciples drew different pictures and were preparing another agenda.

In "The United States and Confederation," a paper delivered at the University of Chicago in 1958, Creighton looked back at the abortive British North American union attempt a century earlier in 1858. That was his starting point in explaining the success of the movement that culminated in Confederation. The paper enunciated several of the themes that Creighton and others would expand upon in the years leading up to the Centennial. Political deadlock, western expansionism, British inducement and American militarism combined to make the era one of "prophetic significance in Canadian history." Canadians "had to build a nation" which "had to be built in the midst of a great war."

An extended lull in Confederation studies followed the deluge that preceded the serendipitous Centennial of 1967. In the words of Ged Martin in your second reading, the views of the "four historians of world rank," Creighton, W.L. Morton, J.M.S. Careless and P.B. Waite, bestowed the authorized version on the subject that served for a generation. Despite this, imperfections in the Confederation arrangement occasionally eclipsed the advantages and raised questions about its inevitability. Regional alienation, Francophone discontent, uncertain leadership and ill-defined national aspirations eventually compelled historians to reappraise the union movement and those opposed to Confederation in the 1860s. In March of 1990, for example, the *Canadian*

Historical Review offered a "CHR Dialogue: The Maritimes and Confederation: A Reassessment" which raised several bothersome questions. No academic has stalked the "consensus" canon more aggressively than Ged Martin, the former Director of the Centre of Canadian Studies at the University of Edinburgh. In several prodding articles and books on the Confederation movement of the 1860s he has battered the received dogma, most recently in *Britain and the Origins of Canadian Confederation, 1837–67* (1995), from which your final reading has been taken. Writing from his seat close to the centre of the British Empire, Martin offers his image of Confederation.

Suggestions for Further Reading

Buckner, Phillip, P.B. Waite and William M. Baker, "CHR Dialogue: The Maritimes and Confederation: A Reassessment," *Canadian Historical Review*, LXXI, no. 1 (March 1990), 1–45.

Careless, J.M.S.(ed.), *The Pre-Confederation Premiers: Ontario Government Leaders, 1841–1867*. Toronto: University of Toronto Press, 1980.

Creighton, Donald, *The Road to Confederation: The Emergence of Canada, 1863–1867*. Toronto: Macmillan of Canada, 1964.

Martin, Ged, *Britain and the Origins of Canadian Confederation, 1837–1867*, Vancouver: University of British Columbia Press, 1995, 27–80.

Martin, Ged (ed.), *The Causes of Canadian Confederation*. Fredericton: Acadiensis Press, 1990.

————, "Launching Canadian Confederation: Means to Ends, 1836–64," *Historical Journal*, 27, no. 3 (1984), 575–602.

Moore, Christopher, *1867: How the Fathers Made a Deal*. Toronto: McClelland and Stewart, 1997.

Moore, Christopher, "Objections to Confederation: The Top Ten of 1865," *Beaver*, 76,5, 1996, 12–19.

Morton, W.L., *The Critical Years: The Union of British North America, 1857–1873*. Toronto: McClelland and Stewart, 1964.

Silver, Arthur, *The French-Canadian Idea of Confederation, 1864–1900*. Toronto: University of Toronto Press, 1982.

Smith, Jennifer, "Canadian Confederation and the Influence of American Federalism," *Canadian Journal of Political Science*, XXI, no. 3 (September 1988), 443–463.

Waite, P.B., *The Life and Times of Confederation, 1864–1867: Politics, Newspapers and the Union of British North America*. Toronto: University of Toronto Press, 1962.

Winks, Robin, *Canada and the United States: The Civil War Years*. Montreal, Harvest House, 1960.

THE UNITED STATES AND CANADIAN CONFEDERATION

Donald Creighton

In the next decade both the United States and Canada will face an impressive succession of important centenaries. On 12 April 1961, it will be a hundred years since the Confederate bombardment opened upon Fort Sumter in Charleston harbour. On 22 June 1964, it will be a century since a coalition Government of Reformers and Liberal-Conservatives took office in the Province of Canada with the declared intention of establishing a general federal union of the whole of British North America. Between these two events—the Civil War in the United States and the federation of British North America—there exists an interesting relationship which I should like to explore with you tonight. It is an important, but also a complex, imprecise, and ambiguous relationship; and it seems to me that there might be more enlightenment in approaching its analysis circuitously than directly. These two famous dates and the national dramas which they recall and commemorate will therefore, for the moment, be set aside; and we can go back a little in time. There is an earlier episode in Canadian history, which could be most appropriately examined on this occasion, for its centenary will be reached, though certainly not enthusiastically celebrated, during the summer of 1958. It is an episode much less well known than the foundation of the coalition Government and the declaration of the coalition Government's purpose in June of 1864; but, for all that, it has its own real significance. And an examination of it may throw some light upon the curious relationship between the American Civil War and the federal union of British North America, upon the influence of the United States on Canadian Confederation.

In the summer of 1858—it was in August, to be precise—the government of the Province of Canada came to a momentous decision. It was, in itself, an important decision, and it was much more important simply because it was the Province of Canada which had reached it. In 1858, the province was only a little over fifteen years old, for it had been formed in 1841 by the union of the two older and smaller provinces of Upper and Lower Canada; but already, in size, ambition, political consequence, and political influence, it was clearly the "empire province" of British North America. From the Gulf of St. Lawrence, it extended westward along the whole long line of the great river and the Great Lakes. On the south, its limit was the international boundary between British North America and the United States; to the north, its frontier was that highly uncertain, vaguely defined line which bounded Rupert's Land, the

From *Canadian Historical Review* 39, no. 3 (September 1958), 209–22. Copyright 1958 by University of Toronto Press. Reprinted by permission of the Estate of Donald Creighton and University of Toronto Press Incorporated.

chartered territories of the Hudson's Bay Company. The other British provinces—Nova Scotia, New Brunswick, Prince Edward Island, and Newfoundland in the east, and Vancouver Island and British Columbia in the far west—were undeniably dwarfed in importance by the Province of Canada. Canada was more prosperous than any of them. Canada was more populous than all of them put together.

It was all true, as the other colonies somewhat enviously admitted; but it was also true that the "empire province" was a socially turbulent and politically agitated community, and that the division between its French-speaking and English-speaking citizens had created a cultural cleavage far more serious than existed elsewhere in the North American Empire. The other northern provinces regarded Canada with a measure of doubt and distrust. The eyebrows of sober Nova Scotians, in particular, were lifted often in pained disapproval at its erratic course. It was always in the throes of some political crisis or other; its citizens were invariably at each other's throats; and it had the highly reprehensible habit of breaking its word in cheerful disregard of the interests of the rest of British North America. Its whole record, in fact, was simply deplorable. And yet, the unwelcome but inescapable fact was that Canada counted. However violent its actions and however incomprehensible its purposes, they had to be taken seriously. And once again, during the agitated summer of 1858, the Canadian government had given the other provincial administrations considerable food for thought. On August 16, when, after a long and turbulent session, the Governor, Sir Edmund Head, finally prorogued the session of the Canadian legislature, he made a brief formal announcement of the policy which his new Government intended to follow. "I propose in the course of the recess," he told the Houses, "to communicate with Her Majesty's Government, and with the Governments of the sister Colonies, on another matter of very great importance. I am desirous of inviting them to discuss with us the principles on which a bond of a federal character, uniting the Provinces of British North America, may perhaps hereafter be practicable."

What had happened? What had persuaded this most important of British American governments to adopt, as its declared policy, the plan of a British American federal union? Long before this, of course, British Governors and High Commissioners, colonial statesmen, authors, and public speakers had been talking and writing about federal union; but until Governor Head made his famous announcement on the afternoon of 16 August 1858, the whole question had remained almost entirely academic. Why had George E. Cartier and John A. Macdonald, the leaders of the Canadian Administration, decided to commit themselves to an ambitious policy which no other British American government had ventured to espouse before? Nearly six years later, on 22 June 1864, another Canadian Government, as we have already seen, was to make another open profession of faith in a federal plan and, after an interval, was to succeed in carrying it out. Yet these two general declarations of purpose are very similar; and at first sight, the occasion, if not the cause of both of them seem very much alike. Each appears to have arisen out of the chronic weakness and instability of Canadian politics.

The fact was that the Canadian Union of 1841 had been formal, not real. In theory, the province was a unitary state; in fact it was an unacknowledged federal system. Its two sections, Canada East and Canada West, the one largely French and the other overwhelmingly English, were united economically by the St. Lawrence transport system and divided socially by their two contrasting cultural inheritances. They had found it impossible to live apart as the separate provinces of Upper and Lower Canada; they were finding it almost equally difficult to live together as the two divisions of a single government. It was true, of course, that the Union Act had itself helped to make these difficulties almost insuperable. By its terms, Canada East and Canada West had been given equal representation in the provincial legislature, irrespective of population; and this political equality tended to harden the sectional division of the province and to exacerbate its inevitable cultural misunderstandings. The cabinet and several of the important departments of government were organized on a sectional basis. Much of the legislation that was passed had to be sectional in character; and the political parties, although they tried, of course, to win a following in both French- and English-speaking Canada, had an irresistible tendency to become strong in one section of the province and correspondingly weak in the other. They tended also, as a natural consequence, to reach a level of approximate political equality; and thus the public affairs of the province were characterized both by a permanent state of sectional conflict and a persistent condition of political instability.

During the summer of 1858 this chronic political unsettlement reached a sudden, sharp crisis; and it was this crisis which provided the occasion for the Cartier-Macdonald Government's dramatic announcement of its adoption of the federal plan. Earlier in the session, the Assembly had been discussing the constitutional problem which lay at the root of its sectional difficulties. The Assembly was always discussing the constitutional problem. It was always anxiously reviewing a number of contradictory proposals for constitutional reform—including federal schemes—which, it was argued, would remove the province from the inveterate embarrassments of sectionalism; and this painfully familiar exercise was barely over, when there occurred an episode which was, in effect, a preposterous, almost ludicrous, illustration of the political stalemate which everybody was so anxious to end. Its origins were simple and absurdly characteristic of the province's real nature. The political crisis of the summer of 1858 arose out of the endless and agonizing problem of deciding where the capital of this politically united but sectionally divided province was to be.

Ever since the union in 1841, this question had been arousing the most acrimonious dissension. Originally, the seat of government had been fixed at Kingston in Canada West; it had then been transferred to Montreal, in Canada

East—a distinctly unfortunate removal, as it turned out, for a few years later, in 1849, the enraged Montreal Conservatives burnt the Parliament Buildings to the ground. For some time after this disgrace, the attempt to find a permanent capital was tacitly abandoned; and the seat of government alternated, at intervals, between Quebec, which was the old capital of Lower Canada, and Toronto, which was the old capital of the upper province. Every few years, the cabinet ministers and a small army of civil servants, together with great masses of official records, government furniture, and personal effects, were laboriously transported, up or down the river valley, in trains and steamships, to their new political headquarters. It is hardly surprising that everybody in politics found these fairly regularly recurring removals an intolerable nuisance; and in 1857 John A. Macdonald had hit upon what was thought to be a most ingenious method of securing permanence. Queen Victoria was invited to name a permanent capital for the united province; and Queen Victoria, duly but privately advised from Canada, decided in favour of a little backwoods town, some distance up the Ottawa River, once called Bytown and now Ottawa.

Ottawa had the advantage of a location on the west bank of the river which formed the boundary between the two sections of the province; but it was definitely in Canada West. Still more obviously, it was neither Quebec nor Montreal; and the French-Canadians in the legislature, even though the great majority of them were members of the Conservative party which had referred the problem to the Queen for final decision, regarded the choice of Ottawa with the darkest disapproval. It was always possible, on a question of such enormous sectional prestige, to persuade some of them, at least momentarily, to forswear their Conservative allegiance; and this was exactly what happened on 28 July 1858. An address to the Queen on the subject of the capital was under consideration. An amendment, declaring flatly that Ottawa ought not to be the permanent seat of government was deliberately moved by the opposition. A small, but sufficient bloc of French-Canadian votes changed sides, and the Government was defeated on this issue.

Macdonald and Cartier decided to resign; and George Brown, the leader of the Liberal Opposition, accepted the Governor's invitation to form a new Government. What followed is of considerable interest in the law and custom of parliamentary institutions in the British Commonwealth. The political crisis of the summer of 1858 anticipates, in some measure, though the circumstances were widely different, the much more famous Canadian constitutional crisis of the summer of 1926 and even finds a faint echo in the speculations and discussions which went on for some time in Canada after the general election of June 1957. Our concern here, however, is not with constitutional issues as such, but with the political instability which resulted in part from the defective constitution of the Province of Canada. Rapidly it became apparent that Brown and his associate French-Canadian leader, Dorion, were in a much more precarious position in the Assembly than their predecessors, Macdonald and Cartier, had ever been. The French-Canadian opponents of Ottawa as the Canadian capital would quickly, if sheepishly, return to the Conservative fold; and, by the law as it then stood, George Brown, Dorion, and the other new ministers would be obliged, on accepting office under the Crown, to resign their seats in Parliament and to seek re-election. With numbers so seriously reduced in such an evenly divided Assembly, the new Government would not be able to meet the inevitable want-of-confidence motion; and Brown, with failure staring him in the face, requested the Governor to grant him a dissolution of Parliament. The request was declined; and on August 4, after having held office for only two days, the Brown-Dorion Administration, "Her Majesty's most ephemeral government," as the Conservatives derisively called it, was obliged to resign, and Macdonald and Cartier were back in power once more.

The crisis had not lasted a long time; it had begun on July 28, and it ended, with the installation of the old ministers, on August 6. Yet this short period of fewer than ten days had provided an almost grotesque illustration of the political instability and futility which was sectionalism's evil gift to the Province of Canada. The Conservative ministers did not, of course, admit that the episode had taught them a lesson—their own triumphant return to office precluded any such embarrassing avowal; but, at the same time, their subsequent actions proved only too clearly that they had now decided to escape, if possible, from the existing state of affairs. Up to this time, it had been the Liberals or Reformers, not the Conservatives, who had kept suggesting solutions for the sectional problem—who had kept pointing out possible exits from the constitutional impasse in which the province found itself. Now, for the first time, the Conservatives took their stand also upon a new policy. For a colony such as Canada, whose two sections could not afford to be separated and did not want to be too closely united, what could be more suitable than a federal form of government? On August 7, the day after the Ministry was formed, Cartier briefly alluded to the new policy, and on August 16, when he prorogued Parliament, Head formally committed his cabinet to the federal scheme.

II

Undoubtedly the political crisis of the summer of 1858 had precipitated the Canadian Conservatives' adoption of the plan of a general British North American federal union. A way out of the political deadlock of sectionalism had been proved to be peremptorily necessary; and a federal union was surely the solution best calculated to preserve the essential character of the Province of Canada. Yet what kind of a federal union? Why had Macdonald and Cartier declared themselves in favour of a comprehensive scheme which would embrace not only all the Maritime Provinces but also, at some future date, the enormous territories of the British north-west? Why had they not been content with the project of converting Canada into a federation of two provinces? This second, smaller plan, which was actually adopted a year later by the Reform party as its policy, was a much more manageable enterprise. It could have been carried out by Canada herself, at her own convenience, and without the slightest reference to the other colonies. Yet this was not the plan which the Conservative party adopted. Instead it had accepted a vastly more ambitious, vastly more difficult undertaking, which could only be completed with the concurrence of four other colonial governments. Why? The urgent necessity of finding a solution for sectional problems is not a satisfactory explanation, for the sectional problem could have been solved just as effectively, and much more expeditiously, by "applying the federal princi- ple," as contemporaries called it, to the Province of Canada alone. What were the other purposes and intentions which lay behind Macdonald's decision? Why had he and his colleagues conceived the grandiose design of a transcontinental British North American federation?

Now it is quite obvious that Canada, in contrast with the Maritime Provinces, had always held to a tradition of western empire. The Maritime Provinces— New Brunswick, Prince Edward Island, and, above all, Nova Scotia and Newfoundland—had grown up in a world in which the three words "ships, colonies, and commerce" formed the indissoluble principles, the virtual "holy trinity," of empire. The dominion in which, on the whole, they had been so com- fortably adjusted, was an oceanic dominion; but the empire which Canada had sought to achieve through the centuries had been essentially continental in character. From the days of the French explorers onward, all the political and com- mercial leaders of the community of the St. Lawrence valley had tried to make the Great River and its Great Lakes the basis of an enormous inland empire. The peace treaty of 1783, which cut a line, at that time artificial and almost mean- ingless, through the centre of this vast region, had transferred its south-west sector to the United States; and it was these tragic losses on their left flank which helped to impel the Montreal fur traders, the real westerners of the pe- riod, into the territories north-west of Lake Superior. Here, in a region which could still be made good for the British Empire, the great trader-explorers of the North West Company, Alexander MacKenzie, David Thompson, and Simon Fraser, drove the fur trade across the prairies and through the mountains to the ocean. They clinched the claims of Cook and Vancouver; they helped to give British North America its wide open window on the Pacific. But the terrible struggle with the Hudson's Bay Company, of which these western exploring enterprises were only a part, had exhausted the North West Company; and in 1821 it virtually capitulated to its great rival. From then on, the Hudson's Bay Company held the north-west quarter of the continent in trust for the future Kingdom of Canada; and for a generation the provinces on the St. Lawrence almost forgot their traditional western empire.

Then, fairly suddenly and without much warning, Canadian interest in the region beyond Lake Superior began to revive. The date of the revival is highly significant, for it began just about eighteen months before the Conservatives adopted their federal scheme in the summer of 1858; and this near coincidence in time suggests that, in matters other than its sectional and constitutional problems, the Province of Canada was reaching a species of crisis in its development. It had, in fact, come nearly to the limit of its possibilities of expansion in the circumstances of the moment, and this at the very time when the rule of the Hudson's Bay Company in the north-west was becoming increasingly uncertain and precarious. There was no longer an agricultural frontier in Canada West, for the good lands south of the Precambrian Shield had all been occupied. There was no real prospect of acquiring the bulk of the trade of the international North American west, for the St. Lawrence was obviously losing in its struggle with the American Atlantic ports. The expansive energies of Canada were being held back in frustration and defeat; but far to the north-west, beyond Lake Superior, was an immense and empty territory which lay waiting for both agricultural settlement and commercial exploitation. Why should not the Province of Canada acquire these lands for its own and British North America's good? Why should it not take over from a moribund seventeenth-century commercial company whose chartered claims were fraudulent, whose rule was baneful, and whose feeble authority was quite incapable of protecting the north-west from encroachment?

Macdonald and his colleagues looked both eagerly and dubiously upon the domain of the Hudson's Bay Company. They were both fascinated and frightened by the thought of acquiring Rupert's Land and the North-west Territories. Inside Canada itself, the popular impulses towards its annexation were very strong; and their strength was powerfully increased by pressures in the same direction which came from outside through both the United Kingdom and the United States. There was no doubt at all that Great Britain was anxious to make new arrangements which would enable her to cut her commitments and reduce her contingent liabilities in North America. In 1857, two years before the Hudson's Bay Company's trading licence was to expire, the British government sponsored a parliamentary committee to consider the state and prospects of Rupert's Land; and although the committee's report made simply a guarded and general recommendation in favour of Canadian settlements in suitable parts of the Red and Saskatchewan valleys, it was quite plain that the imperial government was eager to have Canada take over the responsibility for the north-west.

Yet even this was not all. To the spur of British encouragement was added the stimulus of American rivalry. Canada was determined, sooner or later, to acquire Rupert's Land; the United Kingdom was anxious to arrange a secure British North American future for Rupert's Land; and finally, for both British and Canadians, the irrepressible fear that the United States might succeed in forestalling them lent an additional urgency to their plans for Canadian expansion. This fear was, of course, simply a new western variant of a much older fear, which went back as far as 1775 when, nearly a year before they declared their independence, the Thirteen Colonies launched an attack on Quebec. The armed occupation of Quebec in 1775–76 and the repeated American invasions of the War of 1812 had bred in the British colonies the unshakeable conviction that the United States was the one real threat to their survival on the North American continent. The events which had occurred in the forty years since the Peace of Ghent had, in the main, confirmed rather than qualified this view. At every moment of trouble in British North America, on every occasion of dispute between the United Kingdom and the United States, the threat of American intervention or American attack returned. Only two years before, in 1856, the Crimean War had brought a brief renewal of the old danger. The Nova Scotian, Joseph Howe, with some encouragement and assistance from J.F.T. Crampton, the British Minister at Washington, attempted to secure recruits for the Crimea from among the currently unemployed in the republic. This childishly inept and foolhardy venture was discovered in due course; it was described, a little grandiloquently, by the American Administration as "an act of usurpation against the sovereign rights of the United States." Crampton's recall was demanded; the American newspapers fulminated in indignation. And all this occurred, as similar dangers had occurred so often in the past, when the size of the British garrisons in the northern colonies had been sharply reduced and when Great Britain's hands were tied with a war in Europe.

The fear was an old one, frequently renewed. And now it had taken on a new shape and found a fresh expression. The survival of the existing colonies in a continent dominated by the United States was still not entirely certain; but far more uncertain was British North America's acquisition of the north-west and its expansion to the Pacific Ocean. Would the transcontinental dominion, of which people were already dreaming, ever become a triumphant reality? The Convention of 1818 and the Washington Treaty of 1846 had settled the international boundary, at least on paper; but might not the hard, solid facts of human occupation determine it ultimately in a quite different fashion? There were only three tiny British American communities in the whole north-west— at Red River, on Vancouver Island, and on the mainland of British Columbia; and the tide of American frontier settlement, the network of the American communication systems, were creeping steadily closer to them with every year that passed. Minnesota became a state in 1858, Oregon was to follow in 1859. Hudson Bay had ceased to be the sole centre of the Hudson's Bay Company's transport system; and the Red River settlement was becoming an economic outpost of St. Paul, just as the Pacific colonies were becoming economic outposts of San Francisco.

All this was part of the speculations of informed Canadians in the summer of 1858. All this was inevitably present in the minds of Macdonald and his fellow ministers when they decided to adopt the policy of a general British North American federation. The sectional crisis in the Province of Canada had led them to the idea of federal union; but the shape and scope which they gave to their federal plan had been determined with a view to British North America as a whole. They were eager, not only to reconstruct the constitution of a province, but also to lay the foundations of a nation; and they were convinced that this was the only way in which a transcontinental nation in the northern half of North America could be built. Union with the Maritime Provinces was essential to secure the future nation's Atlantic frontage; but union with the Maritime Provinces was almost equally necessary to provide a base broad and strong enough to support the acquisition of the north-west. Alone, the Province of Canada might not have been sufficiently powerful to bear the responsibility; and even if she had been willing to try, the basic division between her French- and English-speaking citizens would almost certainly have prevented her from making the attempt. Even if only a part of Rupert's Land and the North-west Territories had been added to the united province, the addition would simply have emphasized the already existing preponderance of Canada West. It would probably have forced the adoption of representation by population and led to the abandonment of sectional equality in the provincial legislature. It would, in the eyes of French Canadians, have seriously threatened their distinctive culture; and the union might have broken apart in fear and anger.

British North American federation would prevent all this. British North American federation could transform a provincial crisis into a national triumph. It would provide a framework in which French-Canadian culture would be given the protection of provincial status and in which Rupert's Land and the North-west Territories could be gradually organized as they developed. Only in this fashion, in all probability, could a transcontinental nation be created; and the potential strength of transcontinental nationhood would perhaps alone suffice to ensure the survival of British North America.

III

As one looks back, over the intervening century, at the events of the summer of 1858, one cannot help but be impressed by their prophetic significance in Canadian history. As one regards those three years from 1856 to 1859, one feels almost a sense of astonishment at the closeness of their resemblance to another, much more famous three years which began with the formation of the coalition Government in 1864 and ended with Canadian Confederation in 1867. It is almost as if the period from 1856 to 1859 could be looked upon as a preliminary experiment, a species of dress rehearsal, for successful federal union. Many of the actors have already taken their positions on the stage; some of those with star parts are already clearly discernible. And, as one reads over the letters and memoranda in which the Canadians tried to explain their federal plan to the British Colonial Office during the autumn of 1858, one gets the distinct impression that the dialogue is taking shape and that some of the very best lines have already been written. The situations in the years 1856–59 seem vaguely to anticipate those of 1864–67; and the two plots have an odd family relationship as if, at least, they had been contrived by the same author. The scenery in both cases is identical—a few small, underpopulated, staple-producing provinces, set in the howling wilderness of half a continent, with somewhere in the background, lurking menacingly in the shadow, that sinister villain of all Canadian dramas, the United States.

And yet the dress rehearsal of 1856–59 was not the immediate prelude to a real production. The famous announcement of the summer of 1858 had no direct consequences, while the declared purpose of the summer of 1864 was achieved three years later in Canadian Confederation. How is the success of the one and the failure of the other to be explained? The two episodes lie before us, implying contrasts, inviting comparisons; and one is inevitably tempted to use that method, regarded so fondly by sociologists in general and logical positivists in particular, and, in my opinion at least, so properly distrusted by historians. If we embark on an exercise in the comparative method, we shall probably not discover a general law about movements towards federal union, or even, to narrow the field very sharply indeed, about Canadian movements towards federal union. We may discover that the apparent resemblance between these two examples of the same historical species is a superficial resemblance, observable only from the outside; and that, on closer examination from the inside, the two episodes will turn out to be two separate and quite distinct cases.

One important contrast emerges immediately when one compares the purely parliamentary events of July and August 1858, with those of June 1864. The rapidly changing political situation of the summer of 1858 certainly provided a much better illustration of the governmental instability which sectionalism had brought to the Province of Canada. The constitutional crisis of 1858 was far more dramatic than that of 1864. And yet—and this, surely, is the important point—its parliamentary consequences were a good deal less significant. The federal plan of 1858 was adopted by a Conservative Administration; but it was a coalition Government of Conservatives and Reformers, commanding a large majority in the House and formed with the express purpose of attempting constitutional reform, which, in June 1864, announced that it would seek a federal union of the whole of British North America. There was a good deal of truth in the charge of one of the officials in the Colonial Office that in 1858 the Confederation issue was still in "a crude state of party politics." By 1864 it had been lifted out of the crude state of party politics; and both parties, and all but a small minority of the House, had agreed to end a situation from which everybody had suffered.

The agreement of the Canadian parties was not the only new factor in the situation. The attitude of the United Kingdom had altered in an important and striking fashion in the short period of six years. It was true, of course, that Great Britain's major objectives in the north remained fundamentally much the same. Labouchere and Bulwer-Lytton, the Colonial Secretaries of the late

1850s did not differ materially in purpose from Cardwell and Carnarvon who held office at the time of Canadian Confederation. All of them wished equally to cut British commitments in North America; all of them hoped to persuade the colonies in general, and the Province of Canada in particular, to assume a larger part of the responsibility of government in the new world. Here they were agreed; but Cardwell and Carnarvon realized, as Bulwer-Lytton most emphatically did not, that a British North American federal union would be of immense assistance in achieving these purely imperial objectives. The temperamental Bulwer-Lytton, who, one sometimes suspects, carried the melodrama of his romances into the conduct of the Colonial Office, was at one and the same time hotly insistent that Canada should take over Rupert's Land and the Northwest Territories, and coldly discouraging to the plan of federal union. It was Cardwell and Carnarvon, not Bulwer-Lytton, who understood the essential connection between the west and Confederation. It was Cardwell and Carnarvon who sensibly realized that if Great Britain wished to get rid of some of her burdens in North America, she must help to found a British American state which was strong enough to bear them. From the moment when the new Confederation scheme was first broached in 1864, Cardwell, and later Carnarvon, supported it with conviction and vigour.

British encouragement was much stronger in 1864 than it had been in 1858. And so also, in the eyes of Canadians, was pressure from the United States. The increasing weight of this negative influence, of which British Americans were becoming more and more anxiously conscious during the early 1860s, is attributable largely to the American Civil War. The danger of the encroachment of American settlement and exploitation on the tiny British outposts in the north-west was much as it had been a few years before; it may, indeed, have been developing a little more slowly, as a result, in part, of the republic's concentration on its own desperate domestic struggle. But there was no real reason for assurance here; and there was much cause for disquiet elsewhere. The special peril which threatened Rupert's Land and the new colonies on the Pacific coast might not have increased very noticeably; but the general danger facing British North America as a whole was greater than any of its citizens then living could remember its ever having been before. It is here, perhaps, that we touch upon one of the greatest, if not the greatest of the differences between the situation of 1858 and that of 1864. The Crimean enlistment controversy of 1856 had produced a short, sharp explosion of American annoyance; but the Civil War led to a steady and ominous deterioration of the relations between the United Kingdom and the United States.

British North America was inevitably involved in this mounting antagonism, either directly through the breaches of neutrality which the United States alleged she had committed, or indirectly through the controversies which arose between the United Kingdom and the republic. The *Trent* incident, which led John A. Macdonald to propose a militia force of 100,000 men for Canada alone, provoked the first of these angry quarrels; but the *Trent* incident, for all its seriousness, occurred early, when the hands of the North were more than full and when the outcome of the struggle was still far from certain. In June 1864, when the Canadian coalition Government was formed and when the battle of Gettysburg was nearly a year in the past, the situation had greatly changed. It had changed still more by the autumn of the same year, when a handful of Confederate soldiers launched, from the Province of Canada, their stupid and ineffective raid upon the town of St. Albans in Vermont. By that time the United States was ready and eager for reprisals. It announced the abrogation of the Reciprocity Treaty with British North America; it threatened—and, in the circumstances, no more sinister threat could have been imagined—to suspend the Rush-Bagot agreement limiting naval armaments on the Great Lakes.

It is easy to exaggerate the influence of the American Civil War upon the movement for Canadian Confederation. It is easy, in particular, to overestimate the effects of the St. Albans Raid. The coalition Government of June 1864, was formed and its purpose declared in direct response to a domestic, not an international, crisis. The Quebec Conference, which laid the bases of the federal constitution, met nine days before the St. Albans Raid occurred and the British government's favourable attitude to Confederation had been decided upon even earlier. The American Civil War did not inspire the Canadian desire for constitutional reform or the British wish for retrenchment; but it did help to give both amplitude and urgency to the Anglo-Canadian plans for achieving their objectives. For both Canadians and British it was not enough to do a little constitutional tinkering and make a few budget cuts. They had to build a nation. And their nation had to be built in the midst of a great war which had convulsed the North American continent and threatened to embroil the English-speaking world.

BRITISH NORTH AMERICA ON THE EVE OF CONFEDERATION

Ged Martin

In February and March 1867, the British parliament passed legislation to unite Canada, New Brunswick and Nova Scotia into a single Dominion. The preamble to the British North America Act stated that 'such a Union would conduce to the Welfare of the Provinces and Promote the Interests of the British Empire'.[1] It is not always noted that Confederation passed through Westminster in the midst of the crisis of the Second Reform Act, the most divisive domestic political upheaval in the four decades between the repeal of the Corn Laws in 1846 and the defeat of the Irish Home Rule in 1886. Yet the British North America Act was not passed in an imperial fit of absent-mindedness; the British were active participants in the process of Confederation, not mere onlookers. The main thesis of this study may be reduced to a single statement: between 1837 and 1867, the British came to favour the eventual creation of a union of British North America.[2]

Preliminary statements of this thesis have been summarised by one historian as meaning that 'while British support was essential for Confederation, it was circumstances within British North America which gave the British something to support'.[3] In fact, if British North America and its people are placed within the context of a wider Atlantic world, the British role may be seen to have been more dynamic. Even if viewed as mainly reactive, it is still necessary to explain why the British seem to have been so united in their response to the movement for political union of the provinces. Of course, a bare statement of the thesis is not enough, and its meaning is best explored by asking six questions of the text: who? where? what? why? when? and how? Who were 'the British'? Where were they referring to when they talked of 'Canada' or 'British North America': were their perceptions and understanding of the provinces superficial or profound? What form of government did they believe might be appropriate to such diverse communities? Why did they feel that the provinces should be united? When did they envisage that a union might be brought about? How did they expect the process to occur? The answers to these questions suggest that the British were not simply spectators of a Canadian drama as they have so often been portrayed, but played an active and necessary role in defining and achieving the aim of Confederation.

The role of the British in the achievement of British North American union cannot be fully assessed without a wider examination of the way in which historians have predominantly explained the coming of Confederation in the 1860s. Here it is necessary to say something in defence of the notion that there is a shared corpus, a tendency to consensus, in the way in which historians have treated Confederation. It is argued in the present study that merely to meld words into phrases such as 'British pressure' does not in itself establish that the British had any leverage to contribute, and still less that any efforts they may have made were effective. It would be inconsistent to take such a position on the one hand while on the other simply hiding behind identically constructed allusions to scholarly consensus, interlocking explanatory packages and so forth. Above all, it would be pointed out that Canadian Confederation has attracted the attention of at least four historians of world rank, and that it is an unnecessary slight to their originality to shoe-horn them into a constructed and averaged viewpoint. The birth of the Dominion of Canada inspired a grandeur of imaginative empathy in D.G. Creighton, and a controlled passion of commitment in W.L. Morton. J.M.S. Careless and P.B. Waite combined sensitivity to the subtlety of the options facing British North America with a mastery of sources upon which the subsequent student can only draw with grateful respect.[4] To appear to lump such scholars together, and furthermore to cite them alongside the necessary simplifications of textbooks written for classroom use may seem both a scholarly discourtesy as well as intellectually pointless. Equally, a study which asserts that we should adopt a certain reserve in assessing the statements of the Fathers of Confederation should be wary of pouncing upon every eccentricity or passing error by individual historians as if to imply that each and every scholar who has considered the subject must embrace the same viewpoint.

It may also be objected that some of the works cited are now so dated that it would be kinder to leave them in the peaceful repose. For instance, A.R.M. Lower's *Colony to Nation* first appeared in 1946, and even then went little further than 1939, Lower himself permitted its reissue in 1977 largely as 'a document in its own right'. His description of French Canadians as 'a feminine people' who should be wooed 'as a very womanly woman' was by the standards of 1946 a sympathetic attempt by an English Canadian to bridge the country's great internal divide, but if reflects stereotypes of culture and gender which would now be widely regarded as too embarrassing even to discuss.[5] Why, then, bother to consider Lower's assessment of Confederation? Overall, it may seem tempting to dismiss the notion of an inherited consensus of explanation and attitudes in the historical writing on Confederation as a straw target, lifeless, stuffed with shavings and far too easy to hit.

Yet it is possible to discern areas of predominant consensus and shared attitude in the way in which most historians write about major topics, in all countries and all centuries, and some of this—as Chapter Two discusses—has to do with methodological pitfalls in the craft of history itself. Take, for example, Canada's National Policy, the combined strategy of tariff protection and railway construction adopted in 1879 and seen by Creighton, and many others, as the natural fulfilment of the political union of 1867. In 1966, J.H. Dales attempted to strip the emperor's clothes from this national shibboleth. On the basis of quotation from five works, one of which he had perpetrated himself, Dales identified a 'historians' stereotype' which he attacked both for ignoring internal inconsistencies in its package of arguments and for overlooking the 'awkward gap' of twenty years between the introduction of the policy and the results claimed for it. In positing a historical 'stereotype', Dales did not imply absolute and uniform orthodoxy. Indeed, he was specific in his praise for the way in which Lower impatiently brushed aside 'the standard patter'.[6]

A similar tendency to shared viewpoint—based on the repetition of inconsistent argument and unconvincing assertion—may be discerned in the way historians have discussed Canadian Confederation. Commenting on three studies of the issue in New Brunswick and Prince Edward Island, Phillip Buckner found it 'difficult not to come away from these works with the impressions that there was virtually no support for Confederation in the Maritimes, except for a handful of prescient individuals who had the imagination to accept the leadership of a more far-sighted and progressive Canadians'. This is a point of great importance for the present study, since a tendency among historians to exaggerate opposition to Confederation in the Maritimes has required a similar distortion to present the British as the countervailing force wheeled in to overcome bovine resistance. Buckner identified a tendency to patronise Maritimers as a common theme in the studies he criticised, even when written by scholars who were themselves natives of the region. He also found it significant that all three studies were products of the early 1960s. 'Since most Canadian historians were still influenced by the consensus approach, which minimized the significance of internal conflicts by focusing on the things which united Canadians...they tended to downplay regional concerns and to interpret the making of Confederation as a success story of which all Canadians should be proud.'[7]

Thus it is possible not only to recognise originality and at the same time to honour grace and incisiveness in scholarly work, but also to point to shared assumptions which may colour and unwittingly distort the interpretation of a major episode. Since history is—or should be—written in multiple dialogue, it would indeed be surprising not to find both diversity and consensus, and the existence of the one does not invalidate the identification of the other. Here, the humble textbook may provide an illustrative role, since classroom texts usually represent a distillation and thereby to some extent a simplification of received opinion. Indeed, as the focus of historical scholarship in Canada has tended to shift to new and exciting themes in regional and social history, so the tried and true tale of Confederation seems to be squeezed into increasingly sparse outline. Thus the textbooks of yesteryear retain their place in any discussion of the way in which historians have treated the subject. Lower's structure for explaining Confederation was methodologically impressive, starting with the 'large factors' or long-term predisposing influences, and moving through intermediate causes to immediate circumstances and the role of personalities. Two shortcomings reduced the overall value of his interpretation. One lay in some of the insights which animated the structure he designed, and the other was his verdict that Confederation was a miracle.[8] However, those who teach history have a vested interest in assuming that its influence on those who study the subject lingers after they have completed their courses. In the Canada of the 1990s, both those who claim the country's system of government has failed and those who believe it can be renewed have appealed to the inspiring story of Confederation in the 1860s.[9] This will include an appeal to notions formed by adult citizens in earlier decades. It should be also noted that relatively little has been written on Confederation since the 1960s—itself a kind of testimony to the existence of a satisfactory historical consensus on the subject.

This study challenges a number of the elements which go to make up the generally accepted picture of the coming of Confederation. Briefly, the Union of the Canadas was not a political failure which had to be swept away in favour of the new British North American structure. It was anything but 'deadlocked' in 1864, although its politics had tangled into a short-term log-jam. One issue and one issue alone made its reconstruction overwhelmingly necessary, and that was the rapid population growth of Upper Canada, which rendered untenable the artificially equal representation of the two sections of the province in the Assembly. Some form of representation by population was virtually unavoidable, since Upper Canada was almost united in its demand, and English-speaking Lower Canadians were moving towards joining forces with them to resolve the issue once and for all. The Great Coalition formed in the province of Canada in June 1864 was by no means united in its determination to secure British North American union: the arch-enemies John A. Macdonald and George Brown attempted to seize each other not by the hand but rather by the throat. Brown aimed at trapping Macdonald into delivering a federation simply composed of Upper and Lower Canada, a cosmetic version of outright representation by population, but one which offered a measure of damage-limitation to Cartier and his French Canadian Bleus. Macdonald desperately needed the wider union for the exercise of his political talents of balancing and blandishment.

Confederation emerged as the solution in 1867 not because it was the right answer and inevitable destiny of the provinces. In reality, many of the arguments advanced for Confederation were exaggerated and even downright misleading. It was not necessary for the provinces to unite in order to build the Intercolonial railway, which was in any case a project of doubtful utility. Confederation had almost nothing to offer by way of improvement in local defence, and was equally irrelevant to—if not diversionary from—westward expansion. Arguments about interprovincial trade or appeals to an emerging British North American nationality were based on foundations too weak to provide credible historical explanations. Of course, it is still possible to invert the argument at each point, and conclude that Confederation was carried because enough contemporaries saw sufficient prospect of personal gain in any one of the individual arguments advanced to ignore disadvantages or bogus claims and get behind the proposal. Yet one reason why it was Confederation which triumphed, and not any alternative framework which might equally have opened opportunities, was because Macdonald exploited the fact that British legislation would be required for the reshaping of the province of Canada, and the British were committed to the wider union.

Nova Scotians and New Brunswickers—even if reluctantly—recognised that the time had come to accept a solution which the British had long defined as an eventual target, Ironically, the portrayal of Confederation as primarily the achievement of a farsighted Canadian coalition has actually required the interposition of an imperial and imperious Britain to force a change of heart in the Maritimes in 1865 and 1866. In reality, the imperial contribution after 1864 was little more than bluff and hint, and by portraying the British as the trump card against Maritime reluctance, historians have not merely distorted the record of the mid-1860s, but failed to appreciate the importance of the earlier British contribution in defining the aim and clearing the way to the union of the provinces in the years before 1864. It is necessary to move away from mechanistic ideas of threats and 'pressure', towards a wider appreciation of the position of the British North American provinces within a context framed by the United States and shaped by Britain, towards seeing Confederation not as a solution dictated by the specific circumstances of the mid-1860s, but rather as a long-maturing idea which came to blanket the political discourse of that era because it could be argued—however spuriously and probably with some degree of pardonable insincerity—that its time had come.

***

In 1861, the British railway entrepreneur, Edward Watkin, was glad to find that both the premier of New Brunswick, Leonard Tilley, and the colonial secretary, the Duke of Newcastle, shared his vision of a united transcontinental dominion in British North America.[10] To cite Watkin's enthusiasm as symbolic of the way in which an unofficial British observer could link the imperial government with provincial leadership is not to endorse the myth, which he created in his own autobiography, that he was the crucial progenitor of Confederation: at one time, Watkin made a regular appearance in accounts of the coming of Confederation, presumably to personify a sophisticated element of financial imperialism.[11] Latterly, he has been less visible, probably because it is no longer seemly for an Englishman to have played a key role in a Canadian national achievement, although he is probably the 'Edward Watkins' of a recent textbook.[12] More valuable to a stocktaking than Watkin's boosting of his own importance in the story of Confederation was his subsequent recollection that 'in 1861, this great idea seemed like a mere dream of the uncertain future'.[13]

However, though the future was opaque, it is possible to reconstruct something of the British North American present as it was in 1861, since most provinces imitated Britain in holding a census that year, and all dutifully submitted miscellaneous statistics for publication in London.[14] These statistics may not be perfect, but they are sufficient to demonstrate the position of British North America as a vigorous but still comparatively small segment within a wider Atlantic world. In 1861, the eastern third of British North America was divided into five provinces, with a settler population of about three and a third million. Further west, the land was almost empty. Even by the end of the 1860s, there were barely 25000 settlers in the whole of British Columbia and at the Red River, while native populations probably numbered less than 100000. The North-West loomed large in the imaginations of some British North American leaders, but played almost no part in the events leading to Confederation.[15] For most practical purposes, British North America meant the Atlantic region, the St Lawrence valley and the settled areas to the north of the Great Lakes.

One province dominated British North America in 1861. Canada recorded two and a half million people, three quarters of the total. Moreover, Canada was growing fast: four years later, it was estimated to have added the equivalent of New Brunswick and Prince Edward Island to its population. Indeed, its rapid growth was imposing strains on its internal duality. The province had been created by the British in 1841 by legislating a union of the colonies of

Upper and Lower Canada, which would emerge again in 1867 as Ontario and Quebec. The intention had been to use the English-speaking colonists to control the French, and since Lower Canada then had the larger population, Upper Canadian interests had been weighted by giving the two sections of the new province equal representation in the Assembly.[16] For a brief period, the two sections had been renamed Canada West and Canada East, but the old names soon resurfaced and here will be used throughout.[17] By 1861, Upper Canada (usually pronounced 'Up Canada'[18]) had pulled far ahead, with a shade under 1.4 million people, against the 1.1 million of Lower Canada. Around one fifth of the people of Lower Canada were of British or American origin: the French-speaking population probably fell just short of 900000—enough for cultural survival, but too few to encourage any dreams of an independent state.[19] The remaining provinces were dwarfed by Canada. The three Maritime provinces collectively numbered half the population of Upper Canada, with a third of a million people in Nova Scotia, a quarter of a million in New Brunswick and a mere eighty thousand in Prince Edward Island. Newfoundland did not count its people in 1861, but there was little reason to think that is population had grown much since the previous census, in 1857, had reported 122000 inhabitants.

While the province of Canada overshadowed the remaining colonies of British North America, it looked a good deal less impressive when viewed within a North Atlantic context. To the south, the United States had enumerated over 31 million people at its census of 1860.[20] The raw figure was awe-inspiring, although in 1861 its full import could not be guessed since the great republic was embarking on a civil war which many thought would end in its disruption. Still, even fragmented, the numbers put British North America into a small perspective. The Southern States, seen by many as the gallant underdogs, had a white population of five and a half million, more than double that of the province of Canada, while Black slaves alone outnumbered all British North Americans. the twenty million people of the Northern States would soon show a frightening determination to fight for the Union cause, backed by an even more terrifying industrial might. The other external pole of the British North American world was Britain itself, where in 1861 the census counted 23 million people in England, Wales and Scotland, plus almost six million more in Ireland.[21] Certainly with nine times as many people living in the crowded British Isles as in all the British North American provinces combined, it is hardly surprising that the colonies not only remained dominated by Britain culturally and politically, but were content to be subordinate for purposes of defence and investment as well.

Comparative population figures help to explain the tiny part which British North America played in British affairs. A critic of Confederation warned the Canadian Assembly not to entertain inflated ideas of undertaking the defence of half a continent 'with a population less than that of the city of London'.[22] New Brunswick's governor Arthur Gordon was as usual exaggerating when he impatiently noted that his province was 'little exceeding in population an English manufacturing town', but it was true that there were more people in

Liverpool, Manchester or Birmingham, and indeed in Dublin and Glasgow as well, than in New Brunswick. In the 1860s, Britain's great provincial towns were knocking on the doors of power, and it cannot be said that the politicians within were rushing to admit them. Colonies across a wide ocean could hardly be expected to have much more impact. The contrast became even more striking when towns were matched against towns. Montreal, by common consent the metropolis of Canada, was equal in population to Dundee, the sixteenth largest town in Britain. Toronto, the rising and ambitious centre of the upper province, was smaller than the Black Country town of Dudley, while Quebec ranked a shade ahead of neighbouring Wolverhampton. Saint John, the largest city in the Maritimes, had the same population as the Suffolk port of Ipswich. These comparisons are not intended to denigrate, but merely to stress the point that the Dundees and the Dudleys had little enough political impact inside Britain. Their equivalents overseas were almost invisible. In 1842, MPs packed the House of Commons to discuss the bribery of voters at Ipswich, because electoral corruption touched them all. When the colonial secretary attempted—with apologies 'that it might not excite much interest'—to follow the debate by introducing a measure for the government of Newfoundland, his words were drowned by the noise of MPs streaming from the chamber.[23]

British North American trade figures similarly illustrated the twin pulls of Britain and the United States. The provinces predominantly exported raw materials to Britain and the United States—the latter helped by the Reciprocity Treaty concluded in 1854—and carried on very little trade among themselves. Canada sent 51 per cent of its exports by value to Britain in 1861, and 44 per cent to the United States. The rest of British North America accounted for under 3 per cent of Canadian export trade—and even then Canada had a substantial trade balance with the other provinces. Agricultural products and timber constituted by far the largest categories of exports from Canada. Fish, minerals and manufactures came well behind, each amounting to around 2 per cent of total exports. Unprocessed lumber tended to go to Britain, timber products and animals to the United States, which also absorbed most of Canada's barley. Flour and wheat exports were more evenly divided.

Each of the Atlantic provinces had its own distinct pattern of trade. Timber in various forms made up 70 per cent of New Brunswick's exports. Britain was the destination of two-thirds of its produce, with just under one-fifth going to the United States. Canada barely featured as a destination for New Brunswick exports, and even Nova Scotia took only 6 per cent of its total, although there may have been some under-recording here. Prince Edward Island alone had a trade pattern dominated by British North America, feeding its neighbours with the corn and potatoes which accounted for two-third of its exports. Almost half of its exports went to the other provinces, but only the tiniest trickle found its way to Canada, while the United States was a large market. Fish accounted for two-fifths of Nova Scotian exports—mostly to the West Indies—with coal following at 10 per cent, then timber and a re-export trade in Caribbean sugar.

In sharp contrast to neighbouring New Brunswick, Nova Scotia sent only 5 per cent of its exports by value to Britain, and its external trade was roughly equally divided among the United States, the other provinces and the Caribbean. Newfoundland's trading pattern was different again, Cod in one form or another accounted for 72 per cent of exports by value, and seal products—oil and skins—for 21 per cent. Two-fifths of Newfoundland exports consisted of dried cod shipped to Spain, Portugal and Italy, while Britain was the destination of a further third. Newfoundland did very little trade with the United States, while the rest of British North America was well-nigh invisible in its statistics.

British North American trade figures certainly do not suggest that in 1861 the provinces were in the process of economic integration as the precursor of political unity.[24] Nor would they constitute in any way a predictor of reactions to Confederation when the issue became a practical proposition three years later. By and large, the provinces did not trade with each other at all, and critics of Confederation in Canada argued that it was unlikely that they ever would, simply because they produced virtually identical products. The province which was most dependent on exports to its neighbours was Prince Edward Island, which doggedly refused to merge with them. Compared with Nova Scotia, New Brunswick was more than ten times as reliant upon the British market, yet it can hardly be argued that New Brunswick proved to be ten times more malleable to British wishes.

Yet the trade figures do offer some clues to the way in which the provinces would respond to the Confederation issue. For instance, they draw attention to the dominance of Halifax within Nova Scotia. In 1861 Halifax handled over half the external trade of the province. It is not surprising that there would be more support for Confederation in Halifax than in the rest of the province, for political union and improved communications might make the city the funnel for trade and the fulcrum of communications between British North America and Europe. In the long run, the interests of Halifax were likely to be those of the province. Certainly Yarmouth, the centre of hardline resistance to union with Canada, ranked a poor third, handling less than 3 per cent of Nova Scotia's trade. The importance of coal in the Nova Scotian export trade is also striking, and once the end of reciprocity threatened the United States market, it is understandable that eyes might be turned if not to Canada, then at least to any structure which might bring coal-consuming railways.

Once again, the overall importance of British North American trade needs to be assessed by placing it in a wider Atlantic context. The provinces accounted for around 3 per cent of Britain's total export trade, and supplied in return commodities which would for the most part be obtained elsewhere. By contrast, one-fifth of all British imports came from the United States, including four-fifths of the raw cotton which supplied Lancashire. 'Though with the North we sympathise,' sang *Punch* in 1861, 'it must not be forgotten that with the South we've stronger ties which are composed of cotton'.[25] Despite the steadily increasing obstacle of protectionist tariffs, the United States market remained very important to British industry. 'I leave you to judge how long your large towns would support you in a serious contest with their Customers,' Ashburton warned Howick in 1838.[26] The irony was that Britain was politically committed to the defence of the part of North America which was least valuable to it economically against a possible threat from one of its most important overseas markets. The problem did not greatly matter before 1861, since the British forces in Canada—small though they were—were believed to be superior to the minute United States army, and hence an effective deterrent. By the mid-1860s, a land war with the suddenly militarised United States had become unthinkable—and also terribly likely. From this ambiguity may be traced not the origin but certainly the fervour with which the British endorsed the British North American union: Confederation might not provide the way out of an insoluble trap, but at least it was a step in some direction, even if an unknown one.

One final area of comparison is needed to set British North America into its Atlantic context, and this is perhaps the hardest of all to measure. Comparatively speaking, how rich were the provinces? An attempt at an international league table has been made by two American historians, R.W. Fogel and S.L. Engerman, as part of a controversial project to assess the economic effectiveness of slavery in the American South. Scoring the South at 100, they rated Canada, at 96, as the sixth most prosperous country in the world, behind Australia (144), the North (140), Britain (126) and Switzerland (100). Yet their figures are drawn from the post-Confederation period, and presumably involve an averaging of the diverse regions of the new Dominion.[27] Durham in 1839 had made much play with the contrast between the 'activity and bustle' of the United States and the 'waste and desolate' appearance of the British provinces.[28] Yet some of the perceived backwardness of the provinces was the result of their more recent settlement: for instance, if Upper Canada is compared not with the United States as a whole, but with neighbouring Ohio, Michigan and Indiana, its record of railway construction in the 1850s becomes more impressive.[29] Certainly by 1855, Sir Edmund Head could contrast the '*astounding*' prosperity of Upper Canada with 'the sort of sleepy look which pervades Lower Canada'.[30] The Maritimes, on the other hand, were thought of as poor and sluggish. There was certainly poverty in British North America, but there was comfort and prosperity too. What does seem clear is that British North America was capital-poor. Banks were small and funding for major projects would have to come from outside, and especially from the London money market.[31]

By 1861, all five provinces had achieved an undefined form of self-government, in an imitation of the British parliamentary system which Dickens found like 'looking at Westminster through the wrong end of a telescope'[32] and Cobden 'inherently ludicrous', a travesty 'with its votes of Confidence, its cabinet Ministers, with a mock sovereign dismissing & sending for advisers,—& all about next to nothing.'[33] Party alliances were fluid enough in Britain, but in Canada, commented *The Times*, a politician 'sets about making a party as he would a salad'.[34] There were labels and allegiances, liberal, reform, Clear Grit,

Rouge, conservative and Bleu, but they did not prevent politicians from forming alliances which were sometimes driven by personal ambition and feuds. Presiding over the whole was a governor appointed from Britain, in most cases more than the 'mock sovereign' derided by Cobden, but charged rather with a sensitive task of reconciling local and imperial priorities.[35]

In Canada, the British representative was styled 'governor-general', with the imperial functionaries of the Maritimes technically 'lieutenant-governors' subject to his sway. In practice, the connection was minimal, and for the Maritimes, the less cumbrous style of 'governor' is used throughout this study. Two ex-cabinet ministers, Durham and Sydenham, held office as governor-general of Canada during the crisis years 1838–41, but thereafter the post was held by a series of men who combined some measure of diplomatic, administrative or political experience at home with the financial need for exile in an unprestigious colony. Elgin, who held office from 1847 to 1854, was a Scottish peer who had briefly sat in the Commons. His successor, Sir Edmund Head, was an Oxford don turned administrator, of combined Kentish gentry and South Carolina loyalist stock. Head was succeeded in 1861 by Lord Monck, an Irish peer who had held minor office under Palmerston. For both Elgin and Monck, colonial service held out the attraction of a British peerage, since they were otherwise barred from sitting in the House of Lords.

Perhaps because of its sensitive proximity to the United States, New Brunswick also received socially and politically well-qualified governors between 1848 and 1866, although the last of them, Arthur Gordon, made up for relative lack of experience with a massive shortfall in humility, except in his dealings with the Almighty, to whom, in a much-derided official prayer, he styled himself 'thy servant Arthur'.[36] The actual power of a governor would greatly depend on his personality and local circumstances, but governors had a monopoly on official communications with the Colonial Office, often supplemented by unofficial access to influential figures in London as well.

Cobden was wrong in his scornful claim that British North American politics were 'all about next to nothing'. In Canada, the underlying issue by 1861 was the artificial equality of representation in the Assembly. Grand imperial plans of constitutional engineering had been undermined by the emergence in the 1840s of a system of internal self-government, by which the local affairs of the province were conducted by ministries answerable to the Assembly. Within the supposedly united province, the ministerial system which developed actually enshrined internal duality, partly because the two sections of the province continued to operate distinct legal systems. In a sharp variation from the British model, local ministries were usually led by co-premiers: LaFontaine-Baldwin; Hincks-Morin; Cartier-Macdonald.[37] By the 1850s, rapid immigration had tilted the population balance in favour of Upper Canada, and English-speaking reformers had begun to campaign for representation by population ('rep. by pop.' for short), a redistribution of Assembly seats and voting power which would place Lower Canada in a minority.[38] Alternatives were proposed by a Lower Canada politician, Alexander Galt, a Rouge though of independent leanings, who in July 1858 argued for the reconstruction of the province of Canada as a federation of two or three units, or for a federation of Canada with the North-West, or for a union of all the provinces.[39]

The ministry led by George Cartier and John A. Macdonald had emerged weakened from elections a few months earlier, but had apparently evaded the divisive question of selecting a permanent seat of government for the province (Canada, as a colony, could not aspire to a 'capital') by passing the choice to Queen Victoria. However, the Queen's compromise choice of Ottawa united supporters of other towns, and on 28 July the Assembly voted to ask Victoria to think again. Although undefeated on an issue of confidence, the ministry took the opportunity to resign the next day, thereby forcing the Reform leader, George Brown—who was also proprietor of the *Globe*, Upper Canada's most powerful newspaper—to shoe-horn his francophobic prejudices into an alliance with A.-A. Dorion and the Rouges. On 2 August, the Brown-Dorion ministry was sworn in. By taking office, the new ministers automatically vacated their seats in the Assembly, and had to return to their constituents to fight by-elections. As a result, an already weak combination went down to immediate defeat, and was forced to resign on 4 August following a refusal by the governor-general to call a fresh general election.

Now ensued an element of farce. The law required ministers to fight by-elections on first appointment to office, but it exempted those who accepted a new portfolio within thirty days of resigning an old one: Macdonald had carried the change the previous year to facilitate leisurely reshuffles. Consequently, by swearing themselves into entirely new posts on 6 August, the former Cartier-Macdonald ministers were able to retain their positions in the Assembly, since they had resigned their former offices only a week before.[40] On 7 August, they resigned their new posts and went back to their old ones: John A. Macdonald, formerly Attorney-General West, spent twenty-four hours as postmaster-general before reverting to the position for which his legal skills so well fitted him. So far as the law knew, there had simply been two ministerial reshuffles, both within the permitted thirty-day period. The Reformers remained saddled with the task of fighting by-elections to vindicate their right to hold offices from which they had been summarily ousted. They vented their anger by launching a private prosecution for perjury, claiming that Macdonald had 'insulted the Majesty of Heaven' by swearing to undertake an office which he knew he would abandon the following day. The courts ruled that Macdonald had only sworn to be a diligent postmaster for 'so long as he held the office', but on attempting to recover his legal costs, he found that the prosecution had been undertaken in the name of an undischarged bankrupt.[41] The 'double shuffle' was a squalid episode but one which—as will be argued in Chapter Two—does not merit all the indignation which some historians have poured upon it.

The Cartier-Macdonald combination emerged strengthened from this episode since they persuaded Galt to join them, adopting his policy of British North American union as their own. (This had the incidental advantage of making it less likely that Galt would be lured into alliance with Brown and Dorion, who were vaguely committed to some form of federal restructuring within Canada itself.) However, the Canadian federal initiative of 1858–59 made little progress. The other provinces were reluctant to be dragged into the problems of distant Canada, while the British government treated the whole matter with some reserve—a stance which requires further discussion, since of course it appears to conflict with the thesis of a developing British consensus in favour of a union of the provinces. Nonetheless, the reconstituted ministry proved durable enough, although elections in 1861 once again shook its hold, as Upper Canada became increasingly insistent on securing what it saw as its rightful share of political power. One Reformer, William McDougall, even talked of 'looking below the border for relief'.[42]

The United States, however, provided not a solution but a shock. In November 1861, a Northern warship had stopped a British steamer, the *Trent*, on the high seas and arrested two unofficial Confederate envoys who were on their way to Europe. The British were outraged and the two countries came close to war. Reinforcements were sent to the provinces, but were forced to make an epic journey across New Brunswick to reach Canada, since the St Lawrence was frozen and there was no rail link to the seaboard.[43] The crisis was resolved, but it seemed to point, first, to a reform of Canada's own local defence force, which was called with unconscious but appropriate irony, the 'sedentary' militia and, secondly, to extending Canada's Grand Trunk railway line eastward to Halifax—a project which required a massive capital subsidy, since the Grand Trunk was almost bankrupt and the additional mileage was unlikely to generate much commercial traffic. Arguably, the real lesson of the *Trent* crisis was that Britain simply could not respond in time to defend the provinces against American attack, but in the short term, the militia and the railway were the main items on the political agenda, and historians have generally concluded that not only the politicians but the political system itself failed to respond to the challenge.

The Cartier-Macdonald ministry proposed a reform of the militia which was both extensive and expensive. On 20 May 1862, its bill was rejected in the Assembly. The British were outraged, their disappointment having been fuelled by over-sanguine private reports from the inexperienced governor-general, Lord Monck.[44] In London, both press and parliament accused the Canadians of failing to face reality, of falling down on their obligations. A new ministry was formed, headed by the Reformer, John Sandfield Macdonald, often known simply as 'Sandfield' to distinguish him among Canada's many Macdonalds.[45] His political principle was a primitive form of federalism called the 'double majority': the government would only take action if supported by a majority of members from Upper Canada and a majority of members from Lower Canada.

His stance could variously be regarded as a recognition of basic duality, or as a blind abdication of all leadership.

At least there seemed some prospect of securing the 'Intercolonial' railway, as the line from Halifax to Quebec was coming to be called. In September 1862, the new ministry met representatives of New Brunswick and Nova Scotia to discuss how to apportion the construction costs. The British cabinet had reluctantly agreed in principle to guarantee a loan to finance the work. Two delegates, L.V. Sicotte and W.P. Howland, were then sent to London for further discussions. There, to their dismay, they found that the chancellor of the exchequer, Gladstone, insisted that the loan be accompanied by a sinking fund, that is, that the provinces should take steps to repay the capital borrowed by annual instalments. The Canadians had of course hoped that the entire capital sum would fall due when the loan terminated, so that another generation of politicians would be left to face the task of repayment. Sicotte and Howland withdrew from the London negotiations, but managed to do so in a way which made a reasonable retreat based on lack of money appear as a discreditable lapse from uprightness and common courtesy.[46]

Sandfield's ministry ran into worse trouble the following session, when a private member introduced a bill to extend the degree of public funding to the separate schools of Upper Canada. The issue was apparently semantic but fundamentally sectarian. In Lower Canada, there were two parallel publicly-funded school systems, one Catholic, the other explicitly Protestant. In Upper Canada, there was officially a single system of public schooling. Protestants insisted that the Upper Canadian school system was non-denominational and open to all. Catholics retorted that it was really Protestant and unsuitable for their needs. Hence the development of separate (or Catholic) schools, which clamoured for a share of tax money. Upper Canadian opinion was predominantly opposed to any extension of Catholic privileges, but when the bill came to a vote, many members found it prudent to absent themselves, and the measure was imposed on the upper province by the votes of Catholic French Canadians. What became of the double majority if the principle could be pushed aside on such a sensitive matter? Sandfield replied that it did not extend to private members' bills.[47]

Not surprisingly, a resurgent John A. Macdonald was able to carry a motion of no confidence in May 1863, but narrowly enough to entitle Sandfield to take his case to the voters. The elections were hardly conclusive, although Upper Canadian feeling was hardening in favour of representation by population. Sandfield dropped Sicotte from his ministry, along with two Irishmen, Michael Foley and D'Arcy McGee, but failed to secure the compensating support of his Reform rival, George Brown, who had returned to active politics after a sabbatical business trip to Britain.[48] Both the colonial secretary and the governor-general began to hope that parties might be brought together in a strong government under a neutral leader.[49] Brown, on the other hand, approached the problem from the opposite end, arguing that the most prominent politicians should meet in conclave to review the options for the future of the province.[50] Meanwhile, Sandfield struggled on, to win a place in folklore of Canadian politics as the premier whose ministry lacked even a 'drinking majority': its supporters dared not leave the chamber for a drink for fear that it would be defeated in their absence.[51] They were relieved from this onerous deprivation in March 1864 when Sandfield resigned, undefeated but unsustainable.

Lord Monck secured his elder statesman, but not the broad coalition the British had hoped for. Sir Etienne Taché agreed to come out of semi-retirement—he had dropped out of active politics in 1857 and sat in the Legislative Council—but he formed a ministry around the core of John A. Macdonald, Cartier and Galt which looked very like the combination defeated in 1862. However, the ministry was joined by Michael Foley and D'Arcy McGee, Sandfield's colleagues in 1862–63, notwithstanding the fact that Foley had earlier been characterised by John A. Macdonald as 'Lying Mike' and McGee as a 'ruffian'.[52] The new ministry offered a number of worthy policies, but it could not be said to be built around any overarching crusade for change: on representation by population, for instance, it had no policy at all. It was claimed that Foley had 'temporarily hesitated' on being invited to join, and 'insisted on knowing what the policy of the new Administration was to be'. John A. Macdonald slapped him playfully on the knee and replied, 'D—n it, Foley, join the Government and then help to make the policy.'[53] Parliament reassembled on 4 May 1864, and the new ministry duly went down to defeat on 14 June.

Brown had proposed his committee on the state of the province shortly before Sandfield's resignation in March 1864, but did not secure approval until mid-May. It proved to be unexpectedly harmonious, although this was partly because it also agreed to differ. At its first meeting, a veteran French Canadian, Joseph Turcotte, who had spoken of 'wading knee-deep in blood' to bar representation by population, astonished Brown by announcing that 'the war between Upper and Lower Canada must now cease'.[54] On 14 June, the new committee reported in favour of reconstructing the province on federal lines, although it left open whether this should be British North American in scope or merely confined to the province of Canada. Consensus was still not complete, for three of the twenty members refused to sign the report, and these included Sandfield Macdonald, still wedded to the double majority, his namesake John A. on the grounds that a British North America should adopt the unitary structure of the United Kingdom. Significantly, however, Cartier parted company with his erstwhile ally to sign the report, thereby signalling that he was ready to respond to Brown's reported 'squinting' towards an alliance with the Bleus.[55]

After prolonged negotiations, Taché reconstructed his ministry in the form which became known as the Great Coalition.[56] Brown reluctantly entered, along with Mowat and McDougall, who had both served under Sandfield Macdonald. The Great Coalition is usually described as being committed to the achievement of a British North American union, a fair enough simplification since Confederation was to be its triumph, but in reality it had a dual aim: the union of the whole of British North America if possible, but the reconstruction of the province of Canada if the wider aim proved unattainable. Chapter Two argues that this divergent target was more significant than has usually been recognised.

On the face of it, during the closing months of 1864, the Canadians seemed to be leading a triumphant pageant along what Donald Creighton called 'the road to Confederation'. By useful coincidence, representatives of the Maritime provinces had planned to meet at Charlottetown in September to discuss a union among themselves. While with hindsight this may seem like a natural step towards Confederation, the meeting was in fact undertaken partly in reaction to the perceived bad faith of the Canadians at the Intercolonial negotiations of 1862. The Canadians did not actually gate-crash Charlottetown, but they were energetic in inviting themselves, and quickly won approval in principle for a union of all the provinces. A more formal conference followed at Quebec in October, where a series of resolutions was drawn up. This, the Quebec plan or scheme, became the basis of the eventual British North America Act. Throughout, the Canadians were the driving force, and the bonhomie of the two gatherings masked something of a take-it-or-leave-it attitude to the Maritimers, which soon ensured that neither Prince Edward Island nor Newfoundland would become founders of the new polity. It was the Canadian coalition which sent Brown as its representative to London in December 1864 to enlarge upon the proposals, and the year closed with enthusiastic expressions of support from both government and press in Britain.[57]

There were critics of the scheme in the province of Canada, and their cogency has been underestimated, but when the legislature debated Confederation in February and March 1865, it seemed clear enough that most French Canadians were acquiescent and most English Canadians enthusiastic about the opportunities it would offer.[58] Botched responses by local law-enforcement agencies to desperate raids by Confederate sympathisers from Canadian territory into the Northern States had once again inflamed cross-border relations, and Canadians debated constitutional change in an atmosphere of menace overshadowed by the awful prospect of a vengeful and victorious Northern army invading their province. In the Maritimes, however, a reaction seemed to set in. Joseph Howe was a giant among Nova Scotians, if sometimes a malign one. He emerged from his poor reward for a lifetime's voluble devotion to the empire, a roving post as a fisheries commissioner, to denounce the 'Botheration' scheme with characteristic bombast.[59] Charles Tupper, Nova Scotia's premier, remained committed to Confederation, but prudently refrained from pressing the issue in the Assembly. Worse still, New Brunswick's premier Leonard Tilley decided to go to the polls, and in March 1865 was soundly defeated.[60] The incoming New Brunswick ministry was by no means totally opposed to the union of the provinces—it too was a coalition laced with opportunism—but it seemed at first to be totally united in its dislike for the Quebec scheme. Confederation seemed to be at a standstill.

British North American politicians appeared to respond with a flurry of missions to Britain, and historians have tended to assume that if the principal players thought it appropriate to take their case to London, then the imperial factor must have had a crucial contribution to make. Macdonald, Cartier, Galt and Brown were the first off the mark: John A. himself immodestly styled them 'the big 4',[61] and Creighton dubbed their mission 'Appeal to Caesar'.[62] New Brunswick's A.J. Smith was quick to follow, and Arthur Gordon came home on leave, although in his case with the excuse that he had finally located a bride.[63] The British government made some threatening noises, including disapproving allusions to the problem of colonial defence.[64]

It seemed to work. In November 1865, the Smith ministry in New Brunswick began to fracture, with one member, R.D. Wilmot, converted to Confederation and another, T.W. Anglin, forced out for fundamentalist opposition. Charles Fisher won a symbolic by-election for the cause of Confederation, by the subtle device of promising not to raise the issue if he was elected. By the spring of 1866, Gordon had ousted Smith (something he was not really supposed to do) and both New Brunswick and Nova Scotia fell into line and passed resolutions accepting British North American union in principle. It was now the turn of the Maritimes to discuss the issue in a framework of fear. Demobilised Irish-Americans had proved a fertile recruiting ground for the Fenians, Irish nationalists who aimed to free Ireland by attacking British North America. They were no mean military force, as they proved when they invaded the Niagara peninsula in June 1866, but they were unable to maintain a long-term threat simply because there was a limit to the number of blind eyes the United States government could turn to their activities. Fenian schemes to attack New Brunswick conveniently preceded a second Confederation election in May 1866, and even more conveniently were conducted with minimal regard for confidentiality. For the Irish-born Timothy Anglin, New Brunswick's most fervent anti-Confederate, the Fenians were a disaster. It was not only paranoid Protestantism which came to equate opposition to Confederation with Fenianism: Catholic bishops also supported the constitutional change while damning the revolutionary threat. However, if the Americans showed only limited tolerance towards the Fenians, they vented their disapproval of the provinces by terminating Reciprocity: from St Patrick's Day 1866, British North American produce entering the United States would have to pay customs duties.[65]

The final stages of the road to Confederation led back to Britain. In the autumn and winter of 1866–7, Joseph Howe led a last-ditch campaign to persuade British opinion to grant a reprieve or at least a stay of execution to his province: an election would be due in Nova Scotia in 1867, and Howe hoped to repeat the New Brunswick experience and so block Confederation. Given the disturbed state of British domestic politics at the time, it is notable that Howe's campaign was so unsuccessful, especially as the delegates from Canada did not trouble to arrive until November. In December and January the final details were hammered out, and both the British North America bill and accompanying legislation to provide finance for the Intercolonial railway passed easily through a parliament which was tearing itself apart over changes to Britain's own system of government.[66]

There is admirable artistry in the way in which conventional historical accounts weave together the elements leading to Confederation. From the double
shuffle onwards, the reader sees the crumbling of the existing Canadian Union
through a series of sorry episodes, and watches it sink into helpless deadlock,
as burgeoning Upper Canada demanded an additional share of power which
stagnating Lower Canada could not concede. The *Trent* crisis introduces the
element of external threat, and the defeat of the Militia Bill is presented as a further demonstration of the inability of the existing structure to rise to the
challenge of British North American defence. Upper Canada's spectacular population growth also introduces another element, that of westward expansion. The
demographic explosion of Upper Canada, where population trebled in twenty
years, brought a sensation of impending land shortage, especially as new settlement ran up against the harsh rock of the Canadian Shield. By the mid-1850s,
some Upper Canadians were casting covetous eyes on the largely empty western territories of the Hudson's Bay Company. By coincidence, a gold rush in
the Fraser valley brought about the creation in 1858 of a Pacific coast colony,
British Columbia, supplying a distant focus for expansionist vision. These vast
western territories, it is sometimes asserted,[67] could only be absorbed through
a wholly, new, continental framework of government.

If some eyes in the province of Canada were looking west, others were
drawn eastward, to the Atlantic seaboard, by means of the proposed Intercolonial
railway. The 1850s were a golden age of railway construction, and by the end of
the decade the province of Canada could boast the longest railway line in the
world, running all the way from Sarnia in south-western Upper Canada, to
Rivière-du-Loup, one hundred miles below the city of Quebec. In fact, length
apart, there was not much to boast of about the Grand Trunk. It was widely associated with a lowering of standards of honesty in politics, and its commercial
performance was poor: 'the Grand Trunk was, by 1860, virtually bankrupt'.[68] It
ran parallel to one of the finest waterways in the world: in summer, it could
hardly compete with the St Lawrence route on freight costs, and even for speed,
let alone comfort, it had little to offer. Rivière-du-Loup was its eastern terminus
mainly because the money had finally run out there. The Intercolonial fits into
the explanatory package twice over: first, as a defence project, and secondly
through the argument that such an eastward extension of the Canadian railway
system could only be achieved if balanced by westward expansion to the prairies.
Here again, the *Trent* crisis plays a vital role in the story, since the cameo of
British troops sledging through the snowy interior of New Brunswick seemed
to underline the defence argument for the railway. Moreover, the American
Civil War also introduces an economic motive: Northern resentment at British
North America sympathy for the South led to the termination of Reciprocity, and
so forced the provinces to turn to each other. All in all, the moment was right for
British North Americans to assert a sense of their own nationhood.

In summary, historians have presented five major reasons why
Confederation came about in 1867—with, of course, variation in emphasis and

interpretation. The first was the need for defence against the United States, an argument which underlines the central role of the Intercolonial railway: 'a route for troops from one colony to another, if the Americans attacked'.[69] 'A federation of the British North American colonies could lead to the construction of an intercolonial railway, and to the organisation of a united colonial army'.[70] Secondly, the Intercolonial was also seen as a means of promoting trade among the provinces.[71] Thirdly, the end of Reciprocity provided a further motive 'for the colonies to look to each other, if only as substitute markets'.[72] This seemed to be 'a strong factor in Canada: a larger market had to be obtained somehow and if the United States would not provide it, perhaps the Maritimes would'.[73] Fourthly, Upper Canadians in particular wanted to annex the North-West, and it is asserted that a mere federation of the two Canadas 'could hardly have met the need for expansion'.[74] Lastly, the package is sometimes spiced with a delicate flavour of British North American nationhood, 'a nascent national feeling among English-speaking Canadians'.[75] 'In its emphasis upon expansion, national unification, and independence,' Creighton concluded, 'Canadian Confederation was a typical experiment in nineteenth-century nation-building.'[76] Perhaps this element has appealed to subsequent generations of Canada's historians, enabling them to draw retrospective comfort and inspiration in periods when their country's unity and identity has seemed under threat.[77]

These arguments for Confederation form not simply a series of individually cogent points, but tend to be fused together through the historian's trade of pattern-making into an interlocking package, in which elements are balanced, or traded off, one against another to create a watertight structure of explanation. Thus, according to Morton, 'Lower Canada could scarcely agree to the annexation of the north-west unless this were offset by guarantees of its historic rights in the new union, and by the adherence of the Atlantic provinces to the union to balance the indefinitely growing population of Upper Canada'. Furthermore, French Canadians and Maritimers would not accept 'the cost of building a Pacific railway unless that were matched by the building of the Intercolonial'. Where Creighton thought of the nineteenth century's nation-builders, Garibaldi and Bismarck, Morton was evidently inspired by its engineers, Brunel and Stephenson: 'Only a general union, balanced with all the care and precision of a cantilever, was practical in 1865'.[78] Perhaps the most elegant aspect of the interlocking package is the way in which it integrates nation-building with empire. Confederation is seen as the visionary initiative of the Canadian ministry, supported by a minority of far-sighted politicians in New Brunswick and Nova Scotia. When other Maritimers refused to recognise their destiny, the British are invoked as *deus ex machina* to force them to accept inevitability. The cumulative result constitutes a very attractive and satisfying scholarly analysis of the reasons for Confederation, one which appears to account for every element of a complex continental situation, neatly interweaving them all into a pattern which explains not simply why the provinces decided to unite, but why they decided to unite at a particular moment in the 1860s. It is, however, possible to suggest that the picture is too satisfying, and that in a number of respects it is open to challenge.

Conclusion

The chief shortcoming of the Quebec resolutions, in the opinion of Frederic Rogers, was that so many interests had to be accommodated in a British North American union that the proposed scheme of government was 'rather wanting in neatness and scientific character'.[79] Historians should certainly beware of implying neatness and scientific precision in attempting to explain why Confederation occurred in the 1860s. In the end, politicians in Canada, New Brunswick and Nova Scotia were able to put together majorities in favour of union. Various motives, different cocktails of incentive, played their part in each province, perhaps even in each individual. Arguments were advanced to state the case in as many different ways as possible in order to appeal to people who thought in many different ways. Some arguments were plausible and effective, some merely effective, others were tried but discarded when no roof resounded with appreciative cheers. To carry Confederation by majorities was to carry Confederation by coalitions, and coalition armies march to a cacophony of drumbeats. Historians can reconstruct the cut-and-thrust of debate and note that in 1867 those who favoured Confederation overcame those who opposed it, in the mainland provinces at least. Yet it can never be proved that Confederation triumphed on account of any one of those arguments, or of all of them woven into a package.

The story was told in the 1860s of the principle on which one of the members for the New Brunswick county of Charlotte always decided to cast his vote. 'When a bill's before this house I always asks whats it going to do for Charlotte. I ain't got anything to do with the Province—I sits here for Charlotte and if they tells me it'll do good to the Province but do harm to Charlotte then says I "I go in for Charlotte". And if they tells me it'll harm the Province but do good to Charlotte then too says I "I go in for Charlotte".[80] British North America was composed of many Charlottes, not all of them represented by such frank legislators. Yet the story is not just a cameo of localism but also a reminder of expectations. It is relatively easy to reconstruct why supporters of Confederation claimed that it was the right answer to the problems of the 1860s, but much harder to reconstruct where they thought British North America might be ten or twenty years ahead. Cobden felt that they did not know themselves, that Confederation was 'a device of the Canadian politicians for escaping from themselves into a new & enlarged political arena...few of the prominent actors look beyond this immediate object'.[81] Cobden was habitually unsympathetic in his assessments of Canadian motives. It is much more likely that the prominent actors had notions about the future which were shifting, imprecise but nonetheless in large measure shared. Galt was unusual in believing—as he admitted two years later—that Confederation 'must ultimately lead' to independence from

Britain, although this did not prevent him from accepting a knighthood.[82] Others envisaged an early expansion into a transcontinental union, although the enthusiasm which enticed British Columbia into Confederation in 1870–1 was not fully matched by a determination to keep it in the decade which followed.

Yet it would be ungenerous for historians to abuse the luxury of hindsight by damning the politicians of British North America for their failure to foresee the future, and still less for their inability to find solutions which could impose themselves fully on events. As premier of Nova Scotia, Joseph Howe once justified a piece of legislation as 'framed on the principle, if you can't do all the good you wish, do all you can'.[83] The novelist E.M. Forster once waspishly described the attraction of becoming a historian as like being 'transferred from an office where one is afraid of a sergeant-major into an office where one can intimidate generals'.[84] Historians have no right to censure past politicians for supporting projects which did not solve every difficulty, but might eventually help to solve some—especially if the alternative would be to blame them for inactivity. Yet equally it is important to avoid the trap of assuming that merely because those past politicians advanced large claims in support of any particular project, it must have been the answer to all their problems and prayers.

By the 1860s, the idea of a British North American union had come to be seen not as a distant vision but as a vehicle by which more specific aims might be realised. In 1849, Grey had described federation as an 'old idea'[85] but dismissed it as a practical proposition because of 'an absence of any sufficient common interests to form the ground work of the union'.[86] Thirteen years later, the *Saturday Review* could also describe it as an 'idea, which so far from being novel, has long attracted the attention of Imperial and colonial statesmen' but significantly it had now become something which might facilitate other changes, 'holding out a prospect, however remote, of the reconstruction on a basis more equal, and therefore more likely to be lasting, of those bonds which connect us with our Transatlantic fellow-subjects'.[87]

A few historians have considered the role of Confederation as an idea. Brebner baldly excluded 'the quite natural, if impractical' proposals of earlier times in order to confine the movement for Confederation to the nine years between the depression of 1857 and the departure of delegates for London in 1866.[88] Morton, on the other hand, acknowledged that the 'sudden and dramatic' Canadian mission to Charlottetown could only be 'explained by the long years of germination of the idea of British North American union,' which had 'recurred steadily and rhythmically' at least since the annexationist talk of 1849.[89] Yet the predominant tendency has been to assume that Confederation was deduced from the immediate circumstances of 1864. Upton complained that Canadian history tended to be presented as a pedestrian saga of pragmatic problem-solving, 'so that it often appears that our present form of government was devised overnight by one or two politicians. John A. Macdonald and George Brown, we might be excused for believing, went to Charlottetown in 1864 and placed their daring innovation before an astonished group of lesser men quite unprepared to cope with such intellectual giants.'[90] Put in that form, it becomes comprehensible that some historians have regarded the outcome as miraculous.

Contemporaries were aware that the idea had a prehistory, although they had their own motives for emphasising its existence. The *Westminster Review*, for instance, sought to dismiss the notion that 'the scheme of confederation is the offspring of fear' since its origins could be 'traced much further back than the civil war in the United States'.[91] 'We know that the idea exists in a defined form', the *Daily Telegraph* wrote in 1864, 'but we cannot point to the time or place of its first existence.'[92]

The task of the historian is thus not so much to explain why British North American union was seized upon as the answer to the challenges facing the provinces in 1864—indeed in some respects it was not a very obvious answer at all—but rather why an idea which, as the *Westminster Review* put it in 1865, 'had never been extinct in any of the provinces, although it has taken Rip van Winkle slumbers'—should suddenly flare into life in 1864.[93] 'Colonists are the last people in the world to do or suffer anything for an idea,' lamented *The Times* in September 1865 as Confederation seemed to be slipping away, 'and must have something more solid to reward them for their devotion.'[94] The precise origin of the idea is of less importance than the fact that it had come to take so firm a hold on the British mind in the quarter century before Charlottetown. To say this is not to attempt an imperial recolonisation of Canadian history by seizing the credit for the birth of the Canadian state. The *Edinburgh Review* was surely right in asserting that 'the mainspring of the Federative Movement must be sought not in any past or present impulse from Imperial authorities, but in the political circumstances, necessities, and instincts of the provinces',[95] although as the details emerged, both *The Times* and the *Saturday Review* expressed surprise at the active involvement of the imperial factor.[96]

Fundamentally, Confederation was the creation of a vigorous and confident Upper Canada, which saw it as the best way of escaping from a political log-jam of the existing province, and as an acceptable framework for the prosecution of other projects. Without that dynamic Upper Canadian push, the British would no doubt have continued to wait in the wings for something in British North America to support. Yet equally, without the pre-existing British support for a union of the provinces, vague and illogical though it may have been, there is no reason to suppose that it would have made sense for the ambitious Upper Canadians to have adopted the Confederation of all the provinces as their way forward in 1864. When Canadian politicians recognised in June 1864 that the reconstruction of their province could no longer be postponed, their best chance of securing the legislative compliance of Westminster lay in pursuing the aim of British North American union. For Macdonald, the adhesion of the Maritimes offered a chance of a balancing element which might save him from being trampled under foot in the unavoidable shift of electoral power towards the Grits and Reformers of Upper Canada. In an age of slow communications, the involvement of the British gave him the precious factor of time.

In a province and an era permeated by the rhetoric of loyalty, British support would give him an asset intangible in itself but embarrassing by its absence to his opponents. The involvement of the British also exposed the complex Brown to the intimidating magic of a social élite, for long enough to inhibit him from demanding action on a purely Canadian reform project instead of Confederation. Perhaps the homilies and reproaches of the British rattled Nova Scotians and New Brunswickers—but not their island neighbours—into doubting their own rejection of the Quebec scheme, but perhaps too Maritime politicians who recognised that their provinces were too small to endure in a world of big battalions found it more convenient to seem to bow the knee to the distant imperial Caesar rather than to their fellow centurions from Canada. *The Times*, of course, was wrong to allege that colonists would not make sacrifices for an idea. In a sense, Confederation itself was a form of sacrificial gesture to British opinion. Galt assured Cardwell in April 1865 that the motive of the Canadian government in pressing for Confederation was 'not in any way to weaken the connection with the Mother County, but rather to remove those causes which now afforded many parties in England arguments for asserting that the connection was mutually disadvantageous'.[97] Visiting London that autumn, Monck concluded that 'the anti Colonial party' were 'for the moment, choked off by the proposal for our Union, but if that fails I believe they will return to the charge with redoubled energy'.[98] The strategy could only work if British North American union was not simply a generally accepted British aim, but one which was seen as a forerunner, substitute or just plain nostrum for solving all the problems of the colonial relationship.

Two elements need to be woven into the march of events and the cavalcade of politicians along the road to Confederation. One is the idea of British North American union, and the other is the imperial factor. Both were pervasive but diffuse rather than precise. The idea of intercolonial union, for instance, took many forms, creating the complication that some of the argument in the middle years of the 1860s was not about the end itself but rather the version which had come to the fore, with some Lower Canadians objecting that Confederation would destroy local autonomy, and a strong strand of Maritime opinion fearing that it was not centralised enough. Similarly, the imperial factor should be considered in the broader but less grandiose terms of a general consensus of British opinion. D'Arcy McGee's role in the opening of the Confederation debates in the Canadian Assembly was to combine an overview of the issue with some oratorical spice. Like Brebner, he was content to 'dismiss the antecedent history of the question' and focus rather on the events since 1858 which had given 'importance to the theory in men's minds', but he traced the idea back to the days of Durham and beyond. 'If we have dreamed a dream of union...it is at least worth while remarking that a dream which has been dreamed by such wise and good men, may...have been a sort of vision, a vision foreshadowing forthcoming natural events in a clear intelligence.'[99] Stripped of its oratorical ornament, McGee's point was that the relationship between events and ideas was not merely one-way: the first and original cause of Confederation was the idea of Confederation itself. Once the basic importance of the idea is recognised, then it is possible to see the British role not as one of pressure and command but rather context and support. As *The Times* commented in reporting the first meeting of the Dominion parliament in November 1867: 'Empire never spoke with so small and still a voice as when England humbly suggested and gently aided the idea of a Canadian Confederation'.[100]

Notes

1. The preamble to the British North America Act (1867) is given in Joseph Pope (ed.), *Confederation*, p. 249 and Browne, p. 302.

2. These issues are also discussed in Ged Martin, 'An Imperial Idea and Its Friends: Canadian Confederation and the British, 1837–1864' in Gordon Martel (ed.), *Studies in British Imperial History: Essays in Honour of A.P. Thornton* (Basingstoke, 1986) pp. 49–94; and Ged Martin, 'Launching Canadian Confederation: Means to Ends', *Historical Journal*, xxvii (1984) pp. 575–602. The present study also draws upon G.W. Martin, 'Britain and the Future of British North America, 1837–1867' (PhD thesis, Cambridge, 1972).

    Various studies discuss the idea of Confederation in the decades before 1867. Older works which remain useful are R.G. Trotter, *Canadian Federation: Its Origins and Achievements. A Study in Nation-Building* (Toronto, 1924) and W.M. Whitelaw, *The Maritimes and Canada before Confederation* (Toronto, 1934). Chester Martin, *Foundations of Canadian Nationhood* (Toronto, 1955) is valuable in placing Confederation in a longer perspective, but its usefulness is reduced by the absence of any citation of sources. For the Loyalist pedigree of Confederation, see Peter J. Smith, 'The Ideological Origins of Canadian Confederation', *Canadian Journal of Political Science*, xx (1987) pp. 3–31; Peter J. Smith, 'The Dream of Political Union: Loyalism, Toryism and the Federal Idea in Pre-Confederation Canada', in Ged Martin (ed.) *Causes*, pp. 148–71. Other essays and articles include James A. Gibson, 'The Colonial Office View of Canadian Federation, 1856–1867', CHR, xxxv (1954), pp. 279–313; L.F.S. Upton, 'The Idea of Confederation, 1754–1858' in W.L. Morton (ed.), *The Shield of Achilles* (Toronto, 1968); Bruce A. Knox, 'The Rise of Colonial Federation as an Object of British Policy, 1850–1870', *Journal of British Studies*, xi (1972), pp. 92–112; Ged Martin, 'Confederation Rejected: the British Debate on Canada, 1837–1840', *JICH*, xi (1982), pp. 33–57; and Ged Martin, 'Britain and the Future of British North America, 1841–1846', *British Journal of Canadian Studies*, ii (1987) pp. 74–96.

3. Phillip A. Buckner, 'The Maritimes and Confederation: A Reassessment', CHR, lxxi (1990) p.21n.

4. The three most authoritative modern studies are D.G. Creighton, *The Road to Confederation: The Emergence of Canada 1863–1867* (Toronto, 1964) [cited as *Road to Confederation*]; W.L. Morton, *The Critical Years: The Union of British North America 1857–1873* (Toronto, 1964) [cited as *Critical Years*]; and P.B. Waite, *The Life and Times* of Confederation 1864–1867: *Politics, Newspapers, and the Union of British North America* (Toronto, 1962) [cited as *Life and Times*]. These should be supplemented by two giant biographies of leading politicians: D.G. Creighton, *John A. Macdonald: The Young Politician* (Toronto, 1952) [cited as *Macdonald*, i] and J.M.S.

Careless, *Brown of the Globe*, i: *The Voice of Upper Canada 1818–1859* (Toronto, 1959) and ii: *Statesman of Confederation 1860–1880* (Toronto, 1963) [cited as *Brown*].

5. Arthur R.M. Lower, *Colony to Nation: A History of Canada* (5th ed., 1977, first published 1946), pp. xiii, 471. Other general works referred to include J.B. Brebner, *Canada: A Modern History* (Ann Arbor, 1960) [cited as *Brebner*]; J.M.S. Careless, *Canada: A Story of Challenge* (rev. ed., Toronto, 1974); D.G. Creighton, *Dominion of the North: A History of Canada* (rev. ed., Toronto, 1962) [cited as *Dominion of the North*]; J.L. Finlay and D.N. Sprague, *The Structure of Canada History* (2nd ed., Scarborough, Ont., 1984) [cited as *Structure of Canadian History*]; R. Douglas Francis, R. Jones and D.B. Smith, *Origins: Canadian History to Confederation* (Toronto, 1988); Edgar McInnis, *Canada: A Social and Political History* (4th ed., Toronto, 1982) [cited as *McInnis*]; Kenneth McNaught, *The Pelican History of Canada* (rev. ed., London, 1978) [cited as *McNaught*]; Desmond Morton, *A Short History of Canada* (rev. ed., Edmonton, 1983); W.L. Morton, *Kingdom of Canada: A General History from Earliest Times* (2nd ed., Toronto, 1969) [cited as *Kingdom of Canada*]. For a selection of articles, see Ramsay Cook (ed.), *Confederation* (Canadian Historical Readings, no. 3, Toronto, 1967).

6. J.H. Dales, *The Protective Tariff in Canada's Development* (Toronto, 1966) pp. 145–9. Dales quoted Innis, Creighton, Brebner, Easterbrook and Aitken but exempted Lower and Chester Martin from his 'historians stereotype'.

7. Buckner argues that opposition to Confederation in the Maritimes has been exaggerated, 'The Maritimes and Confederation', pp. 1–30, esp. 5–7, reprinted in Ged Martin (ed.), *Causes*, pp. 86–113. See also D.A. Muise, 'The Federal Election of 1867 in Nova Scotia: An Economic Interpretation', *Collections of the Nova Scotia Historical Society*, xxxvi (1968), pp. 327–51, and Brian D. Tennyson, 'Economic Nationalism, Confederation and Nova Scotia', in Ged Martin (ed.), *Causes*, pp. 130–41.

8. *Colony to Nation*, ch. 23 ('The Miracle of Union').

9. Ronald L. Watts, 'An Overview', in R.L. Watts and D.M. Brown (eds), *Options for a New Canada* (Toronto, 1991) p. 12; Robert C. Vipond, *Liberty and Community: Canadian Federalism and the Failure of the Constitution* (Albany NY, 1991) p. 17; D.J. Bercuson and B. Cooper, *Deconfederation: Canada Without Quebec* (Toronto, 1991) p. 75.

10. E.W. Watkin, *Canada and the States: Recollections 1851 to 1886* (London, 1886) pp. 2, 65b.

11. Watkin's role was seized upon as early as 1924 by R.G. Trotter, *Canadian Federation*, ch. xiii ('Introducing a Promoter of Empire') and enshrined in *Cambridge History of the British Empire*, vi: *Canada and Newfoundland* (1930) pp. 443–4, 462. Watkin also appears in Brebner, pp. 282–4; Careless, *Canada: A Story of Challenge*, pp. 241–2; *Dominion of the North*, pp. 292–3; *Colony to Nation*, p. 317; McInnis, pp. 344, 363; and *Kingdom of Canada*, p. 312. This is one of several example which call to mind the term 'historians' consensus', as used by Dales. Watkin also figures large in an important economic interpretation, Stanley B. Ryerson, *Unequal Union: Roots of Crisis in the Canadas, 1815–1873* (2nd ed., Toronto, 1973) pp. 322–3, 343. An important attempt to interpret the financial aspect of the British role is D.W. Roman, 'The Contribution of Imperial Guarantees for Colonial Railway Loans to the Consolidation of British North America 1847–1865', (DPhil. thesis, Oxford, 1978).

12. Francis, Jones and Smith, *Origins*, p. 390.

13. Watkin, *Canada and the States*, p. 2.

14. They were published in *British Parliamentary Papers* [cited as *BPP*], 1866, lxxiii, *Colonial Trade Statistics*, pp. 126–81.

15. *Life and Times*, ch. 17.

16. J.M.S. Careless, *The Union of the Canadas: The Growth of Canadian Institutions* (Toronto), 1967.

17. Margaret A. Banks, 'Upper and Lower Canada or Canada West and East?', *CHR*, liv (1973) pp. 473–80.

18. *Monck Letters and Journals*, p. 175.

19. *Critical Years*, pp. 2–3.

20. United States figures from *Historical Statistics of the United States: Colonial times to 1957* (Washington DC, 1960).

21. British figures from B.R. Mitchell with P. Deane, *Abstract of British Historical Statistics* (Cambridge, 1962).

22. *CD*, p. 763. The speaker was John A. Macdonald, Reform Members for Toronto West, not to be confused with the better-known John A. Macdonald and John Sandfield Macdonald.

23. Quoted in Monck A-755, Cardwell to Monck, private, 1 September 1865. For Newfoundland and the Ipswich election, *Hansard*, lxiii (26 May 1842) col. 875.

24. As argued by R.C. Nelson, W.C. Soderlund, R.H. Wagenberg and E.D. Briggs, 'Canadian Confederation as a Case Study in Community Formation', in Ged Martin (ed.), *Causes*, pp. 50–85, esp. 59–60, 75–6. Compare S.A. Saunders, *The Economic History of the Maritime Provinces* (Fredericton, 1984) pp. 98–100.

25. *Punch*, 30 March 1861, p. 134.

26. Grey Papers, Ashburton to Howick, 10 April 1838.

27. R.W. Fogel and S.L. Engermann, *Time on the Cross* (2 vols, London, 1974) i, p. 250; ii, p. 163. Sharp differences in per capita commodity income by region in 1870 are demonstrated by the maps in Kris Inwood and James Irwin, 'Canadian Regional Commodity Income Differences at Confederation', in Kris Inwood (ed.), *Farm, Factory and Fortune: New Studies in the Economic History of the Maritime Provinces* (Fredericton, 1993) pp. 99–100.

28. Lucas, ii, p. 212; A. Trollope, *North America* (2 vols, London, 1968 ed., first published 1861) i, p. 55.

29. Douglas McCalla, 'Railways and the Development of Canada West, 1850–1870' in A. Greer and I. Radforth (eds), *Colonial Leviathan: State Formation in Mid-Nineteenth Century Canada* (Toronto, 1992) pp. 192–229.

30. HCC 1543, Head to Lewis, 20 October, 1855.

31. Perceptions of the Maritimes are discussed in Chapter Four. There is some emerging difference of emphasis among economic historians about the dependence of the province of Canada on imported British capital. For an effective summary of the view that British governments manipulated the colonial need for access to capital to

sustain a British North America separate from the United States, see P.J. Cain and A.G. Hopkins, *British Imperialism: Innovations and Expansion 1688–1914* (London, 1993) pp. 258–73. Douglas McCalla has argued that much of the capital required for the development of Upper Canada was locally generated, and that comparison with adjoining American states suggests that larger projects could have been financed independently of the colonial connection. While accepting that Canada benefited from indirect British subsidies, notably through expenditure on garrison, McCalla also suggests that the three largest British-financed transportation projects were of limited benefit. The Rideau Canal, a defence project, quickly became irrelevant. The Grand Trunk Railway was 'neither the only nor even the best possibility for completing the core Canadian railway system'. Most notably, the enlargement of the Welland Canal, financed by the loan which the British government used as a carrot for securing Upper Canadian acquiescence in the Union of 1841, was an 'inappropriate strategy', creating a waterway which rarely functioned above 15 per cent of its capacity. (Douglas McCalla, *Planting the Province: The Economic History of Upper Canada 1748–1870* (Toronto, 1993) esp. pp. 202, 126). What McCalla terms the 'overbuilding' of the Welland as a ship canal is of some importance in this discussion, since Cain and Hopkins revealingly talk of the 'St. Lawrence Seaway as a conduit for trade between Britain and the mid-west of America'. (Cain and Hopkins, *British Imperialism: Innovations and Expansion*, p. 259.) The Seaway was opened in 1959, and the Oxford English Dictionary cites the earliest use of the term from 1921.

32. C. Dickens, *Pictures from Italy and American Notes* (London, 1859 ed.) p. 205. The description was of Halifax in 1842.

33. Gladstone, 44136, Cobden to Gladstone, 24 February 1865, fos 275–8.

34. *The Times*, 26 January 1850.

35. For the evolution of colonial self-government, see Phillip A. Buckner, *The Transition to Responsible Government: British Policy in British North America 1815–1850* (Westport, Conn. 1985); Ged Martin, 'The Canadian Rebellion Losses Bill of 1849 in British Politics', *JICH*, vi (1977) pp. 3–22.

36. J. Pope, *Correspondence of Sir John Macdonald* (Garden City NY ed., 1921) p. 29n.

37. Careless, *Union of the Canadas*.

38. Brown, i, esp. chs 6–8.

39. The resolutions are given in O. D. Skelton, *Life and Times of Sir Alexander Tilloch Galt* (ed. G. MacLean, Toronto, 1966) pp. 283–4.

40. *Critical Years*, pp. 16–20; *Macdonald*, i, pp. 261–70; *Brown*, i, pp. 254–80.

41. Pope, *Memoirs*, pp. 216–17; *Canadian Presbyter*, September 1858, quoted R.W. Vaudry, *The Free Church in Victorian Canada* (Waterloo, Ont. 1989) p. 76.

42. *Brown*, ii, p. 47.

43. For the *Trent* crisis and its political implications, see W. L. Morton, *Critical Years*, ch. 6, and R.W. Winks, *Canada and the United States: The Civil War Years* (rev. ed., Montreal, 1971) ch. 6. For the military problems, see Kenneth Bourne, *Britain and the Balance of Power in North America* (London, 1967) ch. 7, and J. Mackay Hitsman, *Safeguarding Canada 1763–1871* (Toronto, 1968) ch. 8.

44. For example, Newcastle 11413, Monck to Newcastle, private, 8 March 1862.

45. Bruce W. Hodgins, *John Sandfield Macdonald 1812–1872* (Toronto, 1971).

46. *Critical Years*, pp. 121–5.

47. *Ibid.*, p. 125.

48. *Ibid.*, pp. 128–9; *Brown*, ii, pp. 92–5.

49. Newcastle 10887, Newcastle to Monck (copy), private, 18 September 1863, pp. 47–52; Monck to Henry Monck, 28 March 1864, in *Monck Letters and Journals*, pp. 42–3.

50. *Brown*, ii, pp. 127–9.

51. J. Young, *Public Men and Public Life in Canada: The Story of the Canadian Confederacy* (2 vols, Toronto, 1912) i, pp. 197–8.

52. Macdonald to Lindsey, confidential, 24 September 1858; same to same, 14 June 1860, in J.K. Johnson and C.B. Stelmack (eds), *The Papers of the Prime Ministers: The Letters of Sir John A. Macdonald 1858–1861* (Ottawa, 1969) pp. 84, 214.

53. Young, *Public Men and Public Life*, i. p. 201.

54. *Ibid.*, i, p. 211. Young claimed to have had the story from Brown.

55. *Brown*, ii, pp. 129, 124.

56. For an attempted revision of the politics of the Great Coalition, see Ged Martin, *Faction and Fiction in Canada's Great Coalition of 1864* (Sackville, New Brunswick, 1993). For examples of emphasis upon the aim of British North American union, see McNaught, p. 122 and *Structure of Canadian History*, p. 174.

57. *Road to Confederation*, chs 3–7; *Critical Years*, pp. 151–70; *Life and Times*, chs 4–7.

58. *Road to Confederation*, pp. 234–7; A.I. Silver, *The French- Canadian Idea of Confederation 1864–1900*, (Toronto, 1982) ch. 2. A selection of *The Confederation Debates in the Province of Canada 1865* (Toronto, 1963) was edited by P.B. Waite. Citations in this work are to the full edition of 1865 (*CD*).

59. *Road to Confederation*, chs 708; *Critical Years*, pp. 170–81; Beck, *Howe*, ii, ch. 9.

60. W.M. Baker, *Timothy Warren Anglin 1822–1896: Irish Catholic Canadian* (Toronto, 1977) pp. 69–79; A.G. Bailey, 'Railways and the Confederation Issue in New Brunswick, 1863–1865', *CHR*, xxi (1940) pp. 367–83, and 'The Basis and Persistence of Opposition to Confederation in New Brunswick', *CHR*, xxiii (1942) pp. 374–97; J.K. Chapman, 'Arthur Gordon and Confederation', *CHR*, xxxvii (1956) pp. 142–57.

61. Macdonald Letter Book, 8 Macdonald to Watkin (copy), private, 27 March 1865.

62. *Road to Confederation*, ch.9.

63. Baker, *Anglin*, ch. 7; J.K. Chapman, *The Career of Arthur Hamilton Gordon, First Land Stanmore 1829–1912* (Toronto, 1964) ch. 2, esp. pp. 36–7.

64. The British role is discussed in Chapter Seven.

65. Baker, *Anglin*, ch. 7; *Road to Confederation*, chs 10–12; *Critical Years*, ch. 10.

66. *Road to Confederation*, ch. 14; *Critical Years*, ch. 11; Beck, *Howe*, ii, pp. 202–18.

67. For example, *Critical Years*, p. 149; *Structure of Canadian History*, p. 171.

68. G.P. de T. Glazebrook, *A History of Transportation in Canada* (2 vols, Toronto, 1964 ed.) i, p. 172.

69. *Colony to Nation*, p. 316.

70. Francis, Jones and Smith, *Origins*, p. 379.

71. For example, McNaught, pp. 125–6, but compare the note of doubt in *Dominion of the North*, p. 301.

72. Desmond Morton, *Short History of Canada*, p. 71.

73. *Colony to Nation*, p. 323.

74. *Critical Years*, p. 149.

75. McNaught, p. 122.

76. *Dominion of the North*, p. 305.

77. For an example of pride in the achievement of Confederation: Careless, *Canada: A Story of Challenge*, pp. 230, 245.

78. *Kingdom of Canada*, p. 317.

79. Rogers to Miss Rogers, 23 December 1864, in Marindin (ed.), *op. cit.*, pp. 252–3.

80. Story told in Gordon to Gladstone, January 1864, in Knaplund (ed.), *Gladstone-Gordon Correspondence*, pp. 42–3.

81. Gladstone 44136, Cobden to Gladstone, 26 February 1865, fos 275–8.

82. Galt to Sir John Young, 15 May 1869, in Skelton, *op. cit.*, pp. 221–2.

83. Quoted, Beck, Howe, ii, p. 169.

84. Quoted, R. Fitzhenry (ed.), *The Fitzhenry & Whiteside Book of Quotations* (Toronto, 1981) p. 134.

85. *Elgin-Grey Papers*, Grey to Elgin (copy), 8 August 1849, i, p. 437.

86. Russell 8A, Grey to Russell, 8 August 1849, fos 62–5.

87. *Saturday Review*, 4 October 1862, p. 397.

88. Brebner, p. 283.

89. *Kingdom of Canada*, p. 317.

90. Upton, 'Idea of Confederation', p. 184.

91. *Westminster Review*, xxvii (1865), p. 536.

92. *Daily Telegraph*, 25 November 1864.

93. *Westminster Review*, xxvii (1865) p. 540.

94. *The Times*, 14 September 1865.

95. *Edinburgh Review*, cxxxi (1865) p. 184.

96. *The Times*, 9 January 1865; *Saturday Review*, 14 January 1865, p. 37, both commenting on Cardwell's despatch of 3 December 1864.

97. Macdonald 161, report of Galt's statement to Cardwell, p. 65222.

98. Galt 3, Monck to Galt, 26 October 1865, pp. 1057–61.

99. *CD*, pp. 126.

100. *The Times*, 22 November 1867.

Index